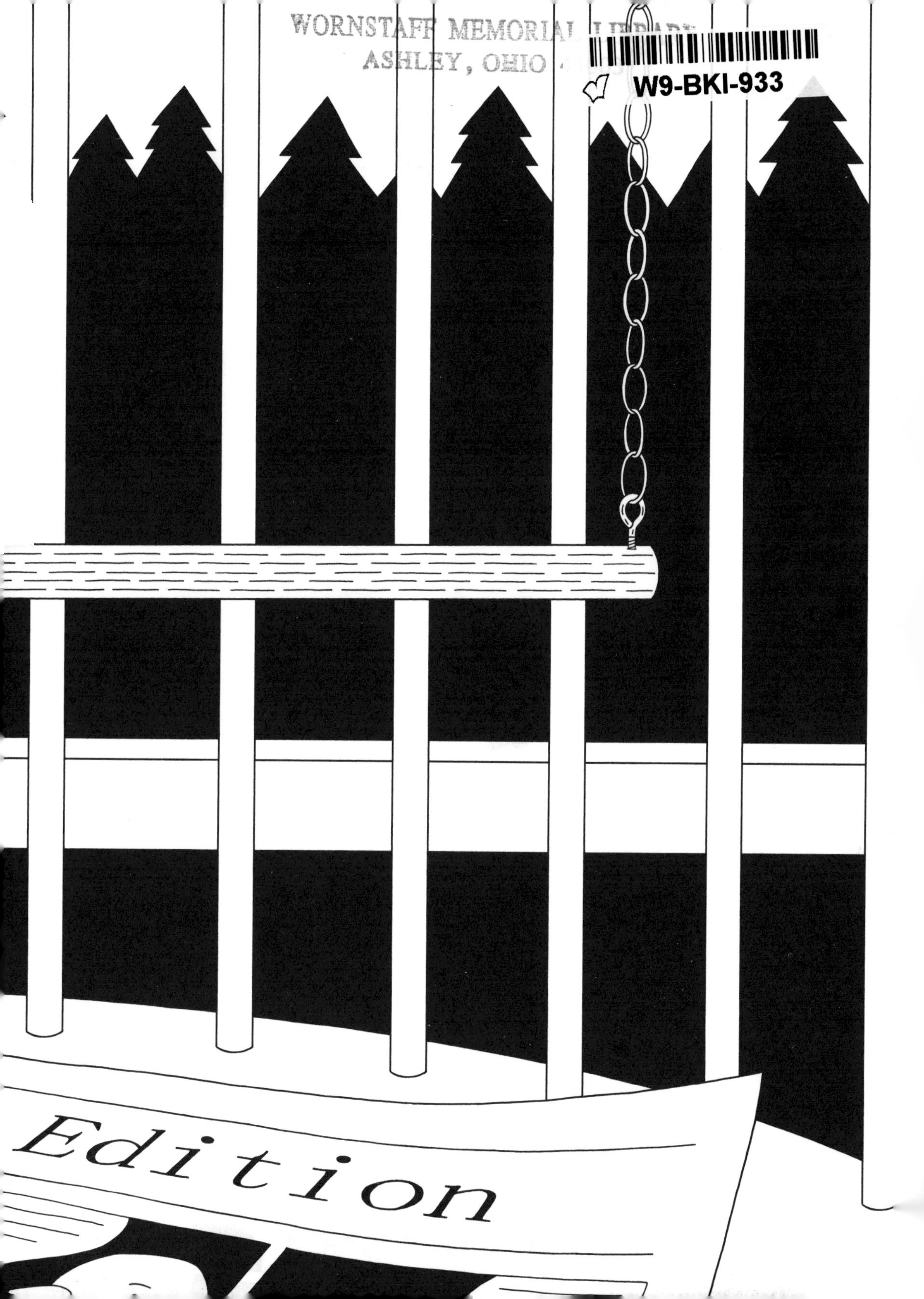
Edition

THE BEST AMERICAN

Comics 2011

GUEST EDITORS OF
THE BEST AMERICAN COMICS

2006 HARVEY PEKAR
2007 CHRIS WARE
2008 LYNDA BARRY
2009 CHARLES BURNS
2010 NEIL GAIMAN
2011 ALISON BECHDEL

THE BEST AMERICAN

Comics

2011

EDITED *and with an*
INTRODUCTION *by* Alison Bechdel

JESSICA ABEL & MATT MADDEN,
series editors

HOUGHTON MIFFLIN HARCOURT
BOSTON ▪ NEW YORK   2011

www.hmhbooks.com

Library of Congress Cataloging-in-Publication Data is available.

ISBN 978-0-547-33362-5

Book design: Robert Overholtzer   Cover design: Gillian Tamaki   Endpaper art: Robert Sergel

PRINTED IN THE UNITED STATES OF AMERICA

DOC 10 9 8 7 6 5 4 3 2 1

Permissions credits are located on page 332.

Contents

Foreword

COMICS IS A PRINTED MEDIUM. And now it's also a digital medium. What it isn't is a *direct* medium, like drawing or painting: there is no "original" comic to read. The pages that have the ink on them may be beautiful to look at and they may offer loads of information for fans and researchers, but most people will agree that it's not really a comic until it has been reproduced.

Reproduction: the simple fact that comics is a medium that's reproduced has worked in tandem with the impulses and interests of the artists themselves to make comics the art form we know today. The earliest comics and protocomics appeared in newspapers or broadsheets, or used novel printing technologies such as the "autography" printing that Rodolphe Töppfer employed for his extremely modern comics back in the 1840s, and those formats and printing technologies helped mold comics into its current form: black linework and noncontinuous tone (like that created by crosshatching and stippling) are robust enough to withstand all but the crudest reproduction techniques, and they do a pretty good job even with those.

The fact that comics were given a certain size and shape (and frequency) in the Sunday pages and daily comic strips also influenced the way that comic art and storytelling evolved. Daily strips were (and remain) short bursts of story often punctuated by humor. Long sagas were serialized day by day or else a theme was riffed on until it was exhausted. The Sunday pages were an opportunity for the artist to experiment with layout and show off the art. The stories would often stand alone, outside or parallel to the daily continuity. In the 1930s, the comic book magazine was introduced and the canvas available for storytelling expanded (while the conventions of comics drawing scrambled to keep up the pace). This pamphlet form became all-dominant in the U.S., and that and the newspaper comic strip continue to be the default images of what a Platonic "comic" looks like. Along the way there have been many variations on those formats, each producing a new twist on visual and narrative style, such as the "little big books" of the 1920s, newspaper insert sections like Will Eisner's *Spirit*, and the two-tier "alternative newspaper strip" format used by Lynda Barry, Jules Feiffer, and Ben Katchor, among others. And of course today the dominant form is the graphic novel, with all the new possibilities this longer and more durable format offers us and challenges us with.

Alongside (under? behind? in front of? upside-down from?) "official" formats used by newspapers and publishers, there has been a crucial parallel development for the art form of comics, dating back to the early twentieth century, and that is the self-published fanzine. The fanzine originated in the 1930s in the science-fiction community as a way for fans to share appreciations of and arcane knowledge related to their favorite writers. Comics were mentioned in these early publications, and soon had their own fanzines devoted to topics such as superheroes and EC titles. Comic fanzines often featured strips and pinup art by nonprofessional comics fans as well as future professionals. Of course, today blogs and social media make this kind of sharing par for the course, but back in the '60s and '70s it was a vital but mostly overlooked movement.

The 'zine scene really took off in the late 1970s and into the '80s, inspired by the DIY ethos of punk rock. With their mostly prose copy (letters, articles, ads) supplemented with a few comics and pinups, fanzines set the stage—and created the readership—for self-published comics. Starting in the early '80s, cartoonists began photocopying, folding, and stapling "minicomics" in a variety of shapes and sizes. They would swap these and sell them through the mail or at comics conventions.

Minicomics offer a format and a forum outside the mainstream—not just the superhero "mainstream" but also independent publishers and the mainstream of culture. To this day, despite the easy availability of online platforms, artists continue using minicomics to explore, experiment with, and develop their craft in an off-the-grid, semidisposable form. For some artists, the minicomic is a training ground and eventually a steppingstone to finding a publisher. For others, minicomics are an end in themselves. Their goal as authors is simply to share work with friends and peers out of the view of the larger culture.

Parallel to the growth of fanzines and minicomics, the 1980s saw a strong mail art movement in which people traded small-scale art (especially collages) and collaborated through the mail. The creative interchange between all of these authors and artists influenced the rise of the comic-as-art-object. You can see that influence in today's minicomics, which, to a much higher degree than in the '90s, tend to have ambitious and elaborate production values, including silkscreened covers, die cuts, fold-outs, art papers, and more.

Another trend in comics publishing roughly simultaneous to all this is the professional self-publishing movement, kicked into high gear by Kevin Eastman and Peter Laird's (self-published) *Teenage Mutant Ninja Turtles* and championed by artists like

Dave Sim (*Cerebus*) and Jeff Smith (*Bone, RASL*—see the wonderful excerpt in this volume). These authors may have started out small, but even as their work gained popularity and was being sold in traditional comic book stores, they chose to continue self-publishing. This movement brought the autonomy of fanzines into the arena of mainstream publishing, its adherents arguing that artists are better off publishing and promoting their own work than sharing it with a publisher. (The creators' rights movement also plays into this, but we're not going to get into that here.)

Every art form has its platforms for amateurs, students, and self-taught artists, whether those be art-school exhibitions or blog posts. Most, however, don't take those public displays all that seriously, nor do they integrate them in the way that comics do. When it comes to self-publishing, the comics world has a very different attitude than most other sectors of publishing. In prose and poetry, self-publishing is more than a little looked down upon. The term "vanity publishing," which is what self-publishing is often called in those fields, smacks of disdain. In comics, no such stigma exists. When R. Crumb was starting out, a pal published the first issue of *Zap Comics,* and Crumb himself sold it out of a baby carriage on Haight-Ashbury. Since the '80s, self-publishing has been a common option for artists from all over the world of comics. The Xeric Foundation (founded by Peter Laird of Ninja Turtle fame in order to spread the self-publishing gospel) gives out grants twice a year to help author-publishers cover printing and promotion costs. Alternative comics conventions like APE, SPX, and the MoCCA Festival provide regular venues for cartoonists to sell and trade their books, easing the burden of shipping costs or the difficulty of finding distribution. And the self-publishing tradition has made many cartoonists savvier about the entrepreneurial aspect of being an artist than their counterparts in other creative fields.

From the very start, comics self-publishing has been a crucial route to the big-leagues. Comics is a devilishly hard medium to master, and self-publishing can form a sort of internship or apprenticeship. At the same time, those apprentice efforts can be incredibly interesting and worth reading, so the committed comics audience (and there has always been an insanely committed audience for comics) seeks out these small-run efforts and is willing to value them on the same level as comics published by established houses. In fact, it's quite common for self-publishers of 'zines and minicomics to evolve into full-fledged publishers.

It seems to us that the fact that comics is a medium that grew in symbiotic tandem with reproduction technologies and embraces self-publishing has allowed cartoonists to take early and easily to new technologies like the Web and developing digital platforms. Print cartoonists started promoting and putting their work online from the get-go, and Scott McCloud trumpeted the creative potential of comics created specifically for the Web and its "infinite canvas." What's surprising is what a huge world webcomics has become in the last ten years, and how independent of the pre-existing comics scene it is. That is, while certain cartoonists from the print world have certainly established a presence on the Internet, a huge parallel scene has grown up that has very little interaction with the pre-Internet comics world. These young artists are inspired by a variety of sources, including manga and animé, video games, and computer geek culture—much more so, perhaps, than by Spider-Man, Tintin, or Mr. Natural. At this point, there are artists and fans whose frame of reference seems to be entirely composed of webcomics and its immediately associated subcultures. We increasingly encounter students at the School of Visual Arts and other places we teach who are completely unschooled about even the basics of comic book history, yet have encyclopedic knowledge of this still-young webcomics scene. It's exciting, if also a little alarming: we hope that some of this particular subculture's continued growth will include broadening its horizons a little and bridging the gap that seems to separate it from the rest of the comics world.

We are therefore excited that this year's volume features for the first time a piece by an artist who emerged entirely from the webcomics scene (as opposed to a comic by a print-based cartoonist that happened to appear online, such as "Manifesto," by Gabrielle Bell, also in this volume). We checked out Kate Beaton's *Hark! A Vagrant* after hearing buzz about it and were instantly won over by its cleverness and some-times gut-splitting humor. We don't know much about Beaton, but it seems she was beckoned by the same inspired-amateur, DIY spirit that led young artists (your editors included) to minicomics and photocopy machines a generation or so back.

The Best American Comics 2011 represents a selection of the outstanding comics pub-lished in North America between September 1, 2009, and August 31, 2010. As you can tell from the preceding paragraphs, we series editors are forever in search of comics in as many formats and publications as we can find, from hand-produced minicomics to individual pamphlet issues to graphic novels and collections to webcomics. Our goal is to put as much interesting and worthwhile material in front of our guest editors as they can stand to read through. This includes works that we consider to be excel-lent by reasonable objective standards, but it also certainly includes comics we have a particular fondness for, as well as left-field choices that may not be our cup of tea but may turn out to be someone else's "best"—and in particular, the guest editor's. Guest editors will sometimes seek out material on their own as well. The guest editor makes the final selections from this large and varied pool of titles. Idiosyncracy is encouraged.

One of the things we love most about this series is the way it changes from year to year. Each volume is indisputably the best of that year—as seen through one particular pair of eyes. And that vision of the guest editor is the most valuable and intriguing aspect of the ongoing series.

Our quest to bring notice to the very notable list of Notable Comics at the back of each Best American volume continues: this year, we've begun posting mini-reviews, with links to authors' and publishers' sites, cover and interior images, and some note as to age-appropriateness, to our teaching blog, dw-wp.com. As we write this, we're in the midst of posting all of 2010's Notables, and we plan to follow up with 2011. And of course you can also find the complete list on the Best American Comics website with as many links as we could find to help you track down these often-obscure publications. Remember: the idiosyncrasy of guest editors' visions of the "best" means that in another year, any of the Notables might have been one of the main selections.

And speaking of guest editors, every year is an adventure with a new partner, and we can't say enough about what a pleasure it was to share this year with Alison Bechdel. Alison approached the work with purpose and incredible organization (her use of a spreadsheet to keep track of her choices will forever endear her to Jessica's heart). She also allowed us more insight into her thinking than we've had with other editors, and it was fascinating to peep into the kinds of Solomonic judgments that are part and parcel of the guest editor's difficult job.

We're also often starstruck a bit by our guest editors, and Alison, though a friend, is no exception. *Fun Home* is one of the best graphic novels in the English language. In 2006, Jessica had the opportunity to read it prepublication and simply could not shut up about it. It seemed like ages before everyone else had read it and knew what the heck she was talking about. Of course, we knew and admired Alison's excellent comics long before *Fun Home*. Her seminal chronicle of lesbian lives and loves, *Dykes to Watch Out For,* began in 1983 and has appeared in many of the formats we described above: alternative newspaper strip, book collections, and, from early on, as a webcomic.

As always, we hope you'll submit your own comics or spread the word to friends and acquaintances to do so. Here are the submission guidelines: comics eligible for consideration must have been published in the eligibility period either on paper or electronically, in English, by a North American author, or one who makes his or her home here. As this 2011 volume hits the shelves, we will have already passed the deadline for the 2012 volume and will be on to collecting for the 2013 volume, whose eligibility window is September 1, 2011, through August 31, 2012.

A note about webcomics (and comics on the Web): it's especially difficult for us to determine which online comics are eligible based on print date. We appreciate very much, therefore, getting dated submissions from Web cartoonists. Printed submissions can be sent to the address below. Digital submissions can be made in the form of a PDF of comics published in the eligibility window, with each comic labeled with the exact date it was published online. Better yet, you might make a subselection of what you consider to be your best strips from the year or send a self-contained continuity as long as it appeared in the eligibility period. You can mail a CD of the PDF to us, or you can e-mail a download link to bestamericancomics@hmhpub.com.

All comics should be labeled with their release date and contact information and mailed to us at the following address:

Jessica Abel and Matt Madden
Series Editors
The Best American Comics
Houghton Mifflin Harcourt Publishing Co.
215 Park Avenue South
New York, NY 10003

Further information is available on the Best American Comics website: bestamericancomics.com.

We'd like to thank all the people who helped us with this volume, starting with the excellent team at Houghton Mifflin Harcourt: our excellent editor Meagan Stacey, our production team of Christopher Moisan, Beth Burleigh Fuller, and David Futato, and our submissions coordinator Tom Bouman. Thanks also to our great studio assistants, Rel Finkelstein, Leah Perrotta, and especially JP Kim and Hilary Allison; and of course to all the artists and publishers from all over who sent in submissions.

JESSICA ABEL and MATT MADDEN

Introduction

ONE OF THE REASONS I BECAME A CARTOONIST WAS SO THAT I COULD WRITE AND DRAW FREE FROM THE KIND OF CRITICAL SCRUTINY THAT I WAS SURE WOULD WITHER ME IF I DARED TO ENTER THE LISTS OF THE FINE ART OR LITERARY WRITING WORLDS. COMICS WAS A DARK, DISREPUTABLE PLACE, FAR FROM THE GLARE AND SELF-IMPORTANCE OF STUFFY GALLERIES AND LITTLE MAGAZINES. YOU COULD DO WHAT YOU WANTED HERE, AND ALTHOUGH THERE MIGHT BE OCCASIONAL FISTICUFFS, NO TWERP FROM *ARTFORUM* WOULD EVER DISMISS YOU WITH A CAUSTIC REVIEW.

THERE IS A CERTAIN POETIC JUSTICE, THEN, TO FINDING MYSELF IN THE POSITION OF DECIDING WHOSE COMICS MERIT INCLUSION IN THE LATEST HARD-COVER, FULL-COLOR ANNUAL VOLUME OF *BEST AMERICAN COMICS*. THE EMINENTLY REPUTABLE *BEST AMERICAN SERIES*, OF COURSE, IS ONLY ONE OF MANY GUARDIANS OF HIGH CULTURE, ALONG WITH *ARTFORUM* AND INNUMERABLE MUSEUMS, GALLERIES, AND LITERARY QUARTERLIES, TO FLING OPEN THEIR GATES TO THIS NEWLY LEGITIMIZED MEDIUM.

IT'S TEMPTING TO SPEAK WISTFULLY OF THOSE SHADOWY DAYS ON THE MARGINS OF SOCIETY. HOW HEADY IT WAS TO KNOW—ESPECIALLY BECAUSE NO ONE ELSE DID—THAT WE WERE THE FUTURE. THE SENSE OF MISSION, THE TIGHT-KNIT COMMUNITY, THE FURTIVE FORAYS TO THAT SHELF IN THE BACK OF THE SHOP WHERE A HANDFUL OF FAMILIAR TITLES BECKONED. THE LINGERING ACCUSATION THAT WE WERE SEDUCING THE INNOCENT! OH, THE AWKWARD, SENSUOUS CHARM OF SMUDGED BLACK INK ON ALREADY YELLOWING NEWSPRINT!

BUT I WILL NOT INDULGE MY NOSTALGIC YEARNING FOR A LOST, LOWBROW PURITY. LIKE MOST NOSTALGIC YEARNINGS, IT'S FOR SOMETHING THAT WAS NEVER REALLY THERE IN THE FIRST PLACE. AND BESIDES, I'M CERTAIN THAT EVEN THE MOST SMOTHERING ESTABLISHMENT EMBRACE COULD NOT BEGIN TO SQUEEZE THE LIFE OUT OF THIS VITAL MEDIUM. STILL, IT'S A QUESTION WORTH ASKING: IF YOU HAVE SPENT A LONG TIME RESISTING THE STATUS QUO (**SEE FIG. 1**)—WHETHER IT'S IN ART, SOCIETY, OR THE POLITICAL WORLD—WHAT HAPPENS WHEN THAT STATUS QUO AT LAST GIVES WAY? (**SEE FIG. 2**)

Fig. 1.

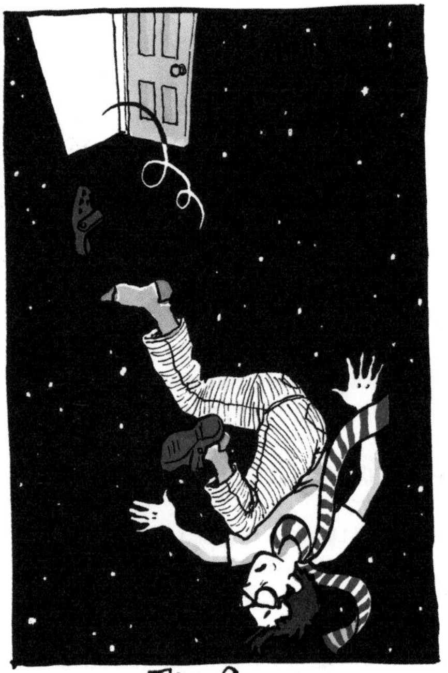

Fig. 2.

A UNIVERSE OF POSSIBILITY OPENS UP—WHICH OF COURSE IS WHAT YOU ALWAYS WANTED, BUT IT CAN STILL BE A SOMEWHAT DISCONCERTING EXPERIENCE. THERE'S A SORT OF NEWTONIAN TENDENCY, ESPECIALLY IF YOU'VE BEEN AT IT A LONG TIME, TO CONTINUE CLINGING BITTERLY TO YOUR RESISTANCE EVEN AFTER THE BATTLE HAS BEEN WON. THE YOUNGER GENERATION, HOWEVER—THE ONE HARD ON YOUR HEELS—WILL HAVE NO QUALMS ABOUT STAKING THEIR CLAIM IN THIS NEW TERRITORY.

IN MY OWN CAREER, I'VE BEEN AT BOTH ENDS OF THIS DIALECTIC PROGRESSION—IT'S VERY CLEAR TO ME THAT THE UNDERGROUND COMICS MOVEMENT MADE MY OWN WORK POSSIBLE. I GOT MY FIRST GLIMPSE OF R. CRUMB AT AGE 8 ON MY FATHER'S *CHEAP THRILLS* ALBUM. I SPENT MY LATENCY STAGE MARINATING IN *MAD* MAGAZINE—OLD COLLECTIONS FROM THE FIFTIES AS WELL AS THE LATEST ISSUES. IN MY ADOLESCENCE I GOT OCCASIONAL GLIMPSES OF THE *FABULOUS FURRY FREAK BROTHERS* AT THE HOME OF AN UNSUPERVISED FRIEND, IN COLLEGE I DISCOVERED *AMERICAN SPLENDOR*, AND AFTER GRADUATION I BEGAN SNAPPING UP LATE-UNDERGROUND TITLES LIKE *GAY COMIX* AND *TITS & CLITS* THE SECOND THEY CAME OFF THE PRESS. BY THE TIME I BEGAN PUBLISHING MY OWN YOUTHFUL EFFORTS A FEW YEARS LATER, *RAW* MAGAZINE AND OTHER ALTERNATIVE COMICS EXPERIMENTS HAD PERMANENTLY ALTERED THE LANDSCAPE.

BUT THE CULTURAL WOODCHIPPER GRINDS ON, CONSUMING EVERYTHING THAT LIES IN ITS PATH AND PULPING IT INTO A FRESH BLANK PAGE FOR THE NEXT GENERATION. GROWING UP ON *MAD* WAS ONE THING. IMAGINE THE SEETHING PHANTASMAGORIC PSYCHE OF THE CARTOONIST EXPOSED AS A TENDER INFANT TO THE PERFIDIOUS POSTMODERN PERMUTATIONS OF GARY PANTER'S SET FOR *PEE-WEE'S PLAYHOUSE*.

WELL, YOU DON'T HAVE TO IMAGINE IT. YOU WILL SEE IT SOMEWHERE IN THESE PAGES. IN JUST THE PAST DECADE, COMICS HAVE UNDERGONE A TRULY ALARMING GROWTH SPURT, NOT JUST IN THE QUANTITY OF NEW WORK COMING OUT, BUT IN THE LEVELS OF FORMAL AND TECHNICAL INNOVATION BEING ATTAINED. IT CAN BE A DAUNTING PLACE TO FIND YOURSELF **(SEE FIG. 3)**, ESPECIALLY IF YOU GOT INTO THIS WHOLE CARTOONING THING BECAUSE IT SEEMED LIKE SUCH A LAID-BACK, AESTHETIC CRITERIA-FREE SCENE. I'M NOT SURE I WOULD HAVE THE NERVE TO ENTER THE FRAY AT THIS POINT IF I WEREN'T ALREADY IN IT. AT MID-CAREER, EVEN WITH SOME

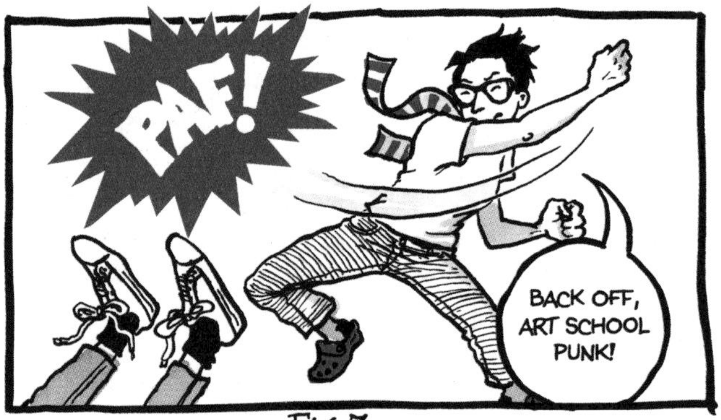
PAF!
BACK OFF, ART SCHOOL PUNK!

Fig. 3.

SUCCESS UNDER MY BELT, I AM OCCASIONALLY PARALYZED WITH ANXIETY.

IN FACT, I WAS IN JUST SUCH A STATE LAST SUMMER, AND FALLING FURTHER AND FURTHER BEHIND SCHEDULE WITH MY OWN WORK **(SEE FIG. 4)**, WHEN THE FIRST BATCH OF *BEST AMERICAN* SUBMISSIONS ARRIVED FROM JESSICA AND MATT.

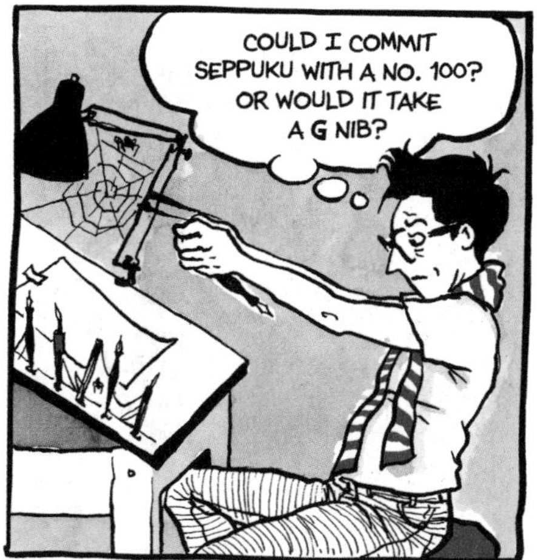
COULD I COMMIT SEPPUKU WITH A NO. 100? OR WOULD IT TAKE A G NIB?

Fig. 4.

IN MY BLOCKED CONDITION, WHAT EXQUISITE AGONY IT WAS TO READ BOOK AFTER ANTHOLOGY AFTER PAMPHLET COMIC AFTER CLEVERLY PACKAGED MINI, EACH ONE MORE VITAL, FRESH, AND INGENIOUS THAN THE LAST. IF I HAD BEEN PARALYZED, NOW I FELT LIKE I'D BEEN TASED. **(SEE FIG. 5)**

I WAS PREPARED FOR POWERFUL WORK BY THE USUAL SUSPECTS, BUT WHO WERE ALL THESE OTHER PEOPLE? APPARENTLY EVERYONE AND HIS BROTHER (AND WITH LESS FREQUENCY, HIS SISTER—MORE ON THIS LATER) WAS KNOCKING OFF GRAPHIC NOVELS, GRAPHIC MEMOIRS, GRAPHIC JOURNALISM, AND WEIRD GENRE-BENDING HYBRIDS OF ALL THESE THINGS, WITH SKILL AND FEROCIOUS INDUSTRY. PERHAPS I HADN'T BEEN KEEPING UP AS CLOSELY AS I SHOULD HAVE. (BUT HONESTLY, WHO HAS TIME TO READ COMICS WHEN IT TAKES SO MUCH TIME TO MAKE THEM?)

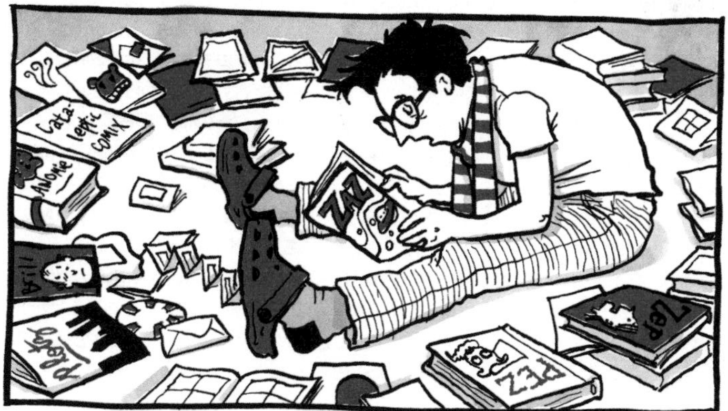

Fig. 5.

IN ANY CASE, I SET ASIDE MY OWN LABORIOUS, CONSTIPATED PROJECT AND PLUNGED FURTHER INTO READING THIS FRESH CROP OF WORK. OVER THE NEXT WEEKS AND MONTHS, MY TORMENT TURNED TO EXHILARATION. SEEING OTHER ARTISTS EXPLOIT THE PECULIAR ALCHEMY OF WORDS AND PICTURES ON THE PAGE IN SUCH VARIETY AND PROFUSION, WITH SUCH JOY AND CONFIDENCE, WAS INFECTIOUS. **(SEE FIG. 6)**

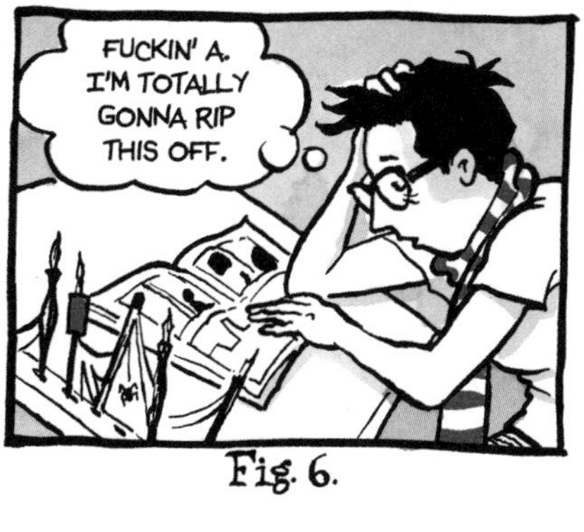
FUCKIN' A. I'M TOTALLY GONNA RIP THIS OFF.

Fig. 6.

ART AND LANGUAGE ARE ALWAYS IN FLUX OF COURSE, BUT THE SOMEWHAT YOUNGER MODE OF COMICS SEEMS TO BE IN A PARTICULARLY MOLTEN STATE. CLOSE READERS MAY OBSERVE RIVULETS OF LAVA COOLING INTO NEW CONVENTIONS RIGHT BEFORE THEIR EYES. THINGS LIKE THE SPEECHLESS ELLIPSIS FROM MANGA, AND THE WAREIAN SOUND EFFECTS "SHUT" AND "STEP," I NOTICED AS I READ,

HAVE BECOME PART OF THE VERNACULAR. **(SEE FIG. 7)**

I FOUND MYSELF RICHLY REWARDED BY GENRES I DON'T NATURALLY GRAVITATE TOWARD, LIKE SCIENCE FICTION. I BECAME SO DISORIENTED BY FUTURISTIC WORLDS, ALTERNATE REALITIES, AND ZOMBIES THAT I WOULD FORGET ABOUT MY OWN PALTRY TROUBLES FOR DAYS AT A STRETCH. **(SEE FIG. 8)**

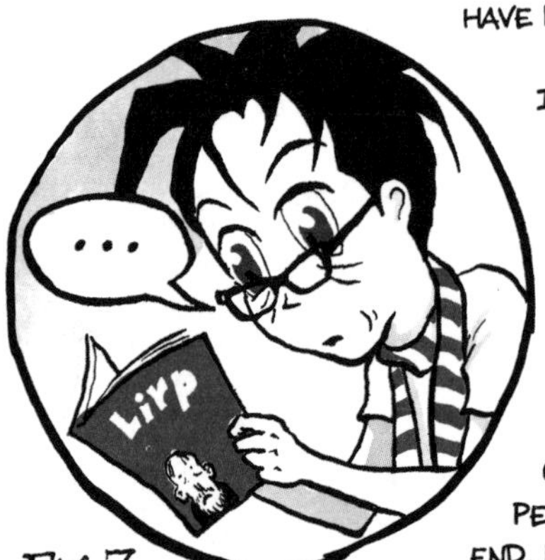
...
LIRP

Fig. 7.

THEN CAME THE HARD PART. THERE WAS ONLY ROOM FOR ABOUT A QUARTER OF THIS STUFF IN THE BOOK. BUT I WILL NOT BORE YOU WITH LAMENTATIONS ABOUT HOW PAINFUL IT WAS TO EXCLUDE SO MUCH GOOD WORK, OR HOW MEANINGLESS AN INDICATOR ONE PERSON'S PECULIAR TASTE IS, OR HOW CAPRICIOUS, IN THE END, MY CHOICES PROBABLY WERE. LET'S TAKE THAT AS READ.

BUT IF YOU LIKE WHAT YOU SEE HERE, PLEASE ALSO CHECK OUT THE NOTABLE COMICS LISTED AT THE BACK OF THE BOOK. AND IF YOU **DON'T** LIKE WHAT YOU SEE HERE, **DEFINITELY** CHECK OUT THE NOTABLE COMICS LISTED AT THE BACK OF THE BOOK. SOMETHING THERE WILL BLOW YOU AWAY.

ONE TRICKY THING ABOUT THIS SERIES IS THAT THE SUBMISSIONS VARY WILDLY IN LENGTH AND FORMAT, AND SOMETIMES THOSE FACTORS MAKE A PIECE IMPOSSIBLE TO INCLUDE, NO MATTER HOW GOOD IT IS. DAN CLOWES'S *WILSON* IS CERTAINLY AMONG THE BEST COMICS OF THE PAST YEAR, BUT NOT EVEN A LENGTHY SWATH OF ITS MORDANT ONE-PAGE GAG STRIPS COULD DO JUSTICE TO THE COMPLEX UNFOLDING OF CLOWES'S FRACTURED NARRATIVE. LIKEWISE, ALEXIS FREDERICK-FROST'S PLAYFUL, BUSINESS-ENVELOPE-SIZED MINICOMIC *THE VOYAGE* WOULD SIMPLY NOT WORK ON THESE VERTICAL PAGES.

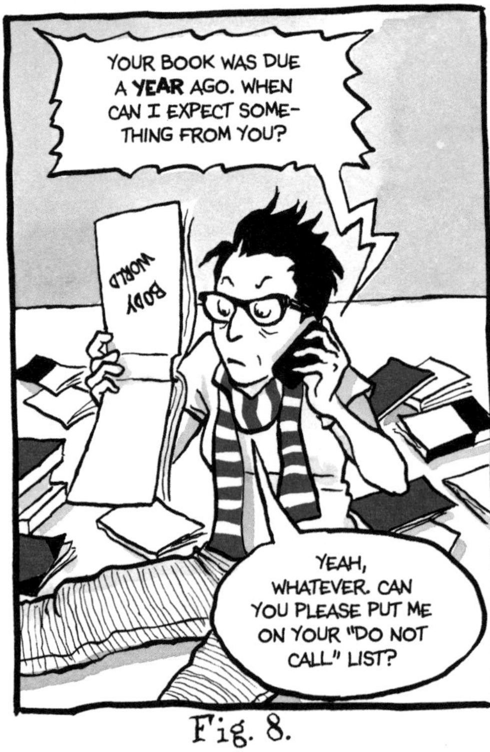
YOUR BOOK WAS DUE A **YEAR** AGO. WHEN CAN I EXPECT SOMETHING FROM YOU?
YEAH, WHATEVER. CAN YOU PLEASE PUT ME ON YOUR "DO NOT CALL" LIST?

Fig. 8.

I FOUND MYSELF GRAVITATING TOWARD WORK THAT DID NOT FIT NEATLY INTO ONE CATEGORY. BRENDAN LEACH'S *PTERODACTYL HUNTERS* IS SURELY FICTION, BUT HIS NEW YORK CITY IN THE YEAR 1904 RESONATES WITH ARCHIVAL VERISIMILITUDE. *MONSTERS,* BY KEN DAHL, IS AN ELASTIC WORK OF CREATIVE NONFICTION THAT COMBINES MEMOIR WITH A GRAPHIC (AND GRAPHICALLY!) EDUCATIONAL TREATISE ON SEXUALLY TRANSMITTED HERPES. GABRIELLE BELL'S *MANIFESTATION* IS A CURIOUS AMALGAM OF AUTOBIOGRAPHY AND THEORETICAL CRITIQUE WITH A LARGE DOLLOP OF FICTION ON TOP. JOE SACCO'S *FOOTNOTES IN GAZA* IS NOT ONLY POWERFUL INVESTIGATIVE JOURNALISM AND A MODERN HISTORY TEXT, IT'S A VIRTUOSIC FEAT OF HISTORIOGRAPHY—A PAINSTAKING DISSECTION OF THE SPACE BETWEEN WHAT REALLY HAPPENED,

AND THE NARRATIVES, OFFICIAL AND UNOFFICIAL, OF WHAT HAPPENED. CHRIS WARE'S *JORDAN W. LINT TO THE AGE 65,* AN EXCERPT FROM THE COMPLETE LIFE OF JORDAN W. LINT, IS A COUP DE MAÎTRE OF FICTIONAL REALIZATION. BUT THIS PASSAGE MAKES A FUNNY AND INCISIVE—YET SOMEHOW AT THE SAME TIME DEEPLY AFFECTING—DETOUR INTO THE PAGES OF THE GRAPHIC MEMOIR LINT'S SON HAS WRITTEN ABOUT *HIS* LIFE.

I STARTED NOTICING THAT IN FACT A LOT OF THESE COMICS WERE COMMENTING ON COMICS IN SOME WAY, AND BEGAN A SEPARATE PILE FOR THEM. THE EXCERPT FROM MICHAEL DE FORGE'S *LOSE #1* DEPICTS A HELLISH DESCENT INTO THE COLLECTIVE CARTOON UNCONSCIOUS. (NOTE: WE HAD TO REPLACE THIS AT THE LAST MINUTE BECAUSE OF PERMISSIONS ISSUES!) JOEY ALISON SAYERS'S *PET CAT* INVESTIGATES THE SOULLESS REITERATIONS THAT HAVE COME TO DEFINE THE MORE COMMERCIAL REACHES OF THE COMICSPHERE. KATE BEATON PITS COMICS AGAINST FICTION IN HER SHRIVELING REDUCTION OF *THE GREAT GATSBY* TO NINE THREE-PANEL GAG STRIPS. I SUPPOSE GABRIELLE BELL'S *MANIFESTATION* COULD ALSO BE INCLUDED IN THIS METACOMIC CATEGORY, GIVEN ITS REFERENCE TO THE POSSIBILITY OF ITS OWN INCLUSION IN THIS VOLUME.

BUT THAT'S NOT WHY I CHOSE TO INCLUDE IT IN THIS VOLUME. I CHOSE IT BECAUSE IT WAS GOOD. AND I DECIDED TO LEAD OFF WITH IT BECAUSE IT SAYS SOME THINGS I WOULD LIKE TO SAY IN THIS INTRODUCTION, ONLY MUCH BETTER. WHY, THIRTY YEARS AFTER THE FIRST ISSUE OF *WIMMEN'S COMIX* APPEARED, IS THERE IS STILL SUCH A MARKED GENDER DISPARITY IN THIS FIELD? **(SEE FIG. 9)** BELL'S FUNNY STORY ISN'T ABOUT COMICS IN PARTICULAR, BUT IT ADDRESSES SOME OF THE ONTOLOGICAL COMPLICATIONS OF BEING A WOMAN WITH A GRACEFUL LUCIDITY OF BOTH THOUGHT AND LINE.

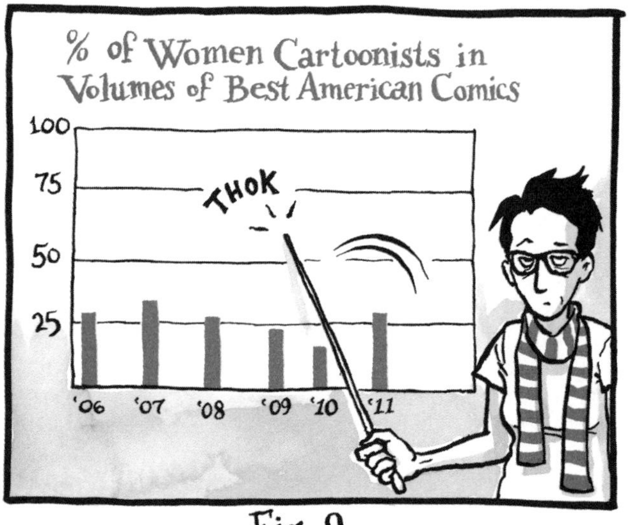
% of Women Cartoonists in Volumes of Best American Comics
100
75
50
25
THOK
'06
'07
'08
'09
'10
'11
Fig. 9.

THERE ARE LOTS OF COMPLICATED REASONS WHY THESE NUMBERS REMAIN SO DISMAL. IT SHOULD ALSO BE NOTED, WHILE I'M AT IT, THAT THERE ARE ZERO AFRICAN-AMERICAN CONTRIBUTORS TO THIS VOLUME. BUT ONE THING THAT'S CLEAR IS THAT CERTAIN KIDS ARE LAYING DOWN THEIR CRAYONS AND MARKERS AT A HIGHER RATE THAN OTHER KIDS. AS LONG AS THE PLAYING FIELD IS WONKY, THIS DISPARITY WILL PERSIST. THE VERY LEAST WE CAN DO IS KEEP CALLING ATTENTION TO IT.

FIVE YEARS AGO I WAS INVITED TO BRYN MAWR COLLEGE TO BE ON A PANEL WITH CARTOONISTS JESSICA ABEL, GABRIELLE BELL, AND LAUREN WEINSTEIN. BRYN MAWR IS A WOMEN'S COLLEGE, AND OBVIOUSLY THE FOUR OF US WERE INVITED, IN PART, BECAUSE WE ARE WOMEN. BUT AFTER THE EVENT WAS OVER, SOMEONE POINTED OUT THAT NOBODY HAD ASKED US THE PERENNIAL QUESTION, "WHY AREN'T THERE MORE WOMEN CARTOONISTS?" WE ALL LAUGHED WITH GIDDY, RETROACTIVE RELIEF. WE HADN'T EVEN NOTICED. WE HAD SPENT THE ENTIRE EVENING *SIMPLY DISCUSSING OUR WORK.*

IT WAS NOT AN EPOCH-MAKING BREAKTHROUGH, JUST A SMALL MOMENT. BUT IT GAVE ME A DELIGHTFUL GLIMPSE OF FREEDOM. AND IT'S THAT KIND OF LIBERATION THAT I WANT FOR

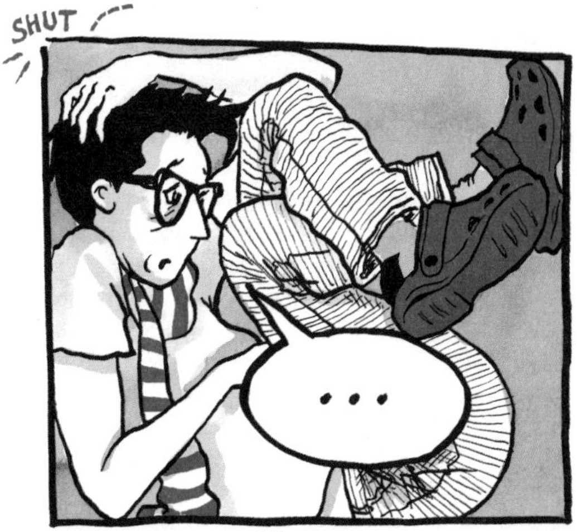
SHUT
...

Fig. 10.

COMICS, TOO. FREEDOM FROM HAVING TO EXPLAIN OR DEFEND OURSELVES. FREEDOM FROM BEING CONFINED TO ONE SECTION OF THE BOOKSTORE. EVEN FREEDOM—ONE DAY, MAYBE—FROM BOOKS LIKE THIS ONE. NO ONE WANTS TO BE PUT IN A BOX, NOT EVEN A CONSTRAINT-LOVING CARTOONIST. **(SEE FIG. 10)**

CATEGORIES, WHETHER THEY'RE DEFINING A GENDER, A GENRE, AN ART FORM, A NATIONALITY, OR A FIT OF JEANS, HAVE THEIR USES. BUT WHEN AS AN ARTIST YOU ALLOW YOURSELF TO REMAIN CIRCUMSCRIBED BY A CATEGORY, WITHOUT SEEING OR UNDERSTANDING ITS RELATION TO OTHER CATEGORIES, YOU'RE PROBABLY NOT DOING YOUR BEST WORK.

IN THE END, THAT WAS ONE OF MY CRITERIA AS I SELECTED THE PIECES IN THIS BOOK. MOST OF THESE CARTOONISTS ARE LOOKING JUST A LITTLE BEYOND THE HORIZON. IT DOESN'T TAKE ANYTHING AWAY FROM COMICS TO RECOGNIZE THAT SOME OF WHAT YOU WILL READ HERE IS ALSO GREAT LITERATURE.

GO AHEAD, DIVE IN. YOU PROBABLY WON'T READ IN ORDER. YOU'LL PROBABLY JUST FLIP THROUGH AND START WITH SOMETHING THAT CATCHES YOUR EYE. YOU'LL FOLLOW A SEQUENCE OF DRAWINGS SEPARATED BY GUTTERS INTO A PARTICULAR PACE AND RHYTHM ON THE PAGE. WHETHER A PANEL INCLUDES WORDS OR NOT, YOU WILL BE READING. WHETHER A PIECE WAS ORIGINALLY PRINTED AND DISTRIBUTED BY A MAJOR PUBLISHING HOUSE OR STAPLED TOGETHER BY ITS CREATOR, IT WILL TELL YOU SOMETHING ABOUT THE WORLD.

THE DARK, DISREPUTABLE PLACE I WAS DRAWN TO IN MY YOUTH HAS GOTTEN PRETTY BRIGHT INDEED. BUT MY EYES ARE STARTING TO ADJUST.

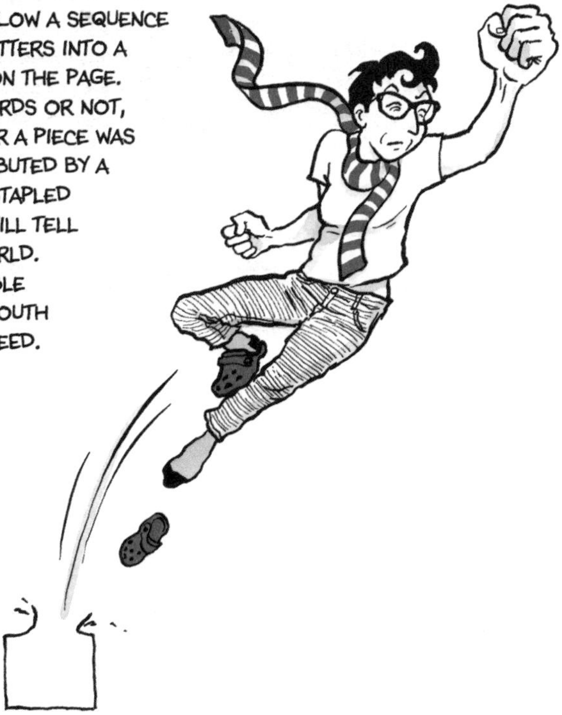

ALISON BECHDEL

THE BEST AMERICAN

Comics 2011

MANIFESTATION

from

gabriellebell.com

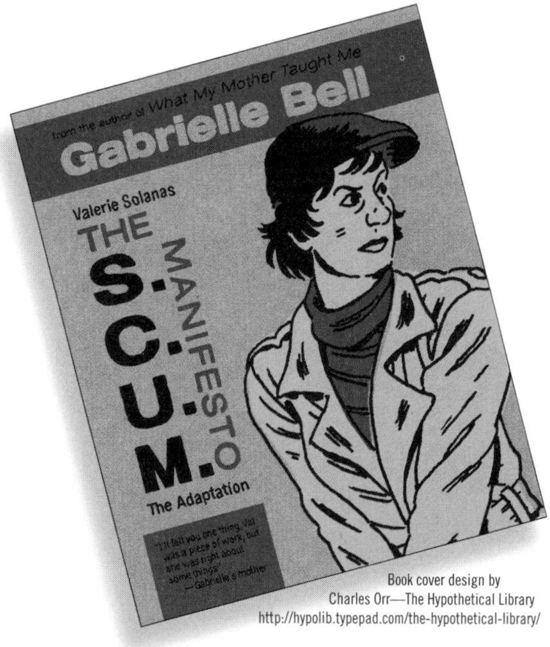
from the author of What My Mother Taught Me
Gabrielle Bell
Valerie Solanas
THE
S.C.U.M.
MANIFESTO
The Adaptation
"I'll tell you one thing, Val was a piece of work, but she was right about some things."
—Gabrielle's mother

Book cover design by
Charles Orr—The Hypothetical Library
http://hypolib.typepad.com/the-hypothetical-library/

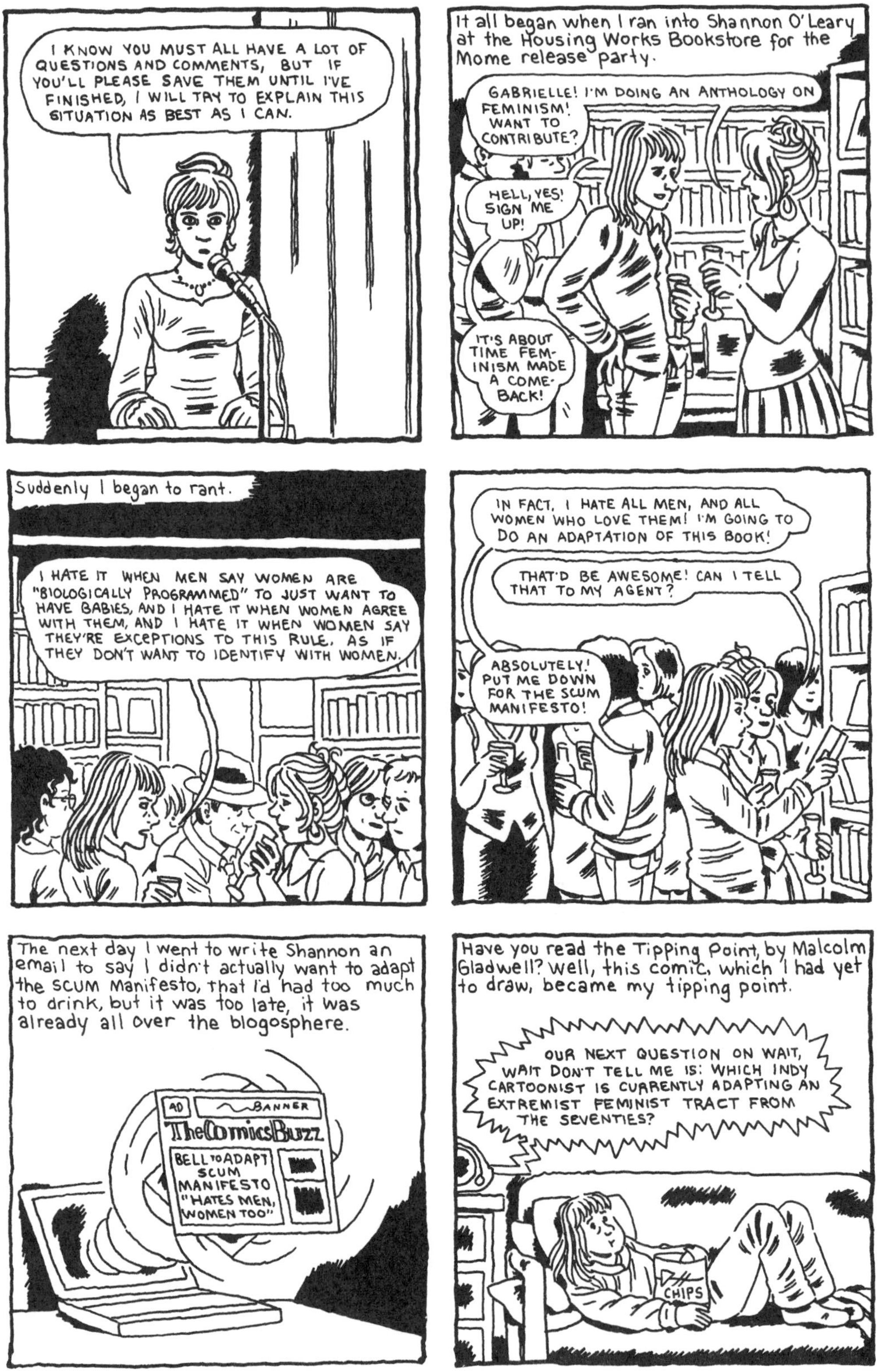
I KNOW YOU MUST ALL HAVE A LOT OF QUESTIONS AND COMMENTS, BUT IF YOU'LL PLEASE SAVE THEM UNTIL I'VE FINISHED, I WILL TRY TO EXPLAIN THIS SITUATION AS BEST AS I CAN.
It all began when I ran into Shannon O'Leary at the Housing Works Bookstore for the Mome release party.
GABRIELLE! I'M DOING AN ANTHOLOGY ON FEMINISM! WANT TO CONTRIBUTE?
HELL, YES! SIGN ME UP!
IT'S ABOUT TIME FEMINISM MADE A COMEBACK!
Suddenly I began to rant.
I HATE IT WHEN MEN SAY WOMEN ARE "BIOLOGICALLY PROGRAMMED" TO JUST WANT TO HAVE BABIES, AND I HATE IT WHEN WOMEN AGREE WITH THEM, AND I HATE IT WHEN WOMEN SAY THEY'RE EXCEPTIONS TO THIS RULE, AS IF THEY DON'T WANT TO IDENTIFY WITH WOMEN.
IN FACT, I HATE ALL MEN, AND ALL WOMEN WHO LOVE THEM! I'M GOING TO DO AN ADAPTATION OF THIS BOOK!
THAT'D BE AWESOME! CAN I TELL THAT TO MY AGENT?
ABSOLUTELY! PUT ME DOWN FOR THE SCUM MANIFESTO!
The next day I went to write Shannon an email to say I didn't actually want to adapt the SCUM Manifesto, that I'd had too much to drink, but it was too late, it was already all over the blogosphere.
AD
BANNER
The Comics Buzz
BELL TO ADAPT SCUM MANIFESTO "HATES MEN, WOMEN TOO"
Have you read the Tipping Point, by Malcolm Gladwell? Well, this comic, which I had yet to draw, became my tipping point.
OUR NEXT QUESTION ON WAIT, WAIT DON'T TELL ME IS: WHICH INDY CARTOONIST IS CURRENTLY ADAPTING AN EXTREMIST FEMINIST TRACT FROM THE SEVENTIES?
CHIPS

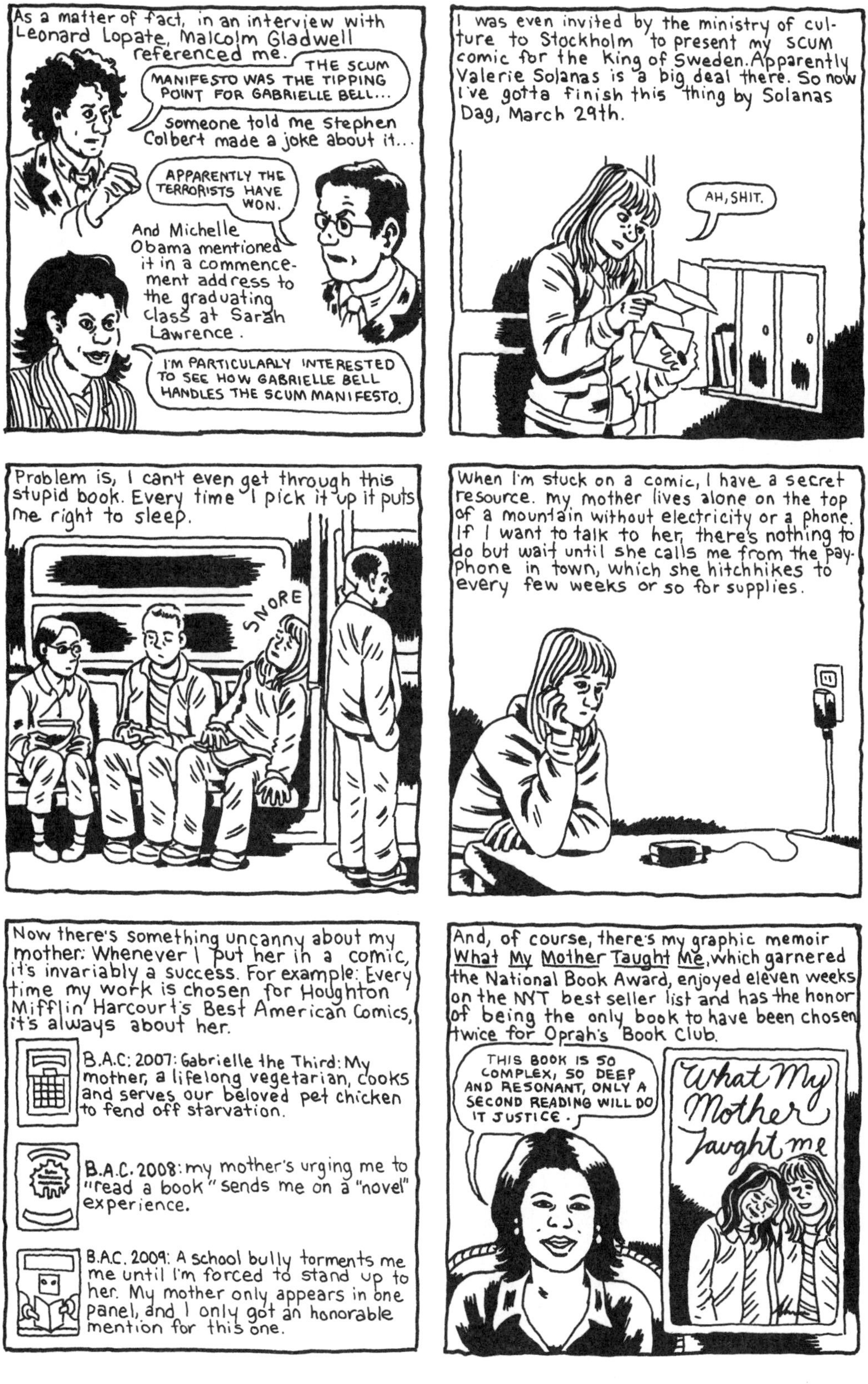
As a matter of fact, in an interview with Leonard Lopate, Malcolm Gladwell referenced me.
THE SCUM MANIFESTO WAS THE TIPPING POINT FOR GABRIELLE BELL...
Someone told me Stephen Colbert made a joke about it...
APPARENTLY THE TERRORISTS HAVE WON.
And Michelle Obama mentioned it in a commencement address to the graduating class at Sarah Lawrence.
I'M PARTICULARLY INTERESTED TO SEE HOW GABRIELLE BELL HANDLES THE SCUM MANIFESTO.
I was even invited by the ministry of culture to Stockholm to present my SCUM comic for the King of Sweden. Apparently Valerie Solanas is a big deal there. So now I've gotta finish this thing by Solanas Dag, March 29th.
AH, SHIT.
Problem is, I can't even get through this stupid book. Every time I pick it up it puts me right to sleep.
SNORE
When I'm stuck on a comic, I have a secret resource. My mother lives alone on the top of a mountain without electricity or a phone. If I want to talk to her, there's nothing to do but wait until she calls me from the payphone in town, which she hitchhikes to every few weeks or so for supplies.
Now there's something uncanny about my mother: Whenever I put her in a comic, it's invariably a success. For example: Every time my work is chosen for Houghton Mifflin Harcourt's Best American Comics, it's always about her.
B.A.C. 2007: Gabrielle the Third: My mother, a lifelong vegetarian, cooks and serves our beloved pet chicken to fend off starvation.
B.A.C. 2008: my mother's urging me to "read a book" sends me on a "novel" experience.
B.A.C. 2009: A school bully torments me until I'm forced to stand up to her. My mother only appears in one panel, and I only got an honorable mention for this one.
And, of course, there's my graphic memoir What My Mother Taught Me, which garnered the National Book Award, enjoyed eleven weeks on the NYT best seller list and has the honor of being the only book to have been chosen twice for Oprah's Book Club.
THIS BOOK IS SO COMPLEX, SO DEEP AND RESONANT, ONLY A SECOND READING WILL DO IT JUSTICE.
What My Mother Taught me

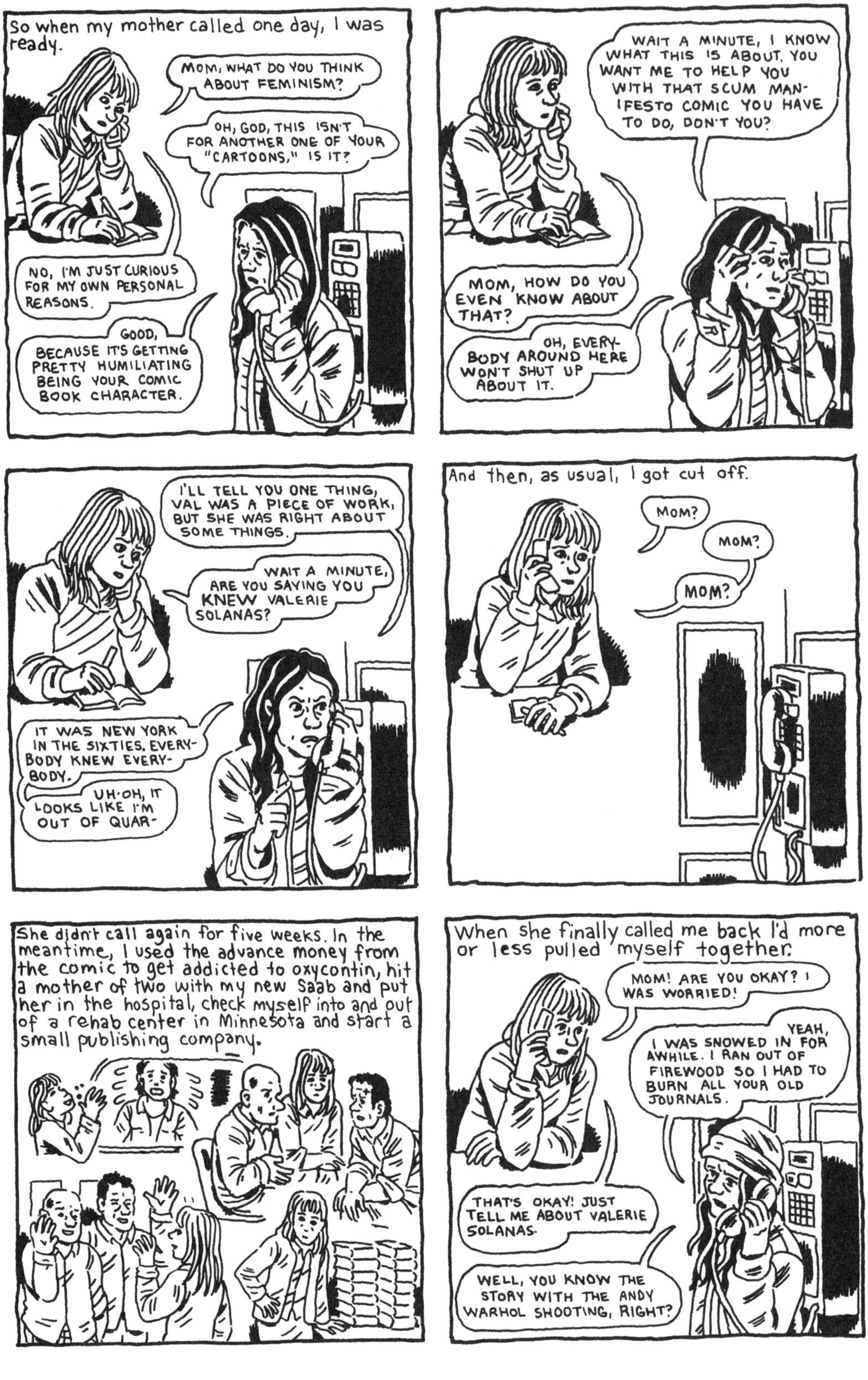
So when my mother called one day, I was ready.
MOM, WHAT DO YOU THINK ABOUT FEMINISM?
OH, GOD, THIS ISN'T FOR ANOTHER ONE OF YOUR "CARTOONS," IS IT?
NO, I'M JUST CURIOUS FOR MY OWN PERSONAL REASONS.
GOOD, BECAUSE IT'S GETTING PRETTY HUMILIATING BEING YOUR COMIC BOOK CHARACTER.
WAIT A MINUTE, I KNOW WHAT THIS IS ABOUT. YOU WANT ME TO HELP YOU WITH THAT SCUM MAN-IFESTO COMIC YOU HAVE TO DO, DON'T YOU?
MOM, HOW DO YOU EVEN KNOW ABOUT THAT?
OH, EVERY-BODY AROUND HERE WON'T SHUT UP ABOUT IT.
I'LL TELL YOU ONE THING, VAL WAS A PIECE OF WORK, BUT SHE WAS RIGHT ABOUT SOME THINGS.
WAIT A MINUTE, ARE YOU SAYING YOU KNEW VALERIE SOLANAS?
IT WAS NEW YORK IN THE SIXTIES. EVERY-BODY KNEW EVERY-BODY.
UH-OH, IT LOOKS LIKE I'M OUT OF QUAR-
And then, as usual, I got cut off.
MOM?
MOM?
MOM?
She didn't call again for five weeks. In the meantime, I used the advance money from the comic to get addicted to oxycontin, hit a mother of two with my new Saab and put her in the hospital, check myself into and out of a rehab center in Minnesota and start a small publishing company.
When she finally called me back I'd more or less pulled myself together.
MOM! ARE YOU OKAY? I WAS WORRIED!
YEAH, I WAS SNOWED IN FOR AWHILE. I RAN OUT OF FIREWOOD SO I HAD TO BURN ALL YOUR OLD JOURNALS.
THAT'S OKAY! JUST TELL ME ABOUT VALERIE SOLANAS.
WELL, YOU KNOW THE STORY WITH THE ANDY WARHOL SHOOTING, RIGHT?

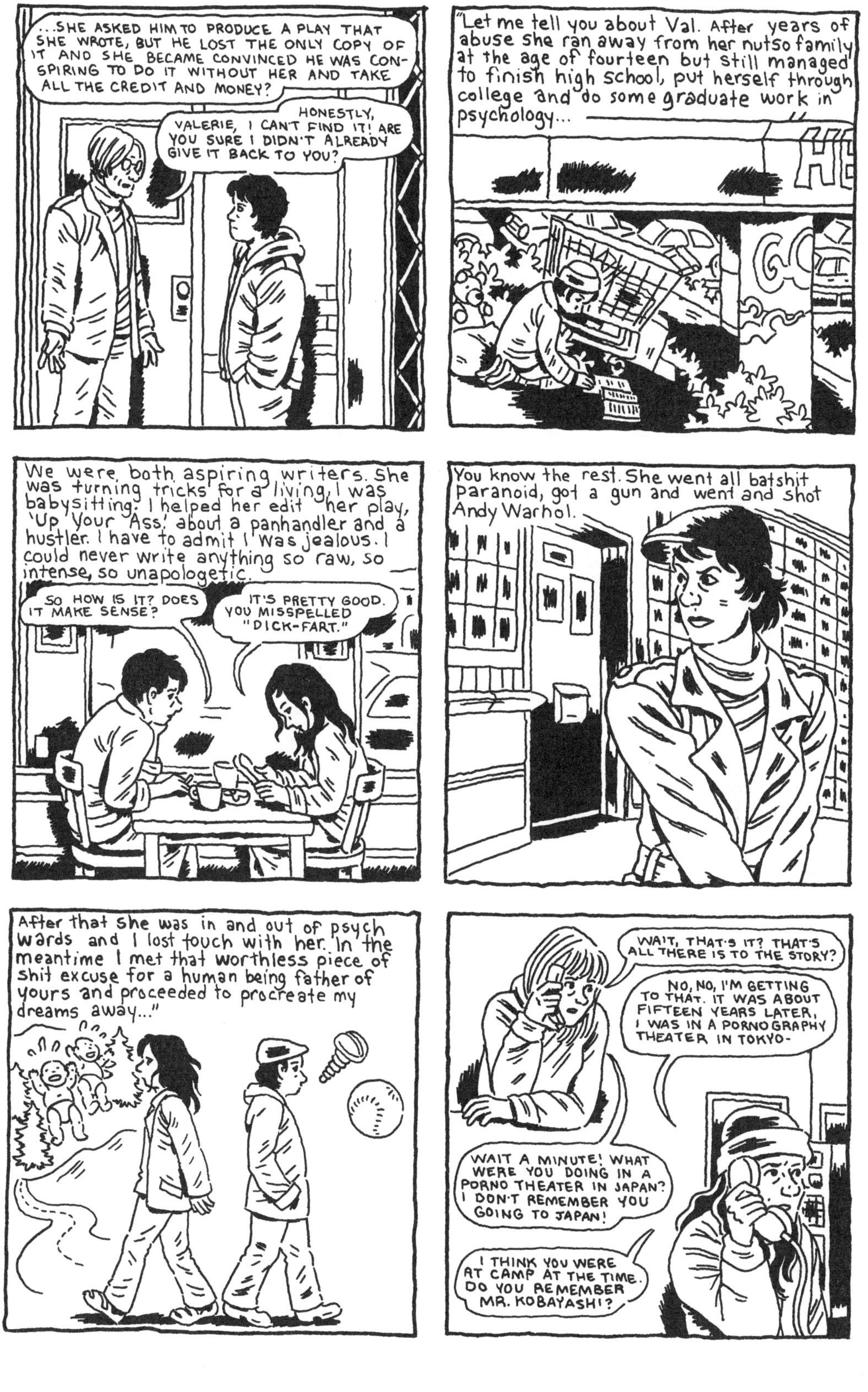
...SHE ASKED HIM TO PRODUCE A PLAY THAT SHE WROTE, BUT HE LOST THE ONLY COPY OF IT AND SHE BECAME CONVINCED HE WAS CONSPIRING TO DO IT WITHOUT HER AND TAKE ALL THE CREDIT AND MONEY?
HONESTLY, VALERIE, I CAN'T FIND IT! ARE YOU SURE I DIDN'T ALREADY GIVE IT BACK TO YOU?
"Let me tell you about Val. After years of abuse she ran away from her nutso family at the age of fourteen but still managed to finish high school, put herself through college and do some graduate work in psychology...
We were both aspiring writers. She was turning tricks for a living, I was babysitting. I helped her edit her play, 'Up Your Ass,' about a panhandler and a hustler. I have to admit I was jealous. I could never write anything so raw, so intense, so unapologetic.
SO HOW IS IT? DOES IT MAKE SENSE?
IT'S PRETTY GOOD. YOU MISSPELLED "DICK-FART."
You know the rest. She went all batshit paranoid, got a gun and went and shot Andy Warhol.
After that she was in and out of psych wards and I lost touch with her. In the meantime I met that worthless piece of shit excuse for a human being father of yours and proceeded to procreate my dreams away..."
WAIT, THAT'S IT? THAT'S ALL THERE IS TO THE STORY?
NO, NO, I'M GETTING TO THAT. IT WAS ABOUT FIFTEEN YEARS LATER, I WAS IN A PORNOGRAPHY THEATER IN TOKYO-
WAIT A MINUTE! WHAT WERE YOU DOING IN A PORNO THEATER IN JAPAN? I DON'T REMEMBER YOU GOING TO JAPAN!
I THINK YOU WERE AT CAMP AT THE TIME. DO YOU REMEMBER MR. KOBAYASHI?

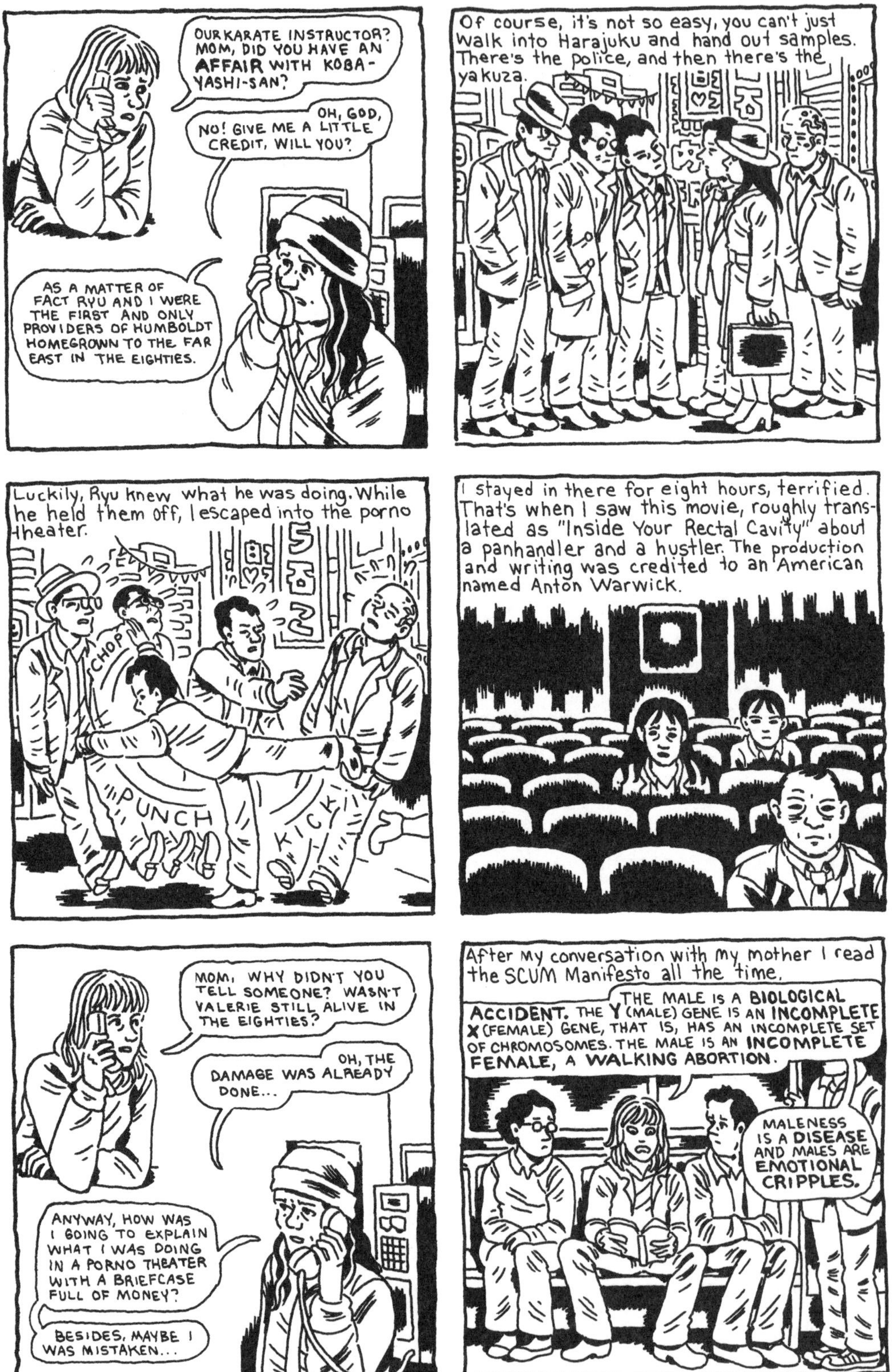

OUR KARATE INSTRUCTOR? MOM, DID YOU HAVE AN AFFAIR WITH KOBAYASHI-SAN?
NO! GIVE ME A LITTLE CREDIT, WILL YOU?
OH, GOD,
AS A MATTER OF FACT RYU AND I WERE THE FIRST AND ONLY PROVIDERS OF HUMBOLDT HOMEGROWN TO THE FAR EAST IN THE EIGHTIES.
Of course, it's not so easy, you can't just walk into Harajuku and hand out samples. There's the police, and then there's the yakuza.
Luckily, Ryu knew what he was doing. While he held them off, I escaped into the porno theater.
CHOP
PUNCH
KICK
I stayed in there for eight hours, terrified. That's when I saw this movie, roughly translated as "Inside Your Rectal Cavity" about a panhandler and a hustler. The production and writing was credited to an American named Anton Warwick.
MOM, WHY DIDN'T YOU TELL SOMEONE? WASN'T VALERIE STILL ALIVE IN THE EIGHTIES?
OH, THE DAMAGE WAS ALREADY DONE...
ANYWAY, HOW WAS I GOING TO EXPLAIN WHAT I WAS DOING IN A PORNO THEATER WITH A BRIEFCASE FULL OF MONEY?
BESIDES, MAYBE I WAS MISTAKEN...
After my conversation with my mother I read the SCUM Manifesto all the time.
THE MALE IS A BIOLOGICAL ACCIDENT. THE Y (MALE) GENE IS AN INCOMPLETE X (FEMALE) GENE, THAT IS, HAS AN INCOMPLETE SET OF CHROMOSOMES. THE MALE IS AN INCOMPLETE FEMALE, A WALKING ABORTION.
MALENESS IS A DISEASE AND MALES ARE EMOTIONAL CRIPPLES.

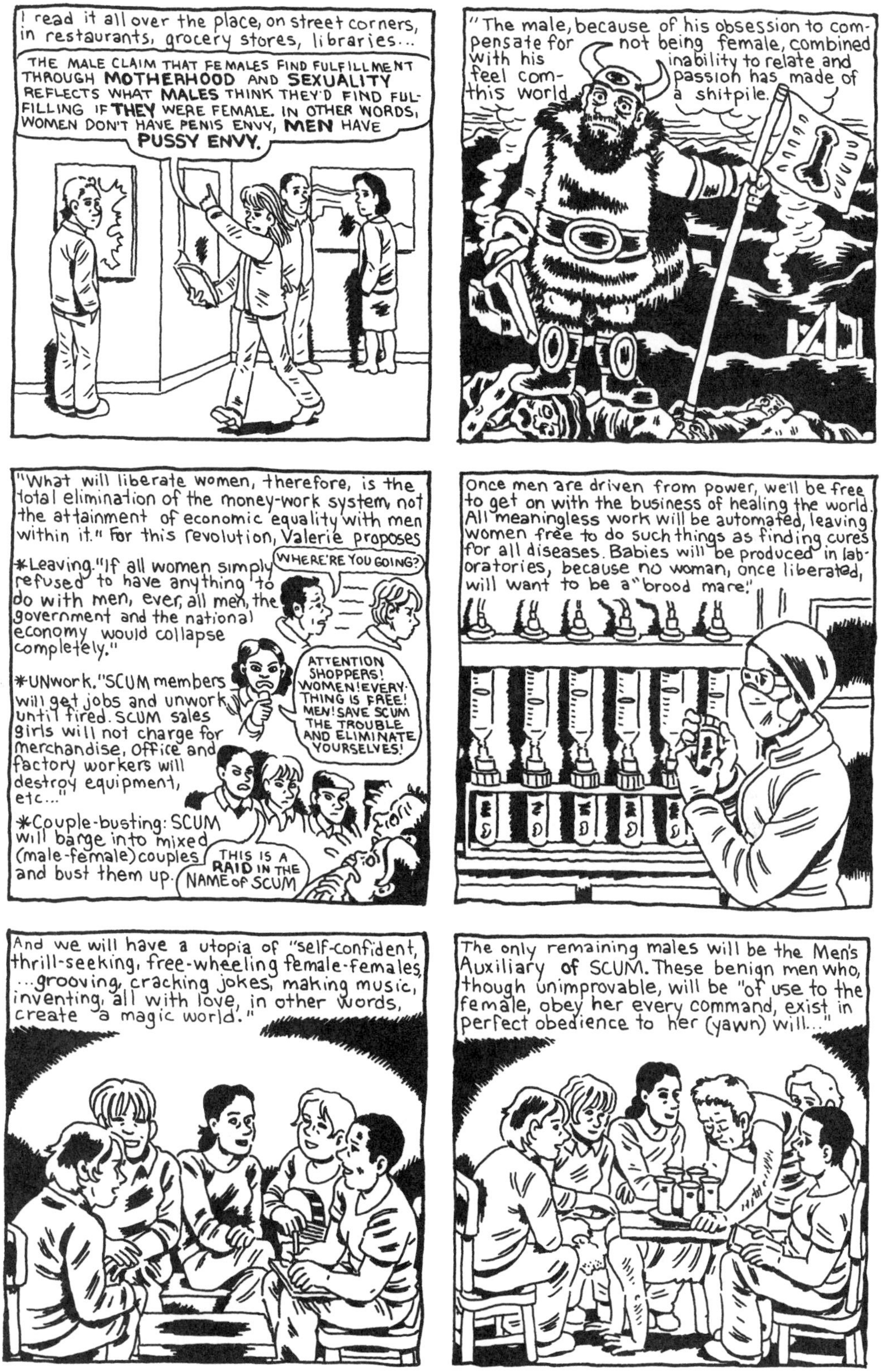
I read it all over the place, on street corners, in restaurants, grocery stores, libraries...
THE MALE CLAIM THAT FEMALES FIND FULFILLMENT THROUGH MOTHERHOOD AND SEXUALITY REFLECTS WHAT MALES THINK THEY'D FIND FULFILLING IF THEY WERE FEMALE. IN OTHER WORDS, WOMEN DON'T HAVE PENIS ENVY, MEN HAVE PUSSY ENVY.
"The male, because of his obsession to compensate for not being female, combined with his inability to relate and feel compassion has made of this world a shitpile.
"What will liberate women, therefore, is the total elimination of the money-work system, not the attainment of economic equality with men within it." For this revolution, Valerie proposes
*Leaving. "If all women simply refused to have anything to do with men, ever, all men, the government and the national economy would collapse completely."
WHERE'RE YOU GOING?
*UNwork. "SCUM members will get jobs and unwork until fired. SCUM sales girls will not charge for merchandise, office and factory workers will destroy equipment, etc..."
ATTENTION SHOPPERS! WOMEN! EVERYTHING IS FREE! MEN! SAVE SCUM THE TROUBLE AND ELIMINATE YOURSELVES!
*Couple-busting: SCUM will barge into mixed (male-female) couples and bust them up.
THIS IS A RAID IN THE NAME OF SCUM
Once men are driven from power, we'll be free to get on with the business of healing the world. All meaningless work will be automated, leaving women free to do such things as finding cures for all diseases. Babies will be produced in laboratories, because no woman, once liberated, will want to be a "brood mare."
And we will have a utopia of "self-confident, thrill-seeking, free-wheeling female-females, ...grooving, cracking jokes, making music, inventing, all with love, in other words, create a magic world'."
The only remaining males will be the Men's Auxiliary of SCUM. These benign men who, though unimprovable, will be "of use to the female, obey her every command, exist in perfect obedience to her (yawn) will..."

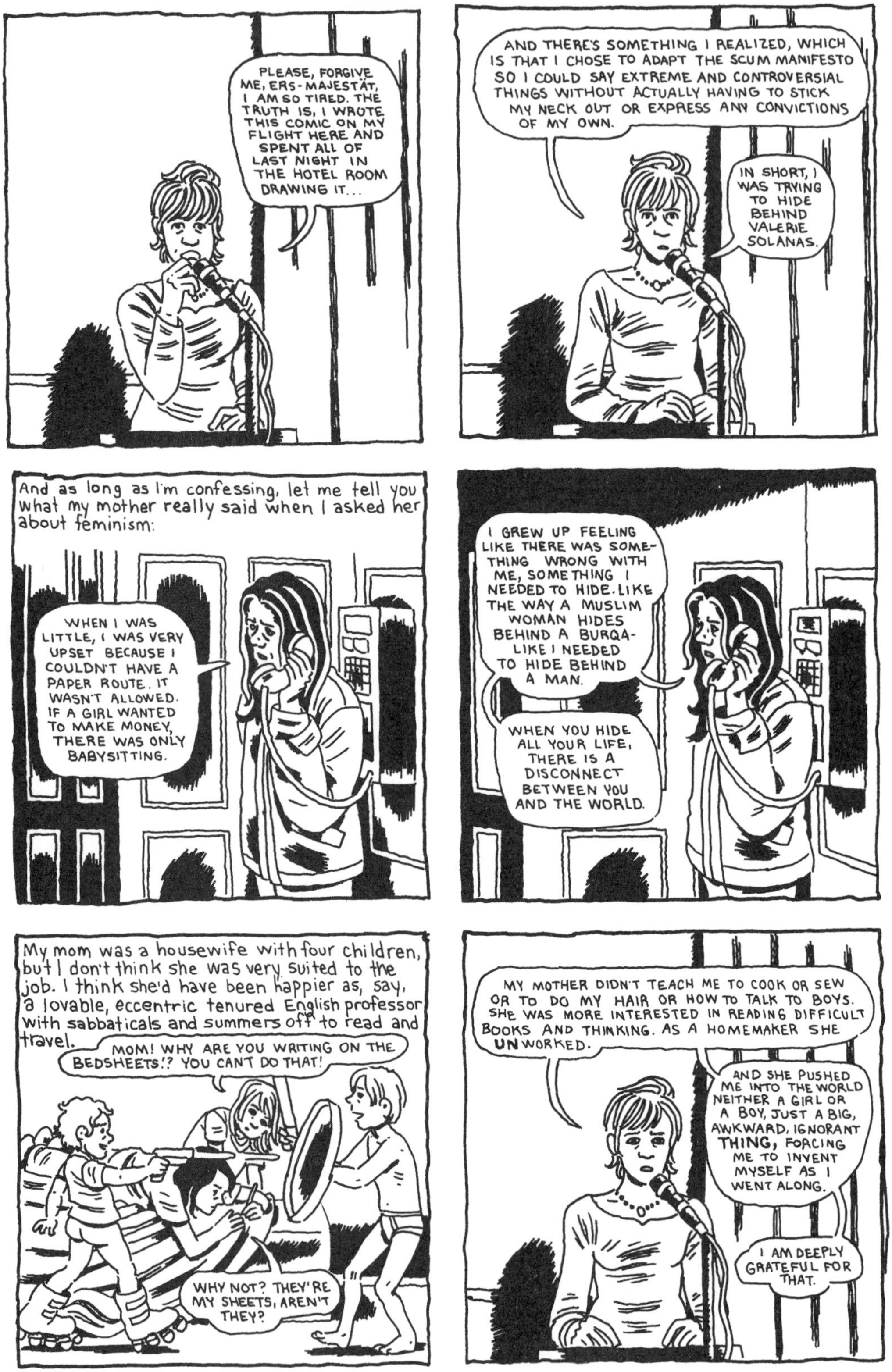
PLEASE, FORGIVE ME, ERS-MAJESTÄT, I AM SO TIRED. THE TRUTH IS, I WROTE THIS COMIC ON MY FLIGHT HERE AND SPENT ALL OF LAST NIGHT IN THE HOTEL ROOM DRAWING IT...
AND THERE'S SOMETHING I REALIZED, WHICH IS THAT I CHOSE TO ADAPT THE SCUM MANIFESTO SO I COULD SAY EXTREME AND CONTROVERSIAL THINGS WITHOUT ACTUALLY HAVING TO STICK MY NECK OUT OR EXPRESS ANY CONVICTIONS OF MY OWN.
IN SHORT, I WAS TRYING TO HIDE BEHIND VALERIE SOLANAS.
And as long as I'm confessing, let me tell you what my mother really said when I asked her about feminism:
WHEN I WAS LITTLE, I WAS VERY UPSET BECAUSE I COULDN'T HAVE A PAPER ROUTE. IT WASN'T ALLOWED. IF A GIRL WANTED TO MAKE MONEY, THERE WAS ONLY BABYSITTING.
I GREW UP FEELING LIKE THERE WAS SOMETHING WRONG WITH ME, SOMETHING I NEEDED TO HIDE. LIKE THE WAY A MUSLIM WOMAN HIDES BEHIND A BURQA-LIKE I NEEDED TO HIDE BEHIND A MAN.
WHEN YOU HIDE ALL YOUR LIFE, THERE IS A DISCONNECT BETWEEN YOU AND THE WORLD.
My mom was a housewife with four children, but I don't think she was very suited to the job. I think she'd have been happier as, say, a lovable, eccentric tenured English professor with sabbaticals and summers off to read and travel.
MOM! WHY ARE YOU WRITING ON THE BEDSHEETS!? YOU CAN'T DO THAT!
WHY NOT? THEY'RE MY SHEETS, AREN'T THEY?
MY MOTHER DIDN'T TEACH ME TO COOK OR SEW OR TO DO MY HAIR OR HOW TO TALK TO BOYS. SHE WAS MORE INTERESTED IN READING DIFFICULT BOOKS AND THINKING. AS A HOMEMAKER SHE UNWORKED.
AND SHE PUSHED ME INTO THE WORLD NEITHER A GIRL OR A BOY, JUST A BIG, AWKWARD, IGNORANT THING, FORCING ME TO INVENT MYSELF AS I WENT ALONG.
I AM DEEPLY GRATEFUL FOR THAT.

excerpt from

Fantastic Life

KEVIN MUTCH

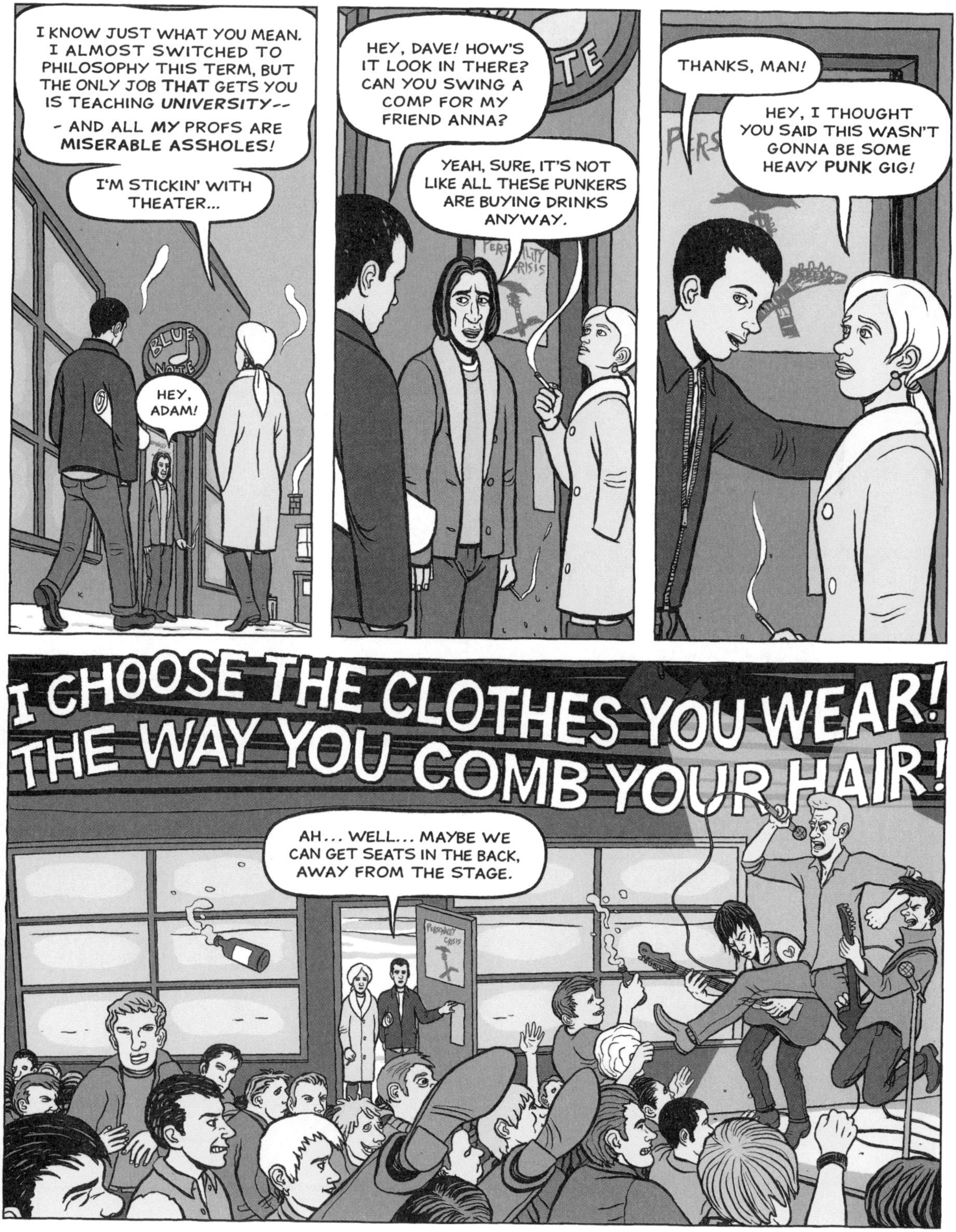
I KNOW JUST WHAT YOU MEAN. I ALMOST SWITCHED TO PHILOSOPHY THIS TERM, BUT THE ONLY JOB THAT GETS YOU IS TEACHING UNIVERSITY--
- AND ALL MY PROFS ARE MISERABLE ASSHOLES!
I'M STICKIN' WITH THEATER...
BLUE NOTE
HEY, ADAM!
HEY, DAVE! HOW'S IT LOOK IN THERE? CAN YOU SWING A COMP FOR MY FRIEND ANNA?
YEAH, SURE, IT'S NOT LIKE ALL THESE PUNKERS ARE BUYING DRINKS ANYWAY.
THANKS, MAN!
HEY, I THOUGHT YOU SAID THIS WASN'T GONNA BE SOME HEAVY PUNK GIG!
I CHOOSE THE CLOTHES YOU WEAR! THE WAY YOU COMB YOUR HAIR!
AH... WELL... MAYBE WE CAN GET SEATS IN THE BACK, AWAY FROM THE STAGE.

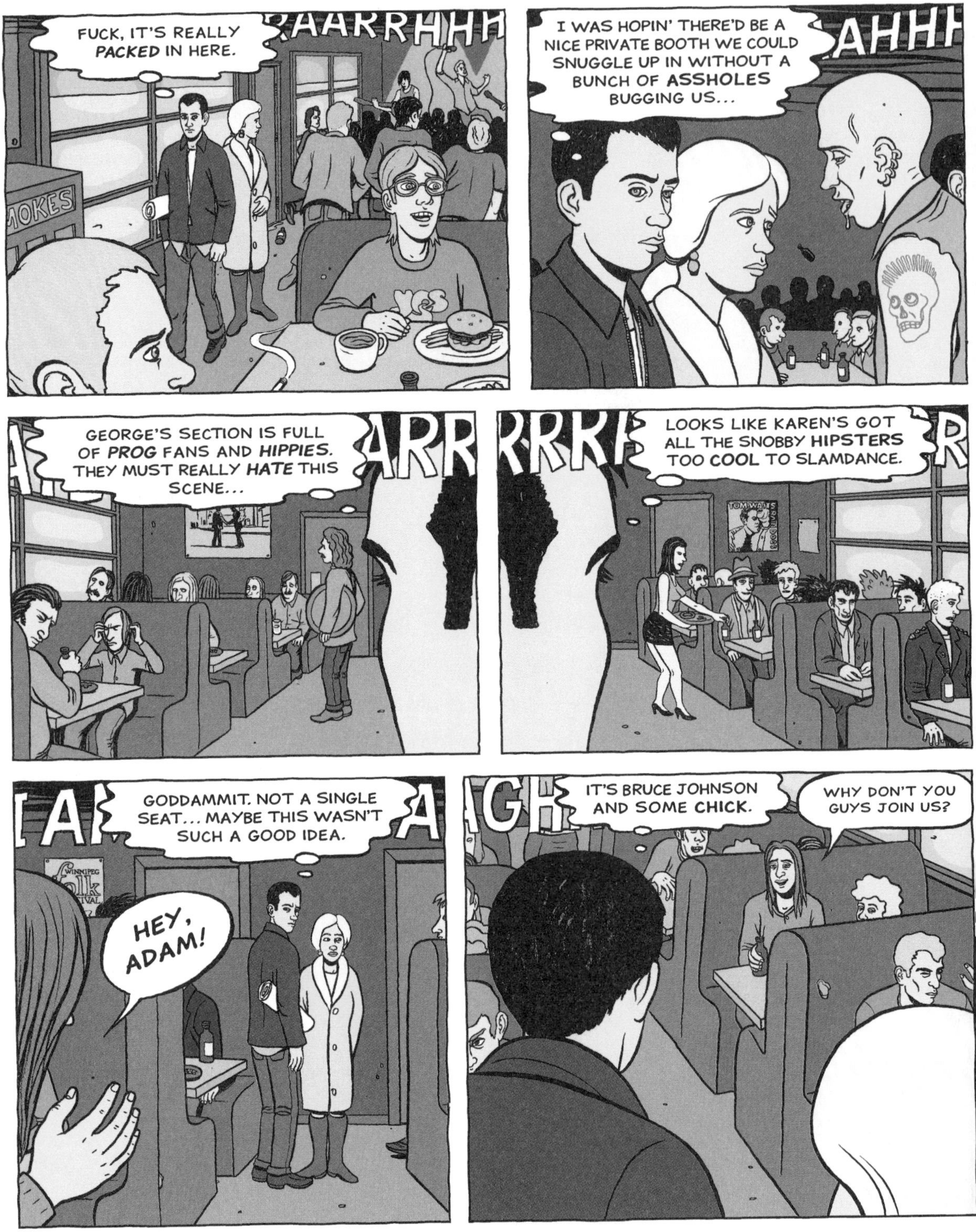
FUCK, IT'S REALLY PACKED IN HERE.
RAARRHHH
MOKES
YES
I WAS HOPIN' THERE'D BE A NICE PRIVATE BOOTH WE COULD SNUGGLE UP IN WITHOUT A BUNCH OF ASSHOLES BUGGING US...
AHHH
GEORGE'S SECTION IS FULL OF PROG FANS AND HIPPIES. THEY MUST REALLY HATE THIS SCENE...
ARR
RRRA
LOOKS LIKE KAREN'S GOT ALL THE SNOBBY HIPSTERS TOO COOL TO SLAMDANCE.
TOM WAITS
GODDAMMIT. NOT A SINGLE SEAT... MAYBE THIS WASN'T SUCH A GOOD IDEA.
WINNIPEG FOLK FESTIVAL
HEY, ADAM!
IT'S BRUCE JOHNSON AND SOME CHICK.
WHY DON'T YOU GUYS JOIN US?

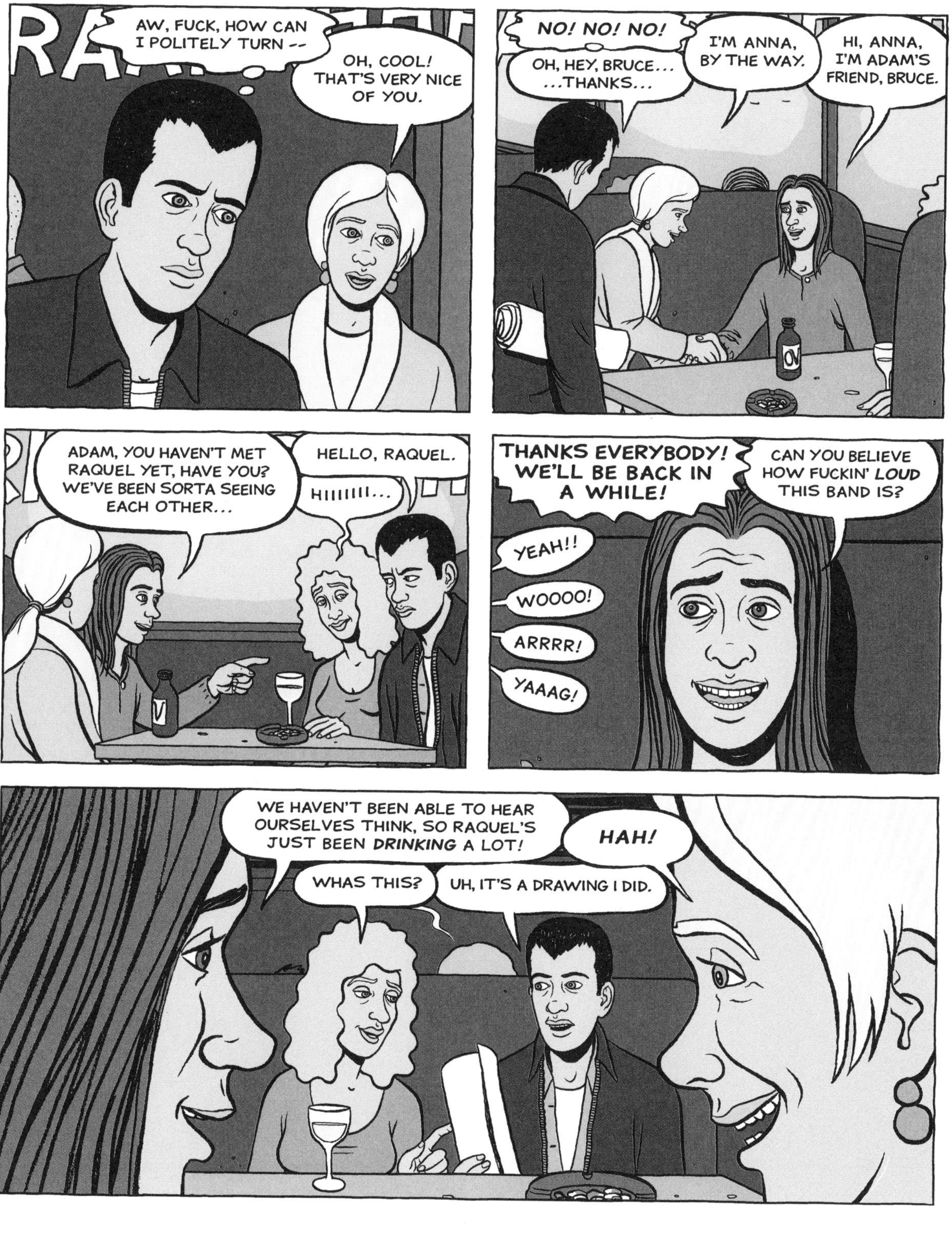

AW, FUCK, HOW CAN I POLITELY TURN --
OH, COOL! THAT'S VERY NICE OF YOU.
NO! NO! NO!
OH, HEY, BRUCE... ...THANKS...
I'M ANNA, BY THE WAY.
HI, ANNA, I'M ADAM'S FRIEND, BRUCE.
ADAM, YOU HAVEN'T MET RAQUEL YET, HAVE YOU? WE'VE BEEN SORTA SEEING EACH OTHER...
HELLO, RAQUEL.
HIIIIIII...
THANKS EVERYBODY! WE'LL BE BACK IN A WHILE!
CAN YOU BELIEVE HOW FUCKIN' *LOUD* THIS BAND IS?
YEAH!!
WOOOO!
ARRRR!
YAAAG!
WE HAVEN'T BEEN ABLE TO HEAR OURSELVES THINK, SO RAQUEL'S JUST BEEN *DRINKING* A LOT!
HAH!
WHAS THIS?
UH, IT'S A DRAWING I DID.

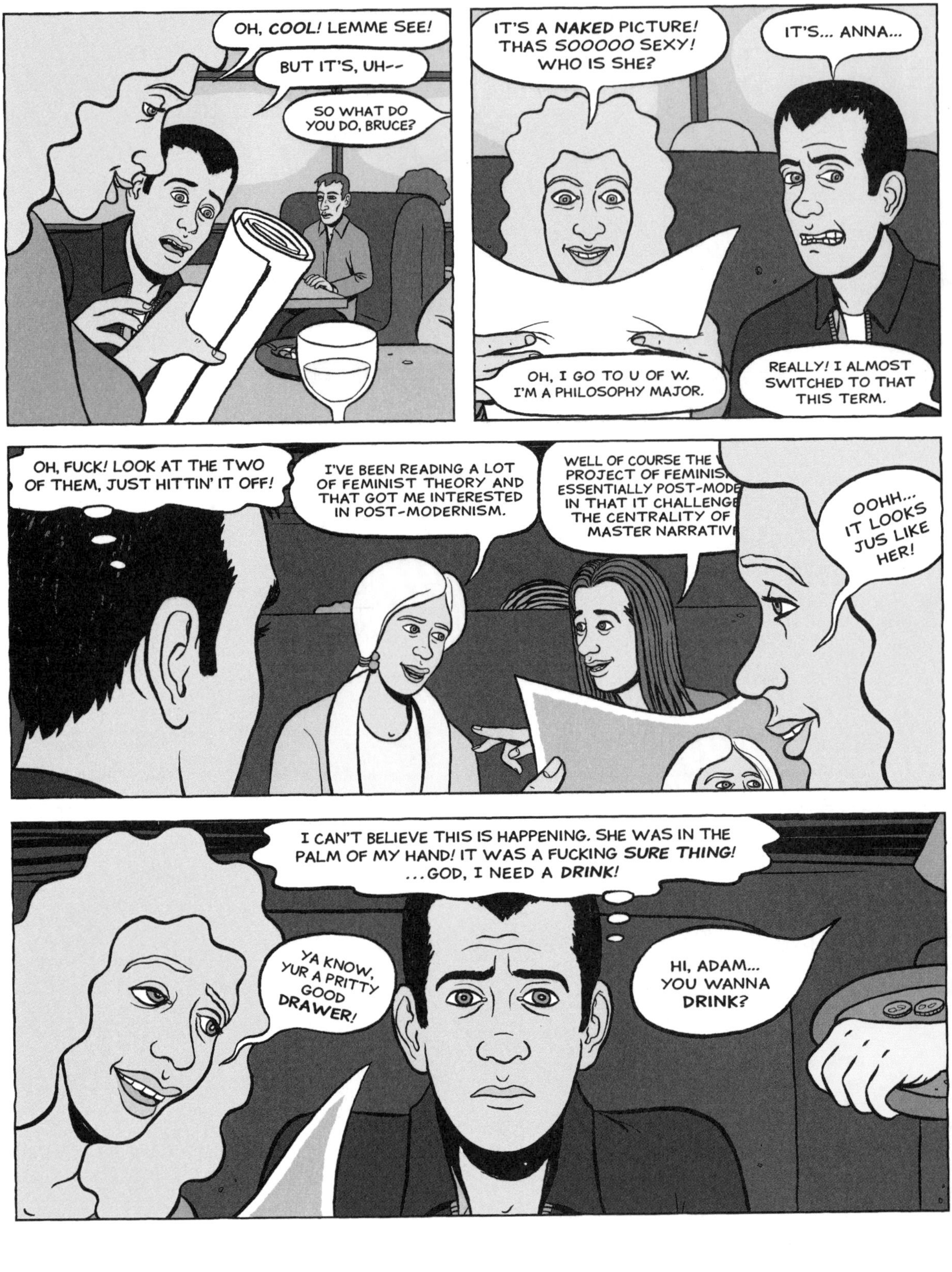
OH, *COOL!* LEMME SEE!
BUT IT'S, UH--
SO WHAT DO YOU DO, BRUCE?
IT'S A *NAKED* PICTURE! THAS *SOOOOO* SEXY! WHO IS SHE?
IT'S... ANNA...
OH, I GO TO U OF W. I'M A PHILOSOPHY MAJOR.
REALLY! I ALMOST SWITCHED TO THAT THIS TERM.
OH, FUCK! LOOK AT THE TWO OF THEM, JUST HITTIN' IT OFF!
I'VE BEEN READING A LOT OF FEMINIST THEORY AND THAT GOT ME INTERESTED IN POST-MODERNISM.
WELL OF COURSE THE PROJECT OF FEMINIS ESSENTIALLY POST-MODE IN THAT IT CHALLENGE THE CENTRALITY OF MASTER NARRATIV
OOHH... IT LOOKS JUS LIKE HER!
I CAN'T BELIEVE THIS IS HAPPENING. SHE WAS IN THE PALM OF MY HAND! IT WAS A FUCKING *SURE THING!* ...GOD, I NEED A *DRINK!*
YA KNOW, YUR A PRITTY GOOD **DRAWER!**
HI, ADAM... YOU WANNA **DRINK?**

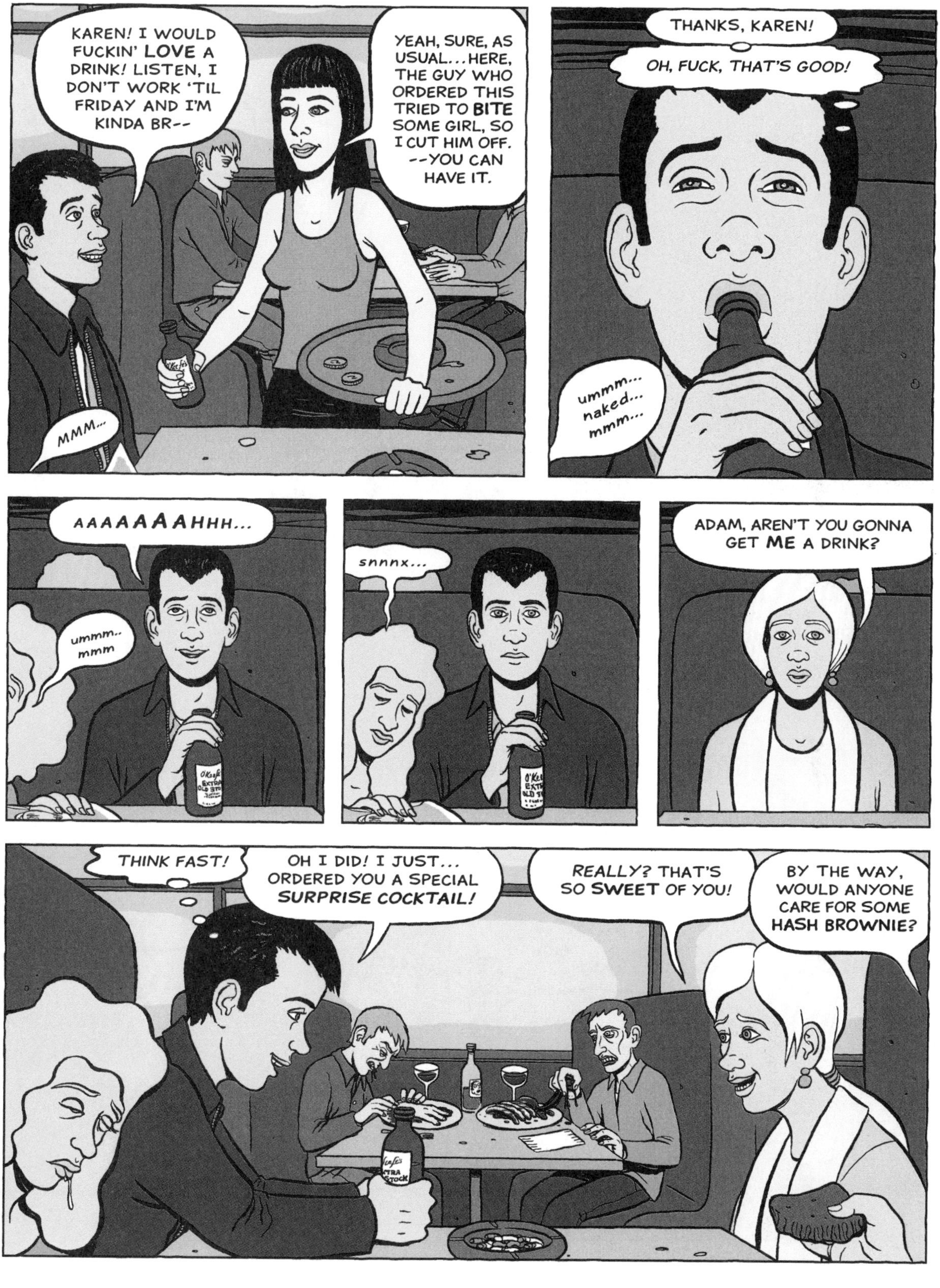
KAREN! I WOULD FUCKIN' LOVE A DRINK! LISTEN, I DON'T WORK 'TIL FRIDAY AND I'M KINDA BR--
YEAH, SURE, AS USUAL... HERE, THE GUY WHO ORDERED THIS TRIED TO BITE SOME GIRL, SO I CUT HIM OFF. --YOU CAN HAVE IT.
MMM...
THANKS, KAREN!
OH, FUCK, THAT'S GOOD!
ummm... naked... mmm...
AAAAAAAHHH...
ummm.. mmm
snnnx...
ADAM, AREN'T YOU GONNA GET ME A DRINK?
THINK FAST!
OH I DID! I JUST... ORDERED YOU A SPECIAL SURPRISE COCKTAIL!
REALLY? THAT'S SO SWEET OF YOU!
BY THE WAY, WOULD ANYONE CARE FOR SOME HASH BROWNIE?

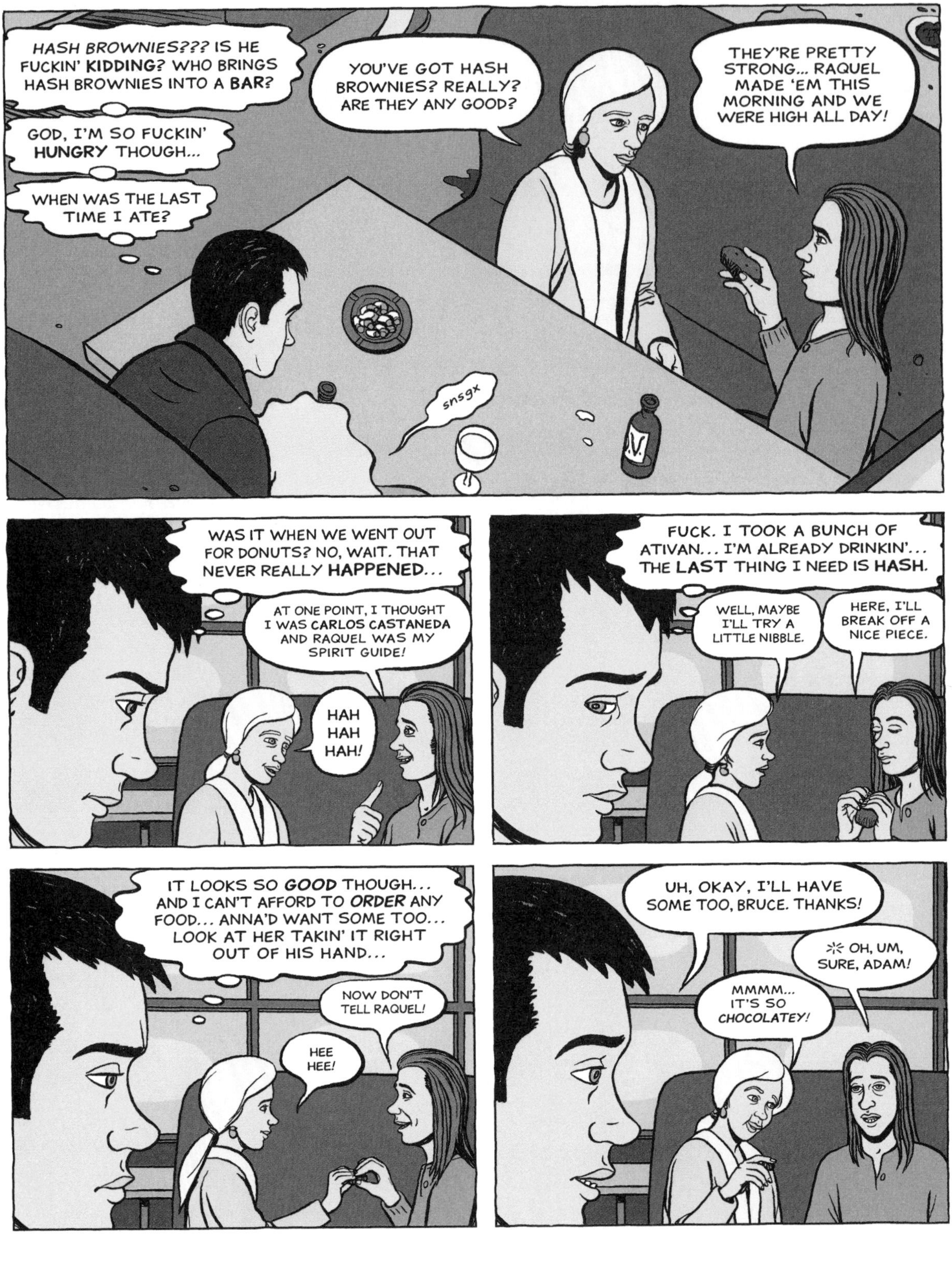
HASH BROWNIES??? IS HE FUCKIN' KIDDING? WHO BRINGS HASH BROWNIES INTO A BAR?
GOD, I'M SO FUCKIN' HUNGRY THOUGH...
WHEN WAS THE LAST TIME I ATE?
YOU'VE GOT HASH BROWNIES? REALLY? ARE THEY ANY GOOD?
THEY'RE PRETTY STRONG... RAQUEL MADE 'EM THIS MORNING AND WE WERE HIGH ALL DAY!
snsgx
WAS IT WHEN WE WENT OUT FOR DONUTS? NO, WAIT. THAT NEVER REALLY HAPPENED...
AT ONE POINT, I THOUGHT I WAS CARLOS CASTANEDA AND RAQUEL WAS MY SPIRIT GUIDE!
HAH HAH HAH!
FUCK. I TOOK A BUNCH OF ATIVAN... I'M ALREADY DRINKIN'... THE LAST THING I NEED IS HASH.
WELL, MAYBE I'LL TRY A LITTLE NIBBLE.
HERE, I'LL BREAK OFF A NICE PIECE.
IT LOOKS SO GOOD THOUGH... AND I CAN'T AFFORD TO ORDER ANY FOOD... ANNA'D WANT SOME TOO... LOOK AT HER TAKIN' IT RIGHT OUT OF HIS HAND...
NOW DON'T TELL RAQUEL!
HEE HEE!
UH, OKAY, I'LL HAVE SOME TOO, BRUCE. THANKS!
OH, UM, SURE, ADAM!
MMMM... IT'S SO CHOCOLATEY!

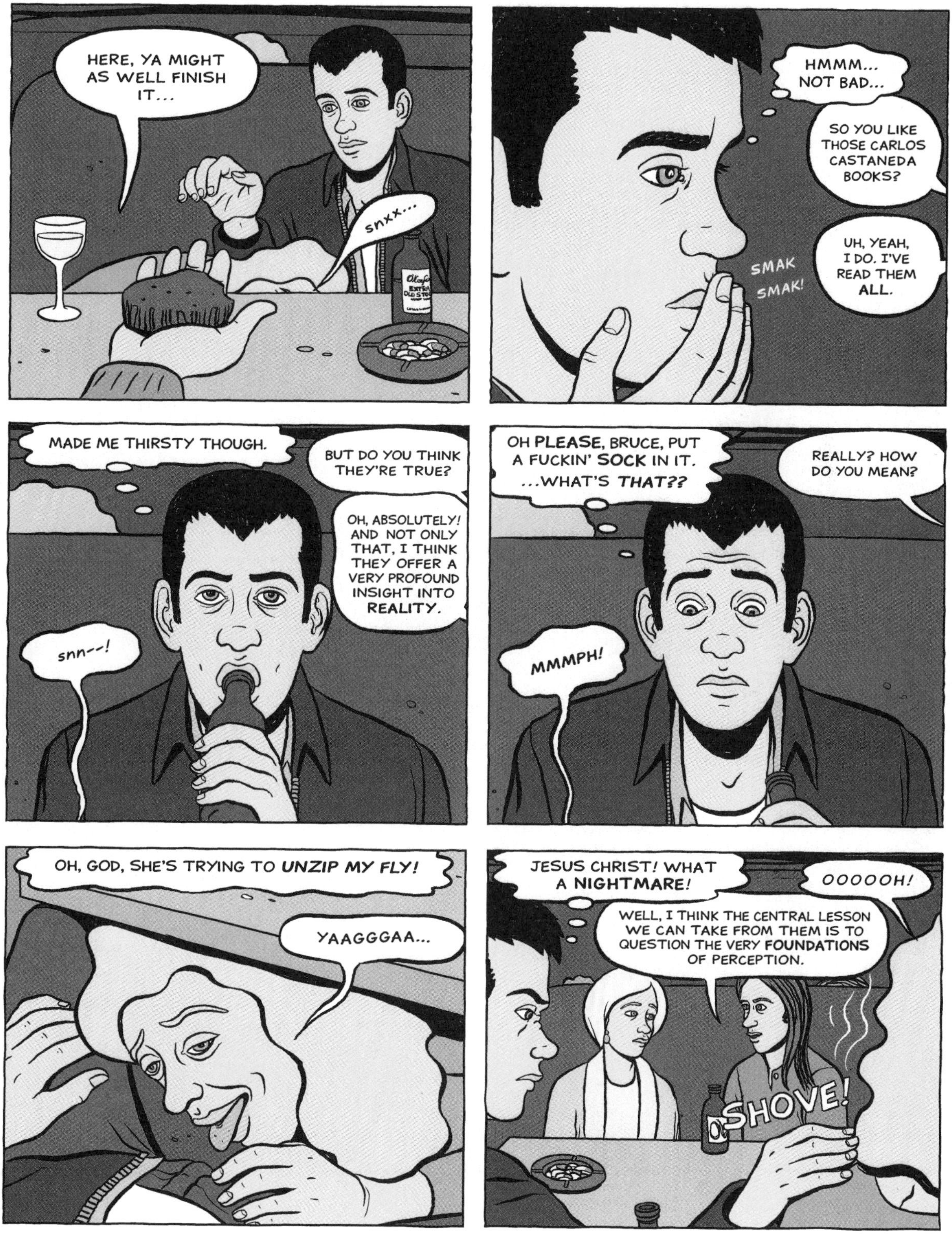
HERE, YA MIGHT AS WELL FINISH IT...
snxx...
HMMM... NOT BAD...
SO YOU LIKE THOSE CARLOS CASTANEDA BOOKS?
SMAK SMAK!
UH, YEAH, I DO. I'VE READ THEM ALL.
MADE ME THIRSTY THOUGH.
BUT DO YOU THINK THEY'RE TRUE?
OH, ABSOLUTELY! AND NOT ONLY THAT, I THINK THEY OFFER A VERY PROFOUND INSIGHT INTO REALITY.
snn--!
OH PLEASE, BRUCE, PUT A FUCKIN' SOCK IN IT. ...WHAT'S THAT??
REALLY? HOW DO YOU MEAN?
MMMPH!
OH, GOD, SHE'S TRYING TO UNZIP MY FLY!
YAAGGGAA...
JESUS CHRIST! WHAT A NIGHTMARE!
OOOOOH!
WELL, I THINK THE CENTRAL LESSON WE CAN TAKE FROM THEM IS TO QUESTION THE VERY FOUNDATIONS OF PERCEPTION.
SHOVE!

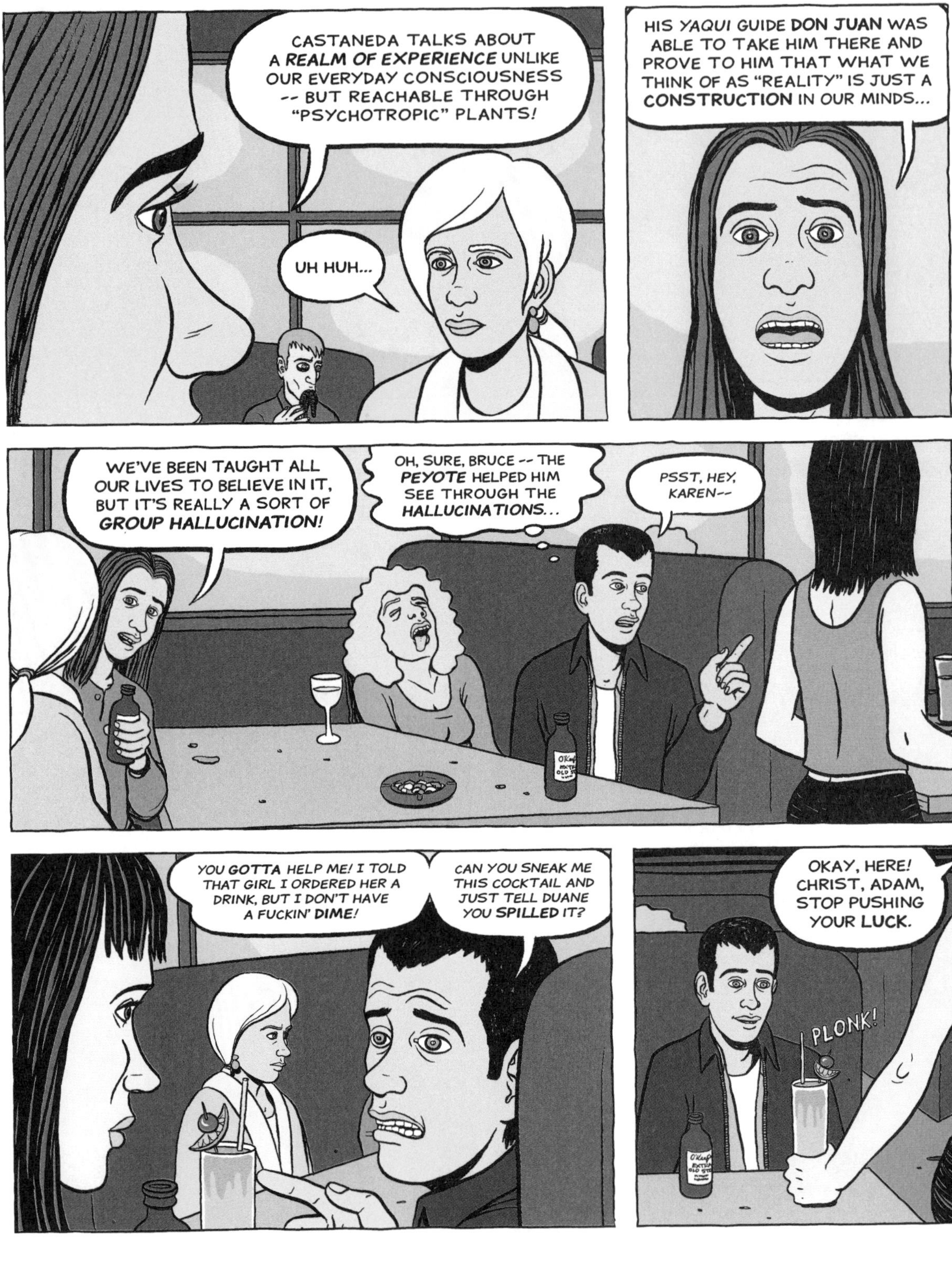
CASTANEDA TALKS ABOUT A REALM OF EXPERIENCE UNLIKE OUR EVERYDAY CONSCIOUSNESS -- BUT REACHABLE THROUGH "PSYCHOTROPIC" PLANTS!
UH HUH...
HIS YAQUI GUIDE DON JUAN WAS ABLE TO TAKE HIM THERE AND PROVE TO HIM THAT WHAT WE THINK OF AS "REALITY" IS JUST A CONSTRUCTION IN OUR MINDS...
WE'VE BEEN TAUGHT ALL OUR LIVES TO BELIEVE IN IT, BUT IT'S REALLY A SORT OF GROUP HALLUCINATION!
OH, SURE, BRUCE -- THE PEYOTE HELPED HIM SEE THROUGH THE HALLUCINATIONS...
PSST, HEY, KAREN--
YOU GOTTA HELP ME! I TOLD THAT GIRL I ORDERED HER A DRINK, BUT I DON'T HAVE A FUCKIN' DIME!
CAN YOU SNEAK ME THIS COCKTAIL AND JUST TELL DUANE YOU SPILLED IT?
OKAY, HERE! CHRIST, ADAM, STOP PUSHING YOUR LUCK.
PLONK!

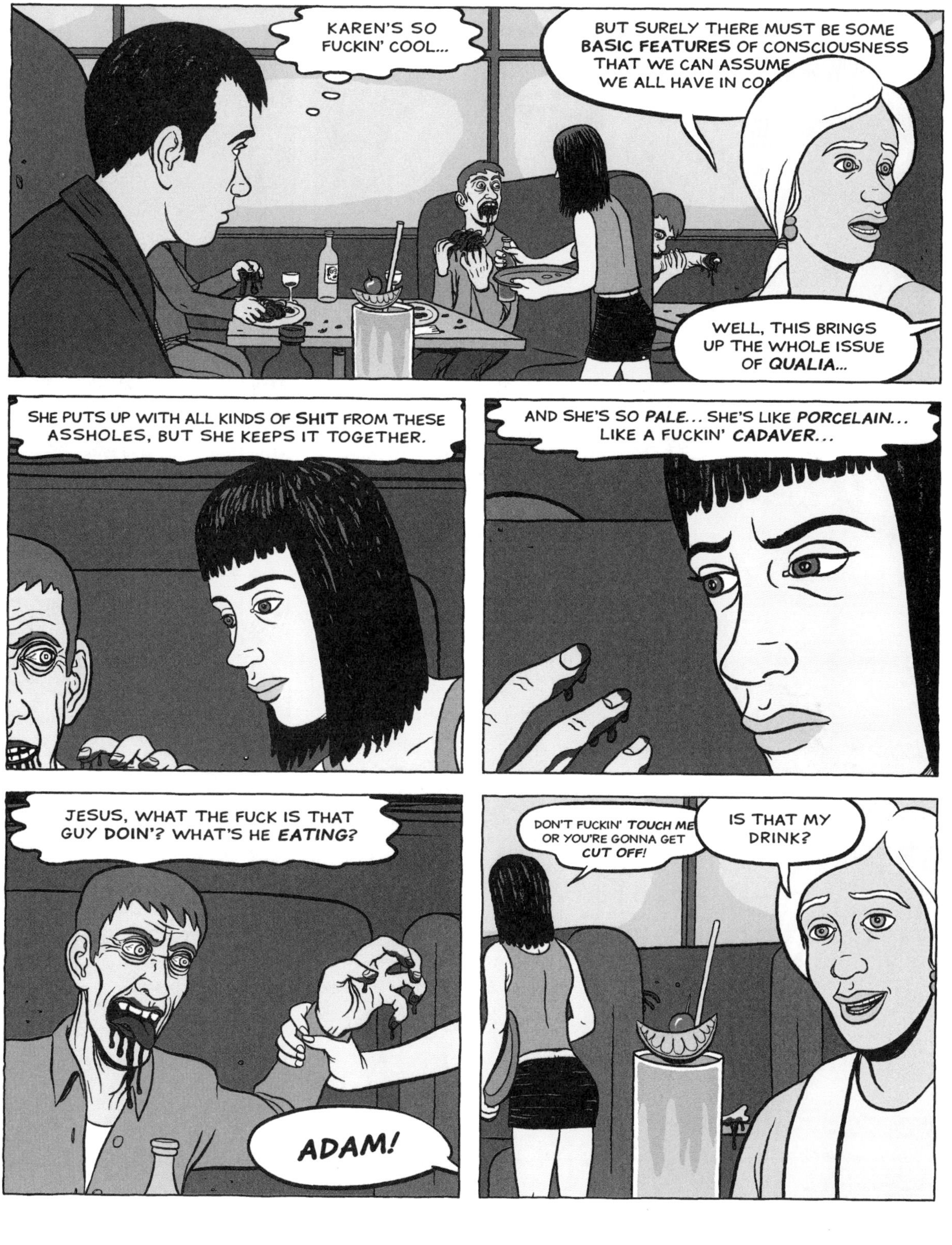

KAREN'S SO FUCKIN' COOL...
BUT SURELY THERE MUST BE SOME BASIC FEATURES OF CONSCIOUSNESS THAT WE CAN ASSUME WE ALL HAVE IN CO
WELL, THIS BRINGS UP THE WHOLE ISSUE OF QUALIA...
SHE PUTS UP WITH ALL KINDS OF SHIT FROM THESE ASSHOLES, BUT SHE KEEPS IT TOGETHER.
AND SHE'S SO PALE... SHE'S LIKE PORCELAIN... LIKE A FUCKIN' CADAVER...
JESUS, WHAT THE FUCK IS THAT GUY DOIN'? WHAT'S HE EATING?
ADAM!
DON'T FUCKIN' TOUCH ME OR YOU'RE GONNA GET CUT OFF!
IS THAT MY DRINK?

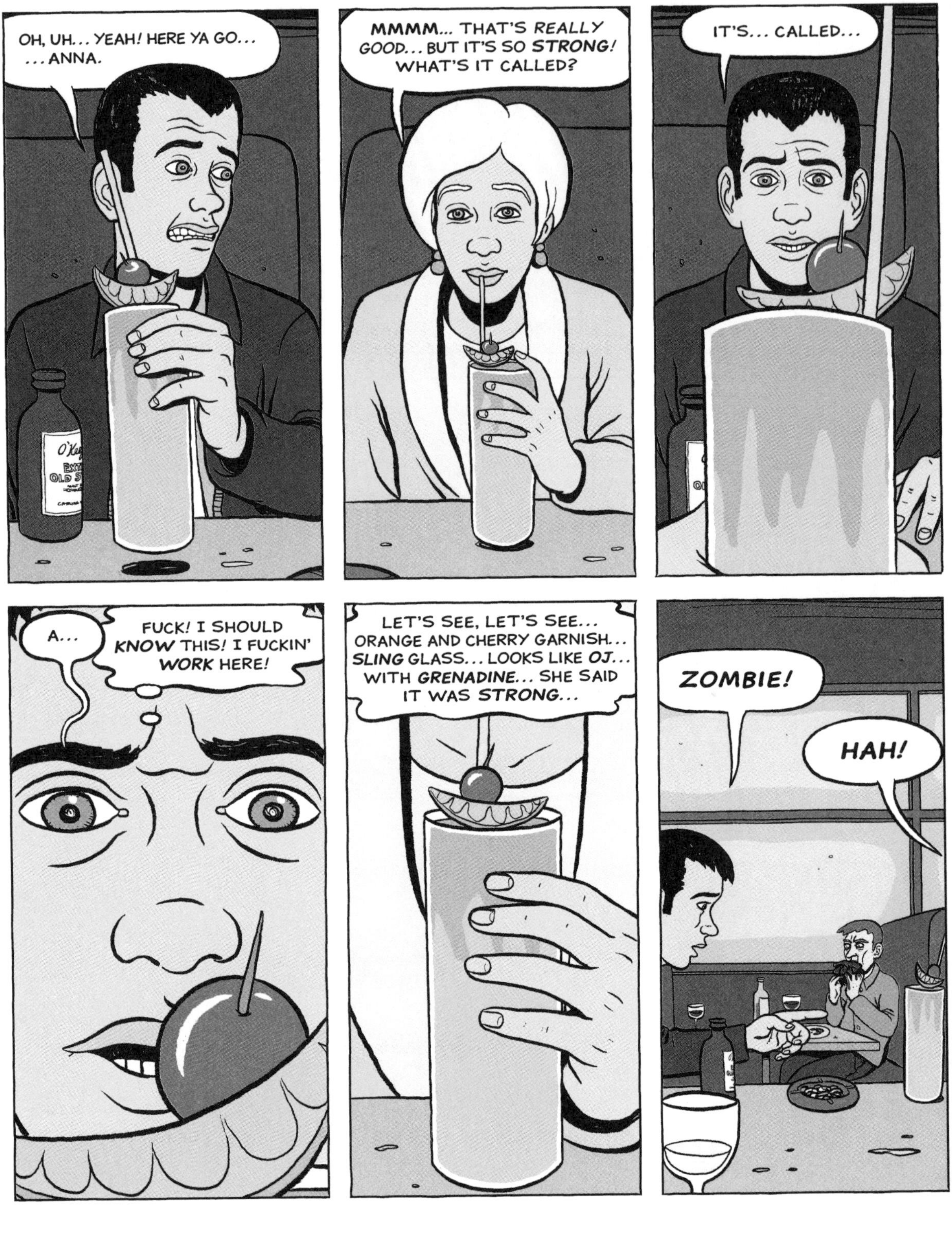
OH, UH... YEAH! HERE YA GO... ...ANNA.
MMMM... THAT'S REALLY GOOD... BUT IT'S SO STRONG! WHAT'S IT CALLED?
IT'S... CALLED...
A...
FUCK! I SHOULD KNOW THIS! I FUCKIN' WORK HERE!
LET'S SEE, LET'S SEE... ORANGE AND CHERRY GARNISH... SLING GLASS... LOOKS LIKE OJ... WITH GRENADINE... SHE SAID IT WAS STRONG...
ZOMBIE!
HAH!

THAT'S SO *PERFECT!* WE WERE JUST *TALKING* ABOUT ZOMBIES!

HUH?

ZZZZZ...

PHILOSOPHICAL ZOMBIES! AUTOMATONS THAT LOOK AND *ACT* LIKE PEOPLE, BUT DON'T REALLY *SEE* OR *HEAR* OR *FEEL*.

--WE USE THEM TO ILLUSTRATE SOME OF THE BASIC PROBLEMS OF CONSCIOUSNESS...

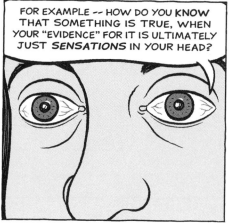

FOR EXAMPLE -- HOW DO YOU **KNOW** THAT SOMETHING IS TRUE, WHEN YOUR "EVIDENCE" FOR IT IS ULTIMATELY JUST *SENSATIONS* IN YOUR HEAD?

THIS IS WHY I FIND **CASTANEDA** SO COMPELLING - HE DEMONSTRATES THAT THERE'S **NO ULTIMATE TRUTH,** JUST SHIFTING SETS OF PERCEPTIONS, ALL OF WHICH ARE EQUALLY TRUE - OR **UNTRUE!**

MOTHERFUCKER! ANNA'S READY TO *SUCK HIS DICK*

...AND I'M GETTIN' TOO WASTED TO TALK!

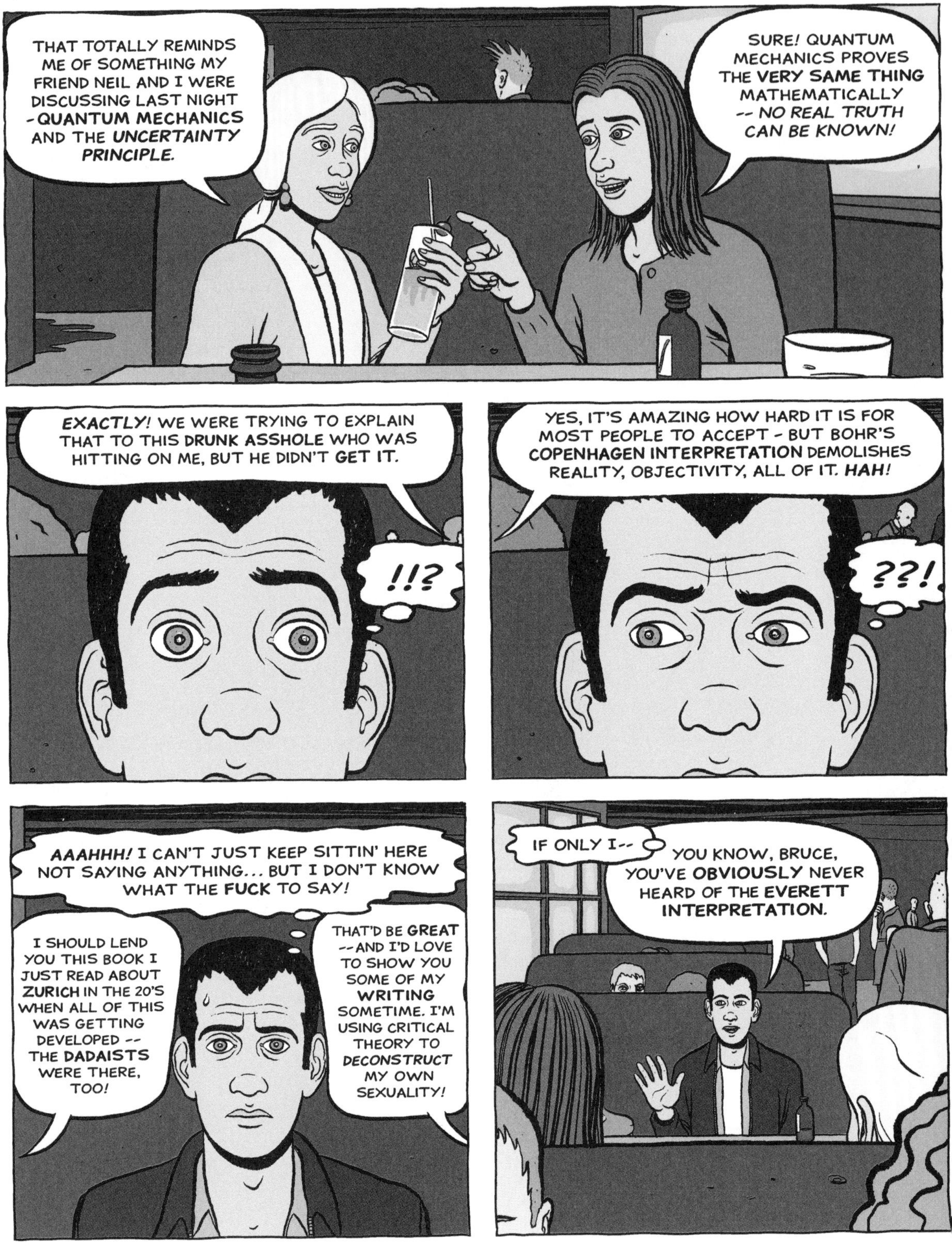
THAT TOTALLY REMINDS ME OF SOMETHING MY FRIEND NEIL AND I WERE DISCUSSING LAST NIGHT - QUANTUM MECHANICS AND THE UNCERTAINTY PRINCIPLE.
SURE! QUANTUM MECHANICS PROVES THE VERY SAME THING MATHEMATICALLY -- NO REAL TRUTH CAN BE KNOWN!
EXACTLY! WE WERE TRYING TO EXPLAIN THAT TO THIS DRUNK ASSHOLE WHO WAS HITTING ON ME, BUT HE DIDN'T GET IT.
!!?
YES, IT'S AMAZING HOW HARD IT IS FOR MOST PEOPLE TO ACCEPT - BUT BOHR'S COPENHAGEN INTERPRETATION DEMOLISHES REALITY, OBJECTIVITY, ALL OF IT. HAH!
??!
AAAHHH! I CAN'T JUST KEEP SITTIN' HERE NOT SAYING ANYTHING... BUT I DON'T KNOW WHAT THE FUCK TO SAY!
I SHOULD LEND YOU THIS BOOK I JUST READ ABOUT ZURICH IN THE 20'S WHEN ALL OF THIS WAS GETTING DEVELOPED -- THE DADAISTS WERE THERE, TOO!
THAT'D BE GREAT -- AND I'D LOVE TO SHOW YOU SOME OF MY WRITING SOMETIME. I'M USING CRITICAL THEORY TO DECONSTRUCT MY OWN SEXUALITY!
IF ONLY I--
YOU KNOW, BRUCE, YOU'VE OBVIOUSLY NEVER HEARD OF THE EVERETT INTERPRETATION.

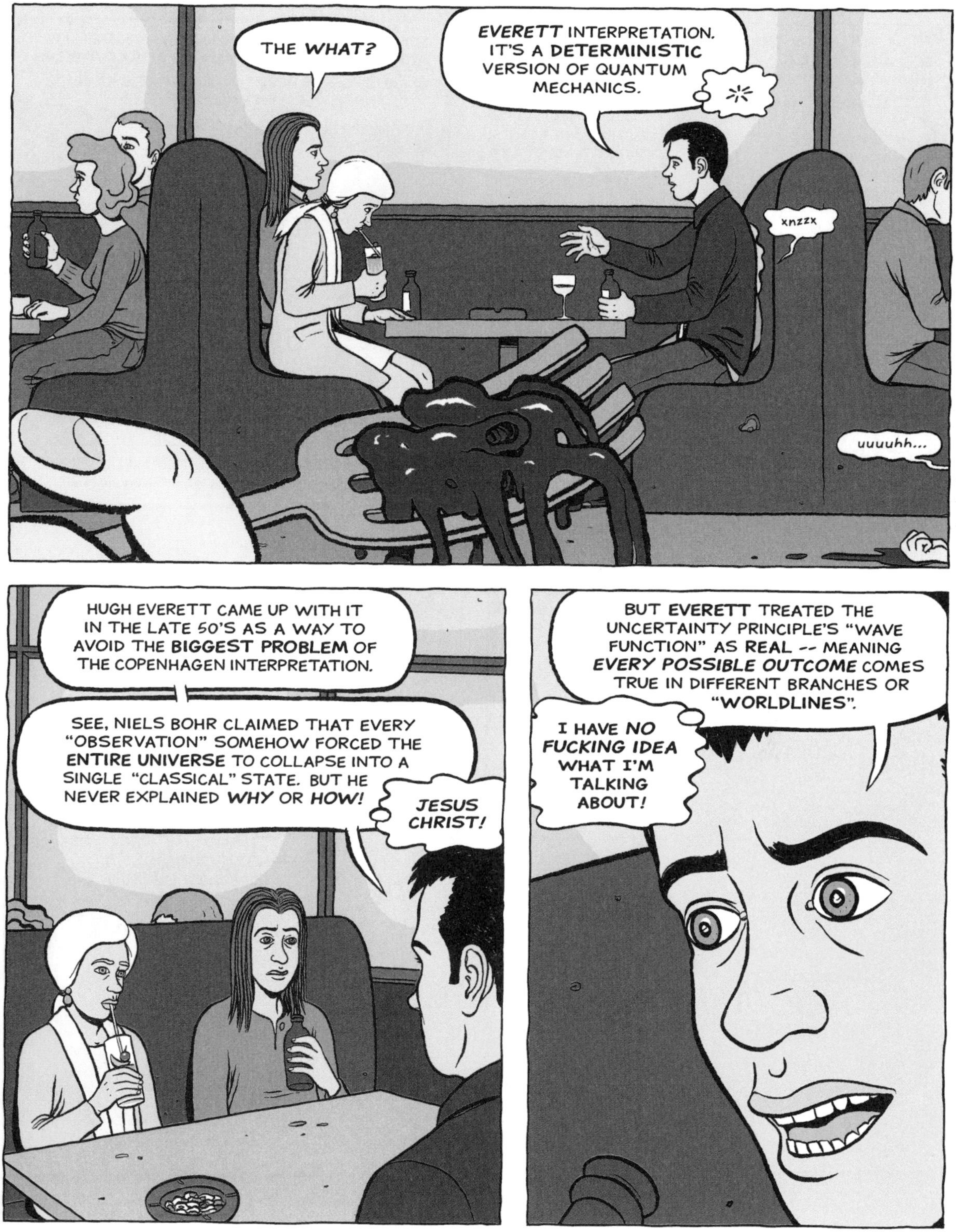
THE WHAT?
EVERETT INTERPRETATION. IT'S A DETERMINISTIC VERSION OF QUANTUM MECHANICS.
xnzzx
uuuuhh...
HUGH EVERETT CAME UP WITH IT IN THE LATE 50'S AS A WAY TO AVOID THE BIGGEST PROBLEM OF THE COPENHAGEN INTERPRETATION.
SEE, NIELS BOHR CLAIMED THAT EVERY "OBSERVATION" SOMEHOW FORCED THE ENTIRE UNIVERSE TO COLLAPSE INTO A SINGLE "CLASSICAL" STATE. BUT HE NEVER EXPLAINED WHY OR HOW!
JESUS CHRIST!
BUT EVERETT TREATED THE UNCERTAINTY PRINCIPLE'S "WAVE FUNCTION" AS REAL -- MEANING EVERY POSSIBLE OUTCOME COMES TRUE IN DIFFERENT BRANCHES OR "WORLDLINES".
I HAVE NO FUCKING IDEA WHAT I'M TALKING ABOUT!

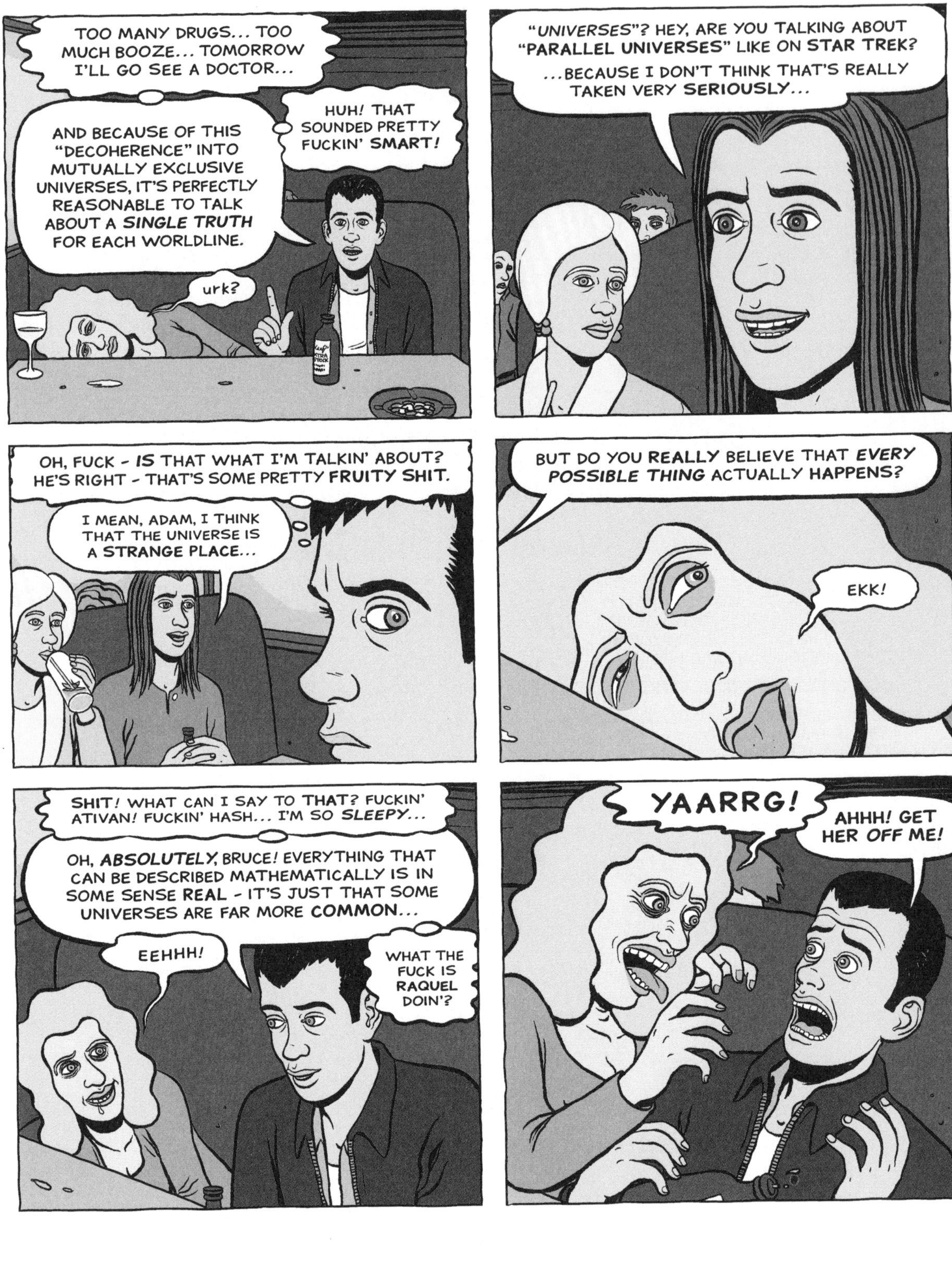

TOO MANY DRUGS... TOO MUCH BOOZE... TOMORROW I'LL GO SEE A DOCTOR...
AND BECAUSE OF THIS "DECOHERENCE" INTO MUTUALLY EXCLUSIVE UNIVERSES, IT'S PERFECTLY REASONABLE TO TALK ABOUT A SINGLE TRUTH FOR EACH WORLDLINE.
HUH! THAT SOUNDED PRETTY FUCKIN' SMART!
urk?
"UNIVERSES"? HEY, ARE YOU TALKING ABOUT "PARALLEL UNIVERSES" LIKE ON STAR TREK?
...BECAUSE I DON'T THINK THAT'S REALLY TAKEN VERY SERIOUSLY...
OH, FUCK - IS THAT WHAT I'M TALKIN' ABOUT? HE'S RIGHT - THAT'S SOME PRETTY FRUITY SHIT.
I MEAN, ADAM, I THINK THAT THE UNIVERSE IS A STRANGE PLACE...
BUT DO YOU REALLY BELIEVE THAT EVERY POSSIBLE THING ACTUALLY HAPPENS?
EKK!
SHIT! WHAT CAN I SAY TO THAT? FUCKIN' ATIVAN! FUCKIN' HASH... I'M SO SLEEPY...
OH, ABSOLUTELY, BRUCE! EVERYTHING THAT CAN BE DESCRIBED MATHEMATICALLY IS IN SOME SENSE REAL - IT'S JUST THAT SOME UNIVERSES ARE FAR MORE COMMON...
EEHHH!
WHAT THE FUCK IS RAQUEL DOIN'?
YAARRG!
AHHH! GET HER OFF ME!

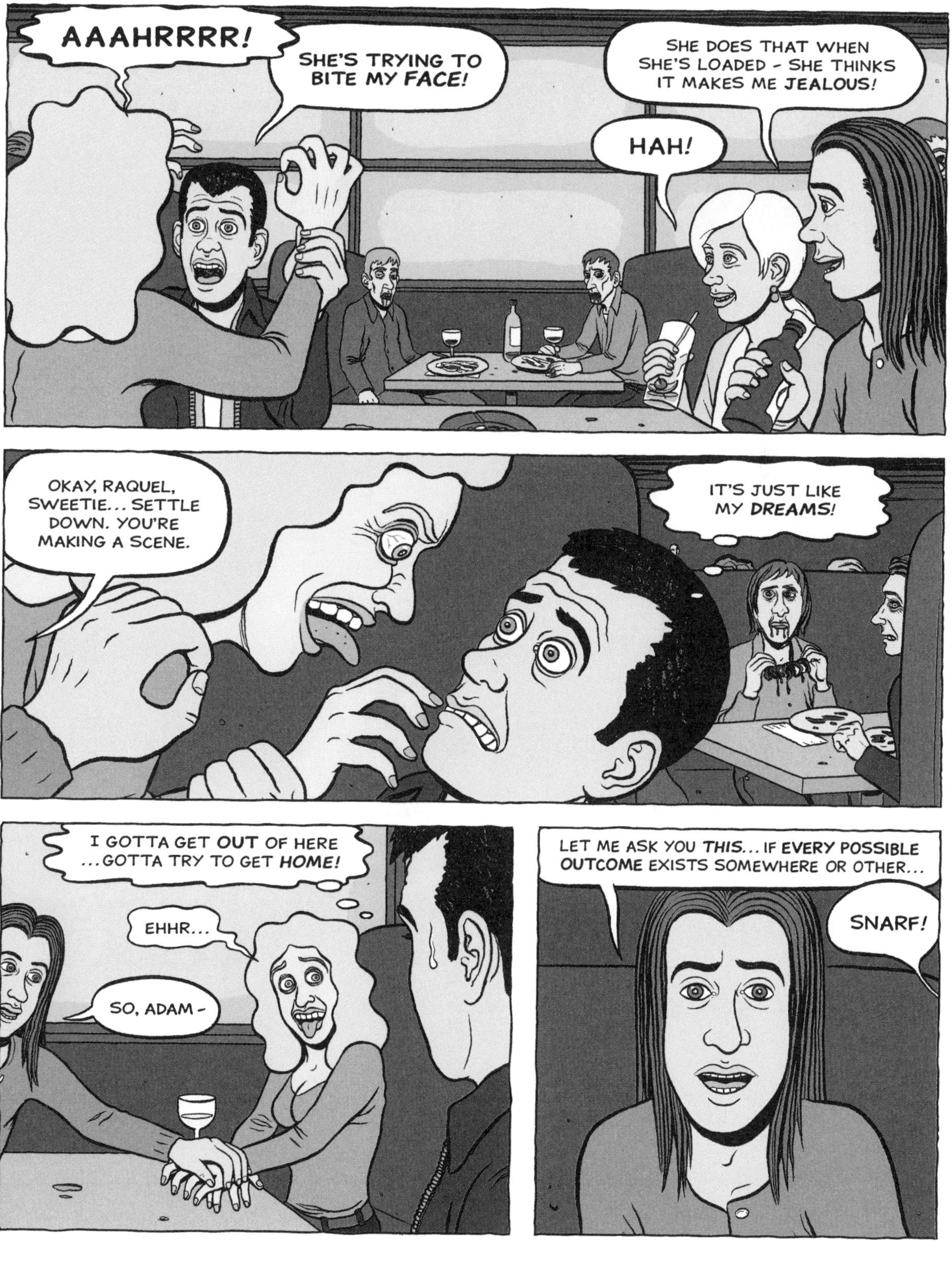
AAAHRRRR!
SHE'S TRYING TO BITE MY FACE!
SHE DOES THAT WHEN SHE'S LOADED - SHE THINKS IT MAKES ME JEALOUS!
HAH!
OKAY, RAQUEL, SWEETIE... SETTLE DOWN. YOU'RE MAKING A SCENE.
IT'S JUST LIKE MY DREAMS!
I GOTTA GET OUT OF HERE ...GOTTA TRY TO GET HOME!
EHHR...
SO, ADAM -
LET ME ASK YOU THIS... IF EVERY POSSIBLE OUTCOME EXISTS SOMEWHERE OR OTHER...
SNARF!

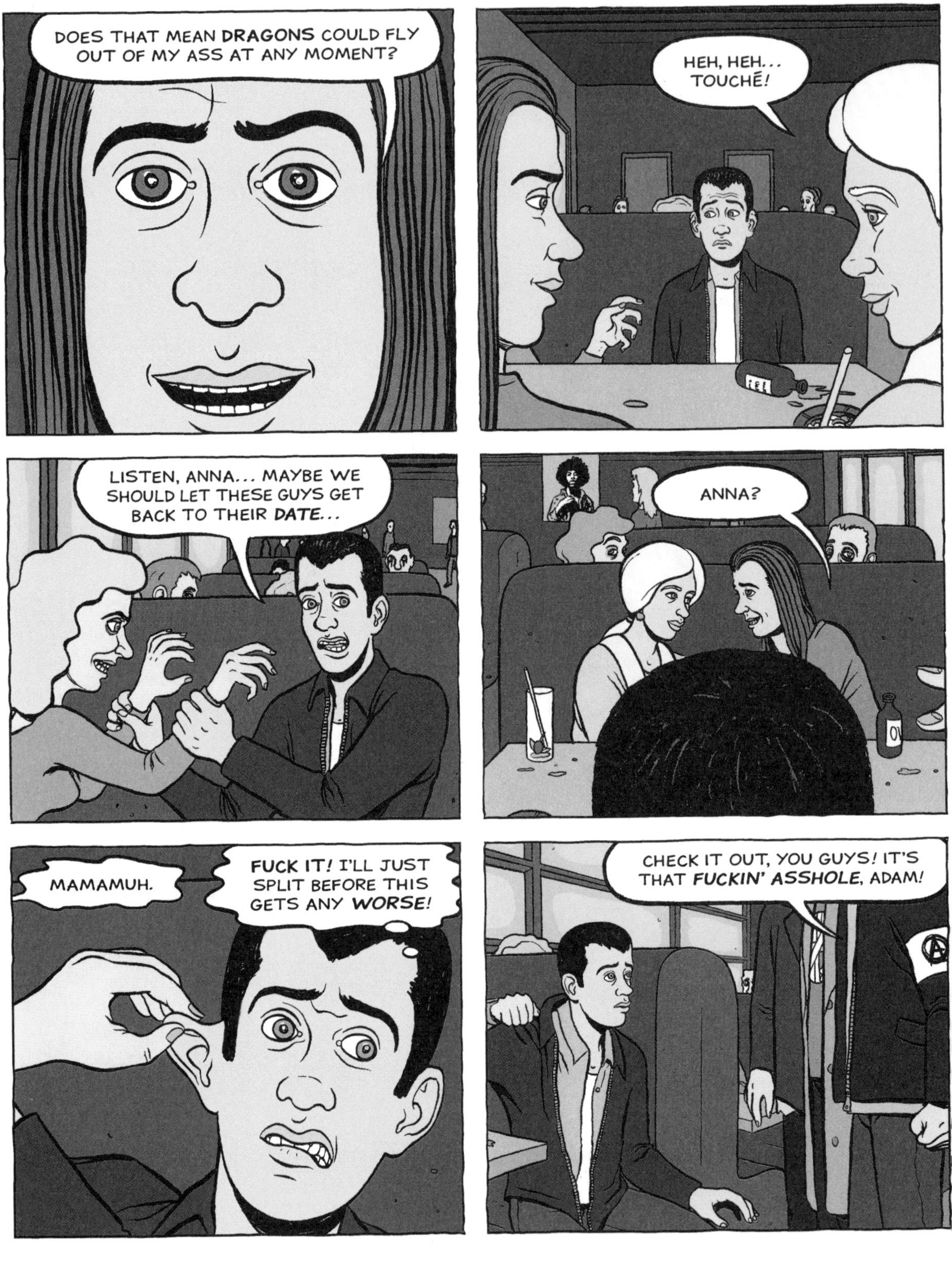
DOES THAT MEAN DRAGONS COULD FLY OUT OF MY ASS AT ANY MOMENT?
HEH, HEH... TOUCHÉ!
LISTEN, ANNA... MAYBE WE SHOULD LET THESE GUYS GET BACK TO THEIR DATE...
ANNA?
MAMAMUH.
FUCK IT! I'LL JUST SPLIT BEFORE THIS GETS ANY WORSE!
CHECK IT OUT, YOU GUYS! IT'S THAT FUCKIN' ASSHOLE, ADAM!

New Year's Eve, 2004

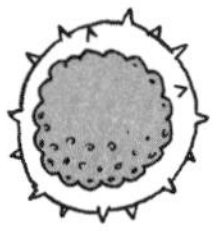

excerpt from *Monsters*

GABBY SCHULZ (AKA KEN DAHL)

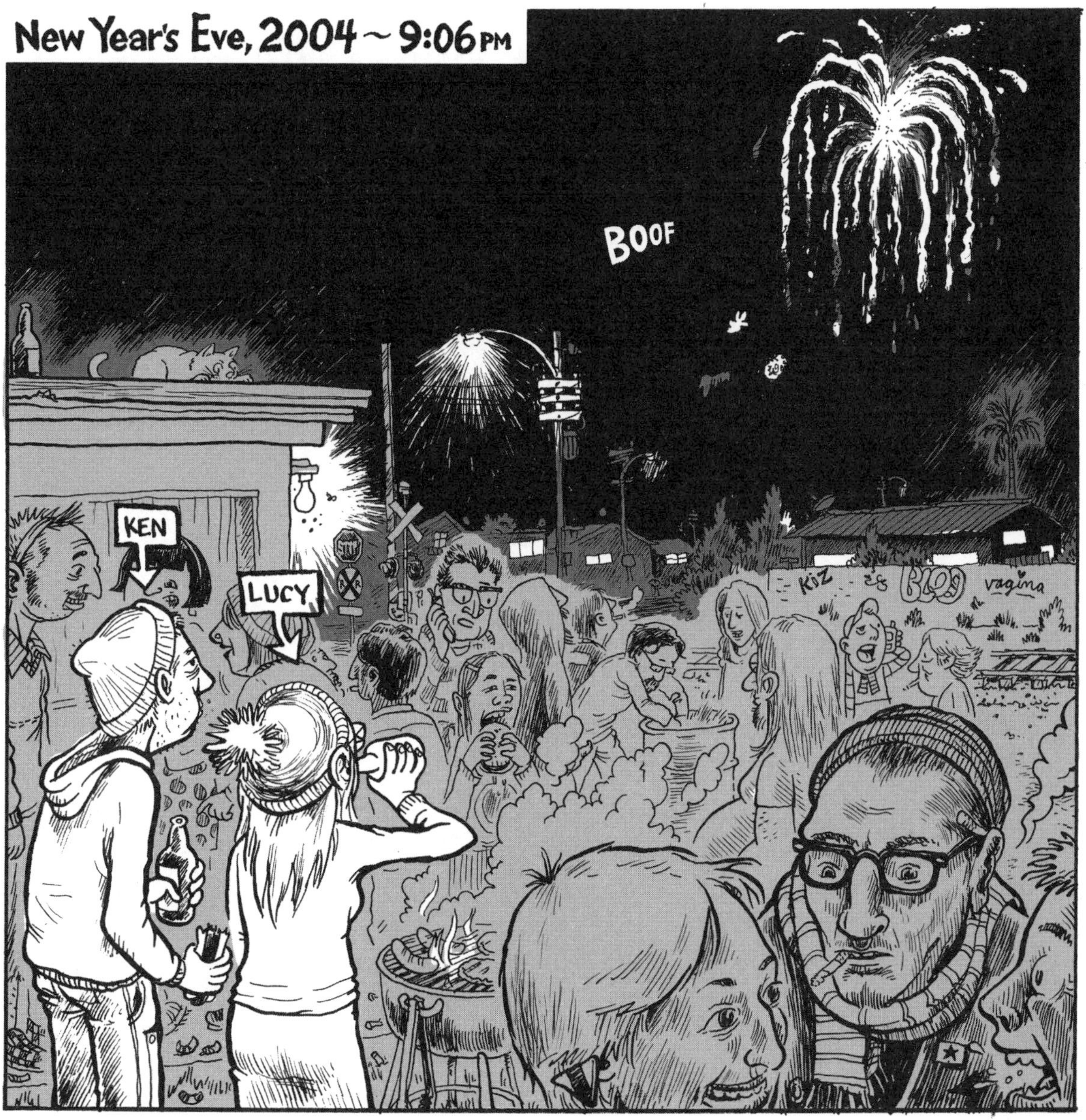
New Year's Eve, 2004 ~ 9:06 PM
BOOF
KEN
LUCY
vagina

HA
HA
PFF
BLAH
BLAH BLAH BLAH
BLAH BLAH
BLAH
BLAH
BLAH
AN ALL MY PEOPLE THAT
DRUUG DEALIN JUST TO GET BAAH
STACK YA MONEY TIL IT GETS SKYY HIIIIGH..

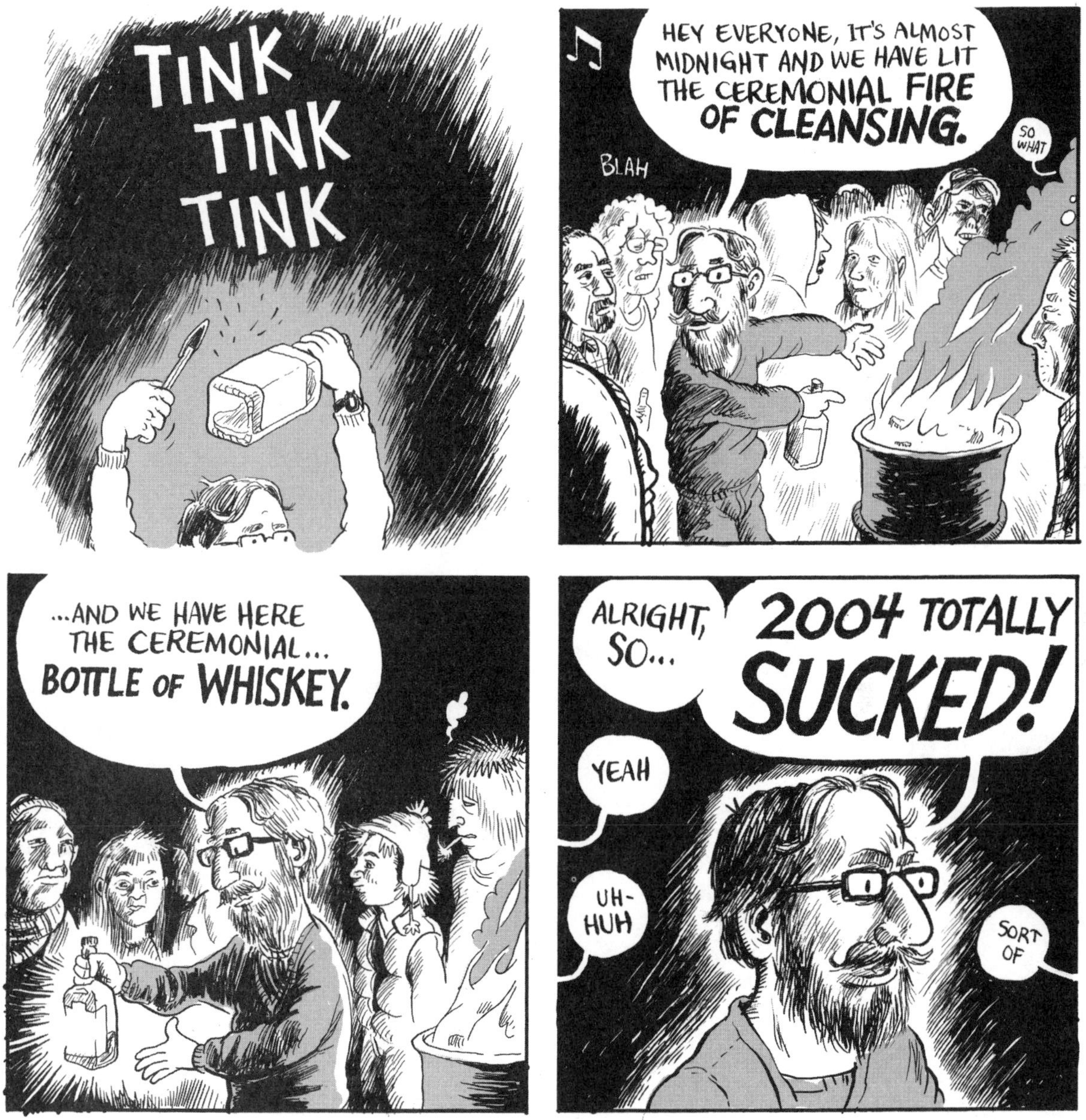

TINK
TINK
TINK
HEY EVERYONE, IT'S ALMOST MIDNIGHT AND WE HAVE LIT THE CEREMONIAL FIRE OF CLEANSING.
BLAH
SO WHAT
...AND WE HAVE HERE THE CEREMONIAL... BOTTLE OF WHISKEY.
ALRIGHT, SO...
2004 TOTALLY SUCKED!
YEAH
UH-HUH
SORT OF

SO, NOW THAT IT'S FINALLY ALMOST **OVER**, WE'RE GOING TO HAVE A RITUAL OF **CLEANSING**.

I'M GOING TO PASS AROUND THESE **PAPERS**, AND ON THEM YOU CAN WRITE DOWN THE **WORST THING** THAT HAPPENED TO YOU THIS YEAR.

YOU MEAN LIKE A POGROM?

... AND THEN YOU TAKE A SIP OF THE **MAGICAL ELIXIR** OF **RENEWAL**...

UNLESS YOU HAVE HERPES.

HA HA

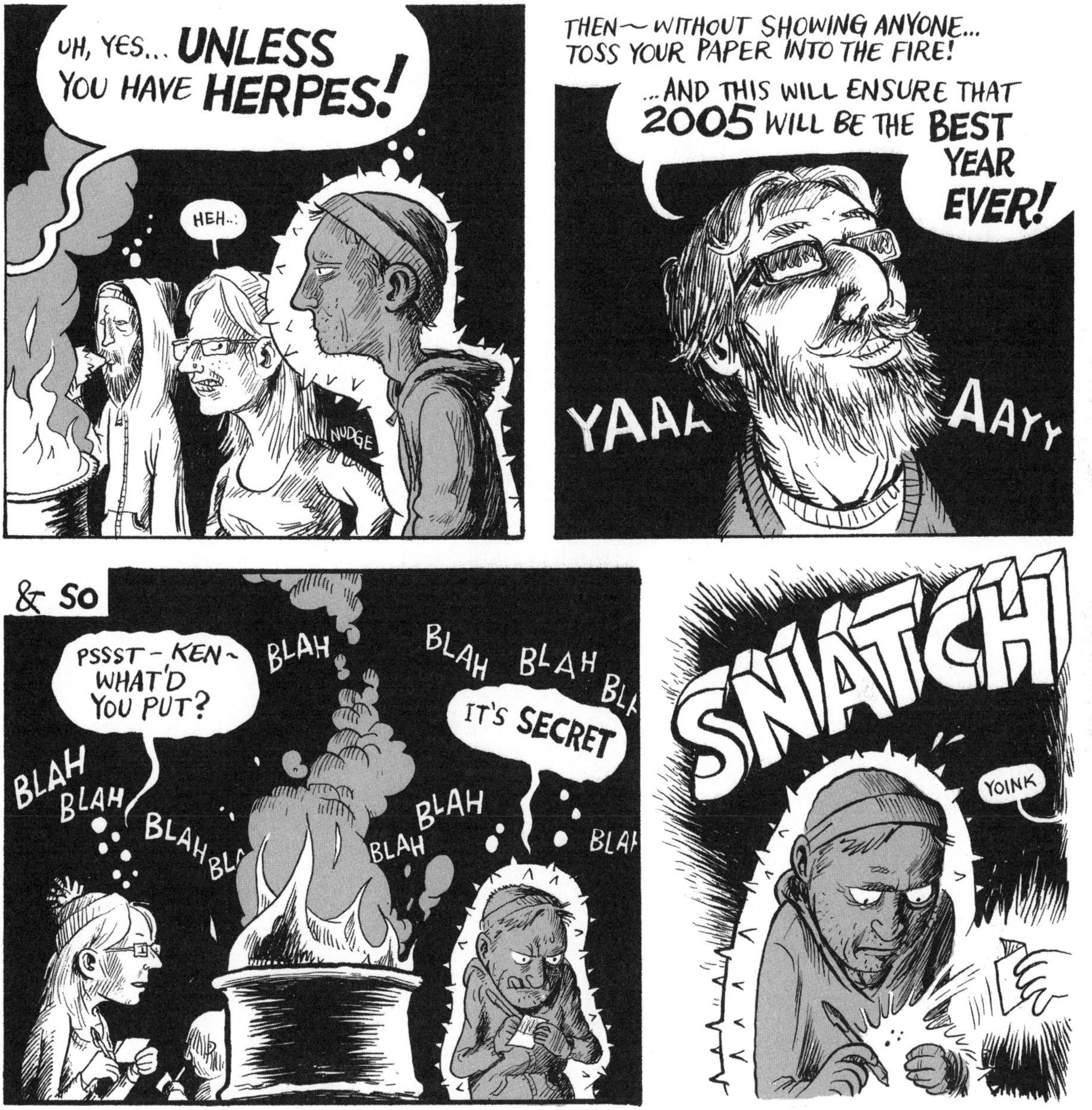
UH, YES... UNLESS YOU HAVE HERPES!
HEH..!
NUDGE
THEN~ WITHOUT SHOWING ANYONE... TOSS YOUR PAPER INTO THE FIRE!
...AND THIS WILL ENSURE THAT 2005 WILL BE THE BEST YEAR EVER!
YAAA
AAYY
& SO
PSSST - KEN~ WHAT'D YOU PUT?
BLAH
BLAH BLAH BL
IT'S SECRET
BLAH BLAH
BLAH BLAH BL
BLAH BLAH
BLAH
SNATCH
YOINK

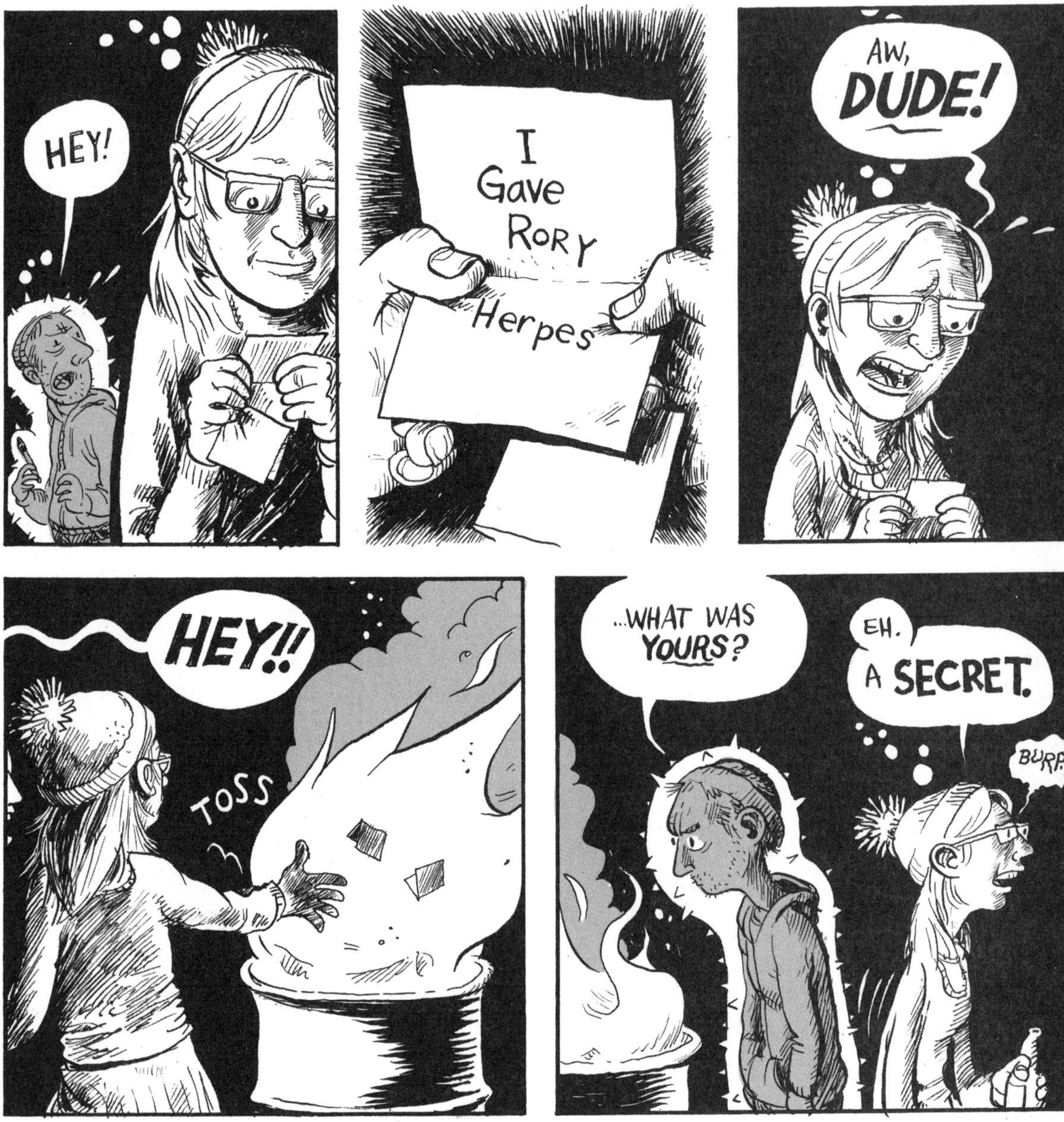
HEY!
I Gave Rory Herpes
AW, DUDE!
HEY!!
TOSS
...WHAT WAS YOURS?
EH.
A SECRET.
BURP.

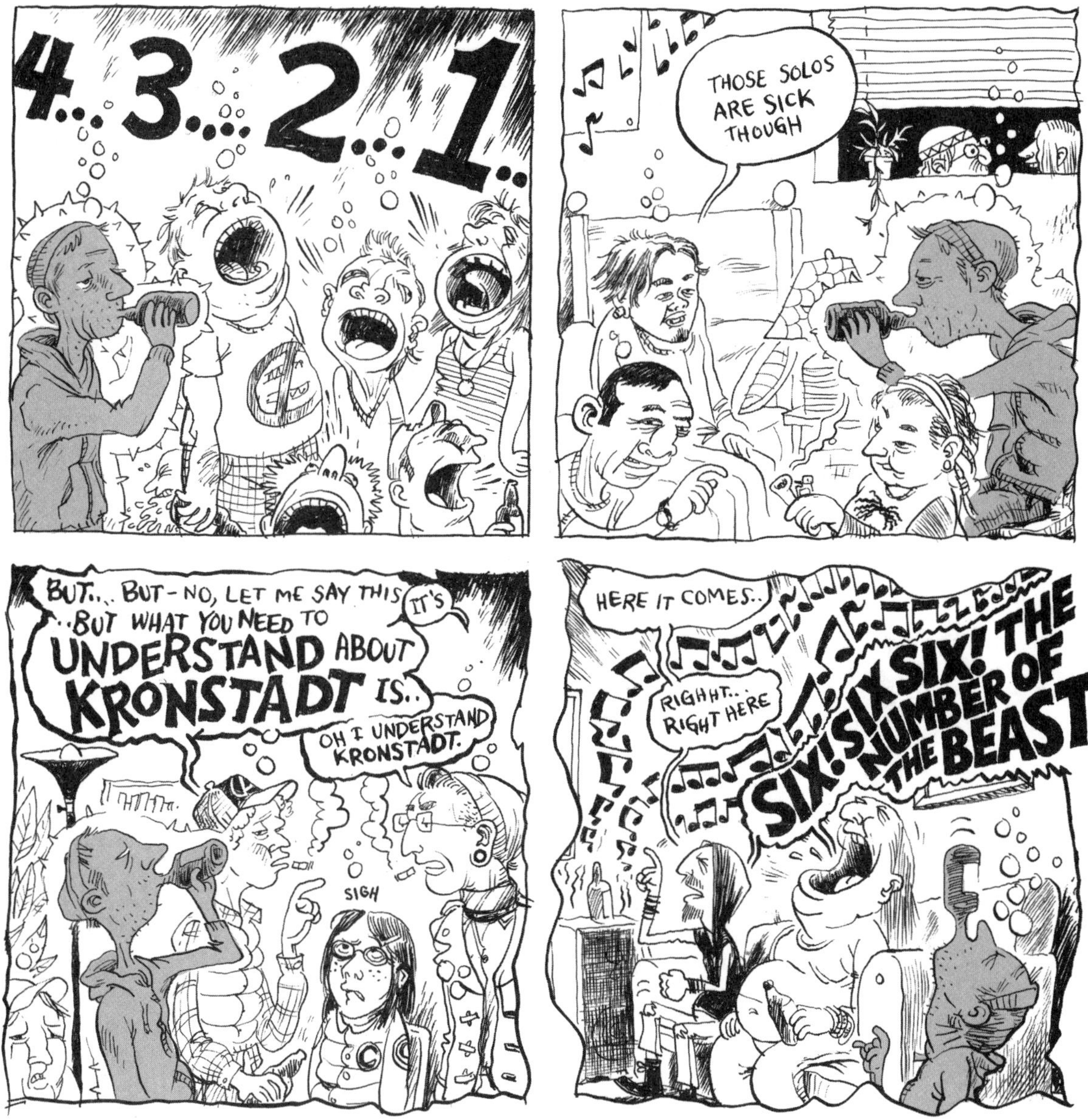
4...3...2...1...
THOSE SOLOS ARE SICK THOUGH
BUT... BUT - NO, LET ME SAY THIS ..BUT WHAT YOU NEED TO UNDERSTAND ABOUT KRONSTADT IS..
IT'S
OH I UNDERSTAND KRONSTADT.
SIGH
HERE IT COMES..
RIGHHT... RIGHT HERE
SIX! SIX SIX! THE NUMBER OF THE BEAST

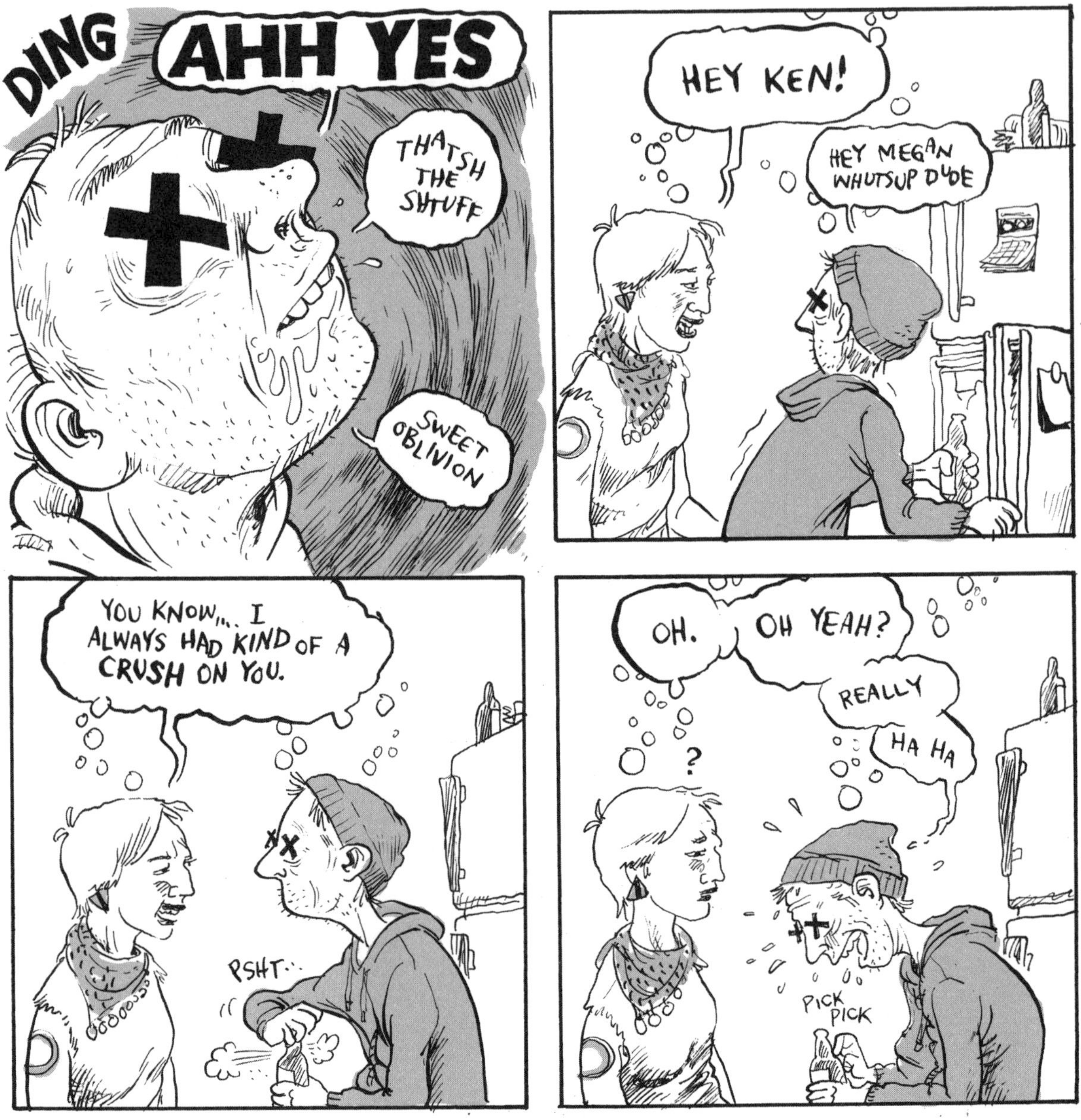
DING
AHH YES
THATSH THE SHTUFF
SWEET OBLIVION
HEY KEN!
HEY MEGAN WHUTSUP DUDE
YOU KNOW.... I ALWAYS HAD KIND OF A CRUSH ON YOU.
PSHT..
OH.
OH YEAH?
REALLY
HA HA
?
PICK PICK

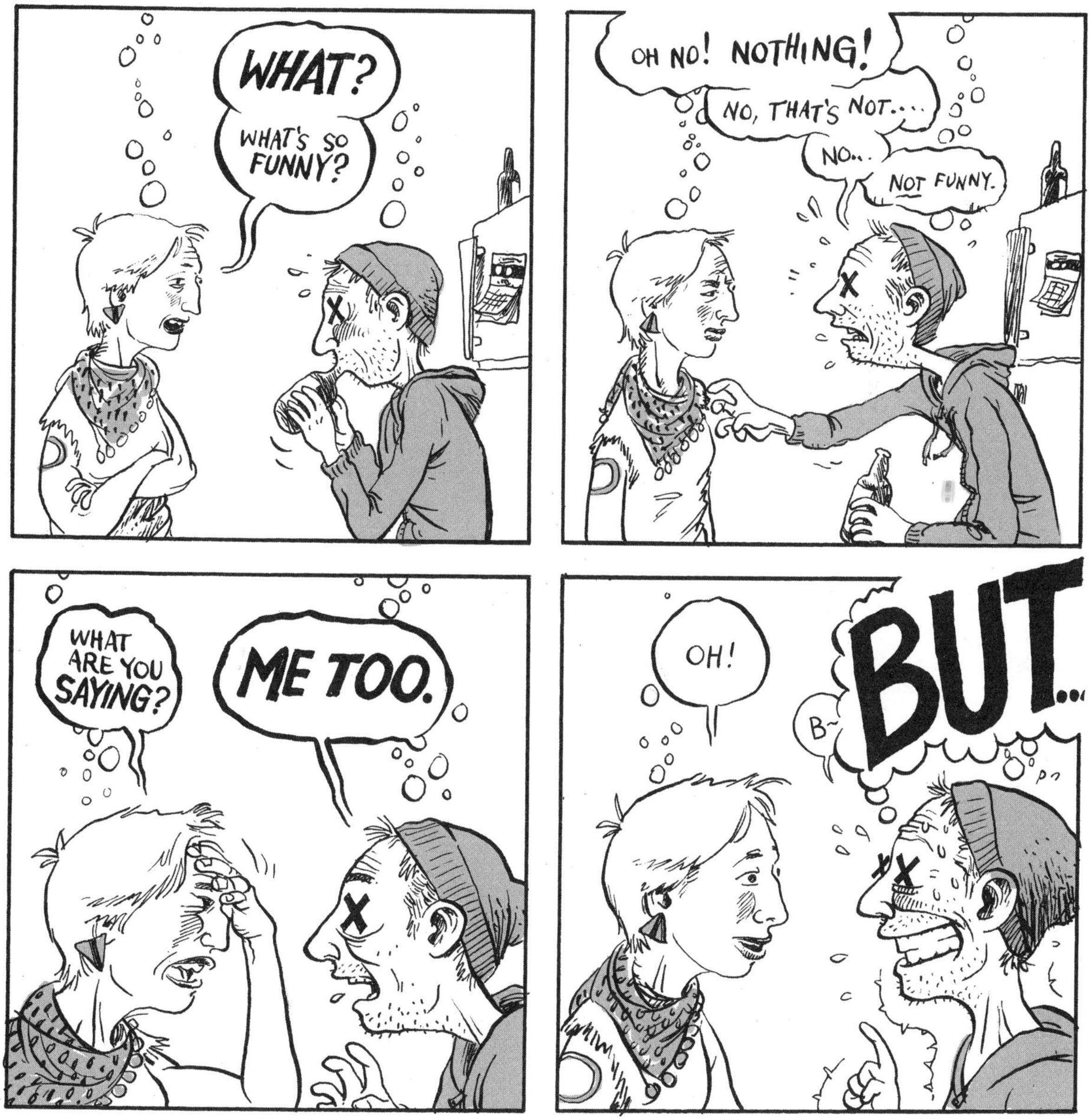
WHAT?
WHAT'S SO FUNNY?
OH NO! NOTHING!
NO, THAT'S NOT....
NO..
NOT FUNNY.
WHAT ARE YOU SAYING?
ME TOO.
OH!
B~
BUT...

HEY... DO YOU WANNA MAKE OUT?
UHHHHHHHHHHH.. ..THAT WOULD BE NICE, BUT...
..BUT...
BBUT..
...BUT WHAT?
LOOK AT HER.... LOOK AT HOW CUTE SHE IS... AND SHE WANTS TO KISS US!

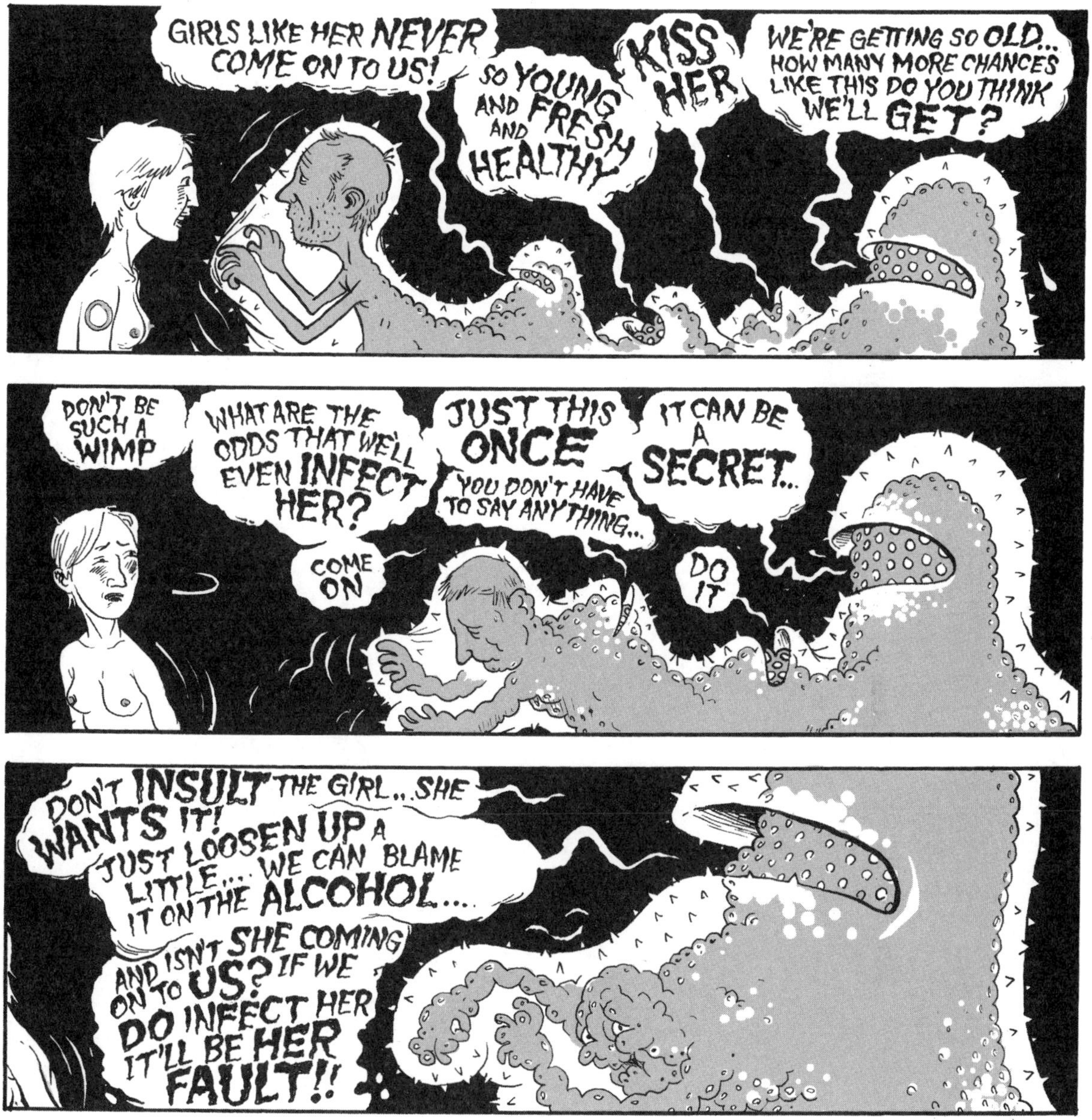
GIRLS LIKE HER NEVER COME ON TO US!
SO YOUNG AND FRESH AND HEALTHY
KISS HER
WE'RE GETTING SO OLD... HOW MANY MORE CHANCES LIKE THIS DO YOU THINK WE'LL GET?
DON'T BE SUCH A WIMP
WHAT ARE THE ODDS THAT WE'LL EVEN INFECT HER?
JUST THIS ONCE
YOU DON'T HAVE TO SAY ANYTHING...
IT CAN BE A SECRET...
COME ON
DO IT
DON'T INSULT THE GIRL.. SHE WANTS IT!
JUST LOOSEN UP A LITTLE... WE CAN BLAME IT ON THE ALCOHOL...
AND ISN'T SHE COMING ON TO US? IF WE DO INFECT HER IT'LL BE HER FAULT!!

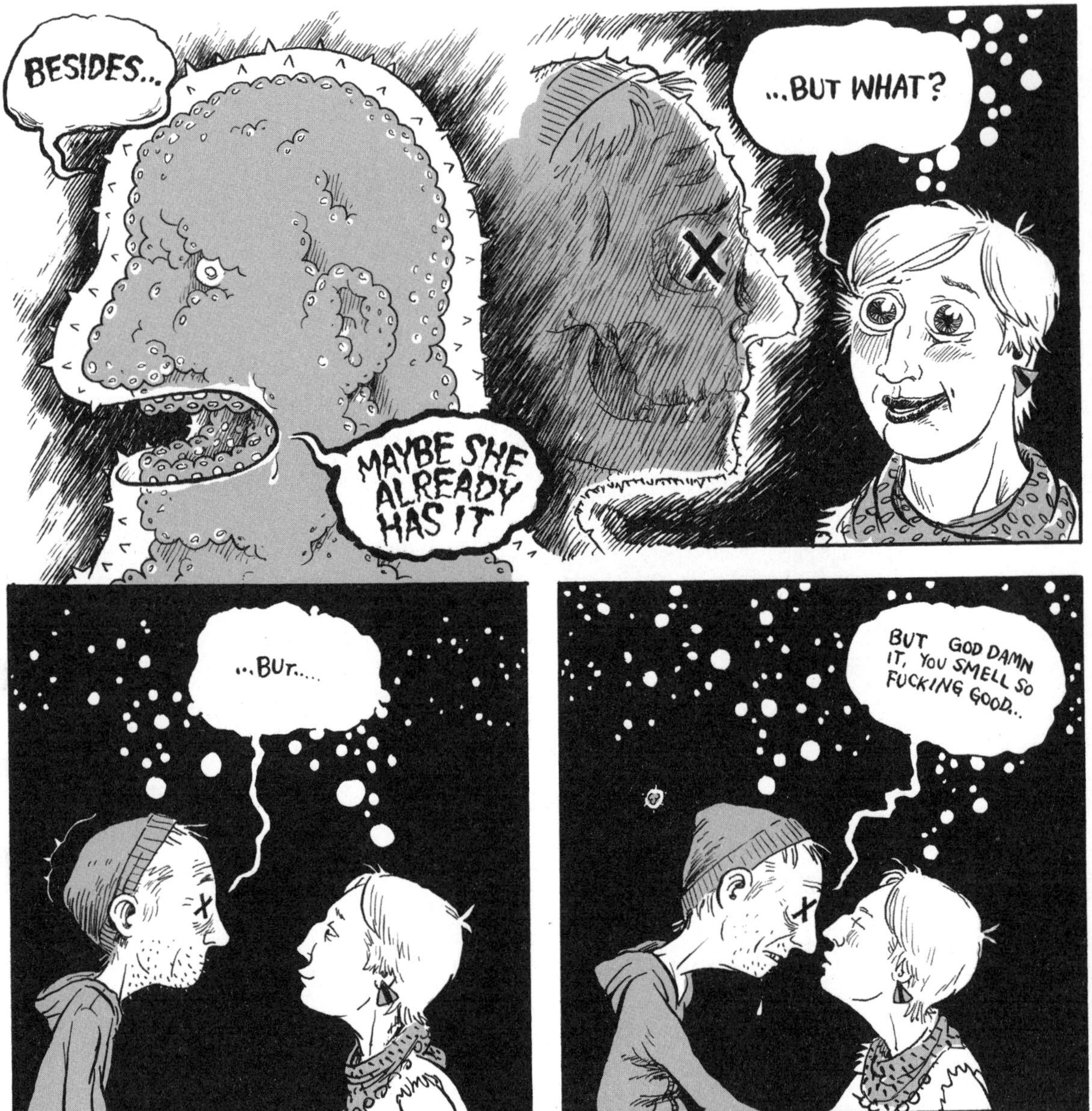
BESIDES...
MAYBE SHE ALREADY HAS IT
...BUT WHAT?
...BUT....
BUT GOD DAMN IT, YOU SMELL SO FUCKING GOOD..

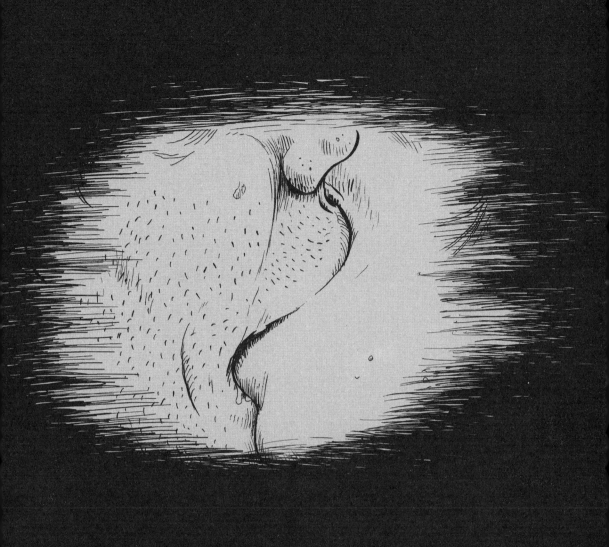

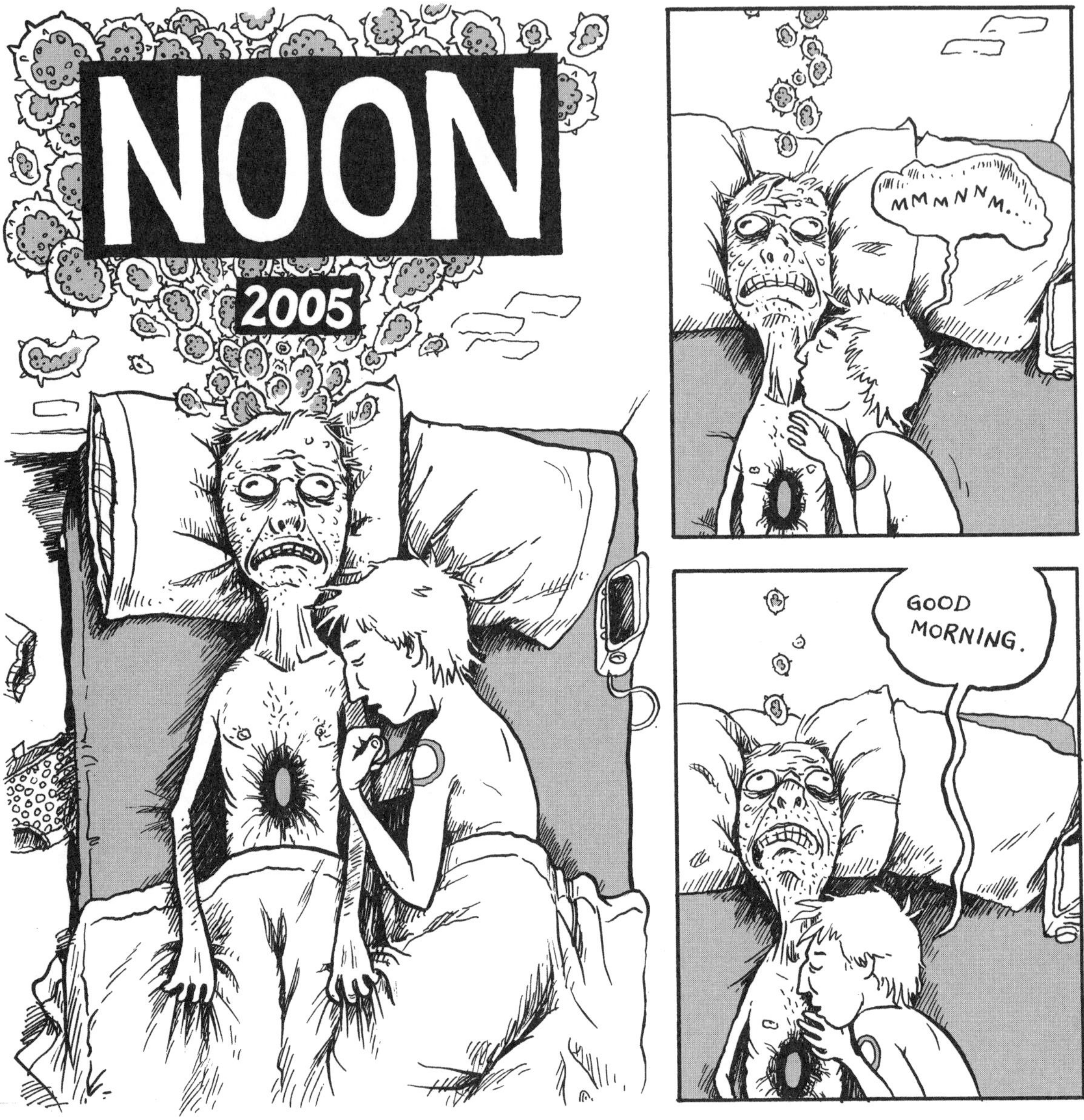
NOON
2005
MMMNNM...
GOOD MORNING.

... ARE YOU OK?
YEAH...
JUST....
HUNGOVER.
OH.

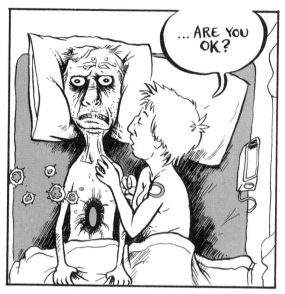

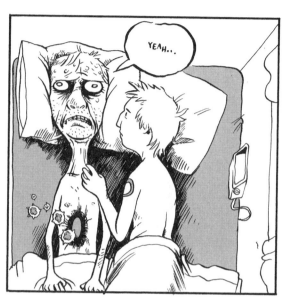

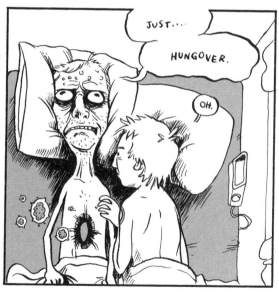

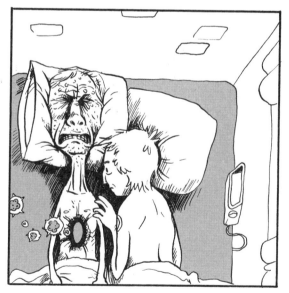

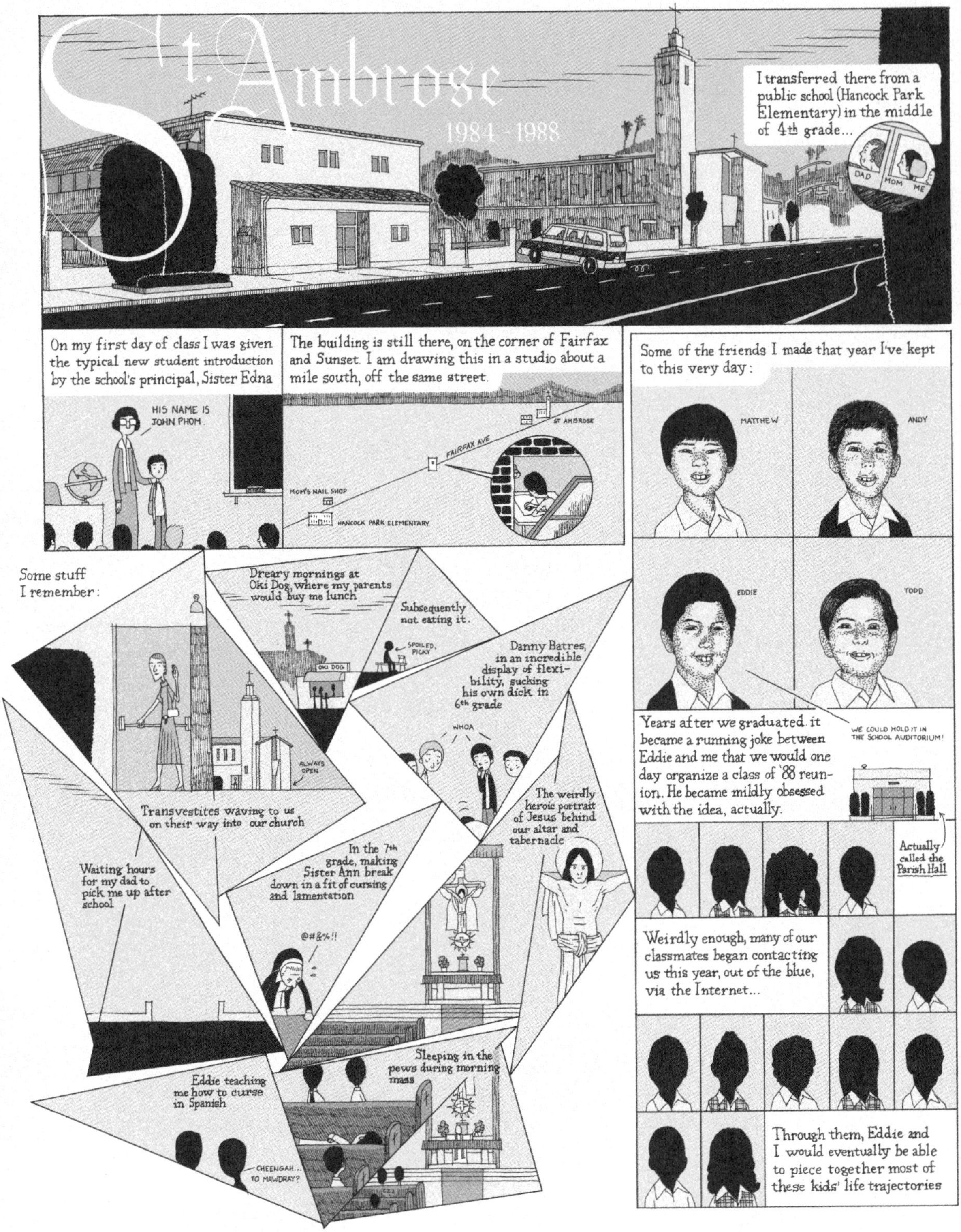
St. Ambrose
1984 - 1988
I transferred there from a public school (Hancock Park Elementary) in the middle of 4th grade...
DAD
MOM
ME
On my first day of class I was given the typical new student introduction by the school's principal, Sister Edna
HIS NAME IS JOHN PHOM.
The building is still there, on the corner of Fairfax and Sunset. I am drawing this in a studio about a mile south, off the same street.
ST AMBROSE
FAIRFAX AVE
MOM'S NAIL SHOP
HANCOCK PARK ELEMENTARY
Some of the friends I made that year I've kept to this very day:
MATTHEW
ANDY
EDDIE
TODD
Years after we graduated it became a running joke between Eddie and me that we would one day organize a class of '88 reunion. He became mildly obsessed with the idea, actually.
WE COULD HOLD IT IN THE SCHOOL AUDITORIUM!
Actually called the Parish Hall
Weirdly enough, many of our classmates began contacting us this year, out of the blue, via the Internet...
Through them, Eddie and I would eventually be able to piece together most of these kids' life trajectories
Some stuff I remember:
Dreary mornings at Oki Dog, where my parents would buy me lunch
OKI DOG
Subsequently not eating it.
SPOILED, PICKY
Transvestites waving to us on their way into our church
ALWAYS OPEN
Danny Batres, in an incredible display of flexibility, sucking his own dick in 6th grade
WHOA
The weirdly heroic portrait of Jesus behind our altar and tabernacle
Waiting hours for my dad to pick me up after school
In the 7th grade, making Sister Ann break down in a fit of cursing and lamentation
@#&%!!
Eddie teaching me how to curse in Spanish
CHEENGAH... TO MAWDRAY?
Sleeping in the pews during morning mass
zzz

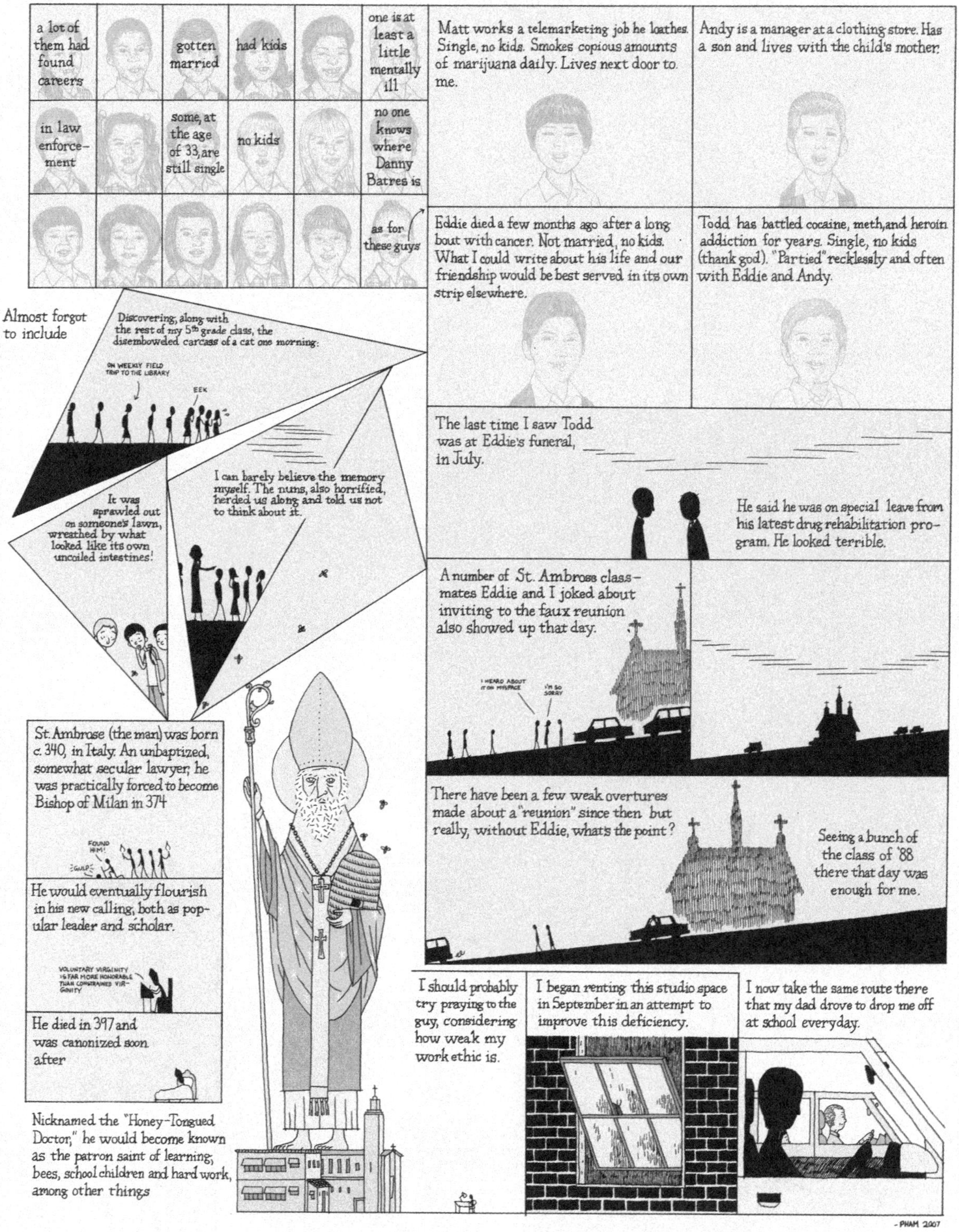

a lot of them had found careers
gotten married
had kids
one is at least a little mentally ill
in law enforce-ment
some, at the age of 33, are still single
no kids
no one knows where Danny Batres is
as for these guys
Matt works a telemarketing job he loathes. Single, no kids. Smokes copious amounts of marijuana daily. Lives next door to me.
Andy is a manager at a clothing store. Has a son and lives with the child's mother.
Eddie died a few months ago after a long bout with cancer. Not married, no kids. What I could write about his life and our friendship would be best served in its own strip elsewhere.
Todd has battled cocaine, meth, and heroin addiction for years. Single, no kids (thank god). "Partied" recklessly and often with Eddie and Andy.
Almost forgot to include
Discovering, along with the rest of my 5th grade class, the disemboweled carcass of a cat one morning:
ON WEEKLY FIELD TRIP TO THE LIBRARY
EEK
It was sprawled out on someone's lawn, wreathed by what looked like its own uncoiled intestines!
I can barely believe the memory myself. The nuns, also horrified, herded us along and told us not to think about it.
The last time I saw Todd was at Eddie's funeral, in July.
He said he was on special leave from his latest drug rehabilitation program. He looked terrible.
A number of St. Ambross class-mates Eddie and I joked about inviting to the faux reunion also showed up that day.
I HEARD ABOUT IT ON MYSPACE
I'M SO SORRY
There have been a few weak overtures made about a "reunion" since then but really, without Eddie, what's the point?
Seeing a bunch of the class of '88 there that day was enough for me.
St. Ambrose (the man) was born c. 340, in Italy. An unbaptized, somewhat secular lawyer, he was practically forced to become Bishop of Milan in 374
FOUND HIM!
GULP
He would eventually flourish in his new calling, both as pop-ular leader and scholar.
VOLUNTARY VIRGINITY IS FAR MORE HONORABLE THAN CONSTRAINED VIR-GINITY
He died in 397 and was canonized soon after
Nicknamed the "Honey-Tongued Doctor," he would become known as the patron saint of learning, bees, school children and hard work, among other things
I should probably try praying to the guy, considering how weak my work ethic is.
I began renting this studio space in September in an attempt to improve this deficiency.
I now take the same route there that my dad drove to drop me off at school everyday.
- PHAM 2007

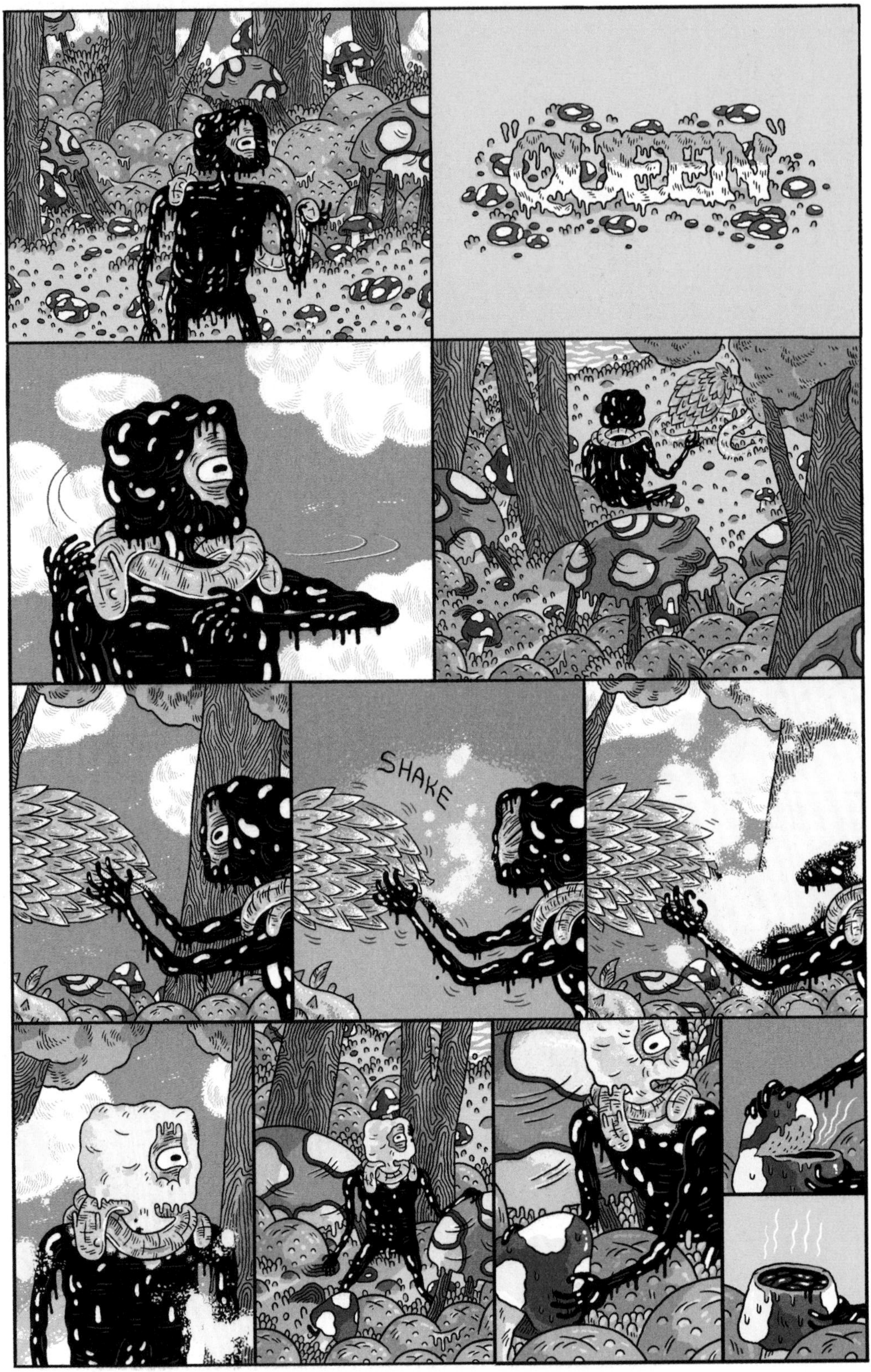
SHAKE

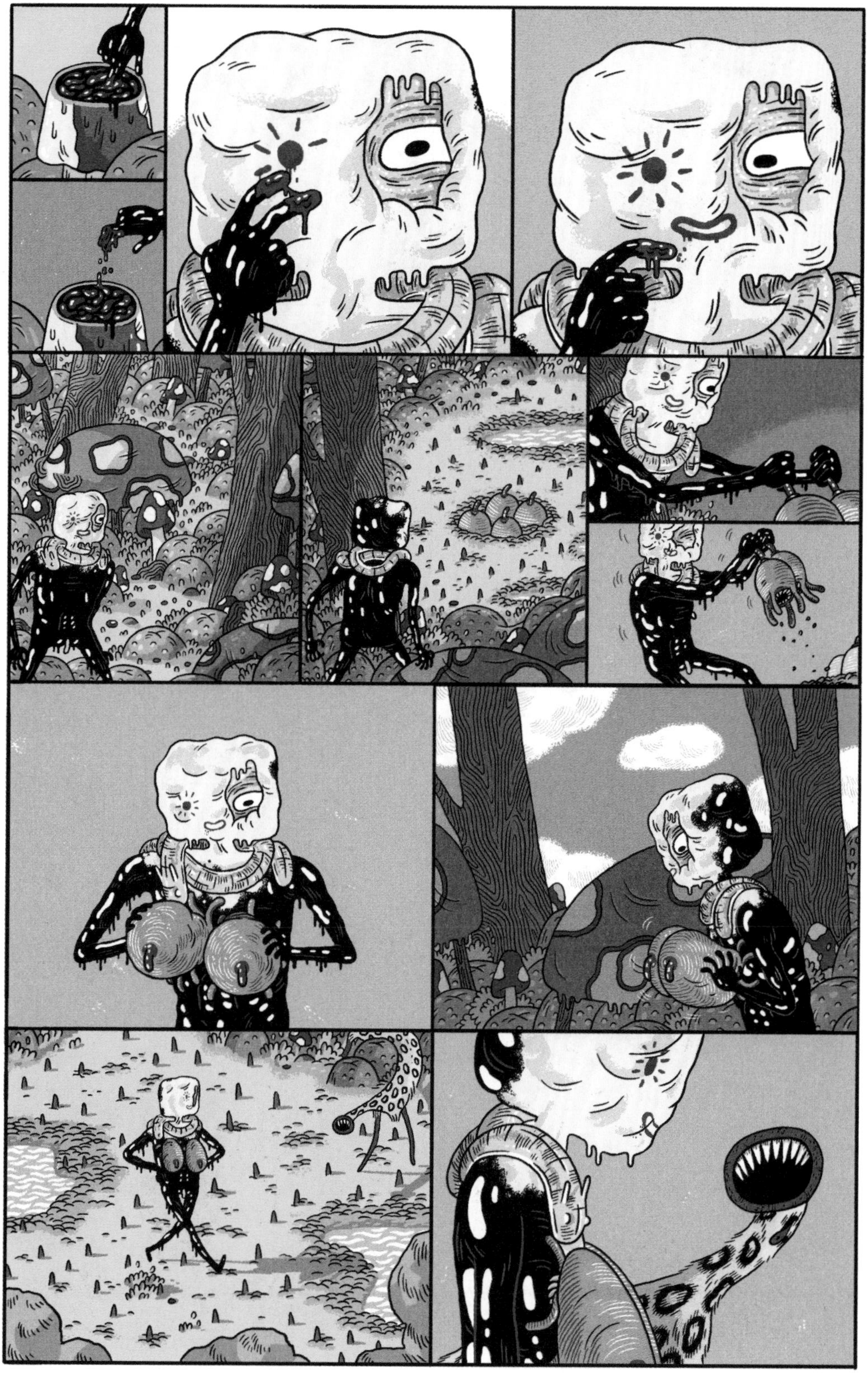

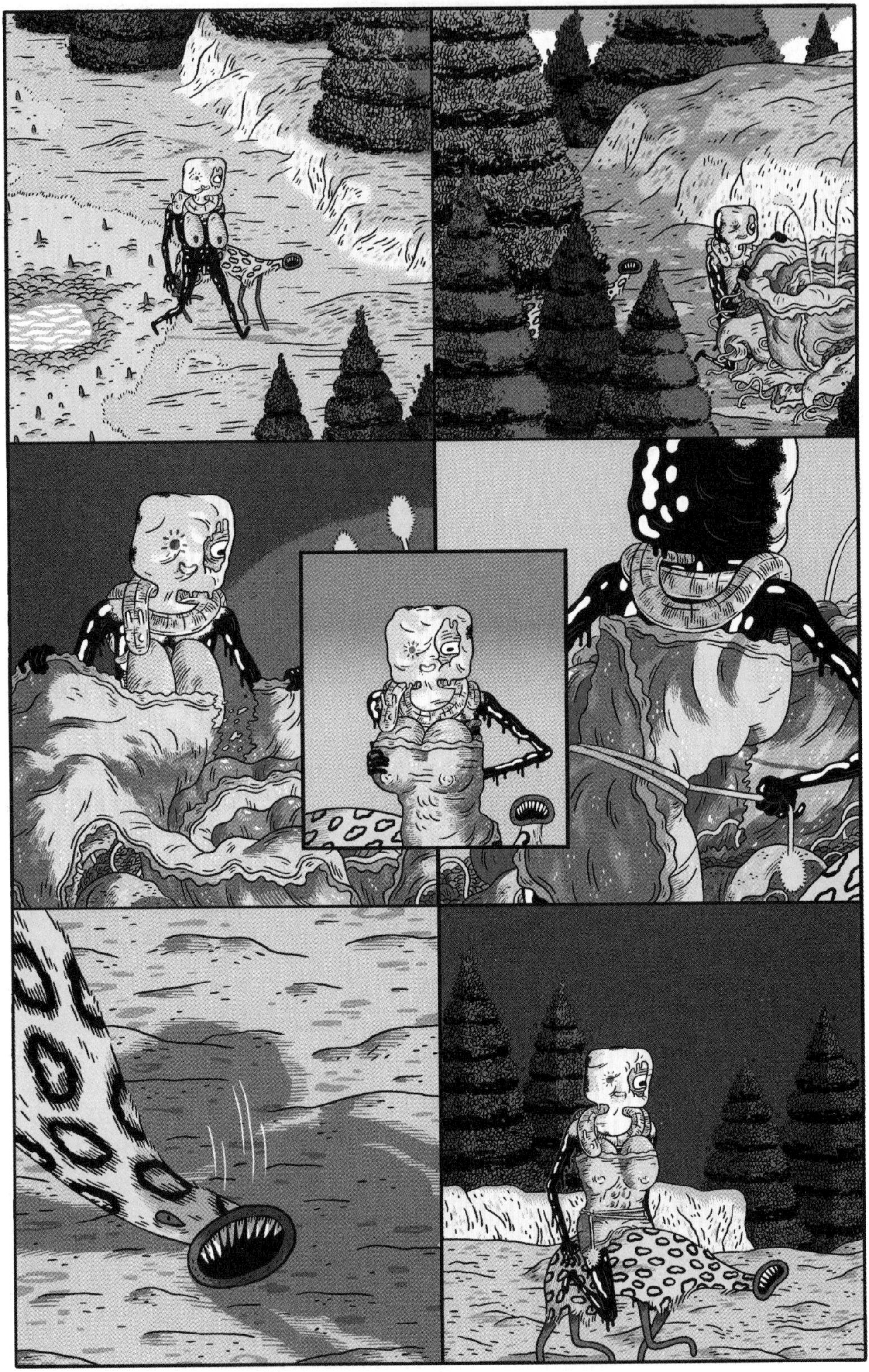

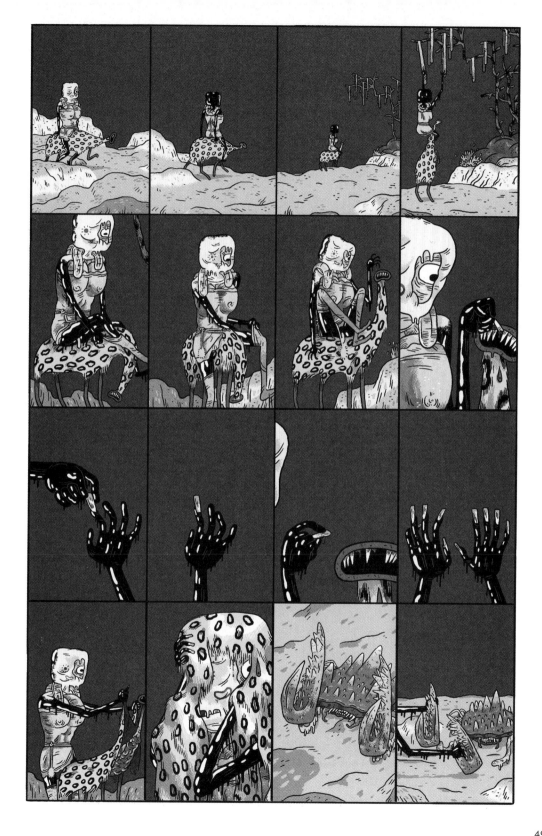

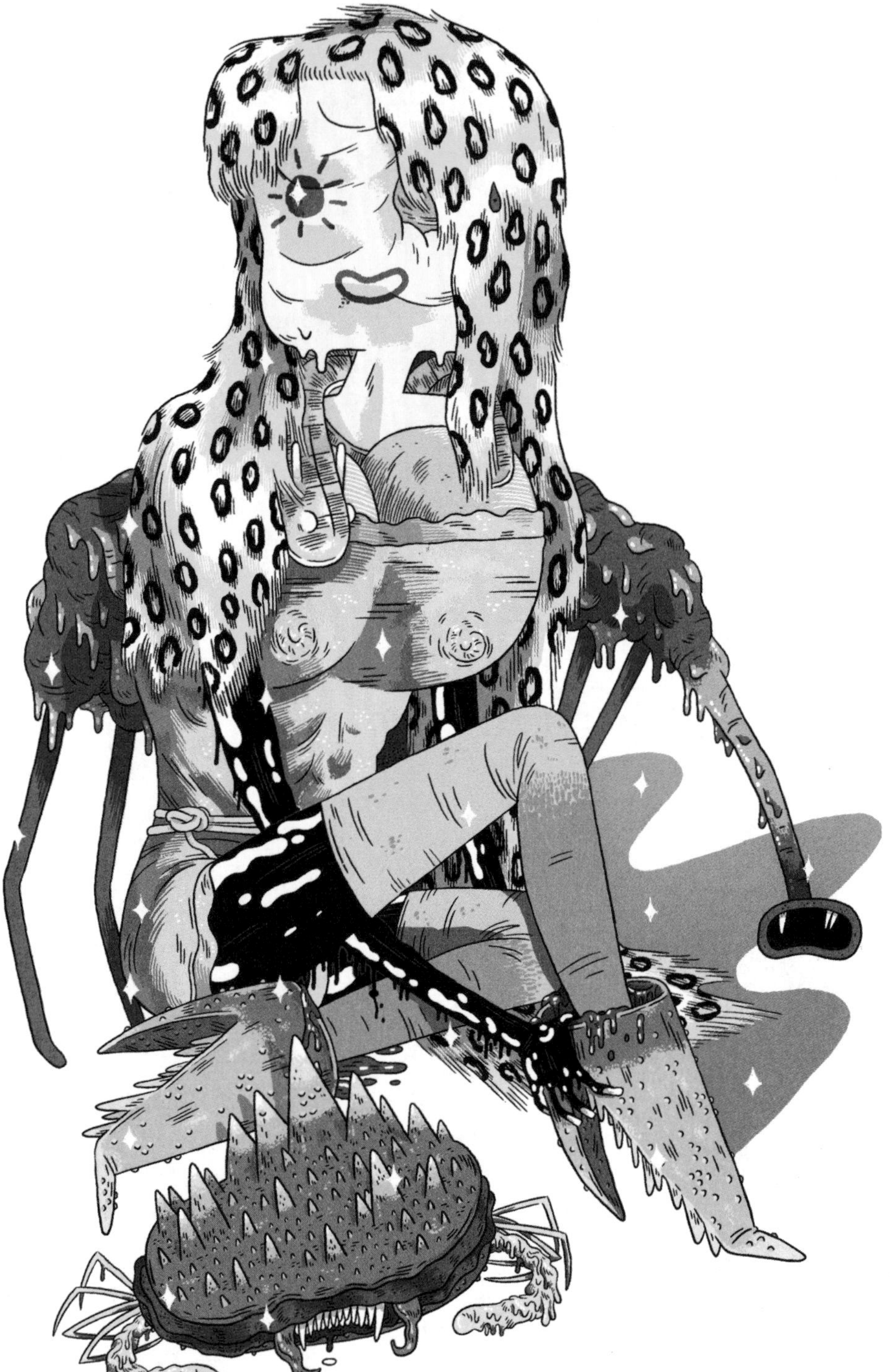

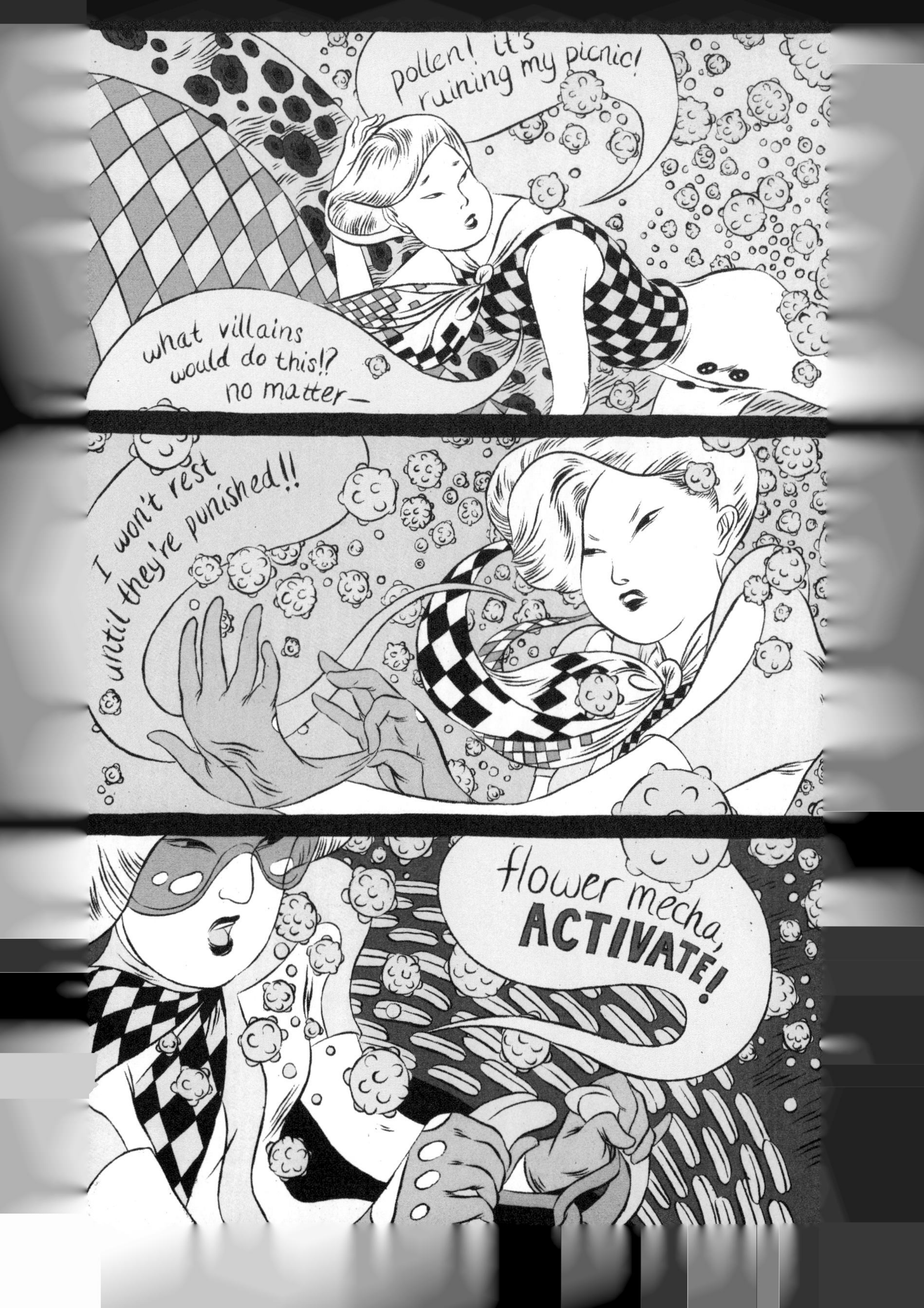
pollen! it's ruining my picnic!
what villains would do this!? no matter—
I won't rest until they're punished!!
flower mecha, ACTIVATE!

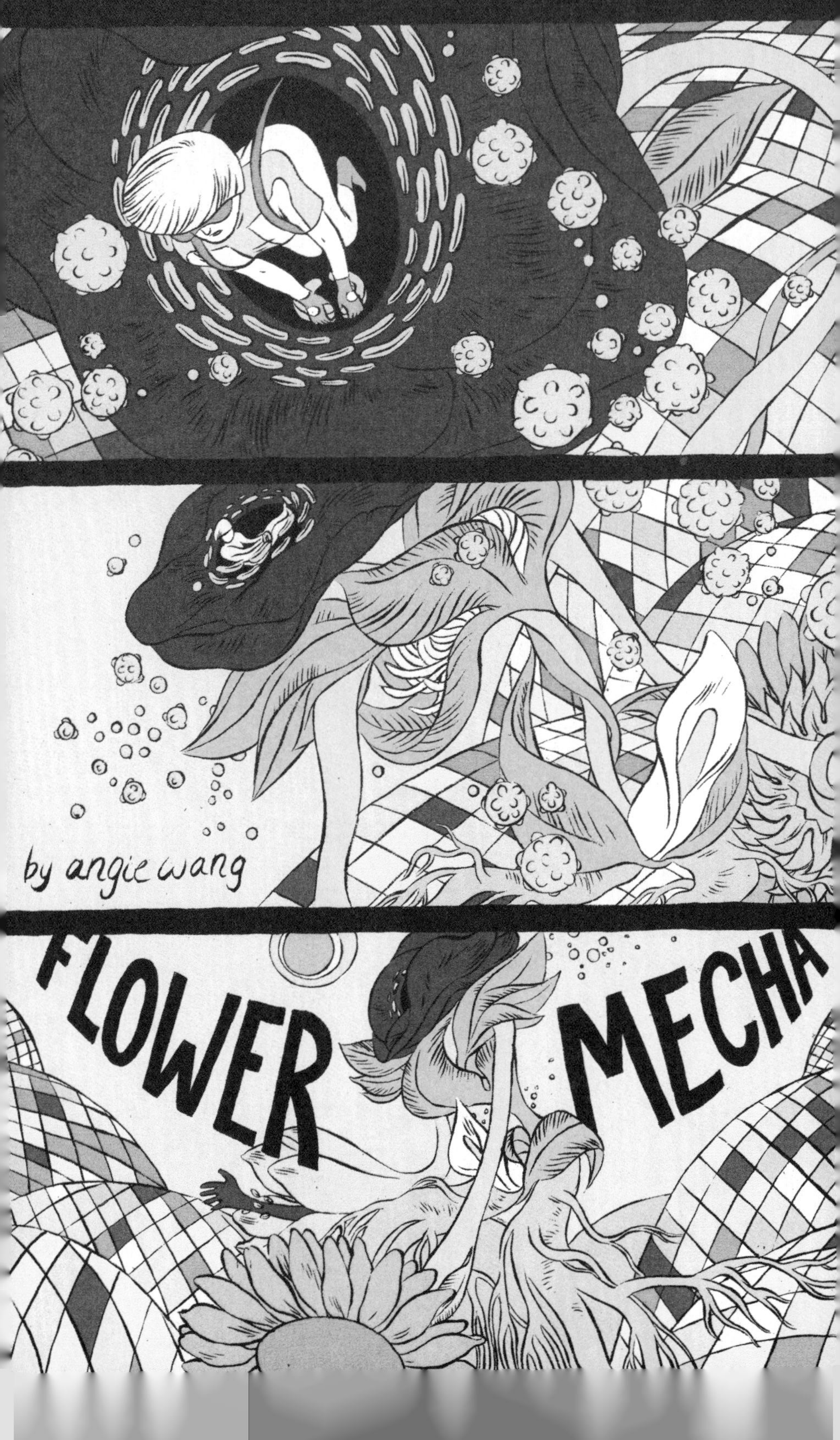

by angie wang
FLOWER MECHA

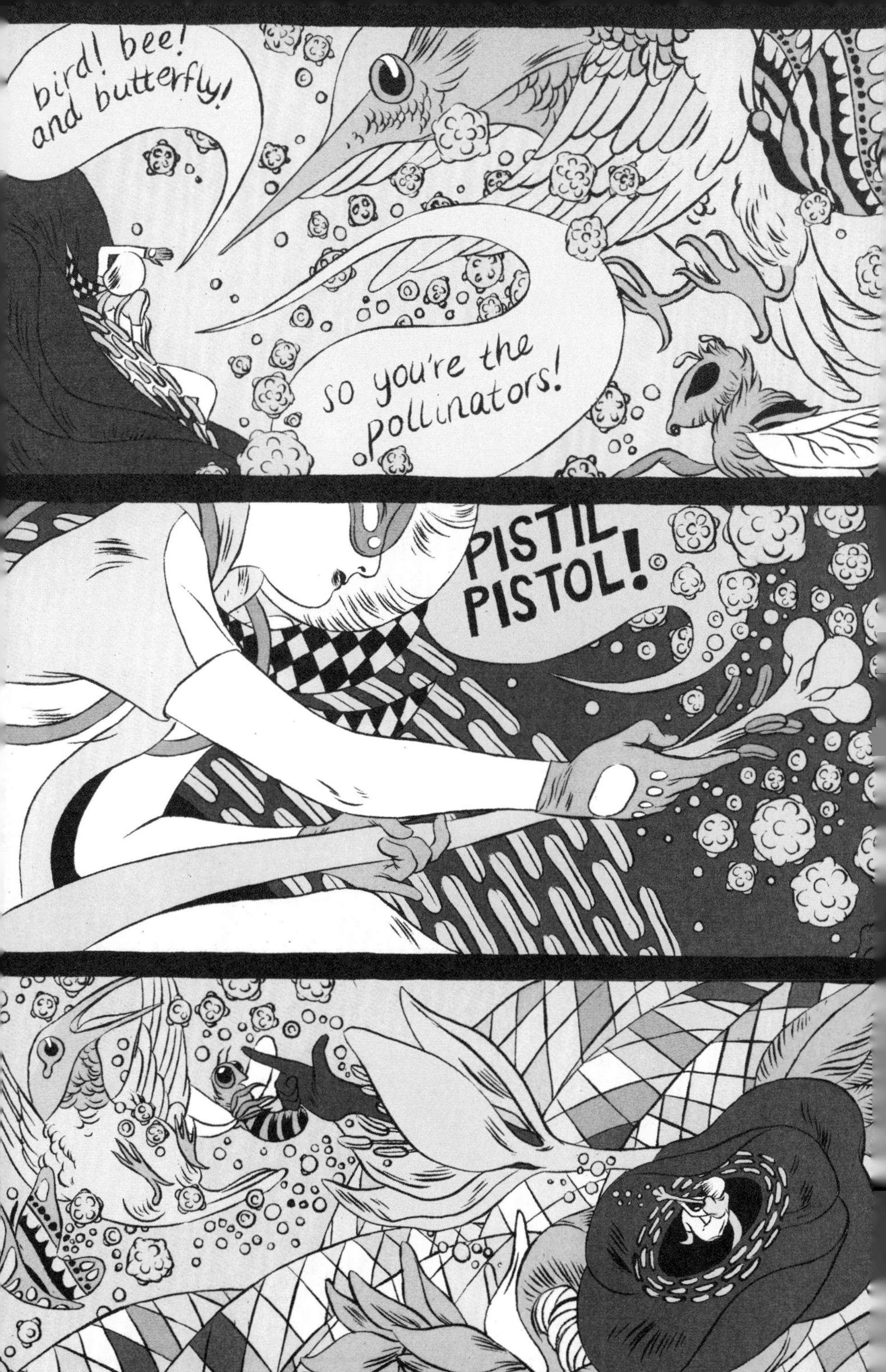
bird! bee! and butterfly!
so you're the pollinators!
PISTIL PISTOL!

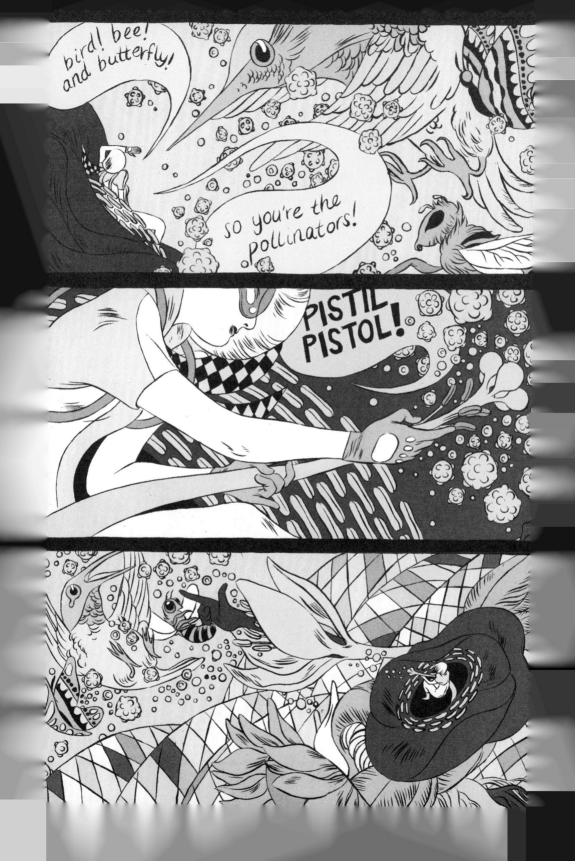

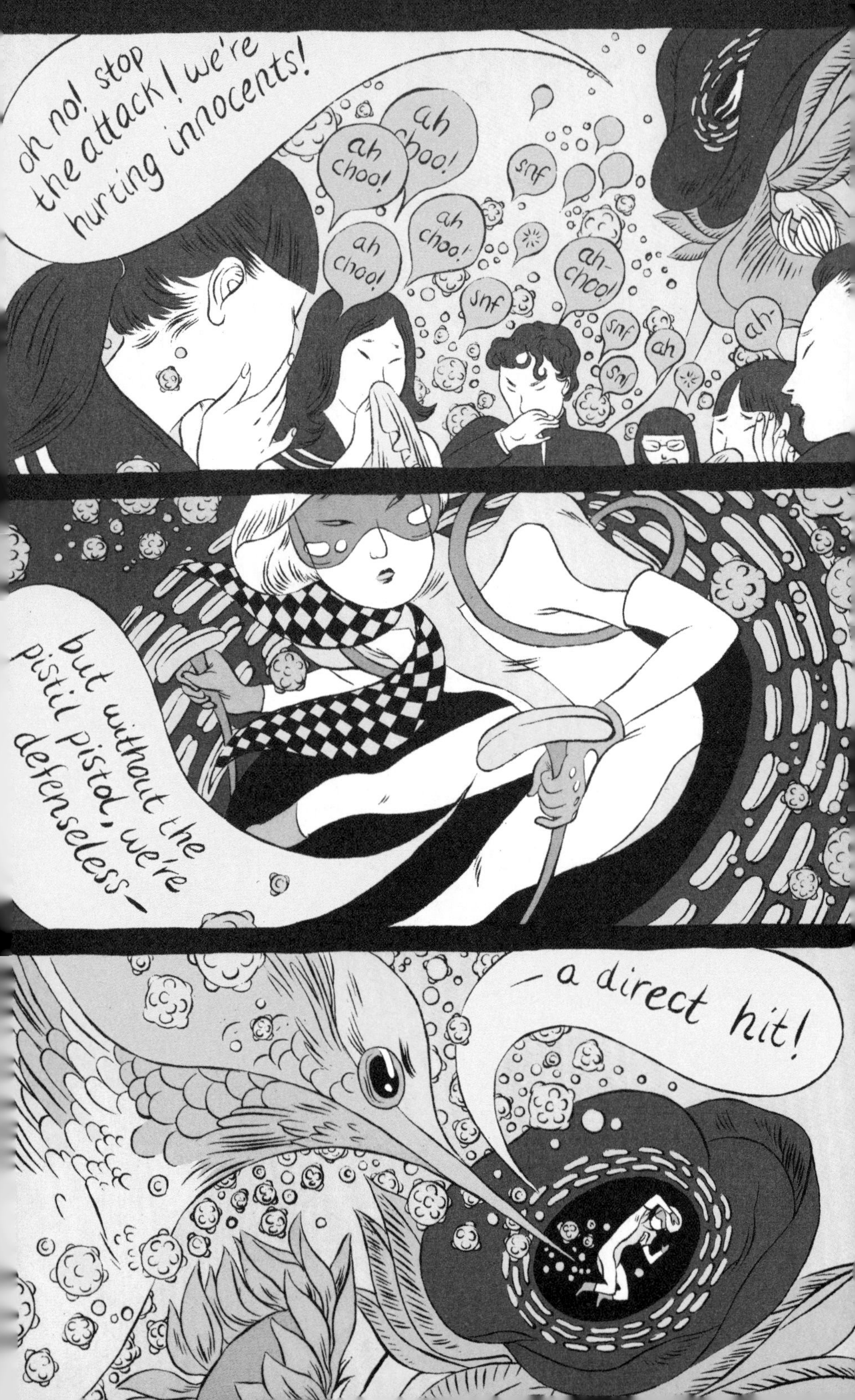
oh no! stop the attack! we're hurting innocents!
ah choo!
ah choo!
snf
ah choo!
ah choo!
ah-choo!
snf
snf
ah
snf
ah-
but without the pistil pistol, we're defenseless-
-a direct hit!

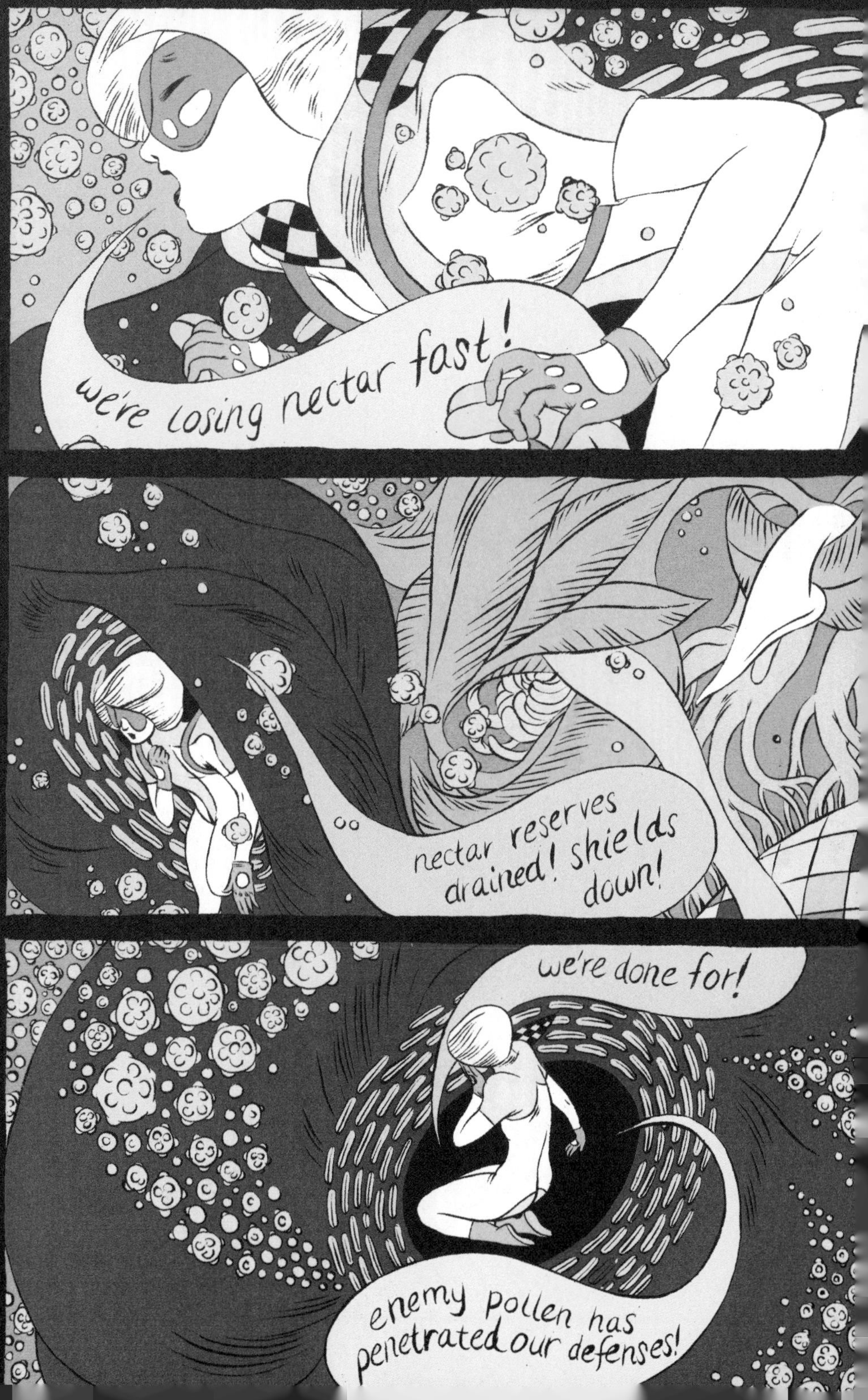
we're losing nectar fast!
nectar reserves drained! shields down!
we're done for!
enemy pollen has penetrated our defenses!

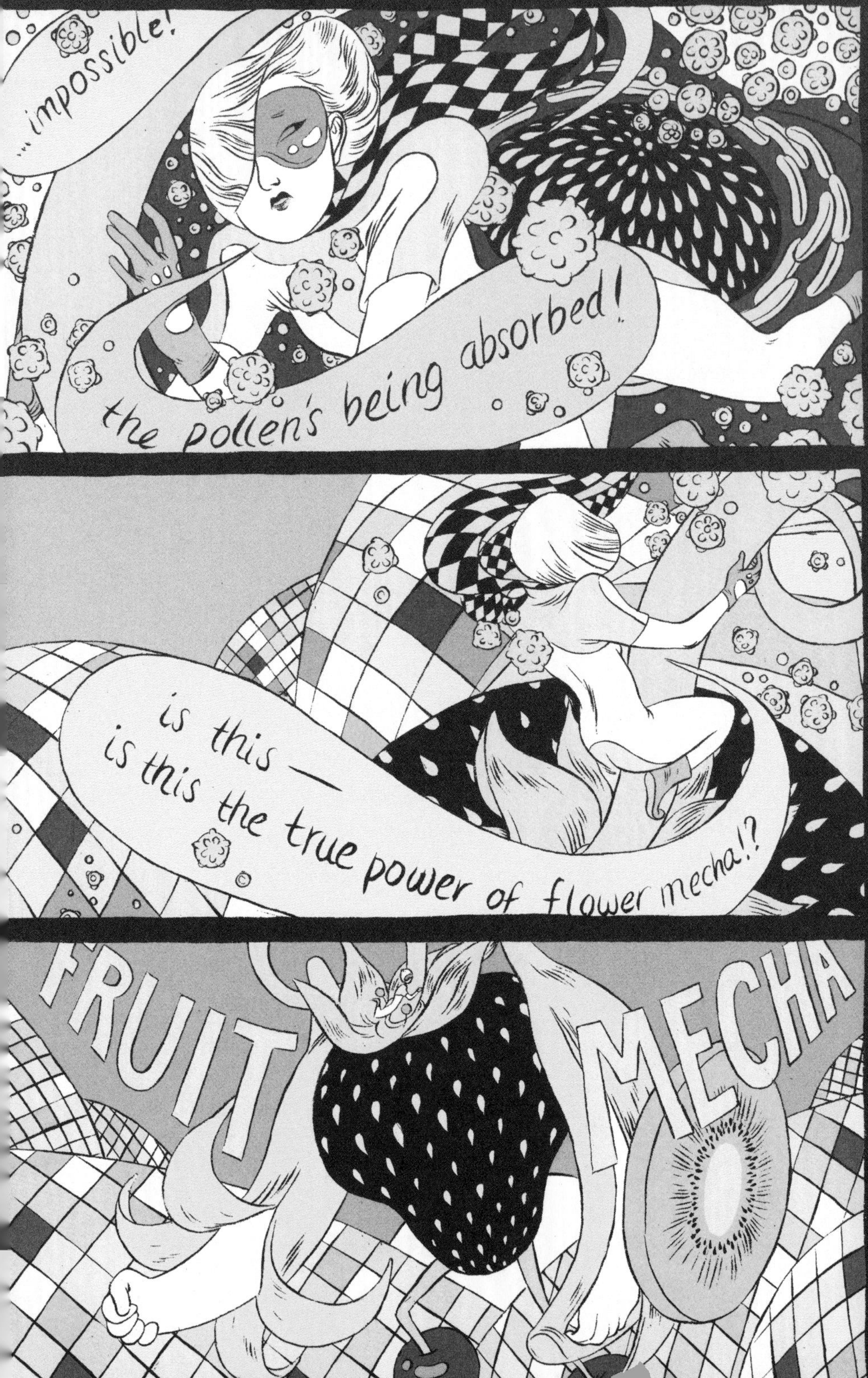
...impossible!
the pollen's being absorbed!
is this—
is this the true power of flower mecha!?
FRUIT MECHA

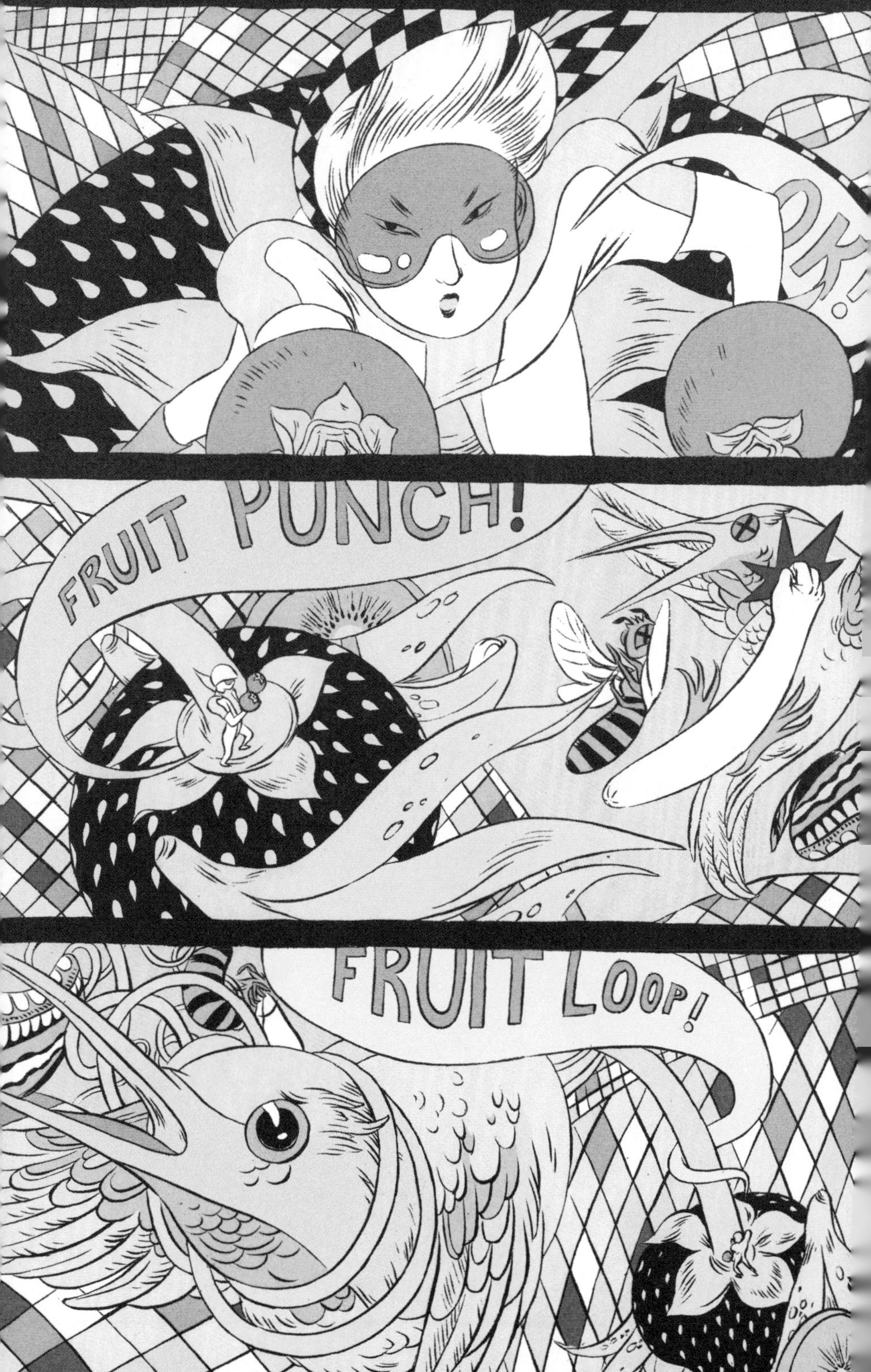
OK!
FRUIT PUNCH!
FRUIT LOOP!

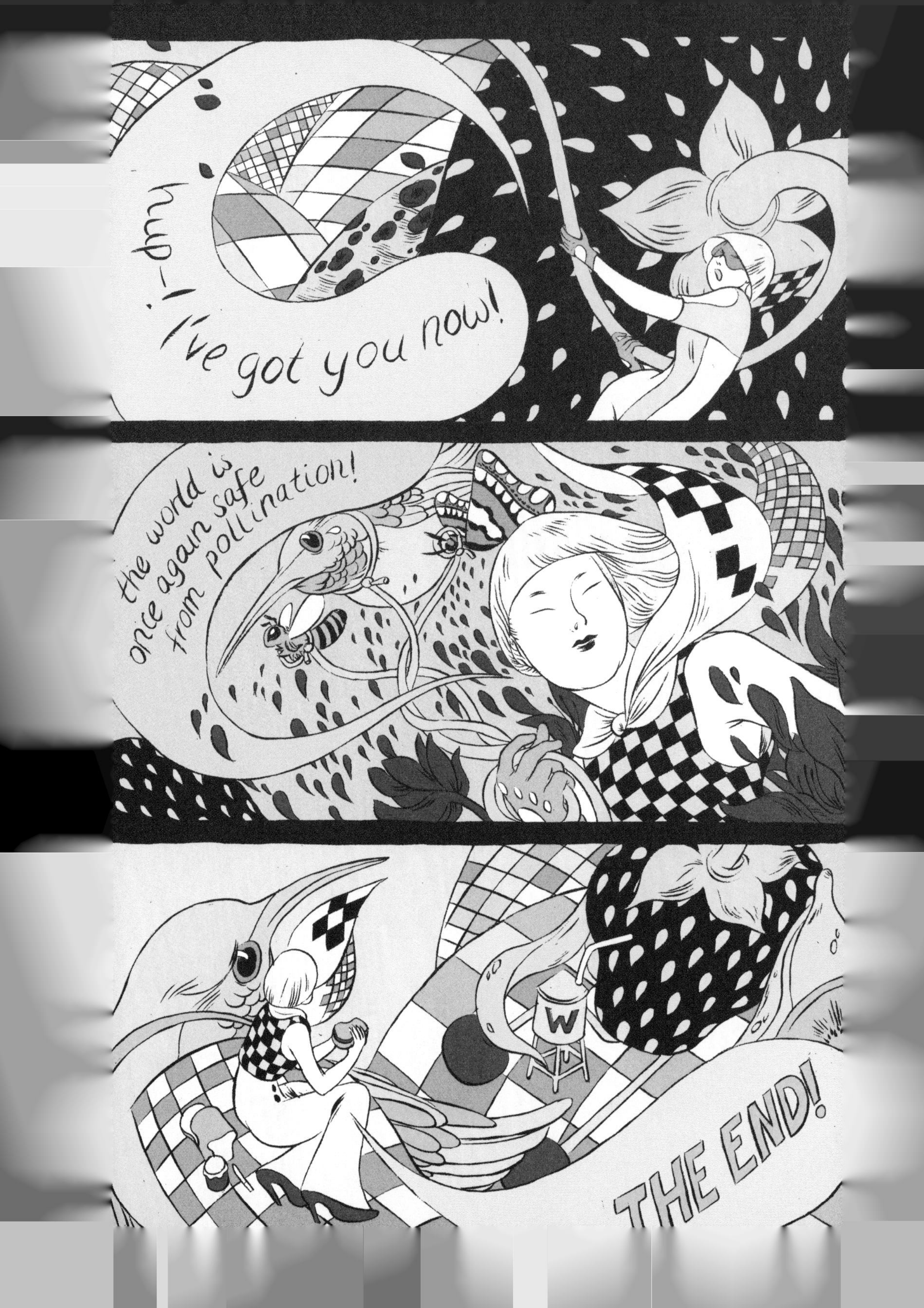
hup—! I've got you now!
the world is once again safe from pollination!
THE END!

CLICK

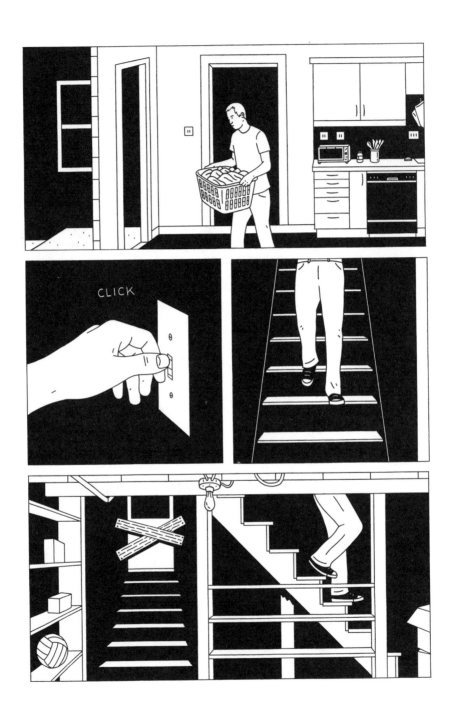

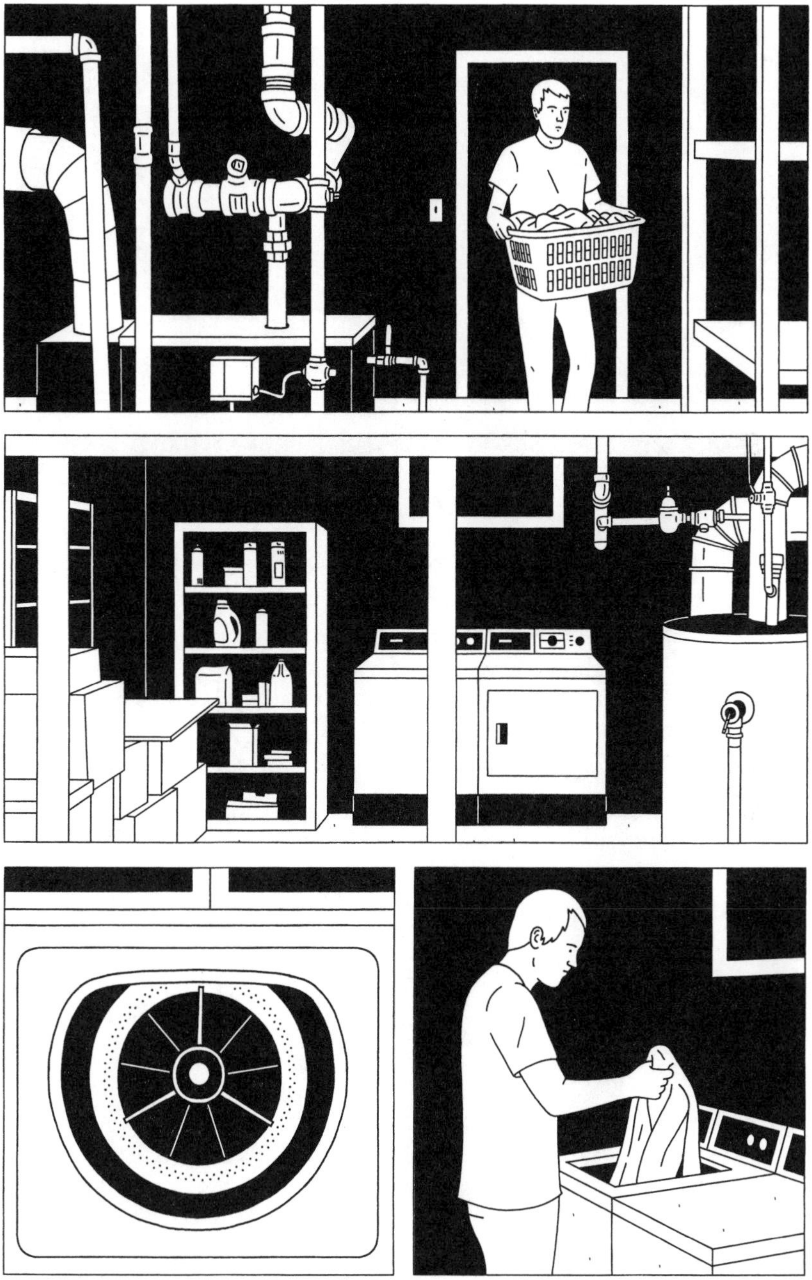

RUMBLE
RUMBLE

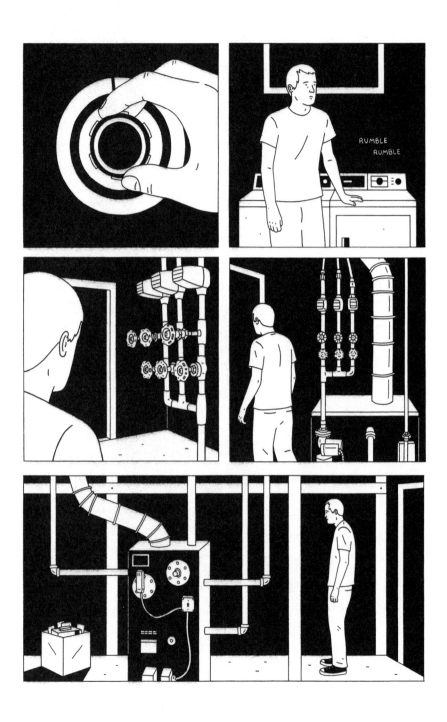

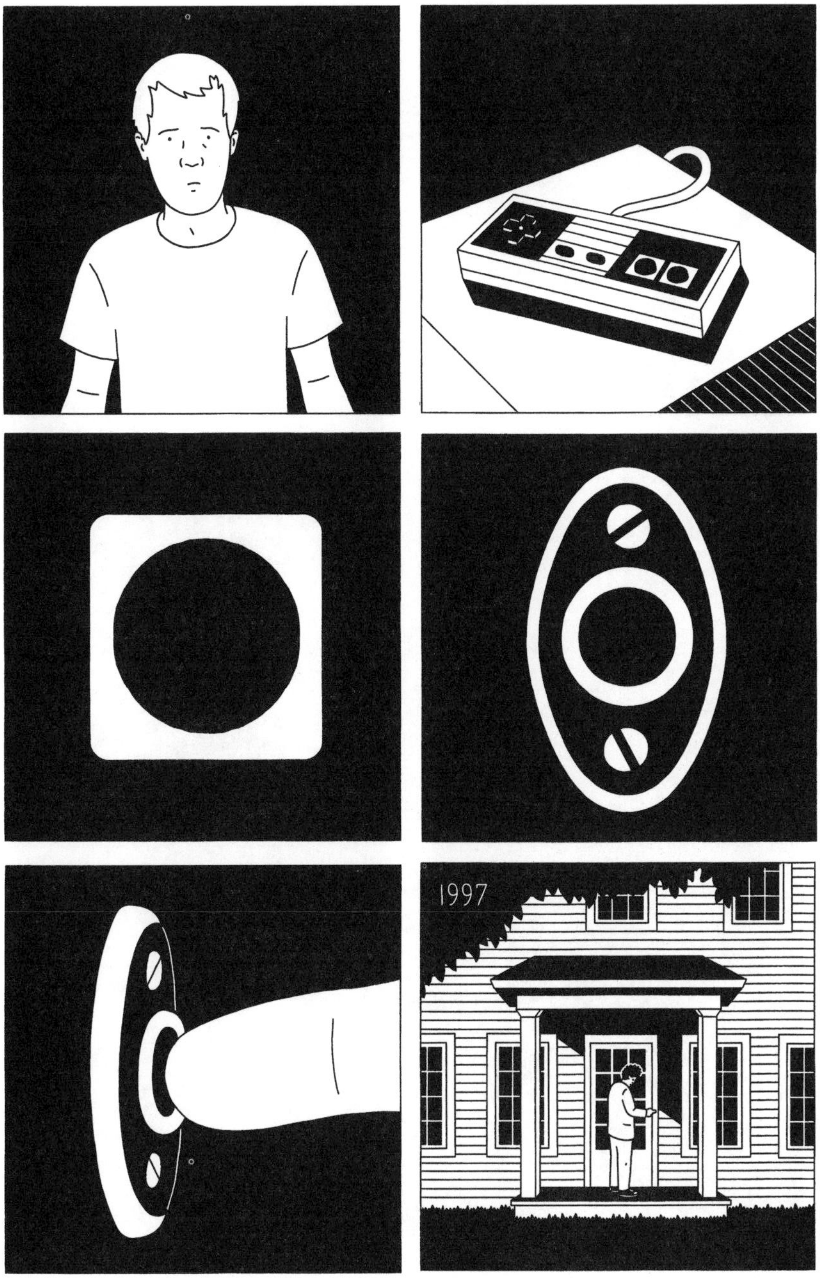
1997

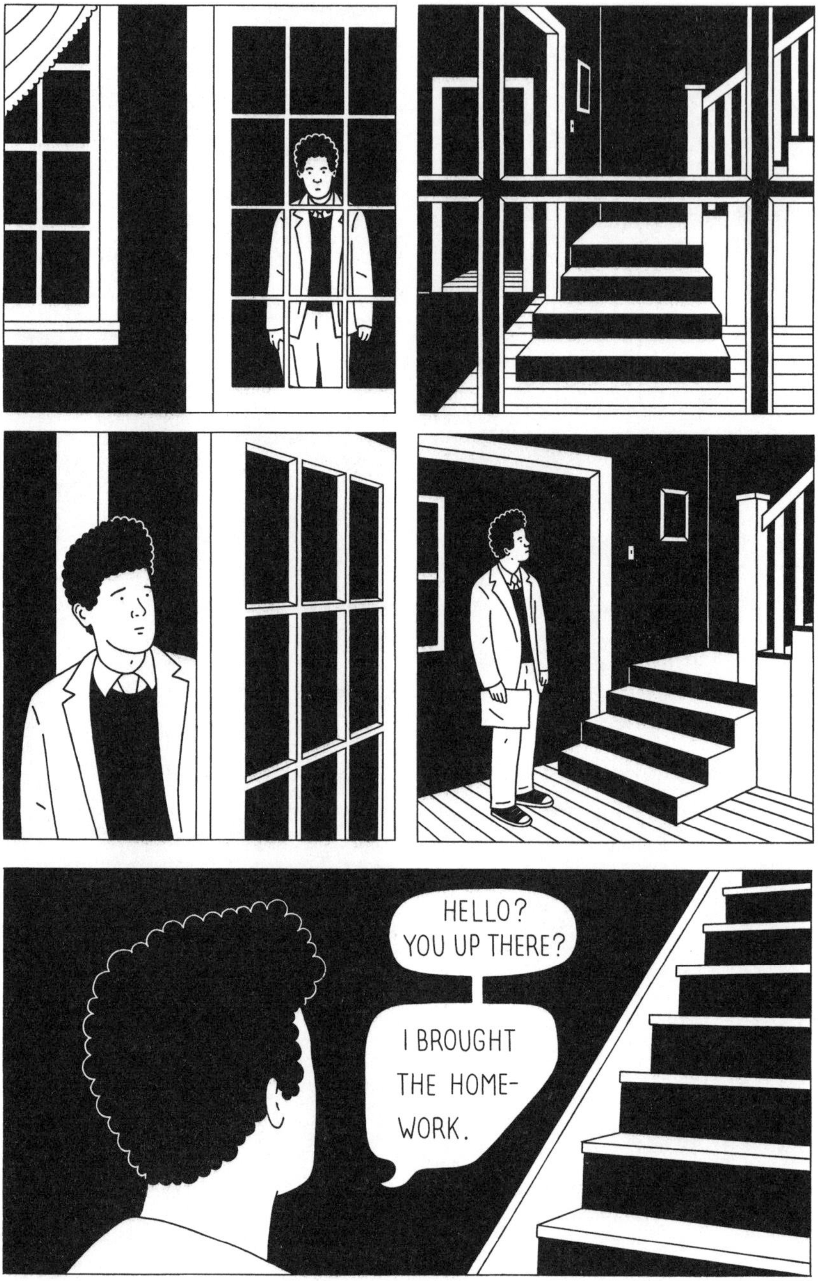
HELLO? YOU UP THERE?
I BROUGHT THE HOME-WORK.

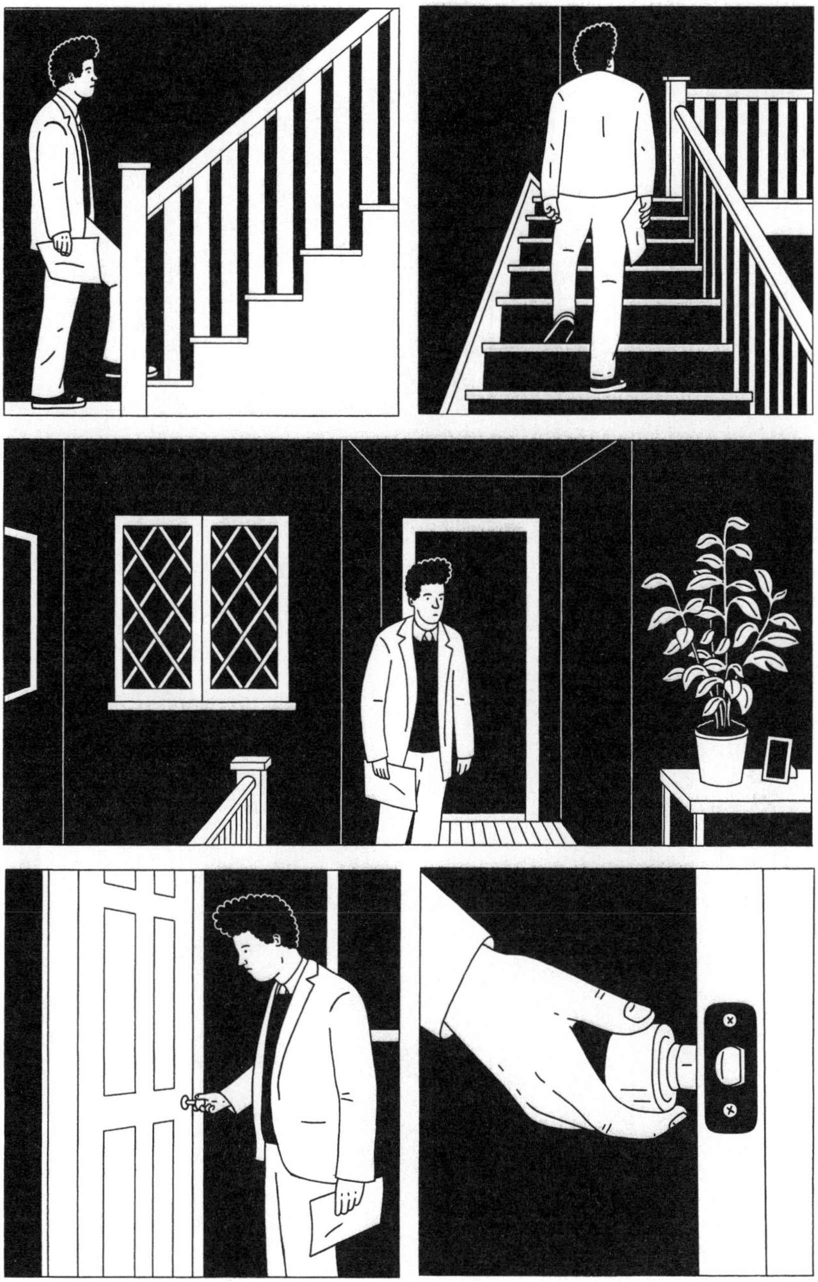

WHO LET YOU IN?
HOW'S YOUR HEAD?
IT'S FINE.
NO THANKS TO YOU.
I GUESS YOU'RE STILL MAD AT ME?

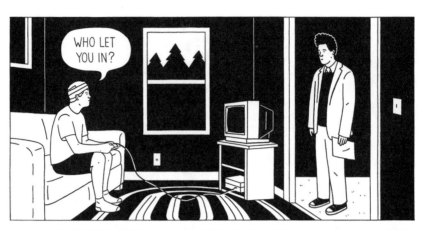

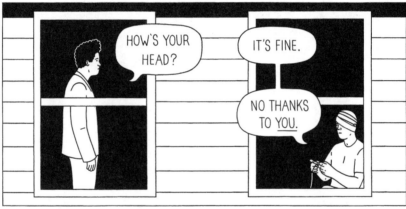

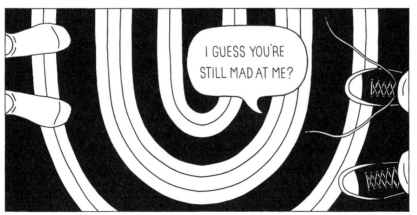

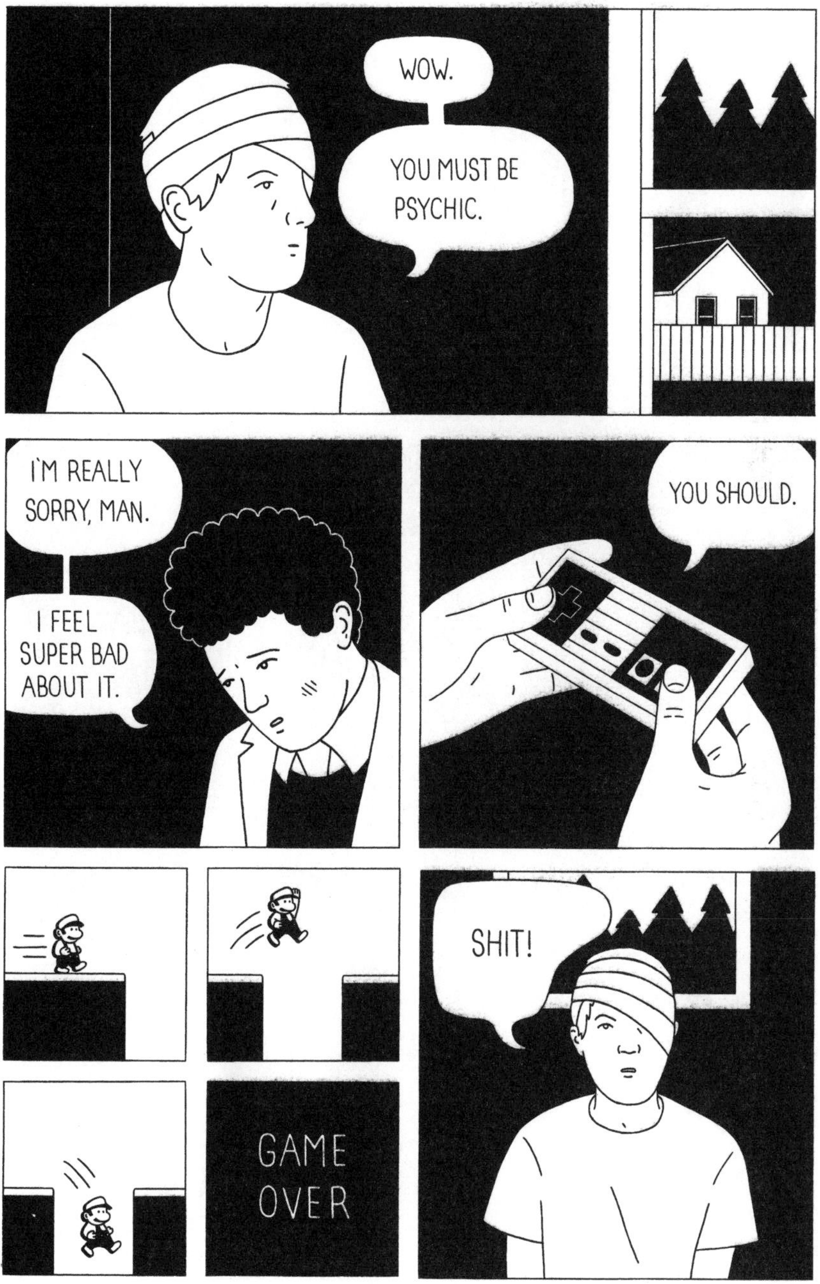
WOW.
YOU MUST BE PSYCHIC.
I'M REALLY SORRY, MAN.
I FEEL SUPER BAD ABOUT IT.
YOU SHOULD.
GAME OVER
SHIT!

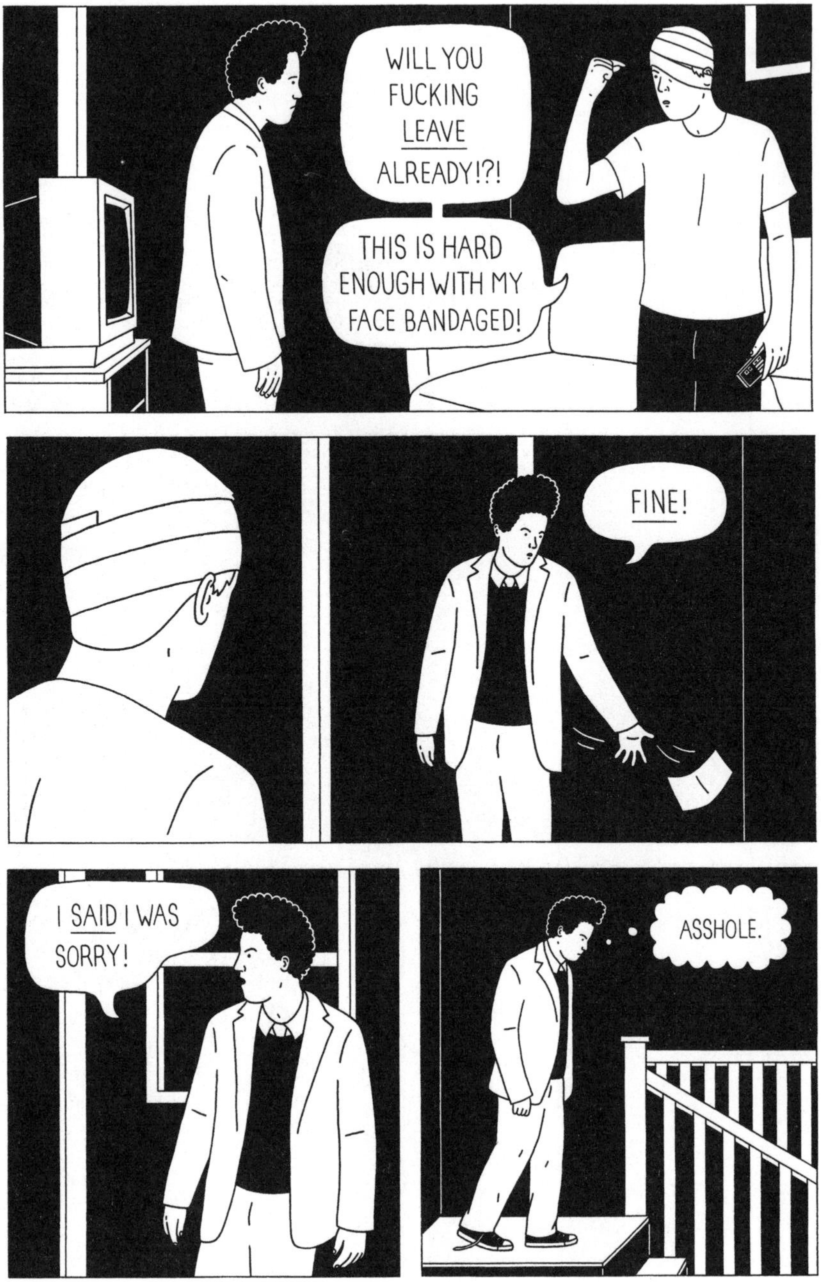

WILL YOU FUCKING LEAVE ALREADY!?!
THIS IS HARD ENOUGH WITH MY FACE BANDAGED!
FINE!
I SAID I WAS SORRY!
ASSHOLE.

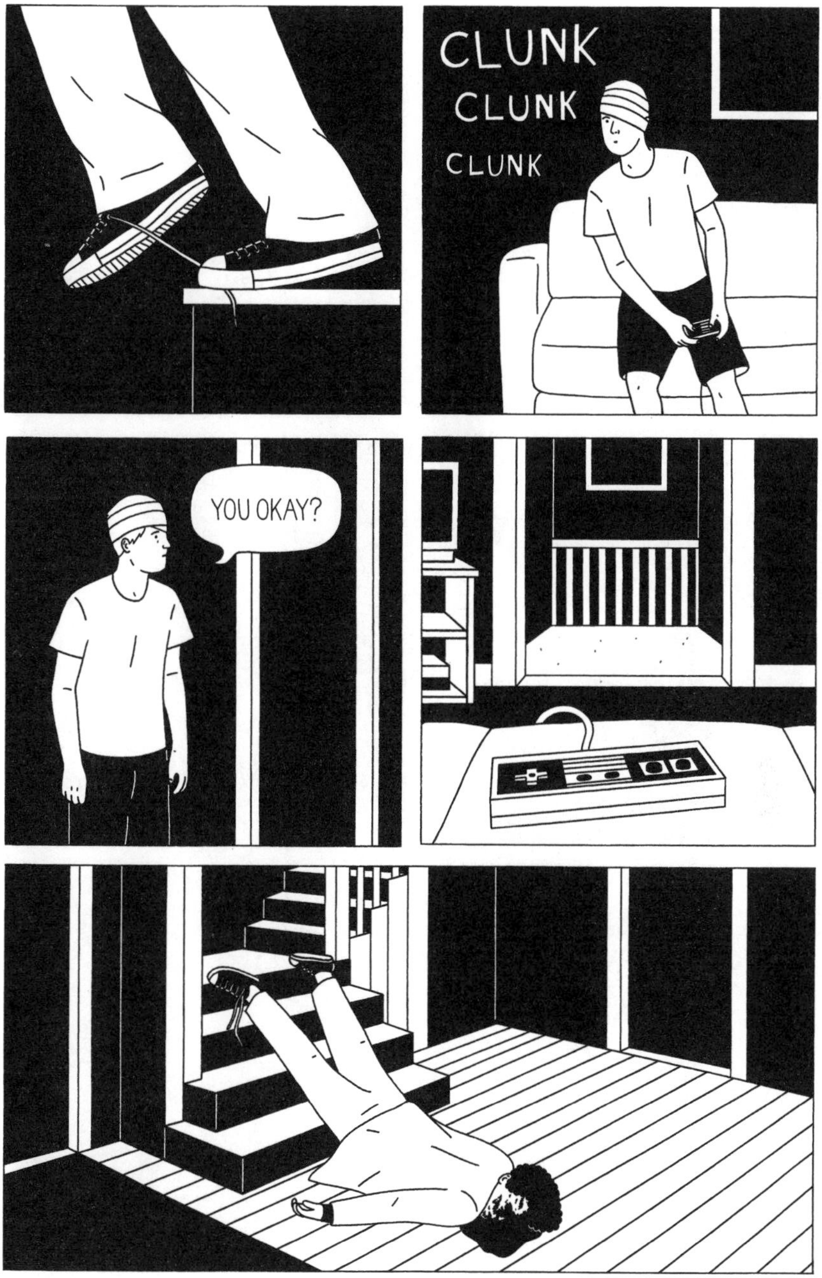
CLUNK
CLUNK
CLUNK
YOU OKAY?

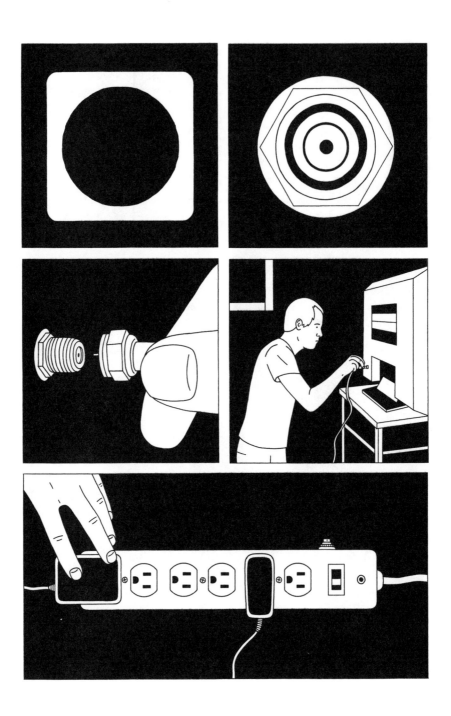

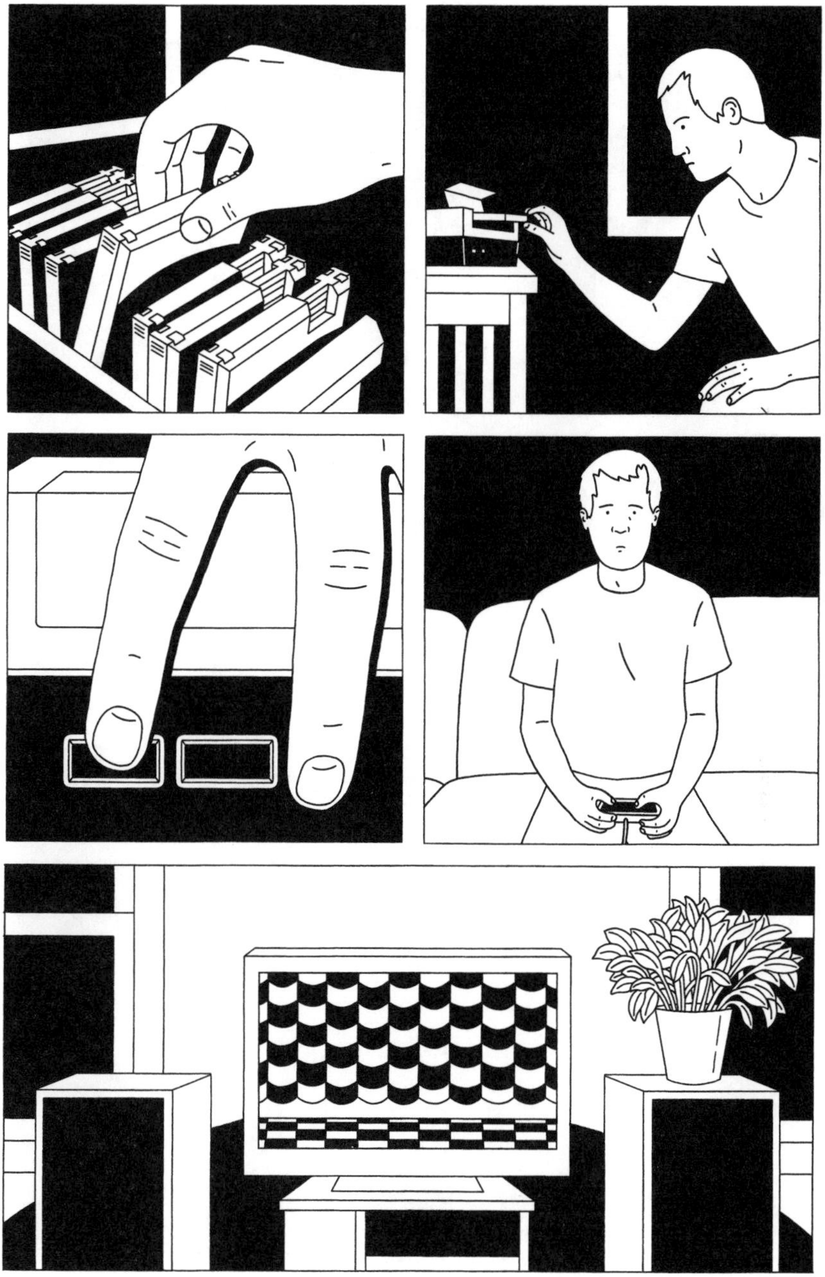

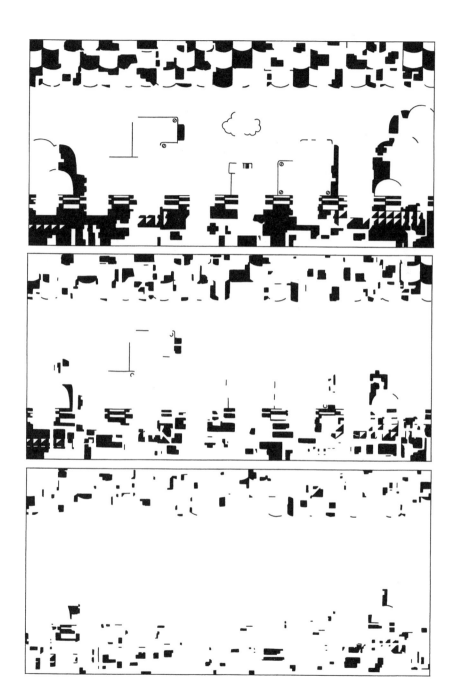

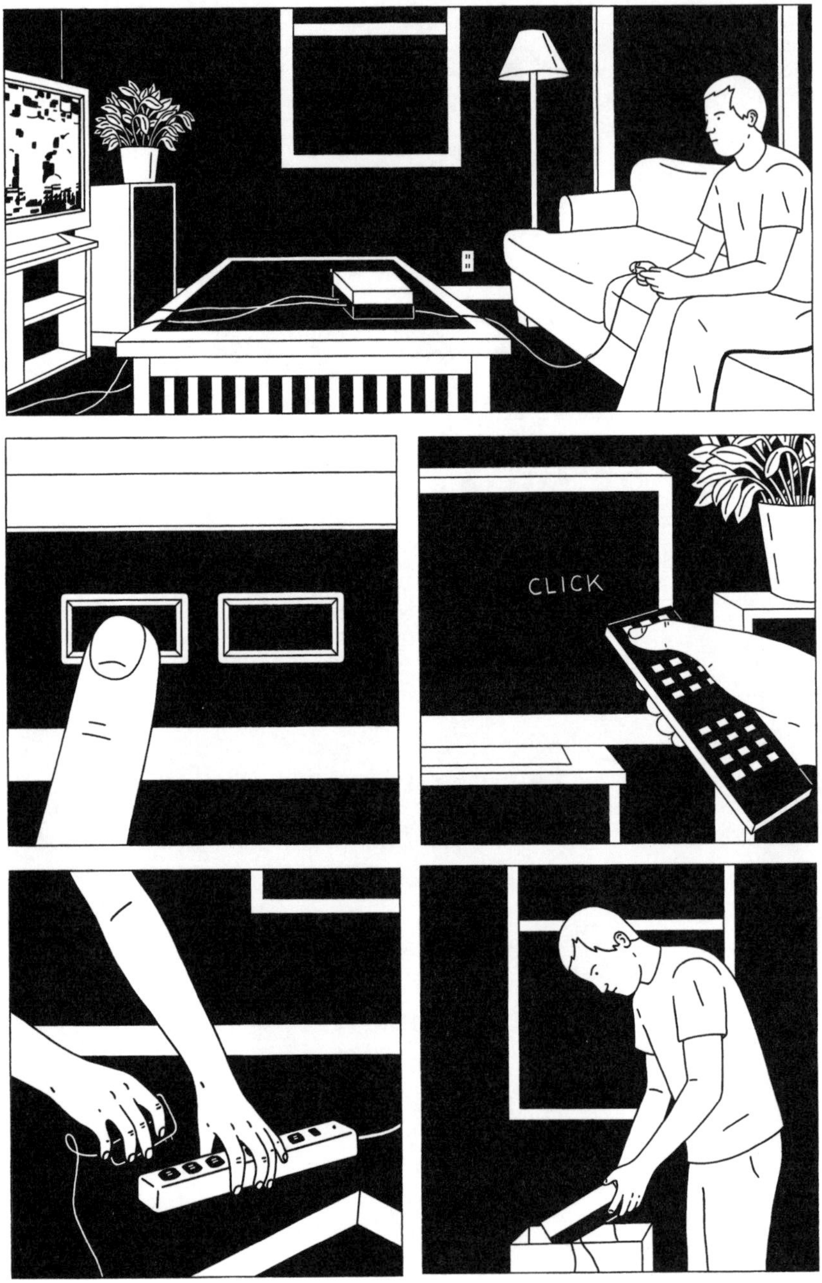
CLICK

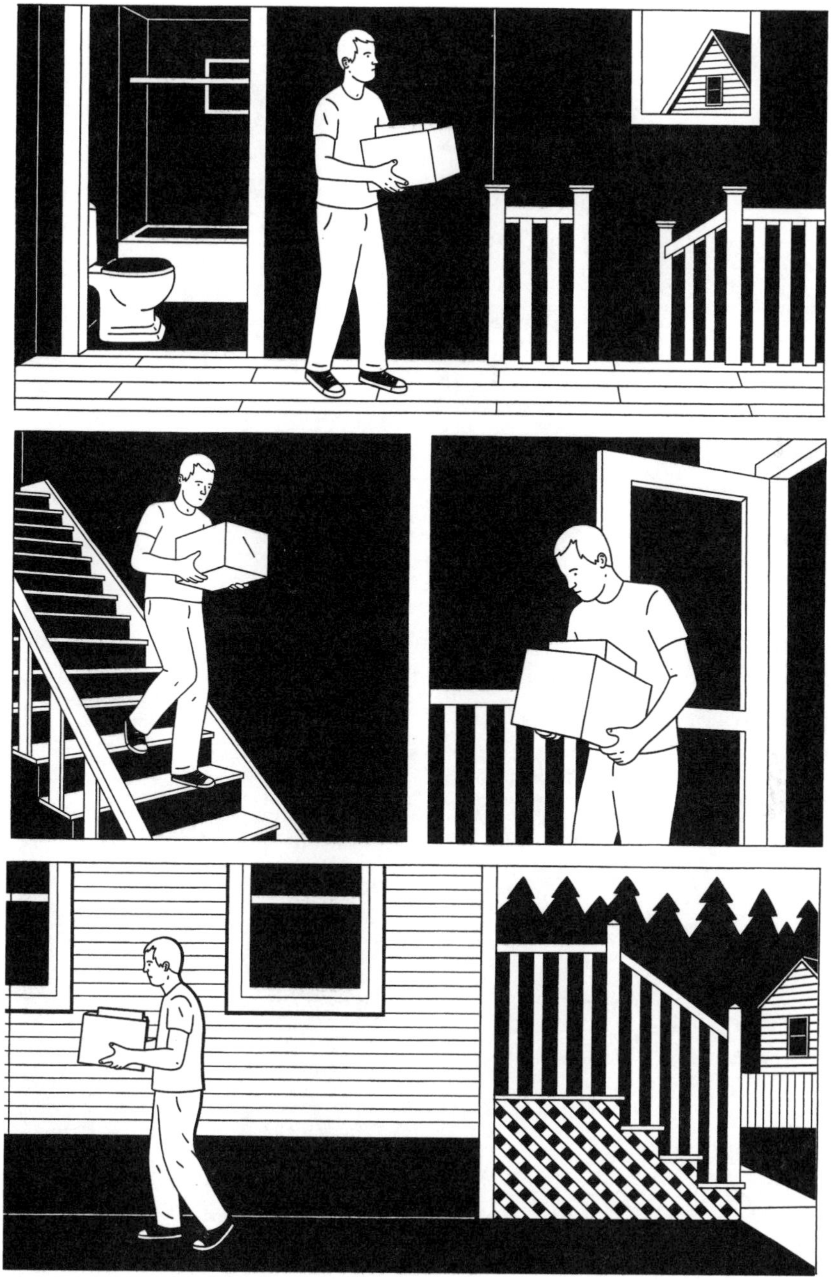

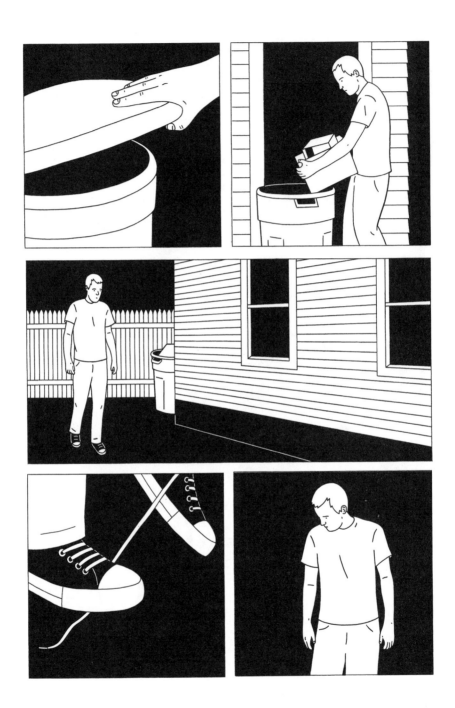

end.

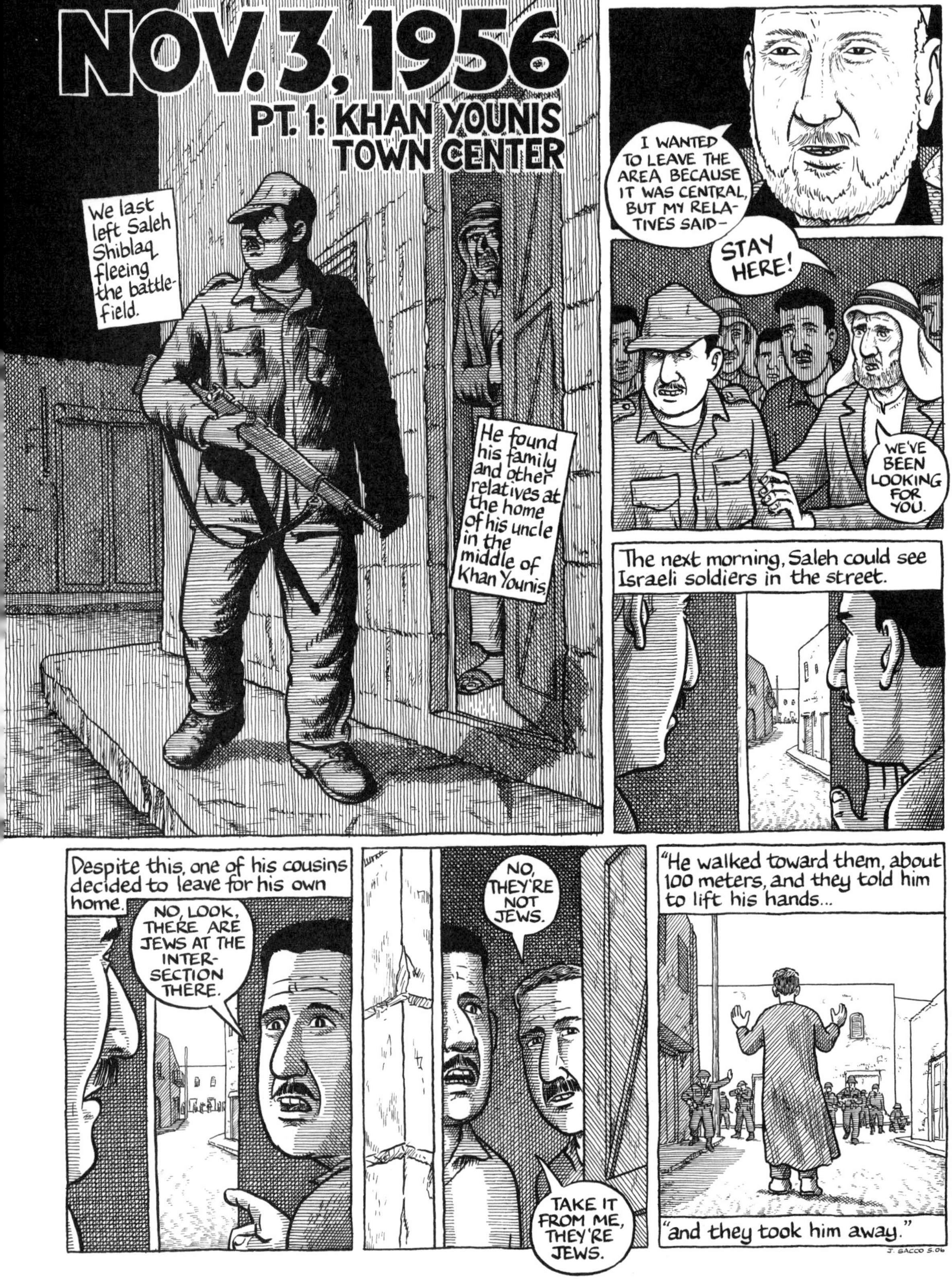
NOV. 3, 1956
PT. 1: KHAN YOUNIS TOWN CENTER
We last left Saleh Shiblaq fleeing the battle-field.
He found his family and other relatives at the home of his uncle in the middle of Khan Younis.
I WANTED TO LEAVE THE AREA BECAUSE IT WAS CENTRAL, BUT MY RELA-TIVES SAID-
STAY HERE!
WE'VE BEEN LOOKING FOR YOU.
The next morning, Saleh could see Israeli soldiers in the street.
Despite this, one of his cousins decided to leave for his own home.
NO, LOOK, THERE ARE JEWS AT THE INTER-SECTION THERE.
NO, THEY'RE NOT JEWS.
TAKE IT FROM ME, THEY'RE JEWS.
"He walked toward them, about 100 meters, and they told him to lift his hands...
"and they took him away."
J. SACCO 5.06

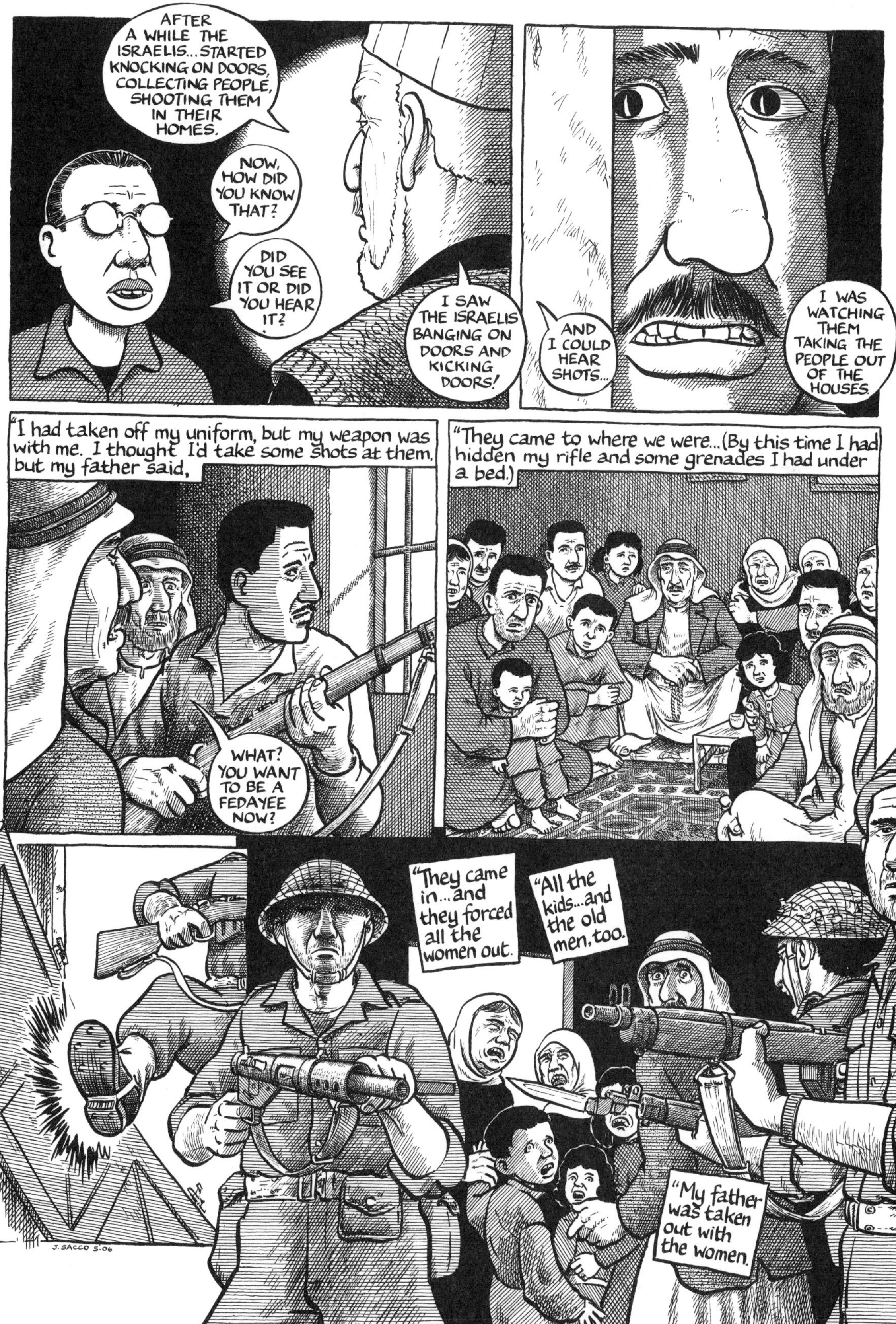
AFTER A WHILE THE ISRAELIS...STARTED KNOCKING ON DOORS, COLLECTING PEOPLE, SHOOTING THEM IN THEIR HOMES.
NOW, HOW DID YOU KNOW THAT?
DID YOU SEE IT OR DID YOU HEAR IT?
I SAW THE ISRAELIS BANGING ON DOORS AND KICKING DOORS!
AND I COULD HEAR SHOTS...
I WAS WATCHING THEM TAKING THE PEOPLE OUT OF THE HOUSES.
"I had taken off my uniform, but my weapon was with me. I thought I'd take some shots at them, but my father said,
WHAT? YOU WANT TO BE A FEDAYEE NOW?
"They came to where we were...(By this time I had hidden my rifle and some grenades I had under a bed.)
"They came in...and they forced all the women out.
"All the kids...and the old men, too.
"My father was taken out with the women.
J. SACCO 5.06

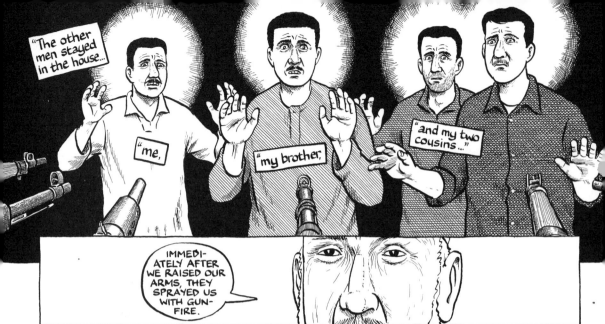

"The other men stayed in the house...

"me,

"my brother,

"and my two cousins..."

IMMEDIATELY AFTER WE RAISED OUR ARMS, THEY SPRAYED US WITH GUNFIRE.

"I was unconscious maybe half an hour, 45 minutes... I saw that the ones in the room were dead.

"I tried to get up and I fell down."

Saleh was wounded in three places. One bullet shattered his forearm.

He still cannot move his arm properly or open his hand fully.

The women of the household carried him to the local clinic the day after the shooting.

From there the Red Cross took him to a hospital in Gaza City.

The cousin who had left the house earlier and been taken by the Israelis was found dead near the Khan Younis castle, one of the town's landmarks.

J. SACCO 5·06

80

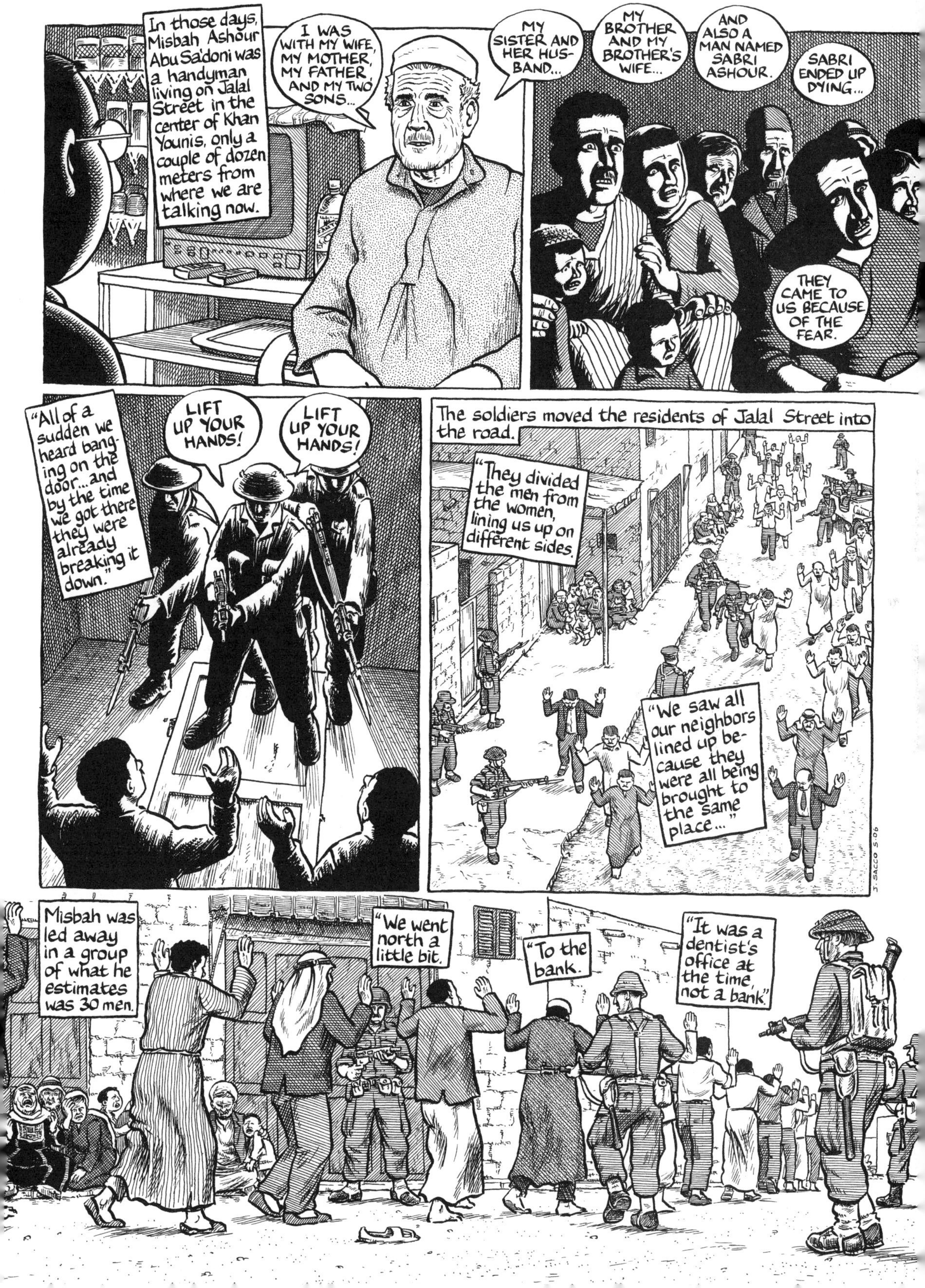

In those days, Misbah Ashour Abu Sa'doni was a handyman living on Jalal Street in the center of Khan Younis, only a couple of dozen meters from where we are talking now.
I WAS WITH MY WIFE, MY MOTHER, MY FATHER, AND MY TWO SONS...
MY SISTER AND HER HUS-BAND...
MY BROTHER AND MY BROTHER'S WIFE...
AND ALSO A MAN NAMED SABRI ASHOUR.
SABRI ENDED UP DYING...
THEY CAME TO US BECAUSE OF THE FEAR.
"All of a sudden we heard bang-ing on the door... and by the time we got there they were already breaking it down."
LIFT UP YOUR HANDS!
LIFT UP YOUR HANDS!
The soldiers moved the residents of Jalal Street into the road.
"They divided the men from the women, lining us up on different sides.
"We saw all our neighbors lined up be-cause they were all being brought to the same place..."
J. SACCO 5.06
Misbah was led away in a group of what he estimates was 30 men.
"We went north a little bit.
"To the bank.
"It was a dentist's office at the time, not a bank."

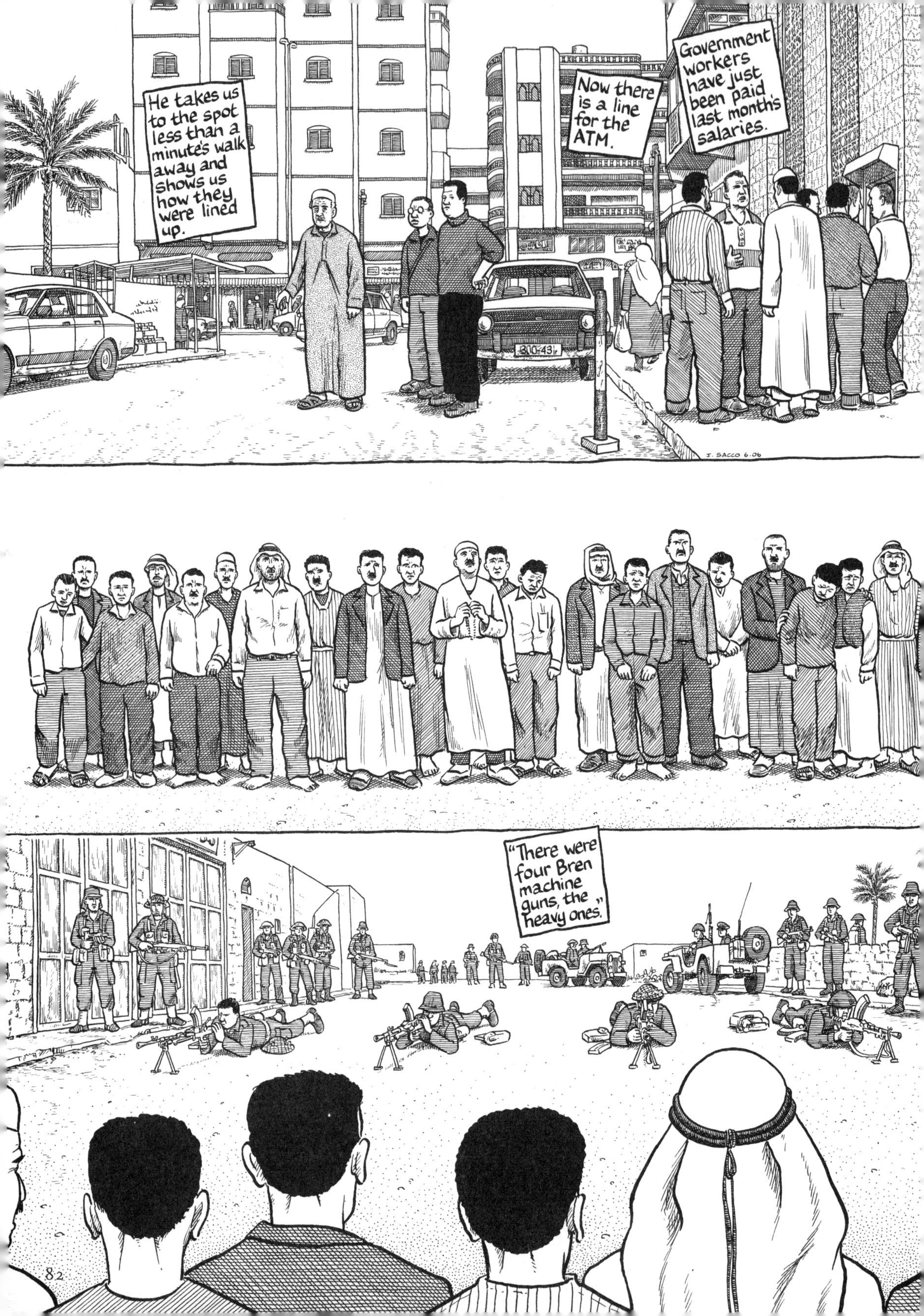
He takes us to the spot less than a minute's walk away and shows us how they were lined up.
Now there is a line for the ATM.
Government workers have just been paid last month's salaries.
J. SACCO 6.06
"There were four Bren machine guns, the heavy ones."

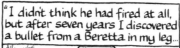
In addition, he says, a soldier was standing there with an Egyptian-issue Beretta sub-machine gun.

"I didn't think he had fired at all, but after seven years I discovered a bullet from a Beretta in my leg...

"I sort of went off to the side. I was thinking of escaping.

"Then they started firing.

"I fell down and the bodies be-gan to fall on top of me."

THE SMELL HURT.

THE SMELL OF WHAT? COR-DITE?

YES, FROM SO MUCH FIRING.

IT HURT OUR NOSES.

THEY FIRED A LOT.

"And then there was silence.

"And then we heard them... putting in new maga-zines.

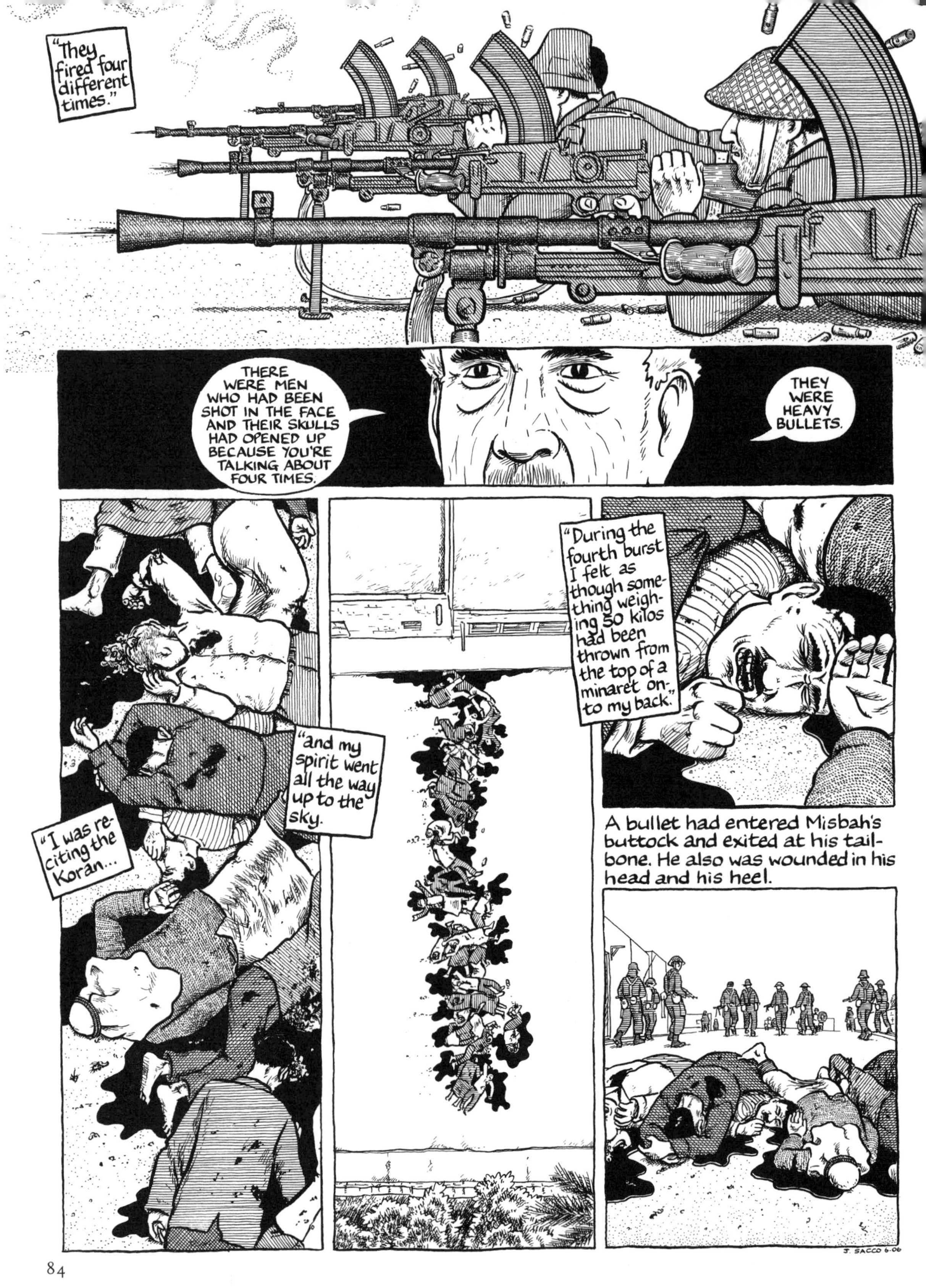
"They fired four different times."
THERE WERE MEN WHO HAD BEEN SHOT IN THE FACE AND THEIR SKULLS HAD OPENED UP BECAUSE YOU'RE TALKING ABOUT FOUR TIMES.
THEY WERE HEAVY BULLETS.
"I was reciting the Koran...
"and my spirit went all the way up to the sky.
"During the fourth burst I felt as though something weighing 50 kilos had been thrown from the top of a minaret onto my back."
A bullet had entered Misbah's buttock and exited at his tailbone. He also was wounded in his head and his heel.
J. SACCO 6.06

"After it happened, we waited... and then we heard someone say,

NOBODY'S HERE.

"We got up...

"my brother,

"this guy Fayeq,

"and me.

"And there were other people who lived [and] were wounded, but they eventually died.

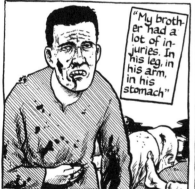

"My brother had a lot of injuries. In his leg, in his arm, in his stomach"

The brothers fled the area and hid in a hole in the ground, but they could see Israeli soldiers nearby.

LET'S GO. LET'S RUN.

"I didn't really want to go. And my brother started to run...

"I tried to start running and would...fall every few meters.

I CAN'T RUN, BUT TAKE CARE OF MY SONS.

THERE'S NO HOPE FOR ME.

J. SACCO 6-06

85

"My brother went...toward the sea. He found someone with a donkey cart who took him to Mawasi.*"

*MAWASI: A NARROW STRIP OF LAND ALONG THE SOUTHERN GAZA COAST.

"Three or four months later he died from his injuries."

Misbah made his way to the entrance of the refugee camp, where he hid among cactus plants until he could bear his pain no longer.

"I didn't care what happened... I didn't care if someone came and shot me.

"So I started crawling... to get to the road to be face to face with the Israelis."

Instead, Misbah was found by women who had ventured forth to find their male relatives...

GIVE ME SOME WATER.

and soon he was discovered by his own family...

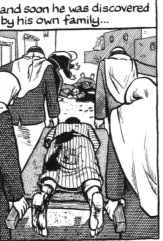

who tried tending to his injuries the best they could.

PUT COFFEE GROUNDS ON HIS WOUND.

PRESS THE WOUND WITH A HOT IRON...

After three days he was taken to a hospital in Gaza City where he had four operations over four months.

86

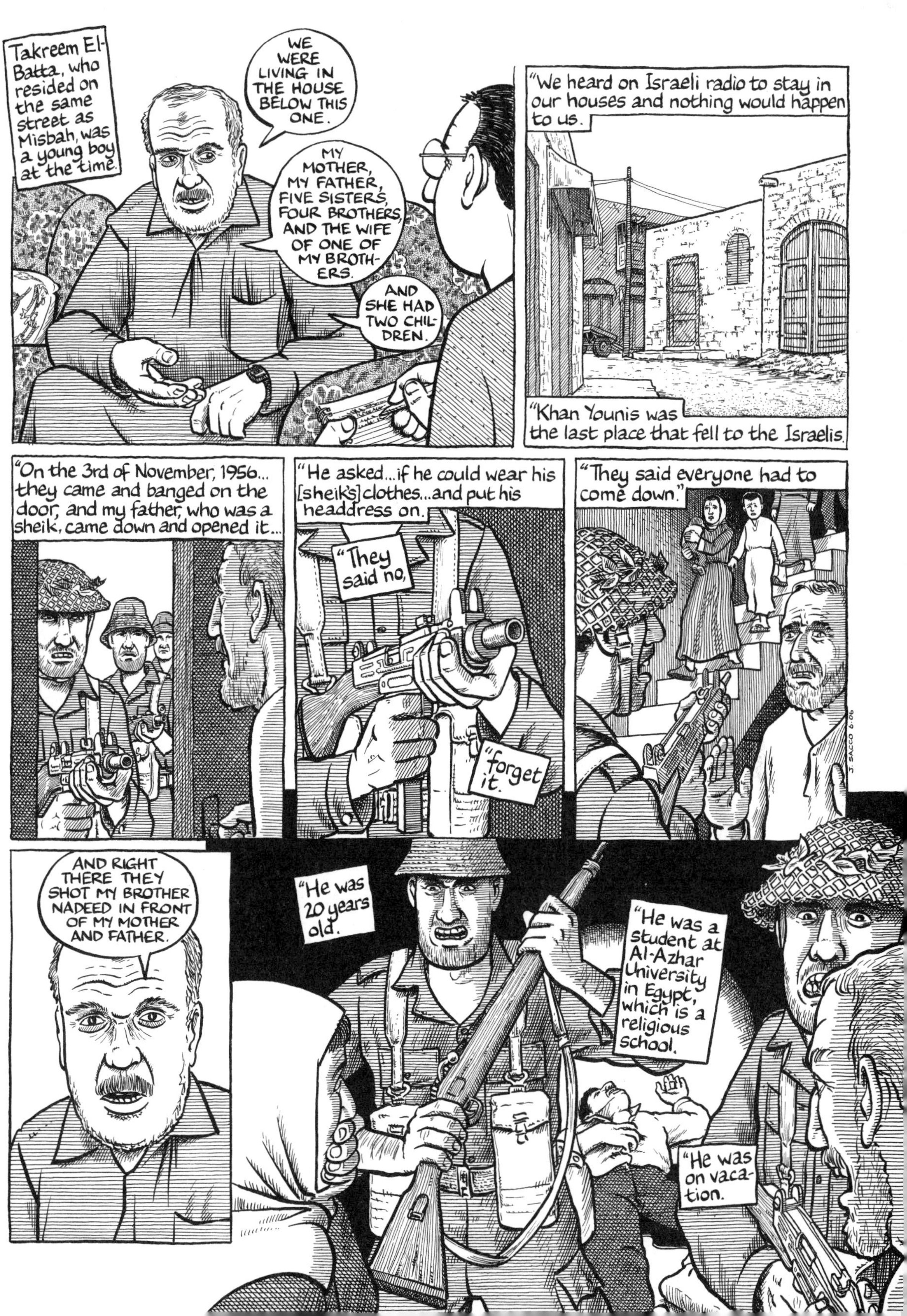
Takreem El-Batta, who resided on the same street as Misbah, was a young boy at the time.
WE WERE LIVING IN THE HOUSE BELOW THIS ONE.
MY MOTHER, MY FATHER, FIVE SISTERS, FOUR BROTHERS, AND THE WIFE OF ONE OF MY BROTHERS.
AND SHE HAD TWO CHILDREN.
"We heard on Israeli radio to stay in our houses and nothing would happen to us.
"Khan Younis was the last place that fell to the Israelis.
"On the 3rd of November, 1956... they came and banged on the door, and my father, who was a sheik, came down and opened it...
"He asked... if he could wear his [sheik's] clothes... and put his headdress on.
"They said no,
"forget it.
"They said everyone had to come down."
J. SACCO 6.06
AND RIGHT THERE THEY SHOT MY BROTHER NADEED IN FRONT OF MY MOTHER AND FATHER.
"He was 20 years old.
"He was a student at Al-Azhar University in Egypt, which is a religious school.
"He was on vacation.

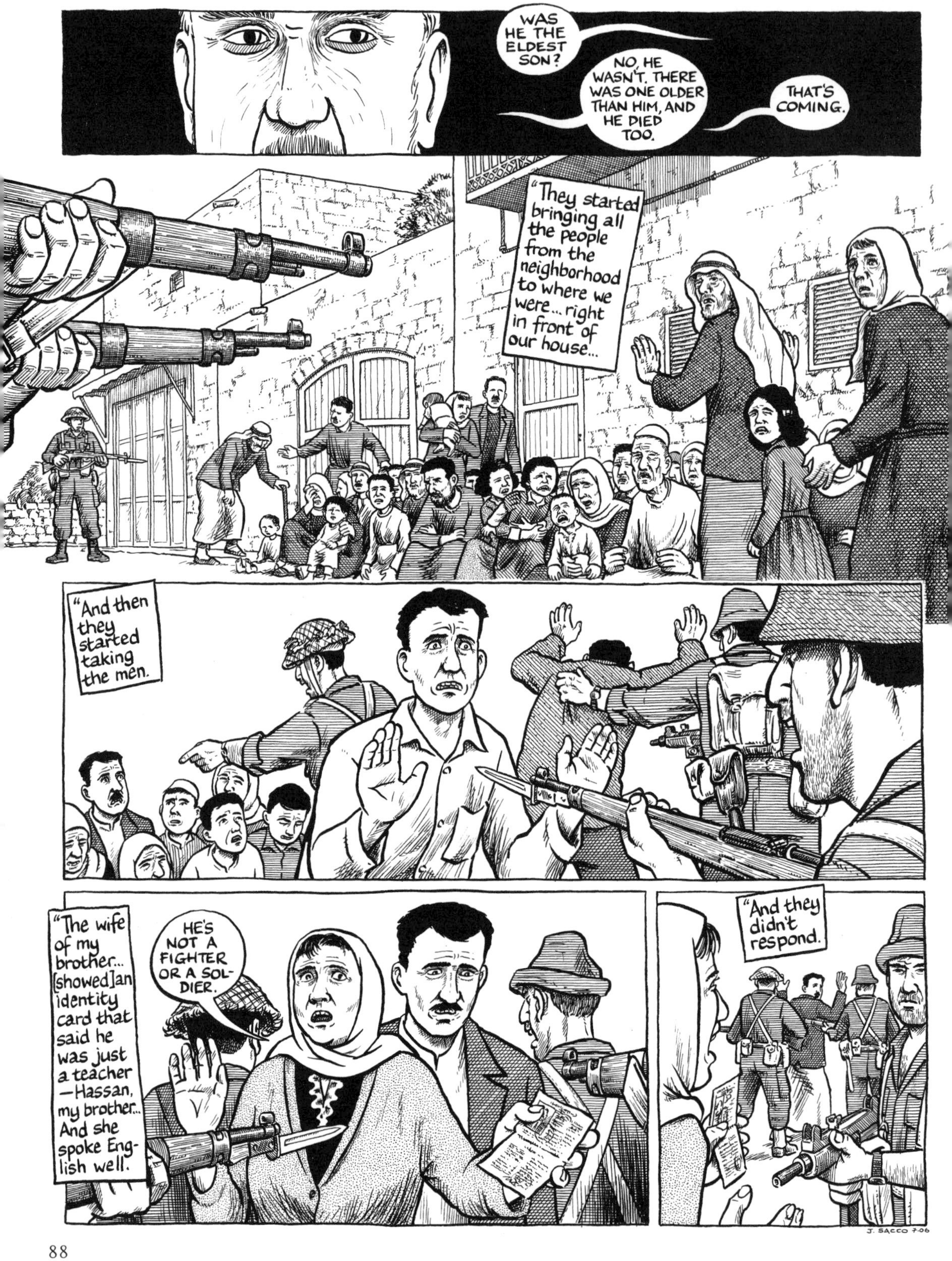
WAS HE THE ELDEST SON?
NO, HE WASN'T. THERE WAS ONE OLDER THAN HIM, AND HE DIED TOO.
THAT'S COMING.
"They started bringing all the people from the neighborhood to where we were... right in front of our house...
"And then they started taking the men.
"The wife of my brother... [showed] an identity card that said he was just a teacher —Hassan, my brother... And she spoke English well.
HE'S NOT A FIGHTER OR A SOLDIER.
"And they didn't respond.
J. SACCO 7·06

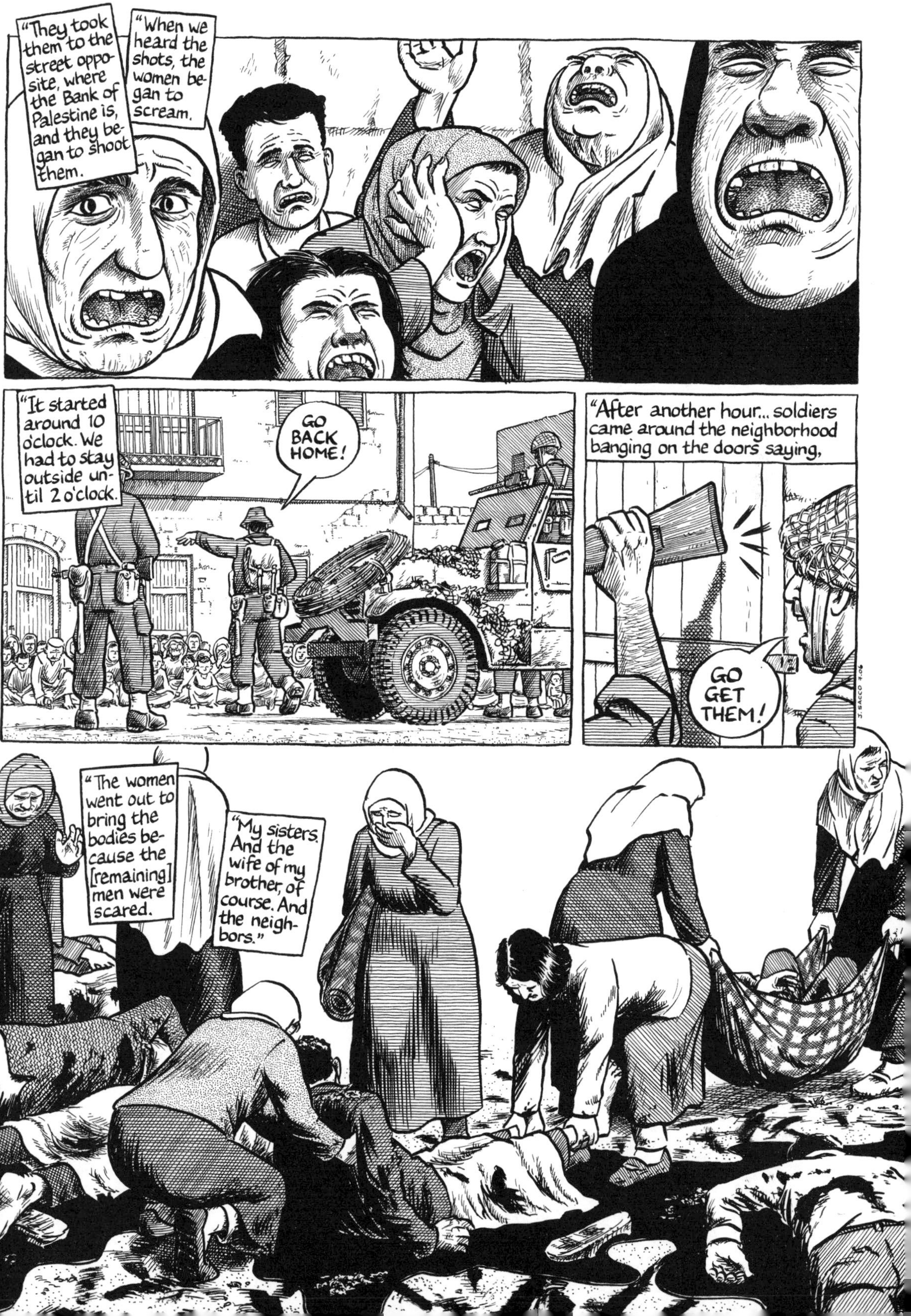
"They took them to the street opposite, where the Bank of Palestine is, and they began to shoot them.
"When we heard the shots, the women began to scream.
"It started around 10 o'clock. We had to stay outside until 2 o'clock.
GO BACK HOME!
"After another hour... soldiers came around the neighborhood banging on the doors saying,
GO GET THEM!
J. SACCO 7.06
"The women went out to bring the bodies because the [remaining] men were scared.
"My sisters. And the wife of my brother, of course. And the neighbors."

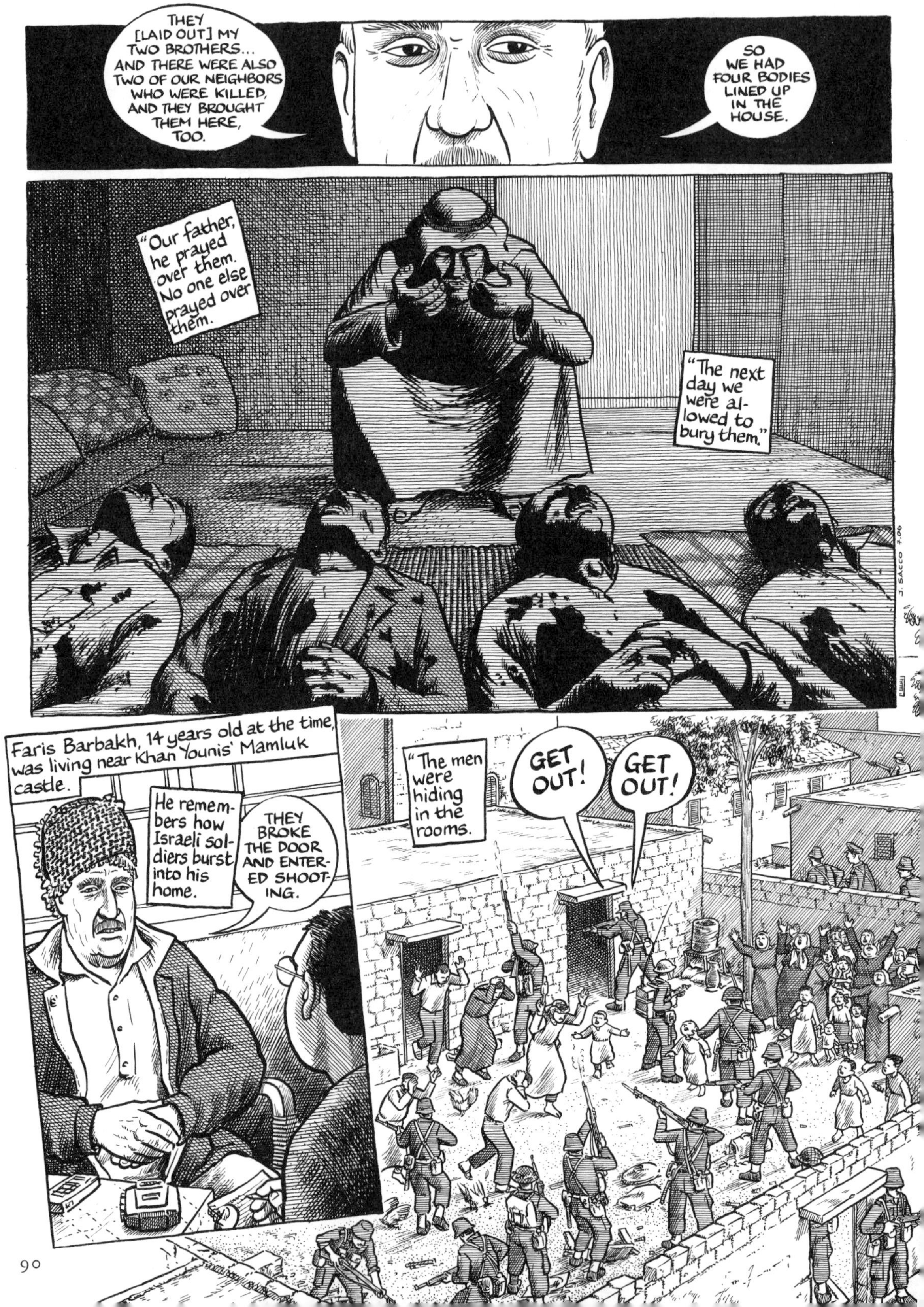
THEY [LAID OUT] MY TWO BROTHERS... AND THERE WERE ALSO TWO OF OUR NEIGHBORS WHO WERE KILLED, AND THEY BROUGHT THEM HERE, TOO.
SO WE HAD FOUR BODIES LINED UP IN THE HOUSE.
"Our father, he prayed over them. No one else prayed over them.
"The next day we were allowed to bury them."
J. SACCO 7.06
Faris Barbakh, 14 years old at the time, was living near Khan Younis' Mamluk castle.
He remembers how Israeli soldiers burst into his home.
THEY BROKE THE DOOR AND ENTERED SHOOTING.
"The men were hiding in the rooms.
GET OUT!
GET OUT!

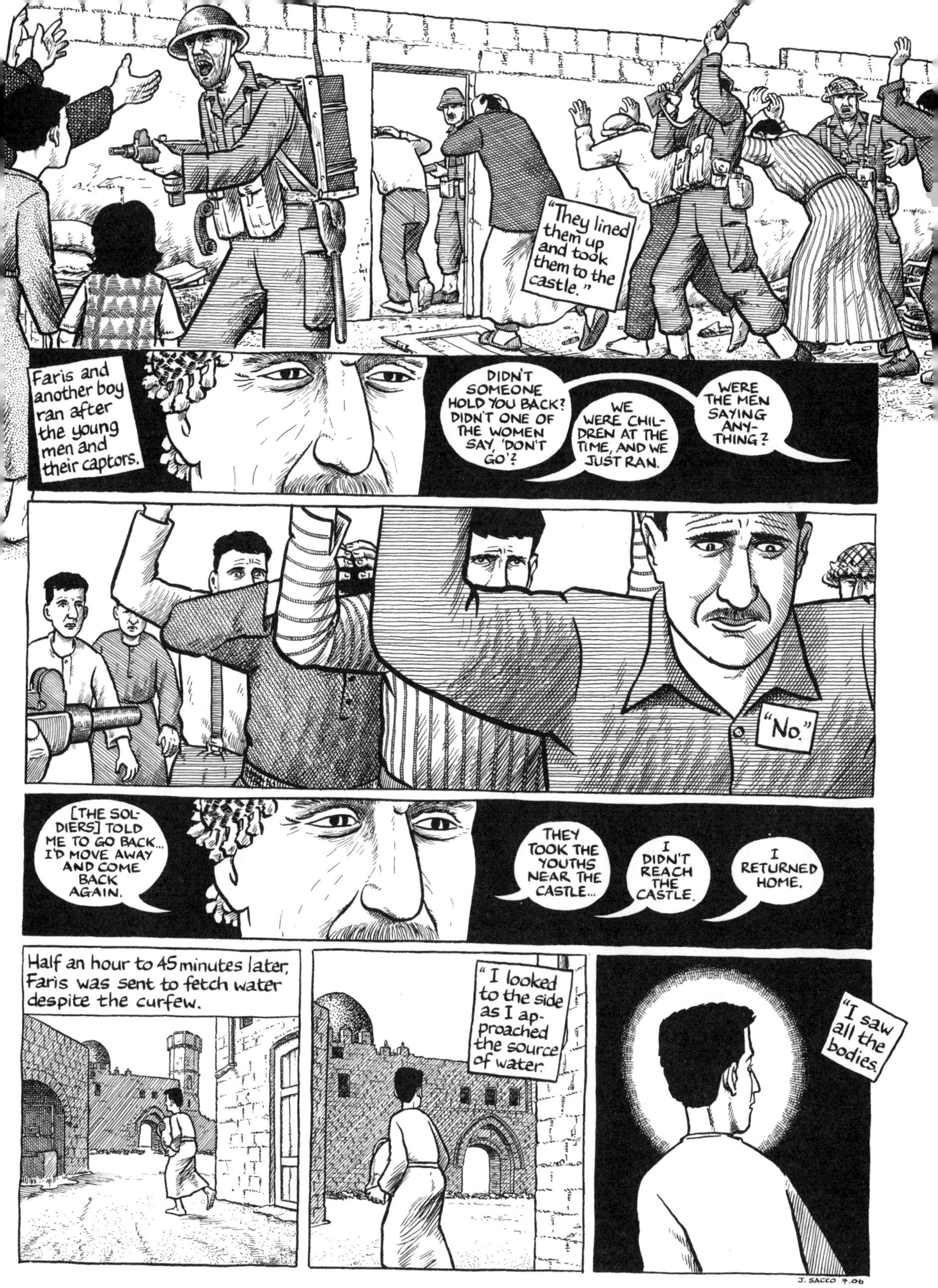
"They lined them up and took them to the castle."
Faris and another boy ran after the young men and their captors.
DIDN'T SOMEONE HOLD YOU BACK? DIDN'T ONE OF THE WOMEN SAY, 'DON'T GO'?
WE WERE CHILDREN AT THE TIME, AND WE JUST RAN.
WERE THE MEN SAYING ANYTHING?
"No."
[THE SOLDIERS] TOLD ME TO GO BACK... I'D MOVE AWAY AND COME BACK AGAIN.
THEY TOOK THE YOUTHS NEAR THE CASTLE...
I DIDN'T REACH THE CASTLE.
I RETURNED HOME.
Half an hour to 45 minutes later, Faris was sent to fetch water despite the curfew.
"I looked to the side as I approached the source of water.
"I saw all the bodies.
J. SACCO 7.06

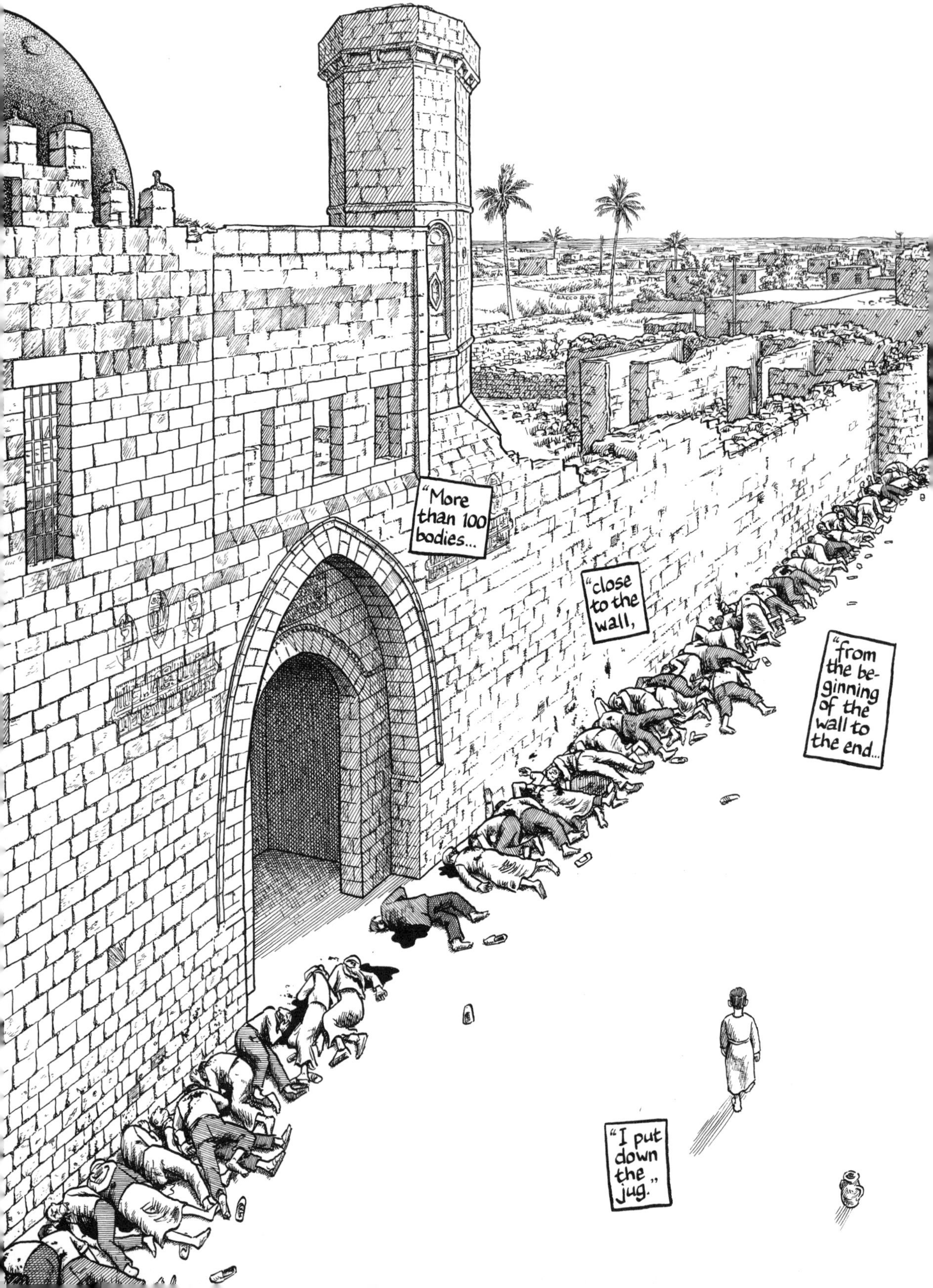
"More than 100 bodies...
"close to the wall,
"from the beginning of the wall to the end...
"I put down the jug."

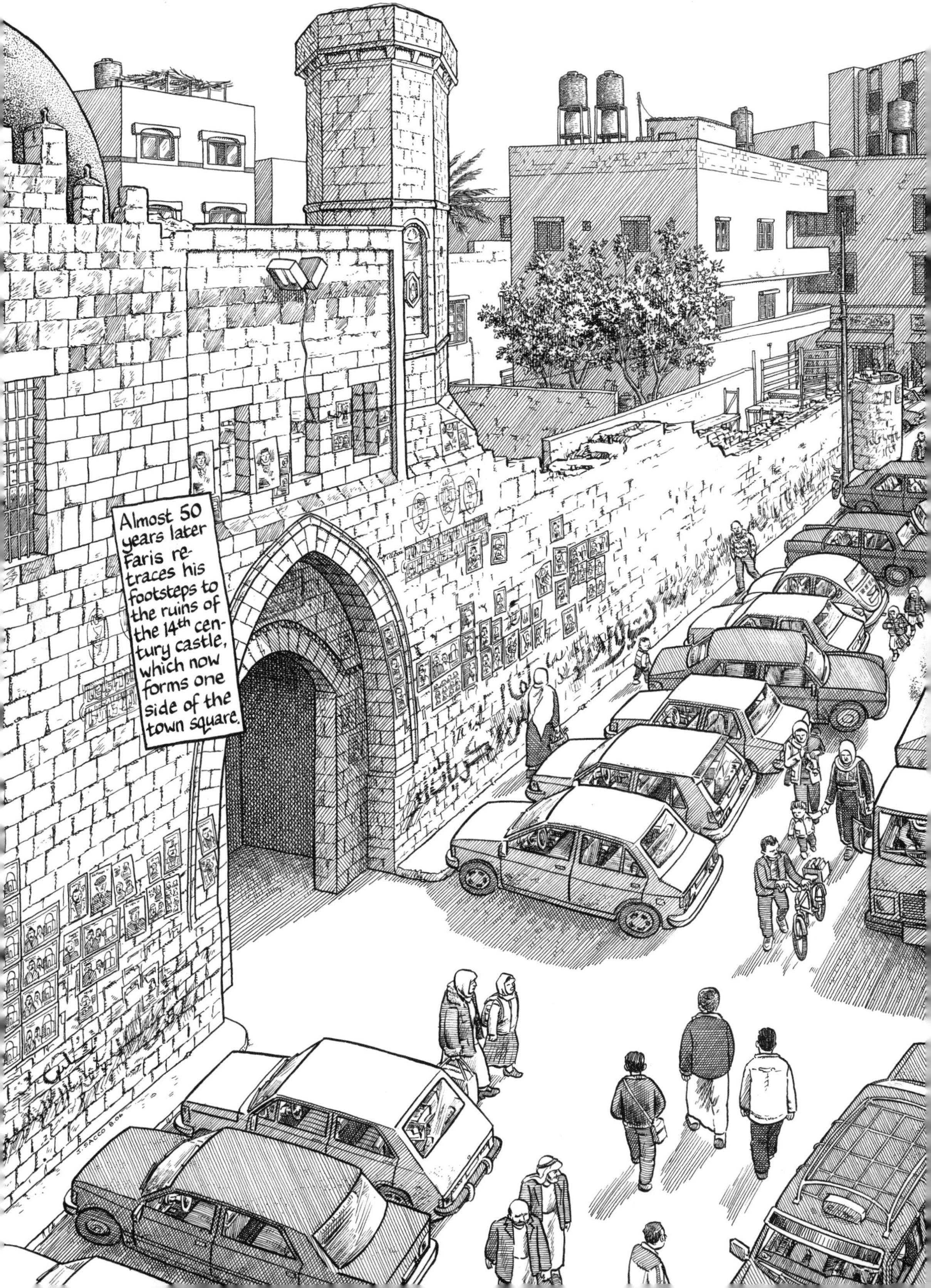
Almost 50 years later Faris re-traces his footsteps to the ruins of the 14th century castle, which now forms one side of the town square.
J. SACCO 8.06

"I went to the house of one of my relatives, El-Hajj Abdullah. His house was very close to the area.

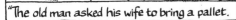

"The old man asked his wife to bring a pallet.

"This is Abdel."

"This is Anwar."

"This is Abed."

"The old man was checking their faces."

J. SACCO 8-06

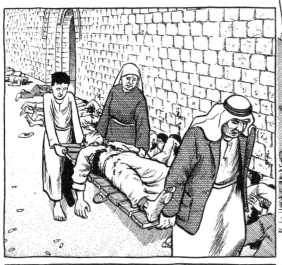

Faris leads us through a market, where there was once an open area, to the cemetery where they took the bodies one by one.

I ask him how he feels now, decades later.

I FEEL LIKE I AM THAT CHILD AGAIN.

We arrive at the common family grave—called a fusgeya—into which his cousins were lowered.

"At that time there were hundreds of bodies in one area. You can't bury them individually. You have to hurry and bury the bodies.

J. SACCO 8-06

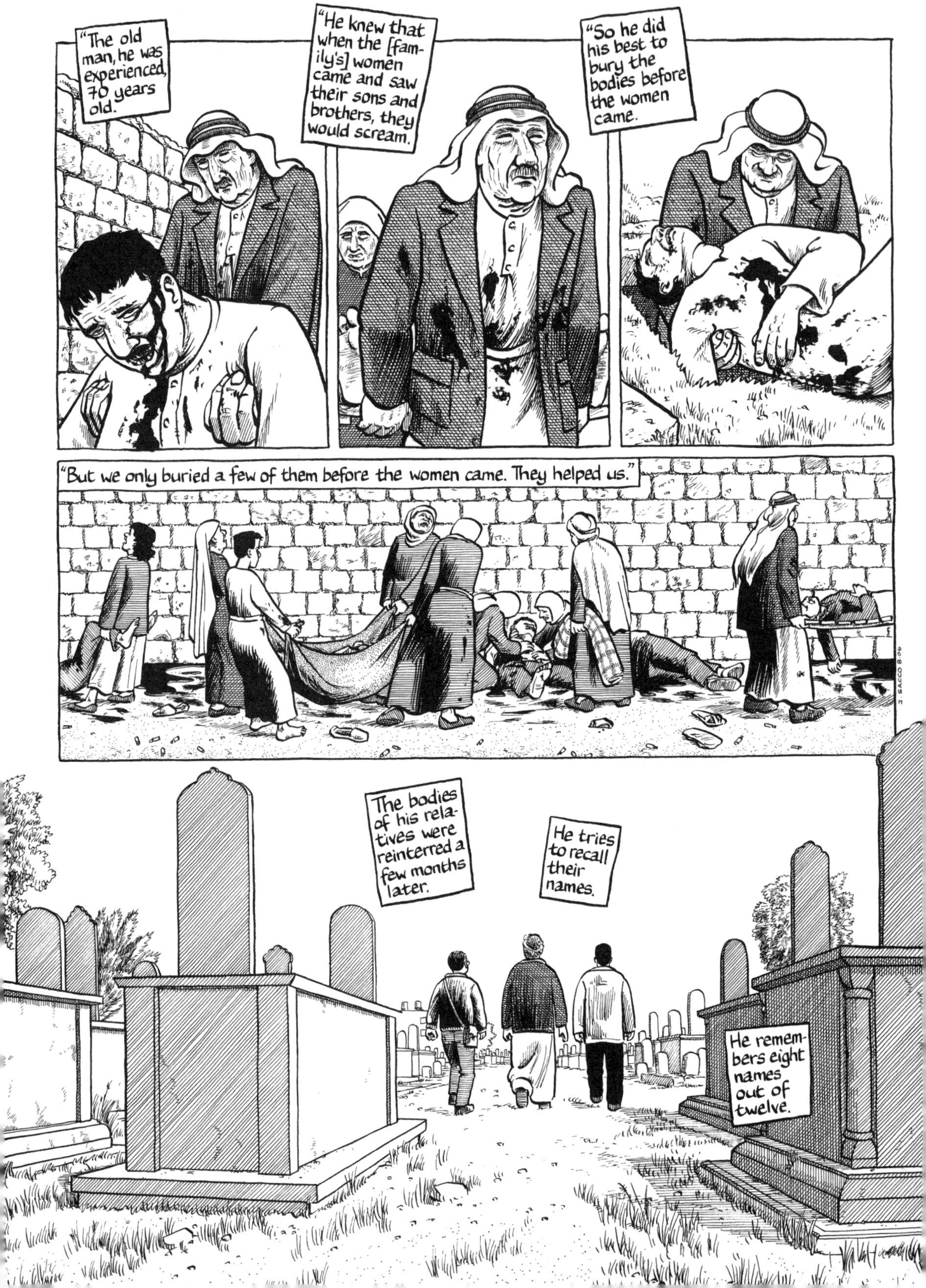
"The old man, he was experienced, 70 years old.
"He knew that when the [family's] women came and saw their sons and brothers, they would scream.
"So he did his best to bury the bodies before the women came.
"But we only buried a few of them before the women came. They helped us."
J. SACCO 8.06
The bodies of his relatives were reinterred a few months later.
He tries to recall their names.
He remembers eight names out of twelve.

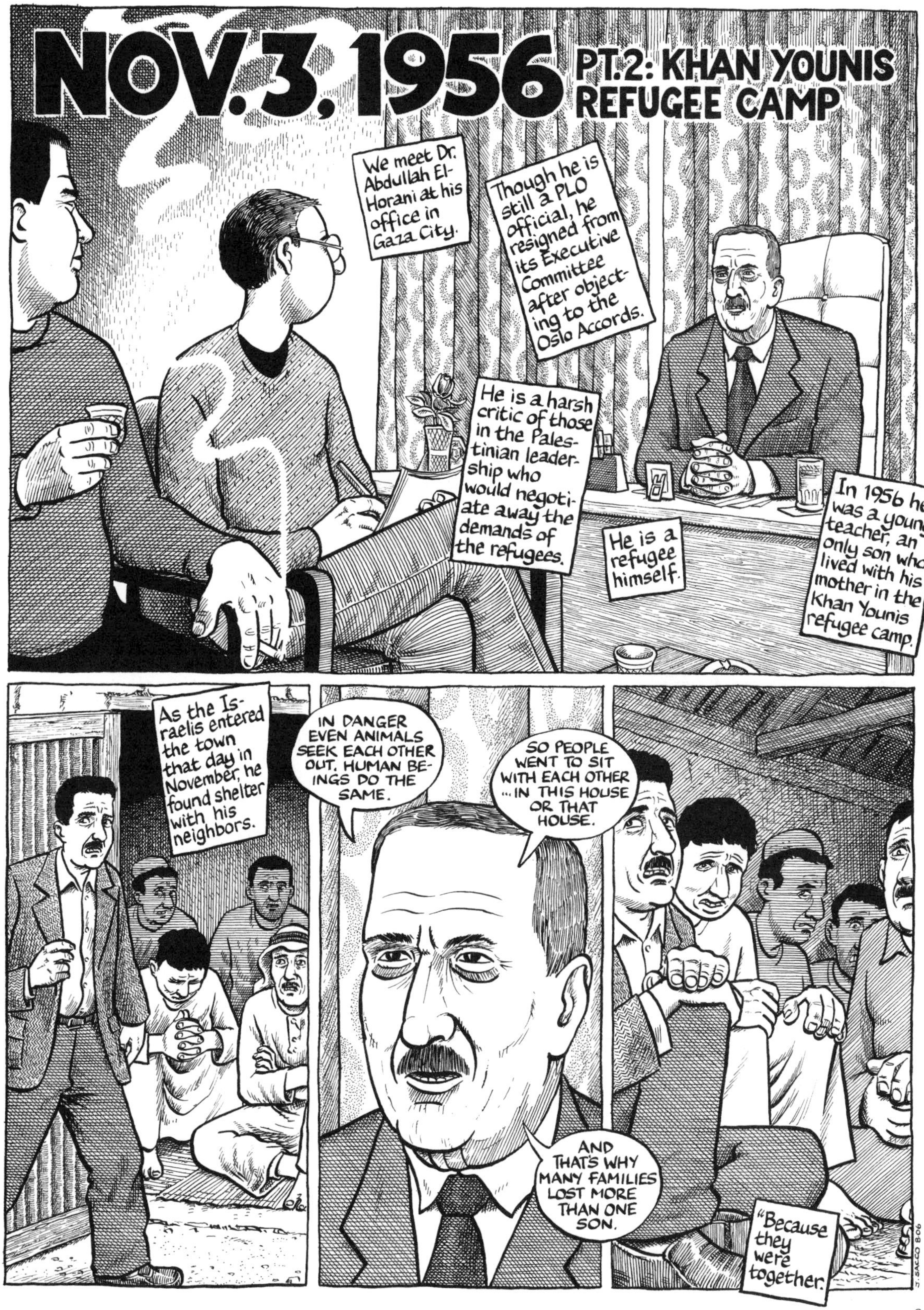
NOV. 3, 1956
PT. 2: KHAN YOUNIS REFUGEE CAMP
We meet Dr. Abdullah El-Horani at his office in Gaza City.
Though he is still a PLO official, he resigned from its Executive Committee after objecting to the Oslo Accords.
He is a harsh critic of those in the Palestinian leadership who would negotiate away the demands of the refugees.
He is a refugee himself.
In 1956 he was a young teacher, an only son who lived with his mother in the Khan Younis refugee camp.
As the Israelis entered the town that day in November, he found shelter with his neighbors.
IN DANGER EVEN ANIMALS SEEK EACH OTHER OUT. HUMAN BEINGS DO THE SAME.
SO PEOPLE WENT TO SIT WITH EACH OTHER ...IN THIS HOUSE OR THAT HOUSE.
AND THAT'S WHY MANY FAMILIES LOST MORE THAN ONE SON.
"Because they were together.
J. SACCO 8.06

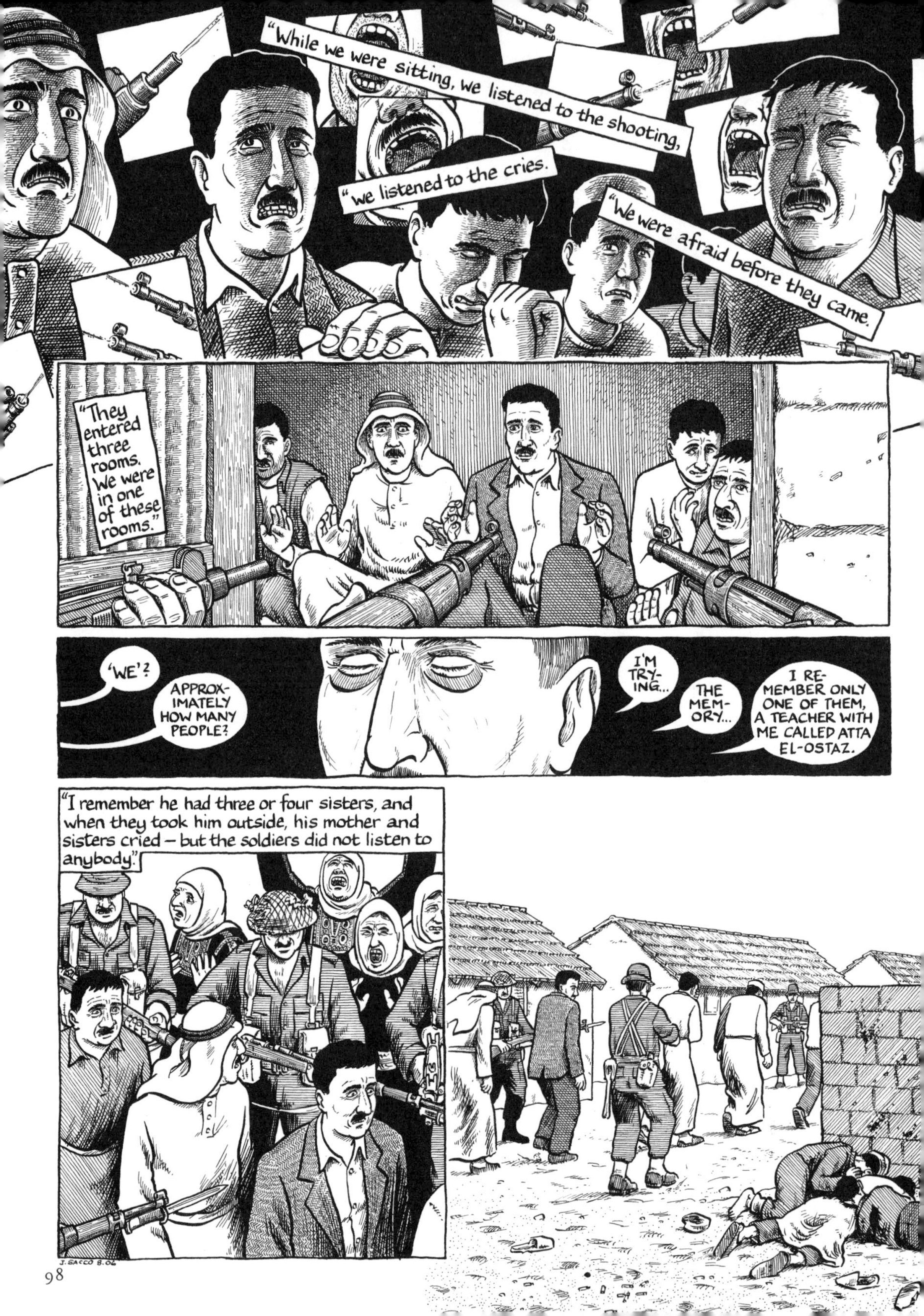
"While we were sitting, we listened to the shooting,
"we listened to the cries.
"We were afraid before they came.
"They entered three rooms. We were in one of these rooms."
'WE'?
APPROX-IMATELY HOW MANY PEOPLE?
I'M TRY-ING...
THE MEM-ORY...
I RE-MEMBER ONLY ONE OF THEM, A TEACHER WITH ME CALLED ATTA EL-OSTAZ.
"I remember he had three or four sisters, and when they took him outside, his mother and sisters cried – but the soldiers did not listen to anybody."
J. SACCO 8.06

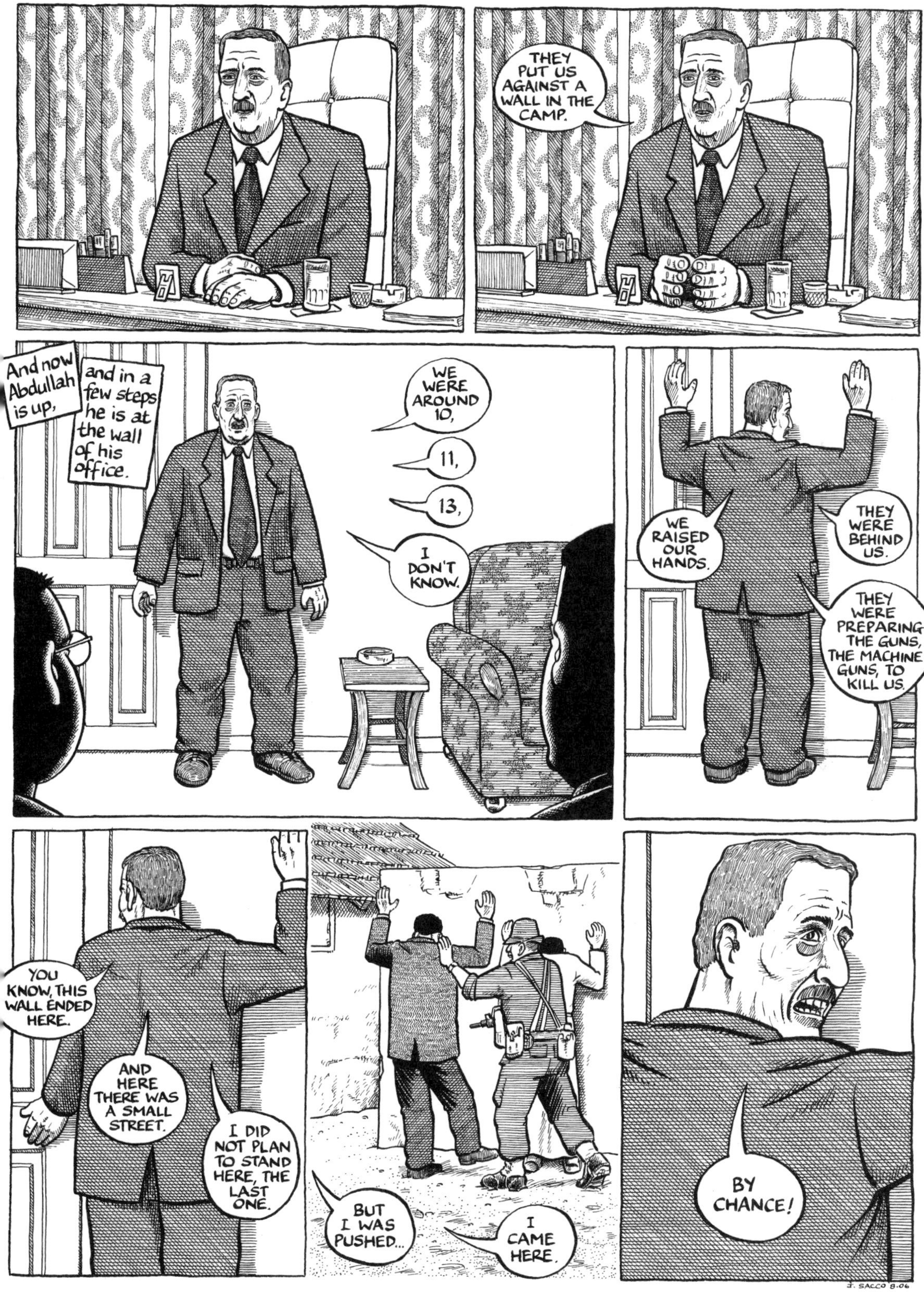
THEY PUT US AGAINST A WALL IN THE CAMP.
And now Abdullah is up,
and in a few steps he is at the wall of his office.
WE WERE AROUND 10,
11,
13,
I DON'T KNOW.
WE RAISED OUR HANDS.
THEY WERE BEHIND US.
THEY WERE PREPARING THE GUNS, THE MACHINE GUNS, TO KILL US.
YOU KNOW, THIS WALL ENDED HERE.
AND HERE THERE WAS A SMALL STREET.
I DID NOT PLAN TO STAND HERE, THE LAST ONE.
BUT I WAS PUSHED...
I CAME HERE.
BY CHANCE!
J. SACCO 8.06

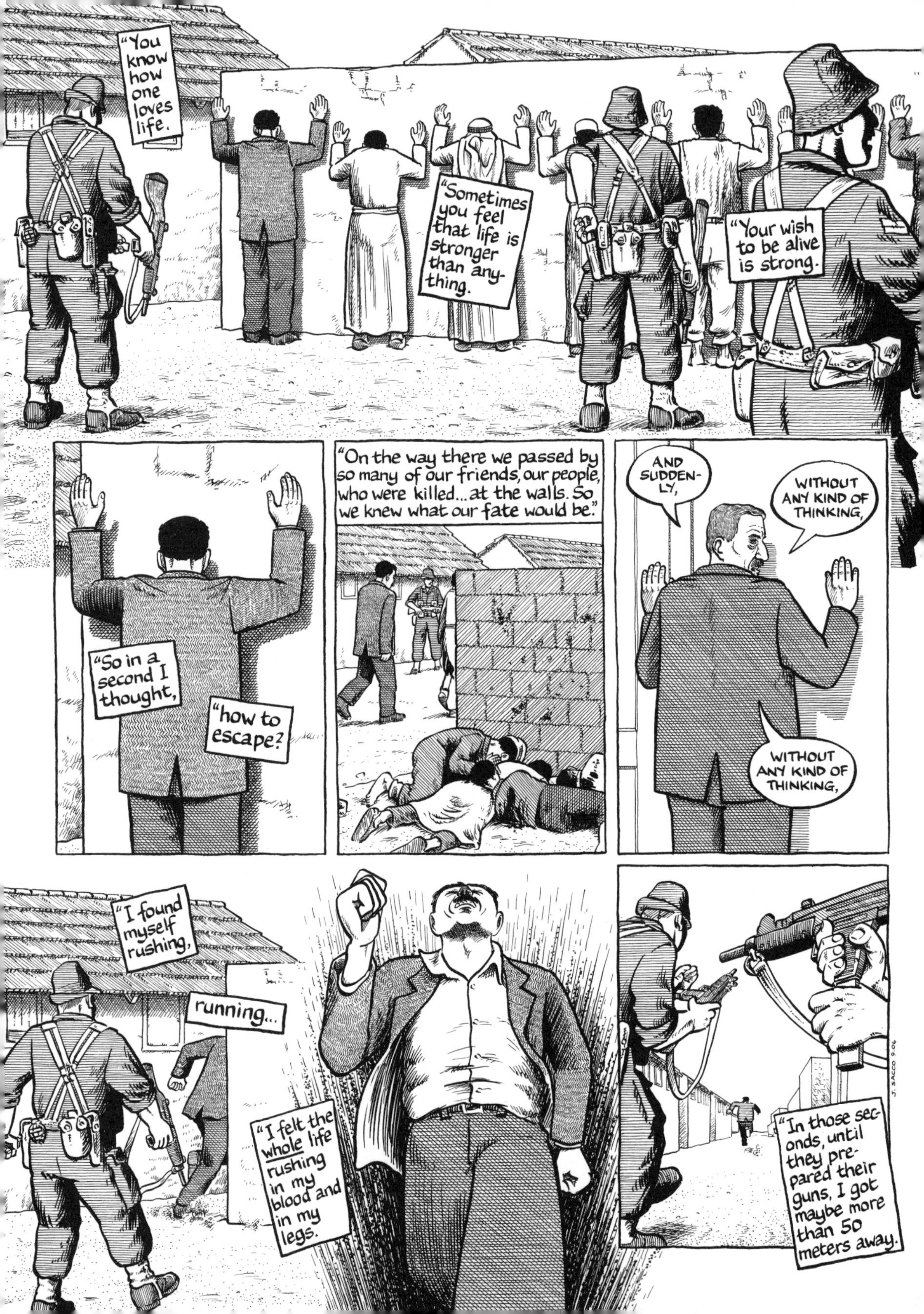
"You know how one loves life.
"Sometimes you feel that life is stronger than anything.
"Your wish to be alive is strong.
"So in a second I thought,
"how to escape?
"On the way there we passed by so many of our friends, our people, who were killed... at the walls. So we knew what our fate would be."
AND SUDDENLY,
WITHOUT ANY KIND OF THINKING,
WITHOUT ANY KIND OF THINKING,
"I found myself rushing,
running...
"I felt the whole life rushing in my blood and in my legs.
"In those seconds, until they prepared their guns, I got maybe more than 50 meters away.
J. SACCO 9.06

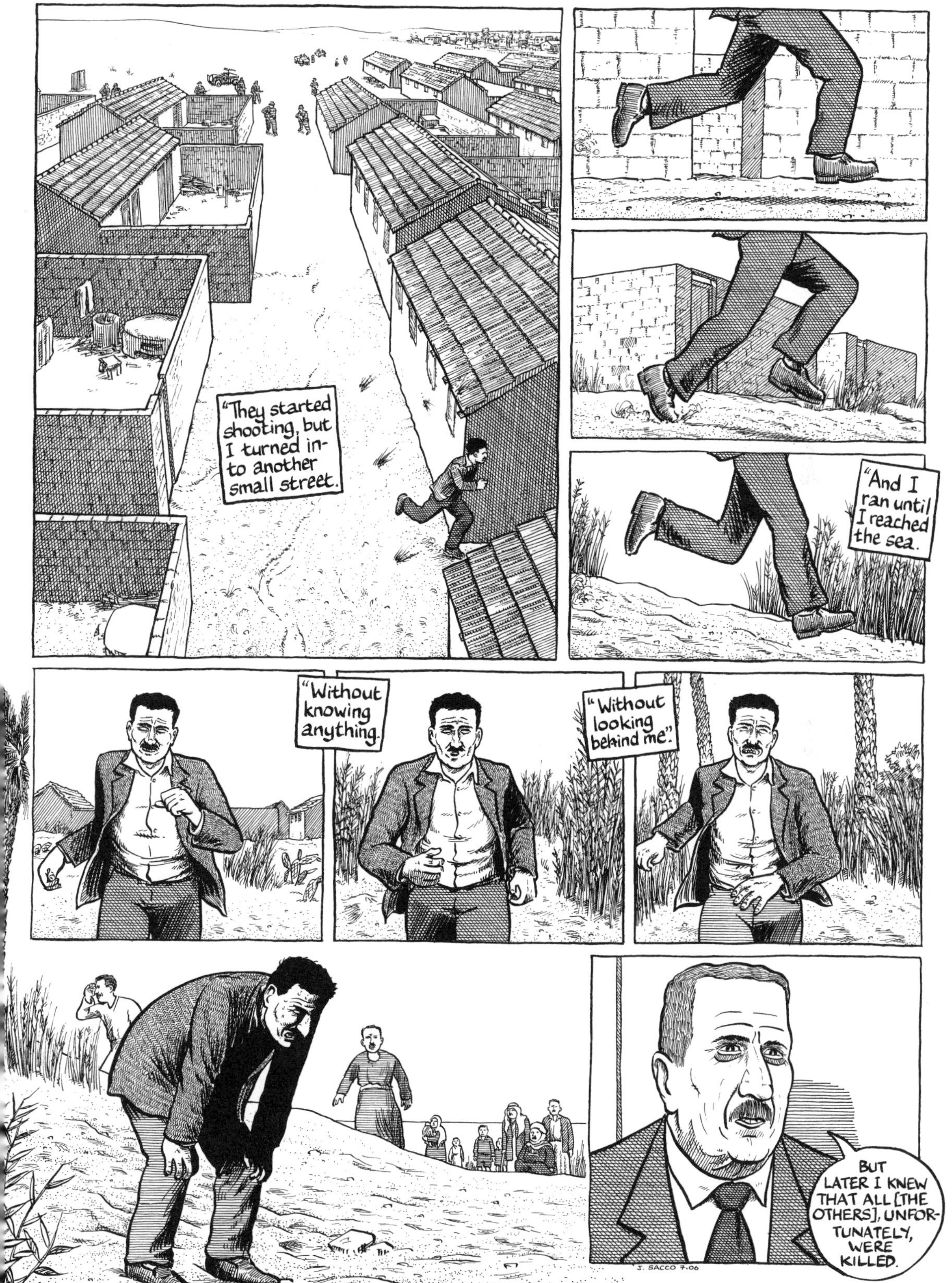
"They started shooting, but I turned into another small street.
"And I ran until I reached the sea.
"Without knowing anything.
"Without looking behind me".
BUT LATER I KNEW THAT ALL [THE OTHERS], UNFORTUNATELY, WERE KILLED.
J. SACCO 7.06

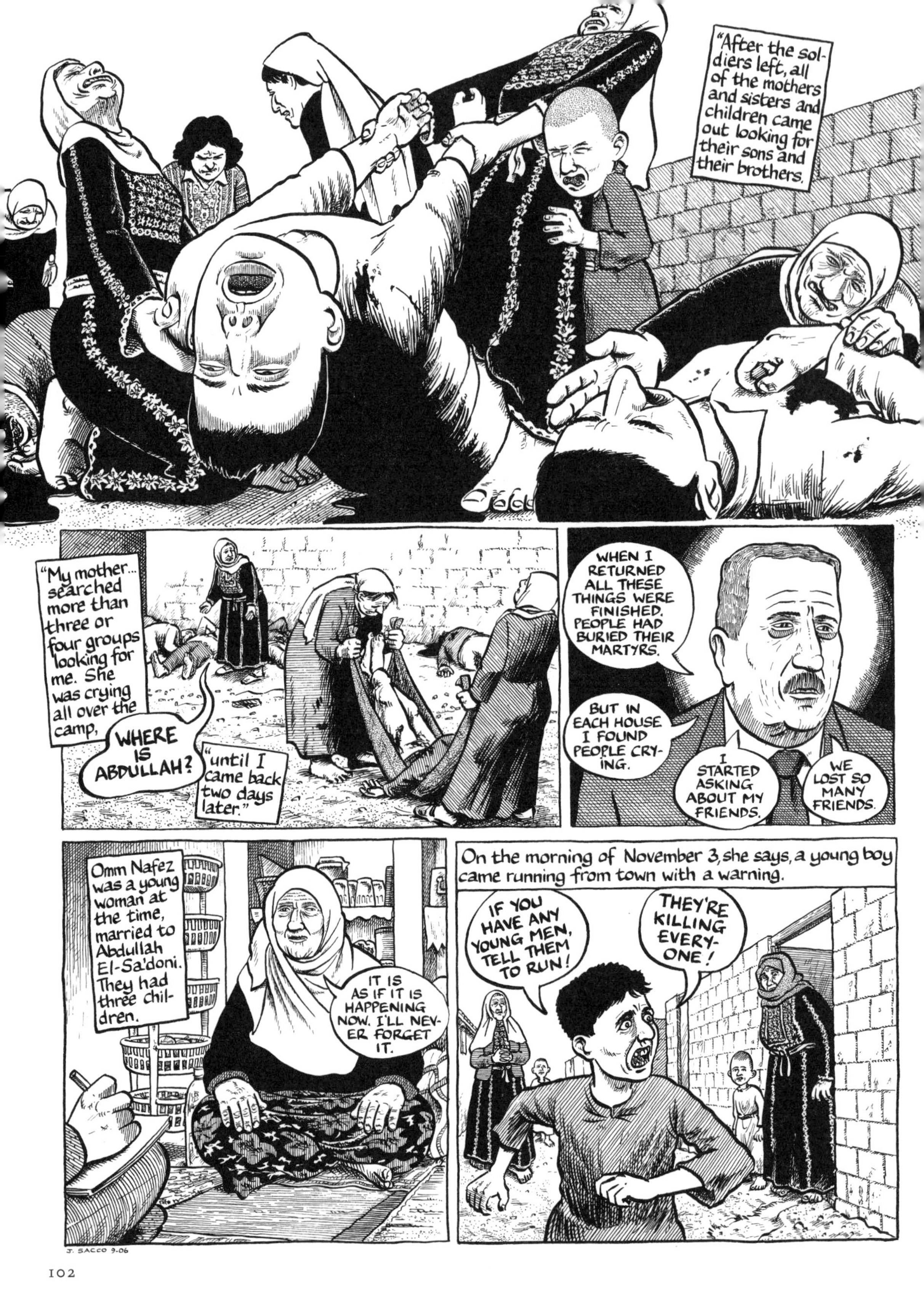
"After the soldiers left, all of the mothers and sisters and children came out looking for their sons and their brothers.
"My mother... searched more than three or four groups looking for me. She was crying all over the camp,
WHERE IS ABDULLAH?
"until I came back two days later."
WHEN I RETURNED ALL THESE THINGS WERE FINISHED. PEOPLE HAD BURIED THEIR MARTYRS.
BUT IN EACH HOUSE I FOUND PEOPLE CRYING.
I STARTED ASKING ABOUT MY FRIENDS.
WE LOST SO MANY FRIENDS.
Omm Nafez was a young woman at the time, married to Abdullah El-Sa'doni. They had three children.
IT IS AS IF IT IS HAPPENING NOW. I'LL NEVER FORGET IT.
On the morning of November 3, she says, a young boy came running from town with a warning.
IF YOU HAVE ANY YOUNG MEN, TELL THEM TO RUN!
THEY'RE KILLING EVERYONE!
J. SACCO 9-06

But Abdullah and three of his brothers were still in the camp, huddled with their families, when the Israelis arrived.

"Two Israeli soldiers stood outside the door, and one came in to get the boys out."

"The first brother who came out was Ibrahim.

"They killed him.

"The next was Subhi. Subhi held a child in his arms.

"They shot Subhi, and as he [fell] they shot the boy, too.*

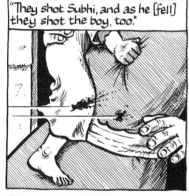

"Then came Abdullah and Khamis. I called:"

MY HUSBAND!

At that point, Khamis made a run for it.

"He jumped over the wall and escaped.

"Abdullah...was trying to escape, but they caught him.

"They took him outside the door ...and they shot him in his side."

* THE INJURED BOY, A NEPHEW OF THE BROTHERS, WOULD LOSE HIS LEG.

J. SACCO 9·06

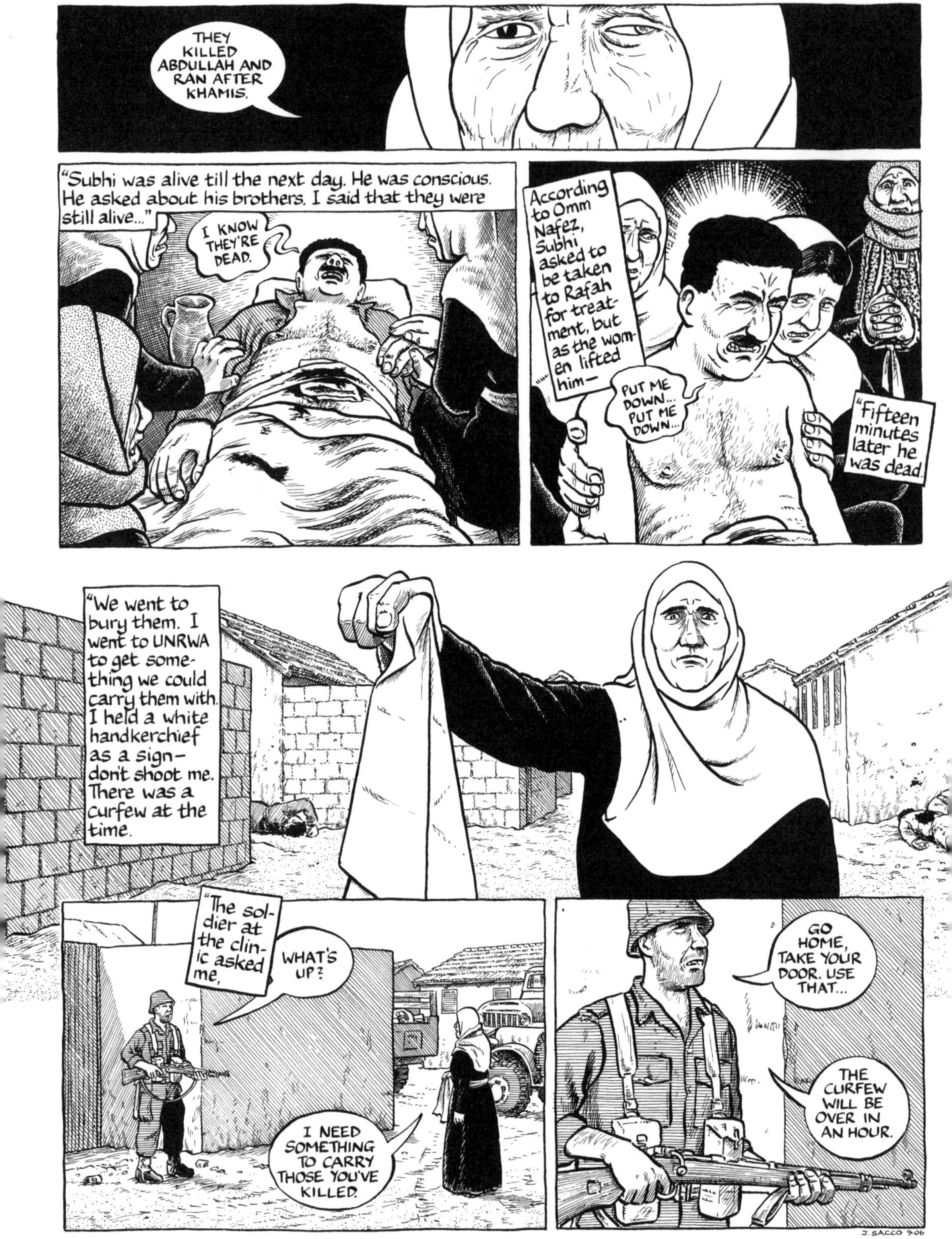
THEY KILLED ABDULLAH AND RAN AFTER KHAMIS.
"Subhi was alive till the next day. He was conscious. He asked about his brothers. I said that they were still alive..."
I KNOW THEY'RE DEAD.
According to Omm Nafez, Subhi asked to be taken to Rafah for treatment, but as the women lifted him—
PUT ME DOWN... PUT ME DOWN...
"Fifteen minutes later he was dead.
"We went to bury them. I went to UNRWA to get something we could carry them with. I held a white handkerchief as a sign—don't shoot me. There was a curfew at the time.
"The soldier at the clinic asked me,
WHAT'S UP?
I NEED SOMETHING TO CARRY THOSE YOU'VE KILLED.
GO HOME, TAKE YOUR DOOR. USE THAT...
THE CURFEW WILL BE OVER IN AN HOUR.
J. SACCO 9·06

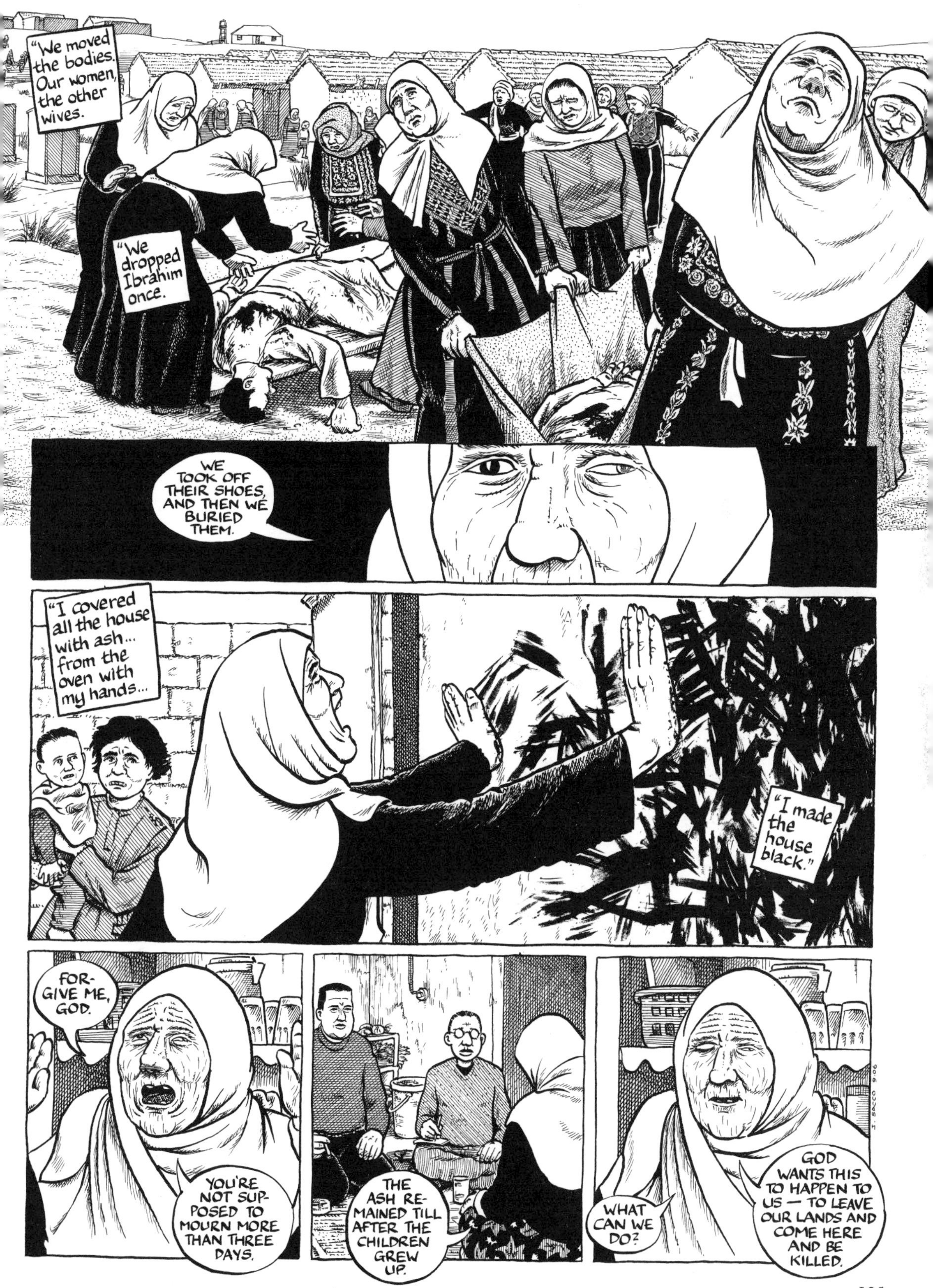
"We moved the bodies. Our women, the other wives.
"We dropped Ibrahim once.
WE TOOK OFF THEIR SHOES, AND THEN WE BURIED THEM.
"I covered all the house with ash... from the oven with my hands...
"I made the house black."
FOR-GIVE ME, GOD.
YOU'RE NOT SUP-POSED TO MOURN MORE THAN THREE DAYS.
THE ASH RE-MAINED TILL AFTER THE CHILDREN GREW UP.
WHAT CAN WE DO?
GOD WANTS THIS TO HAPPEN TO US — TO LEAVE OUR LANDS AND COME HERE AND BE KILLED.
J. SACCO 9.06

MEMORY AND THE ESSENTIAL TRUTH

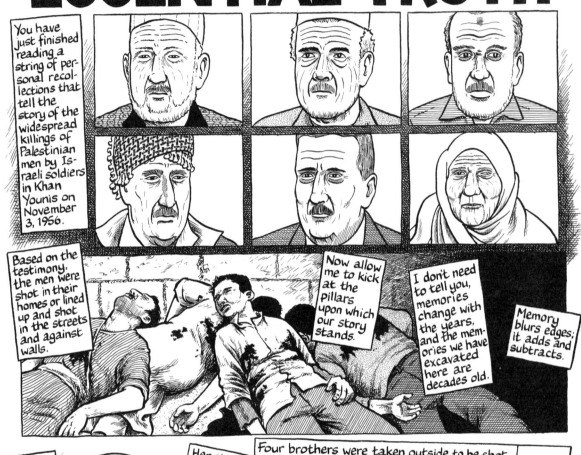

You have just finished reading a string of personal recollections that tell the story of the widespread killings of Palestinian men by Israeli soldiers in Khan Younis on November 3, 1956.

Based on the testimony, the men were shot in their homes or lined up and shot in the streets and against walls.

Now allow me to kick at the pillars upon which our story stands.

I don't need to tell you, memories change with the years, and the memories we have excavated here are decades old.

Memory blurs edges; it adds and subtracts.

Let us take one example, the story of Omm Nafez.

Her story is well known among the camp old-timers because it is particularly tragic.

Four brothers were taken outside to be shot.

Her husband was among them, and he was killed.

One of the brothers, Khamis, escaped.

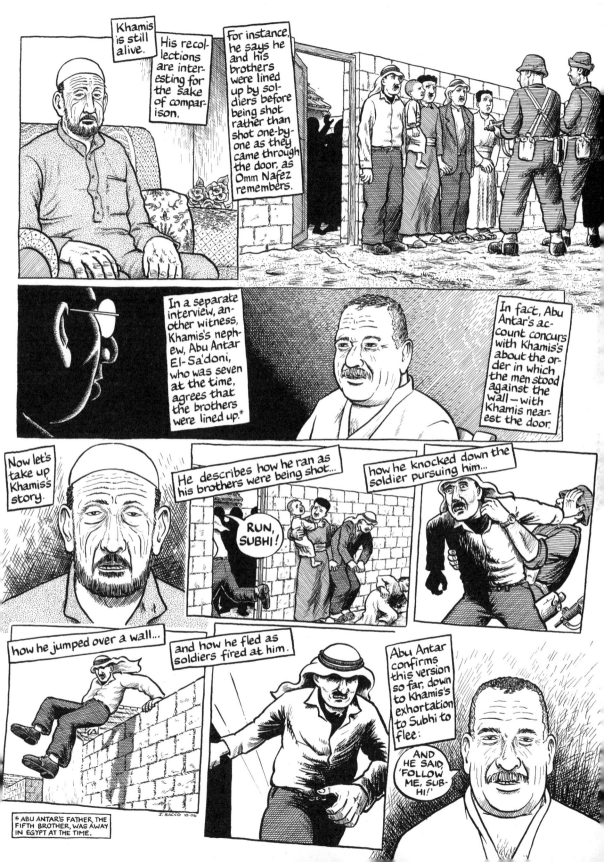

Khamis is still alive.

His recollections are interesting for the sake of comparison.

For instance, he says he and his brothers were lined up by soldiers before being shot rather than shot one-by-one as they came through the door, as Omm Nafez remembers.

In a separate interview, another witness, Khamis's nephew, Abu Antar El-Sa'doni, who was seven at the time, agrees that the brothers were lined up.*

In fact, Abu Antar's account concurs with Khamis's about the order in which the men stood against the wall—with Khamis nearest the door.

Now let's take up Khamis's story.

He describes how he ran as his brothers were being shot...

RUN, SUBHI!

how he knocked down the soldier pursuing him...

how he jumped over a wall...

and how he fled as soldiers fired at him.

Abu Antar confirms this version so far, down to Khamis's exhortation to Subhi to flee:

AND HE SAID, 'FOLLOW ME, SUBHI!'

* ABU ANTAR'S FATHER, THE FIFTH BROTHER, WAS AWAY IN EGYPT AT THE TIME.

J. SACCO 10-06

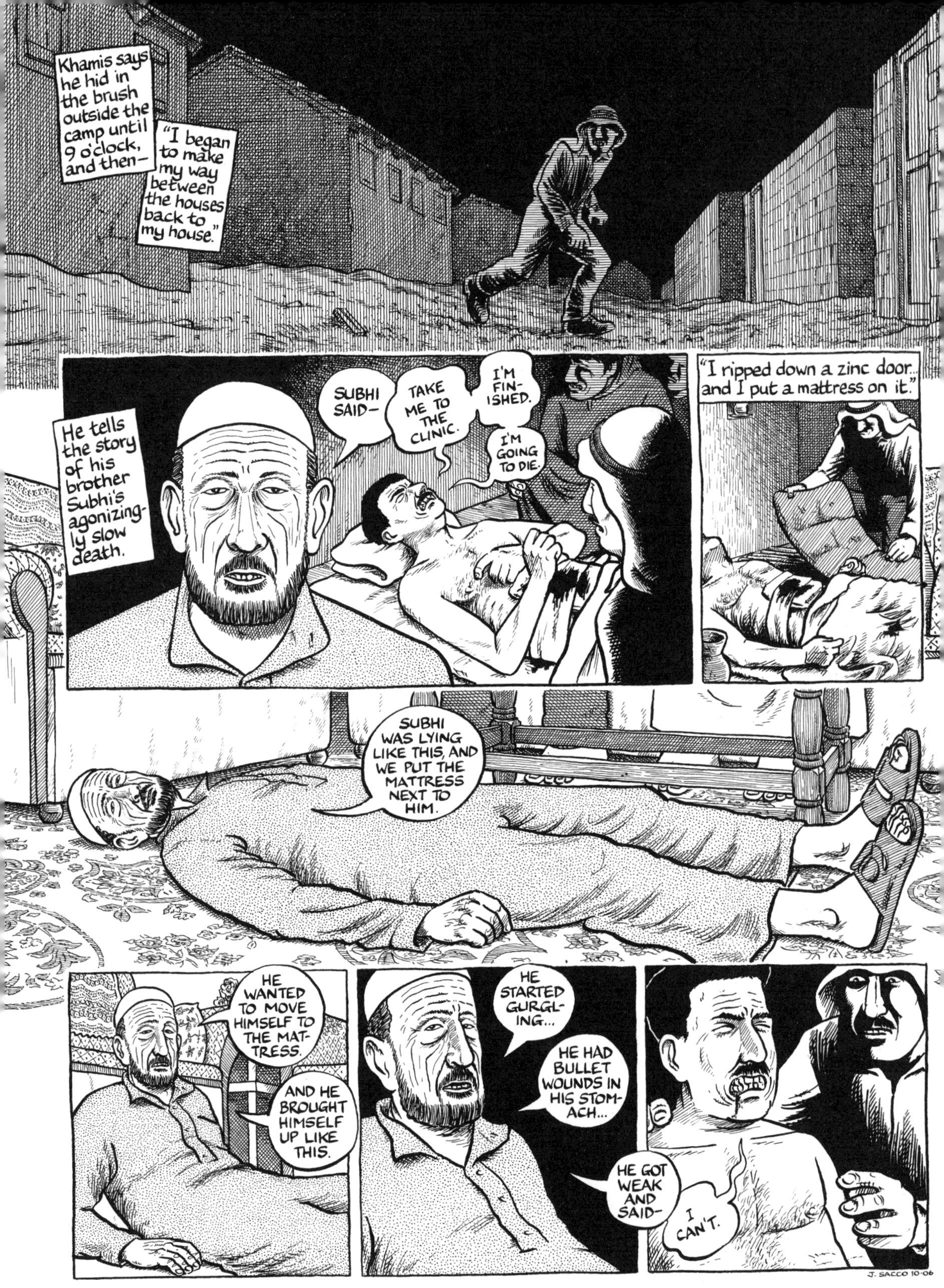
Khamis says he hid in the brush outside the camp until 9 o'clock, and then–
"I began to make my way between the houses back to my house."
He tells the story of his brother Subhi's agonizingly slow death.
SUBHI SAID–
TAKE ME TO THE CLINIC.
I'M FINISHED.
I'M GOING TO DIE.
"I ripped down a zinc door... and I put a mattress on it."
SUBHI WAS LYING LIKE THIS, AND WE PUT THE MATTRESS NEXT TO HIM.
HE WANTED TO MOVE HIMSELF TO THE MATTRESS.
AND HE BROUGHT HIMSELF UP LIKE THIS.
HE STARTED GURGLING...
HE HAD BULLET WOUNDS IN HIS STOMACH...
HE GOT WEAK AND SAID–
I CAN'T.
J. SACCO 10·06

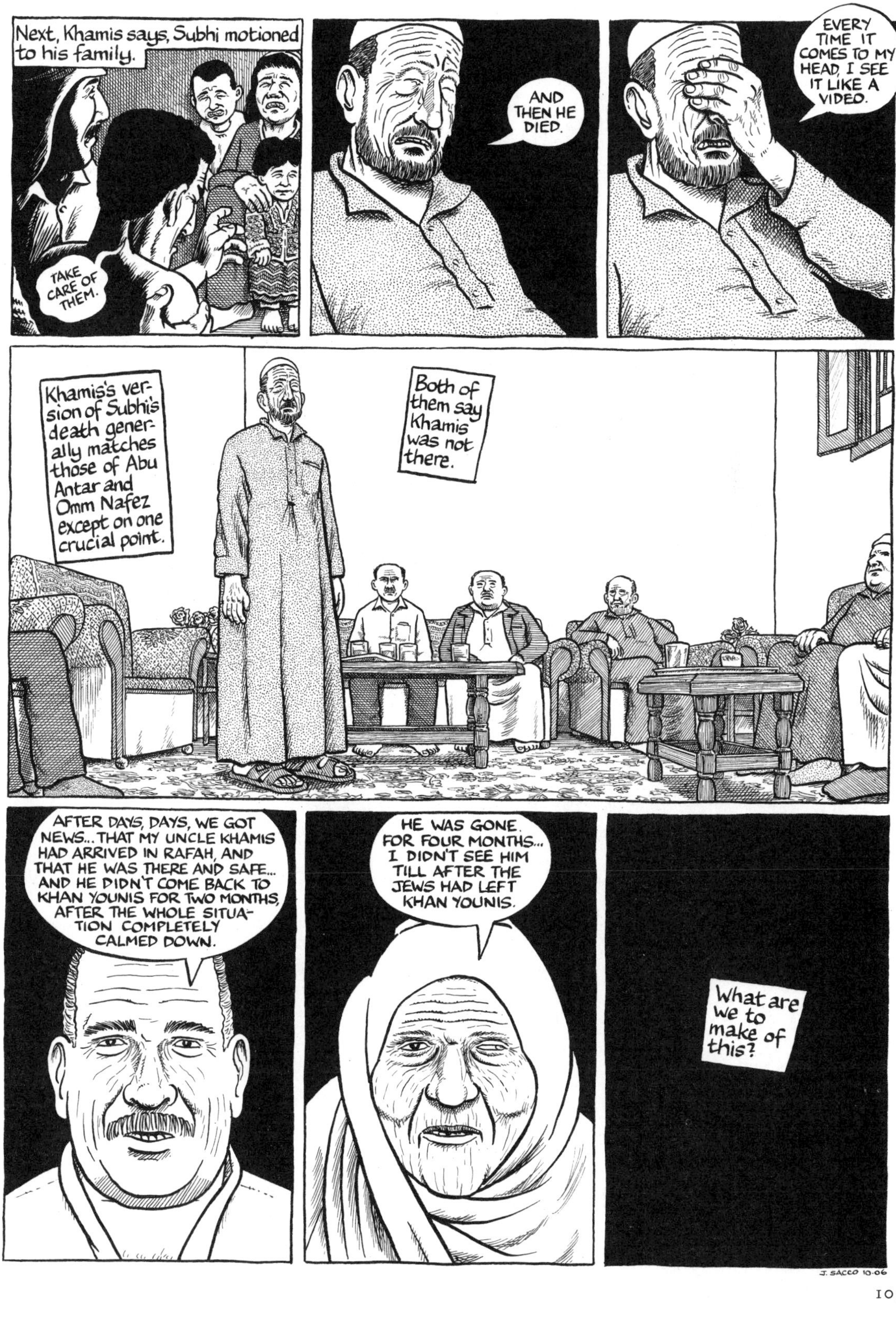
Next, Khamis says, Subhi motioned to his family.
TAKE CARE OF THEM.
AND THEN HE DIED.
EVERY TIME IT COMES TO MY HEAD, I SEE IT LIKE A VIDEO.
Khamis's version of Subhi's death generally matches those of Abu Antar and Omm Nafez except on one crucial point.
Both of them say Khamis was not there.
AFTER DAYS, DAYS, WE GOT NEWS... THAT MY UNCLE KHAMIS HAD ARRIVED IN RAFAH, AND THAT HE WAS THERE AND SAFE... AND HE DIDN'T COME BACK TO KHAN YOUNIS FOR TWO MONTHS, AFTER THE WHOLE SITUATION COMPLETELY CALMED DOWN.
HE WAS GONE FOR FOUR MONTHS... I DIDN'T SEE HIM TILL AFTER THE JEWS HAD LEFT KHAN YOUNIS.
What are we to make of this?
J. SACCO 10·06

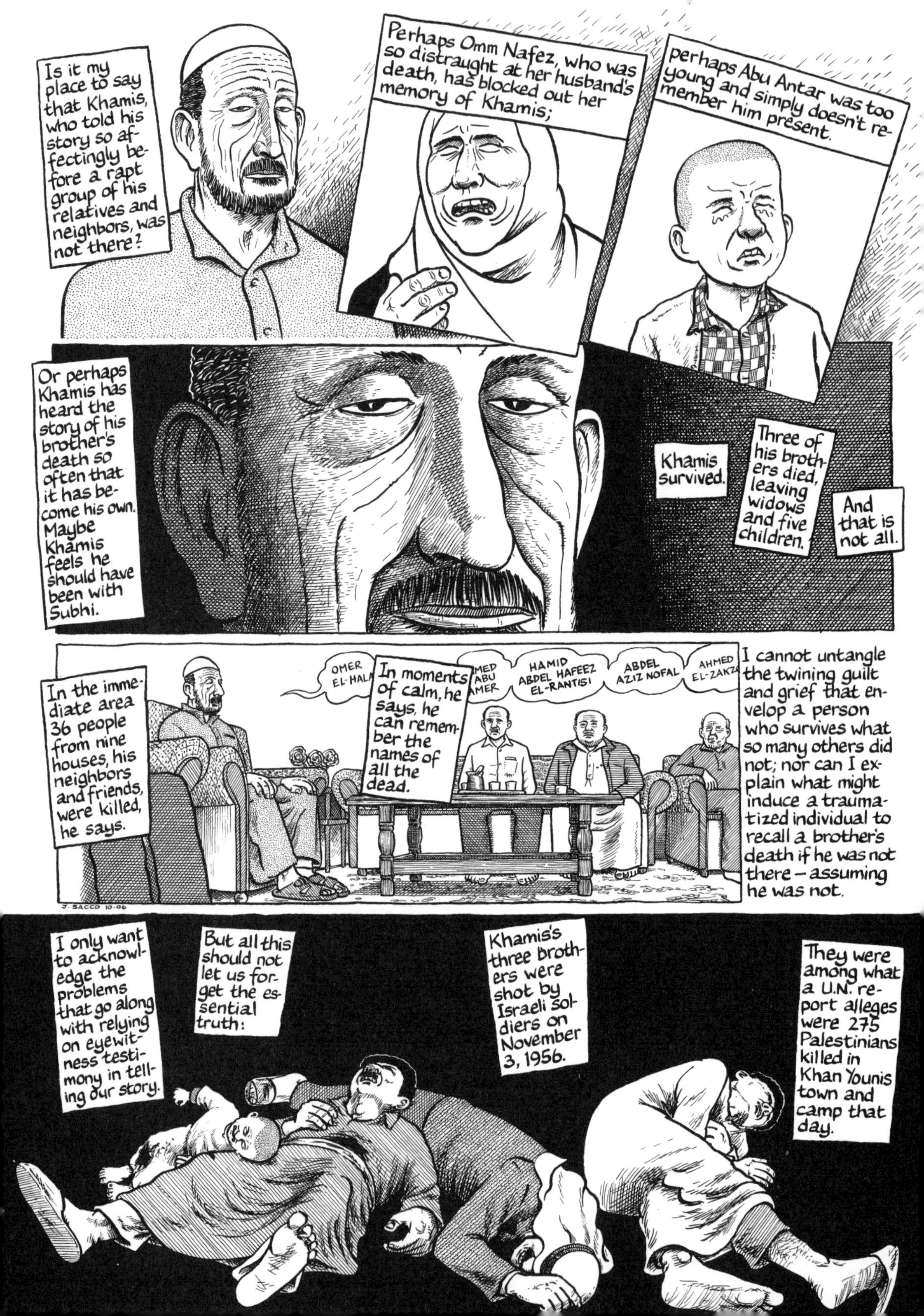
Is it my place to say that Khamis, who told his story so affectingly before a rapt group of his relatives and neighbors, was not there?
Perhaps Omm Nafez, who was so distraught at her husband's death, has blocked out her memory of Khamis;
perhaps Abu Antar was too young and simply doesn't remember him present.
Or perhaps Khamis has heard the story of his brother's death so often that it has become his own. Maybe Khamis feels he should have been with Subhi.
Khamis survived.
Three of his brothers died, leaving widows and five children.
And that is not all.
In the immediate area 36 people from nine houses, his neighbors and friends, were killed, he says.
In moments of calm, he says, he can remember the names of all the dead.
OMER EL-HALA
HAMID ABDEL HAFEEZ EL-RANTISI
ABDEL AZIZ NOFAL
I cannot untangle the twining guilt and grief that envelop a person who survives what so many others did not; nor can I explain what might induce a traumatized individual to recall a brother's death if he was not there—assuming he was not.
J. SACCO 10.06
I only want to acknowledge the problems that go along with relying on eyewitness testimony in telling our story.
But all this should not let us forget the essential truth:
Khamis's three brothers were shot by Israeli soldiers on November 3, 1956.
They were among what a U.N. report alleges were 275 Palestinians killed in Khan Younis town and camp that day.

EXCERPT FROM

BODYWORLD

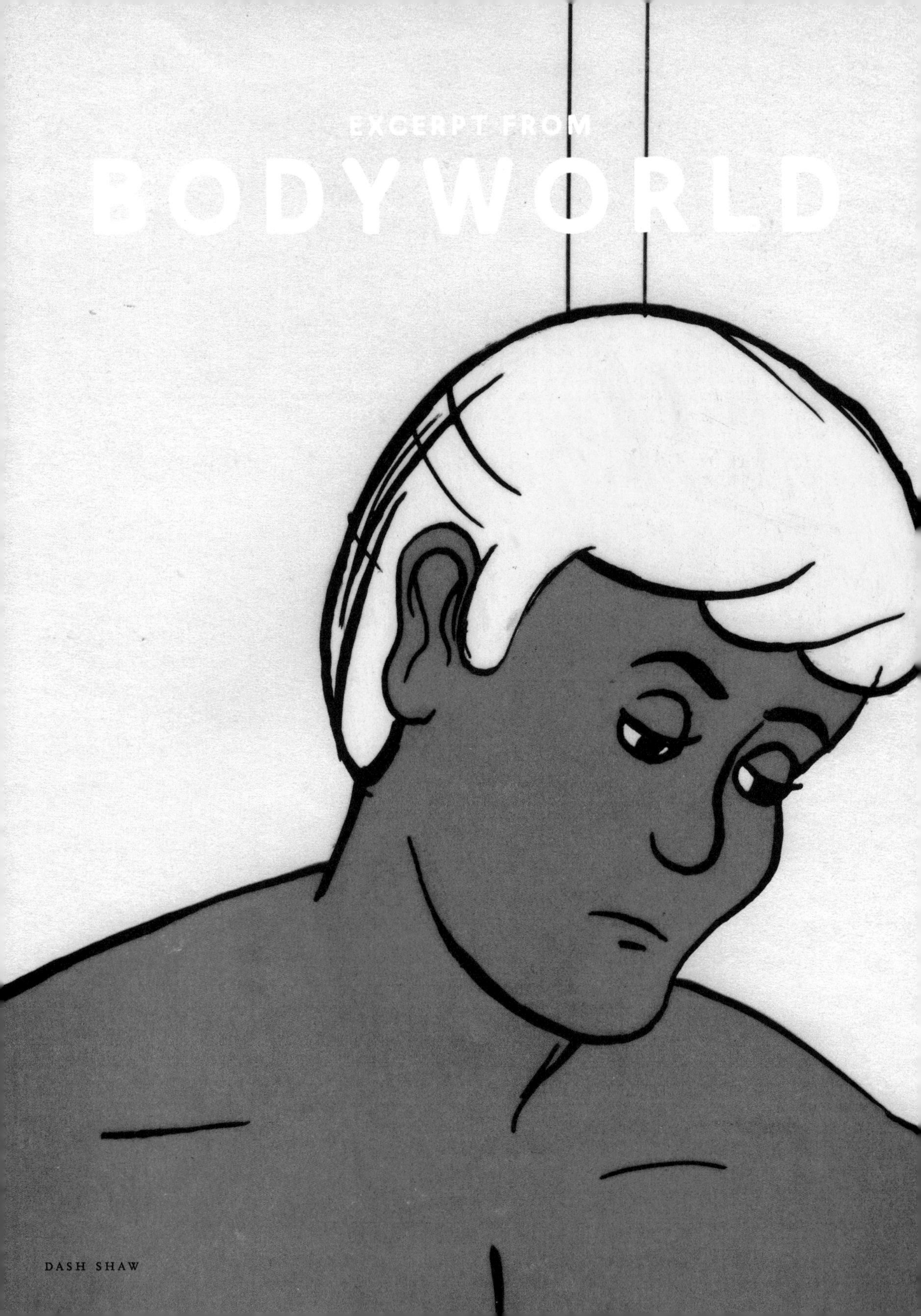

DASH SHAW

CHAPTER THREE

A-B-C,
IT'S AS
KNOCK KNOCK
EASY AS
KNOCK
FWOOSH
1-2-
KNOCK
NNN-
3,
KNOCK
AHHH! AHHH!
AS
KNOCK
STOMP STOMP
SIMPLE

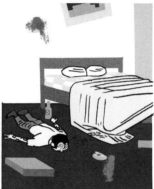

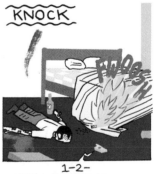

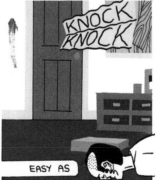

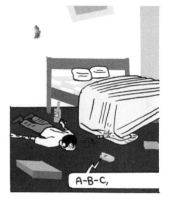

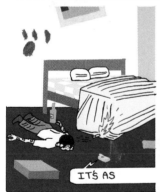

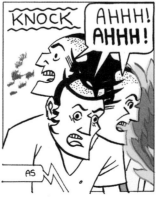

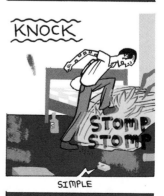

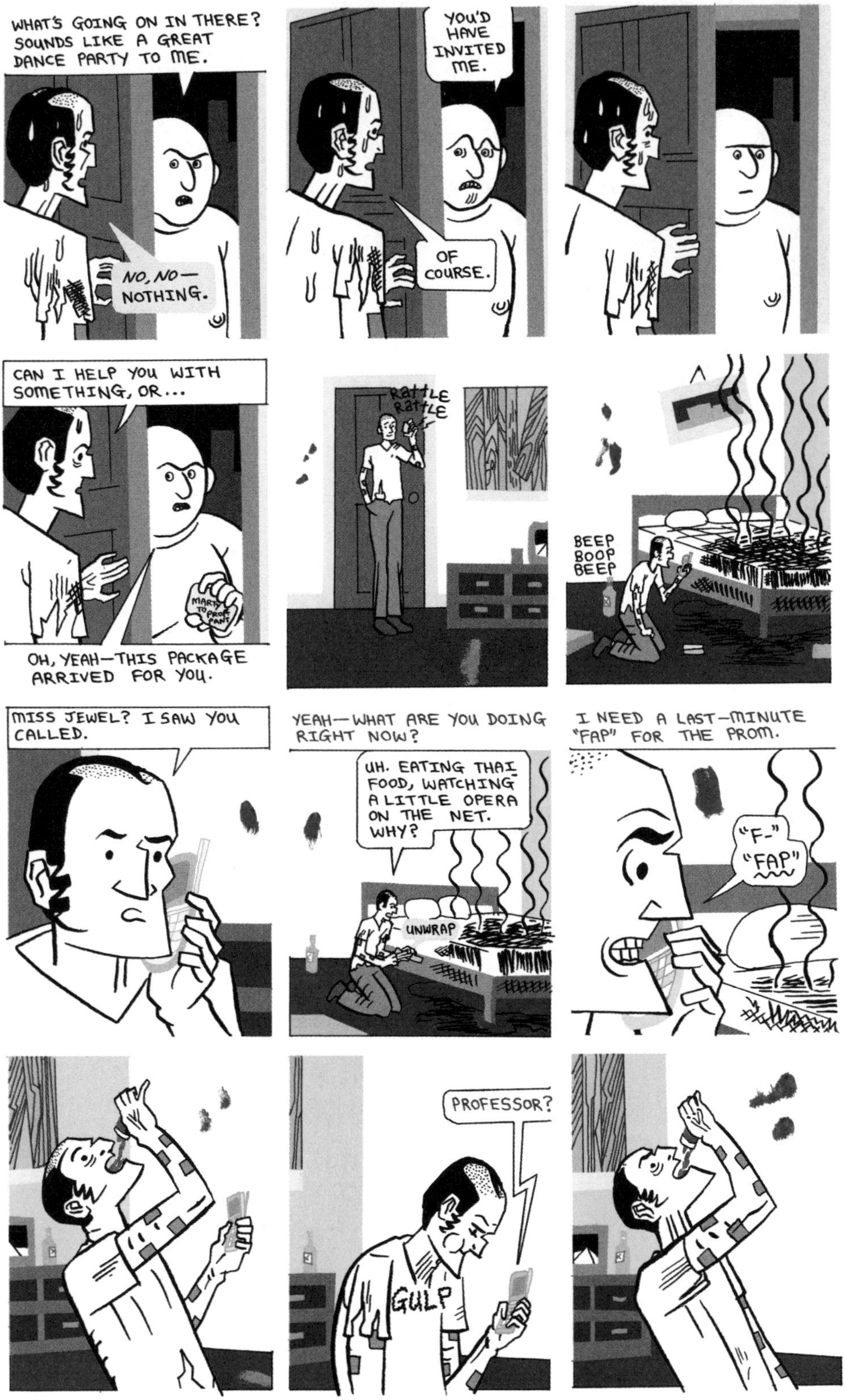
WHAT'S GOING ON IN THERE? SOUNDS LIKE A GREAT DANCE PARTY TO ME.
NO, NO— NOTHING.
YOU'D HAVE INVITED ME.
OF COURSE.
CAN I HELP YOU WITH SOMETHING, OR...
MARTY TO PROF PANT
OH, YEAH—THIS PACKAGE ARRIVED FOR YOU.
RATTLE RATTLE
BEEP BOOP BEEP
MISS JEWEL? I SAW YOU CALLED.
YEAH—WHAT ARE YOU DOING RIGHT NOW?
UH. EATING THAI FOOD, WATCHING A LITTLE OPERA ON THE NET. WHY?
UNWRAP
I NEED A LAST-MINUTE "FAP" FOR THE PROM.
"F-" "FAP"
PROFESSOR?
GULP

"F-A-P" FRIENDLY ADULT PRESENCE

SHAKE (NO RATTLE)

OH. OH, YEAH. SURE.

AT THE SCHOOL GYMNASIUM. WEAR A TIE.

GIVE ME TWENTY MINUTES.

CLICK

OXY PAD

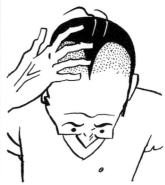

CAN I BUM A NECK TIE AND A DRESS SHIRT OFF OF YOU, FRIEND?

SURE!

I GOT ONE RIGHT OVER HERE.

THANKS. HOW NEIGHBORLY OF YOU.

HA! NO PROB.

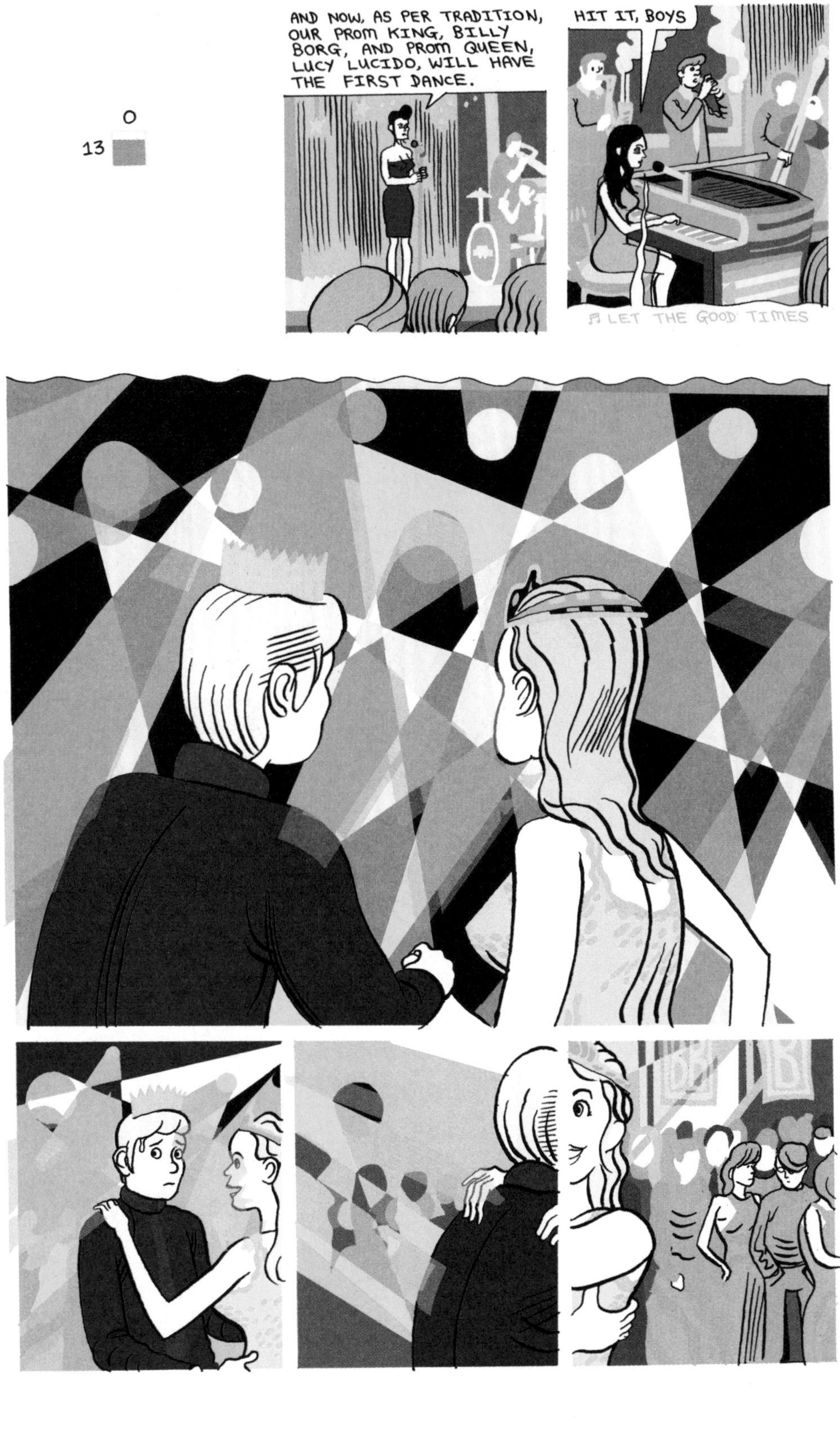
0
13
AND NOW, AS PER TRADITION, OUR PROM KING, BILLY BORG, AND PROM QUEEN, LUCY LUCIDO, WILL HAVE THE FIRST DANCE.
HIT IT, BOYS
♫ LET THE GOOD TIMES

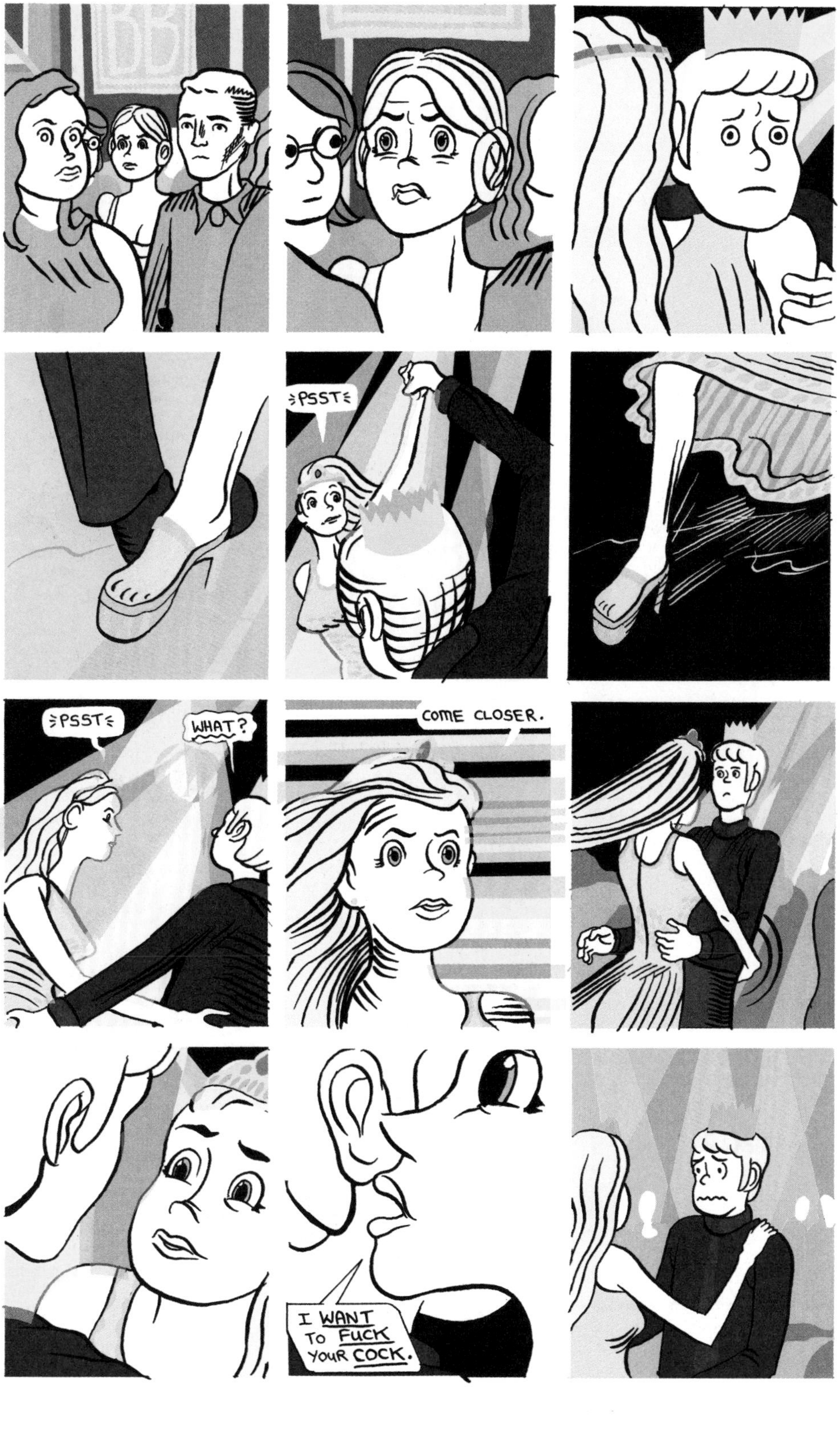
PSST
PSST
WHAT?
COME CLOSER.
I WANT TO FUCK YOUR COCK.

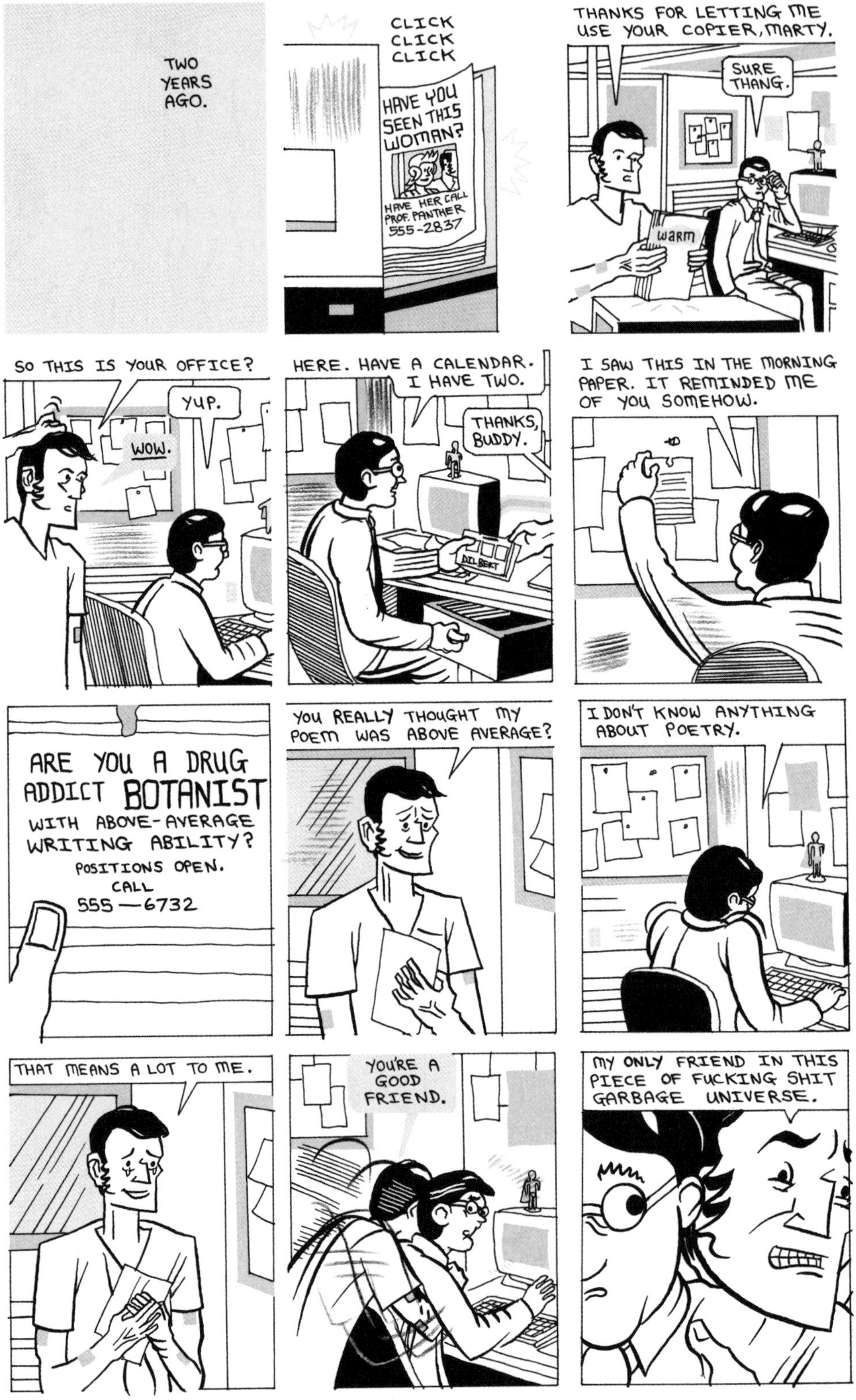
TWO YEARS AGO.
CLICK CLICK CLICK
HAVE YOU SEEN THIS WOMAN?
HAVE HER CALL PROF. PANTHER 555-2837
THANKS FOR LETTING ME USE YOUR COPIER, MARTY.
SURE THANG.
warm
SO THIS IS YOUR OFFICE?
YUP.
WOW.
HERE. HAVE A CALENDAR. I HAVE TWO.
THANKS, BUDDY.
DILBERT
I SAW THIS IN THE MORNING PAPER. IT REMINDED ME OF YOU SOMEHOW.
ARE YOU A DRUG ADDICT BOTANIST WITH ABOVE-AVERAGE WRITING ABILITY?
POSITIONS OPEN.
CALL 555—6732
YOU REALLY THOUGHT MY POEM WAS ABOVE AVERAGE?
I DON'T KNOW ANYTHING ABOUT POETRY.
THAT MEANS A LOT TO ME.
YOU'RE A GOOD FRIEND.
MY ONLY FRIEND IN THIS PIECE OF FUCKING SHIT GARBAGE UNIVERSE.

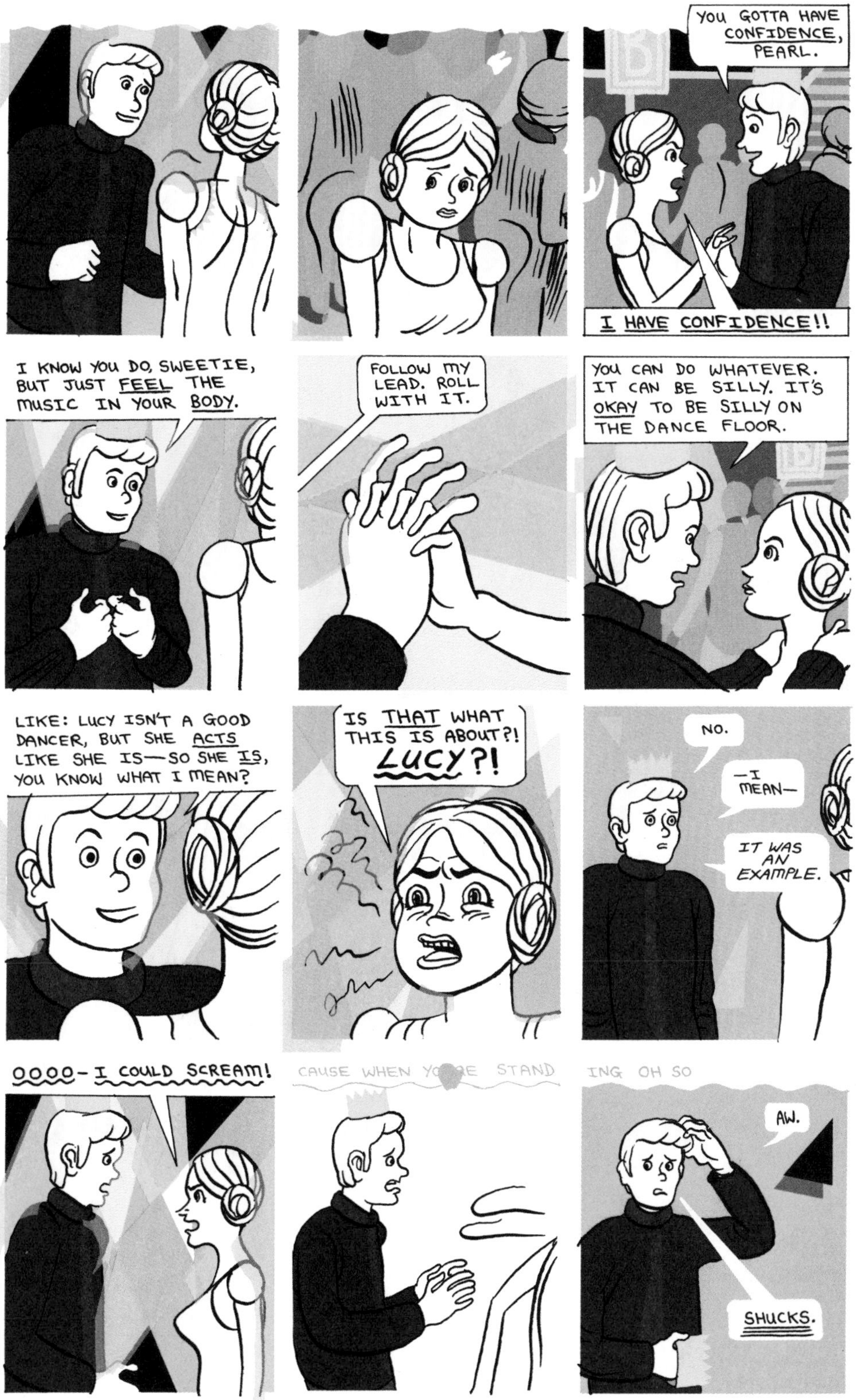
YOU GOTTA HAVE CONFIDENCE, PEARL.
I HAVE CONFIDENCE!!
I KNOW YOU DO, SWEETIE, BUT JUST FEEL THE MUSIC IN YOUR BODY.
FOLLOW MY LEAD. ROLL WITH IT.
YOU CAN DO WHATEVER. IT CAN BE SILLY. IT'S OKAY TO BE SILLY ON THE DANCE FLOOR.
LIKE: LUCY ISN'T A GOOD DANCER, BUT SHE ACTS LIKE SHE IS—SO SHE IS, YOU KNOW WHAT I MEAN?
IS THAT WHAT THIS IS ABOUT?! LUCY?!
NO.
—I MEAN—
IT WAS AN EXAMPLE.
OOOO-I COULD SCREAM!
CAUSE WHEN YOU'RE STAND
ING OH SO
AW.
SHUCKS.

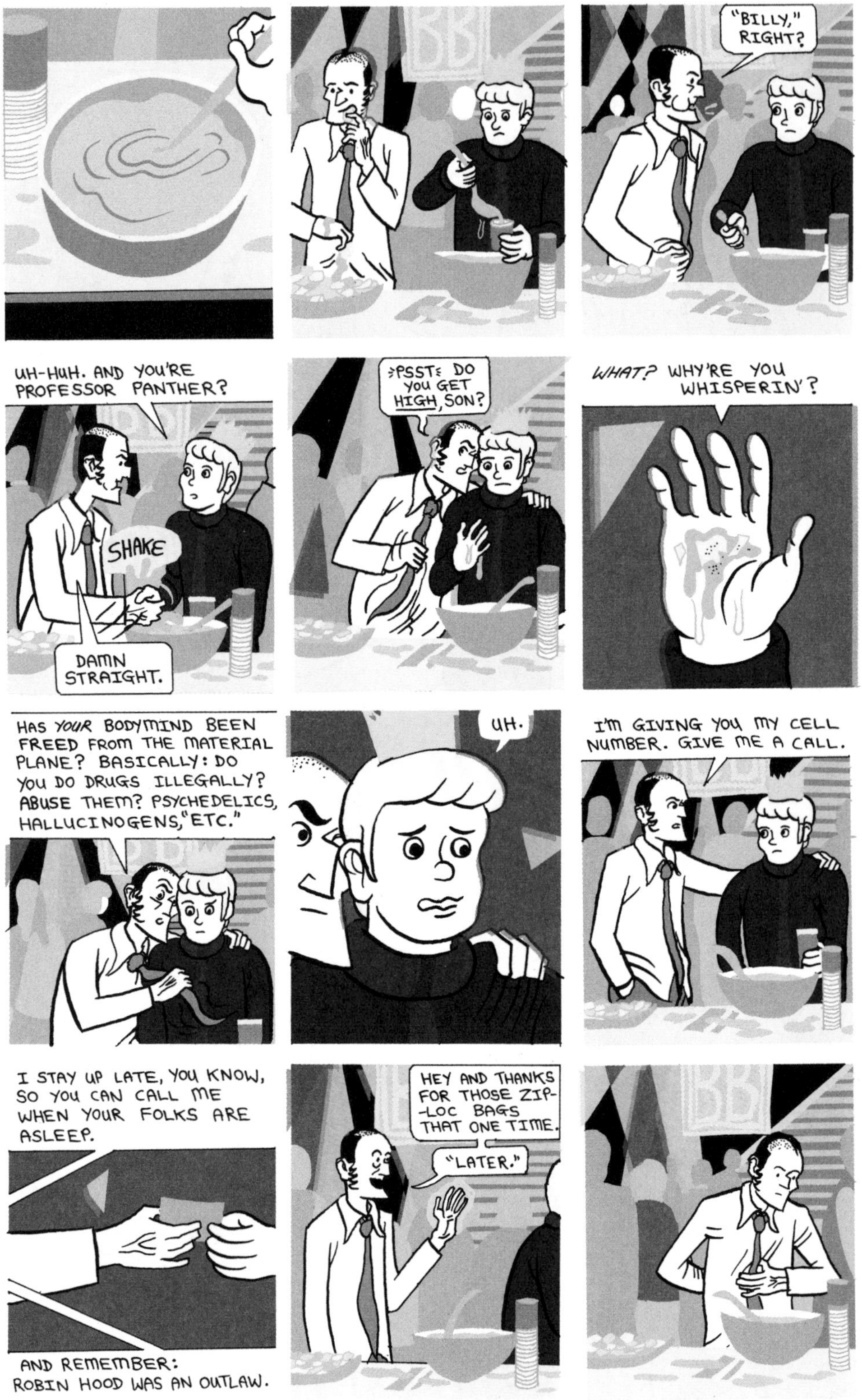
"BILLY," RIGHT?
UH-HUH. AND YOU'RE PROFESSOR PANTHER?
SHAKE
DAMN STRAIGHT.
PSST DO YOU GET HIGH, SON?
WHAT? WHY'RE YOU WHISPERIN'?
HAS YOUR BODYMIND BEEN FREED FROM THE MATERIAL PLANE? BASICALLY: DO YOU DO DRUGS ILLEGALLY? ABUSE THEM? PSYCHEDELICS, HALLUCINOGENS, "ETC."
UH.
I'M GIVING YOU MY CELL NUMBER. GIVE ME A CALL.
I STAY UP LATE, YOU KNOW, SO YOU CAN CALL ME WHEN YOUR FOLKS ARE ASLEEP.
AND REMEMBER: ROBIN HOOD WAS AN OUTLAW.
HEY AND THANKS FOR THOSE ZIP-LOC BAGS THAT ONE TIME.
"LATER."

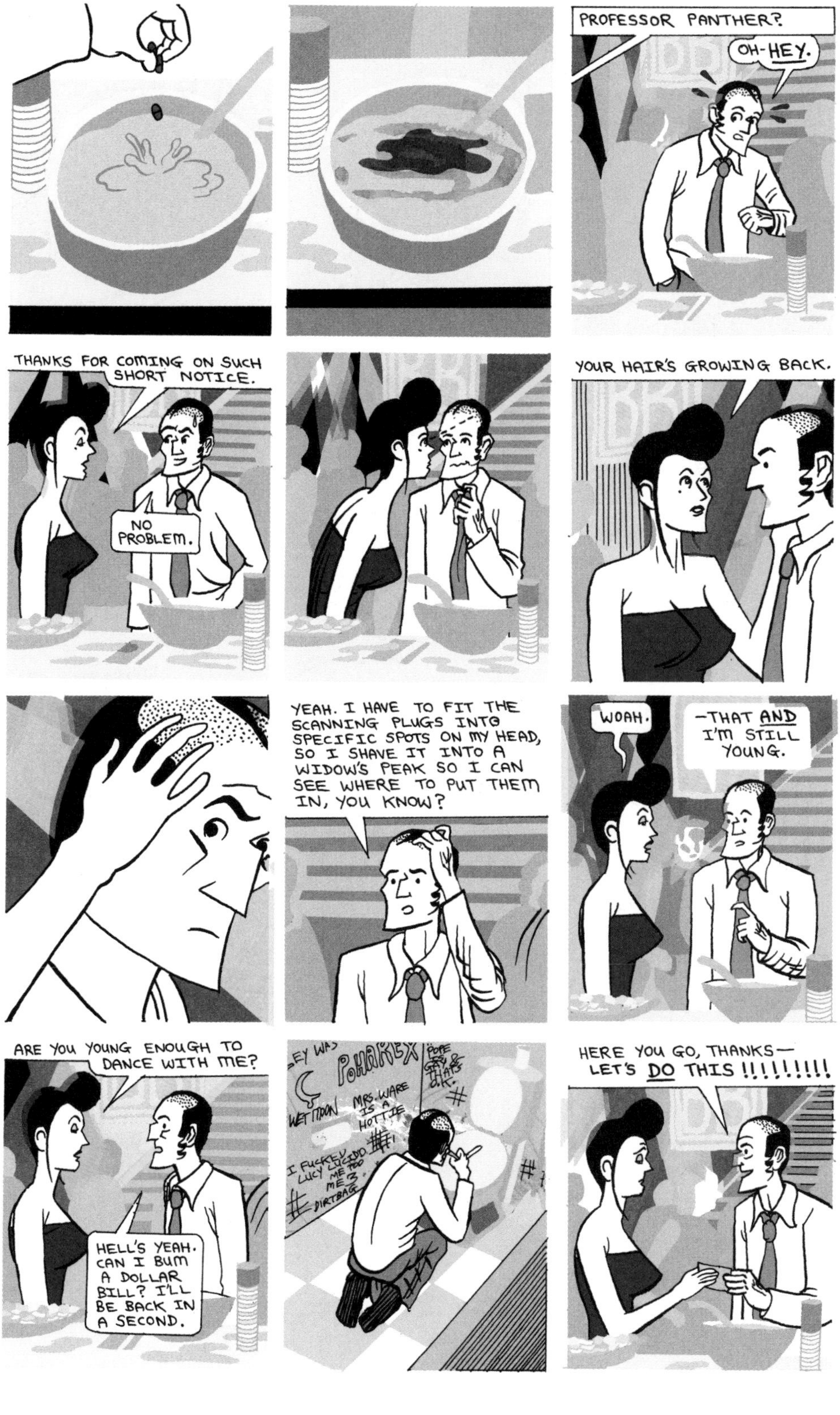
PROFESSOR PANTHER?
OH-HEY.
THANKS FOR COMING ON SUCH SHORT NOTICE.
NO PROBLEM.
YOUR HAIR'S GROWING BACK.
YEAH. I HAVE TO FIT THE SCANNING PLUGS INTO SPECIFIC SPOTS ON MY HEAD, SO I SHAVE IT INTO A WIDOW'S PEAK SO I CAN SEE WHERE TO PUT THEM IN, YOU KNOW?
WOAH.
—THAT AND I'M STILL YOUNG.
ARE YOU YOUNG ENOUGH TO DANCE WITH ME?
HELL'S YEAH. CAN I BUM A DOLLAR BILL? I'LL BE BACK IN A SECOND.
WET MOON
MRS. WARE IS A HOTTIE
DIRTBAG
HERE YOU GO, THANKS—
LET'S DO THIS !!!!!!!!!

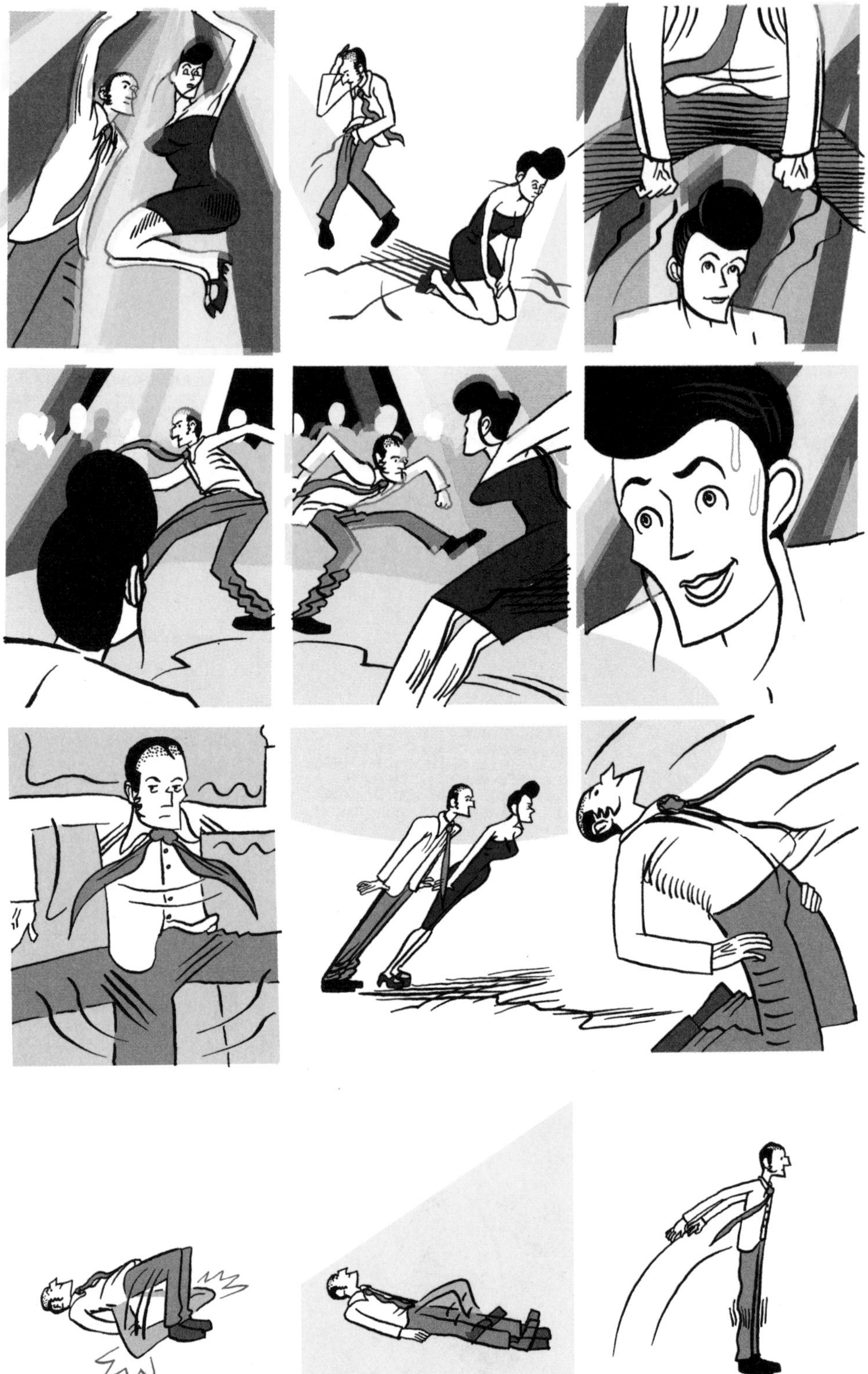

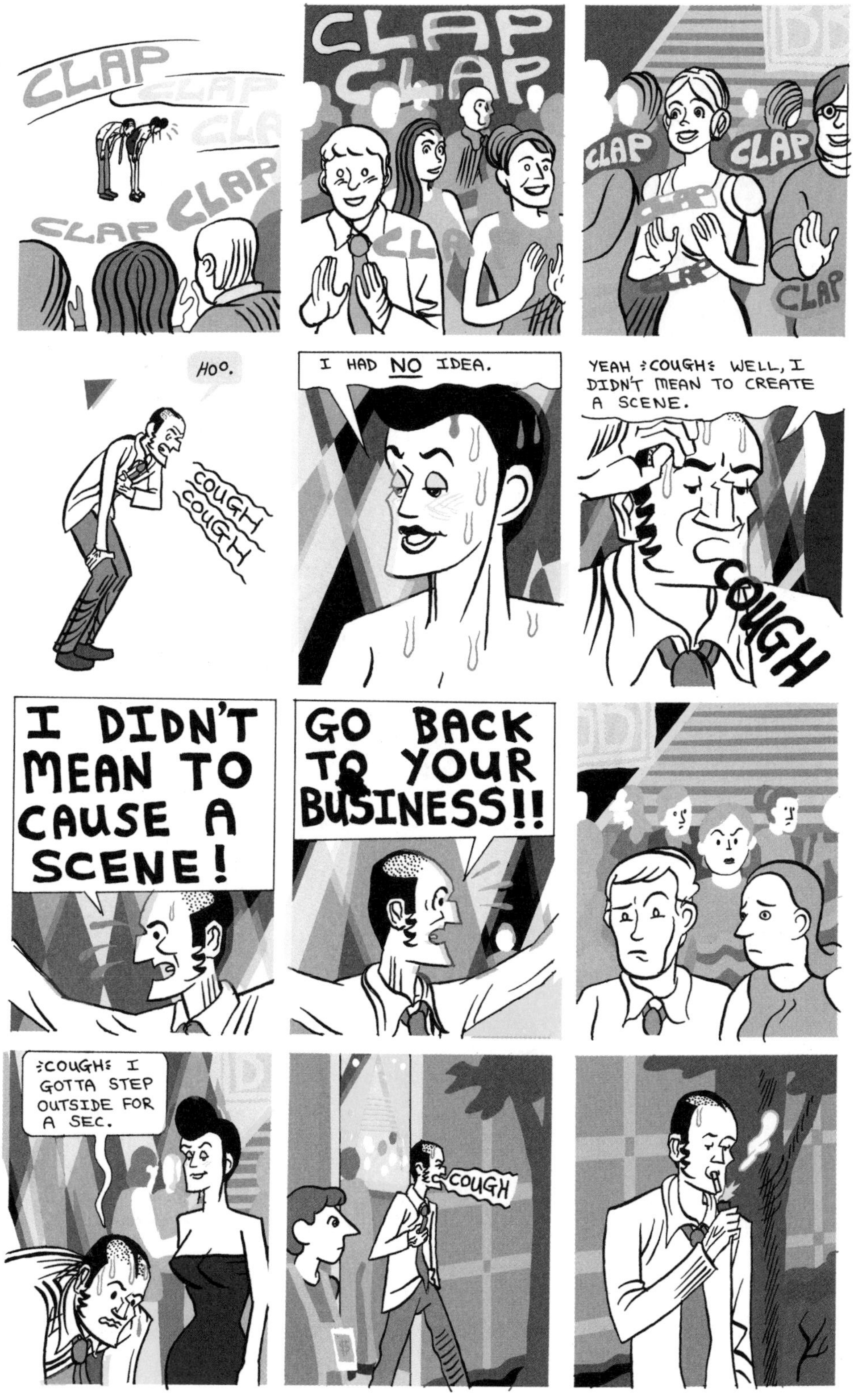
CLAP CLAP CLAP CLAP CLAP CLAP
CLAP CLAP
CLAP CLAP CLAP CLAP
HOO.
COUGH COUGH
I HAD NO IDEA.
YEAH :COUGH: WELL, I DIDN'T MEAN TO CREATE A SCENE.
COUGH
I DIDN'T MEAN TO CAUSE A SCENE!
GO BACK TO YOUR BUSINESS!!
:COUGH: I GOTTA STEP OUTSIDE FOR A SEC.
COUGH

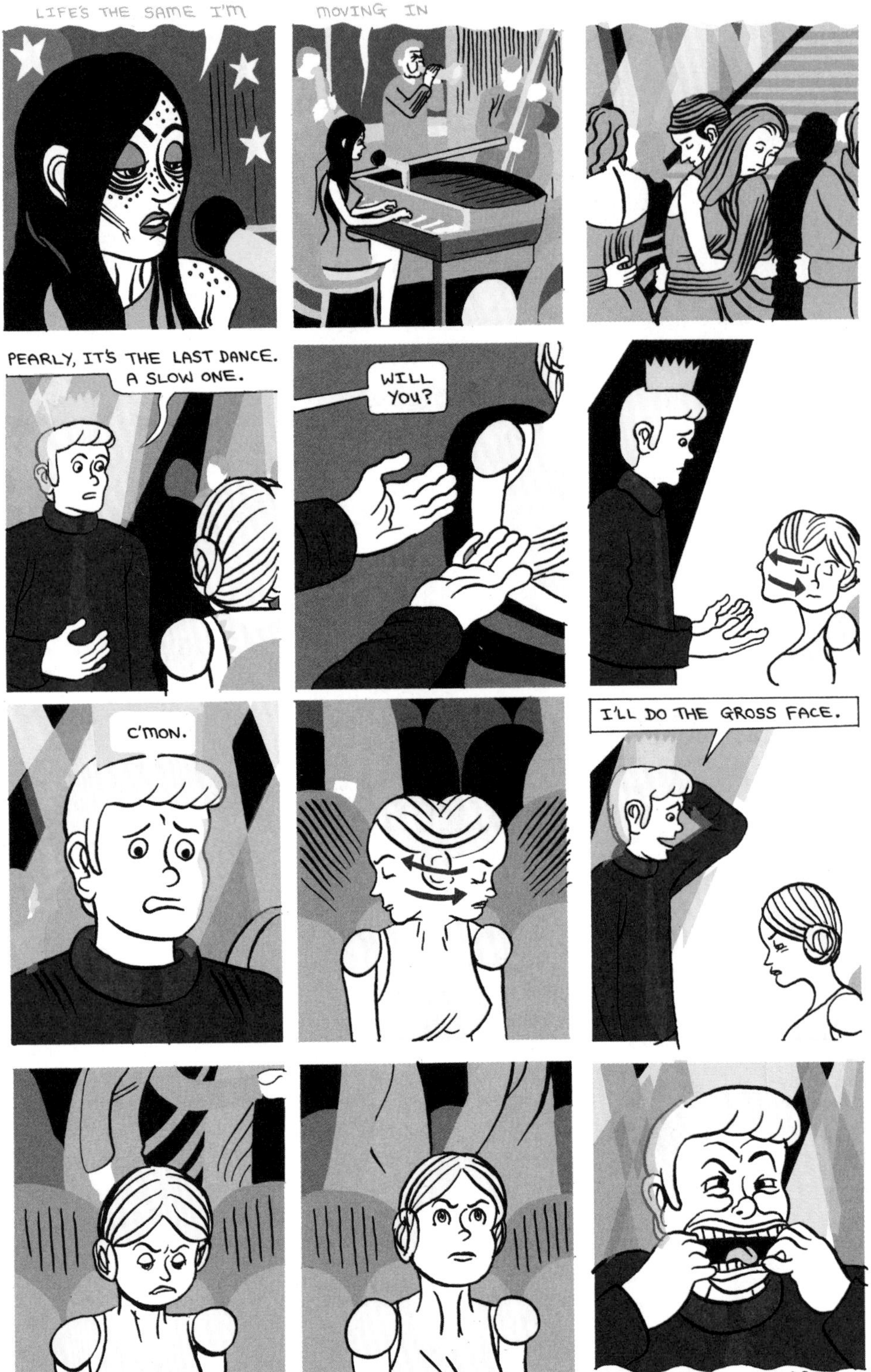
LIFE'S THE SAME I'M
MOVING IN
PEARLY, IT'S THE LAST DANCE. A SLOW ONE.
WILL YOU?
C'MON.
I'LL DO THE GROSS FACE.
HA HA HA HA

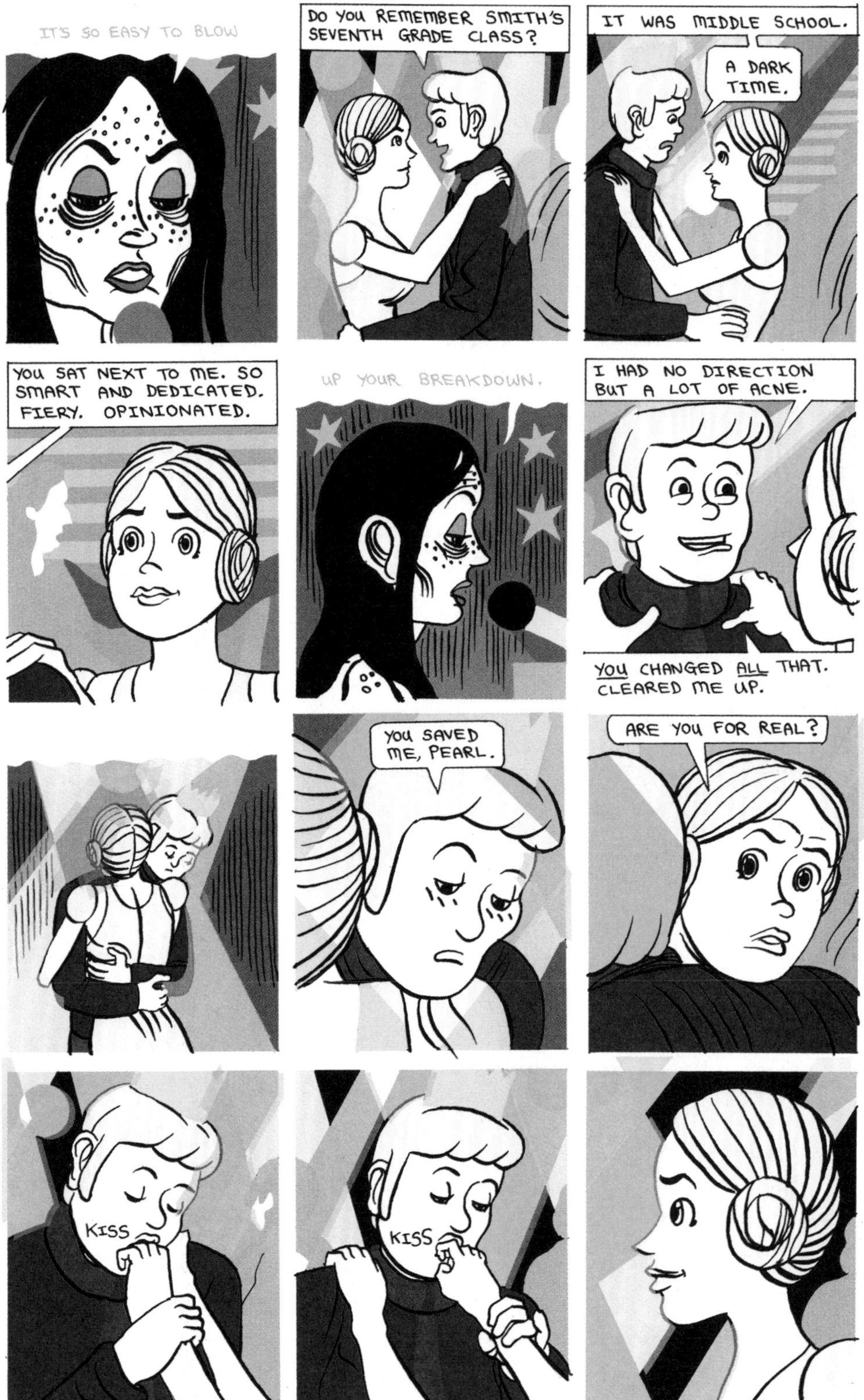
IT'S SO EASY TO BLOW
DO YOU REMEMBER SMITH'S SEVENTH GRADE CLASS?
IT WAS MIDDLE SCHOOL.
A DARK TIME.
YOU SAT NEXT TO ME. SO SMART AND DEDICATED. FIERY. OPINIONATED.
UP YOUR BREAKDOWN.
I HAD NO DIRECTION BUT A LOT OF ACNE.
YOU CHANGED ALL THAT. CLEARED ME UP.
YOU SAVED ME, PEARL.
ARE YOU FOR REAL?
KISS
KISS

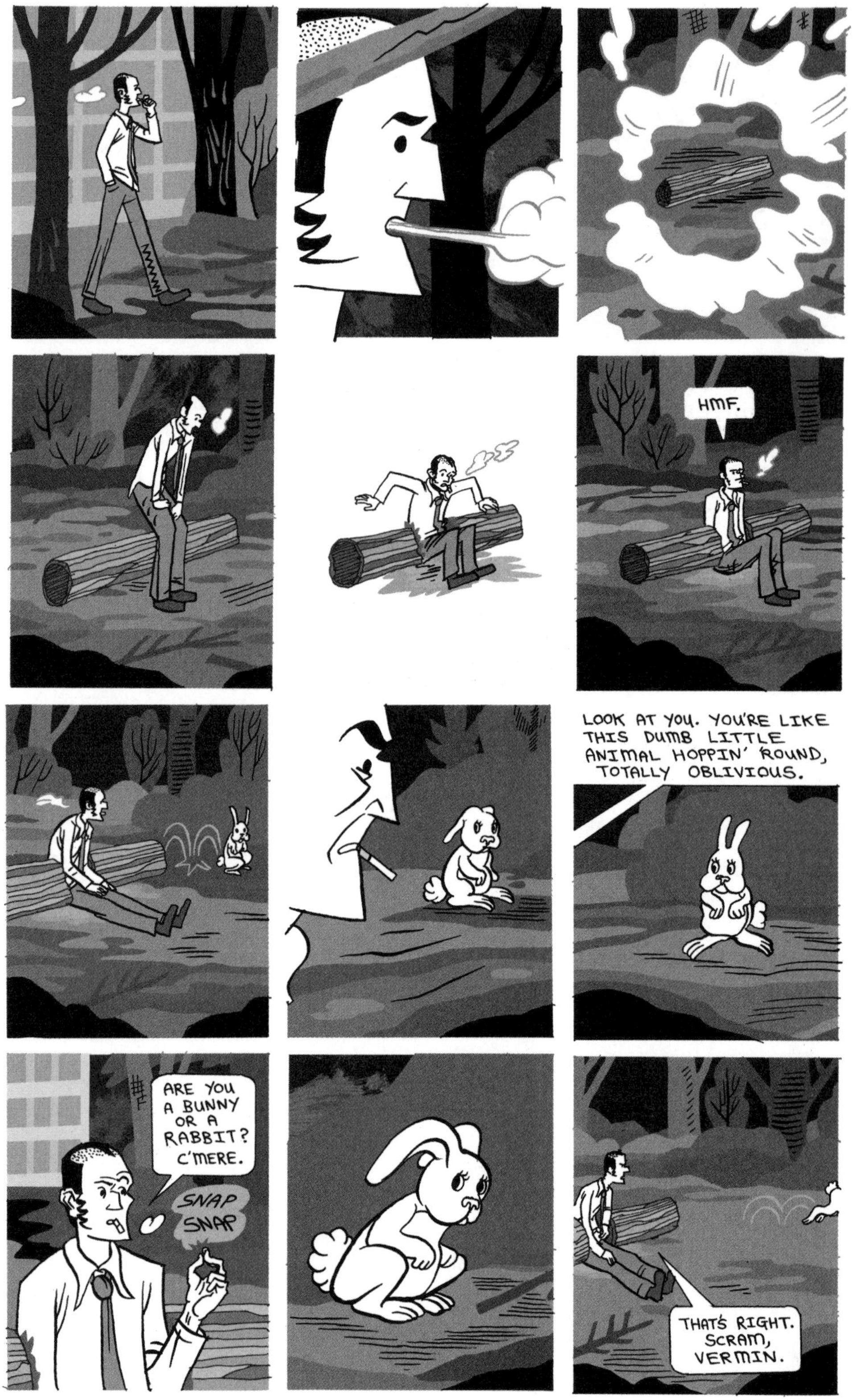
HMF.
LOOK AT YOU. YOU'RE LIKE THIS DUMB LITTLE ANIMAL HOPPIN' 'ROUND, TOTALLY OBLIVIOUS.
ARE YOU A BUNNY OR A RABBIT? C'MERE.
SNAP SNAP
THAT'S RIGHT. SCRAM, VERMIN.

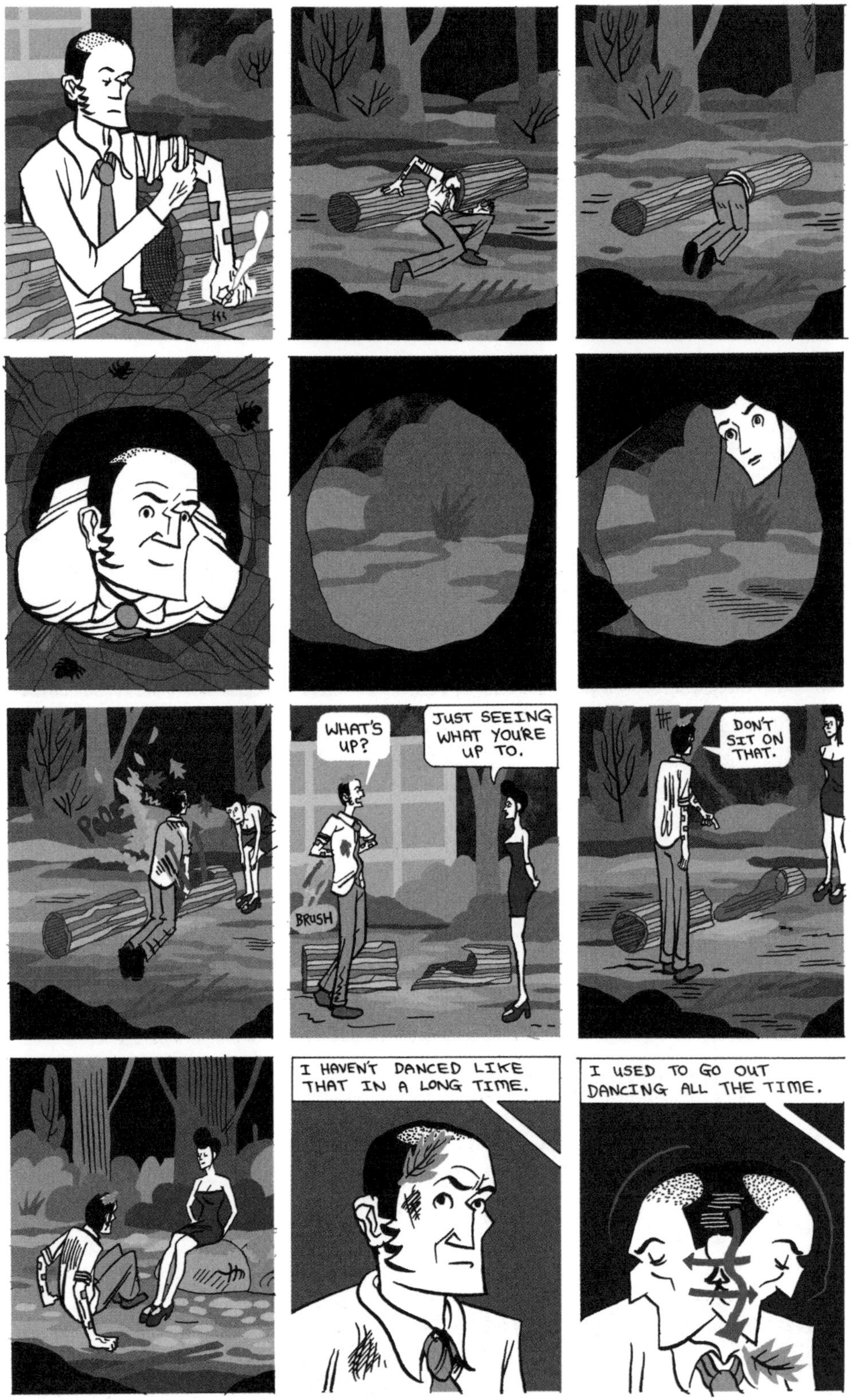
POOF
WHAT'S UP?
JUST SEEING WHAT YOU'RE UP TO.
BRUSH
DON'T SIT ON THAT.
I HAVEN'T DANCED LIKE THAT IN A LONG TIME.
I USED TO GO OUT DANCING ALL THE TIME.

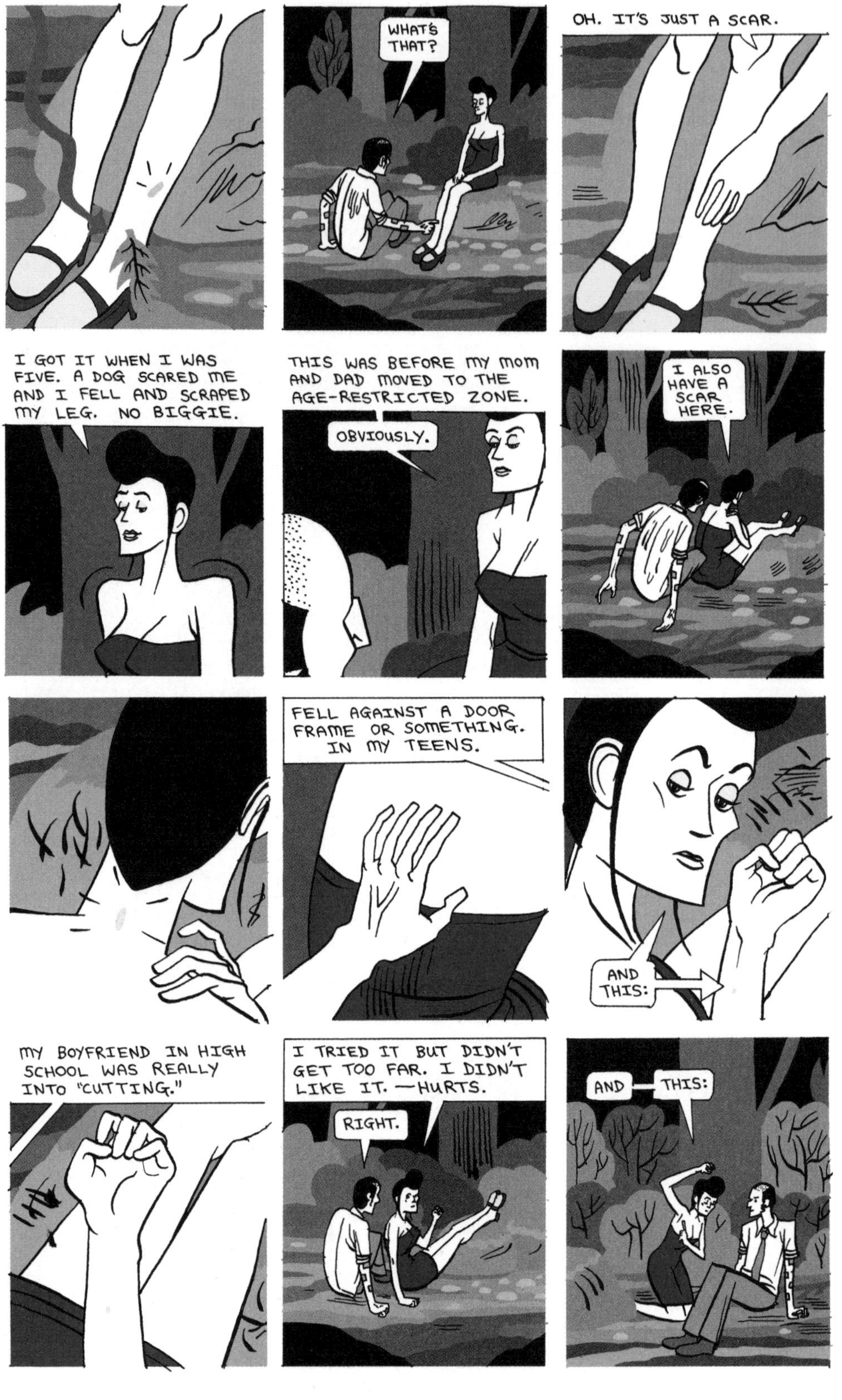
WHAT'S THAT?
OH. IT'S JUST A SCAR.
I GOT IT WHEN I WAS FIVE. A DOG SCARED ME AND I FELL AND SCRAPED MY LEG. NO BIGGIE.
THIS WAS BEFORE MY MOM AND DAD MOVED TO THE AGE-RESTRICTED ZONE.
OBVIOUSLY.
I ALSO HAVE A SCAR HERE.
FELL AGAINST A DOOR FRAME OR SOMETHING. IN MY TEENS.
AND THIS:
MY BOYFRIEND IN HIGH SCHOOL WAS REALLY INTO "CUTTING."
I TRIED IT BUT DIDN'T GET TOO FAR. I DIDN'T LIKE IT. —HURTS.
RIGHT.
AND
THIS:

IN THE ARM PIT

FROM MY DAYS IN THE OUTER RIM. A BOUNCER PUSHED ME AGAINST A METAL FENCE.

Hmm.

TICKLE
TICKLE

HAR HAR HAR!

OH MY GOD. YOU LAUGH LIKE A PIRATE.

YEAH, I KNOW. I TRY NOT TO LAUGH.

YOU HAVE A SCAR, TOO.

I FELL OFF MY TRICYCLE.

I HAVE A SCAR HERE.

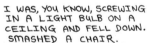

I WAS, YOU KNOW, SCREWING IN A LIGHT BULB ON A CEILING AND FELL DOWN. SMASHED A CHAIR.

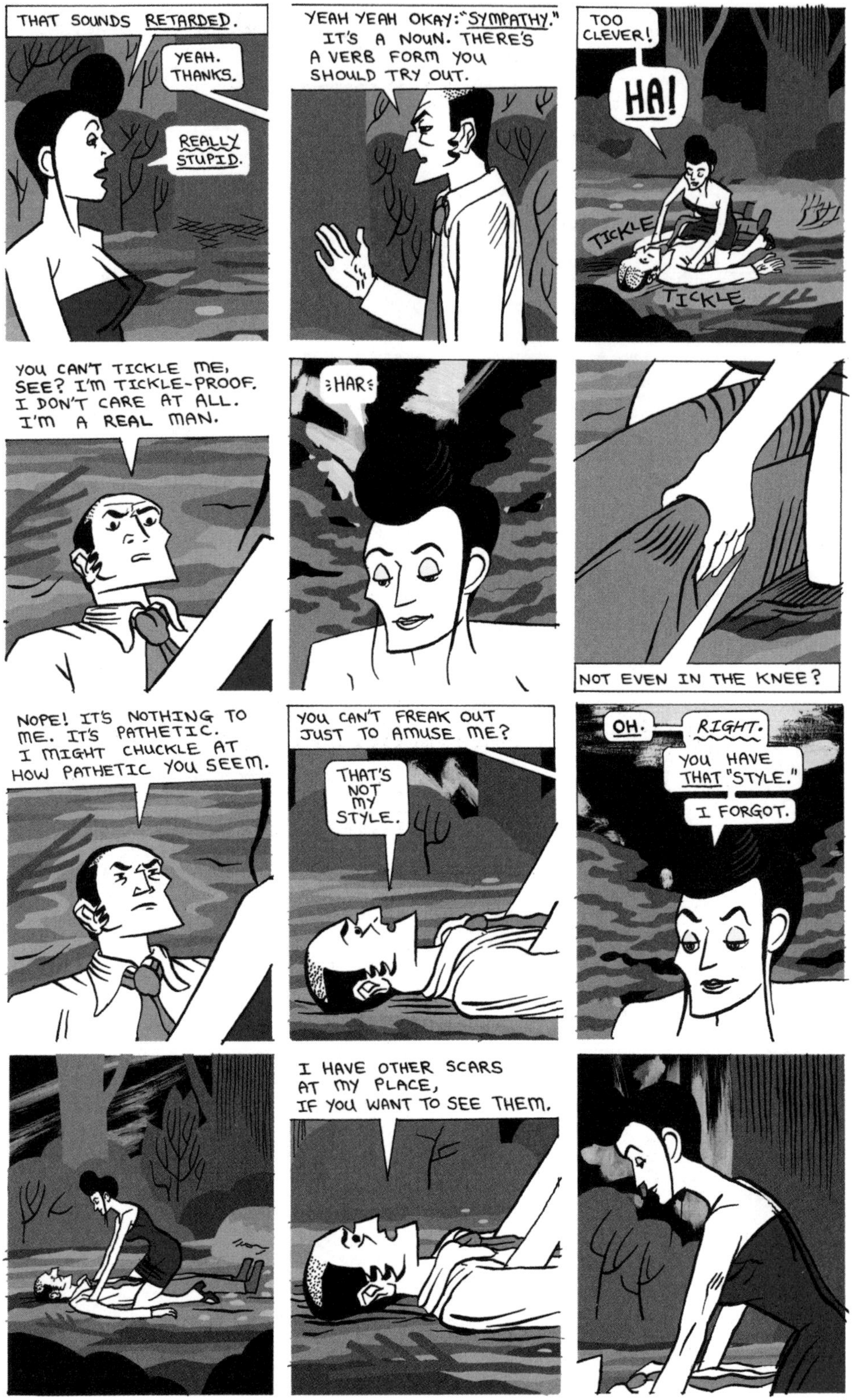
THAT SOUNDS RETARDED.
YEAH. THANKS.
REALLY STUPID.
YEAH YEAH OKAY: "SYMPATHY." IT'S A NOUN. THERE'S A VERB FORM YOU SHOULD TRY OUT.
TOO CLEVER!
HA!
TICKLE
TICKLE
YOU CAN'T TICKLE ME, SEE? I'M TICKLE-PROOF. I DON'T CARE AT ALL. I'M A REAL MAN.
HAR
NOT EVEN IN THE KNEE?
NOPE! IT'S NOTHING TO ME. IT'S PATHETIC. I MIGHT CHUCKLE AT HOW PATHETIC YOU SEEM.
YOU CAN'T FREAK OUT JUST TO AMUSE ME?
THAT'S NOT MY STYLE.
OH.
RIGHT.
YOU HAVE THAT "STYLE."
I FORGOT.
I HAVE OTHER SCARS AT MY PLACE, IF YOU WANT TO SEE THEM.

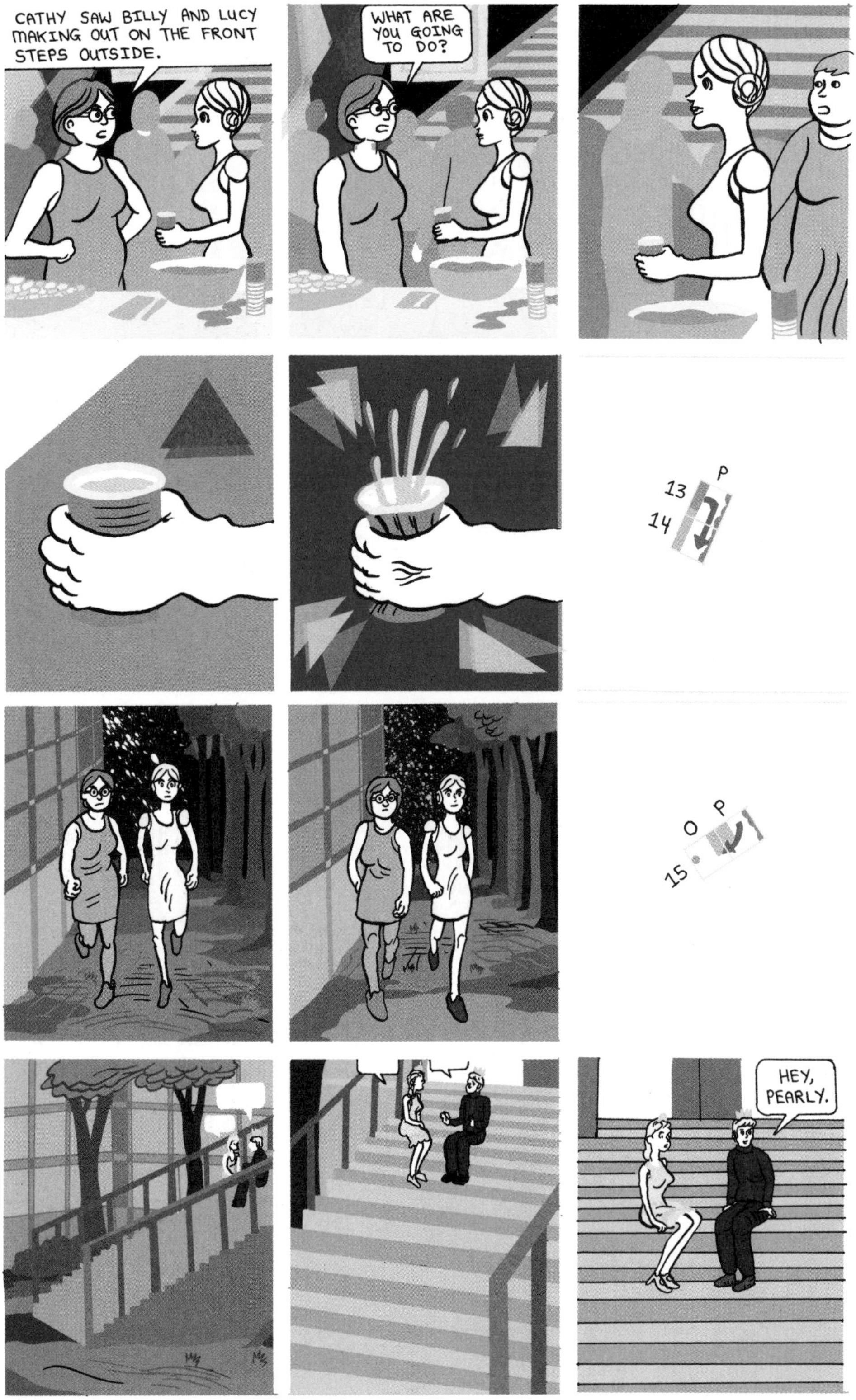
CATHY SAW BILLY AND LUCY MAKING OUT ON THE FRONT STEPS OUTSIDE.
WHAT ARE YOU GOING TO DO?
13
P
14
O
P
15
HEY, PEARLY.

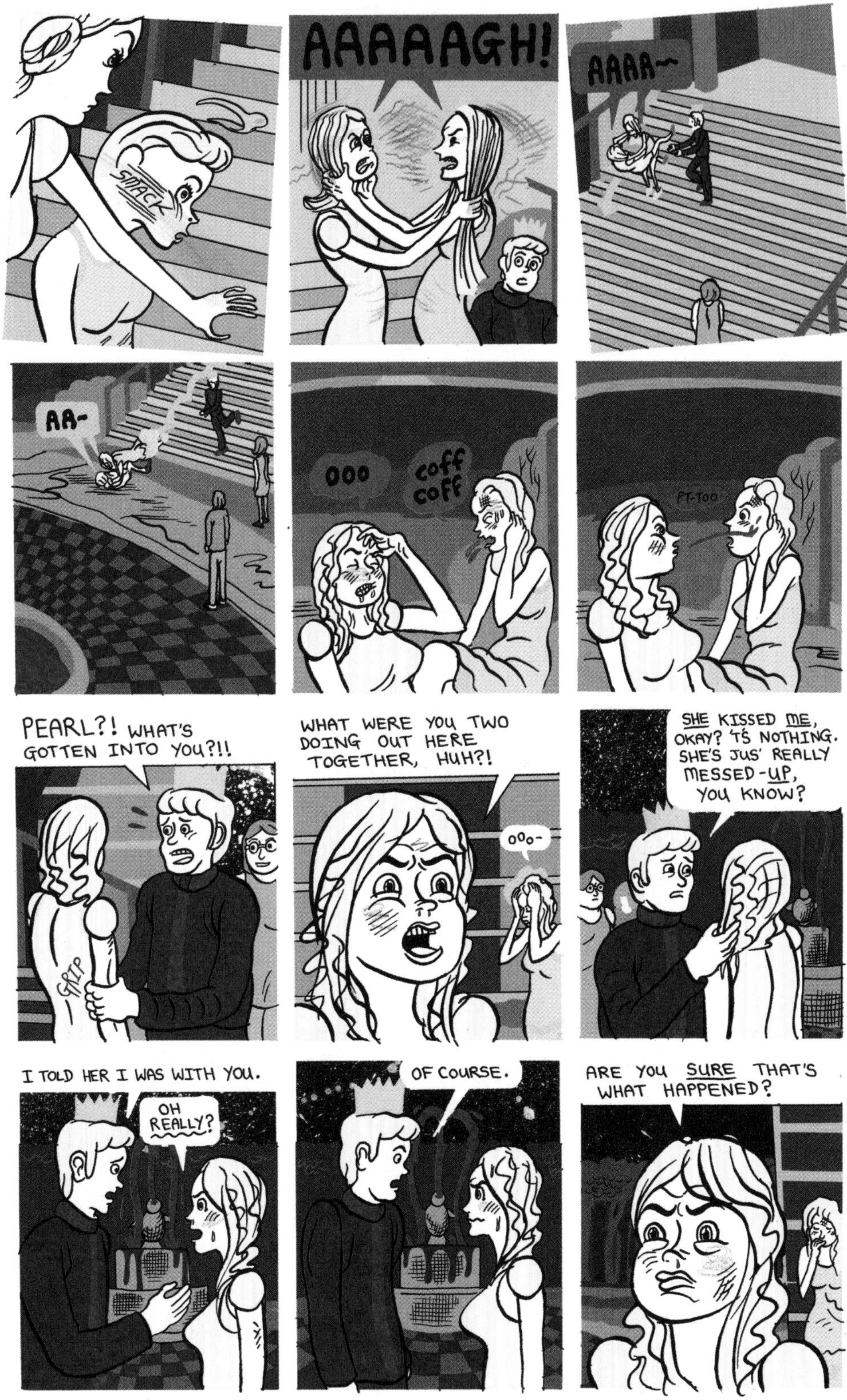
SMACK
AAAAAGH!
AAAA~
AA-
OOO
coff coff
PT-TOO
PEARL?! WHAT'S GOTTEN INTO YOU?!!
GRIP
WHAT WERE YOU TWO DOING OUT HERE TOGETHER, HUH?!
OOo-
SHE KISSED ME, OKAY? 'T'S NOTHING. SHE'S JUS' REALLY MESSED-UP, YOU KNOW?
I TOLD HER I WAS WITH YOU.
OH REALLY?
OF COURSE.
ARE YOU SURE THAT'S WHAT HAPPENED?

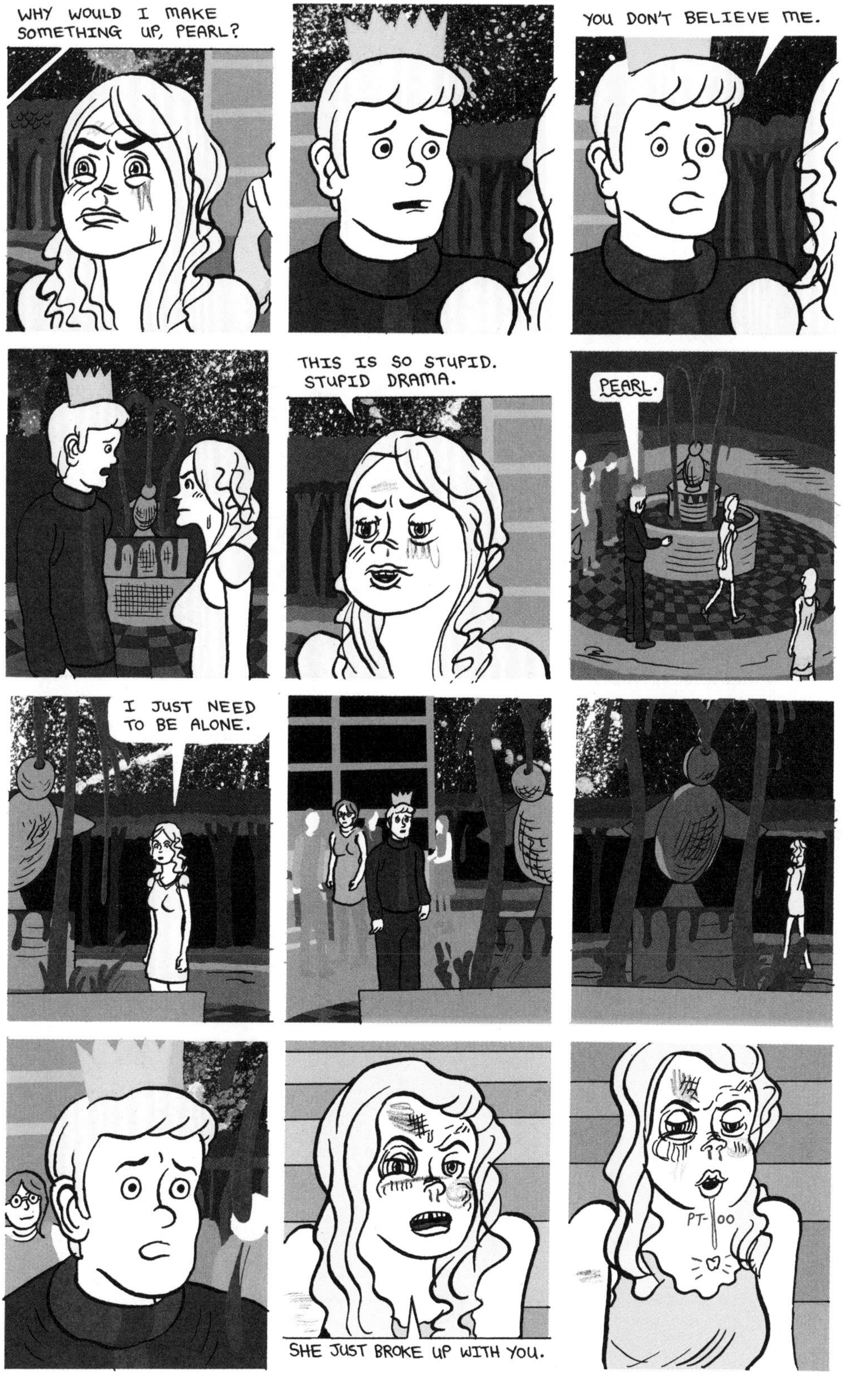
WHY WOULD I MAKE SOMETHING UP, PEARL?
YOU DON'T BELIEVE ME.
THIS IS SO STUPID. STUPID DRAMA.
PEARL.
I JUST NEED TO BE ALONE.
SHE JUST BROKE UP WITH YOU.
PT-OO

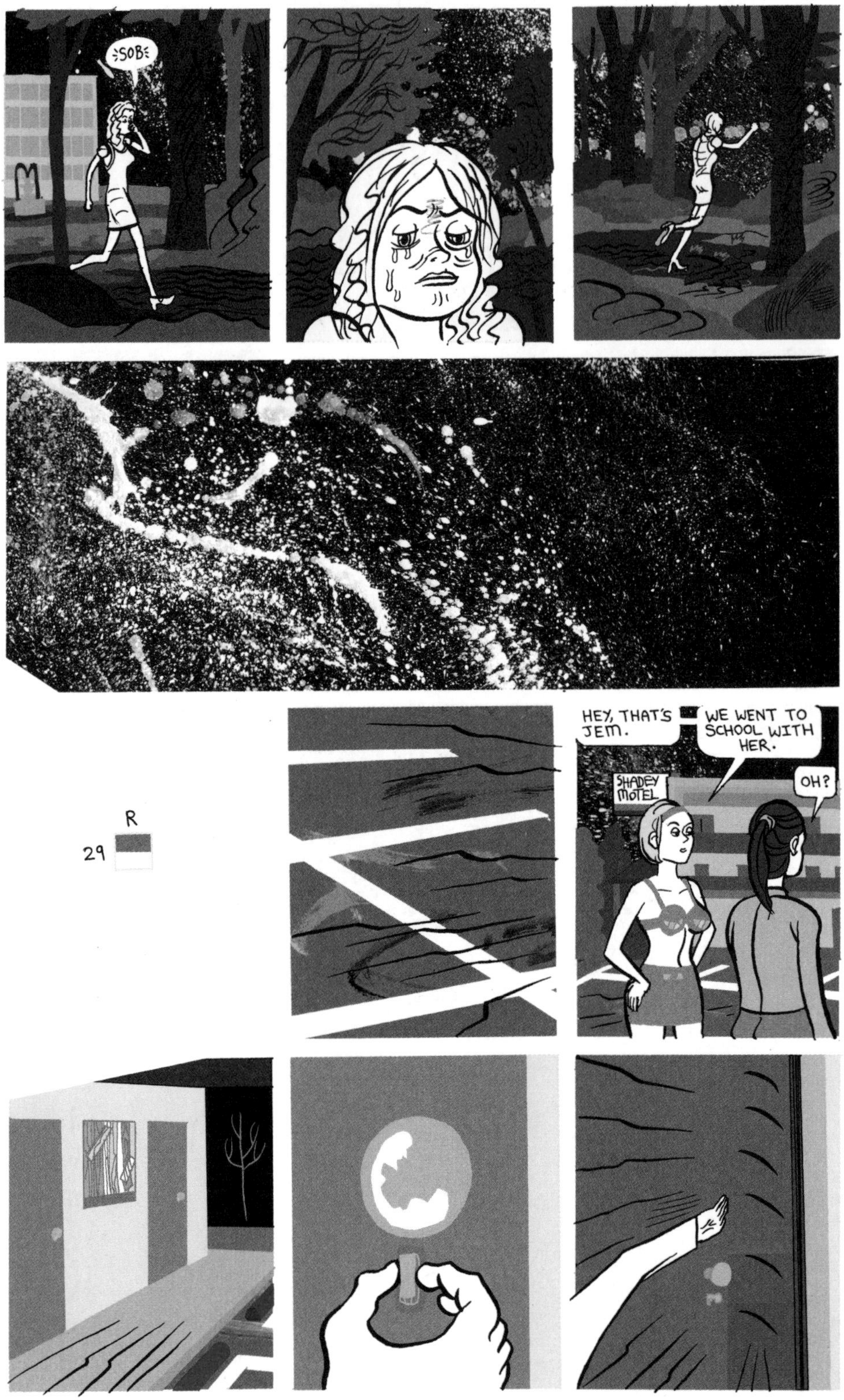
SOB
R
29
HEY, THAT'S JEM.
WE WENT TO SCHOOL WITH HER.
SHADEY MOTEL
OH?

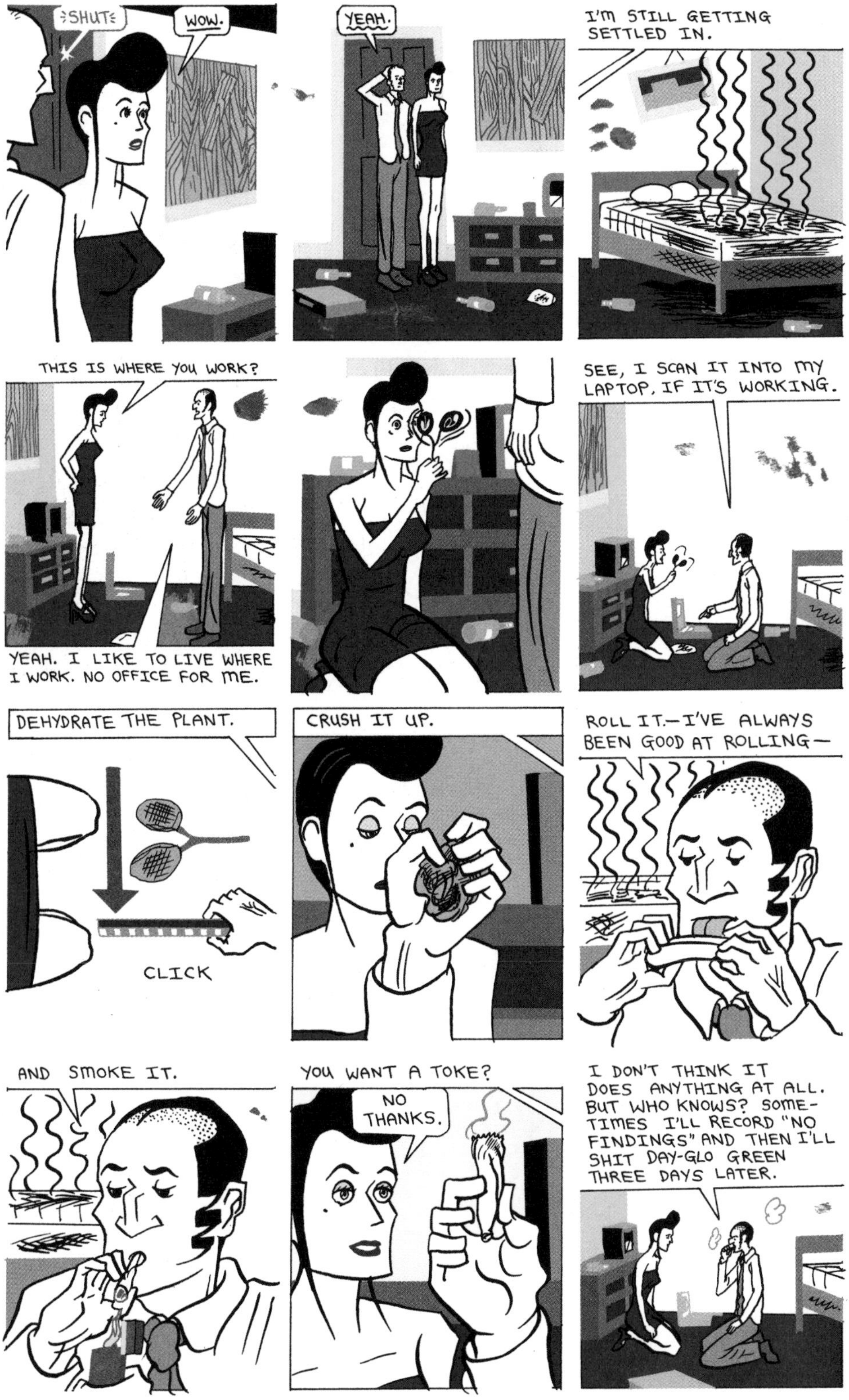
SHUT
WOW.
YEAH.
I'M STILL GETTING SETTLED IN.
THIS IS WHERE YOU WORK?
YEAH. I LIKE TO LIVE WHERE I WORK. NO OFFICE FOR ME.
SEE, I SCAN IT INTO MY LAPTOP, IF IT'S WORKING.
DEHYDRATE THE PLANT.
CLICK
CRUSH IT UP.
ROLL IT.—I'VE ALWAYS BEEN GOOD AT ROLLING—
AND SMOKE IT.
YOU WANT A TOKE?
NO THANKS.
I DON'T THINK IT DOES ANYTHING AT ALL. BUT WHO KNOWS? SOMETIMES I'LL RECORD "NO FINDINGS" AND THEN I'LL SHIT DAY-GLO GREEN THREE DAYS LATER.

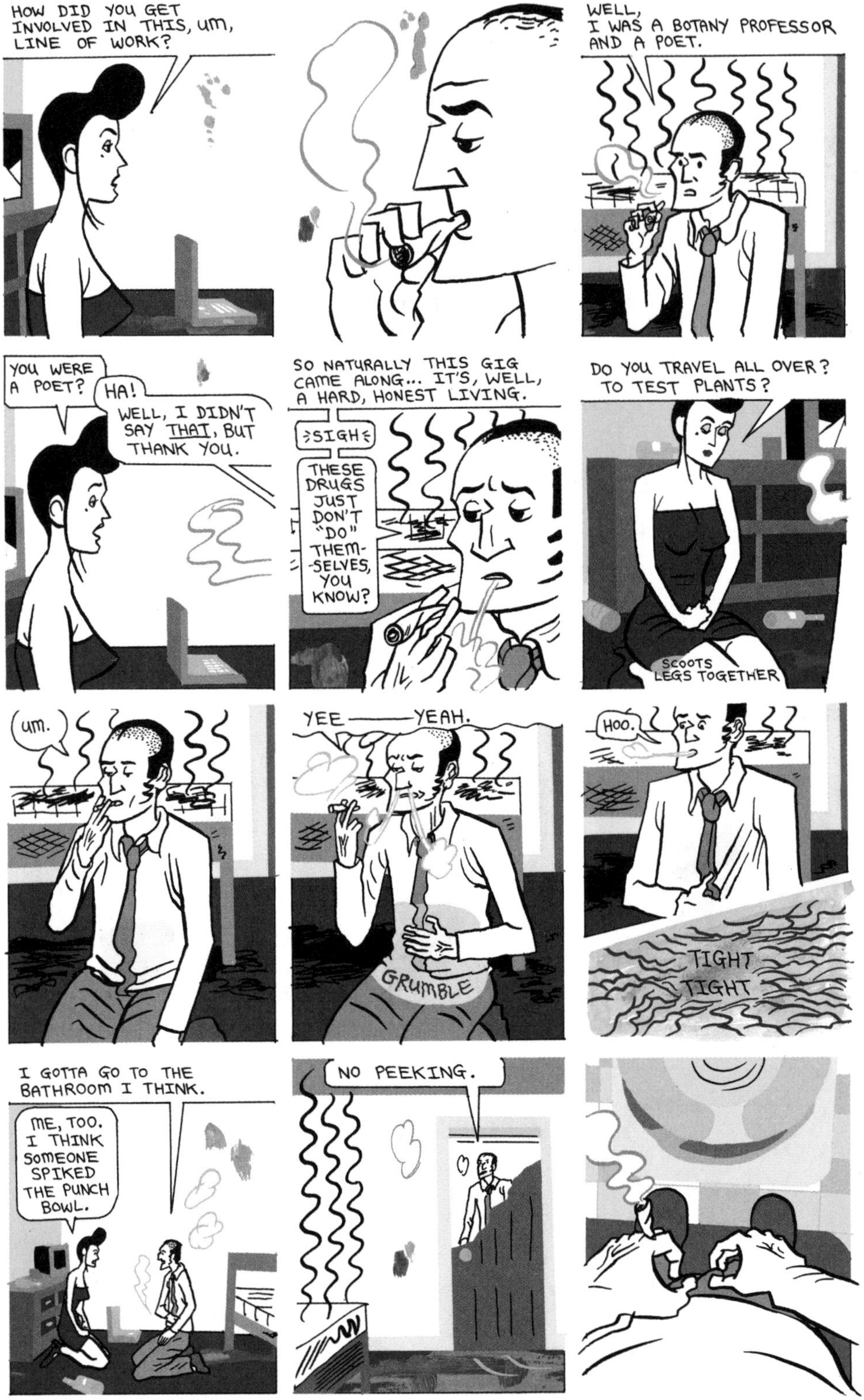
HOW DID YOU GET INVOLVED IN THIS, UM, LINE OF WORK?
WELL, I WAS A BOTANY PROFESSOR AND A POET.
YOU WERE A POET?
HA!
WELL, I DIDN'T SAY THAT, BUT THANK YOU.
SO NATURALLY THIS GIG CAME ALONG... IT'S, WELL, A HARD, HONEST LIVING.
SIGH
THESE DRUGS JUST DON'T "DO" THEM-SELVES, YOU KNOW?
DO YOU TRAVEL ALL OVER? TO TEST PLANTS?
SCOOTS LEGS TOGETHER
UM.
YEE——YEAH.
GRUMBLE
HOO.
TIGHT
TIGHT
I GOTTA GO TO THE BATHROOM I THINK.
ME, TOO. I THINK SOMEONE SPIKED THE PUNCH BOWL.
NO PEEKING.

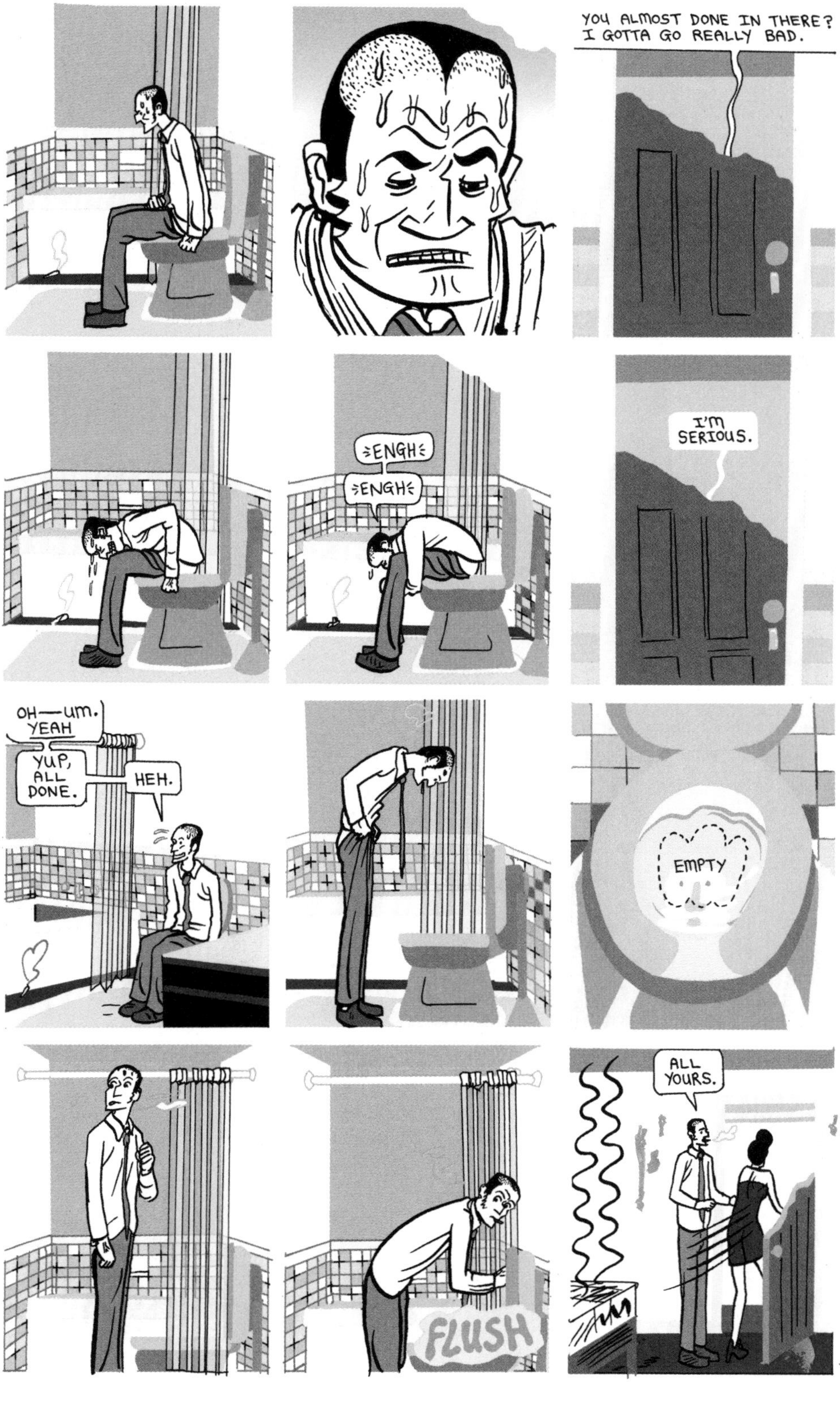
YOU ALMOST DONE IN THERE? I GOTTA GO REALLY BAD.
ENGH
ENGH
I'M SERIOUS.
OH—UM. YEAH
YUP, ALL DONE.
HEH.
EMPTY
FLUSH
ALL YOURS.

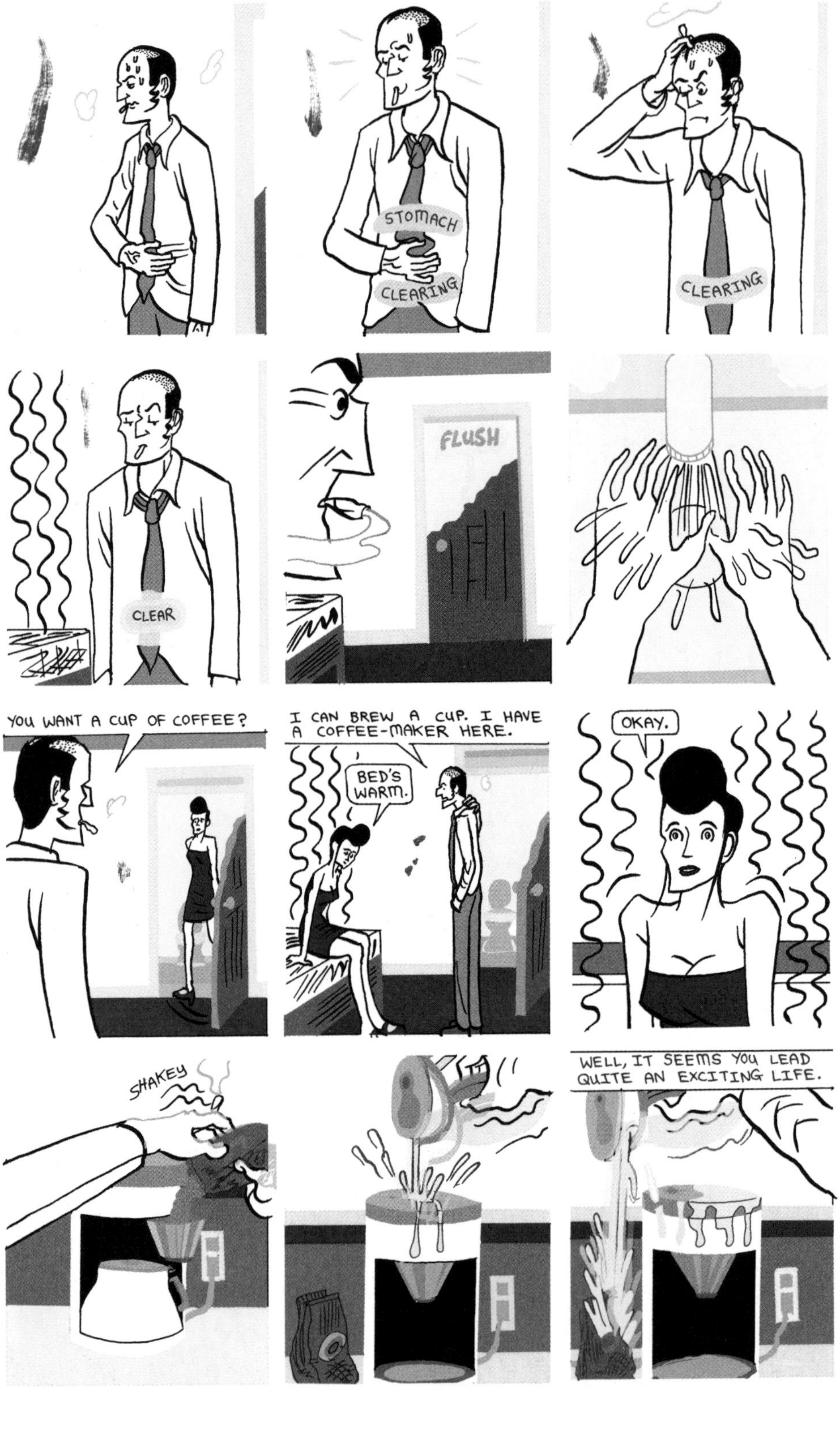
STOMACH
CLEARING
CLEARING
CLEAR
FLUSH
YOU WANT A CUP OF COFFEE?
I CAN BREW A CUP. I HAVE A COFFEE-MAKER HERE.
BED'S WARM.
OKAY.
SHAKEY
WELL, IT SEEMS YOU LEAD QUITE AN EXCITING LIFE.

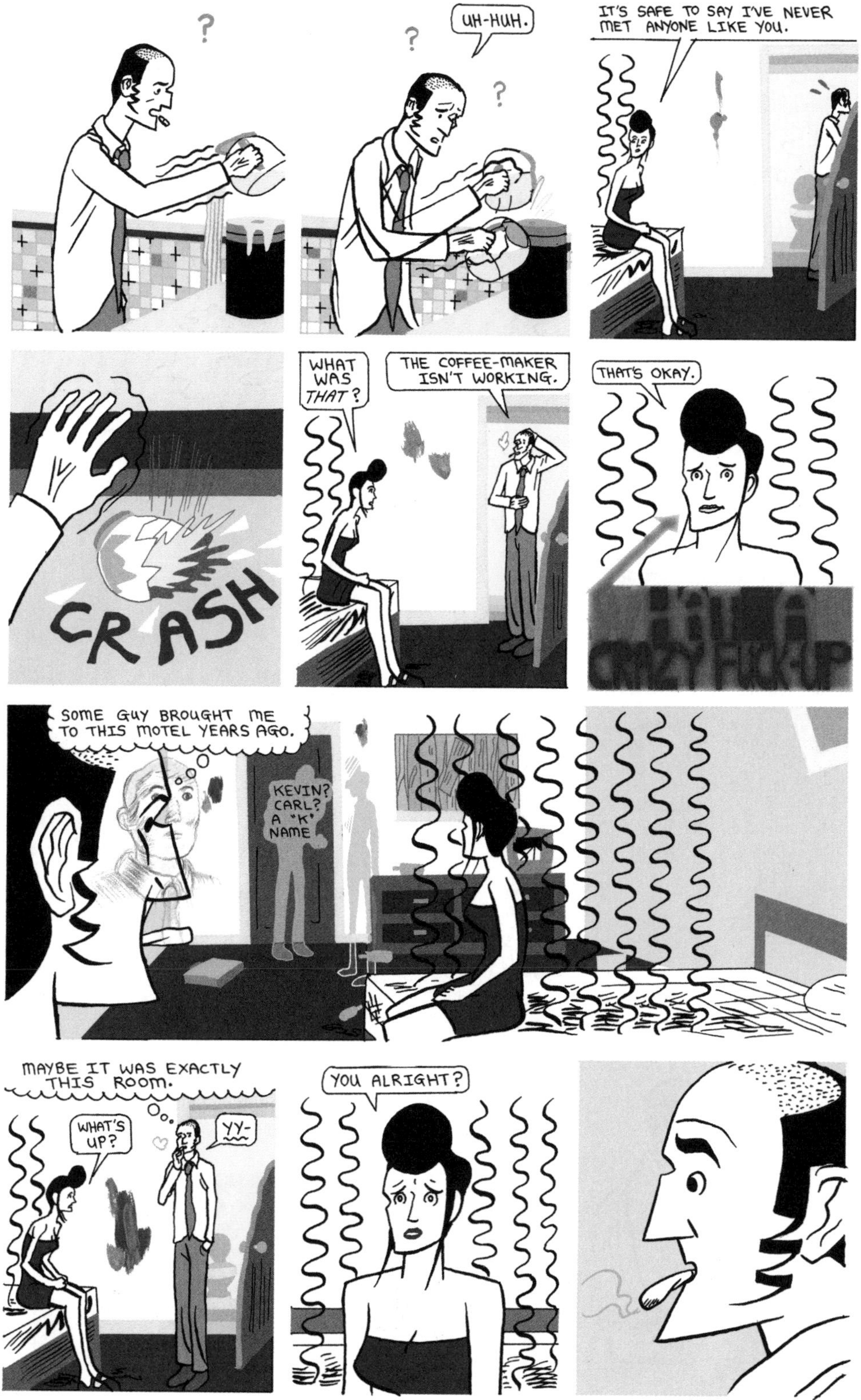
?
?
UH-HUH.
?
IT'S SAFE TO SAY I'VE NEVER MET ANYONE LIKE YOU.
CRASH
WHAT WAS *THAT*?
THE COFFEE-MAKER ISN'T WORKING.
THAT'S OKAY.
CRAZY FUCK-UP
SOME GUY BROUGHT ME TO THIS MOTEL YEARS AGO.
KEVIN? CARL? A "K" NAME
MAYBE IT WAS EXACTLY THIS ROOM.
WHAT'S UP?
YY-
YOU ALRIGHT?

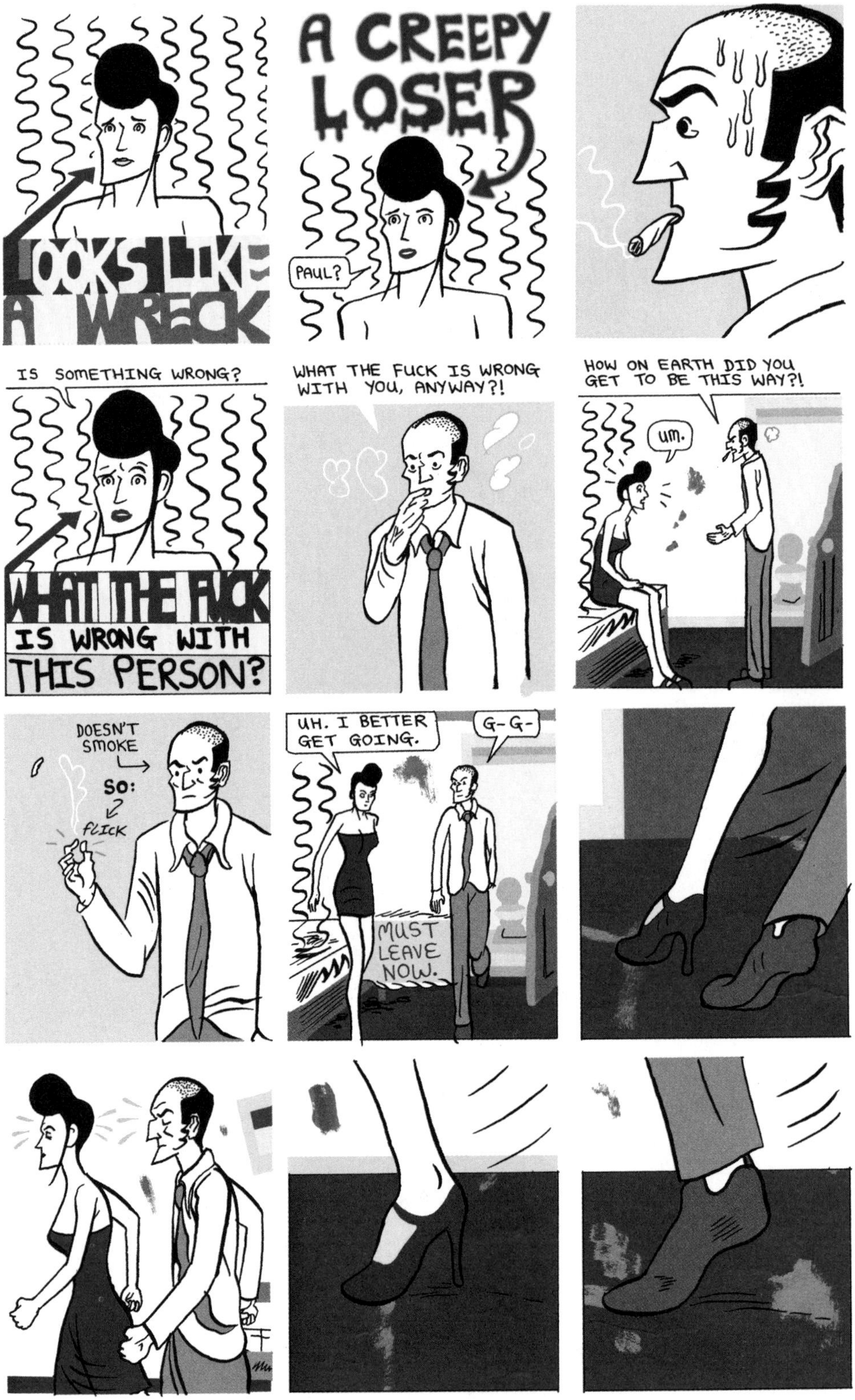

LOOKS LIKE A WRECK
A CREEPY LOSER
PAUL?
IS SOMETHING WRONG?
WHAT THE FUCK IS WRONG WITH THIS PERSON?
WHAT THE FUCK IS WRONG WITH YOU, ANYWAY?!
HOW ON EARTH DID YOU GET TO BE THIS WAY?!
UM.
DOESN'T SMOKE
SO:
FLICK
UH. I BETTER GET GOING.
G-G-
MUST LEAVE NOW.

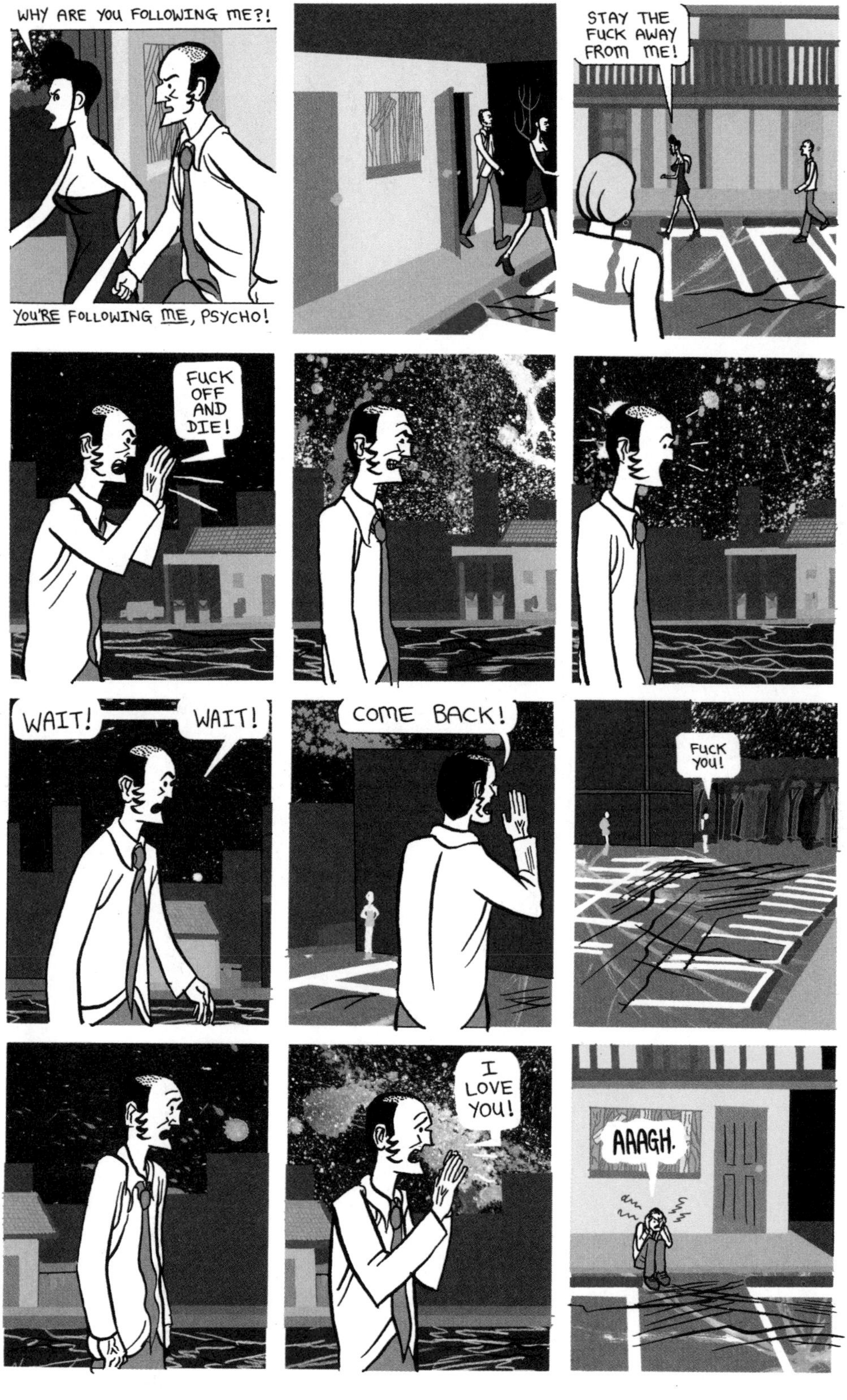
WHY ARE YOU FOLLOWING ME?!
YOU'RE FOLLOWING ME, PSYCHO!
STAY THE FUCK AWAY FROM ME!
FUCK OFF AND DIE!
WAIT!
WAIT!
COME BACK!
FUCK YOU!
I LOVE YOU!
AAAGH.

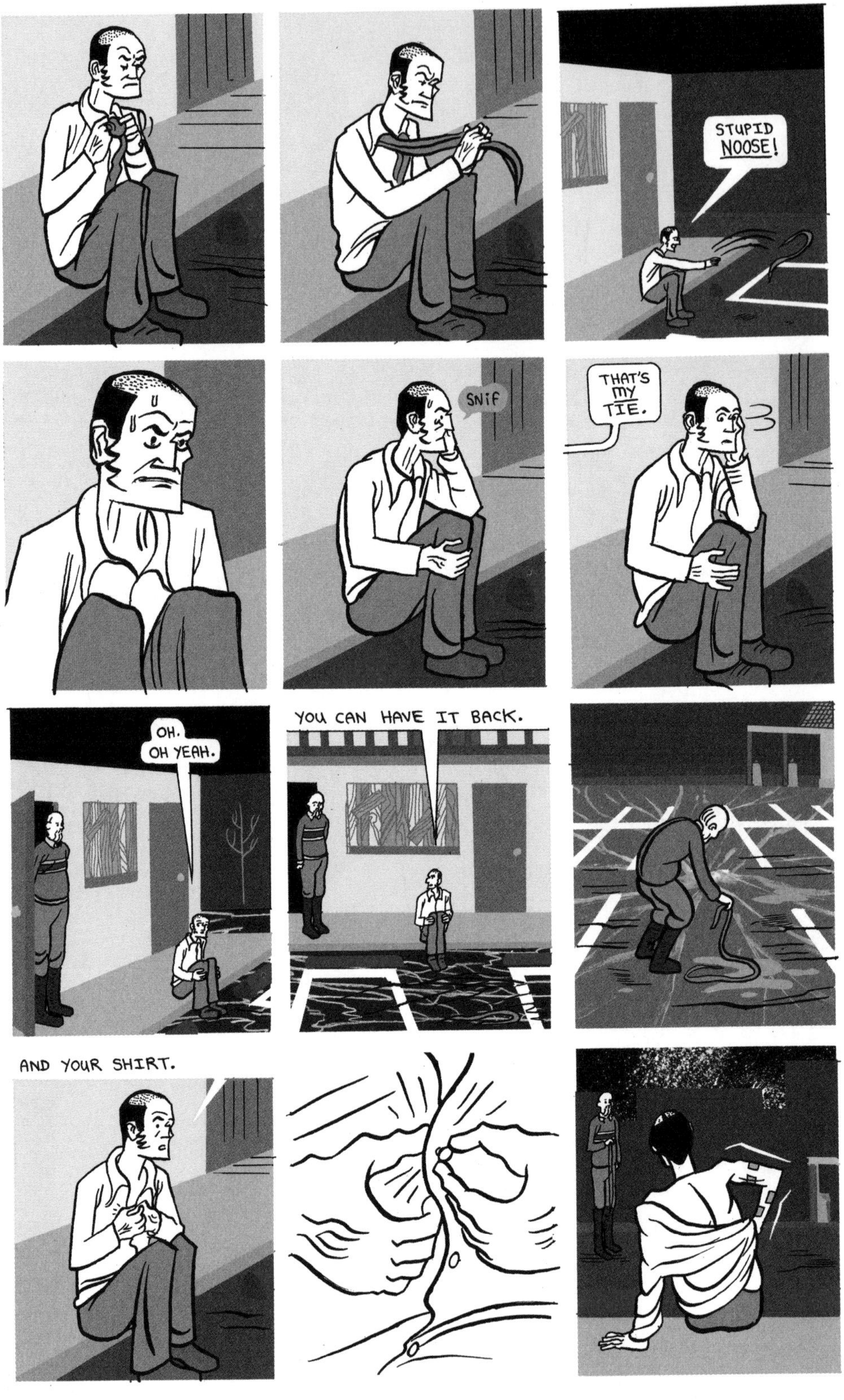

STUPID NOOSE!
SNIF
THAT'S MY TIE.
OH. OH YEAH.
YOU CAN HAVE IT BACK.
AND YOUR SHIRT.

WOAH. IS THAT SOME KIND OF MEDICAL CONDITION YA GOT THERE?

WHAT? THE SHNOZ?

NO.

THOSE

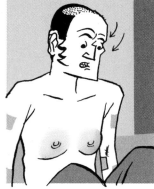

HOLEEE —— SHIT!

END OF CHAPTER THREE.

Pet Cat

joey alison sayers

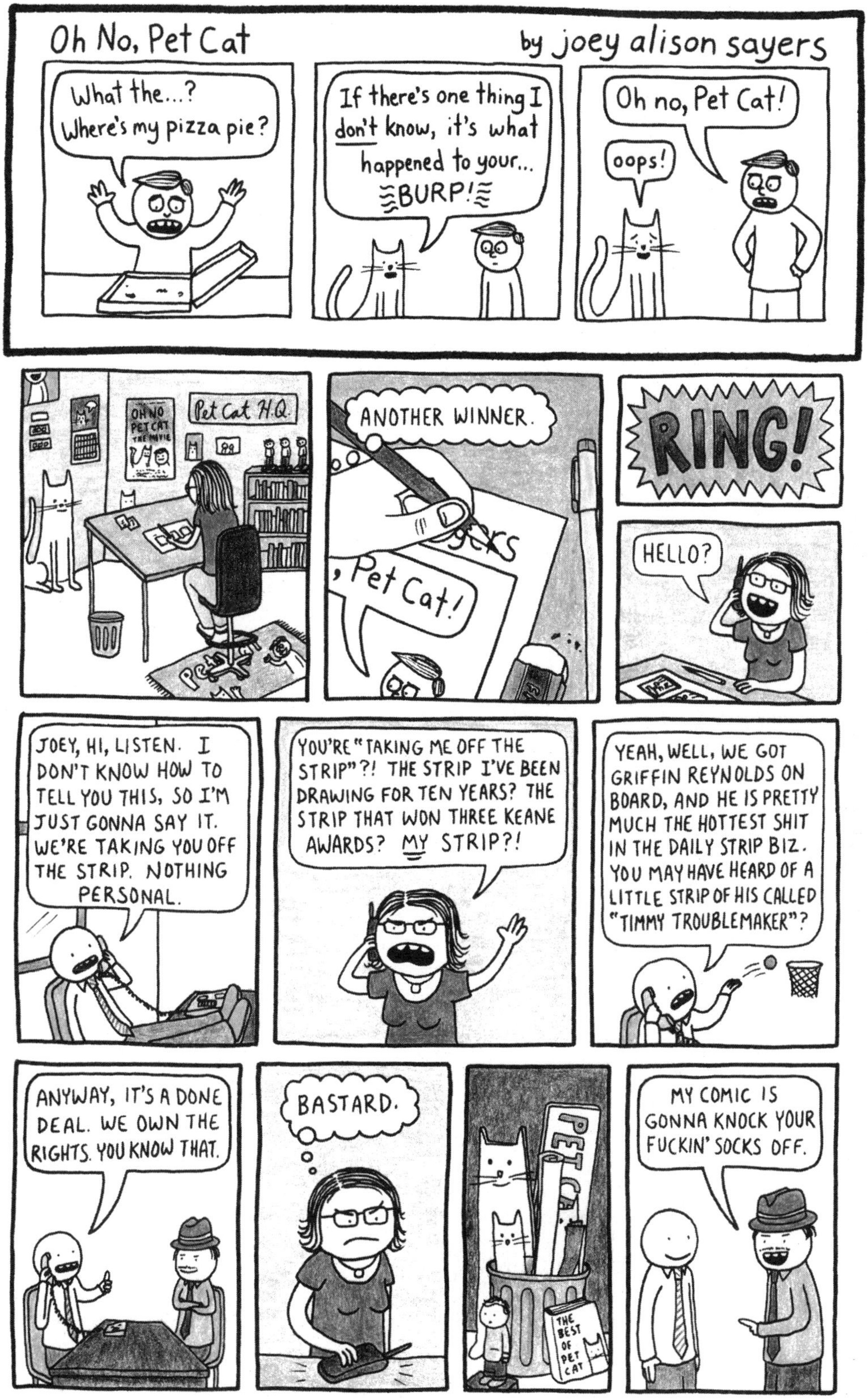

Oh No, Pet Cat
by joey alison sayers
What the...? Where's my pizza pie?
If there's one thing I don't know, it's what happened to your... BURP!
Oh no, Pet Cat!
oops!
OH NO PET CAT THE MOVIE
Pet Cat H.Q.
ANOTHER WINNER.
, Pet Cat!
RING!
HELLO?
JOEY, HI, LISTEN. I DON'T KNOW HOW TO TELL YOU THIS, SO I'M JUST GONNA SAY IT. WE'RE TAKING YOU OFF THE STRIP. NOTHING PERSONAL.
YOU'RE "TAKING ME OFF THE STRIP"?! THE STRIP I'VE BEEN DRAWING FOR TEN YEARS? THE STRIP THAT WON THREE KEANE AWARDS? MY STRIP?!
YEAH, WELL, WE GOT GRIFFIN REYNOLDS ON BOARD, AND HE IS PRETTY MUCH THE HOTTEST SHIT IN THE DAILY STRIP BIZ. YOU MAY HAVE HEARD OF A LITTLE STRIP OF HIS CALLED "TIMMY TROUBLEMAKER"?
ANYWAY, IT'S A DONE DEAL. WE OWN THE RIGHTS. YOU KNOW THAT.
BASTARD.
THE BEST OF PET CAT
MY COMIC IS GONNA KNOCK YOUR FUCKIN' SOCKS OFF.

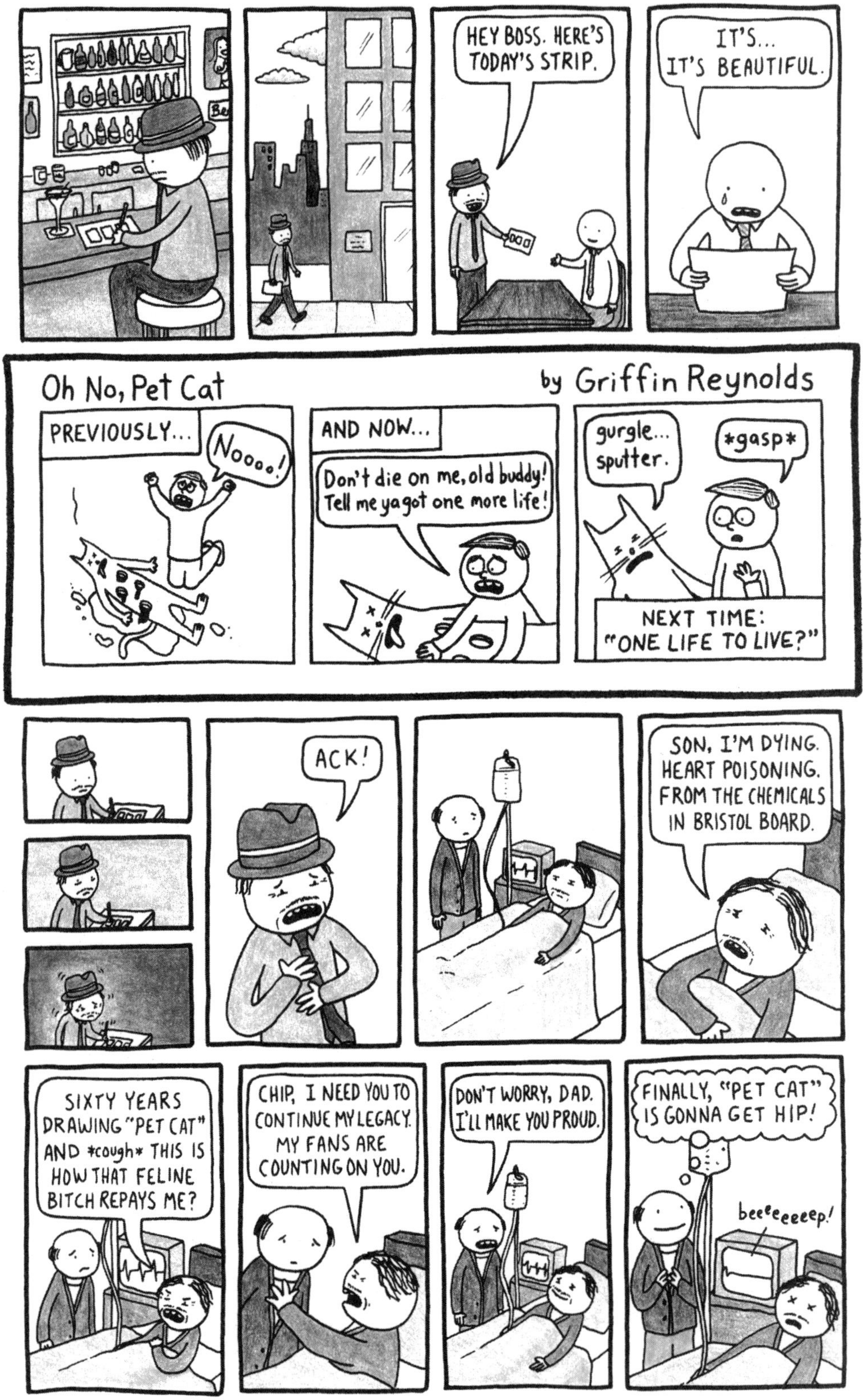
HEY BOSS. HERE'S TODAY'S STRIP.
IT'S... IT'S BEAUTIFUL.
Oh No, Pet Cat
by Griffin Reynolds
PREVIOUSLY...
Noooo!
AND NOW...
Don't die on me, old buddy! Tell me ya got one more life!
gurgle... sputter.
gasp
NEXT TIME: "ONE LIFE TO LIVE?"
ACK!
SON, I'M DYING. HEART POISONING. FROM THE CHEMICALS IN BRISTOL BOARD.
SIXTY YEARS DRAWING "PET CAT" AND *cough* THIS IS HOW THAT FELINE BITCH REPAYS ME?
CHIP, I NEED YOU TO CONTINUE MY LEGACY. MY FANS ARE COUNTING ON YOU.
DON'T WORRY, DAD. I'LL MAKE YOU PROUD.
FINALLY, "PET CAT" IS GONNA GET HIP!
beeeeeeeep!

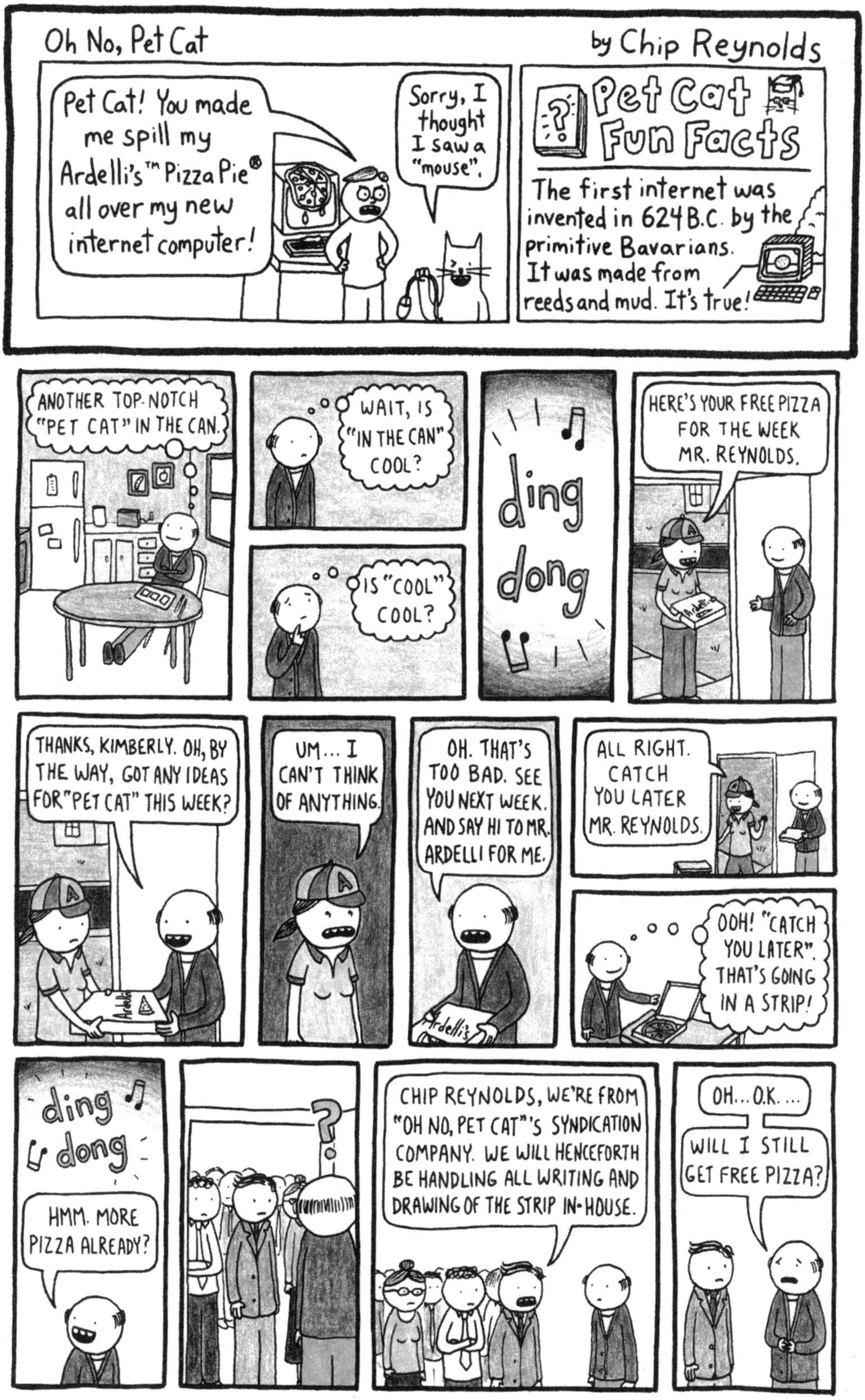

Oh No, Pet Cat
by Chip Reynolds
Pet Cat! You made me spill my Ardelli's™ Pizza Pie® all over my new internet computer!
Sorry, I thought I saw a "mouse".
Pet Cat Fun Facts
The first internet was invented in 624 B.C. by the primitive Bavarians. It was made from reeds and mud. It's true!
ANOTHER TOP-NOTCH "PET CAT" IN THE CAN.
WAIT, IS "IN THE CAN" COOL?
IS "COOL" COOL?
ding dong
HERE'S YOUR FREE PIZZA FOR THE WEEK MR. REYNOLDS.
THANKS, KIMBERLY. OH, BY THE WAY, GOT ANY IDEAS FOR "PET CAT" THIS WEEK?
UM... I CAN'T THINK OF ANYTHING.
OH. THAT'S TOO BAD. SEE YOU NEXT WEEK. AND SAY HI TO MR. ARDELLI FOR ME.
ALL RIGHT. CATCH YOU LATER MR. REYNOLDS.
OOH! "CATCH YOU LATER". THAT'S GOING IN A STRIP!
ding dong
HMM. MORE PIZZA ALREADY?
?
CHIP REYNOLDS, WE'RE FROM "OH NO, PET CAT"'S SYNDICATION COMPANY. WE WILL HENCEFORTH BE HANDLING ALL WRITING AND DRAWING OF THE STRIP IN-HOUSE.
OH... O.K. ...
WILL I STILL GET FREE PIZZA?

OK, IS EVERYBODY HERE?

FIRST OF ALL, I WANT TO CONGRATULATE EVERYONE ON TODAY'S "PET CAT." IT'S DOING GREAT IN VIRTUALLY EVERY DEMOGRAPHIC.

AND NOW, LADIES AND GENTLEMEN: TOMORROW'S STRIP!

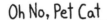
Oh No, Pet Cat   by Cartoon Product Syndicate

Hey, international pop sensation Tammy Wilcox, have you seen Pet Cat?

No I haven't but I sure could go for some pizza pie.

Me too!

Oh no, Pet Cat!

LOOK FOR THE NEW TAMMY WILCOX ALBUM, FEATURING PET CAT in stores March 23!

IT'S LIKE STEINBECK BRILLIANT.

WE ARE CHANGING THE FACE OF POPULAR CULTURE.

FUCKIN' BEAUTIFUL GODDAMN SYNERGY IS WHAT THAT IS!

GREAT, NOW LET'S BRAINSTORM THURSDAY'S STRIP. KYLE, WHAT'VE YOU GOT?

OK, RESEARCH IS SHOWING WOMEN AGE 28-45 ARE MOSTLY INTERESTED IN CHOCOHOLISM AND SWIMSUIT FASHION. AM I RIGHT, CAROL?

YOU GOT THAT RIGHT, KYLE!

PET CAT COULD HAVE A COUSIN FROM ANOTHER...

boom!

HUH... WEIRD. ANYWAY, THIS COUSIN COULD...

BOOM!

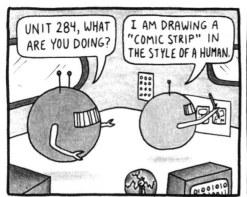

UNIT 284, WHAT ARE YOU DOING?

I AM DRAWING A "COMIC STRIP" IN THE STYLE OF A HUMAN.

HUMANS ARE THOSE STRANGE CREATURES THAT HAVE BEEN EXTINCT FOR 40,000 YEARS. THEY MADE ART?

YES. LIKE THIS.

Oh No, Pet Cat

by Unit 284

 Empathy and an innate desire to nurture small mammals compels me to feed you...

 Even though you are functionally indistinguishable from my own sustenance.

 Perhaps I am increasing your girth with this pizza pie for a ceremonial human feast.

 ...

I DO NOT GET IT.

I WOULD NOT EXPECT YOU TO, UNIT 651172908. IT HAS FEELING AND EMOTION. IT IS LIKE POETRY. IT IS A SONG YOU HEAR WITH YOUR SOUL.

I'M KEEPING THE COMIC ALIVE TO REMIND OUR SPECIES ABOUT THE BEAUTY OF ART.

OH, BY THE WAY, HAVE YOU SEEN THE NEW HUMOROUS SEQUENTIAL HOLO-STORY IN THE DAILY NEWS FEED?

gasp IT IS GORGEOUS. AND... HA HA HA... HILARIOUS.

OH... MY...

GOD, WHAT'S WRONG?

"OH NO, PET CAT", THE BEST COMIC STRIP OF ALL TIME, MIGHT FINALLY BE DONE. WHAT AM I GOING TO READ NOW?

OOH! UNLESS...

CARL. GO GET JOEY ALISON SAYERS.

...AND SO I THOUGHT: WHY LET THE STRIP DIE, WHEN I'M THE MOST POWERFUL, AND DARE I SAY FUNNIEST BEING IN THE UNIVERSE? I'M THE NEW WRITER AND ARTIST OF "PET CAT"! NOT TO TOOT MY OWN HORN, BUT I THINK IT'S THE BEST THING I'VE WILLED INTO EXISTENCE SINCE KITTENS.

HERE. READ IT.

Oh No, Pet Cat   by god

Pet Cat, I am most fulfilled when we share the pizza pie.

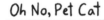

Yes, but something is missing.

UH...

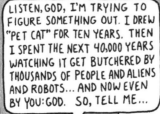

LISTEN, GOD, I'M TRYING TO FIGURE SOMETHING OUT. I DREW "PET CAT" FOR TEN YEARS. THEN I SPENT THE NEXT 40,000 YEARS WATCHING IT GET BUTCHERED BY THOUSANDS OF PEOPLE AND ALIENS AND ROBOTS... AND NOW EVEN BY YOU: GOD. SO, TELL ME...

THIS IS ACTUALLY HELL, RIGHT? I'M IN HELL.

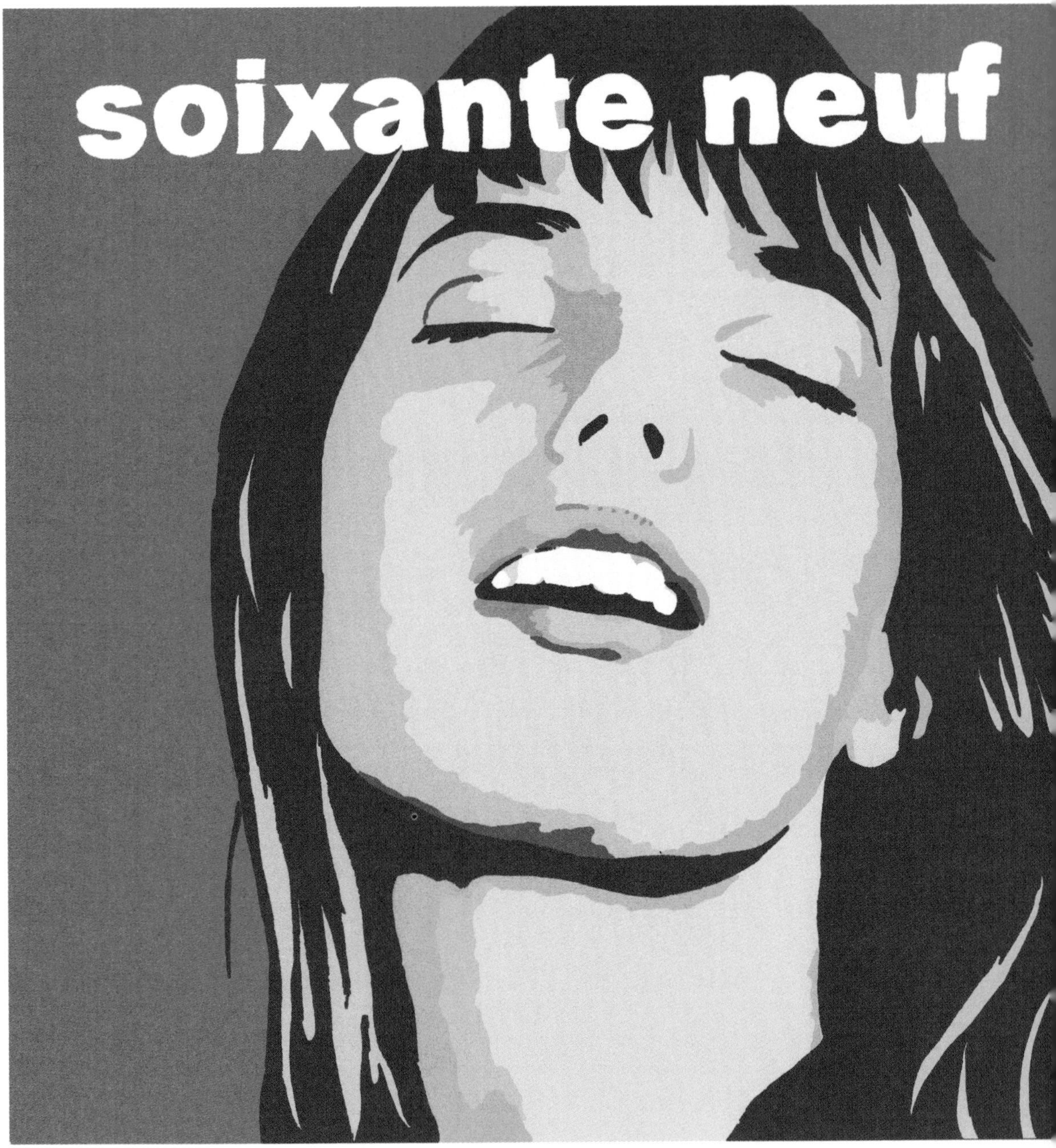
soixante neuf

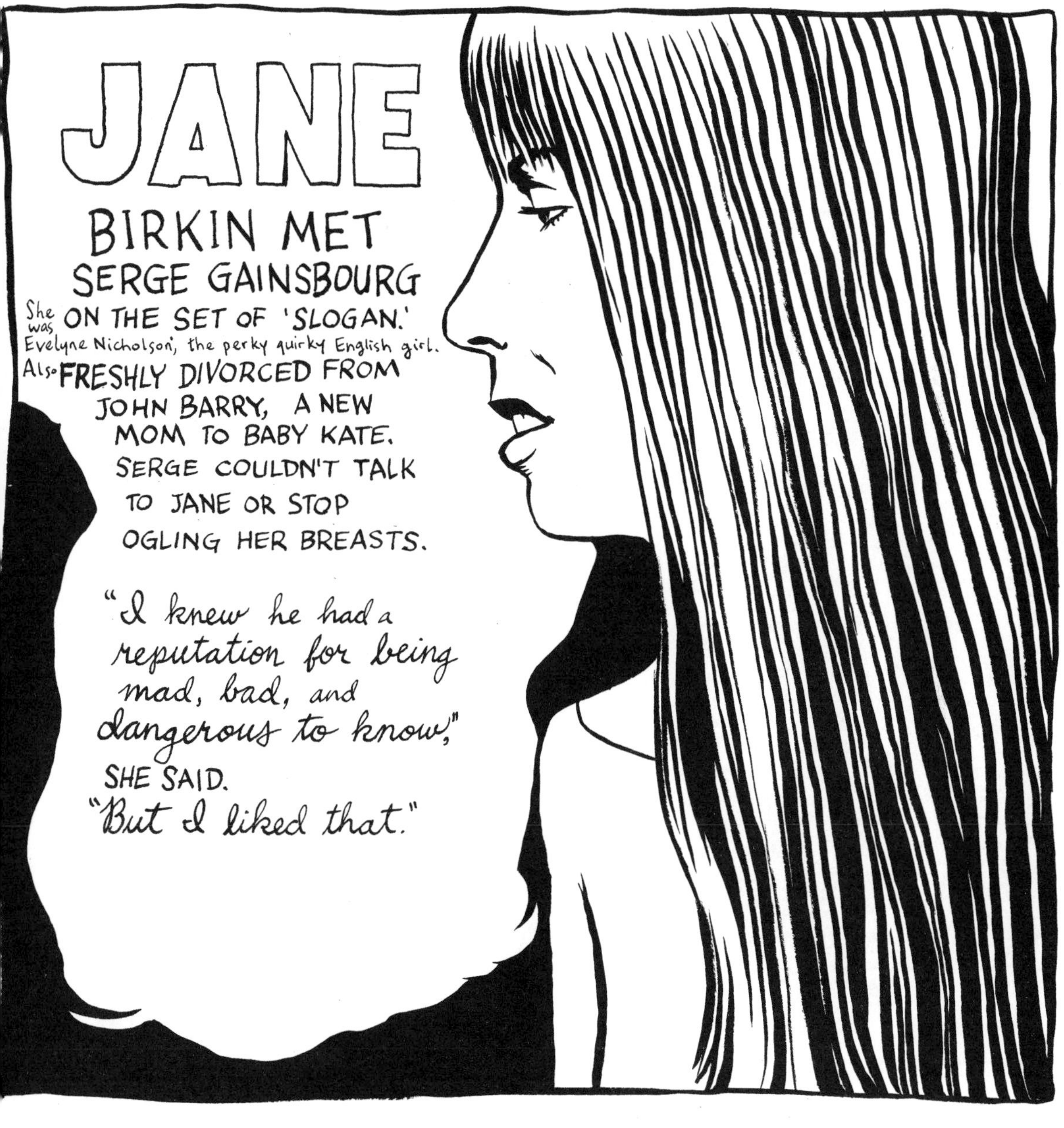
JANE
BIRKIN MET
SERGE GAINSBOURG
She was ON THE SET OF 'SLOGAN.'
Evelyne Nicholson', the perky quirky English girl.
Also FRESHLY DIVORCED FROM
JOHN BARRY, A NEW
MOM TO BABY KATE.
SERGE COULDN'T TALK
TO JANE OR STOP
OGLING HER BREASTS.
"I knew he had a
reputation for being
mad, bad, and
dangerous to know,"
SHE SAID.
"But I liked that."

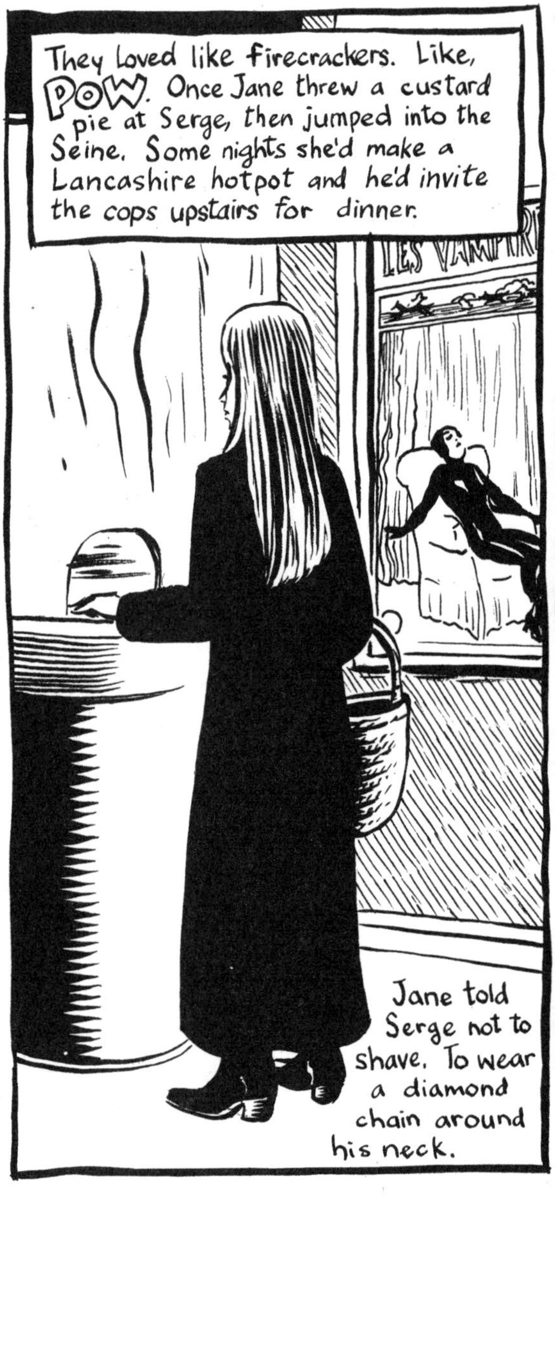

They loved like firecrackers. Like, POW. Once Jane threw a custard pie at Serge, then jumped into the Seine. Some nights she'd make a Lancashire hotpot and he'd invite the cops upstairs for dinner.
LES VAMPIR
Jane told Serge not to shave. To wear a diamond chain around his neck.

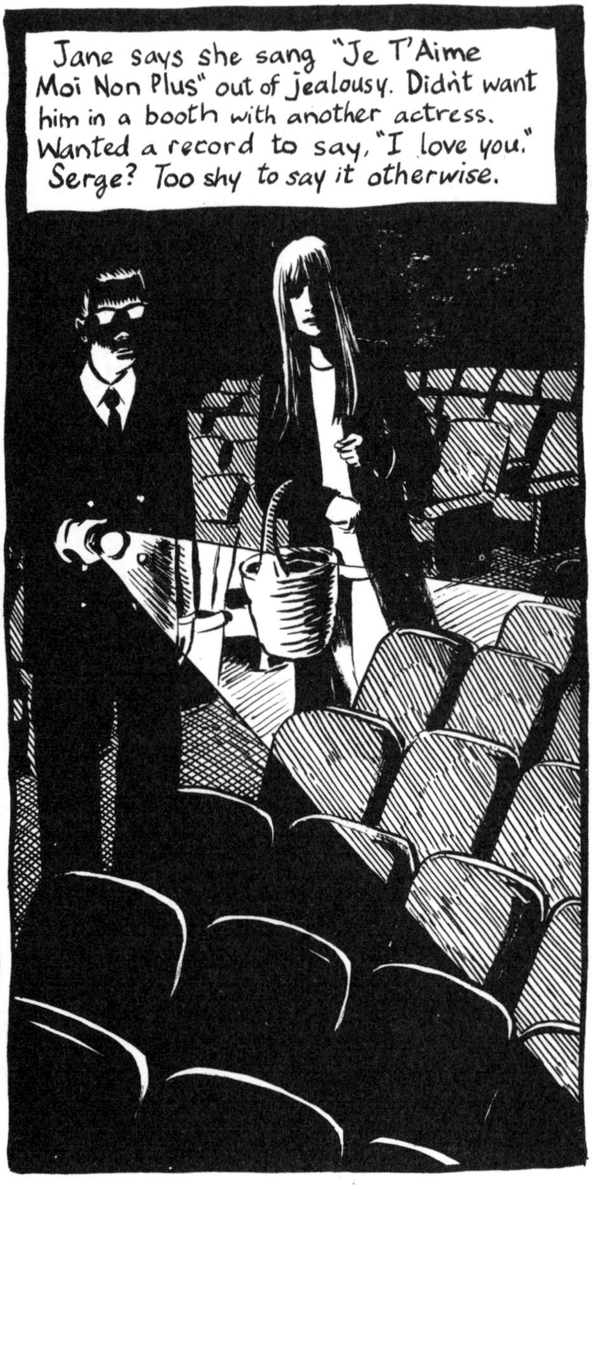

Jane says she sang "Je T'Aime Moi Non Plus" out of jealousy. Didn't want him in a booth with another actress. Wanted a record to say, "I love you." Serge? Too shy to say it otherwise.

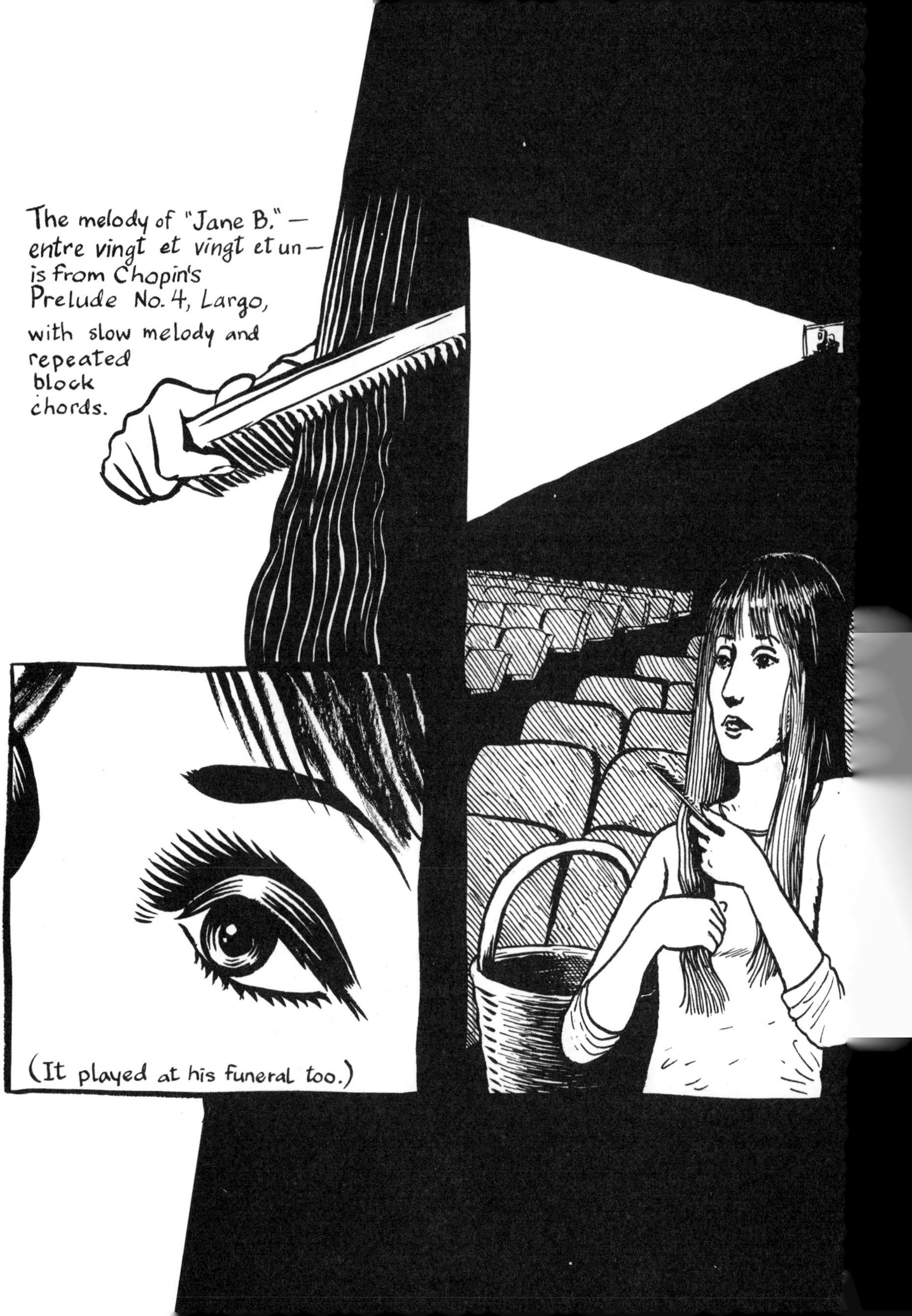
The melody of "Jane B." — entre vingt et vingt et un — is from Chopin's Prelude No. 4, Largo, with slow melody and repeated block chords.
(It played at his funeral too.)

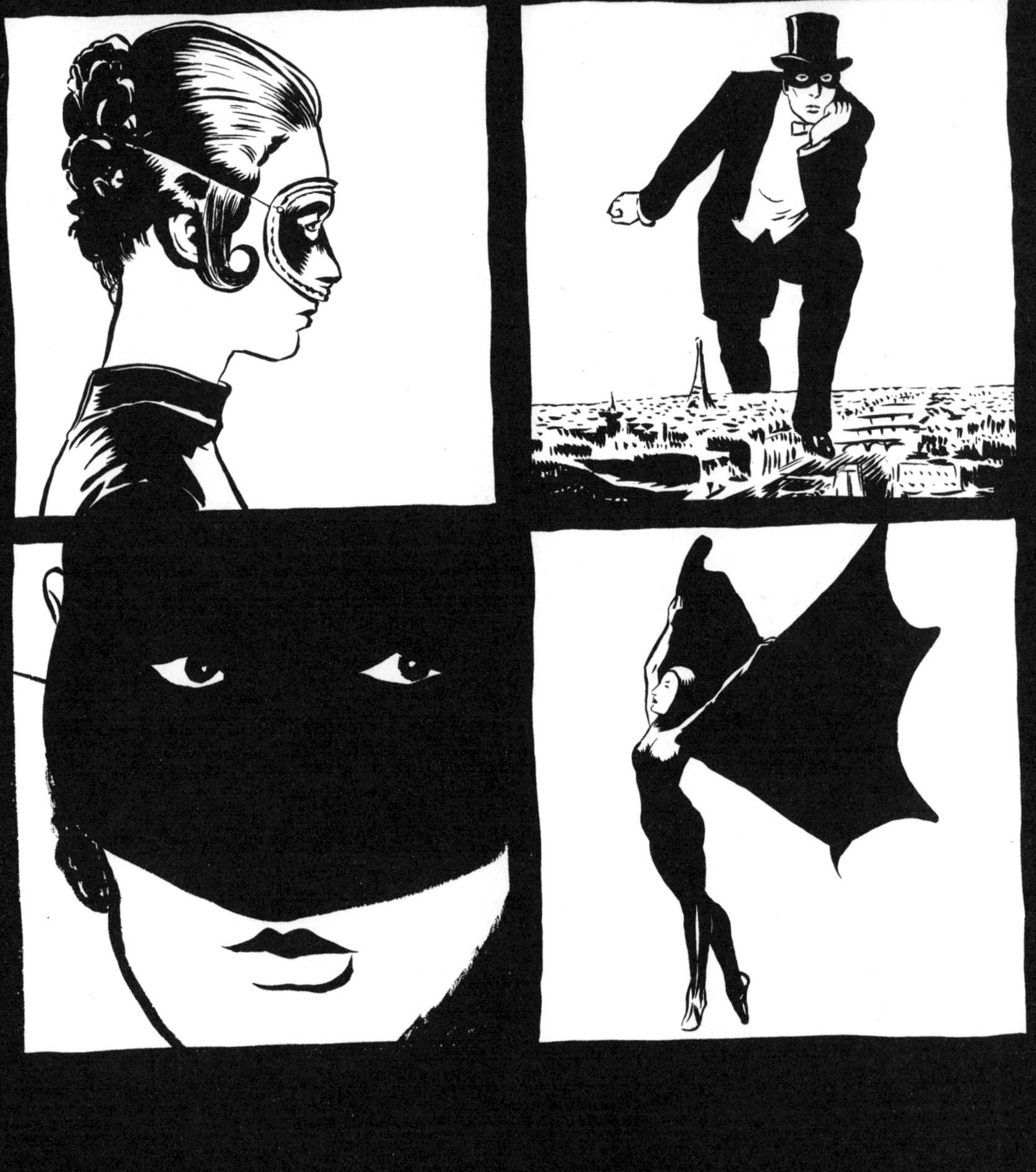

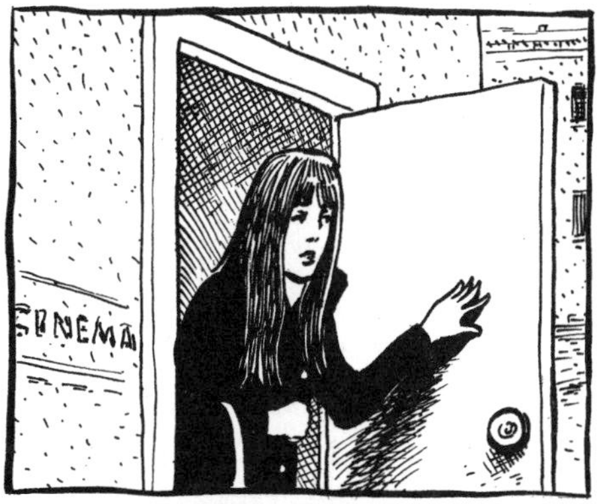
CINEMA

Some songs are for other women, for Françoise Hardy and France Gall.

"Sucettes" has a girl sliding a lollipop down her neck. The candy's liquorice flavored — liquorice for breath, for nausea, for purity.

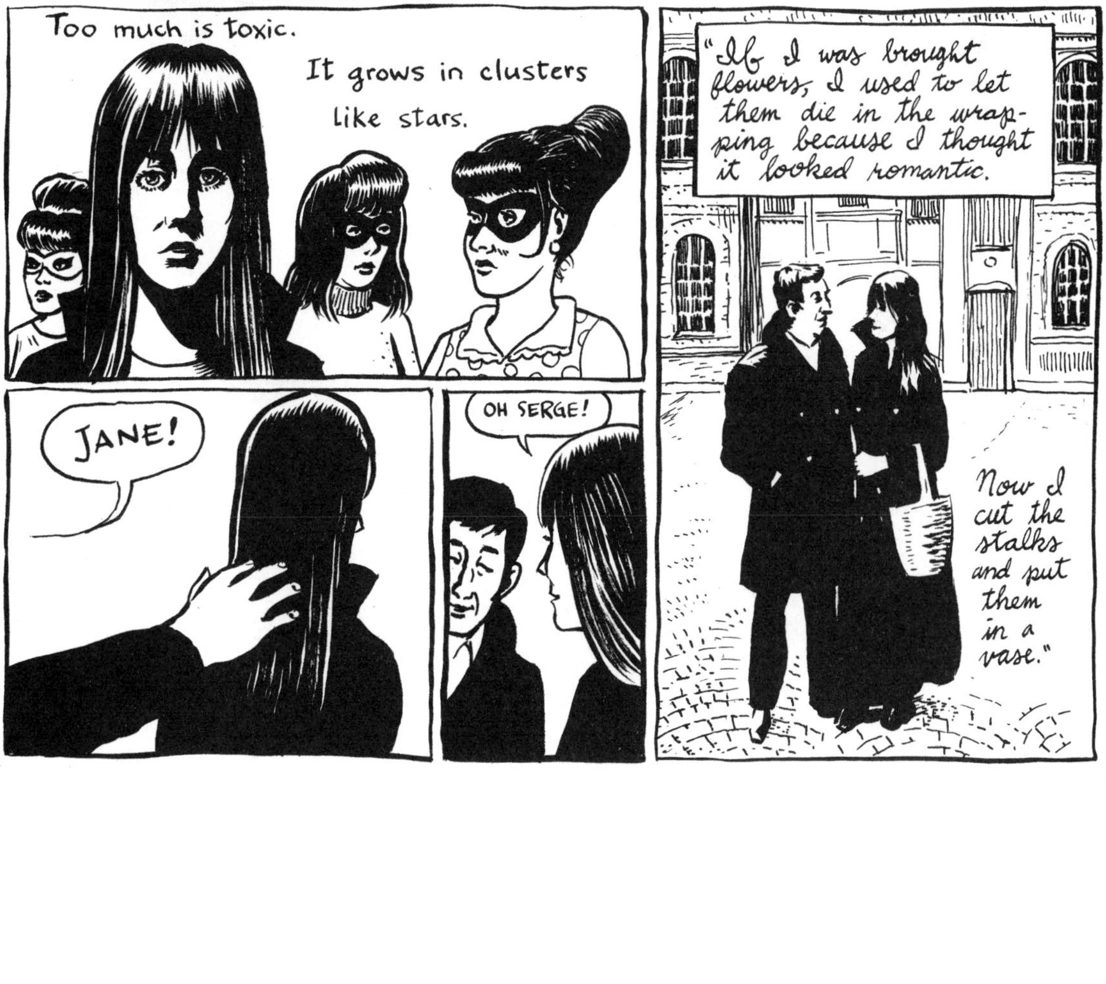
Too much is toxic.
It grows in clusters like stars.
"If I was brought flowers, I used to let them die in the wrapping because I thought it looked romantic.
JANE!
OH SERGE!
Now I cut the stalks and put them in a vase."

"We lived this extraordinary life. We would go out until six in the morning, wake the children up for school, have breakfast with them, then sleep until it was time to pick them up.

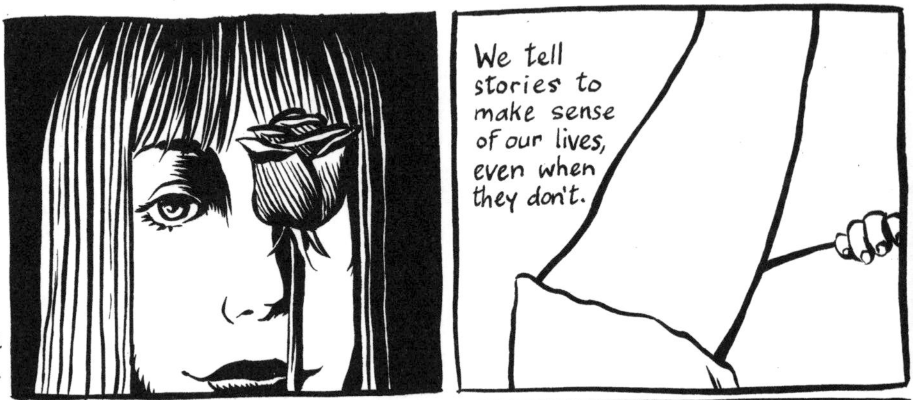
We tell stories to make sense of our lives, even when they don't.

Then we'd take them to the park and at 10 o'clock the whole thing would start again."

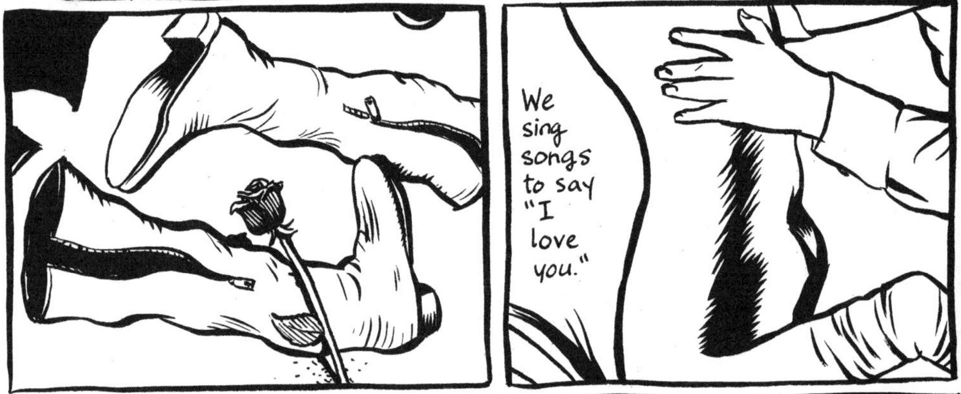
We sing songs to say "I love you."

"Je T'Aime Moi Non Plus" was #1 in Europe and #69 in the U.S.

It was banned by the Pope and the B.B.C.

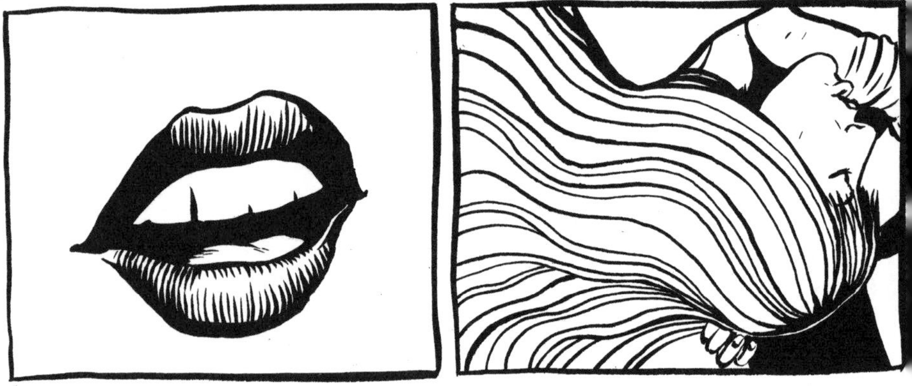

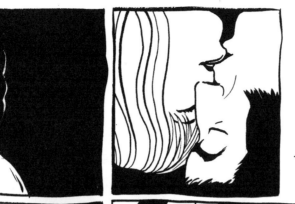

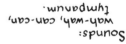

JANE: "Serge was a permanent adolescent. All was impertinent of me to say and change him. Not foolish. Impertinent.

"All he loved somebody, it was definitely Chopin."

Je vais
et
je viens,
entre
tes
reins.

Sounds:
wah-wah, can-can,
tympanum.
Objects:
poppyseeds and monkeys,
propellers and cobblestones.
Fleas, ice, barley sugar.
A canary on a balcony.

Lots of throaty rhymes:
aime, viens, riens.
Gotta sing with your
tongue curled. With your
nose in the air.

Once done, Jane and Serge walked into the Hôtel d'Alsace restaurant to play their song. She was 21, he 40.
Jaws dropped.
Eyes popped.
The guy at Philips said he'd go to jail for a hit record but not a single. So Serge went home to write ten more tunes, and *Jane Birkin/Serge Gainsbourg* streeted in 1969.

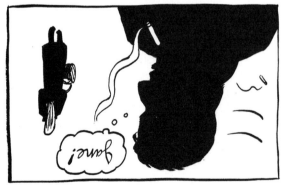

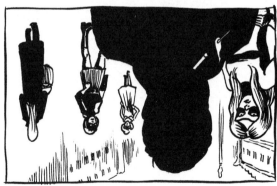

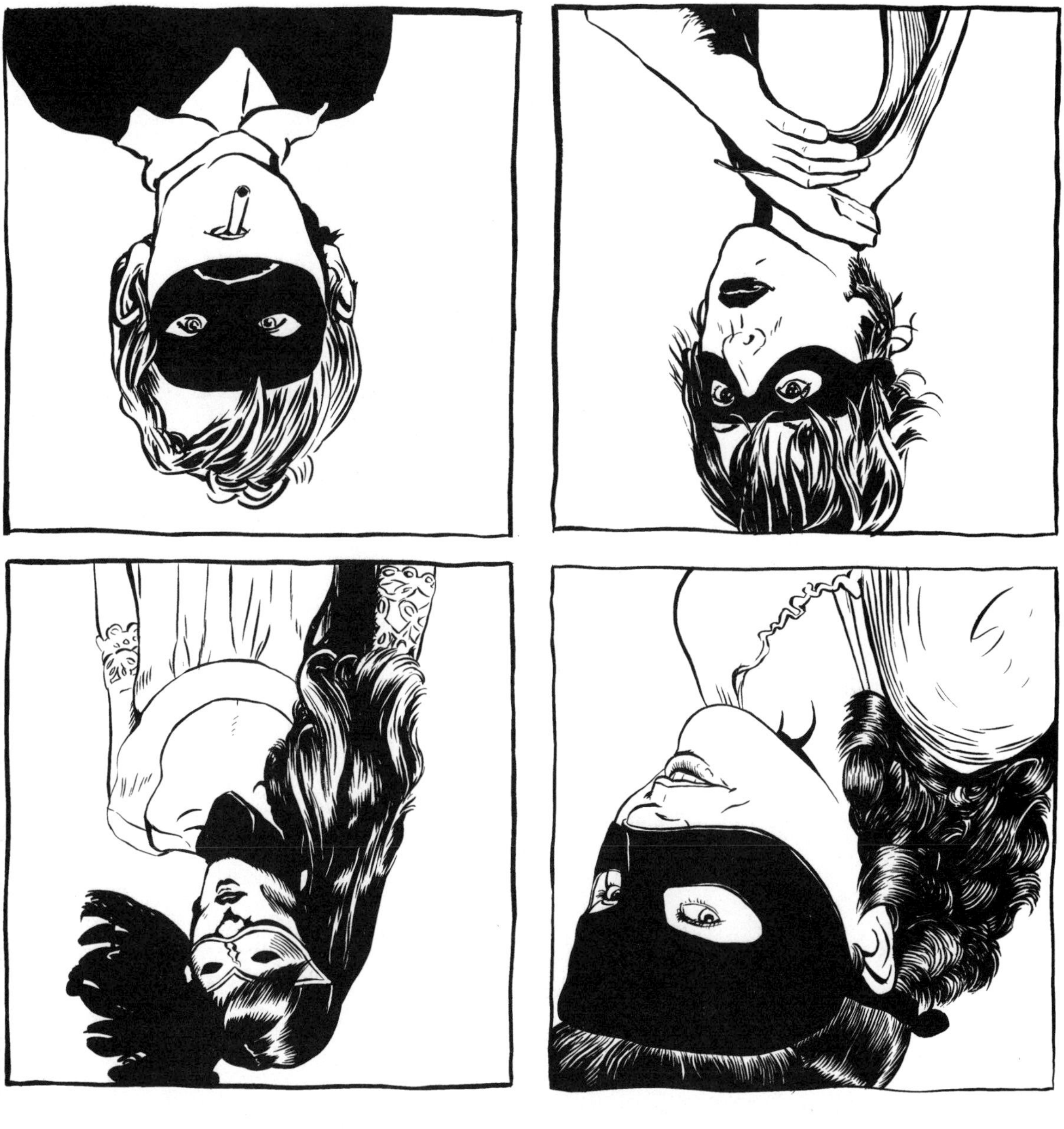

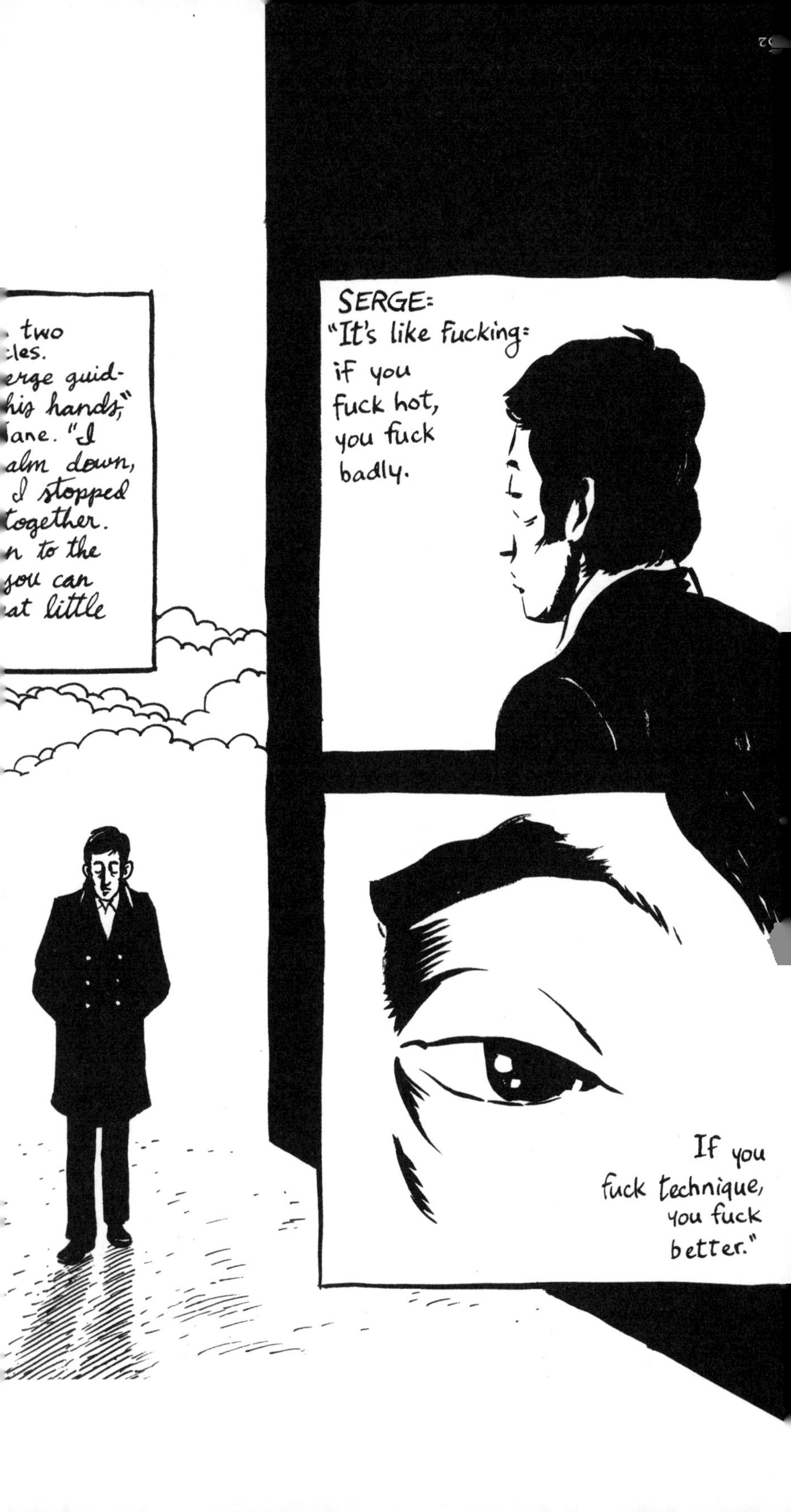
two
cles.
erge guid-
his hands,"
Jane. "I
alm down,
I stopped
together.
n to the
you can
at little
SERGE:
"It's like fucking:
if you
fuck hot,
you fuck
badly.
If you
fuck technique,
you fuck
better."

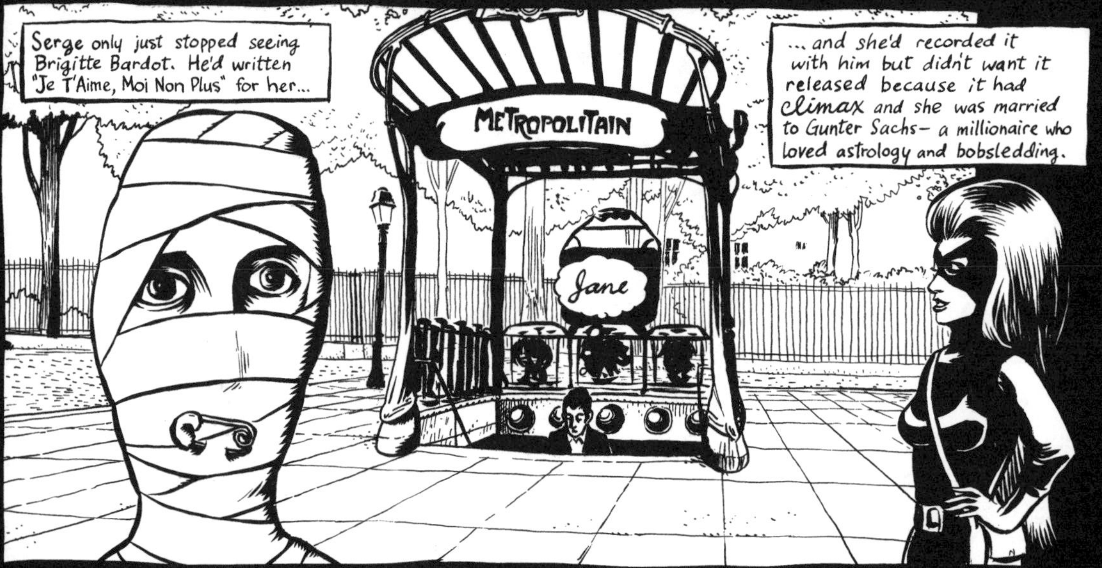
Serge only just stopped seeing Brigitte Bardot. He'd written "Je T'Aime, Moi Non Plus" for her...
METROPOLITAIN
Jane
...and she'd recorded it with him but didn't want it released because it had climax and she was married to Gunter Sachs– a millionaire who loved astrology and bobsledding.

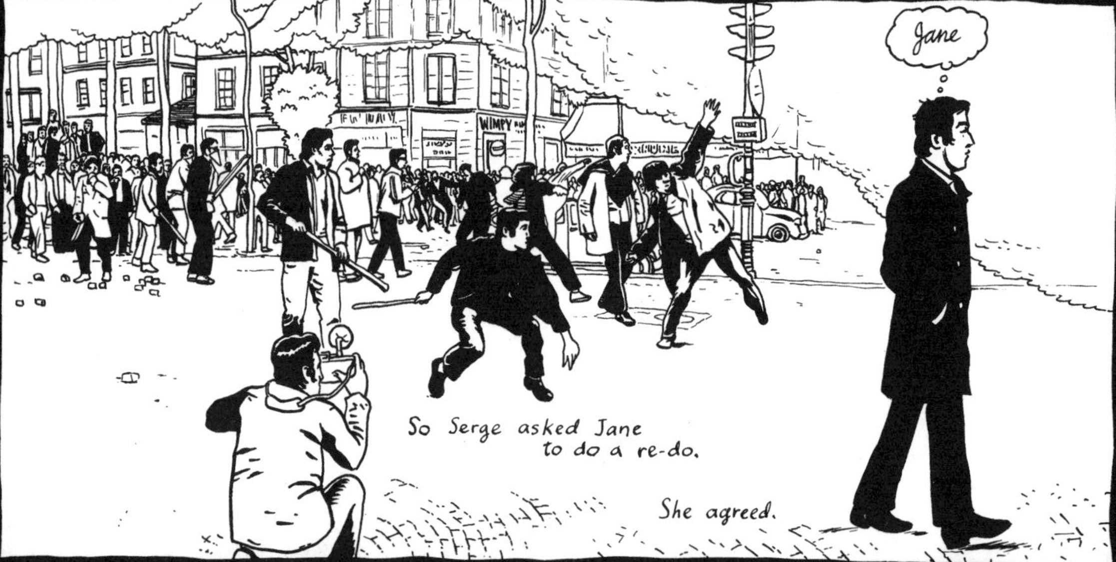
Jane
WIMPY
So Serge asked Jane to do a re-do.
She agreed.

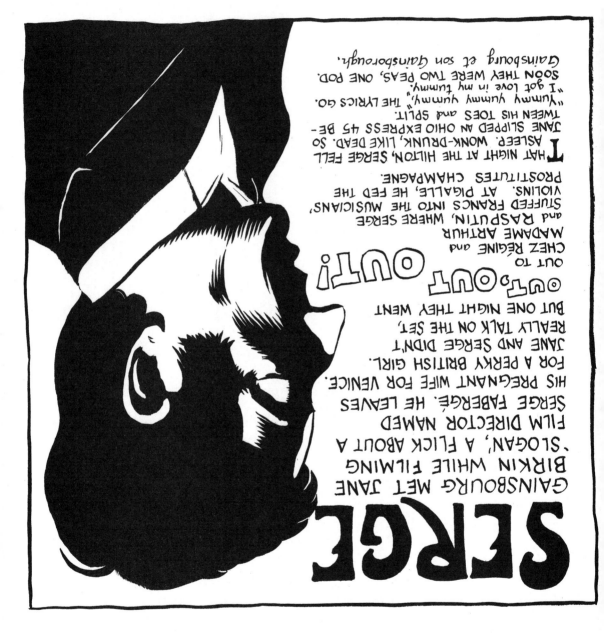

SERGE

GAINSBOURG MET JANE BIRKIN WHILE FILMING 'SLOGAN,' A FLICK ABOUT A FILM DIRECTOR NAMED SERGE FABERGÉ. HE LEAVES HIS PREGNANT WIFE FOR VENICE, FOR A PERKY BRITISH GIRL.

JANE AND SERGE DIDN'T REALLY TALK ON THE SET, BUT ONE NIGHT THEY WENT

OUT, OUT, OUT, OUT!

out to CHEZ RÉGINE and MADAME ARTHUR and RASPUTIN, WHERE SERGE STUFFED FRANCS INTO THE MUSICIANS' VIOLINS. AT PIGALLE, HE FED THE PROSTITUTES CHAMPAGNE.

THAT NIGHT AT THE HILTON, SERGE FELL ASLEEP, WONK-DRUNK, LIKE DEAD. SO JANE SLIPPED AN OHIO EXPRESS 45 BE-TWEEN HIS TOES AND SPLIT.

"Yummy yummy yummy," THE LYRICS GO. "I got love in my tummy." SOON THEY WERE TWO PEAS, ONE POD.

Gainsbourg et son Gainsborough.

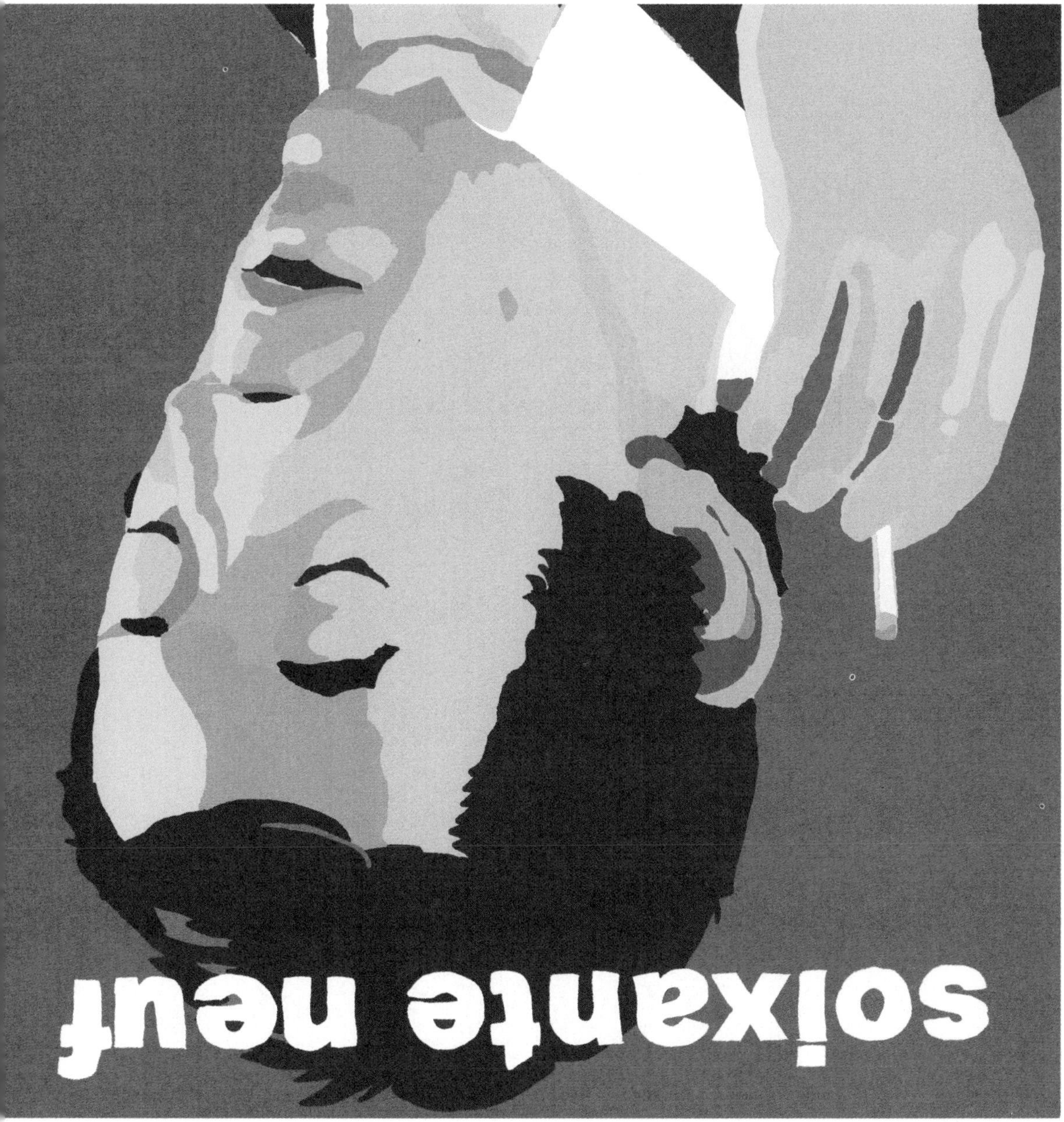
soixante neuf

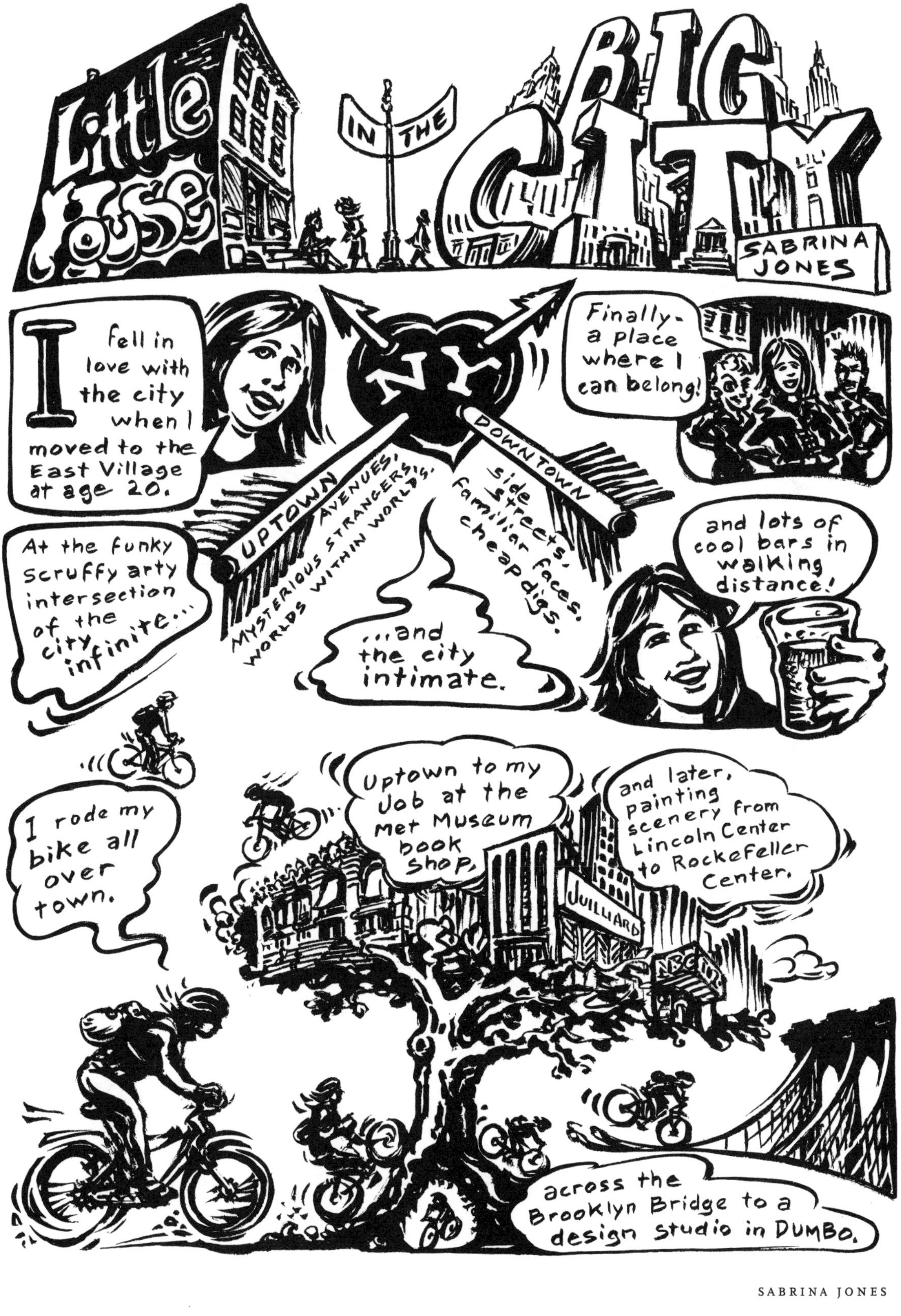
Little House in the Big City
SABRINA JONES
I fell in love with the city when I moved to the East Village at age 20.
NY
UPTOWN
DOWNTOWN
Finally- a place where I can belong!
At the funky scruffy arty intersection of the city infinite...
AVENUES, MYSTERIOUS STRANGERS, WORLDS WITHIN WORLDS
side streets, familiar faces, cheap digs.
...and the city intimate.
and lots of cool bars in walking distance!
I rode my bike all over town.
Uptown to my job at the Met Museum book shop,
and later, painting scenery from Lincoln Center to Rockefeller Center.
JUILLIARD
across the Brooklyn Bridge to a design studio in DUMBO.

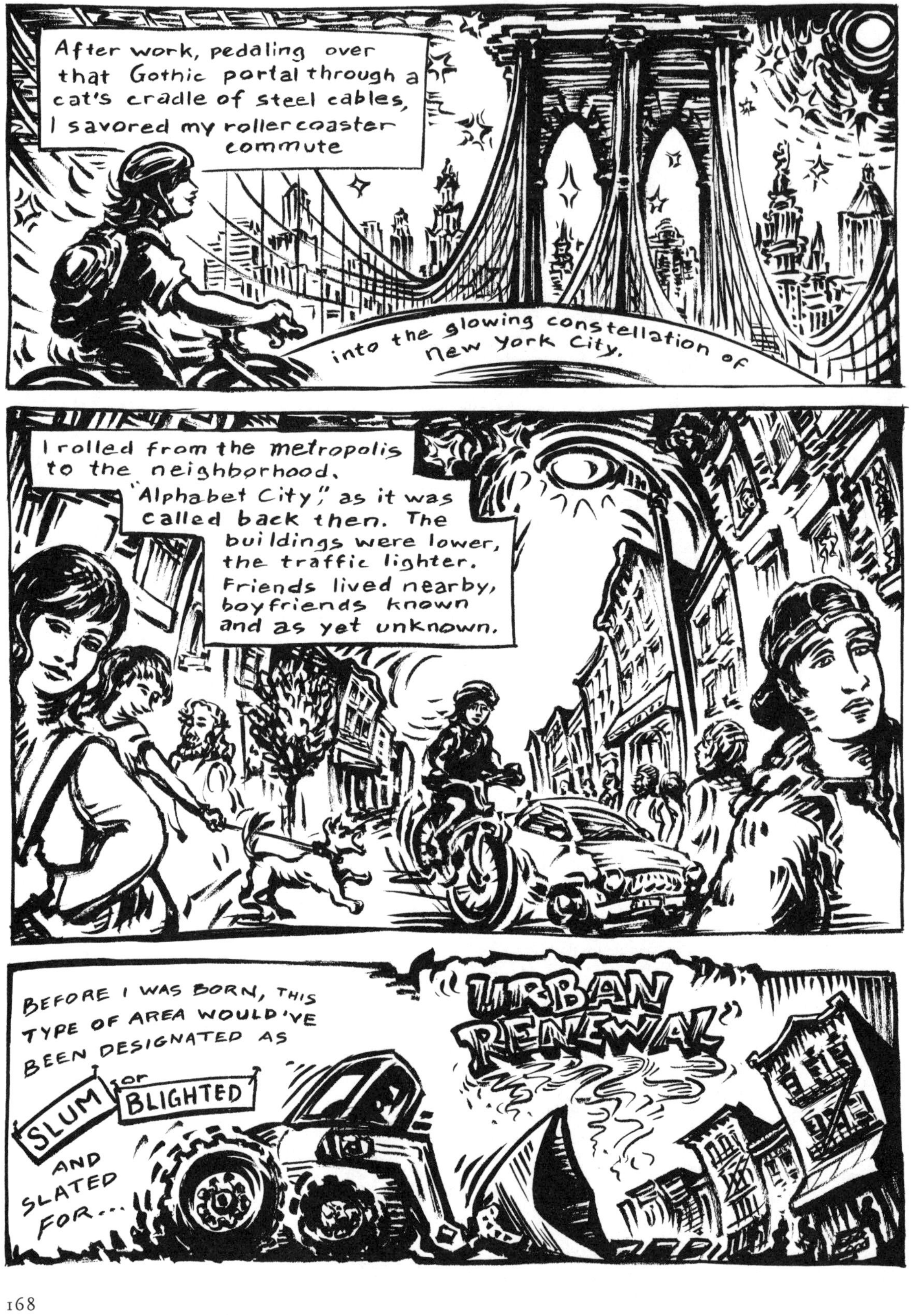
After work, pedaling over that Gothic portal through a cat's cradle of steel cables, I savored my rollercoaster commute
into the glowing constellation of New York City.
I rolled from the metropolis to the neighborhood.
"Alphabet City," as it was called back then. The buildings were lower, the traffic lighter. Friends lived nearby, boyfriends known and as yet unknown.
BEFORE I WAS BORN, THIS TYPE OF AREA WOULD'VE BEEN DESIGNATED AS
SLUM
or
BLIGHTED
AND SLATED FOR...
"URBAN RENEWAL"

WHOLE NEIGHBORHOODS WERE DEMOLISHED.

IN THEIR PLACE ROSE THE NEW SUPERBLOCKS.

UNIFORM TOWERS →

UNUSED OPEN SPACE

← MULTI-LANE EXPRESSWAYS

WHAT WERE THE PLANNERS THINKING? AND HOW WAS THIS SYSTEMATIC ASSAULT ON URBAN LIVING TURNED AROUND?

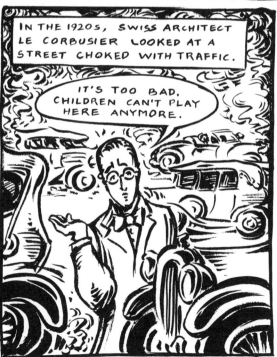

IN THE 1920s, SWISS ARCHITECT LE CORBUSIER LOOKED AT A STREET CHOKED WITH TRAFFIC.

IT'S TOO BAD. CHILDREN CAN'T PLAY HERE ANYMORE.

HIS SOLUTION:

WE CAN NEVER GO BACK, SO...

...WE MUST EMBRACE THE CAR!

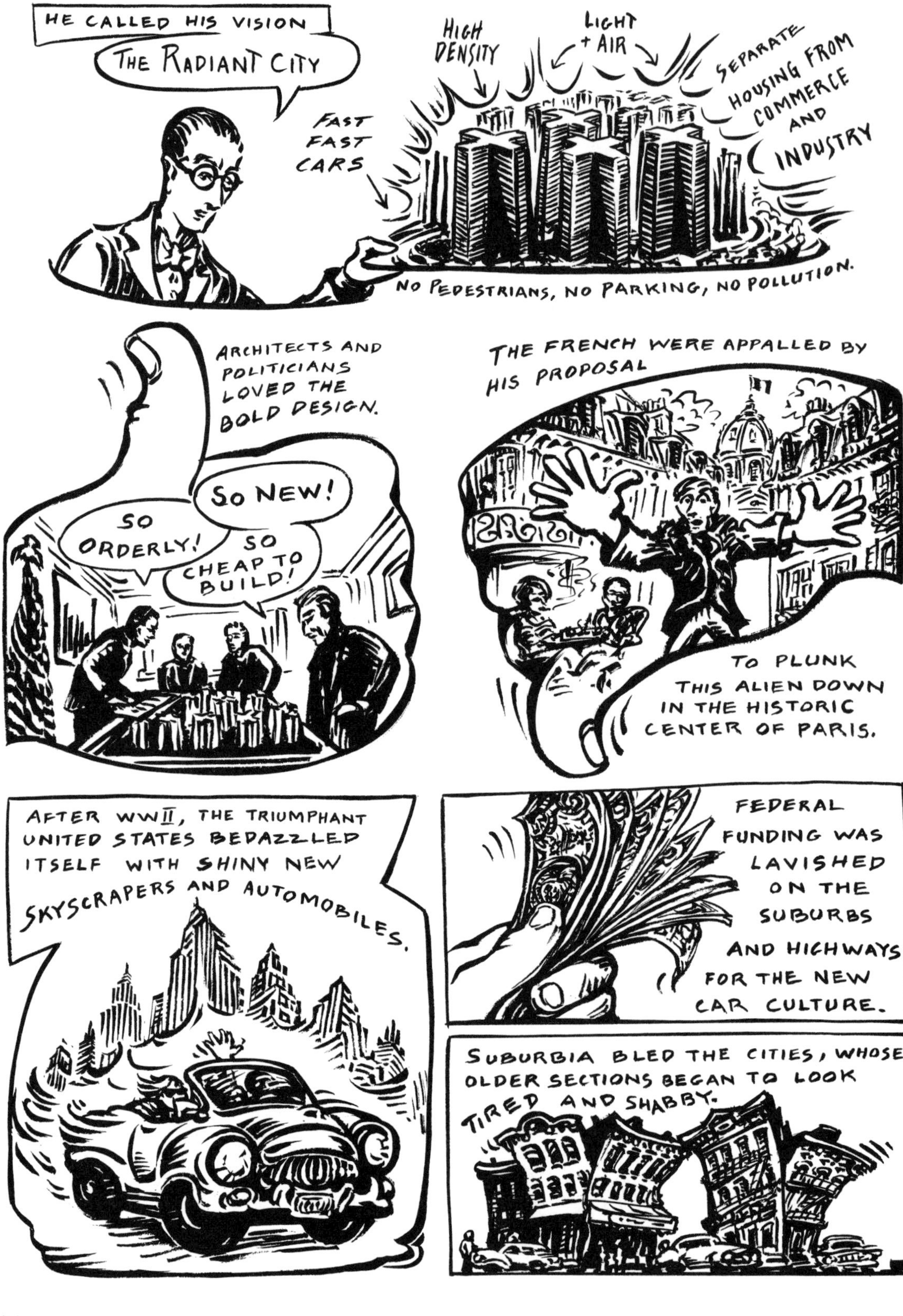
HE CALLED HIS VISION
THE RADIANT CITY
HIGH DENSITY
LIGHT + AIR
SEPARATE HOUSING FROM COMMERCE AND INDUSTRY
FAST FAST CARS
NO PEDESTRIANS, NO PARKING, NO POLLUTION.
ARCHITECTS AND POLITICIANS LOVED THE BOLD DESIGN.
SO ORDERLY!
SO NEW!
SO CHEAP TO BUILD!
THE FRENCH WERE APPALLED BY HIS PROPOSAL
TO PLUNK THIS ALIEN DOWN IN THE HISTORIC CENTER OF PARIS.
AFTER WWII, THE TRIUMPHANT UNITED STATES BEDAZZLED ITSELF WITH SHINY NEW SKYSCRAPERS AND AUTOMOBILES.
FEDERAL FUNDING WAS LAVISHED ON THE SUBURBS AND HIGHWAYS FOR THE NEW CAR CULTURE.
SUBURBIA BLED THE CITIES, WHOSE OLDER SECTIONS BEGAN TO LOOK TIRED AND SHABBY.

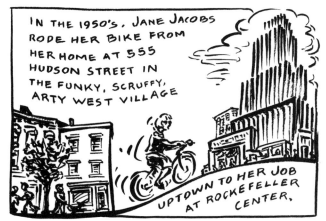

IN THE 1950's, JANE JACOBS RODE HER BIKE FROM HER HOME AT 555 HUDSON STREET IN THE FUNKY, SCRUFFY, ARTY WEST VILLAGE

UPTOWN TO HER JOB AT ROCKEFELLER CENTER,

SHE WAS A WRITER AND EDITOR FOR ARCHITECTURAL FORUM MAGAZINE.

SHE LOVED TO EXPLORE THE CITY AND WRITE ABOUT ITS VARIOUS DISTRICTS— THE DIAMOND DISTRICT, THE FUR DISTRICT, AND THE

FLOWER DISTRICT.

SHE WENT TO PHILADELPHIA TO COVER A HIGHLY PRAISED

RENEWAL PROJECT.

FIRST, CITY PLANNER ED BACON SHOWED HER THE OFFENDING SLUM THAT WAS BEING REPLACED.

THEY'RE OBVIOUSLY POOR, BUT THEY'RE ENJOYING THEMSELVES AND EACH OTHER.

THEN THE BRAND-NEW PROJECT

BUT WHERE ARE THE PEOPLE?

THEY DON'T APPRECIATE THESE THINGS.

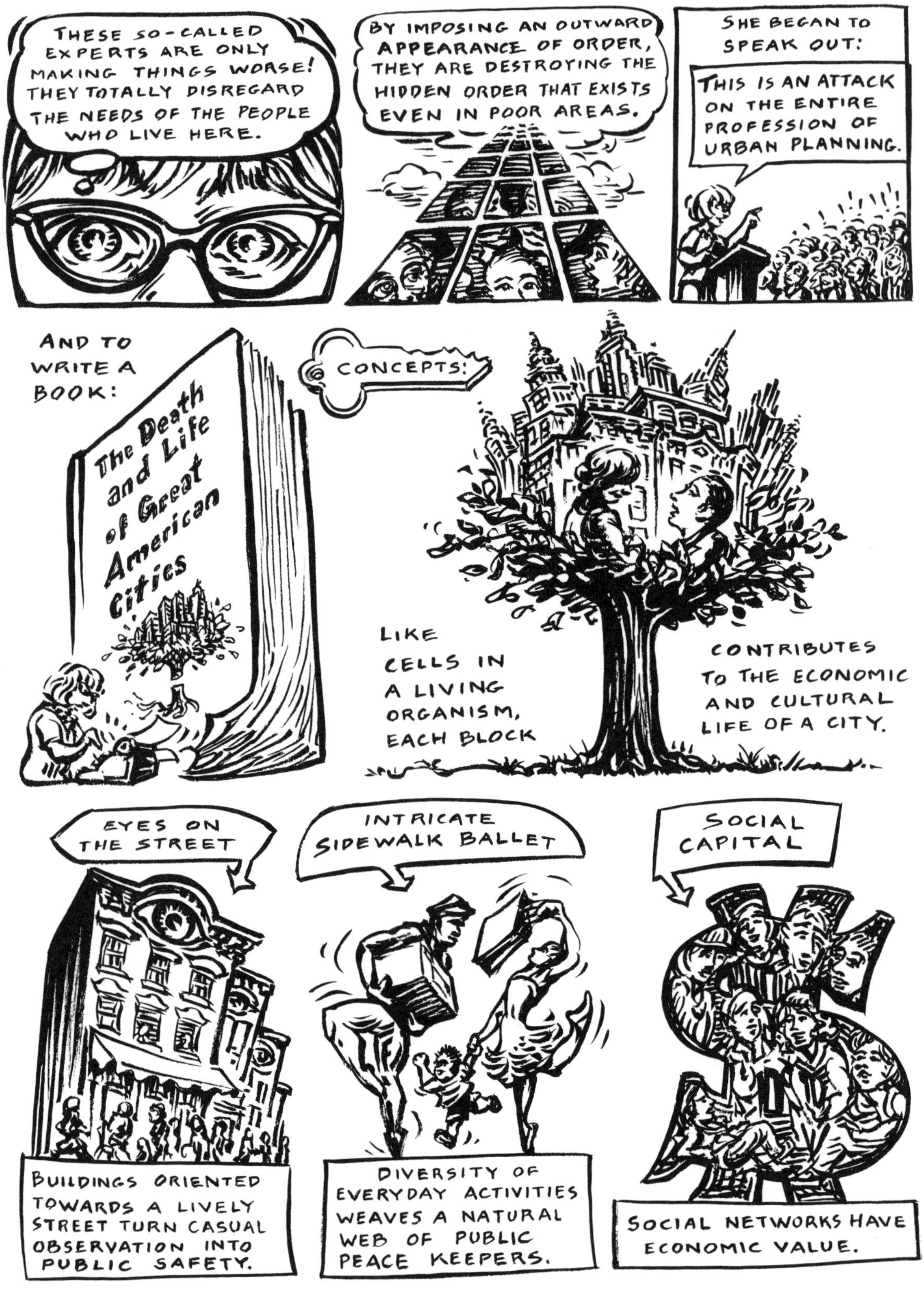

THESE SO-CALLED EXPERTS ARE ONLY MAKING THINGS WORSE! THEY TOTALLY DISREGARD THE NEEDS OF THE PEOPLE WHO LIVE HERE.
BY IMPOSING AN OUTWARD APPEARANCE OF ORDER, THEY ARE DESTROYING THE HIDDEN ORDER THAT EXISTS EVEN IN POOR AREAS.
SHE BEGAN TO SPEAK OUT:
THIS IS AN ATTACK ON THE ENTIRE PROFESSION OF URBAN PLANNING.
AND TO WRITE A BOOK:
The Death and Life of Great American Cities
CONCEPTS:
LIKE CELLS IN A LIVING ORGANISM, EACH BLOCK
CONTRIBUTES TO THE ECONOMIC AND CULTURAL LIFE OF A CITY.
EYES ON THE STREET
BUILDINGS ORIENTED TOWARDS A LIVELY STREET TURN CASUAL OBSERVATION INTO PUBLIC SAFETY.
INTRICATE SIDEWALK BALLET
DIVERSITY OF EVERYDAY ACTIVITIES WEAVES A NATURAL WEB OF PUBLIC PEACE KEEPERS.
SOCIAL CAPITAL
SOCIAL NETWORKS HAVE ECONOMIC VALUE.

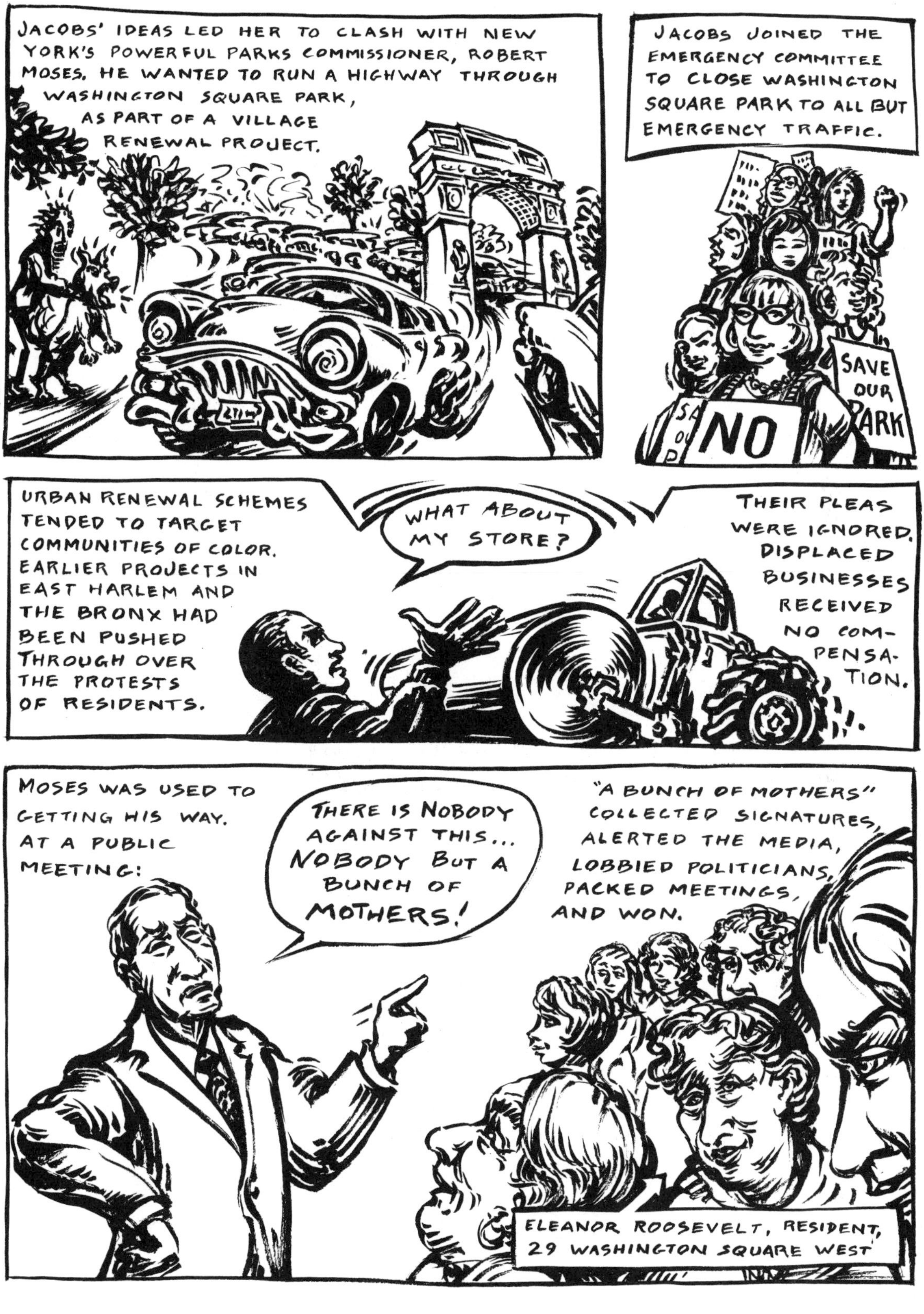
JACOBS' IDEAS LED HER TO CLASH WITH NEW YORK'S POWERFUL PARKS COMMISSIONER, ROBERT MOSES. HE WANTED TO RUN A HIGHWAY THROUGH WASHINGTON SQUARE PARK, AS PART OF A VILLAGE RENEWAL PROJECT.
JACOBS JOINED THE EMERGENCY COMMITTEE TO CLOSE WASHINGTON SQUARE PARK TO ALL BUT EMERGENCY TRAFFIC.
SAVE OUR PARK
NO
URBAN RENEWAL SCHEMES TENDED TO TARGET COMMUNITIES OF COLOR. EARLIER PROJECTS IN EAST HARLEM AND THE BRONX HAD BEEN PUSHED THROUGH OVER THE PROTESTS OF RESIDENTS.
WHAT ABOUT MY STORE?
THEIR PLEAS WERE IGNORED. DISPLACED BUSINESSES RECEIVED NO COMPENSATION.
MOSES WAS USED TO GETTING HIS WAY. AT A PUBLIC MEETING:
THERE IS NOBODY AGAINST THIS... NOBODY BUT A BUNCH OF MOTHERS!
"A BUNCH OF MOTHERS" COLLECTED SIGNATURES, ALERTED THE MEDIA, LOBBIED POLITICIANS, PACKED MEETINGS, AND WON.
ELEANOR ROOSEVELT, RESIDENT, 29 WASHINGTON SQUARE WEST

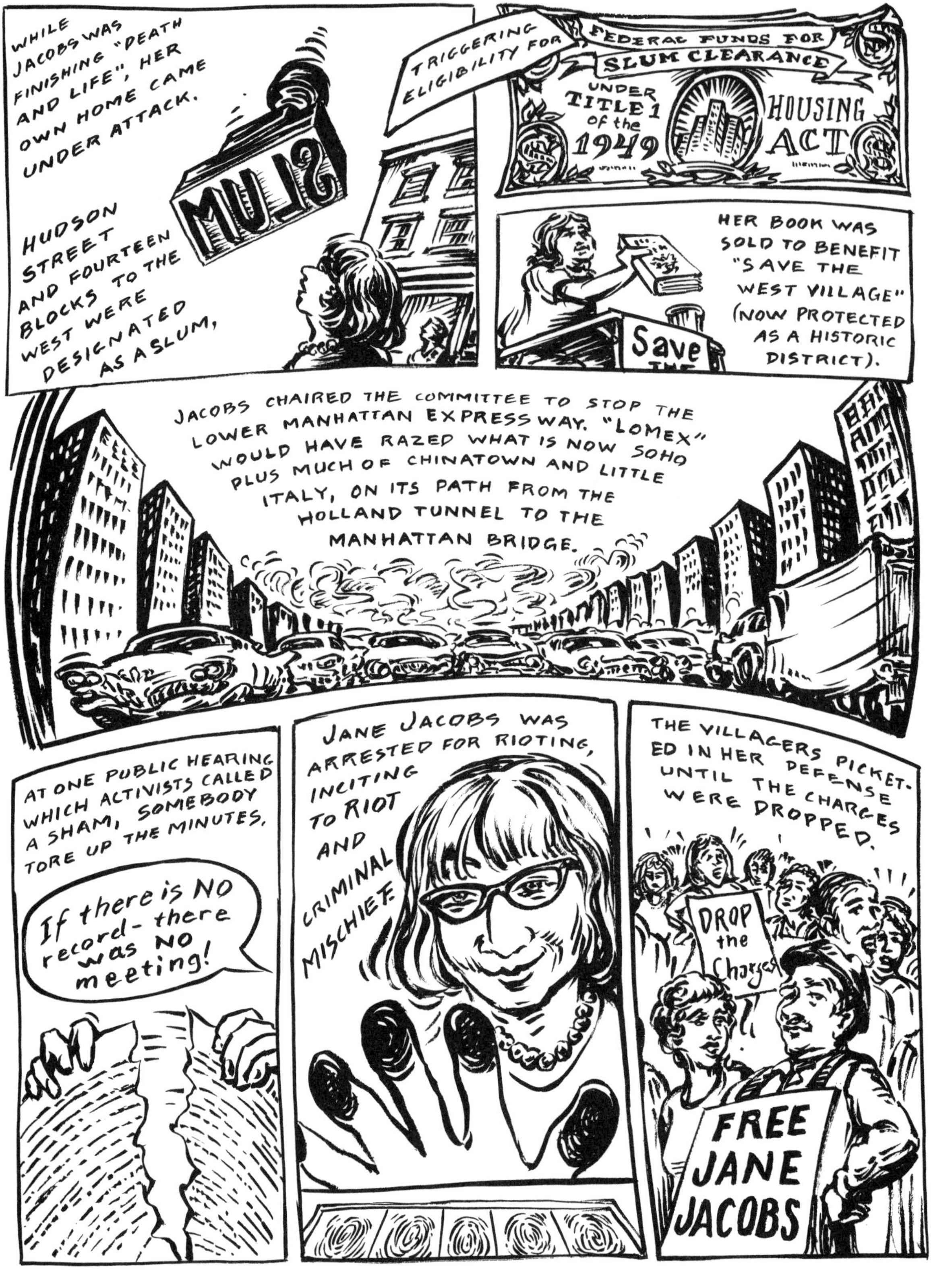
WHILE JACOBS WAS FINISHING "DEATH AND LIFE", HER OWN HOME CAME UNDER ATTACK.
SLUM
HUDSON STREET AND FOURTEEN BLOCKS TO THE WEST WERE DESIGNATED AS A SLUM,
TRIGGERING ELIGIBILITY FOR
FEDERAL FUNDS FOR
SLUM CLEARANCE
UNDER TITLE 1 of the 1949 HOUSING ACT
HER BOOK WAS SOLD TO BENEFIT "SAVE THE WEST VILLAGE" (NOW PROTECTED AS A HISTORIC DISTRICT).
Save
JACOBS CHAIRED THE COMMITTEE TO STOP THE LOWER MANHATTAN EXPRESSWAY. "LOMEX" WOULD HAVE RAZED WHAT IS NOW SOHO PLUS MUCH OF CHINATOWN AND LITTLE ITALY, ON ITS PATH FROM THE HOLLAND TUNNEL TO THE MANHATTAN BRIDGE.
AT ONE PUBLIC HEARING WHICH ACTIVISTS CALLED A SHAM, SOMEBODY TORE UP THE MINUTES.
If there is NO record- there was NO meeting!
JANE JACOBS WAS ARRESTED FOR RIOTING, INCITING TO RIOT AND CRIMINAL MISCHIEF.
THE VILLAGERS PICKETED IN HER DEFENSE UNTIL THE CHARGES WERE DROPPED.
DROP the Charges
FREE JANE JACOBS

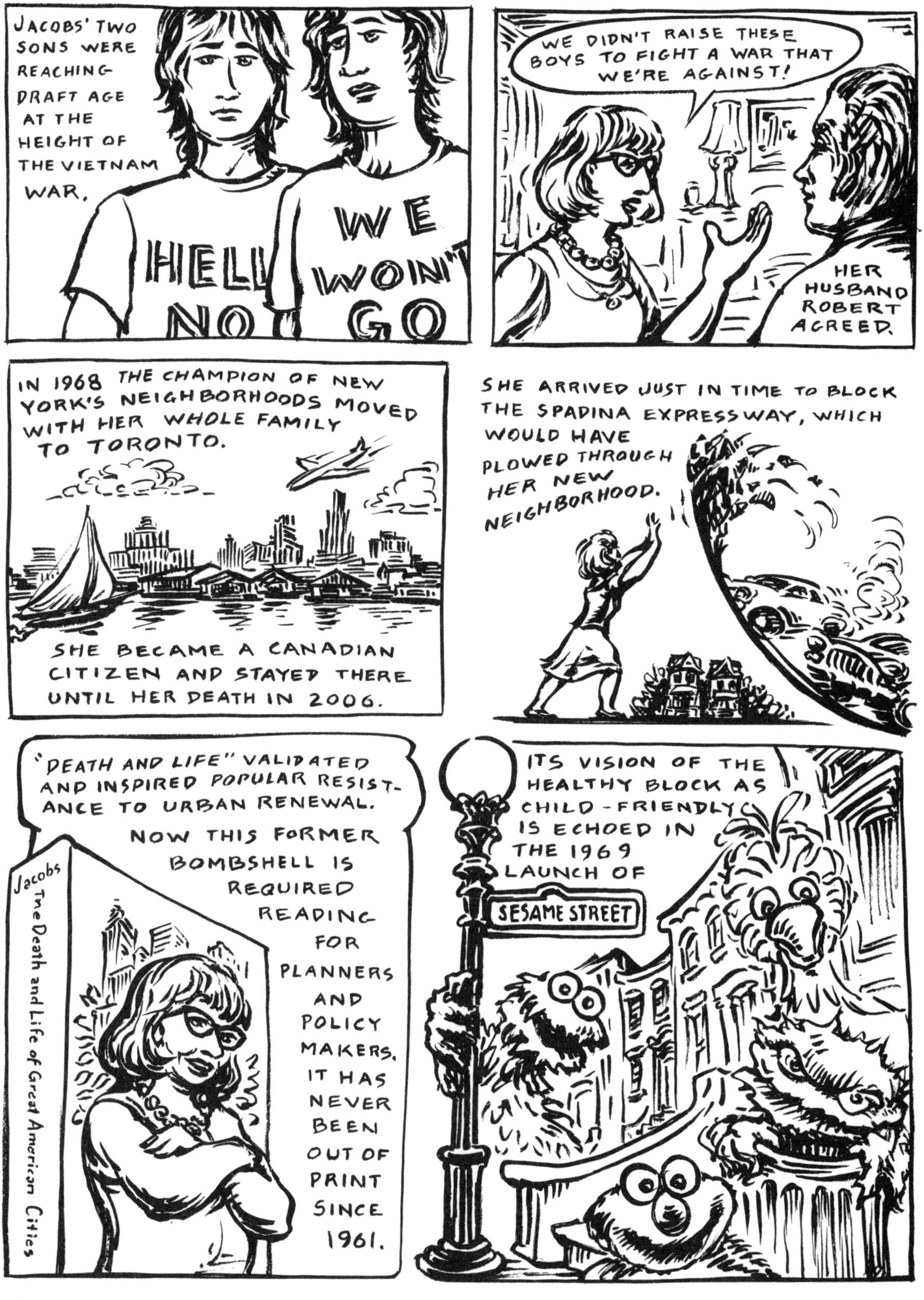
JACOBS' TWO SONS WERE REACHING DRAFT AGE AT THE HEIGHT OF THE VIETNAM WAR.
HELL NO
WE WON'T GO
WE DIDN'T RAISE THESE BOYS TO FIGHT A WAR THAT WE'RE AGAINST!
HER HUSBAND ROBERT AGREED.
IN 1968 THE CHAMPION OF NEW YORK'S NEIGHBORHOODS MOVED WITH HER WHOLE FAMILY TO TORONTO.
SHE BECAME A CANADIAN CITIZEN AND STAYED THERE UNTIL HER DEATH IN 2006.
SHE ARRIVED JUST IN TIME TO BLOCK THE SPADINA EXPRESSWAY, WHICH WOULD HAVE PLOWED THROUGH HER NEW NEIGHBORHOOD.
"DEATH AND LIFE" VALIDATED AND INSPIRED POPULAR RESISTANCE TO URBAN RENEWAL.
NOW THIS FORMER BOMBSHELL IS REQUIRED READING FOR PLANNERS AND POLICY MAKERS. IT HAS NEVER BEEN OUT OF PRINT SINCE 1961.
Jacobs
The Death and Life of Great American Cities
ITS VISION OF THE HEALTHY BLOCK AS CHILD-FRIENDLY IS ECHOED IN THE 1969 LAUNCH OF
SESAME STREET

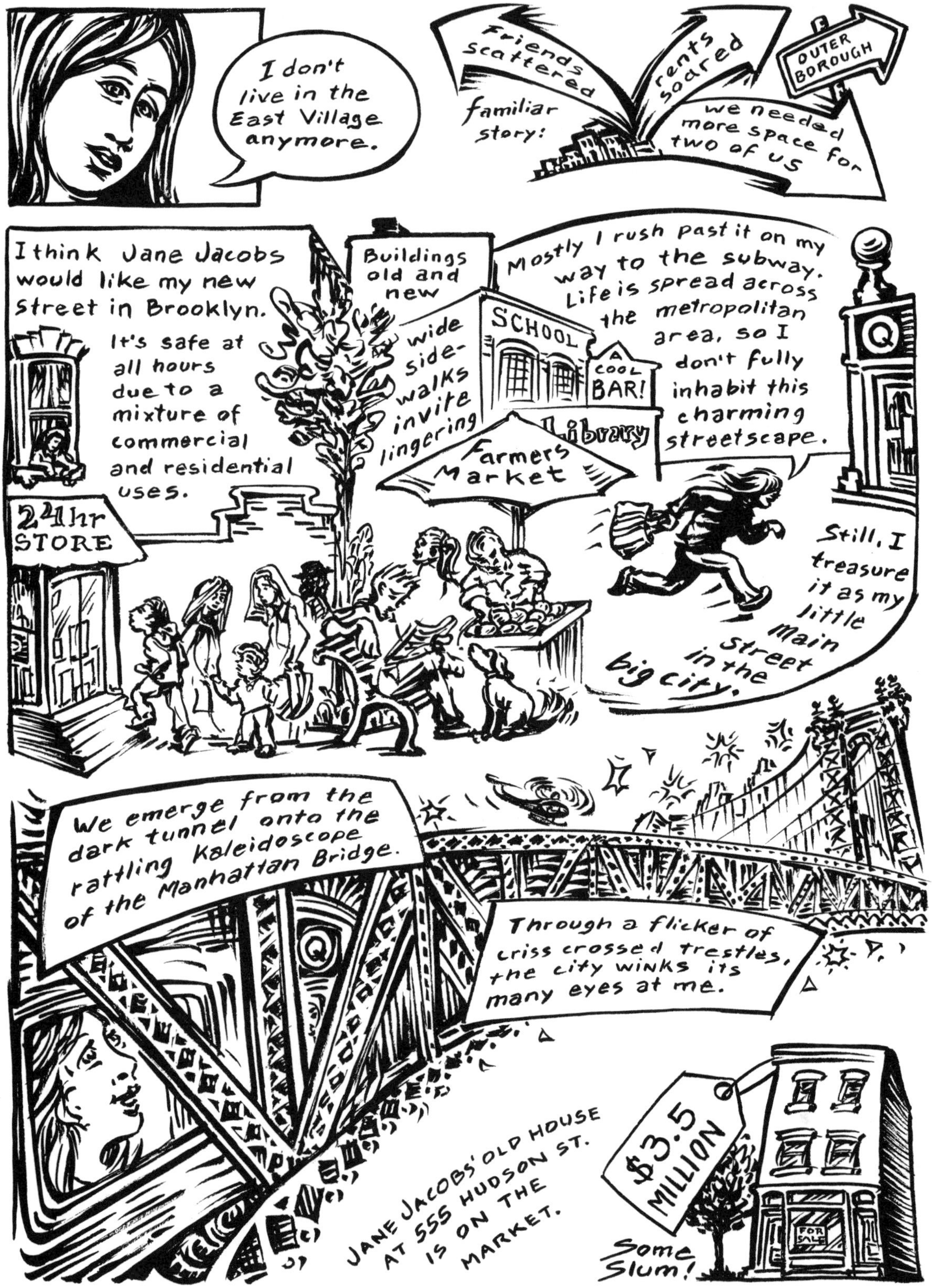

I don't live in the East Village anymore.
familiar story:
Friends scattered
rents soared
OUTER BOROUGH
we needed more space for two of us
I think Jane Jacobs would like my new street in Brooklyn.
It's safe at all hours due to a mixture of commercial and residential uses.
Buildings old and new
wide side-walks invite lingering
SCHOOL
A COOL BAR!
Library
Farmers Market
24hr STORE
Mostly I rush past it on my way to the subway. Life is spread across the metropolitan area, so I don't fully inhabit this charming streetscape.
Q
Still, I treasure it as my little main street in the big city.
We emerge from the dark tunnel onto the rattling kaleidoscope of the Manhattan Bridge.
Q
Through a flicker of criss crossed trestles, the city winks its many eyes at me.
JANE JACOBS' OLD HOUSE AT 555 HUDSON ST. IS ON THE MARKET.
$3.5 MILLION
FOR SALE
Some Slum!

JORDAN W. LINT TO THE AGE 65.

CUT

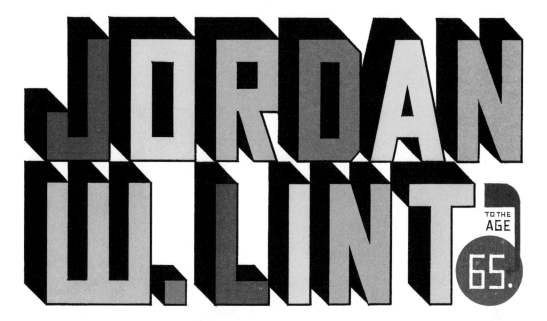

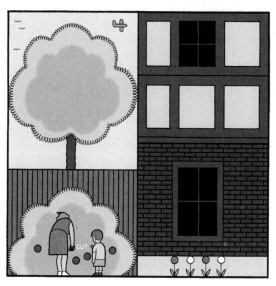

Born: June 27th, 1958, Omaha, Nebraska.

Feared: father.
Most cherished memory of birth mother: picking peonies at northwest corner of house; ants present. Age: five (?)
Disliked: stepmother, father, schoolteachers.
Best friend in grade school: Brett Hornslach (1959 — 1976).
Held back one year in grade school because of: poor academic performance, behavioral problems.
First day capable of sexual reproduction: March 1st, 1971.

College education: 1977 — 1981, The University of Nebraska at Lincoln; BA, Business Management; Lambda Delta Lambda.
Attempted success in the popular music recording industry: Los Angeles, California, 1981 — 1984.
Employed by Lint, Inc.: Omaha, Nebraska, 1984 — 2010.

First Wife: Leslie (1960 —).
Child: Zachary (1988 —).
Stepdaughter: Maria (1987 —).
Grandchild: Javier (2013 —).

Child: Gabriel (1991 —).

Second Wife: Elizabeth Delilah (1974 —).
Stepchild: Olivia (1999 —).
Child: Levi (2016 —).

Father: Richard James Lint (1932 — 2002).
Mother: Mary Elizabeth Narbush (1934 — 1964).
Stepmother: Janet Alpauws (1937 — 2004).

First 13 years of life available in: *The Book of Other People*, Zadie Smith, editor; 2007.

Ages 14 — present: *The Virginia Quarterly Review*, Winter 2007 — present.

Your cartoonist: C. Ware, born December 28th, 1967.

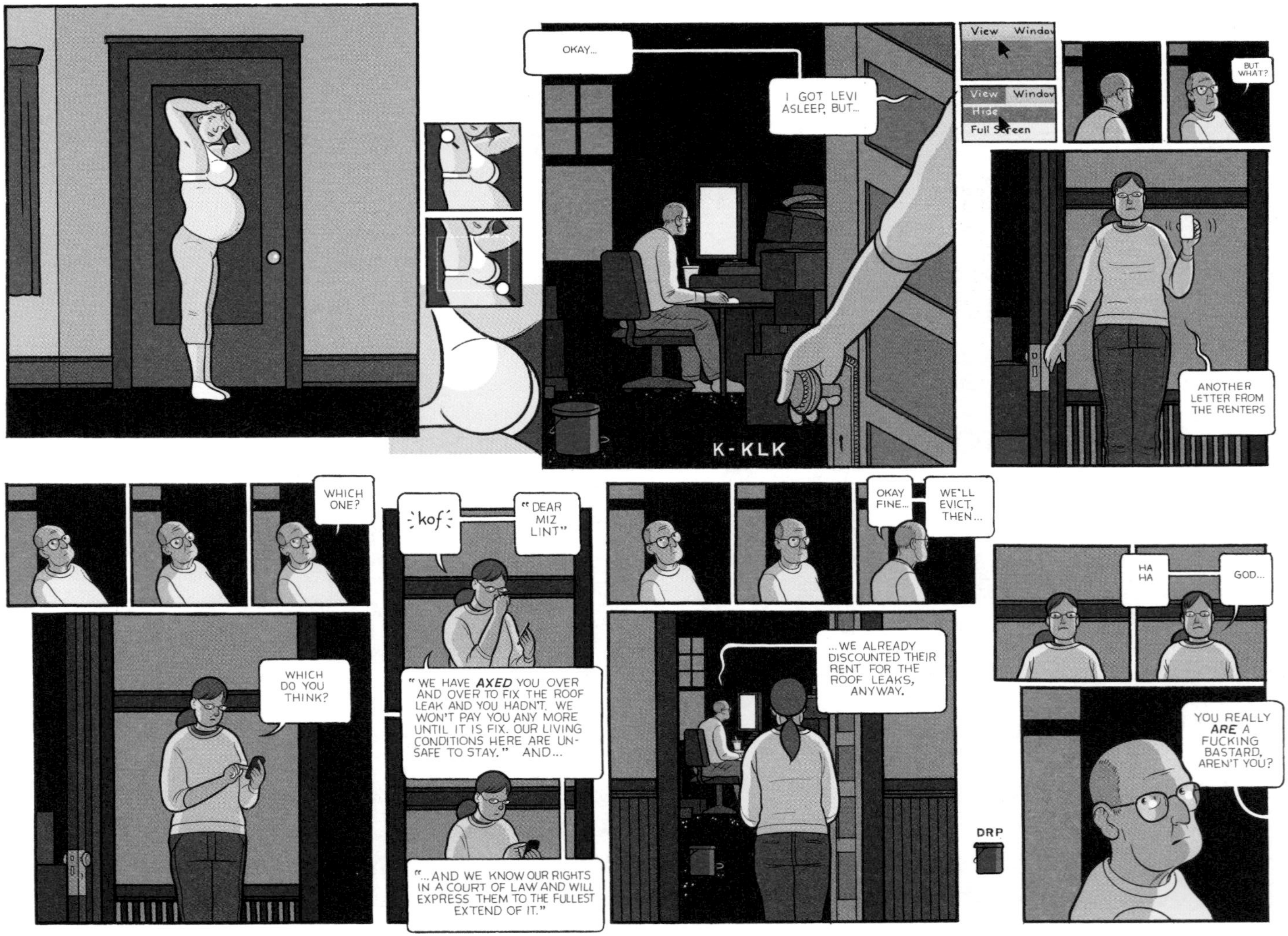
OKAY...
I GOT LEVI ASLEEP, BUT...
K-KLK
View Windo
View Windo
Hide
Full Screen
BUT WHAT?
ANOTHER LETTER FROM THE RENTERS
WHICH ONE?
WHICH DO YOU THINK?
kof
"DEAR MIZ LINT"
"WE HAVE **AXED** YOU OVER AND OVER TO FIX THE ROOF LEAK AND YOU HADN'T. WE WON'T PAY YOU ANY MORE UNTIL IT IS FIX. OUR LIVING CONDITIONS HERE ARE UN-SAFE TO STAY." AND...
"...AND WE KNOW OUR RIGHTS IN A COURT OF LAW AND WILL EXPRESS THEM TO THE FULLEST EXTEND OF IT."
OKAY FINE...
WE'LL EVICT, THEN...
...WE ALREADY DISCOUNTED THEIR RENT FOR THE ROOF LEAKS, ANYWAY.
DRP
HA HA
GOD...
YOU REALLY **ARE** A FUCKING BASTARD, AREN'T YOU?

Google

gabriel lint

Google search | I'm feeling lucky

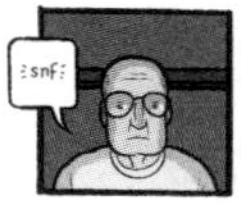
:snf:

Results **1 - 10** of **271,321** for **gabriel lint**. (0.0004 sec)

Author Feels Your...
Grueling memoir of life told...
cached - similar

Omaha's Bestselling...
Writer tells grisly tale of...
cached - similar

Show more results in NEWS

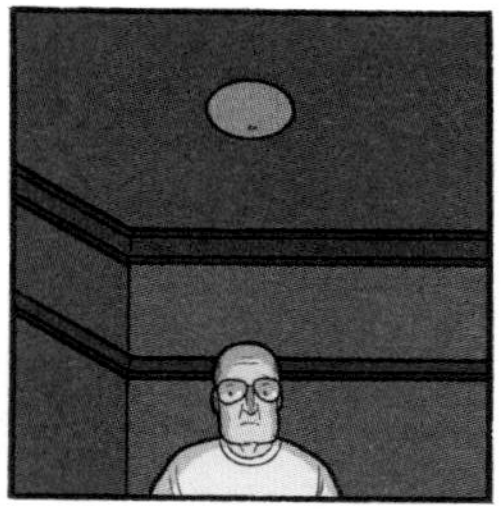

Author Feels Your Pain — and His, Too

New York Times - 59 minutes ago

Young memoirist turns a revealing experimental novel of abusive upbringing and self-destructive loneliness into an inspiring literary achievement.

Don't Sweep This Lint Away Washington Post

Bestseller Highlights Role of Parenting FamilyNews

Reuters - Examiner.com - XinHua - CBS2 - Facebook

all 38 news articles >> **email this story**

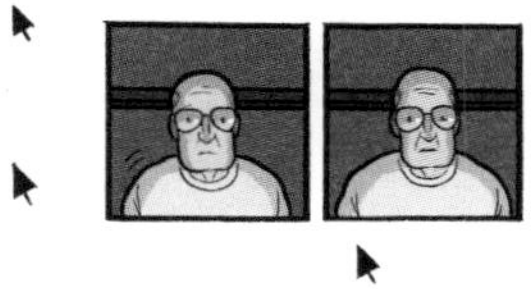

Feelings, Not Words, Tell the Whole Story

By **AGNES KONIGSBERG**

Published November 29, 2019

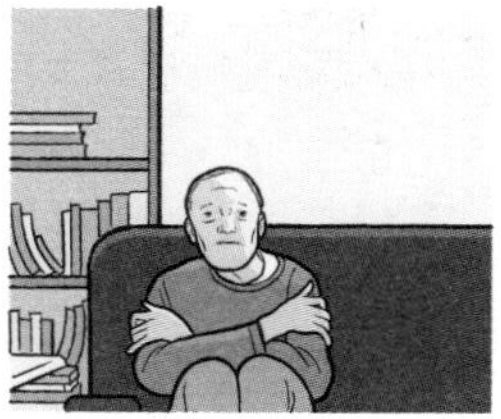

Gabriel Lint

I LOVED YOU
By Gabriel Lint
580 pages. Strathmore Press.
$29 eBook/$59 Paper.

☐ RECOMMEND
☐ TWITTER
☐ MAIL
☐ SEND TO PHONE
☐ PRINT
☐ SHARE

"I've always been a quiet person," says Gabriel Lint, almost inaudibly. "I guess it makes sense that I'm most comfortable in books, or on paper."

Comfortable is hardly a word one would use to describe the slight, headshy 28-year-old, whose bestselling memoir, "I Loved You," has sent him into the spotlight with universally favorable reviews and talk of shortlisting for both the National Book Award and the PEN First Lit prize. "I don't know what to think of it all," says Lint, with a quavering laugh.

Laugh? One might hope to, somewhere, in the midst of this young author's book, but its pages are unrelieved from scenes – or one should really say sensations – of self-laceration, multiple suicide attempts and parental abuse, all rendered in a sometimes disorienting but amazingly discernable language of impressions, phonemes and short bursts of text. One critic has called it "synæsthetic," likening it to Joyce's "revolutionary prose, but in [Mr. Lint's] case one feels as if he's systematically replacing one's memories and feelings with his own." Mr. Lint says more simply, "I guess I just want the reader to feel the things that I did."

Born in Omaha, Nebraska, and raised both there and in Denver, Colorado, Mr. Lint says he always felt out of step with his family and his surroundings. "Back then, especially in the midwest, homosexuality wasn't always something you could discuss. People forget that now. And having deeply religious parents didn't help." Suddenly, his voice fills the Bushwick apartment he's kept since 2017: "I mean, I've forgiven my first Dad. But I don't know why I should." A harrowing account of a broken collarbone opens the book but it's the scene from which the memoir takes its title that has garnered Lint the most glowing praise.

"Early in the story I wanted to depict what it felt like to be in a body that was already losing its will to live, and how an alcoholic personality feeds on that desperation," he says, adding, "particularly since I knew later I'd be depicting my own body as it was losing life itself." Such statements are common for Mr. Lint, who at age 17 left home to live in various Denver squats. He took drugs and played in bands. At the same time he was reading voraciously and keeping a journal. "It was stupid of me, I guess. I was eating out of dumpsters, but I couldn't stop reading and at the same time writing down all of these awful things that'd happened to me."

1 | 2 | 3 NEXT PAGE

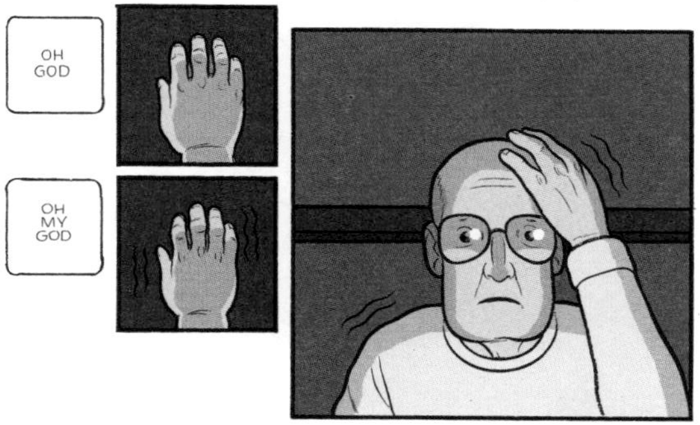
OH GOD
OH MY GOD

BUY "I Loved You" from amazon.com
JOIN "I Loved You" discussion group
READ excerpt of "I Loved You"

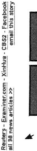

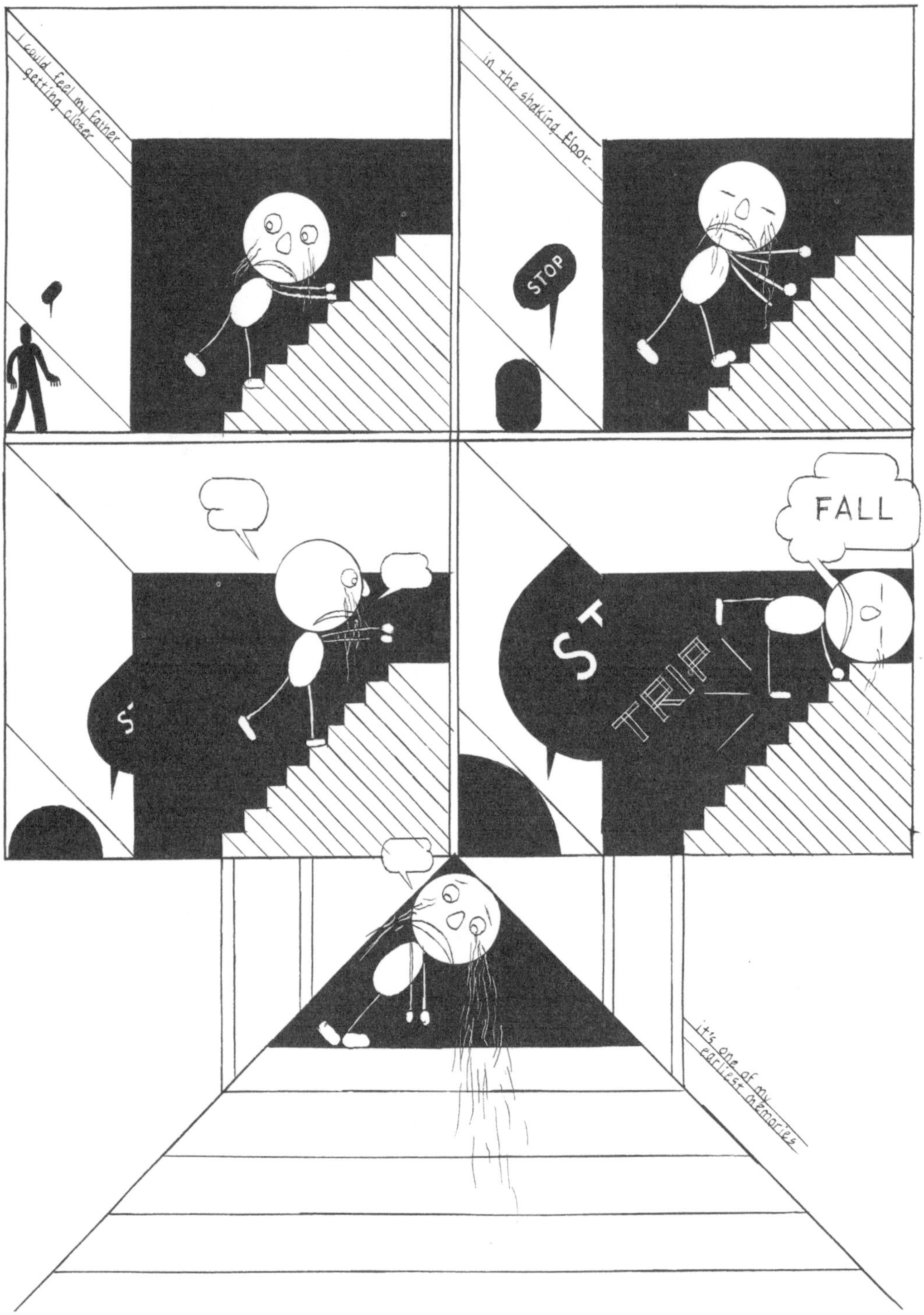
I could feel my father getting closer
in the shaking floor
STOP
S
ST
TRIP
FALL
it's one of my earliest memories

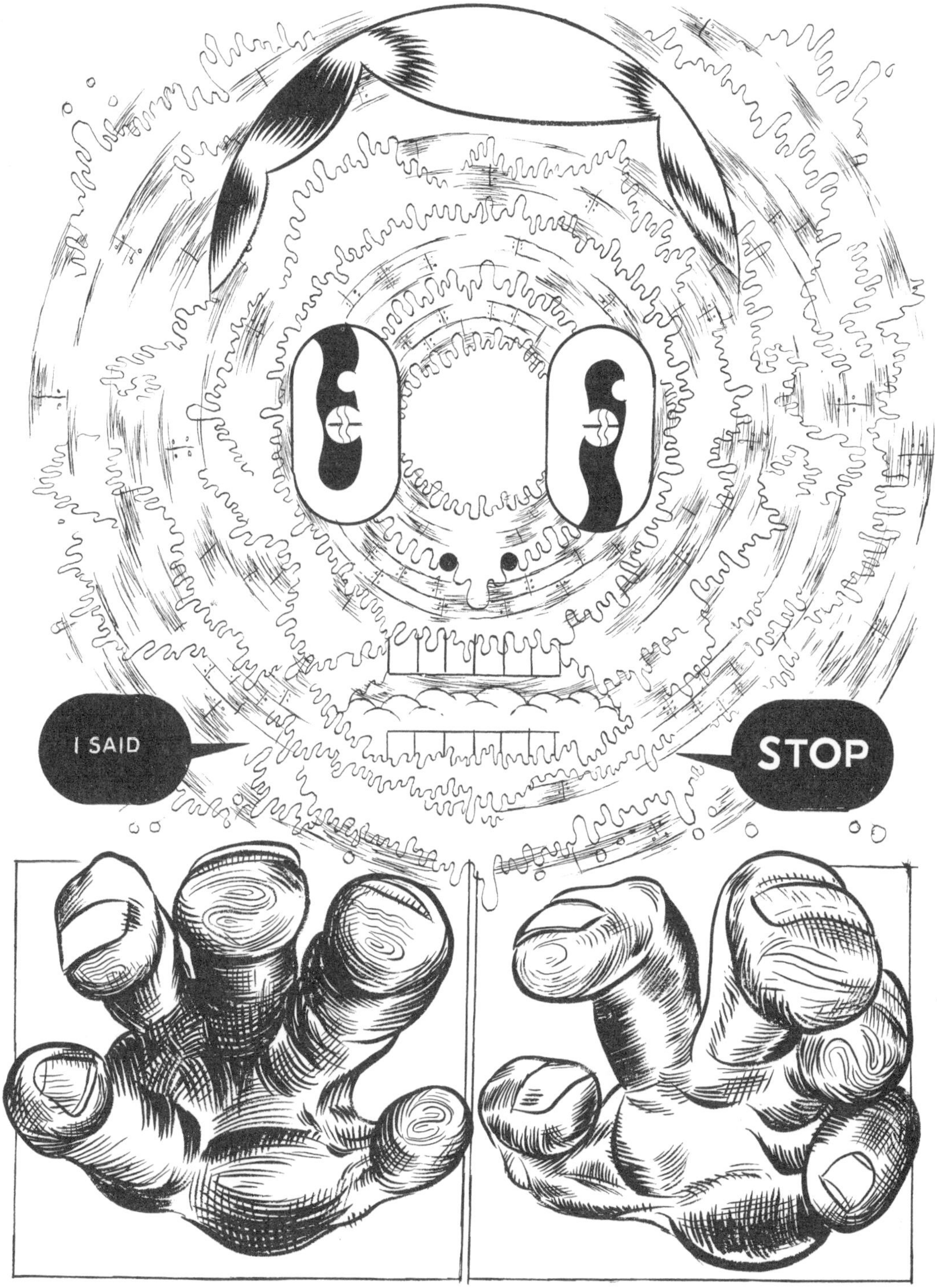
I SAID
STOP

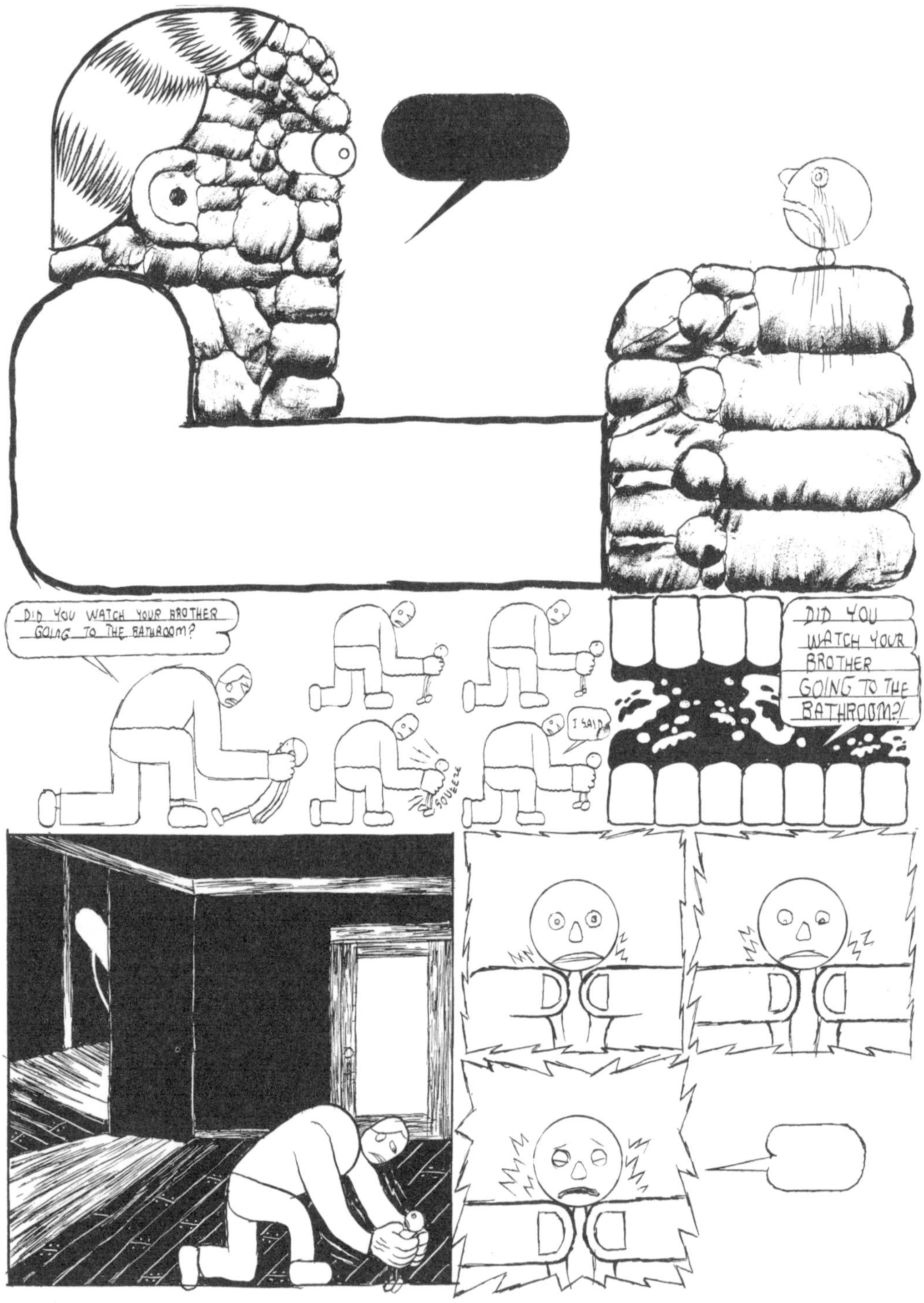
DID YOU WATCH YOUR BROTHER GOING TO THE BATHROOM?
I SAID
SQUEEZE
DID YOU WATCH YOUR BROTHER GOING TO THE BATHROOM?!

It was 1996. Summer, 1996.

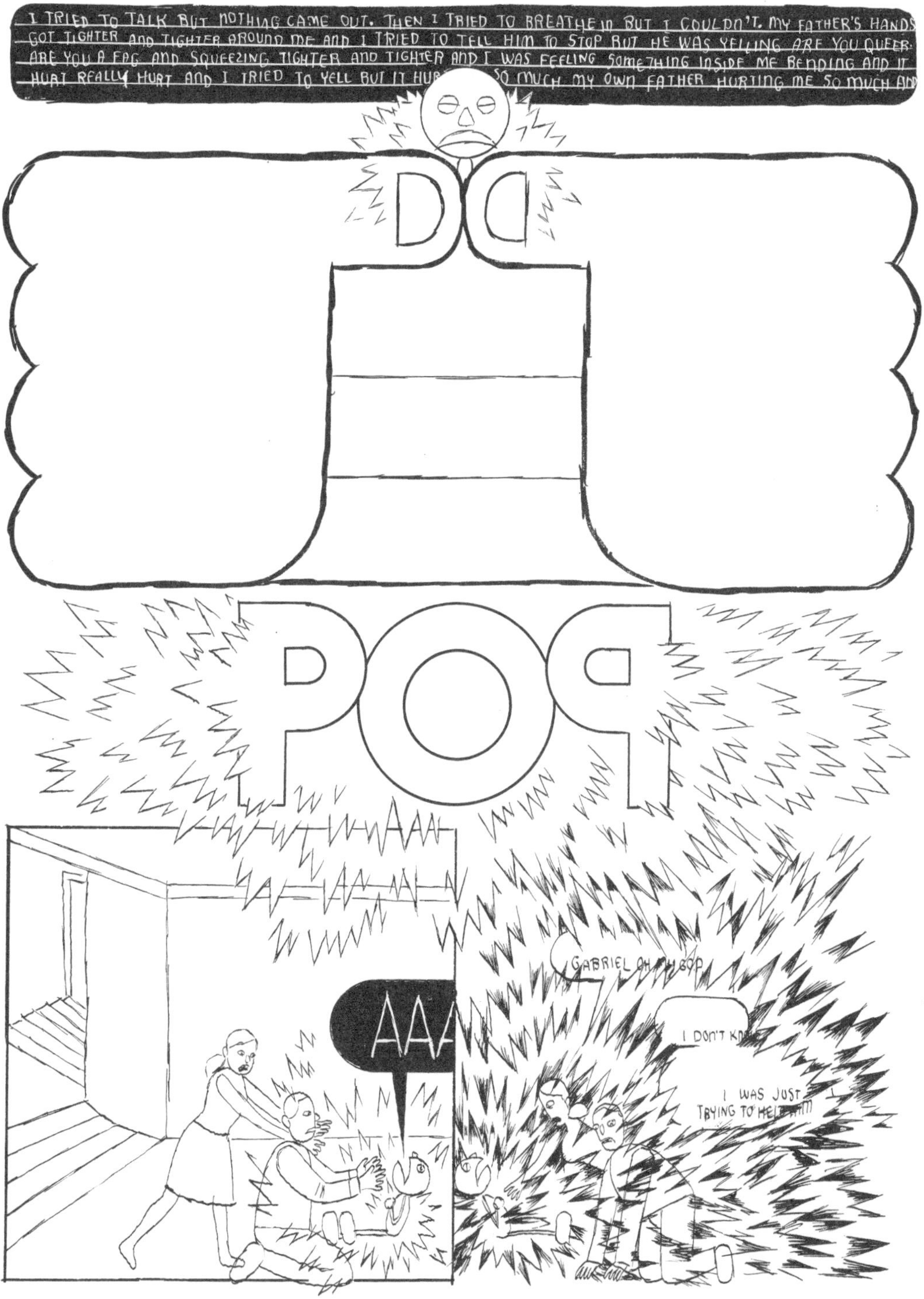
I TRIED TO TALK BUT NOTHING CAME OUT. THEN I TRIED TO BREATHE IN BUT I COULDN'T. MY FATHER'S HANDS GOT TIGHTER AND TIGHTER AROUND ME AND I TRIED TO TELL HIM TO STOP BUT HE WAS YELLING ARE YOU QUEER. ARE YOU A FAG AND SQUEEZING TIGHTER AND TIGHTER AND I WAS FEELING SOMETHING INSIDE ME BENDING AND IT HURT REALLY HURT AND I TRIED TO YELL BUT IT
SO MUCH MY OWN FATHER HURTING ME SO MUCH AND
POP
AAA
GABRIEL OH
I DON'T
I WAS JUST TRYING TO

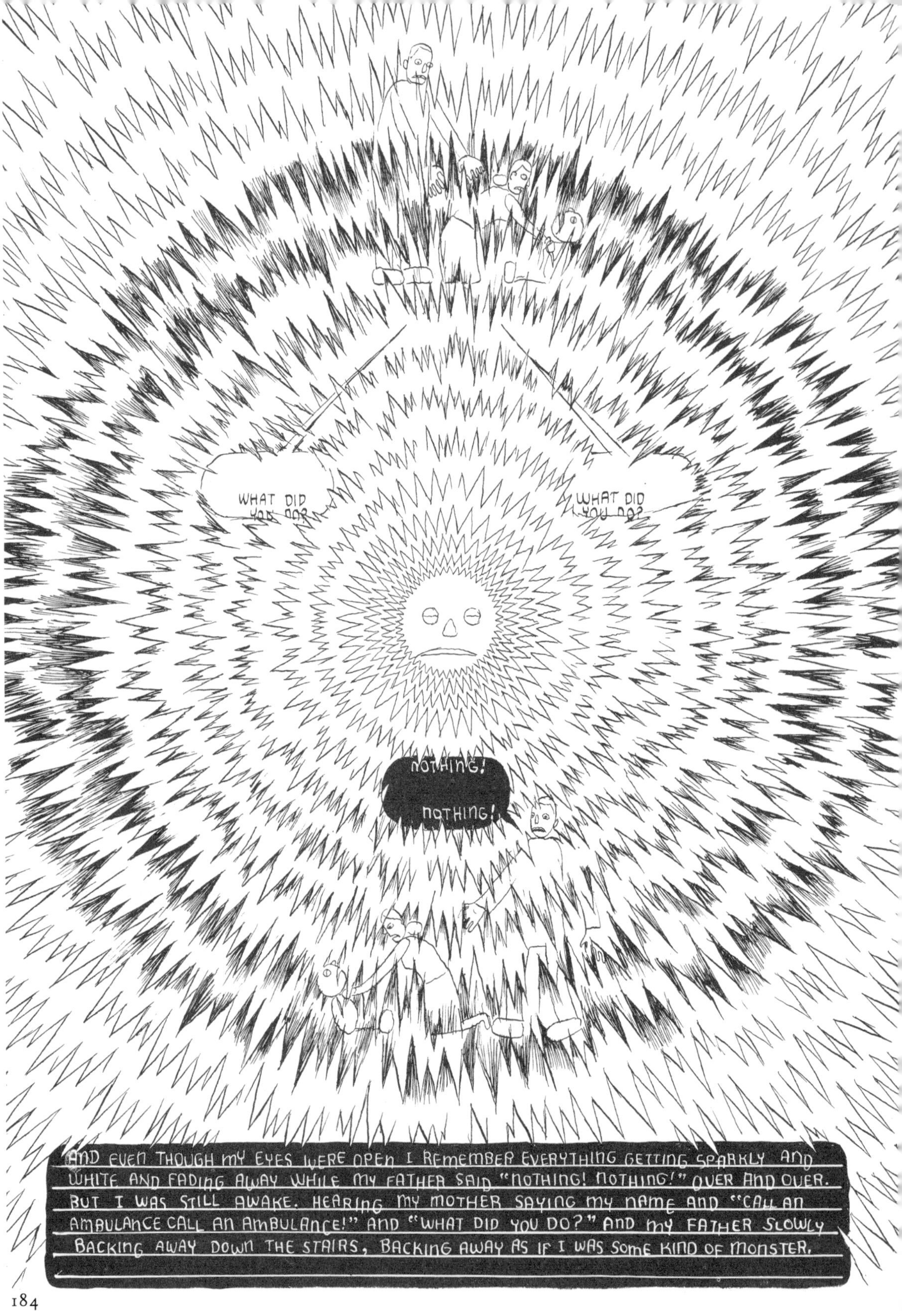
WHAT DID YOU DO?
WHAT DID YOU DO?
NOTHING! NOTHING!
AND EVEN THOUGH MY EYES WERE OPEN I REMEMBER EVERYTHING GETTING SPARKLY AND WHITE AND FADING AWAY WHILE MY FATHER SAID "NOTHING! NOTHING!" OVER AND OVER. BUT I WAS STILL AWAKE. HEARING MY MOTHER SAYING MY NAME AND "CALL AN AMBULANCE CALL AN AMBULANCE!" AND "WHAT DID YOU DO?" AND MY FATHER SLOWLY BACKING AWAY DOWN THE STAIRS, BACKING AWAY AS IF I WAS SOME KIND OF MONSTER.

t did you do?" and
y down the stairs,
kind of monster.
t did you do?" and
y down the stairs,
kind of monster.
POPPA?
POPPA
POPPA WHERE'S MOMMA?
WHERE'S MOMMA, POPPA?

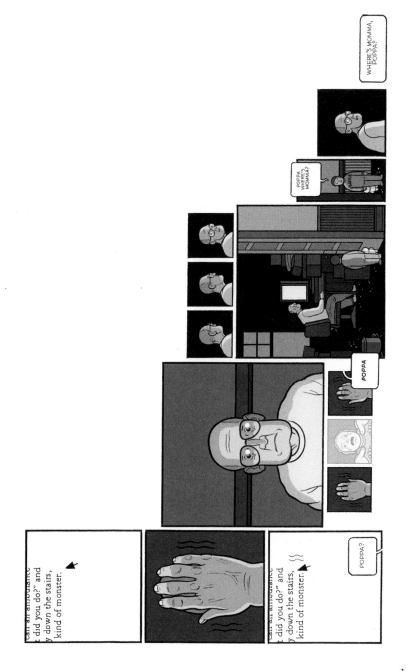

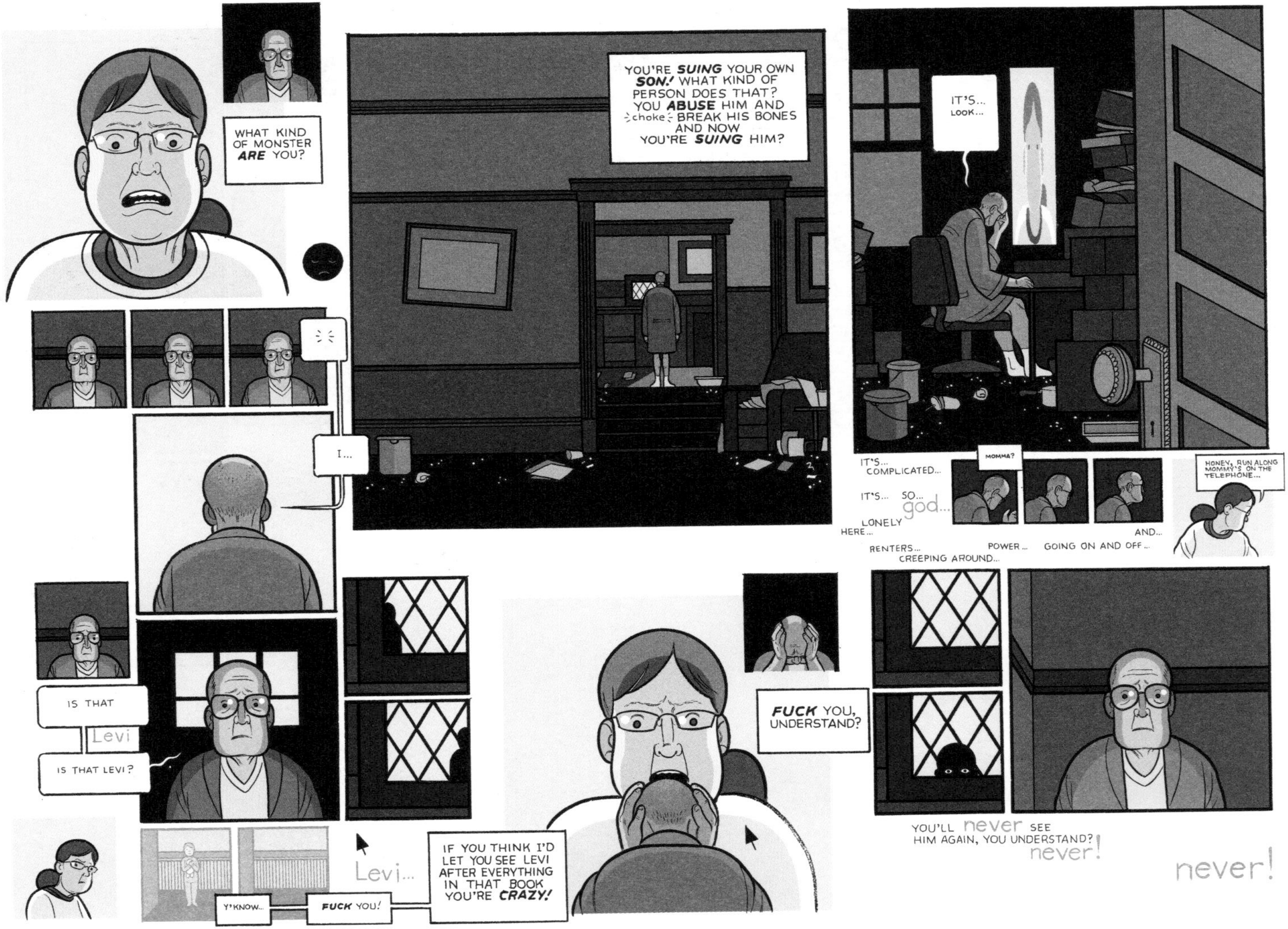
WHAT KIND OF MONSTER ARE YOU?
YOU'RE SUING YOUR OWN SON! WHAT KIND OF PERSON DOES THAT? YOU ABUSE HIM AND choke BREAK HIS BONES AND NOW YOU'RE SUING HIM?
IT'S... LOOK...
I...
IT'S... COMPLICATED...
IT'S... SO... god...
LONELY HERE...
MOMMA?
HONEY, RUN ALONG MOMMY'S ON THE TELEPHONE...
RENTERS... CREEPING AROUND...
POWER...
GOING ON AND OFF...
AND...
IS THAT
Levi
IS THAT LEVI?
Levi...
Y'KNOW...
FUCK YOU!
IF YOU THINK I'D LET YOU SEE LEVI AFTER EVERYTHING IN THAT BOOK YOU'RE CRAZY!
FUCK YOU, UNDERSTAND?
YOU'LL never SEE HIM AGAIN, YOU UNDERSTAND?
never!
never!

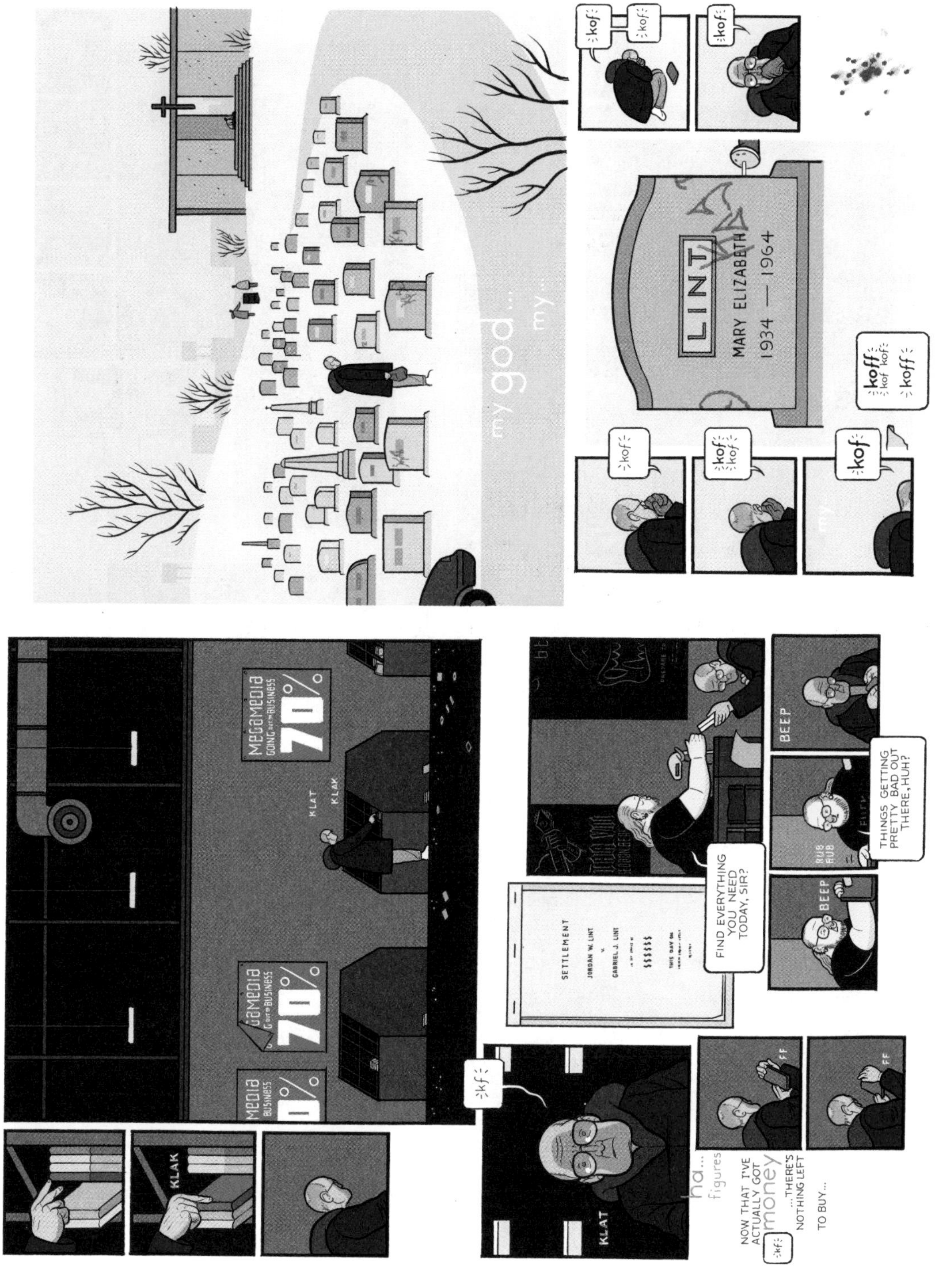
KLAK
MegaMedia GOING OUT OF BUSINESS 70%
KLAT
KLAK
MegaMedia GOING OUT OF BUSINESS 70%
Media BUSINESS
kf
KLAT
ha... figures
kf
NOW THAT I'VE ACTUALLY GOT money
...THERE'S NOTHING LEFT
TO BUY...
FF
FF
SETTLEMENT
JORDAN W. LINT
v.
GABRIEL J. LINT
$$$$$
FIND EVERYTHING YOU NEED TODAY, SIR?
BEEP
RUB RUB
THINGS GETTING PRETTY BAD OUT THERE, HUH?
BEEP
my god... my...
kof
kof kof
my
kof
LINT
MARY ELIZABETH
1934 — 1964
koff kof kof koff
kof
kof
kof

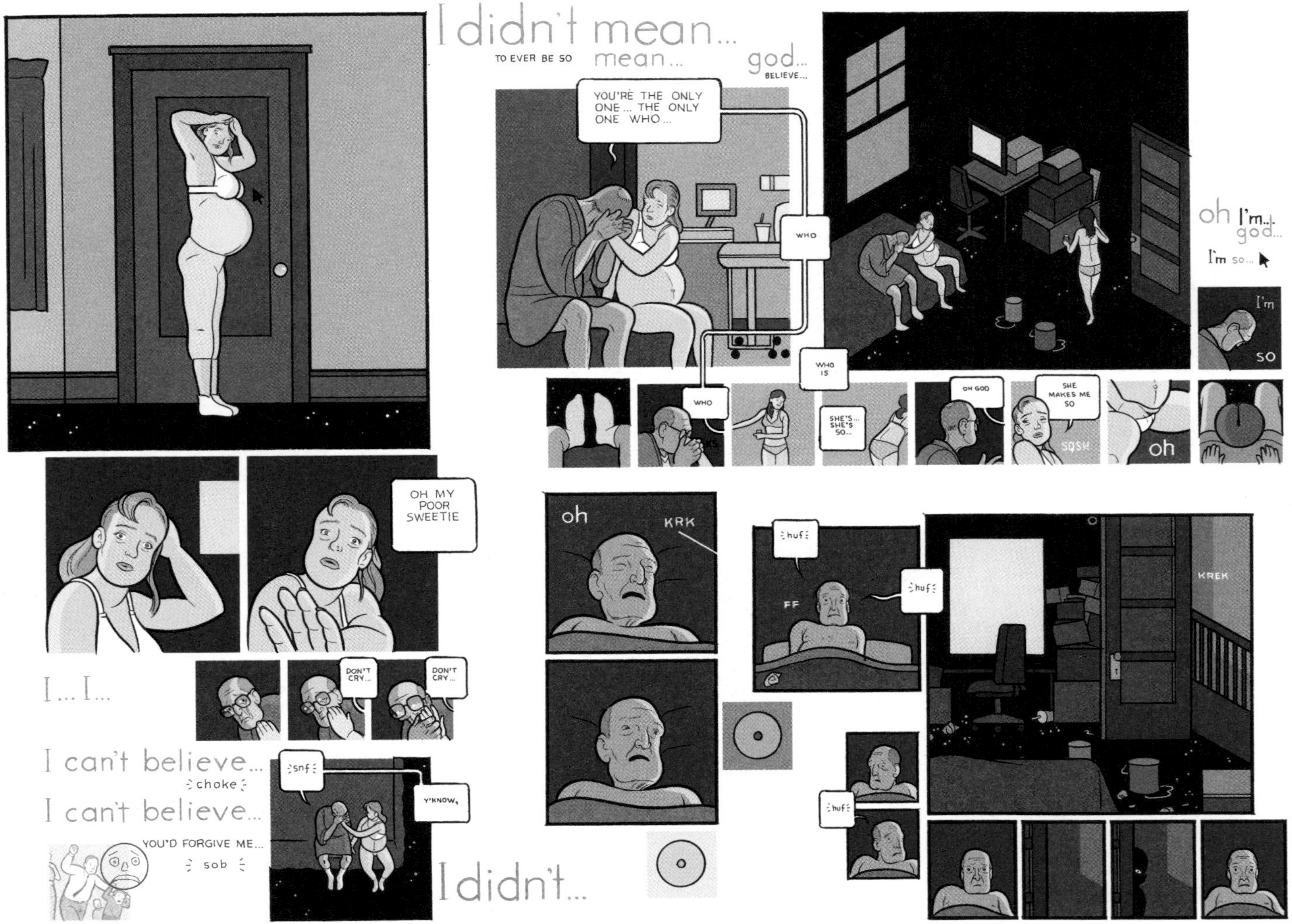
I didn't mean...
TO EVER BE SO
mean...
god...
BELIEVE...
YOU'RE THE ONLY ONE ... THE ONLY ONE WHO ...
WHO
WHO IS
WHO
oh I'm...
god...
I'm so...
I'm
SO
SHE'S... SHE'S SO...
OH GOD
SHE MAKES ME SO
SQSH
oh
OH MY POOR SWEETIE
I... I...
DON'T CRY...
DON'T CRY...
I can't believe...
choke
I can't believe...
YOU'D FORGIVE ME...
sob
snf
Y'KNOW,
I didn't...
oh
KRK
huf
FF
huf
KREK
huf

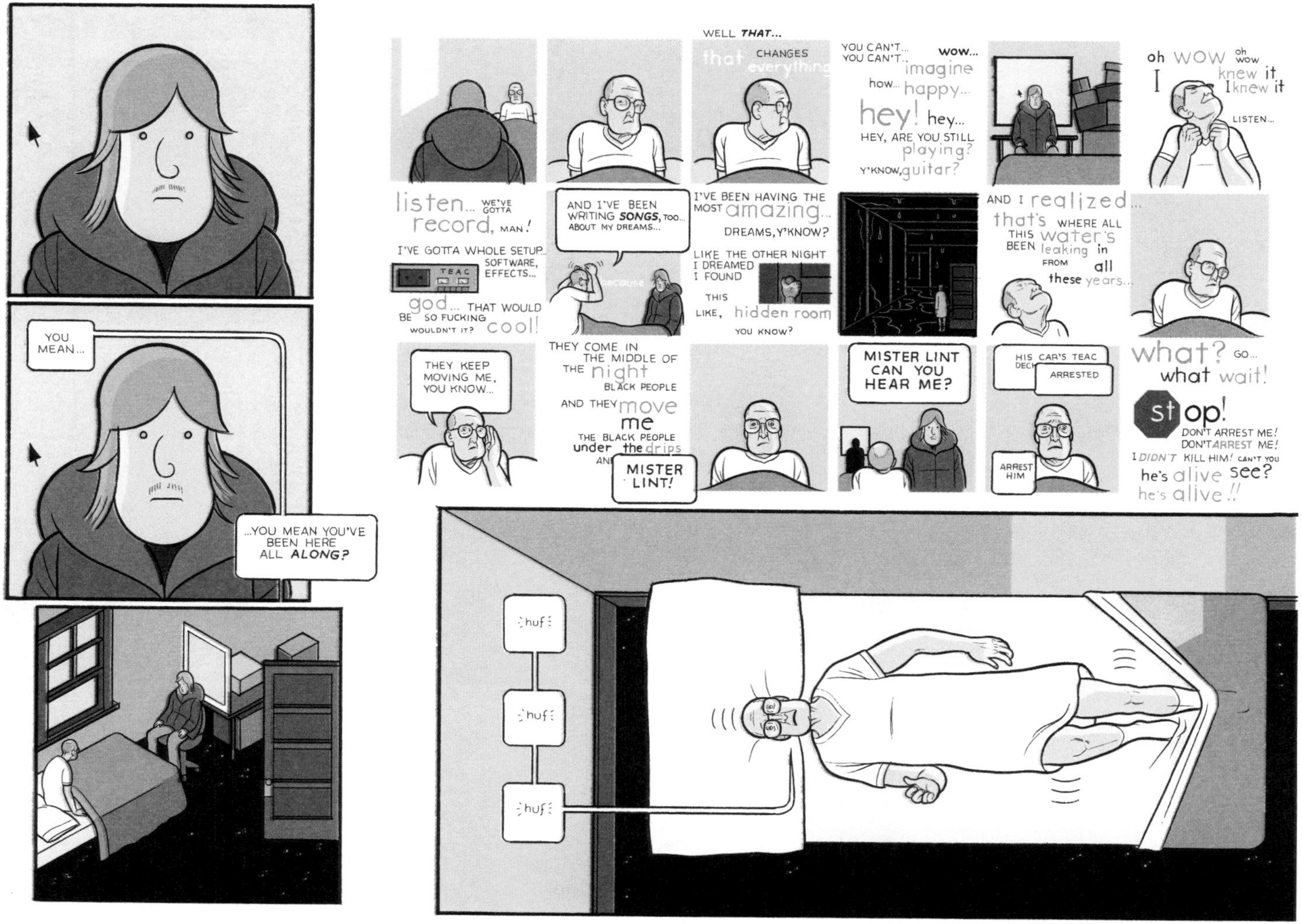
YOU MEAN...
...YOU MEAN YOU'VE BEEN HERE ALL ALONG?
WELL THAT...
that CHANGES everything
YOU CAN'T... YOU CAN'T... imagine how... happy... WOW...
hey! hey...
HEY, ARE YOU STILL playing? Y'KNOW, guitar?
oh WOW oh wow I knew it I knew it
LISTEN...
listen... WE'VE GOTTA record, MAN!
I'VE GOTTA WHOLE SETUP... SOFTWARE, EFFECTS...
TEAC
god... THAT WOULD BE SO FUCKING cool! WOULDN'T IT?
AND I'VE BEEN WRITING SONGS, TOO... ABOUT MY DREAMS...
I'VE BEEN HAVING THE MOST amazing... DREAMS, Y'KNOW?
LIKE THE OTHER NIGHT I DREAMED I FOUND THIS LIKE, hidden room YOU KNOW?
AND I realized... that's WHERE ALL THIS water's BEEN leaking in FROM all these years...
THEY KEEP MOVING ME, YOU KNOW...
THEY COME IN THE MIDDLE OF THE night BLACK PEOPLE AND THEY move me THE BLACK PEOPLE under the drips
MISTER LINT!
MISTER LINT CAN YOU HEAR ME?
HIS CAR'S TEAC
ARRESTED
ARREST HIM
what? GO... what wait!
stop!
DON'T ARREST ME! DON'T ARREST ME!
I DIDN'T KILL HIM! CAN'T YOU SEE? he's alive he's alive!!
huf
huf
huf

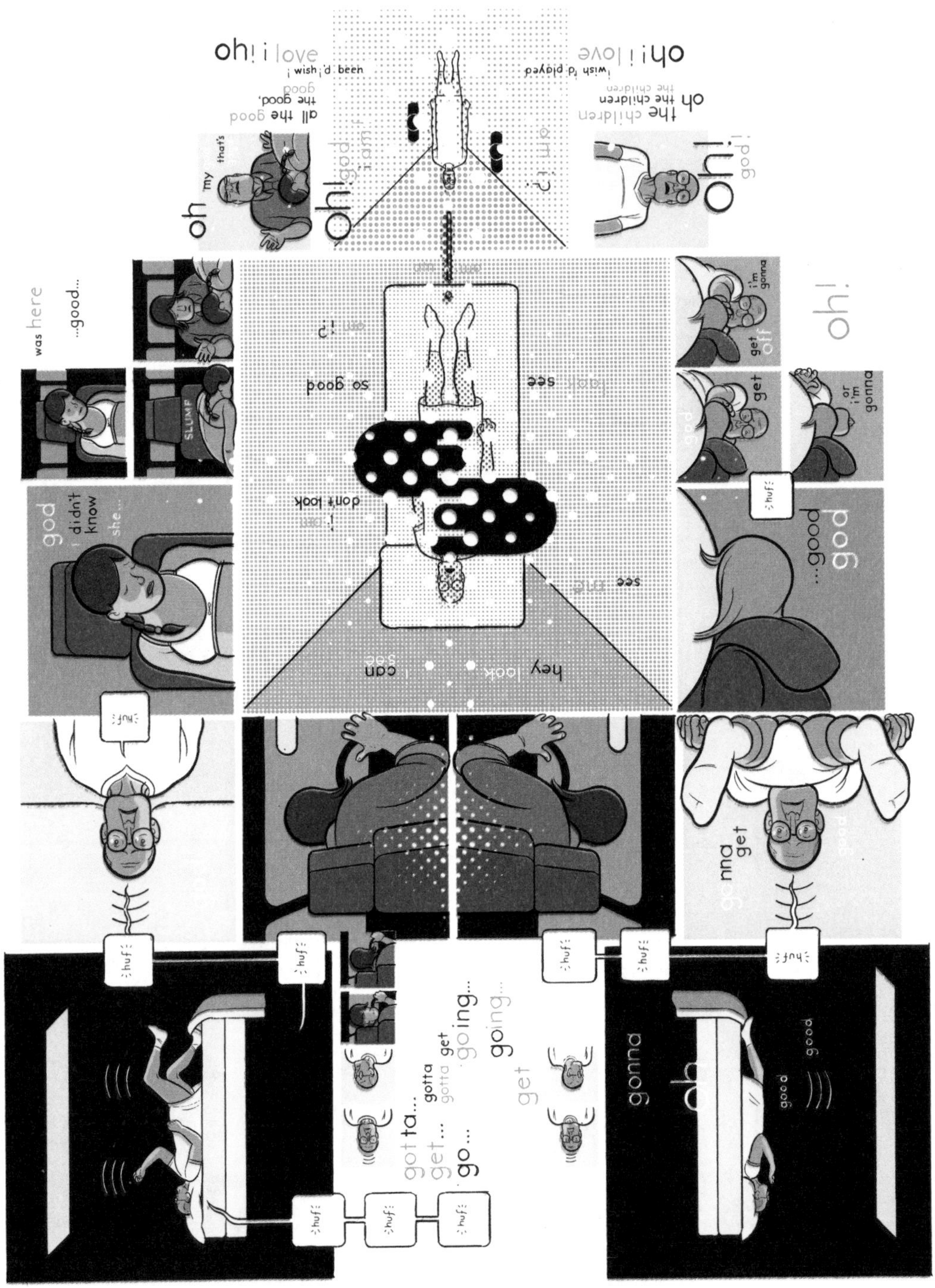
oh my that's
all the good
the good,
good
oh! i love
i wish i'd been
oh the children
the children
i wish i'd played
oh! i love
oh! god
oh! god!
was here
...good...
god
i didn't know
she...
SLUMP
huf
so good
don't look
hey look
can see
see me
oh!
i'm gonna
get off
god
get
or i'm gonna
huf
...good
god
gonna get
good
huf
huf
huf
huf
huf
got ta...
get...
go...
gotta
gotta
get
going...
going...
get
huf
huf
huf
gonna
oh
good
good
good

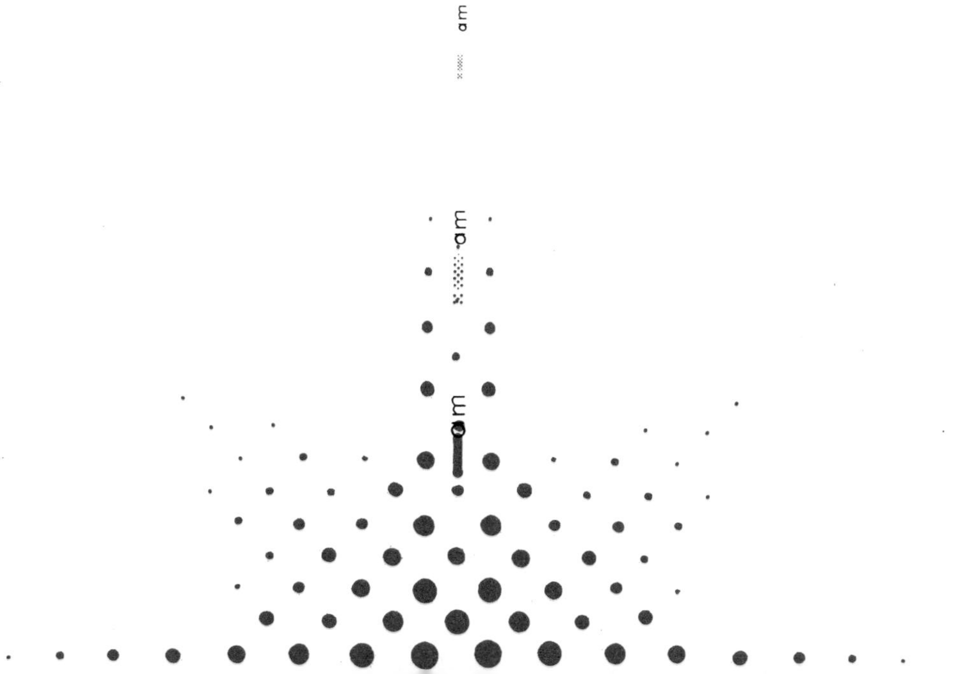
am
am
am

DOMESTIC MEN OF MYSTERY

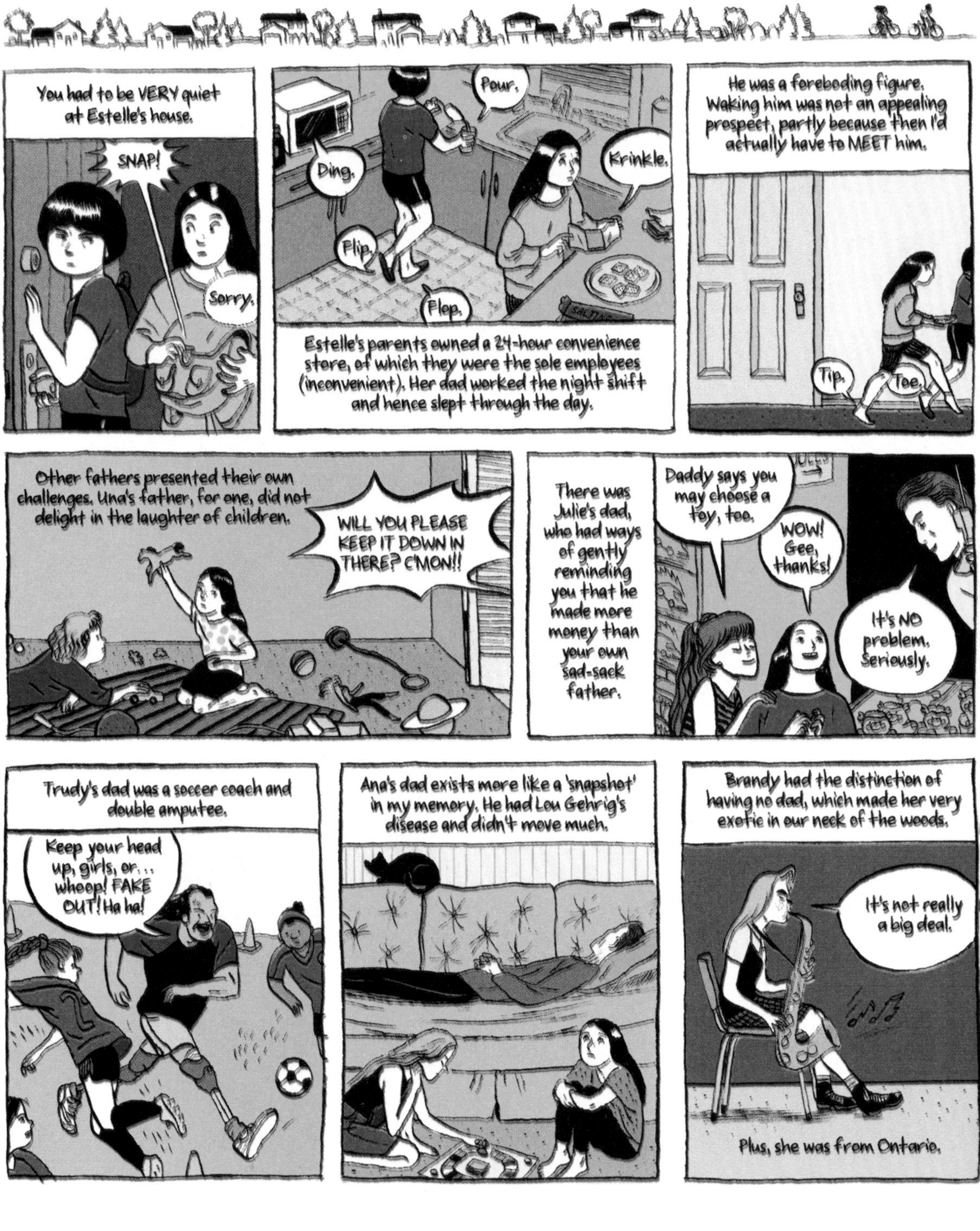

You had to be VERY quiet at Estelle's house.
SNAP!
Sorry.
Pour.
Ding.
Krinkle.
Flip.
Flop.
Estelle's parents owned a 24-hour convenience store, of which they were the sole employees (inconvenient). Her dad worked the night shift and hence slept through the day.
He was a foreboding figure. Waking him was not an appealing prospect, partly because then I'd actually have to MEET him.
Tip.
Toe.
Other fathers presented their own challenges. Una's father, for one, did not delight in the laughter of children.
WILL YOU PLEASE KEEP IT DOWN IN THERE? C'MON!!
There was Julie's dad, who had ways of gently reminding you that he made more money than your own sad-sack father.
Daddy says you may choose a toy, too.
WOW! Gee, thanks!
It's NO problem. Seriously.
Trudy's dad was a soccer coach and double amputee.
Keep your head up, girls, or... whoop! FAKE OUT! Ha ha!
Ana's dad exists more like a 'snapshot' in my memory. He had Lou Gehrig's disease and didn't move much.
Brandy had the distinction of having no dad, which made her very exotic in our neck of the woods.
It's not really a big deal.
Plus, she was from Ontario.

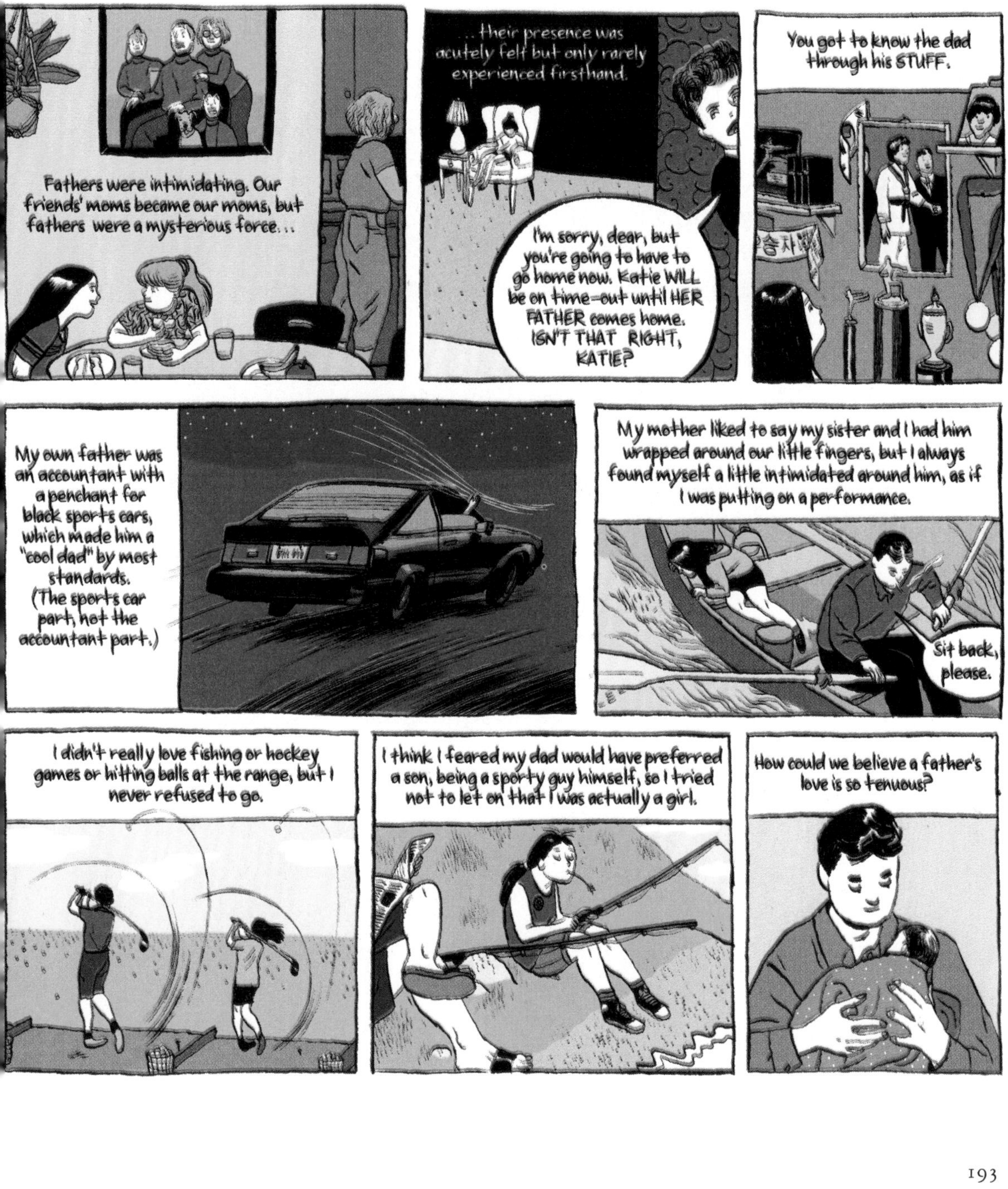
Fathers were intimidating. Our friends' moms became our moms, but fathers were a mysterious force...
...their presence was acutely felt but only rarely experienced firsthand.
I'm sorry, dear, but you're going to have to go home now. Katie WILL be on time-out until HER FATHER comes home. ISN'T THAT RIGHT, KATIE?
You got to know the dad through his STUFF.
My own father was an accountant with a penchant for black sports cars, which made him a "cool dad" by most standards. (The sports car part, not the accountant part.)
My mother liked to say my sister and I had him wrapped around our little fingers, but I always found myself a little intimidated around him, as if I was putting on a performance.
Sit back, please.
I didn't really love fishing or hockey games or hitting balls at the range, but I never refused to go.
I think I feared my dad would have preferred a son, being a sporty guy himself, so I tried not to let on that I was actually a girl.
How could we believe a father's love is so tenuous?

BROWNTOWN

excerpt from
LOVE AND ROCKETS: NEW STORIES

JAIME HERNANDEZ

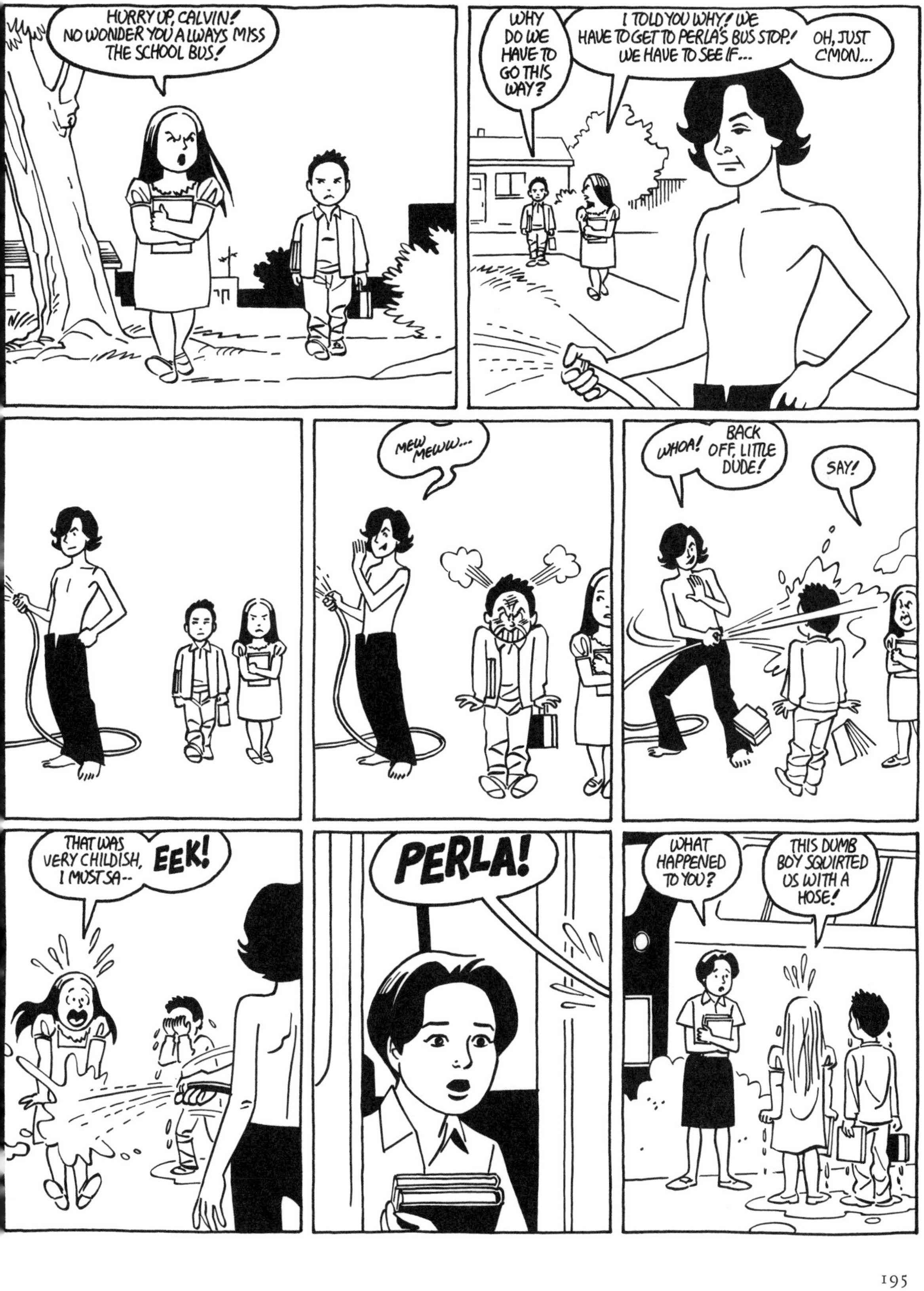
HURRY UP, CALVIN! NO WONDER YOU ALWAYS MISS THE SCHOOL BUS!
WHY DO WE HAVE TO GO THIS WAY?
I TOLD YOU WHY! WE HAVE TO GET TO PERLA'S BUS STOP! WE HAVE TO SEE IF...
OH, JUST C'MON...
MEW MEWW...
WHOA!
BACK OFF, LITTLE DUDE!
SAY!
THAT WAS VERY CHILDISH, I MUST SA--
EEK!
PERLA!
WHAT HAPPENED TO YOU?
THIS DUMB BOY SQUIRTED US WITH A HOSE!

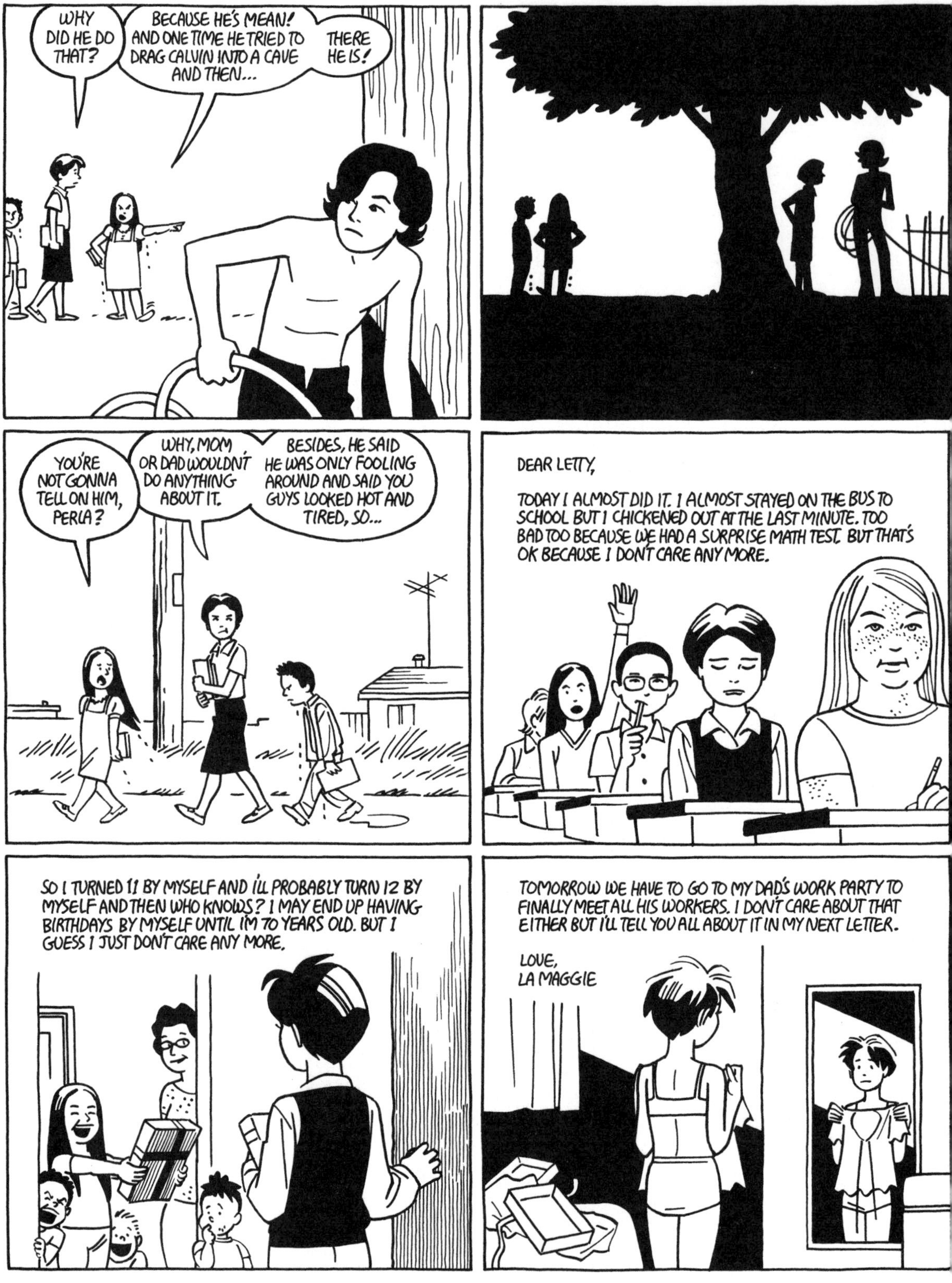
WHY DID HE DO THAT?
BECAUSE HE'S MEAN! AND ONE TIME HE TRIED TO DRAG CALVIN INTO A CAVE AND THEN...
THERE HE IS!
YOU'RE NOT GONNA TELL ON HIM, PERLA?
WHY, MOM OR DAD WOULDN'T DO ANYTHING ABOUT IT.
BESIDES, HE SAID HE WAS ONLY FOOLING AROUND AND SAID YOU GUYS LOOKED HOT AND TIRED, SO...
DEAR LETTY,
TODAY I ALMOST DID IT. I ALMOST STAYED ON THE BUS TO SCHOOL BUT I CHICKENED OUT AT THE LAST MINUTE. TOO BAD TOO BECAUSE WE HAD A SURPRISE MATH TEST. BUT THAT'S OK BECAUSE I DON'T CARE ANY MORE.
SO I TURNED 11 BY MYSELF AND I'LL PROBABLY TURN 12 BY MYSELF AND THEN WHO KNOWS? I MAY END UP HAVING BIRTHDAYS BY MYSELF UNTIL I'M 70 YEARS OLD. BUT I GUESS I JUST DON'T CARE ANY MORE.
TOMORROW WE HAVE TO GO TO MY DAD'S WORK PARTY TO FINALLY MEET ALL HIS WORKERS. I DON'T CARE ABOUT THAT EITHER BUT I'LL TELL YOU ALL ABOUT IT IN MY NEXT LETTER.
LOVE,
LA MAGGIE

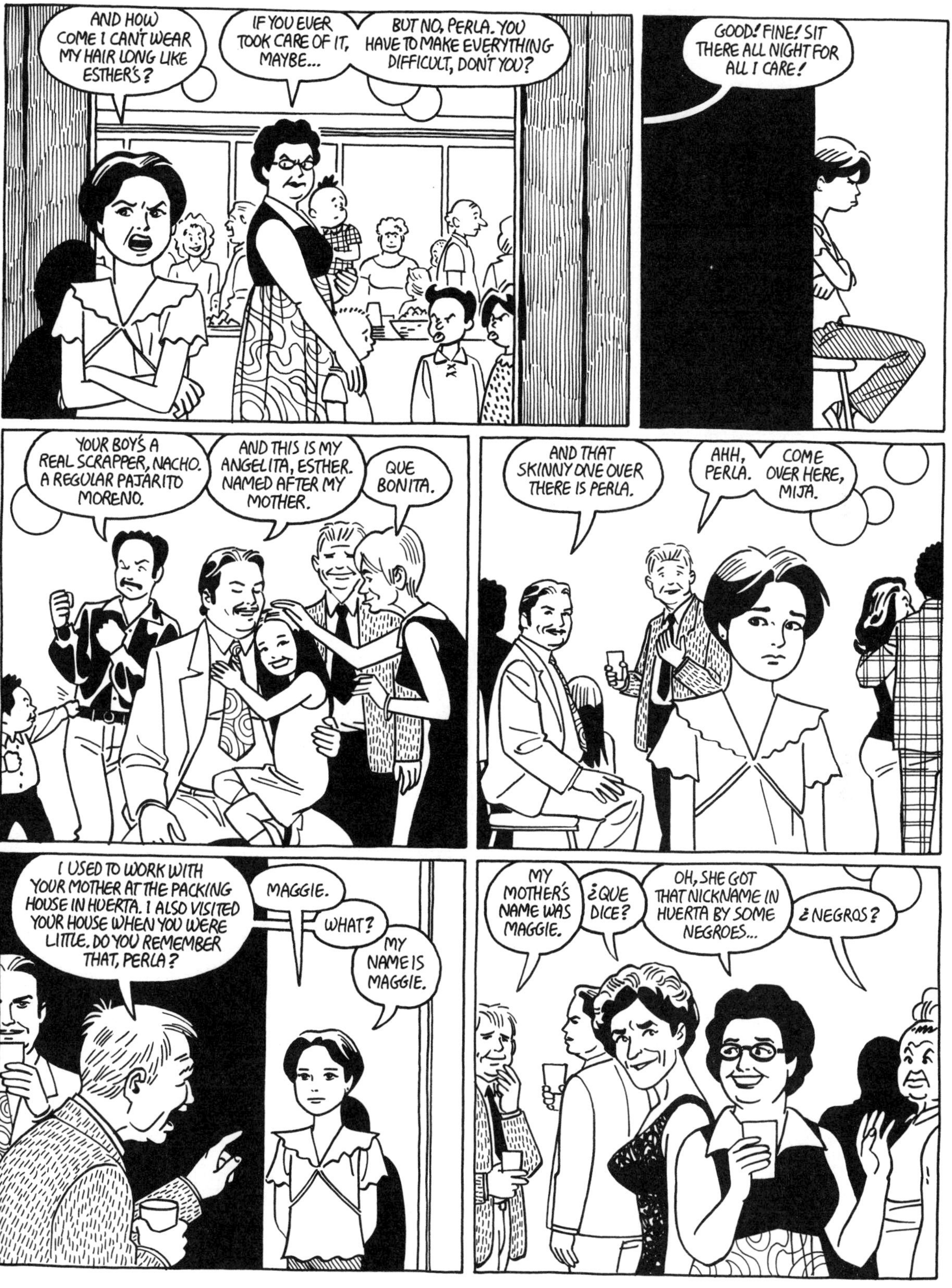
AND HOW COME I CAN'T WEAR MY HAIR LONG LIKE ESTHER'S?
IF YOU EVER TOOK CARE OF IT, MAYBE...
BUT NO, PERLA. YOU HAVE TO MAKE EVERYTHING DIFFICULT, DON'T YOU?
GOOD! FINE! SIT THERE ALL NIGHT FOR ALL I CARE!
YOUR BOY'S A REAL SCRAPPER, NACHO. A REGULAR PAJARITO MORENO.
AND THIS IS MY ANGELITA, ESTHER. NAMED AFTER MY MOTHER.
QUE BONITA.
AND THAT SKINNY ONE OVER THERE IS PERLA.
AHH, PERLA.
COME OVER HERE, MIJA.
I USED TO WORK WITH YOUR MOTHER AT THE PACKING HOUSE IN HUERTA. I ALSO VISITED YOUR HOUSE WHEN YOU WERE LITTLE. DO YOU REMEMBER THAT, PERLA?
MAGGIE.
WHAT?
MY NAME IS MAGGIE.
MY MOTHER'S NAME WAS MAGGIE.
¿QUE DICE?
OH, SHE GOT THAT NICKNAME IN HUERTA BY SOME NEGROES...
¿NEGROS?

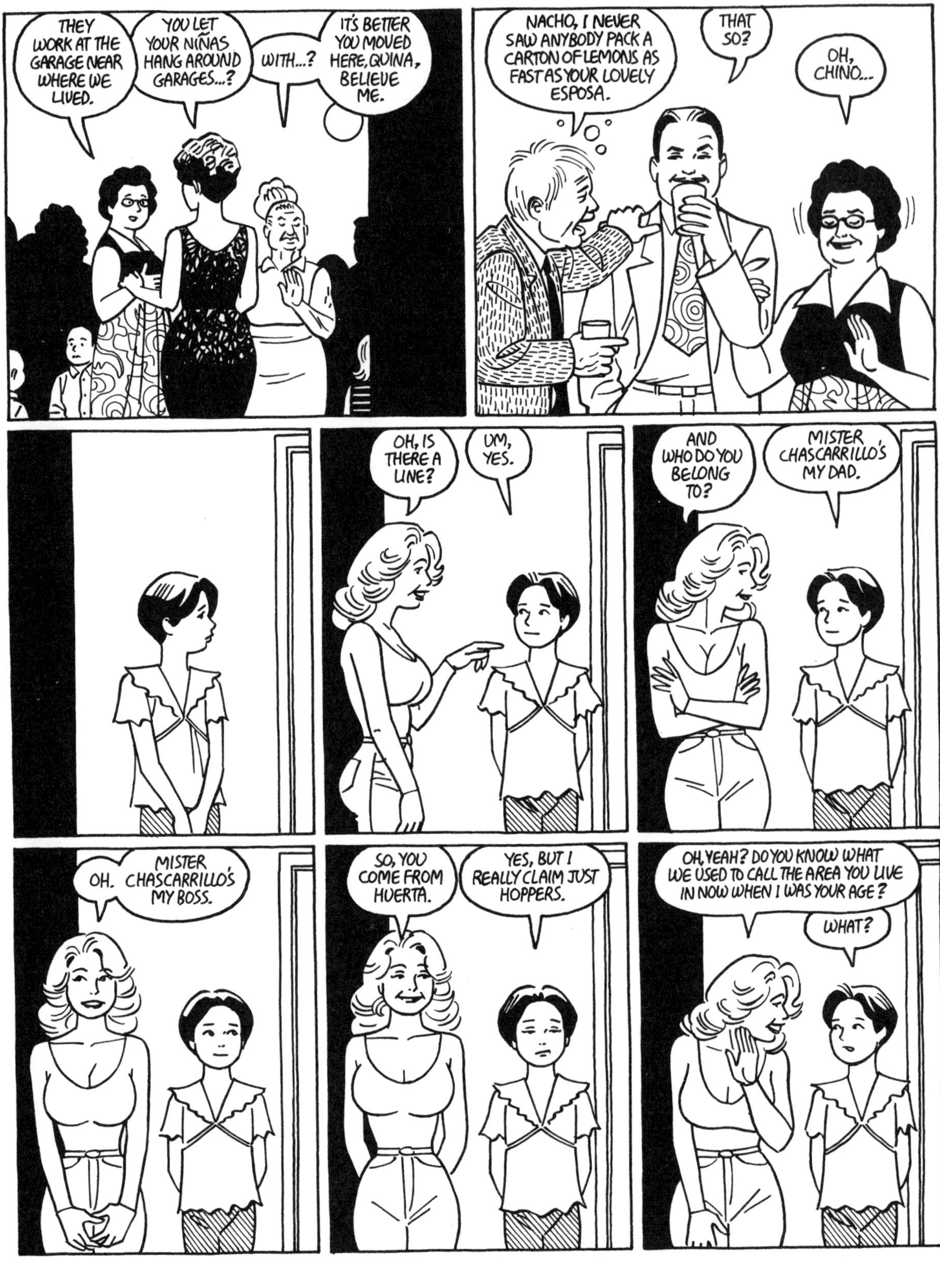
THEY WORK AT THE GARAGE NEAR WHERE WE LIVED.
YOU LET YOUR NIÑAS HANG AROUND GARAGES...?
WITH...?
IT'S BETTER YOU MOVED HERE, QUINA, BELIEVE ME.
NACHO, I NEVER SAW ANYBODY PACK A CARTON OF LEMONS AS FAST AS YOUR LOVELY ESPOSA.
THAT SO?
OH, CHINO...
OH, IS THERE A LINE?
UM, YES.
AND WHO DO YOU BELONG TO?
MISTER CHASCARRILLO'S MY DAD.
OH.
MISTER CHASCARRILLO'S MY BOSS.
SO, YOU COME FROM HUERTA.
YES, BUT I REALLY CLAIM JUST HOPPERS.
OH, YEAH? DO YOU KNOW WHAT WE USED TO CALL THE AREA YOU LIVE IN NOW WHEN I WAS YOUR AGE?
WHAT?

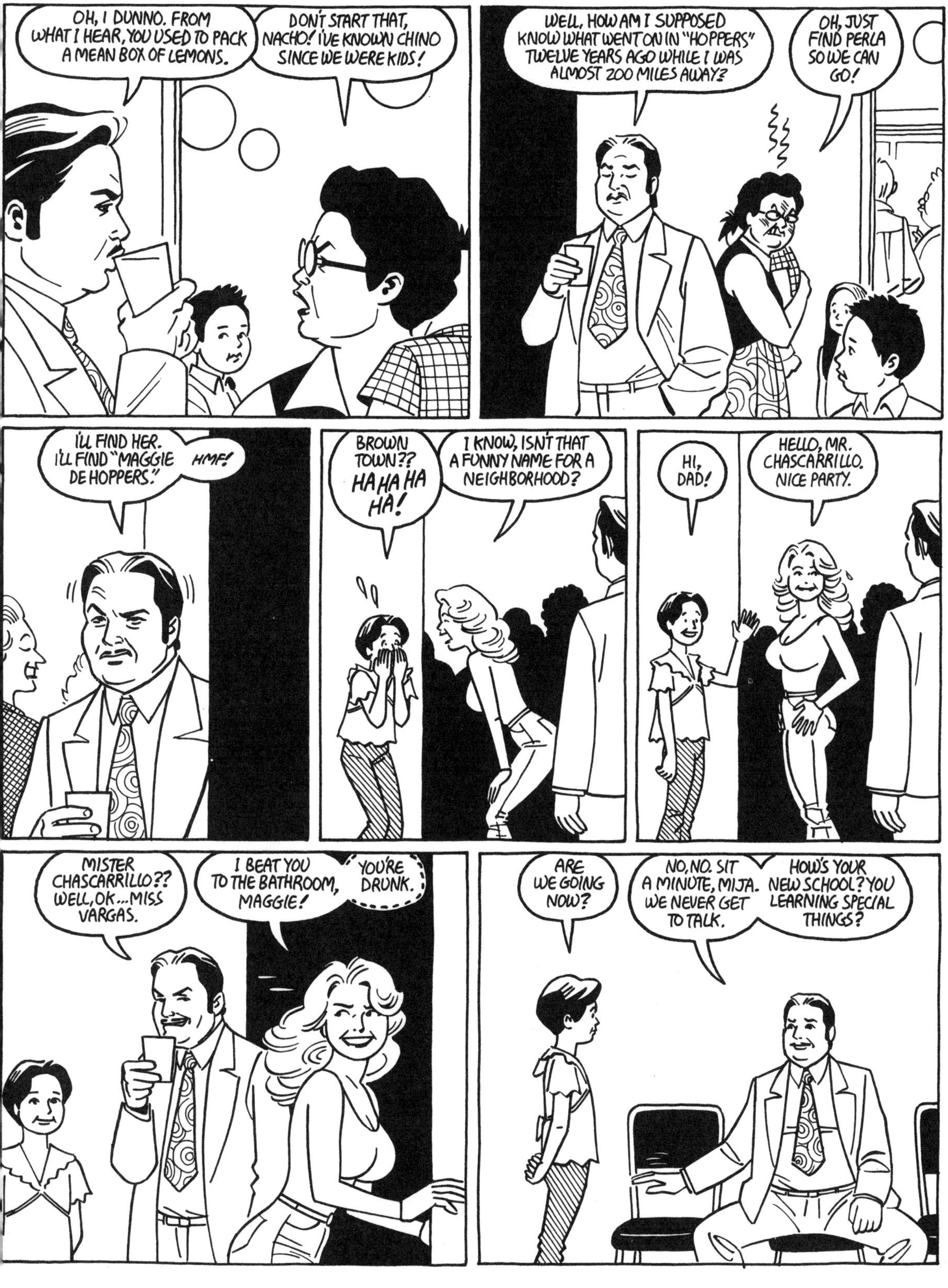

OH, I DUNNO. FROM WHAT I HEAR, YOU USED TO PACK A MEAN BOX OF LEMONS.
DON'T START THAT, NACHO! I'VE KNOWN CHINO SINCE WE WERE KIDS!
WELL, HOW AM I SUPPOSED KNOW WHAT WENT ON IN "HOPPERS" TWELVE YEARS AGO WHILE I WAS ALMOST 200 MILES AWAY?
OH, JUST FIND PERLA SO WE CAN GO!
I'LL FIND HER. I'LL FIND "MAGGIE DE HOPPERS."
HMF!
BROWN TOWN?? HA HA HA HA!
I KNOW, ISN'T THAT A FUNNY NAME FOR A NEIGHBORHOOD?
HI, DAD!
HELLO, MR. CHASCARRILLO. NICE PARTY.
MISTER CHASCARRILLO?? WELL, OK... MISS VARGAS.
I BEAT YOU TO THE BATHROOM, MAGGIE!
YOU'RE DRUNK.
ARE WE GOING NOW?
NO, NO. SIT A MINUTE, MIJA. WE NEVER GET TO TALK.
HOW'S YOUR NEW SCHOOL? YOU LEARNING SPECIAL THINGS?

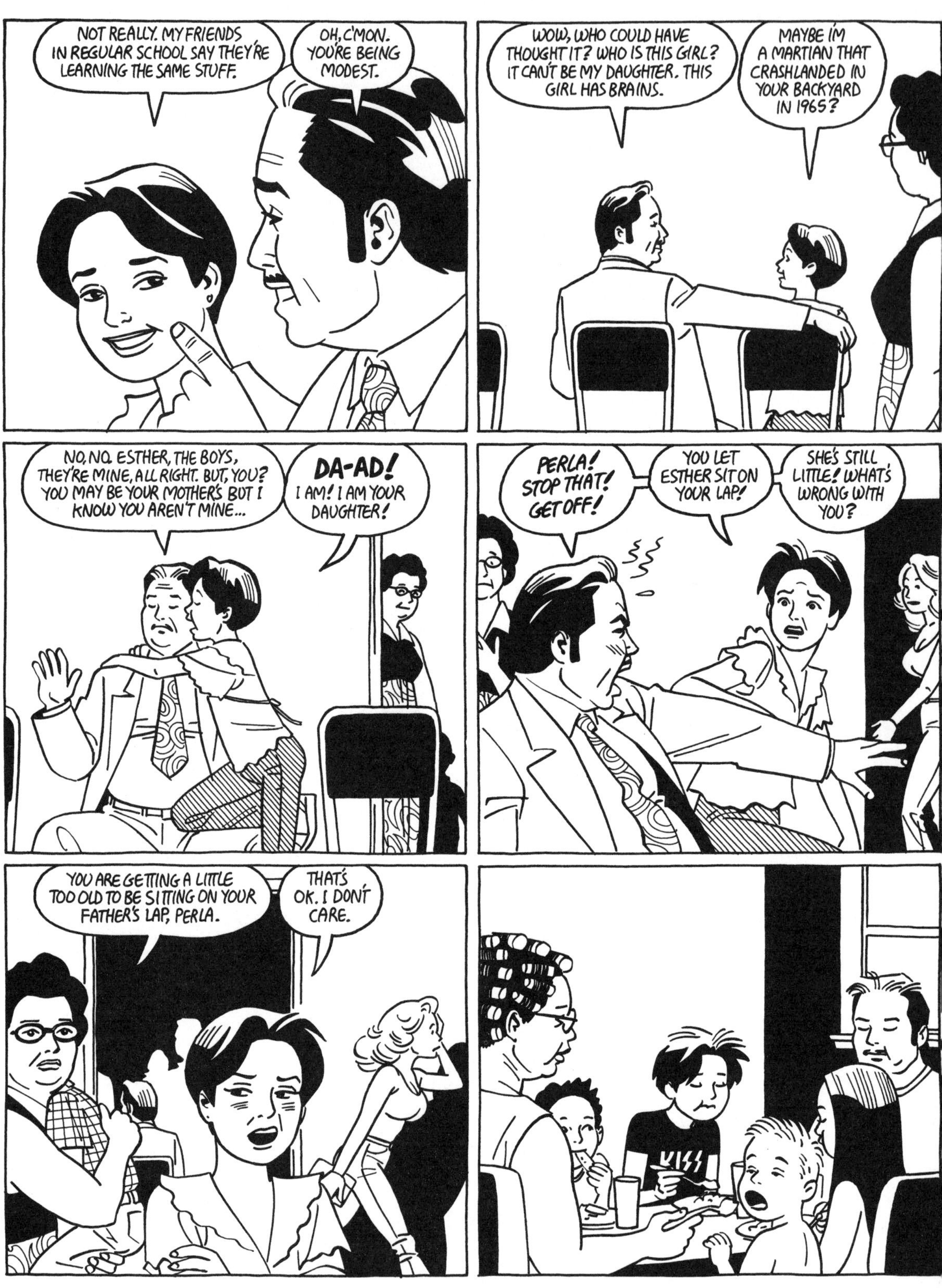
NOT REALLY. MY FRIENDS IN REGULAR SCHOOL SAY THEY'RE LEARNING THE SAME STUFF.
OH, C'MON. YOU'RE BEING MODEST.
WOW, WHO COULD HAVE THOUGHT IT? WHO IS THIS GIRL? IT CAN'T BE MY DAUGHTER. THIS GIRL HAS BRAINS.
MAYBE I'M A MARTIAN THAT CRASHLANDED IN YOUR BACKYARD IN 1965?
NO, NO. ESTHER, THE BOYS, THEY'RE MINE, ALL RIGHT. BUT, YOU? YOU MAY BE YOUR MOTHER'S BUT I KNOW YOU AREN'T MINE...
DA-AD! I AM! I AM YOUR DAUGHTER!
PERLA! STOP THAT! GET OFF!
YOU LET ESTHER SIT ON YOUR LAP!
SHE'S STILL LITTLE! WHAT'S WRONG WITH YOU?
YOU ARE GETTING A LITTLE TOO OLD TO BE SITTING ON YOUR FATHER'S LAP, PERLA.
THAT'S OK. I DON'T CARE.
KISS

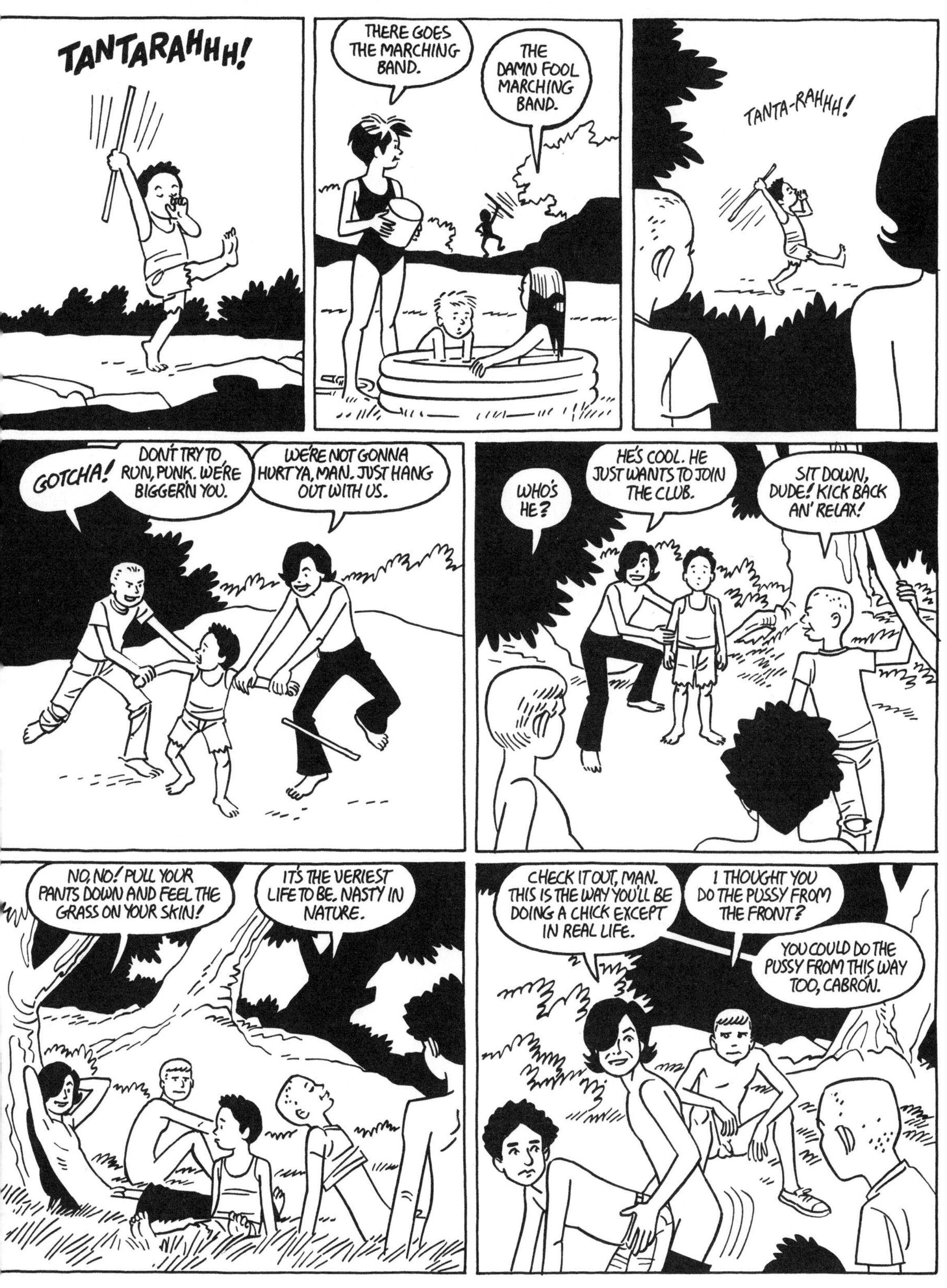
TANTARAHHH!
THERE GOES THE MARCHING BAND.
THE DAMN FOOL MARCHING BAND.
TANTA-RAHHH!
GOTCHA!
DON'T TRY TO RUN, PUNK. WE'RE BIGGER'N YOU.
WE'RE NOT GONNA HURT YA, MAN. JUST HANG OUT WITH US.
WHO'S HE?
HE'S COOL. HE JUST WANTS TO JOIN THE CLUB.
SIT DOWN, DUDE! KICK BACK AN' RELAX!
NO, NO! PULL YOUR PANTS DOWN AND FEEL THE GRASS ON YOUR SKIN!
IT'S THE VERIEST LIFE TO BE. NASTY IN NATURE.
CHECK IT OUT, MAN. THIS IS THE WAY YOU'LL BE DOING A CHICK EXCEPT IN REAL LIFE.
I THOUGHT YOU DO THE PUSSY FROM THE FRONT?
YOU COULD DO THE PUSSY FROM THIS WAY TOO, CABRÓN.

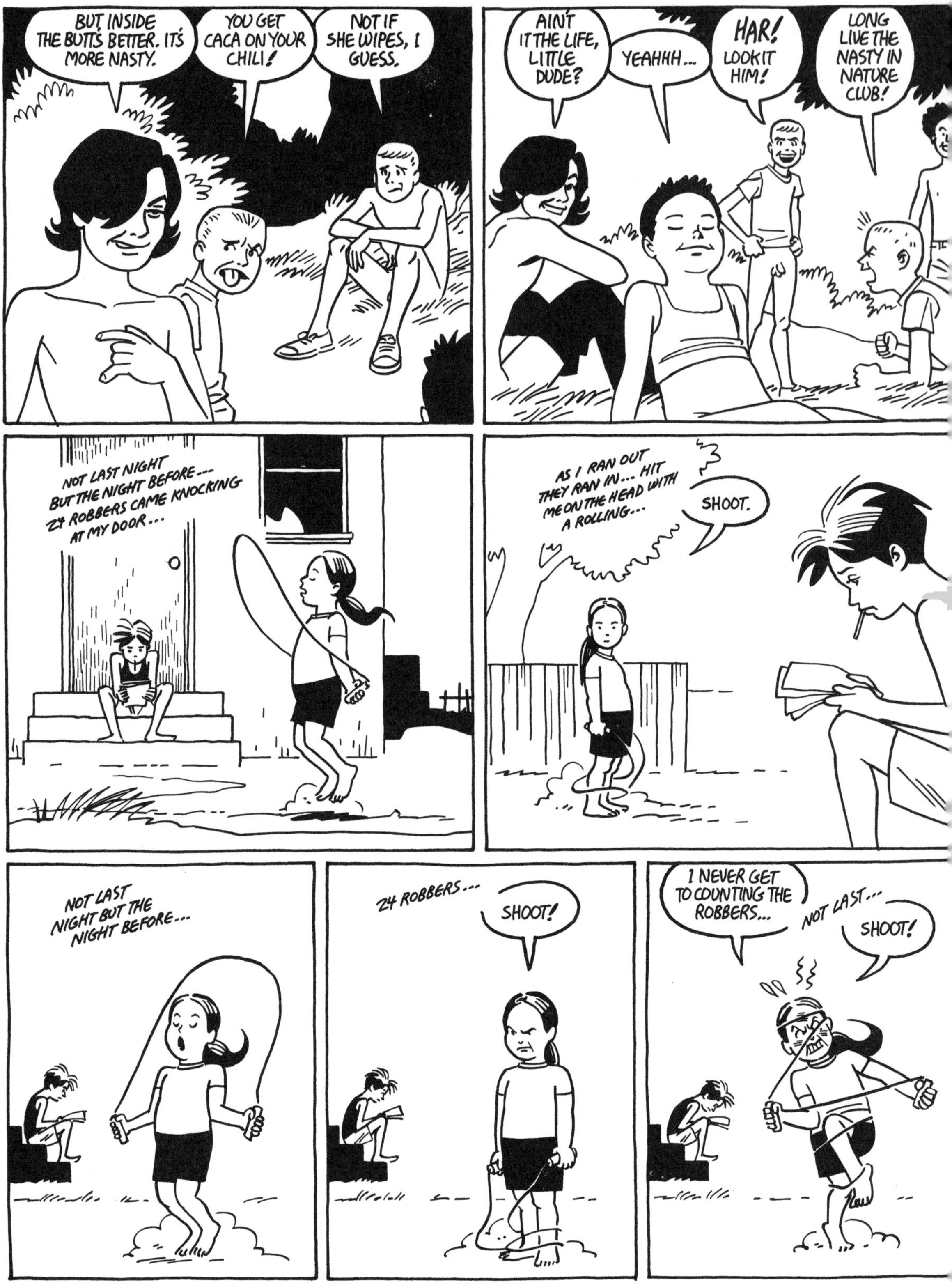
BUT, INSIDE THE BUTT'S BETTER. IT'S MORE NASTY.
YOU GET CACA ON YOUR CHILI!
NOT IF SHE WIPES, I GUESS.
AIN'T IT THE LIFE, LITTLE DUDE?
YEAHHH...
HAR! LOOKIT HIM!
LONG LIVE THE NASTY IN NATURE CLUB!
NOT LAST NIGHT BUT THE NIGHT BEFORE... 24 ROBBERS CAME KNOCKING AT MY DOOR...
AS I RAN OUT THEY RAN IN... HIT ME ON THE HEAD WITH A ROLLING...
SHOOT.
NOT LAST NIGHT BUT THE NIGHT BEFORE...
24 ROBBERS...
SHOOT!
I NEVER GET TO COUNTING THE ROBBERS...
NOT LAST...
SHOOT!

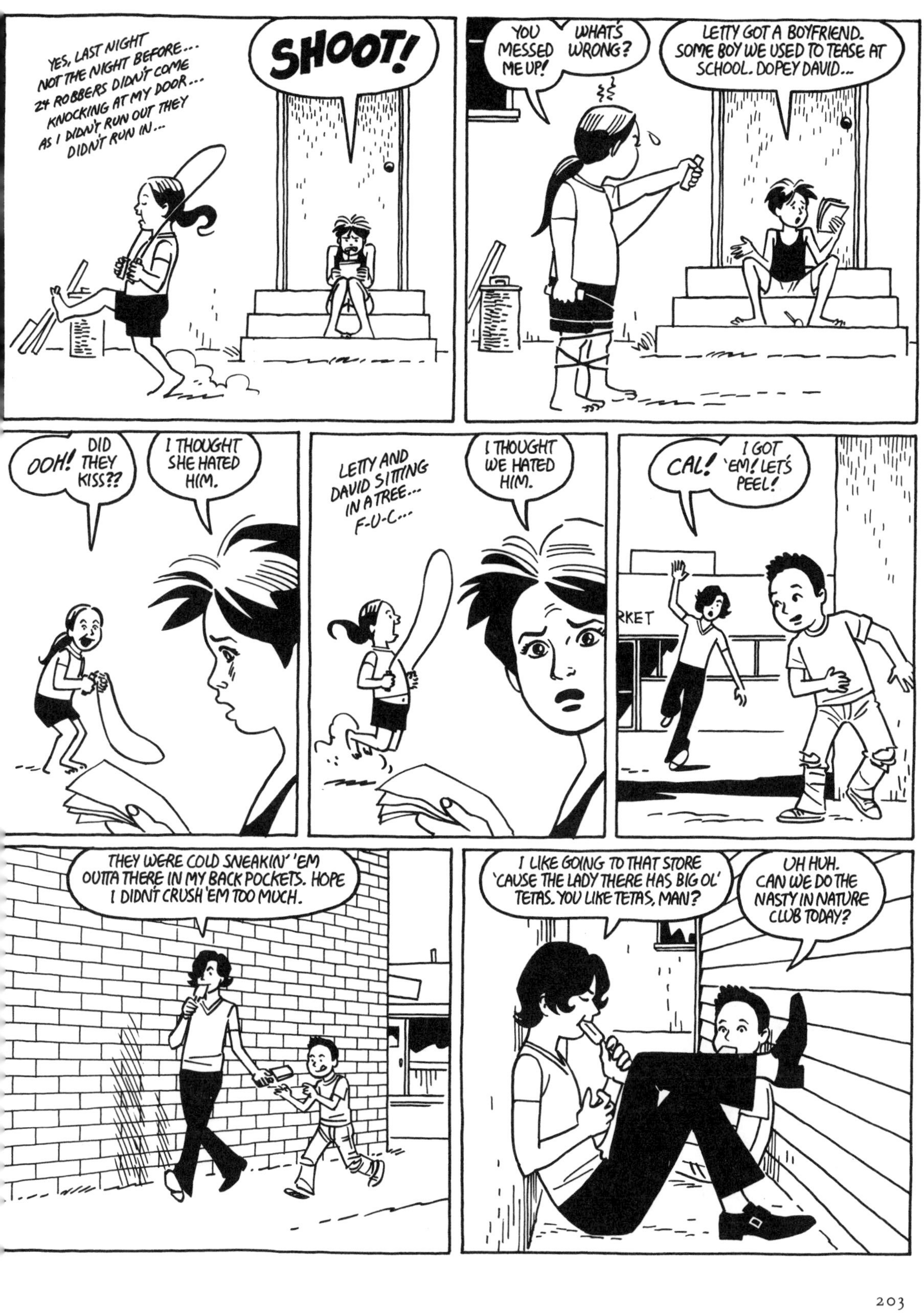
YES, LAST NIGHT NOT THE NIGHT BEFORE... 24 ROBBERS DIDN'T COME KNOCKING AT MY DOOR... AS I DIDN'T RUN OUT THEY DIDN'T RUN IN...
SHOOT!
YOU MESSED ME UP!
WHAT'S WRONG?
LETTY GOT A BOYFRIEND. SOME BOY WE USED TO TEASE AT SCHOOL. DOPEY DAVID...
OOH!
DID THEY KISS??
I THOUGHT SHE HATED HIM.
LETTY AND DAVID SITTING IN A TREE... F-U-C...
I THOUGHT WE HATED HIM.
CAL!
I GOT 'EM! LET'S PEEL!
RKET
THEY WERE COLD SNEAKIN' 'EM OUTTA THERE IN MY BACK POCKETS. HOPE I DIDN'T CRUSH 'EM TOO MUCH.
I LIKE GOING TO THAT STORE 'CAUSE THE LADY THERE HAS BIG OL' TETAS. YOU LIKE TETAS, MAN?
UH HUH. CAN WE DO THE NASTY IN NATURE CLUB TODAY?

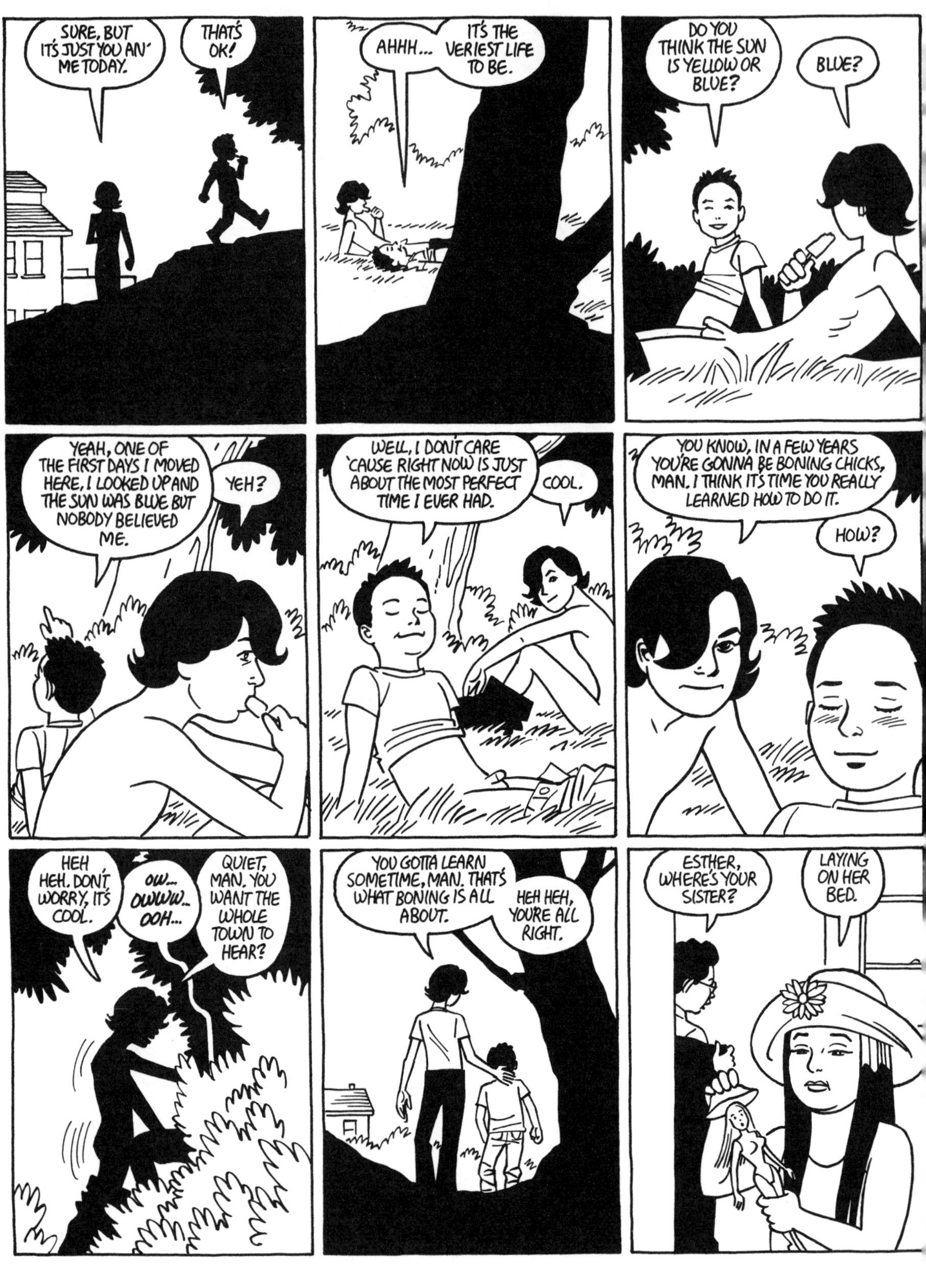

SURE, BUT IT'S JUST YOU AN' ME TODAY.
THAT'S OK!
AHHH...
IT'S THE VERIEST LIFE TO BE.
DO YOU THINK THE SUN IS YELLOW OR BLUE?
BLUE?
YEAH, ONE OF THE FIRST DAYS I MOVED HERE, I LOOKED UP AND THE SUN WAS BLUE BUT NOBODY BELIEVED ME.
YEH?
WELL, I DON'T CARE 'CAUSE RIGHT NOW IS JUST ABOUT THE MOST PERFECT TIME I EVER HAD.
COOL.
YOU KNOW, IN A FEW YEARS YOU'RE GONNA BE BONING CHICKS, MAN. I THINK ITS TIME YOU REALLY LEARNED HOW TO DO IT.
HOW?
HEH HEH. DON'T WORRY, IT'S COOL.
OW... OWWW... OOH...
QUIET, MAN. YOU WANT THE WHOLE TOWN TO HEAR?
YOU GOTTA LEARN SOMETIME, MAN. THAT'S WHAT BONING IS ALL ABOUT.
HEH HEH, YOU'RE ALL RIGHT.
ESTHER, WHERE'S YOUR SISTER?
LAYING ON HER BED.

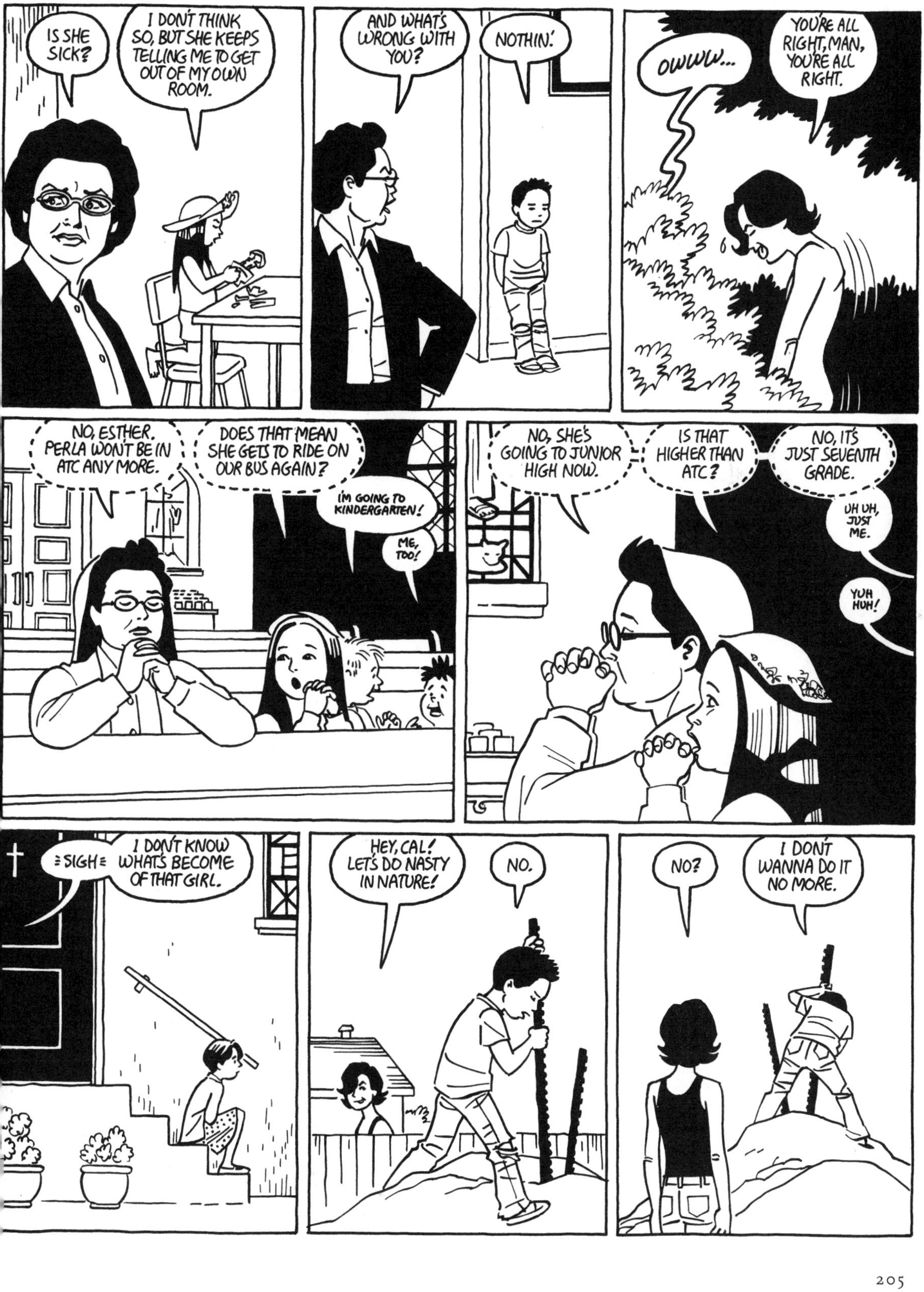
IS SHE SICK?
I DON'T THINK SO, BUT SHE KEEPS TELLING ME TO GET OUT OF MY OWN ROOM.
AND WHAT'S WRONG WITH YOU?
NOTHIN'.
OWWW...
YOU'RE ALL RIGHT, MAN, YOU'RE ALL RIGHT.
NO, ESTHER. PERLA WON'T BE IN ATC ANY MORE.
DOES THAT MEAN SHE GETS TO RIDE ON OUR BUS AGAIN?
I'M GOING TO KINDERGARTEN!
ME, TOO!
NO, SHE'S GOING TO JUNIOR HIGH NOW.
IS THAT HIGHER THAN ATC?
NO, IT'S JUST SEVENTH GRADE.
UH UH, JUST ME.
YUH HUH!
≡SIGH≡
I DON'T KNOW WHAT'S BECOME OF THAT GIRL.
HEY, CAL! LET'S DO NASTY IN NATURE!
NO.
NO?
I DON'T WANNA DO IT NO MORE.

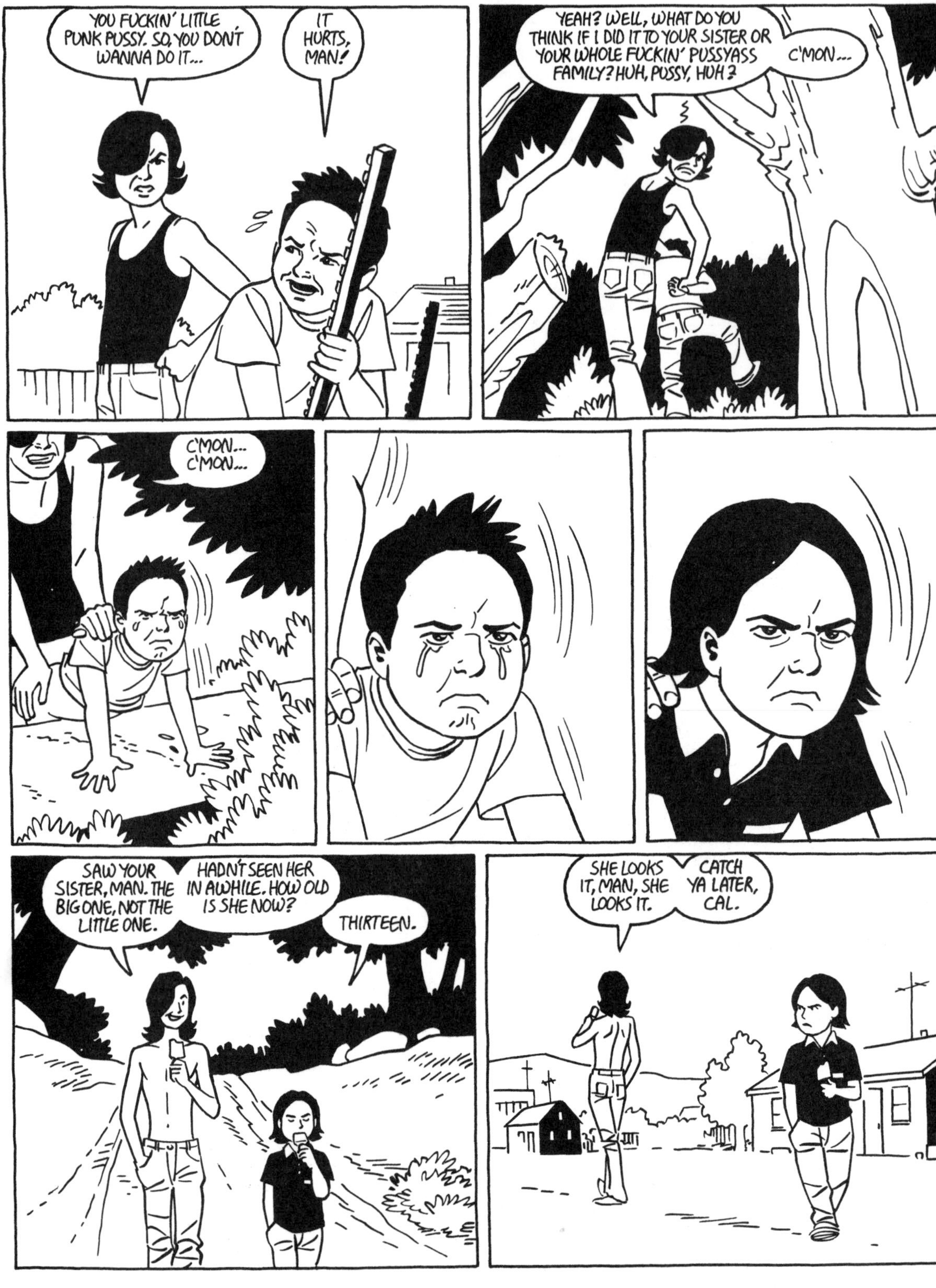
YOU FUCKIN' LITTLE PUNK PUSSY. SO, YOU DON'T WANNA DO IT...
IT HURTS, MAN!
YEAH? WELL, WHAT DO YOU THINK IF I DID IT TO YOUR SISTER OR YOUR WHOLE FUCKIN' PUSSYASS FAMILY? HUH, PUSSY, HUH?
C'MON...
C'MON... C'MON...
SAW YOUR SISTER, MAN. THE BIG ONE, NOT THE LITTLE ONE.
HADN'T SEEN HER IN AWHILE. HOW OLD IS SHE NOW?
THIRTEEN.
SHE LOOKS IT, MAN, SHE LOOKS IT.
CATCH YA LATER, CAL.

FEAR OF FIRE

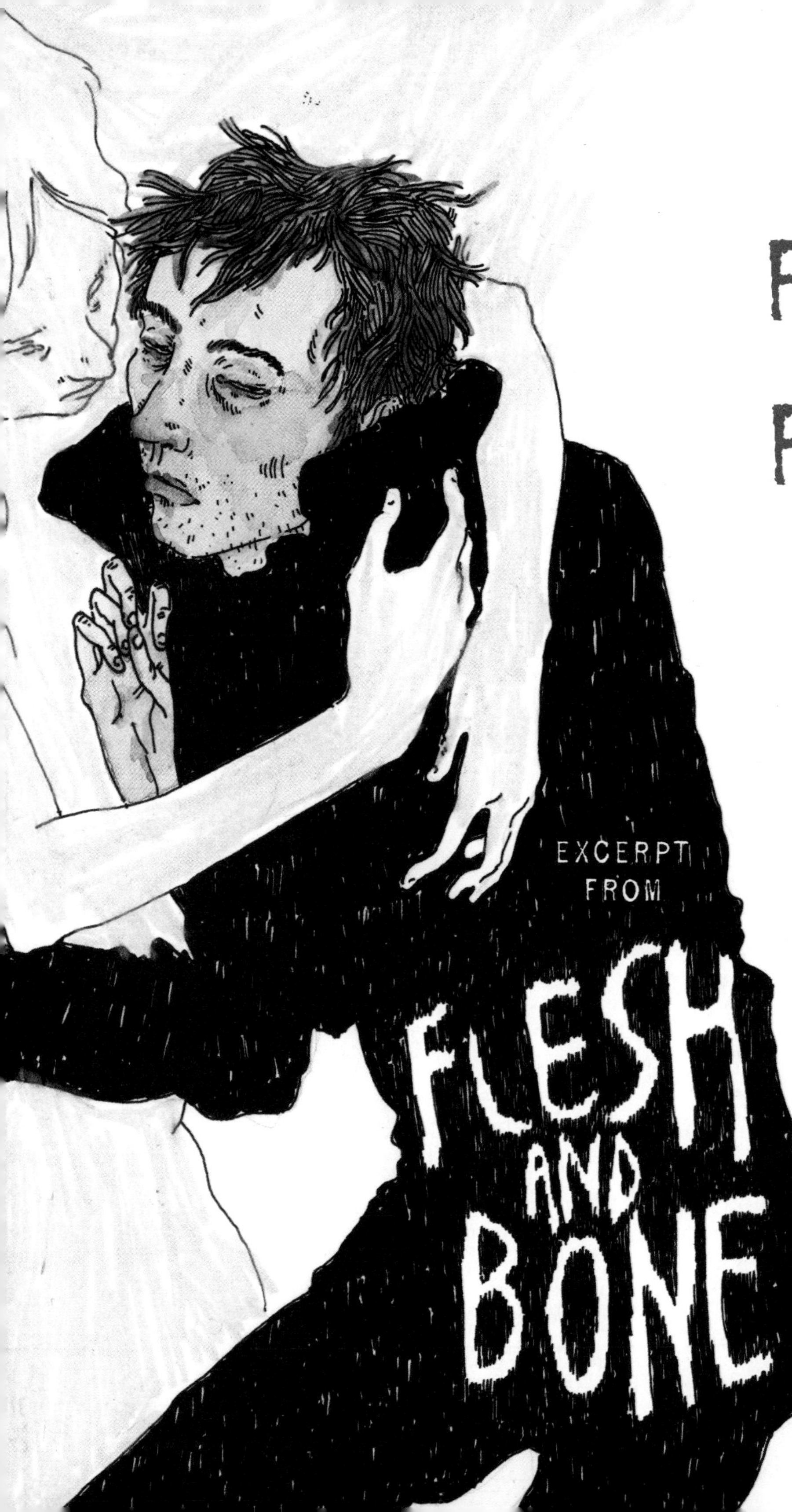
EXCERPT
FROM
FLESH
AND
BONE

JULIA GFRÖRER

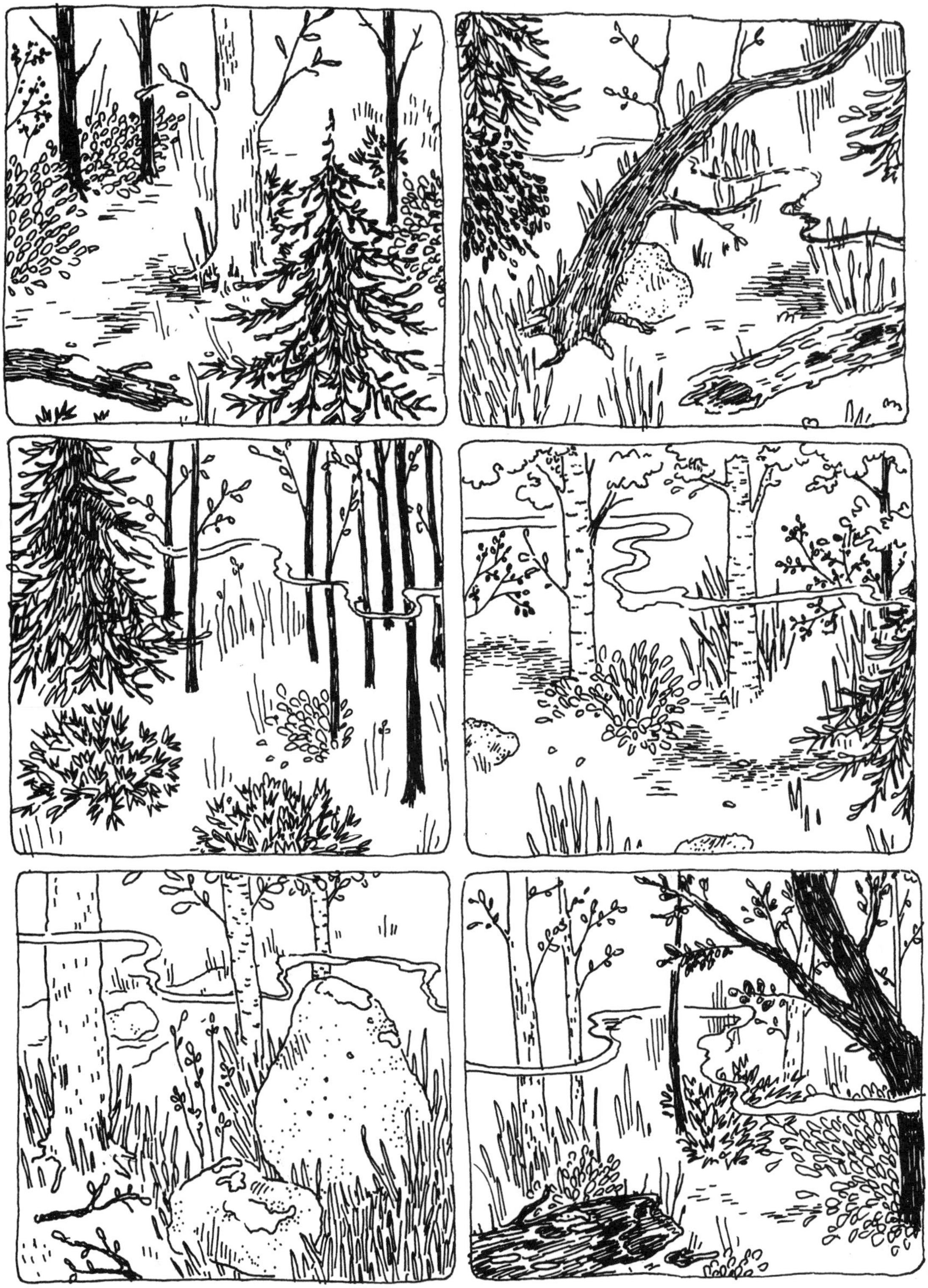

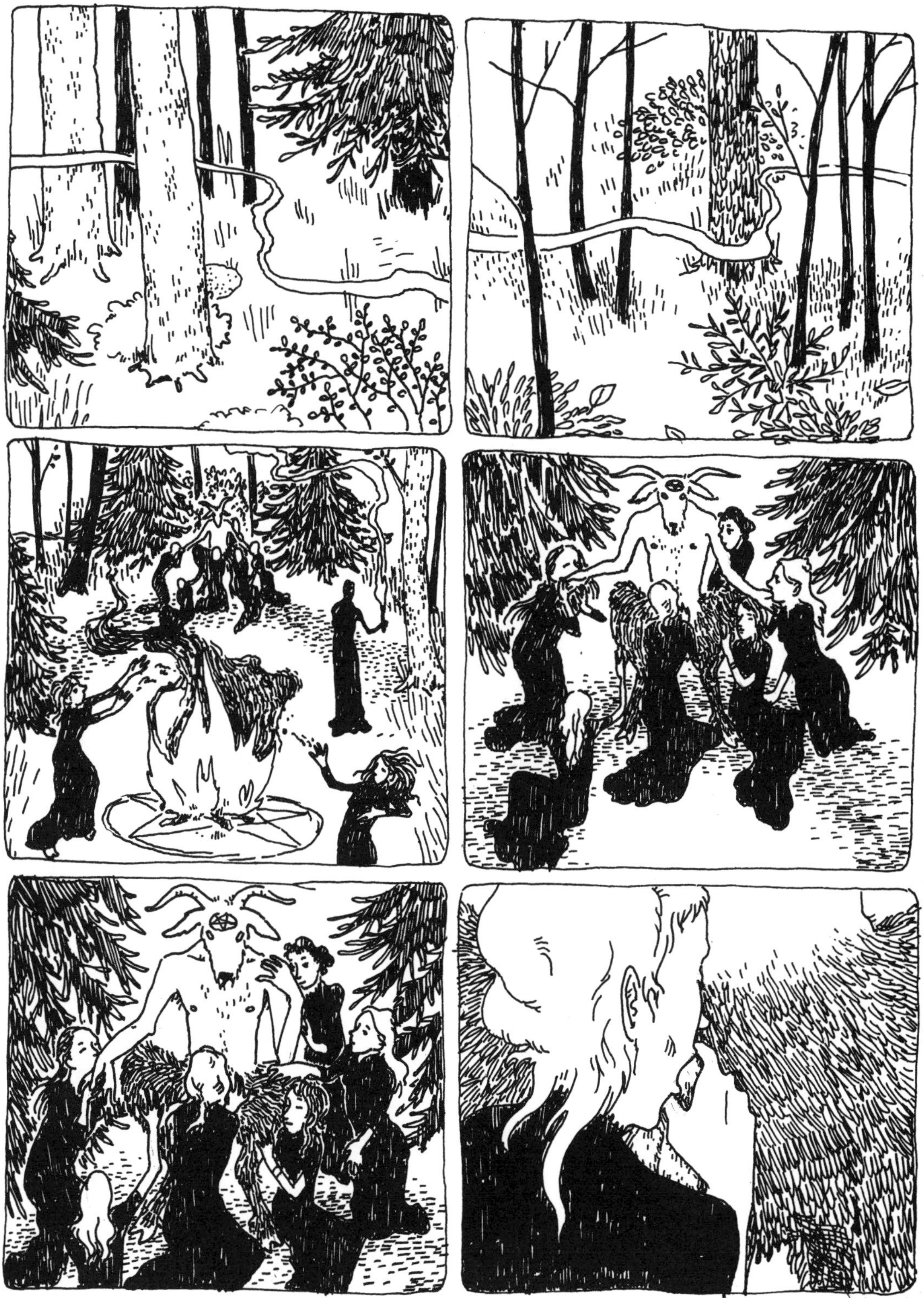

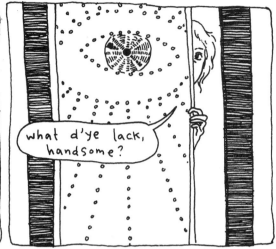

what d'ye lack, handsome?

is it social deviance? a venereal disease?

or maybe you just need a girl to sit on that pretty face.

whatever it is, handsome, you're sick for missing it.

I wish to be reunited with my love who is dead.

of course you do, handsome.

I should have guessed.

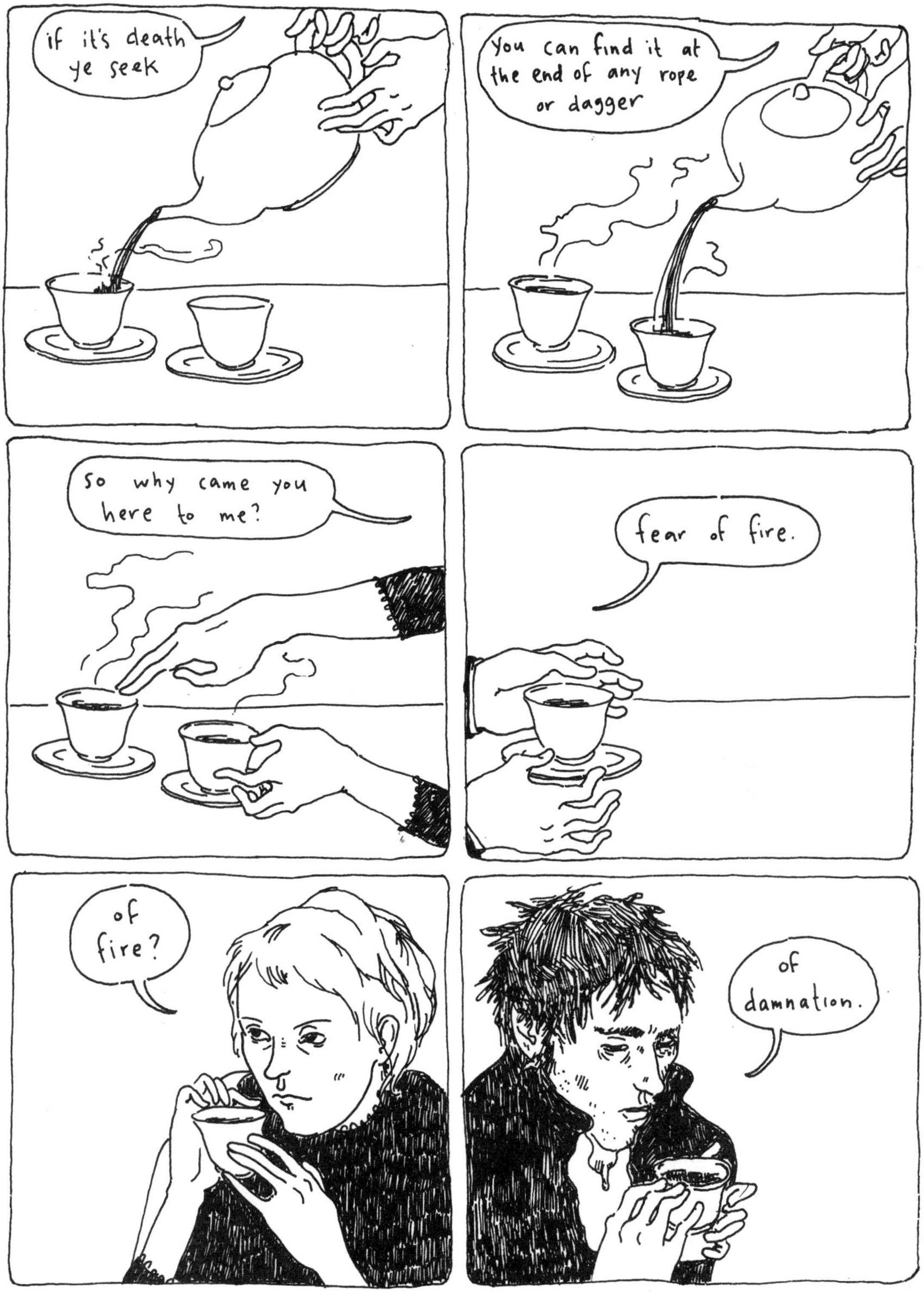
if it's death
ye seek
You can find it at
the end of any rope
or dagger
so why came you
here to me?
fear of fire.
of
fire?
of
damnation.

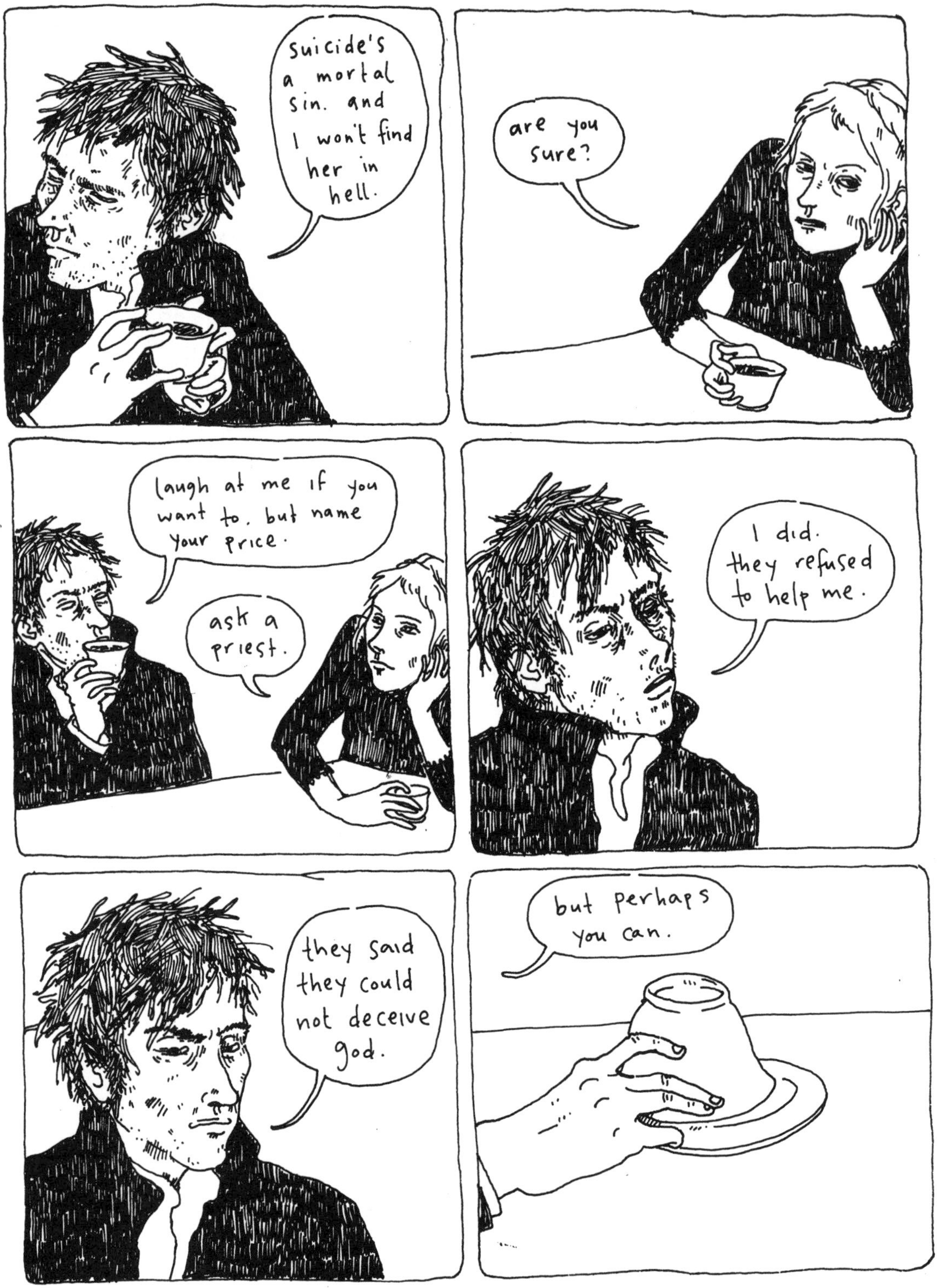
suicide's a mortal sin. and I won't find her in hell.
are you sure?
laugh at me if you want to. but name your price.
ask a priest.
I did. they refused to help me.
they said they could not deceive god.
but perhaps you can.

Yes, perhaps.

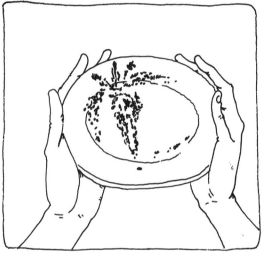

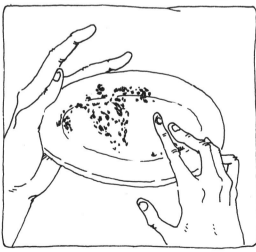

Come back after midnight and I will tell you my price.

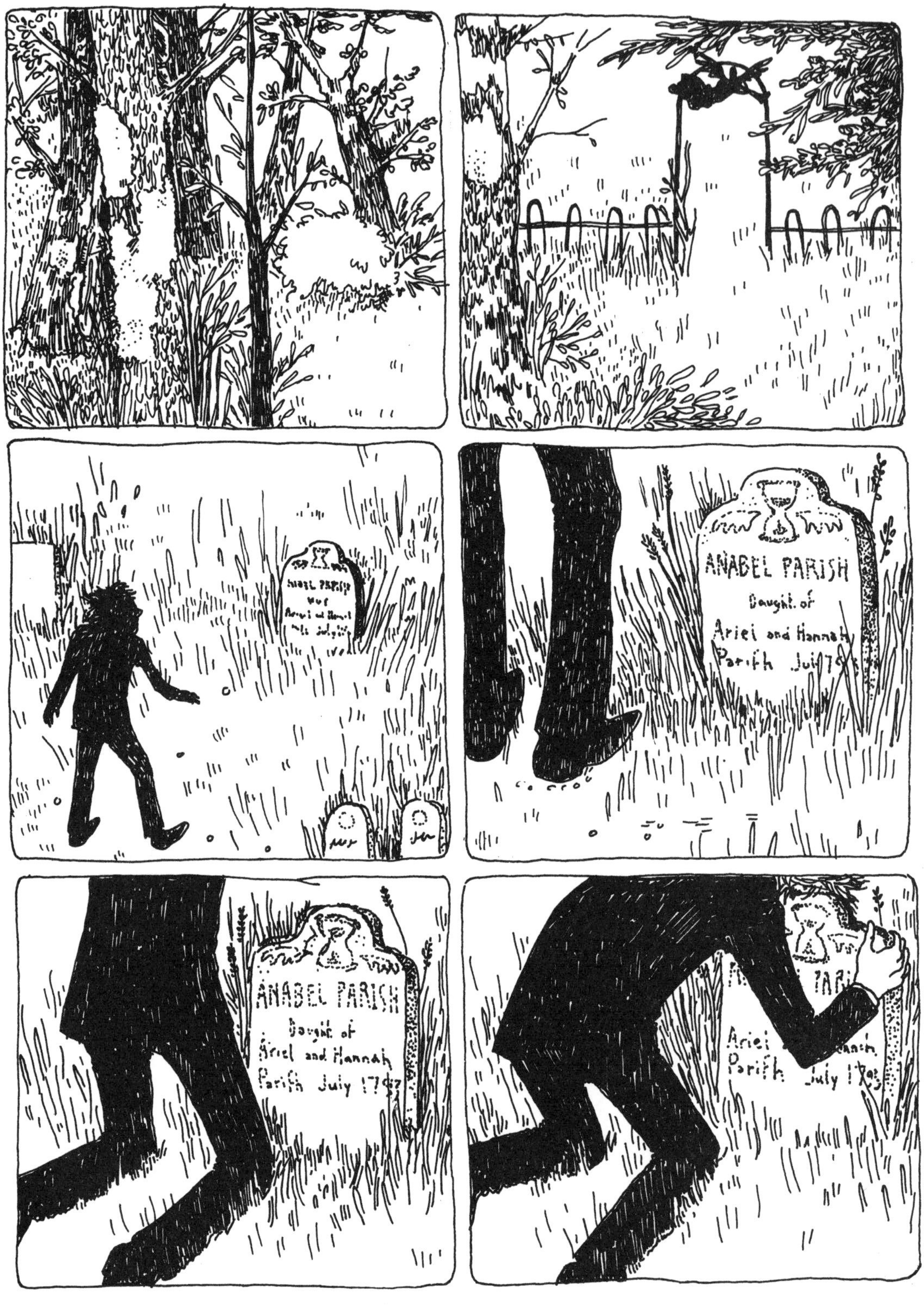
ANABEL PARISH
Daught. of
Ariel and Hannah
Parifh July

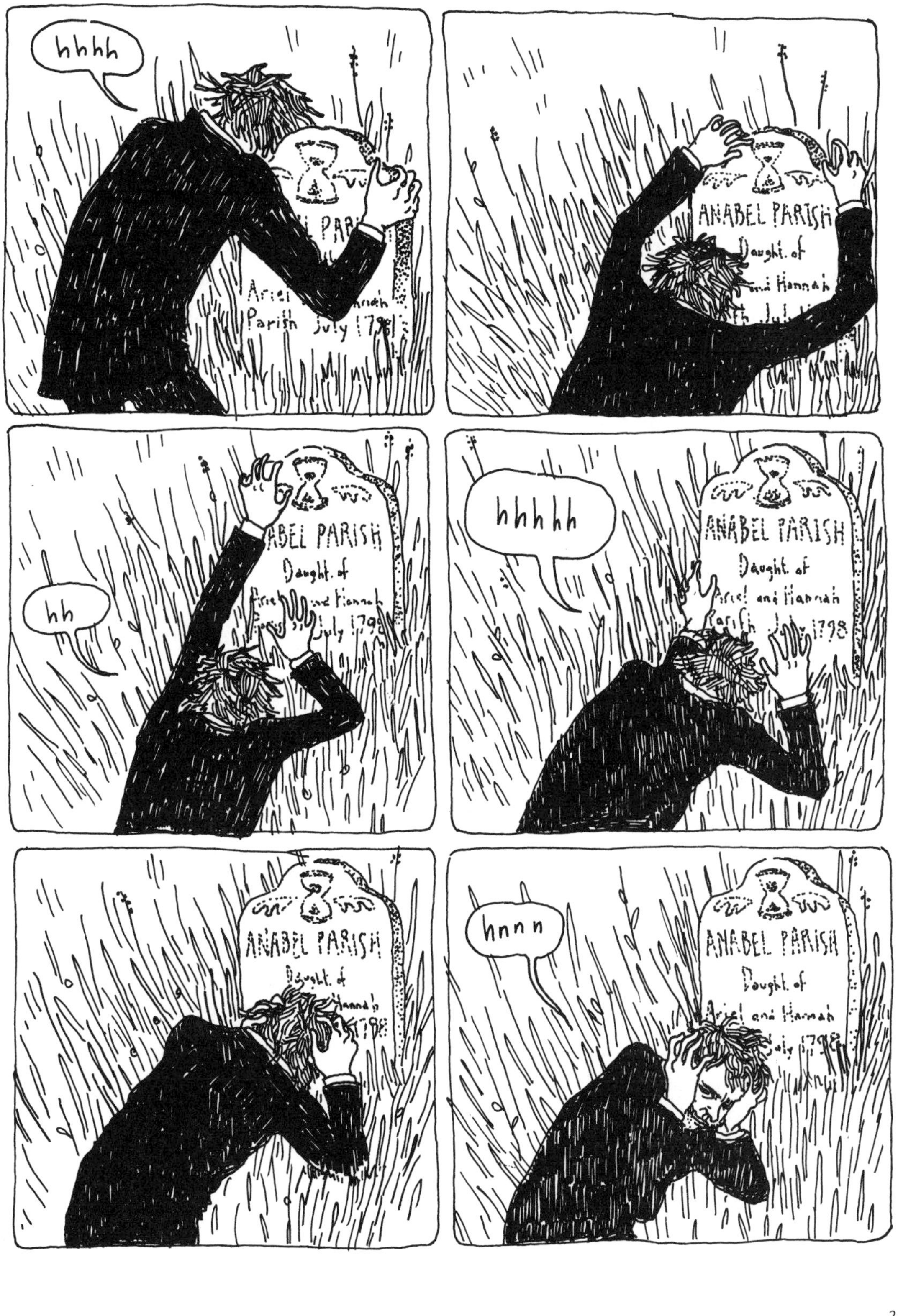
hhhh
ANABEL PARISH
Daught. of
hh
hhhhh
ANABEL PARISH
Daught. of
Ariel and Hannah
Parish July 1798
ANABEL PARISH
Daught. of
hnnn
ANABEL PARISH
Daught. of
Ariel and Hannah

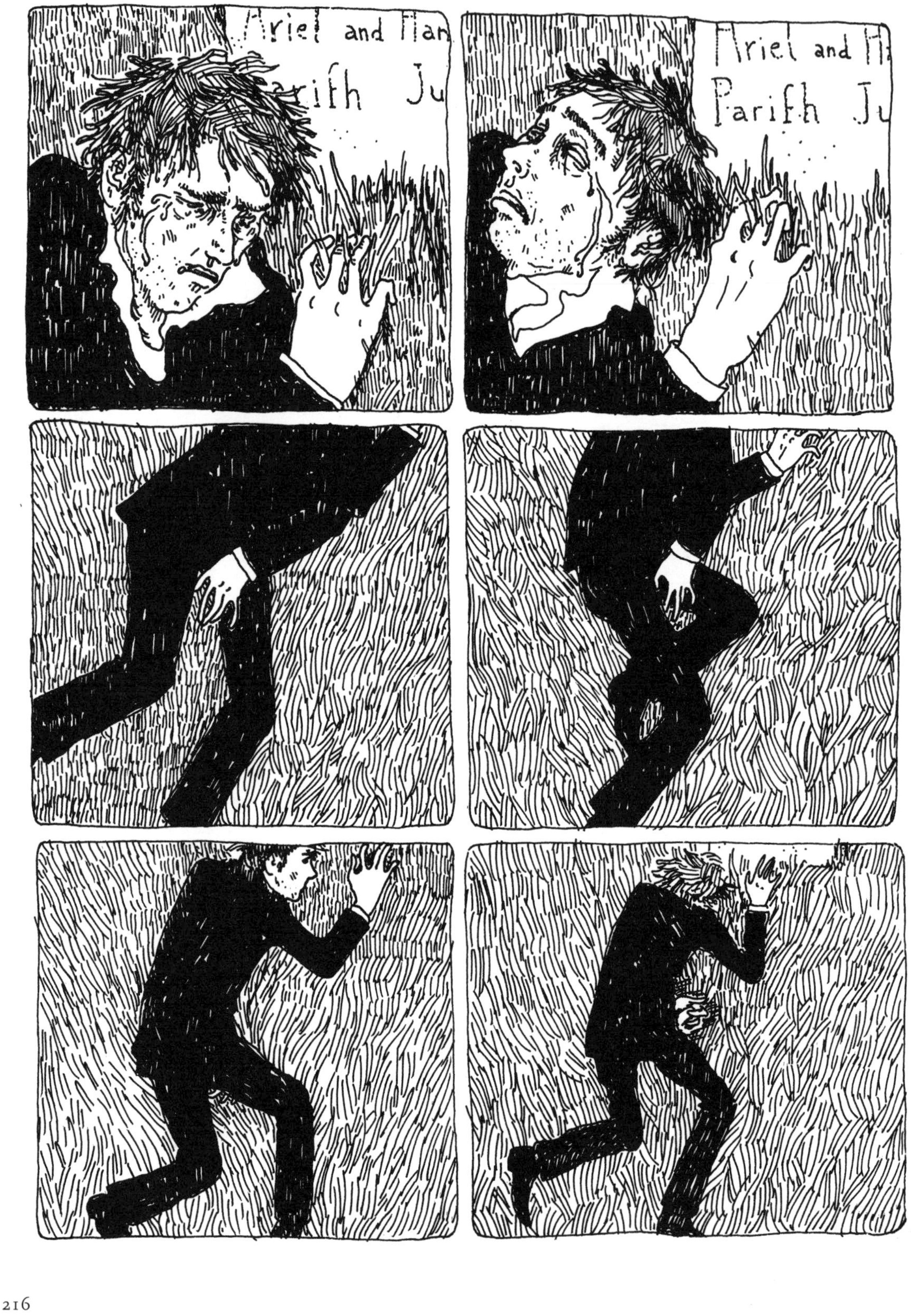
Ariel and Ha
arifh Ju
Ariel and H
Parifh Ju

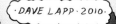

PEOPLE AROUND HERE

PORT BURWELL, ON · DAVE LAPP · 2010 ·

YOU'RE LEAVING ME UP HERE ALL ALONE?

THERE'S NO SHADE DOWN ON THE BEACH. YOU'LL GET BURNED.

BYE SWEETIE!

SEE? WHAT DID I TELL YA? THIS PLACE IS GREAT!

WEE! YAH!

WEE!

C'MON, JUST JUMP DOWN.

AW, MY LEG'S KIND OF SORE.

YAHHH!

LET'S SEE YOU JUMP.

I JUST CAN'T. MY LEG HURTS.

HA HA YOU'RE TOO OLD!

WHEN WE USED TO COME HERE.

WHEN I WAS YOUR AGE...

IT'S TOO HOT. I'M TAKING MY TOP OFF.

YOU CAN'T WEAR JUST YOUR BRA!

THERE'S NO ONE AROUND.

WHAT IF MOM FINDS OUT?

WELL DON'T TELL HER!

How fast can I swim?...

HEY, LET'S BURY HIM!

YAH, YAH! C'MON! LIE DOWN!

HOW'S IT FEEL TO HAVE TWO GIRLS' HANDS ALL OVER YOU?

I'VE HAD BETTER.

HA HA

LOOK WHAT I MADE FOR HIM!

EEEW!

EEEW!

HA HA

GEE, WHAT'S SO BAD ABOUT IT?

RRRR!

IT'S GROSS!

HA HA

MY BRA'S FULL OF SAND AND STUFF... SO DON'T LOOK!

DON'T LOOK!

GIVE IT A REST! NOBODY CARES!

DON'T LOOK...

DAVE LAPP

GREAT GATSBYS

DREAM GIRL

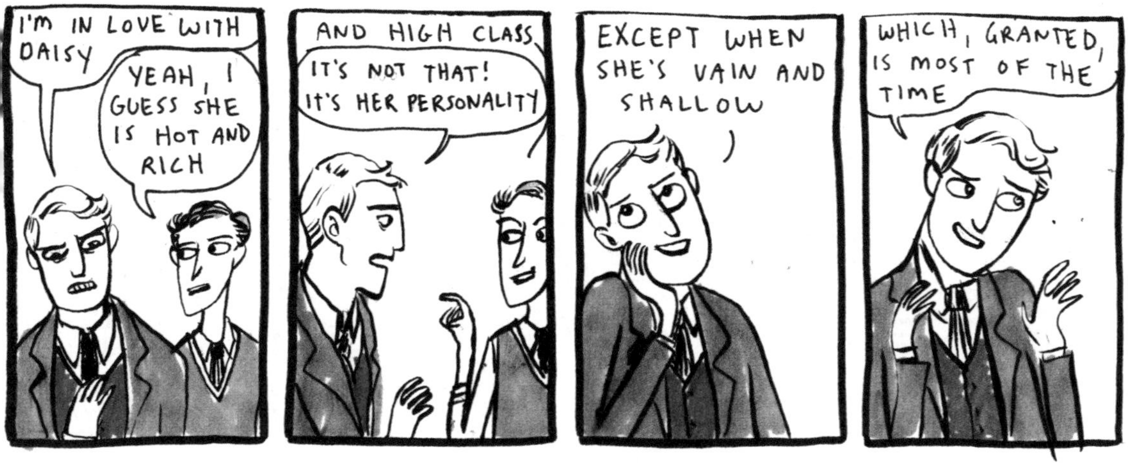
I'M IN LOVE WITH DAISY
YEAH, I GUESS SHE IS HOT AND RICH
AND HIGH CLASS
IT'S NOT THAT! IT'S HER PERSONALITY
EXCEPT WHEN SHE'S VAIN AND SHALLOW
WHICH, GRANTED, IS MOST OF THE TIME

LIKE TOM'S A GOOD FATHER

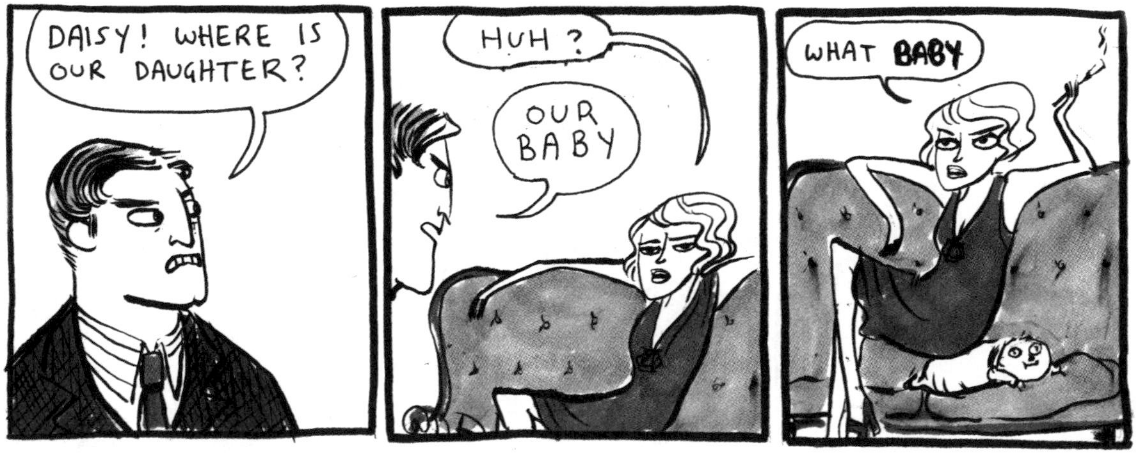
DAISY! WHERE IS OUR DAUGHTER?
HUH?
OUR BABY
WHAT BABY

IN THE VALLEY OF ASHES

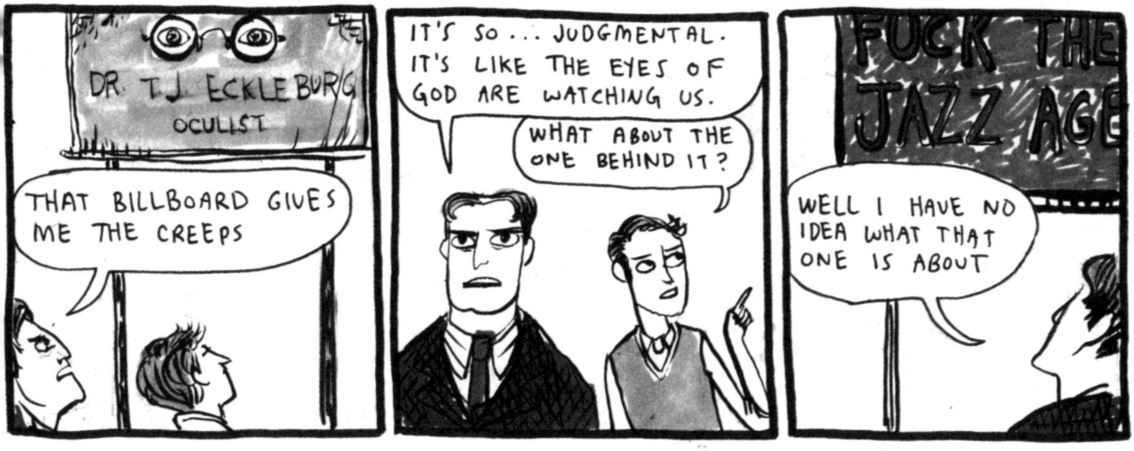
DR. T.J. ECKLEBURG
OCULIST
THAT BILLBOARD GIVES ME THE CREEPS
IT'S SO... JUDGMENTAL. IT'S LIKE THE EYES OF GOD ARE WATCHING US.
WHAT ABOUT THE ONE BEHIND IT?
FUCK THE JAZZ AGE
WELL I HAVE NO IDEA WHAT THAT ONE IS ABOUT

GREEN LIGHT

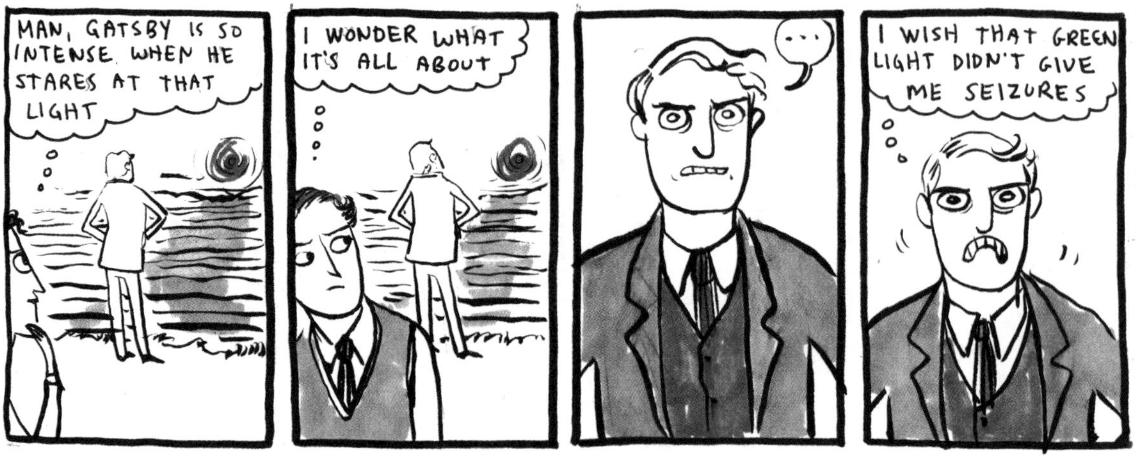
MAN, GATSBY IS SO INTENSE WHEN HE STARES AT THAT LIGHT
I WONDER WHAT IT'S ALL ABOUT
...
I WISH THAT GREEN LIGHT DIDN'T GIVE ME SEIZURES

THE REAL JAY GATSBY

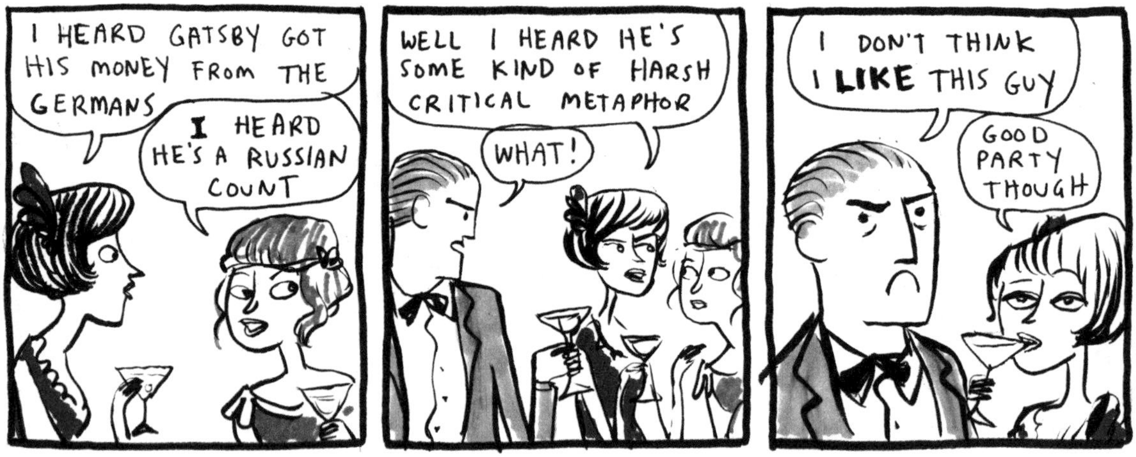
I HEARD GATSBY GOT HIS MONEY FROM THE GERMANS
I HEARD HE'S A RUSSIAN COUNT
WELL I HEARD HE'S SOME KIND OF HARSH CRITICAL METAPHOR
WHAT!
I DON'T THINK I **LIKE** THIS GUY
GOOD PARTY THOUGH

THAT'S PRETTY OLD

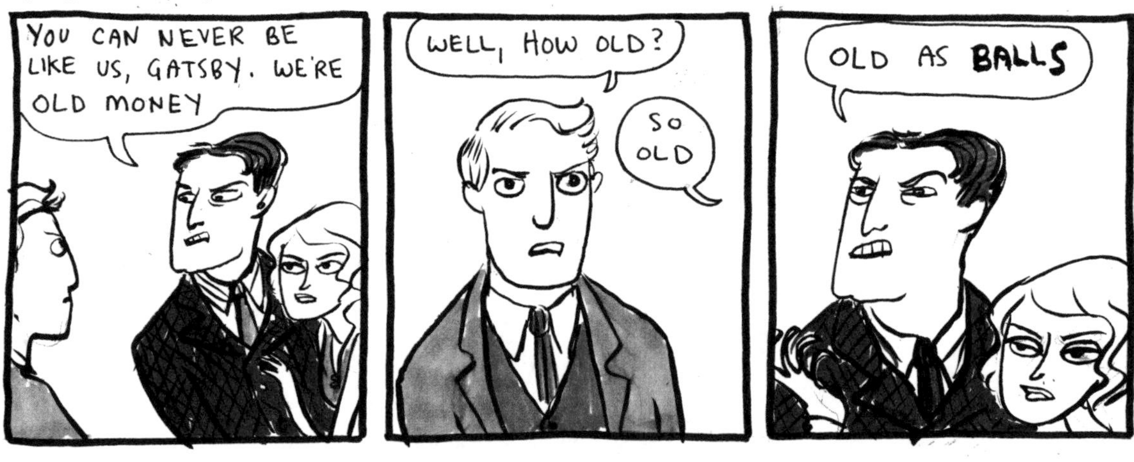
YOU CAN NEVER BE LIKE US, GATSBY. WE'RE OLD MONEY
WELL, HOW OLD?
SO OLD
OLD AS **BALLS**

LATER SHE DUMPS HIM

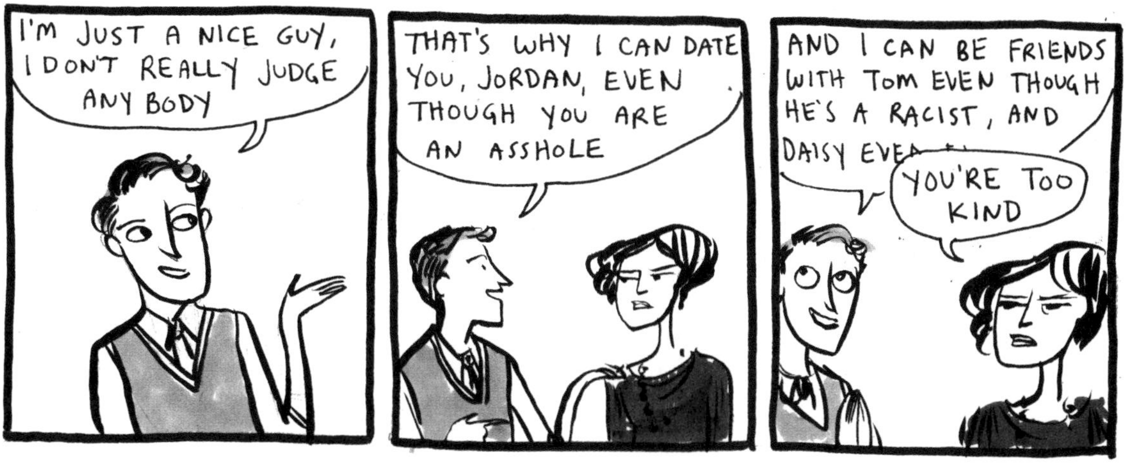
I'M JUST A NICE GUY, I DON'T REALLY JUDGE ANY BODY
THAT'S WHY I CAN DATE YOU, JORDAN, EVEN THOUGH YOU ARE AN ASSHOLE
AND I CAN BE FRIENDS WITH TOM EVEN THOUGH HE'S A RACIST, AND DAISY EV
YOU'RE TOO KIND

JUST AS GOOD THE SECOND TIME

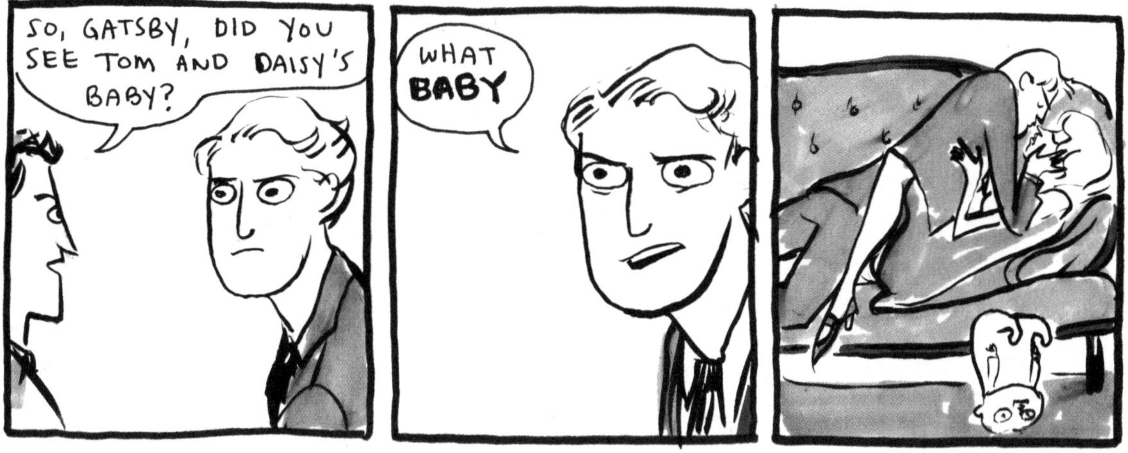
SO, GATSBY, DID YOU SEE TOM AND DAISY'S BABY?
WHAT BABY

NICK'S LUNCH DATE

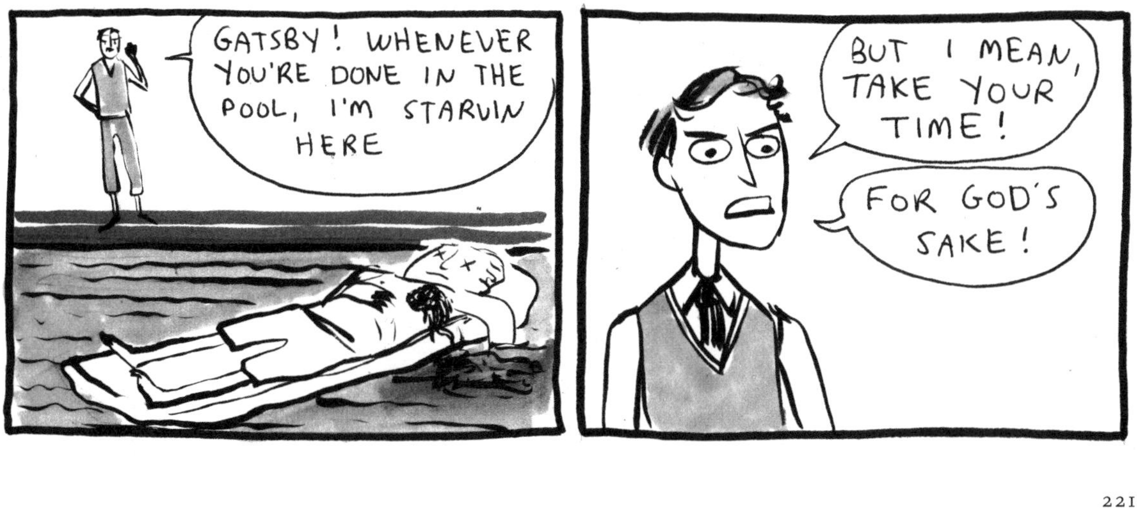
GATSBY! WHENEVER YOU'RE DONE IN THE POOL, I'M STARVIN HERE
BUT I MEAN, TAKE YOUR TIME!
FOR GOD'S SAKE!

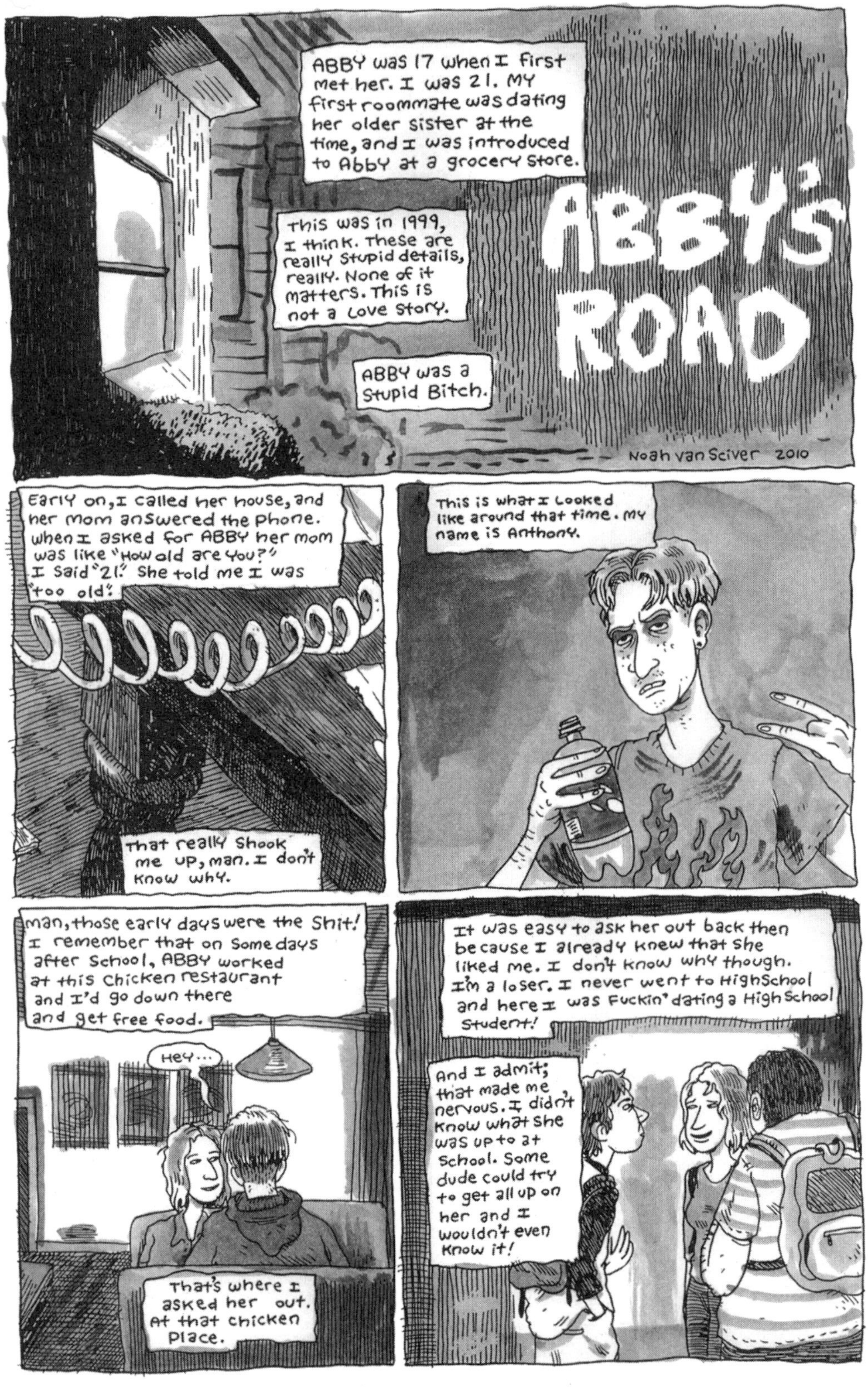
ABBY was 17 when I first met her. I was 21. MY first roommate was dating her older sister at the time, and I was introduced to Abby at a grocery store.
This was in 1999, I think. These are really stupid details, really. None of it matters. This is not a love story.
ABBY was a stupid Bitch.
ABBY'S ROAD
Noah van Sciver 2010
Early on, I called her house, and her mom answered the phone. When I asked for ABBY her mom was like "How old are you?" I said "21." She told me I was "too old".
That really shook me up, man. I don't know why.
This is what I looked like around that time. My name is Anthony.
Man, those early days were the shit! I remember that on some days after school, ABBY worked at this chicken restaurant and I'd go down there and get free food.
Hey...
That's where I asked her out. At that chicken place.
It was easy to ask her out back then because I already knew that she liked me. I don't know why though. I'm a loser. I never went to High School and here I was fuckin' dating a High School student!
And I admit; that made me nervous. I didn't know what she was up to at school. Some dude could try to get all up on her and I wouldn't even know it!

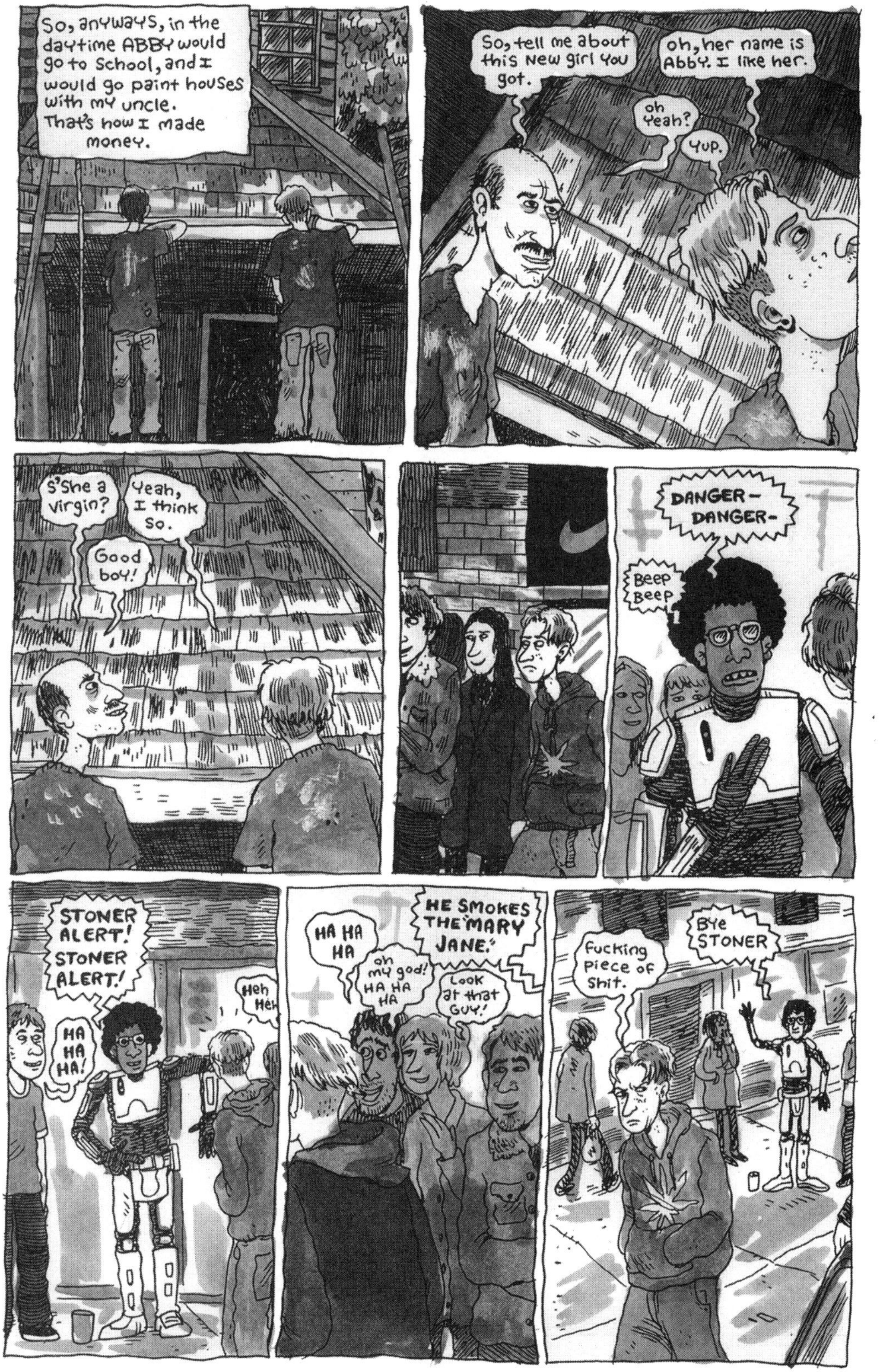
So, anyways, in the daytime ABBY would go to School, and I would go paint houses with my uncle. That's how I made money.
So, tell me about this New girl you got.
oh, her name is Abby. I like her.
oh yeah?
Yup.
S'she a virgin?
Yeah, I think so.
Good boy!
DANGER-DANGER-
Beep Beep
STONER ALERT! STONER ALERT!
HA HA HA!
Heh Heh
HA HA HA
HE SMOKES THE "MARY JANE."
oh my god! HA HA HA
Look at that GUY!
Fucking piece of shit.
BYe STONER

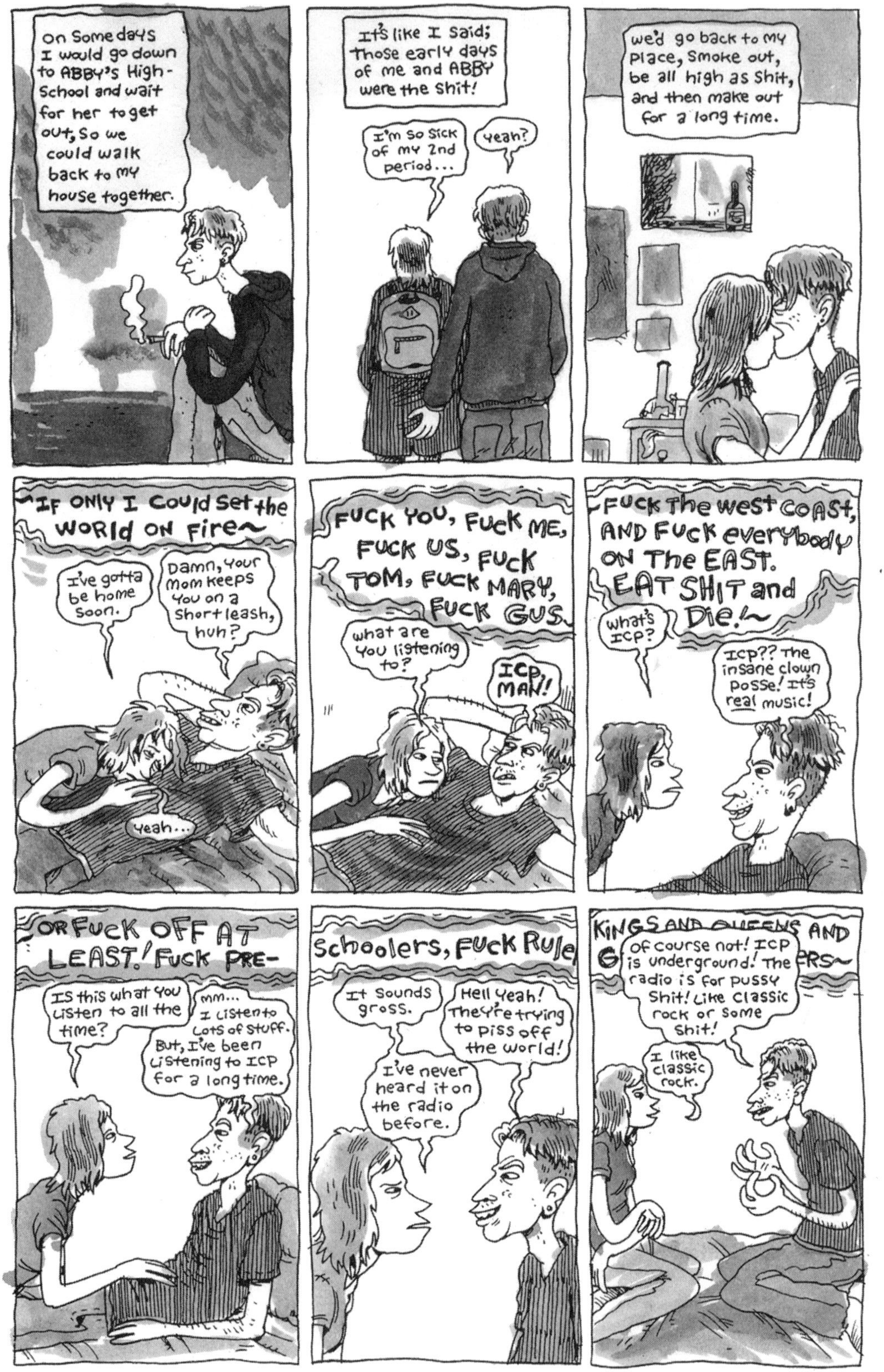
On Some days I would go down to ABBY's High-School and wait for her to get out, So we could walk back to my house together.
It's like I said; Those early days of me and ABBY were the Shit!
I'm so Sick of my 2nd period...
yeah?
we'd go back to my place, Smoke out, be all high as Shit, and then make out for a long time.
~IF ONLY I Could set the WORld ON Fire~
I've gotta be home soon.
Damn, your mom keeps you on a Short leash, huh?
yeah...
FUCK YOU, FUCK ME, FUCK US, FUCK TOM, FUCK MARY, FUCK GUS
what are you listening to?
ICP, MAN!
~FUCK The west COAST, AND FUCK everybody ON The EAST. EAT SHIT and Die!~
what's ICP?
ICP?? The insane clown posse! It's real music!
~OR FUCK OFF AT LEAST! FUCK PRE-
IS this what you listen to all the time?
mm... I listen to lots of stuff. But, I've been listening to ICP for a long time.
Schoolers, FUCK Rule
It Sounds gross.
Hell Yeah! They're trying to piss off the world!
I've never heard it on the radio before.
KINGS AND
AND
ERS~
Of course not! ICP is underground! The radio is for pussy Shit! Like classic rock or Some Shit!
I like classic rock.

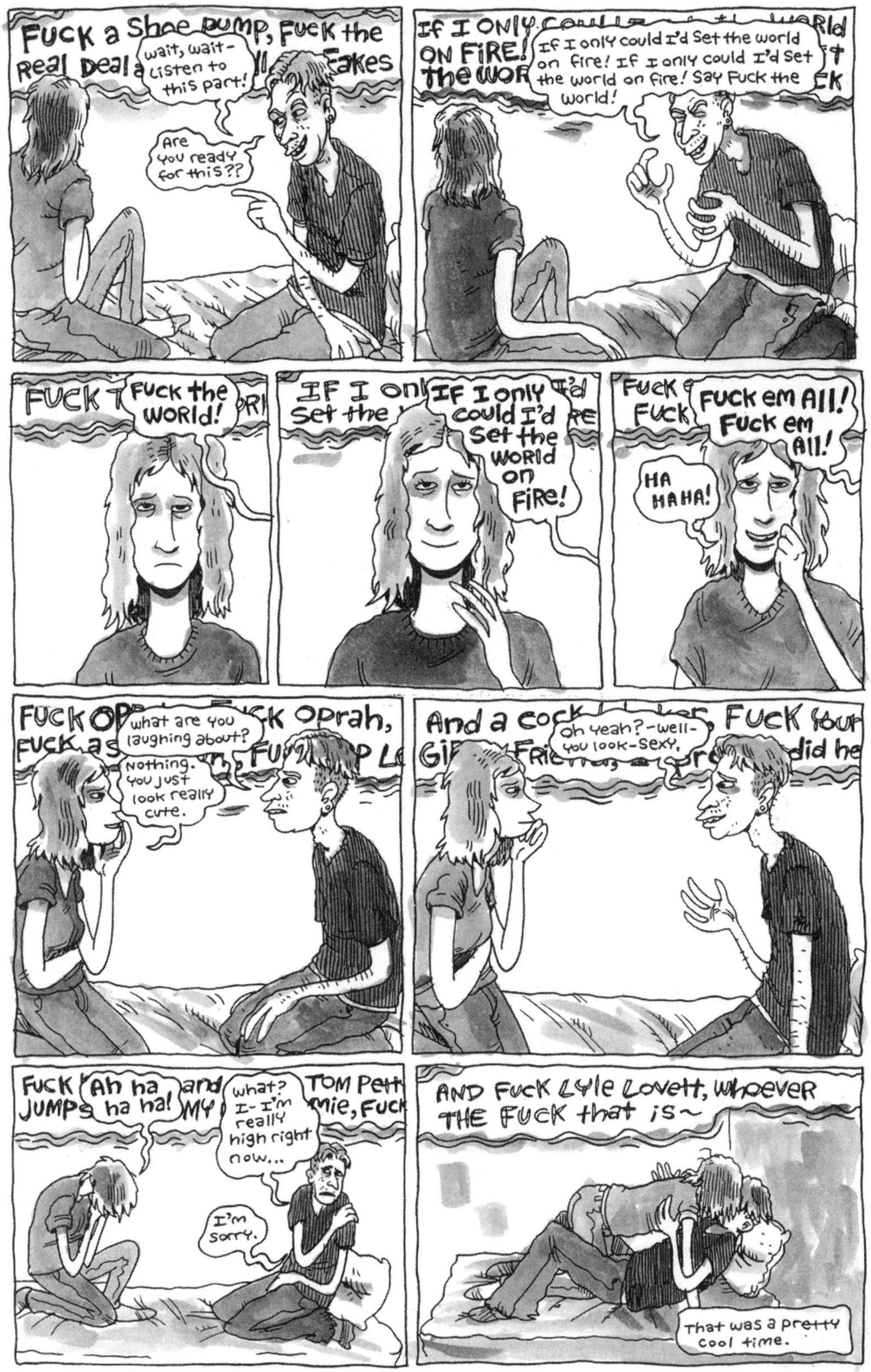
wait, wait- listen to this part!
Are you ready for this??
If I only could I'd set the world on fire! If I only could I'd set the world on fire! Say Fuck the world!
Fuck the WORLD!
IF I only could I'd set the WORLD on Fire!
Fuck em All! Fuck em All!
HA HAHA!
what are you laughing about?
Nothing. You just look really cute.
oh yeah?-well- you look-sexy.
Ah ha ha ha!
what? I-I'm really high right now...
I'm sorry.
AND FUCK LYLE LOVETT, WHOEVER THE FUCK that is~
That was a pretty cool time.

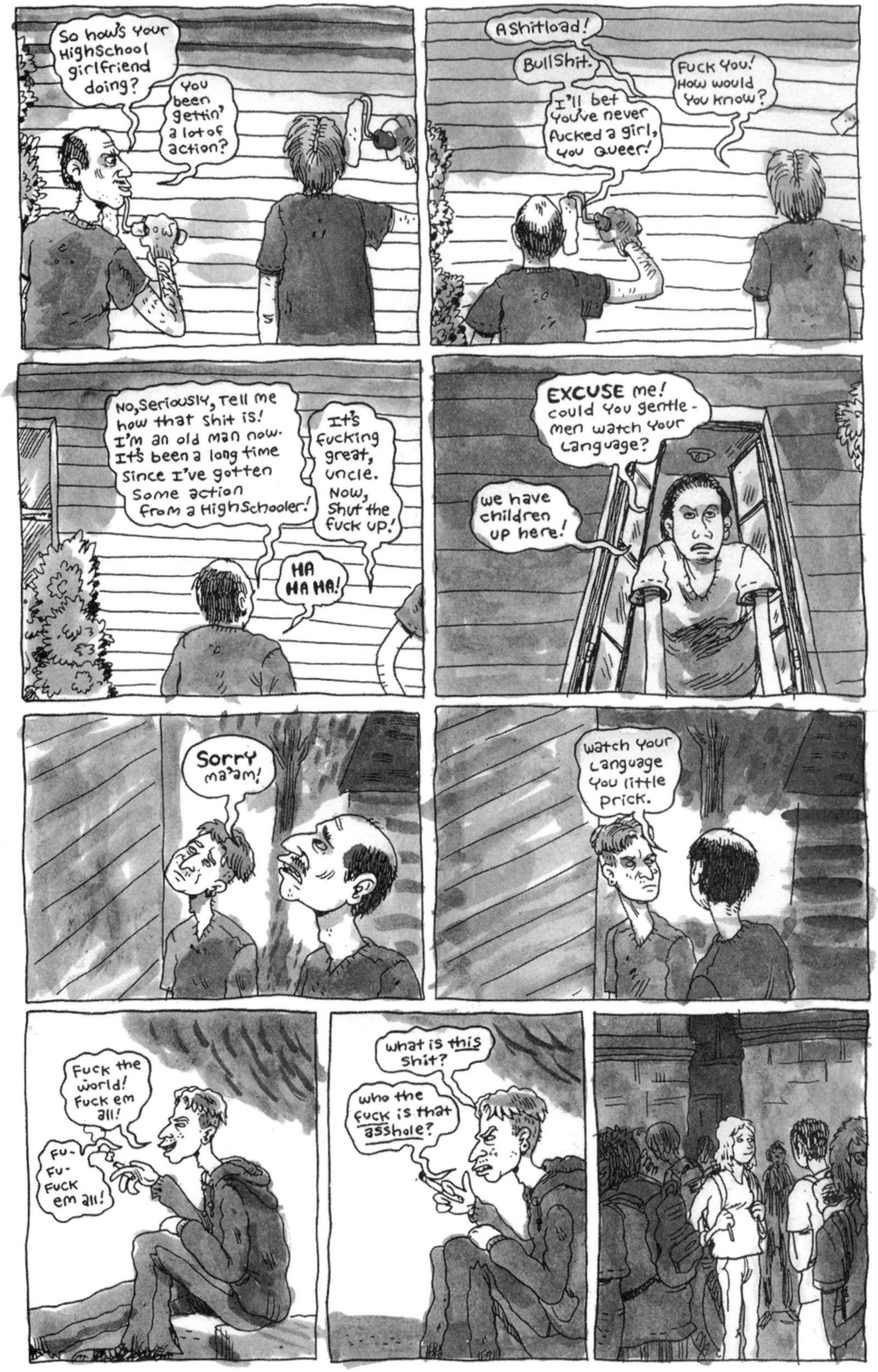
So how's your HighSchool girlfriend doing?
You been gettin' a lot of action?
A Shitload!
BullShit.
I'll bet you've never fucked a girl, you Queer!
Fuck you! How would you know?
No, Seriously, Tell me how that shit is! I'm an old man now. It's been a long time since I've gotten some action from a HighSchooler!
It's fucking great, uncle. Now, Shut the fuck up!
HA HA HA!
EXCUSE me! could you gentle-men watch your Language?
we have children up here!
SORRY ma'am!
watch your Language you little prick.
Fuck the world! Fuck em all!
FU- FU- FUCK em all!
what is this shit?
who the fuck is that asshole?

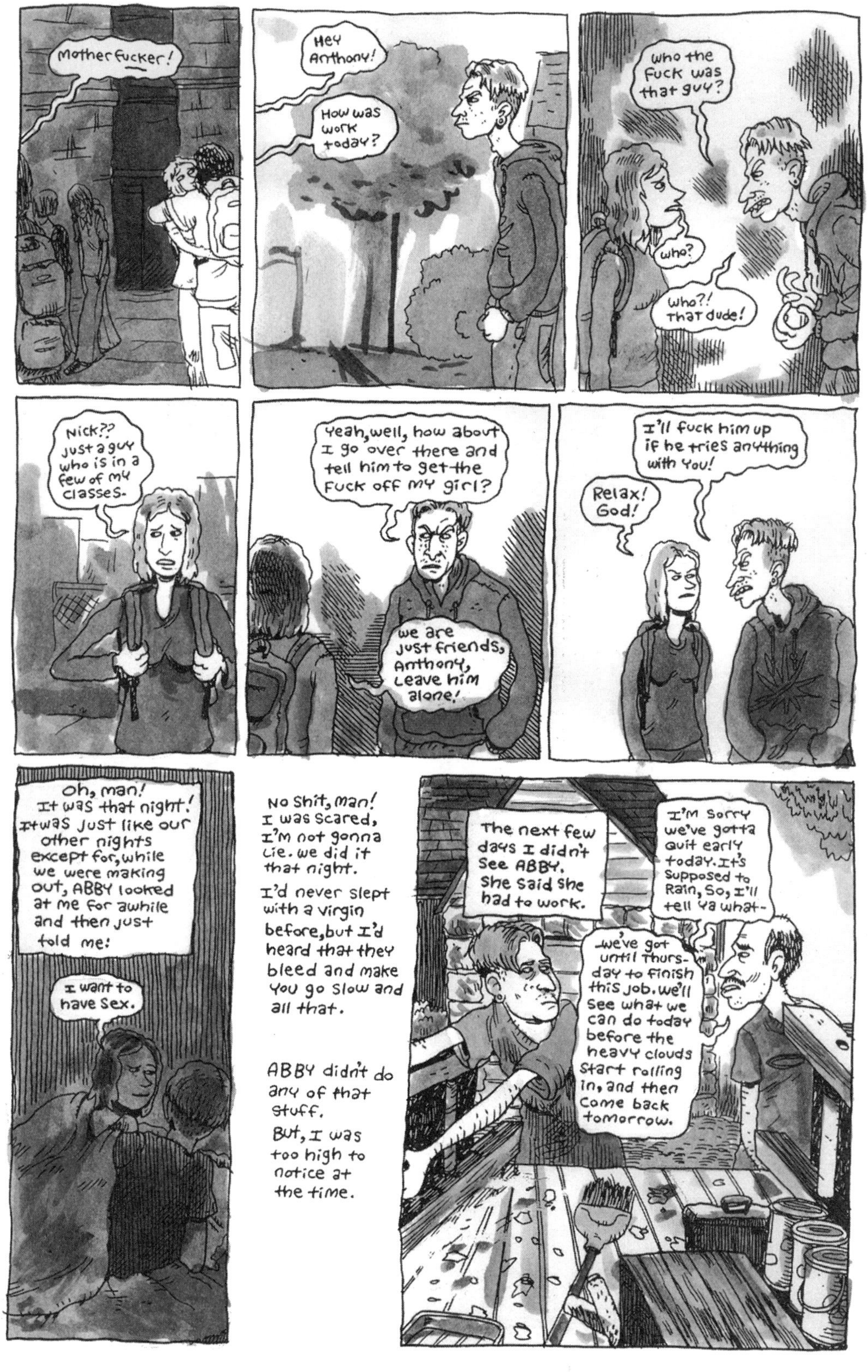

Mother Fucker!
Hey Anthony!
How was work today?
who the Fuck was that guy?
who?
who?! That dude!
Nick?? Just a guy who is in a few of my classes.
Yeah, well, how about I go over there and tell him to get the Fuck off my girl?
we are Just friends, Anthony, Leave him alone!
I'll fuck him up if he tries anything with you!
Relax! God!
Oh, man! It was that night! It was just like our other nights except for, while we were making out, ABBY looked at me for awhile and then just told me:
I want to have sex.
No Shit, man! I was scared, I'm not gonna lie. we did it that night.
I'd never slept with a virgin before, but I'd heard that they bleed and make you go slow and all that.
ABBY didn't do any of that stuff.
But, I was too high to notice at the time.
The next few days I didn't see ABBY. She said she had to work.
I'm sorry we've gotta quit early today. It's supposed to Rain, So, I'll tell ya what-
-we've got until Thursday to finish this job. we'll see what we can do today before the heavy clouds start rolling in, and then come back tomorrow.

Hey Bud— Lemme ask you—

Are you still dating that high-school chick?

Yeah, uncle. And I don't wanna hear any of your shit about it. So, just keep it in your mouth this time.

I'm not gonna kid you, Anthony... All I'm askin' for is cuz I saw her the other night with some other guy...

And I'll tell you what—

The way she was acting with him— Didn't look like you two were dating anymore.

Huh? What the fuck? It was ABBY? You don't even know what she looks like!

But, I know where she works.

And that's where she was. It was her all right.

With some preppy little fucker. I mean, listen, I just saw them talking but when he left he kissed her.

Fuck off.

Anthony...

I didn't know what to say. I guess I didn't really know if he was fucking with me or not. He didn't bring it up again, and I didn't either.

We painted until the clouds were real dark and right above our heads and then we packed up and ducked out.

The next day I waited in a different spot for ABBY to get out of school.

I guess I was really looking for that guy Nick.

That preppy fucker.

And damn, man— I waited for a long fuckin' time! I saw every mother fucking person leave that fucking school and not a single one was ABBY or fucking NICK.

It was stupid as shit.

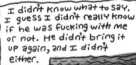

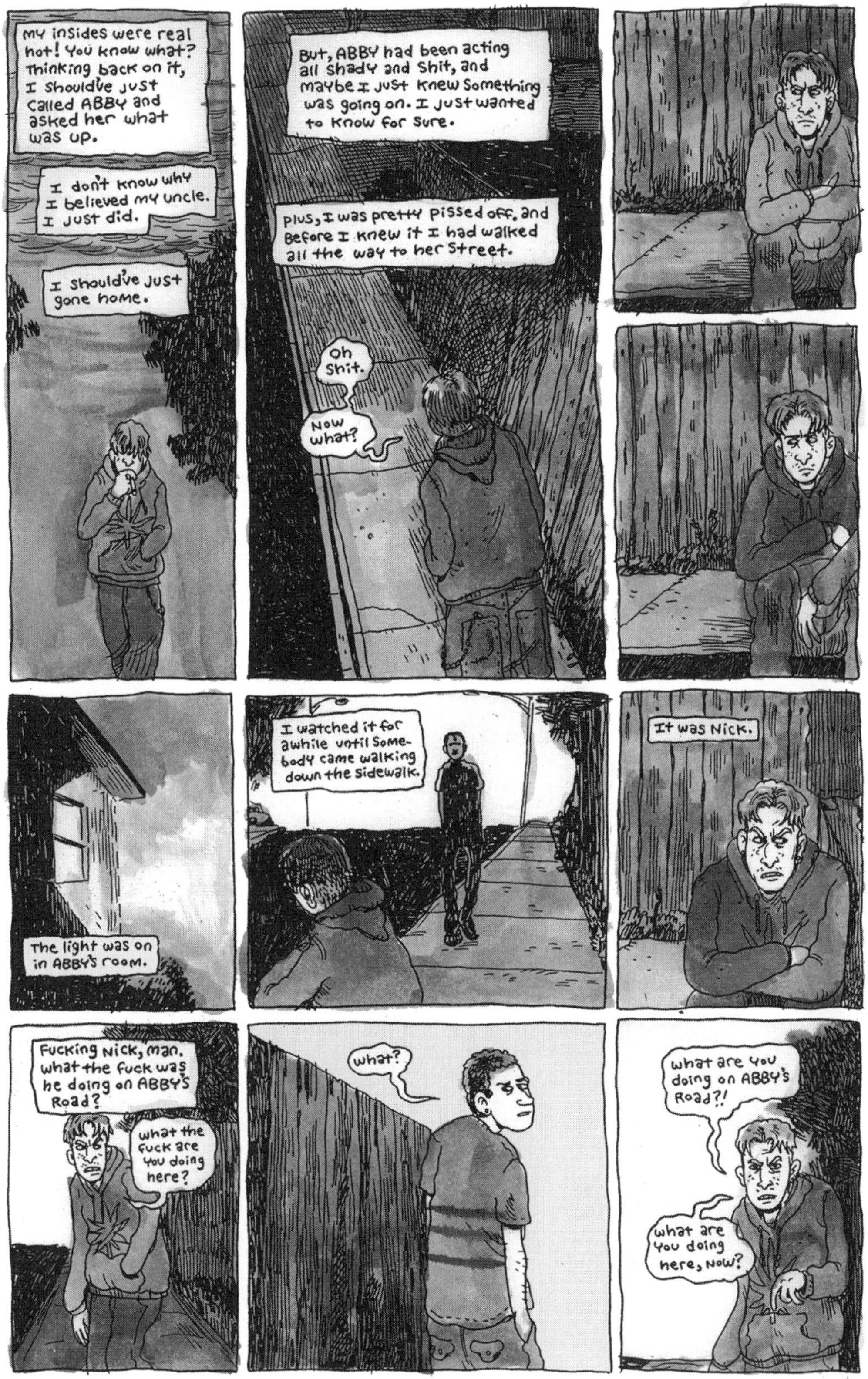
My insides were real hot! You know what? Thinking back on it, I should've just called ABBY and asked her what was up.
I don't know why I believed my uncle. I just did.
I should've just gone home.
But, ABBY had been acting all shady and shit, and maybe I just knew something was going on. I just wanted to know for sure.
Plus, I was pretty pissed off, and before I knew it I had walked all the way to her street.
Oh shit.
Now what?
The light was on in ABBY's room.
I watched it for awhile until somebody came walking down the sidewalk.
It was Nick.
Fucking Nick, man. What the fuck was he doing on ABBY's Road?
What the fuck are you doing here?
What?
What are you doing on ABBY's Road?!
What are you doing here, now?

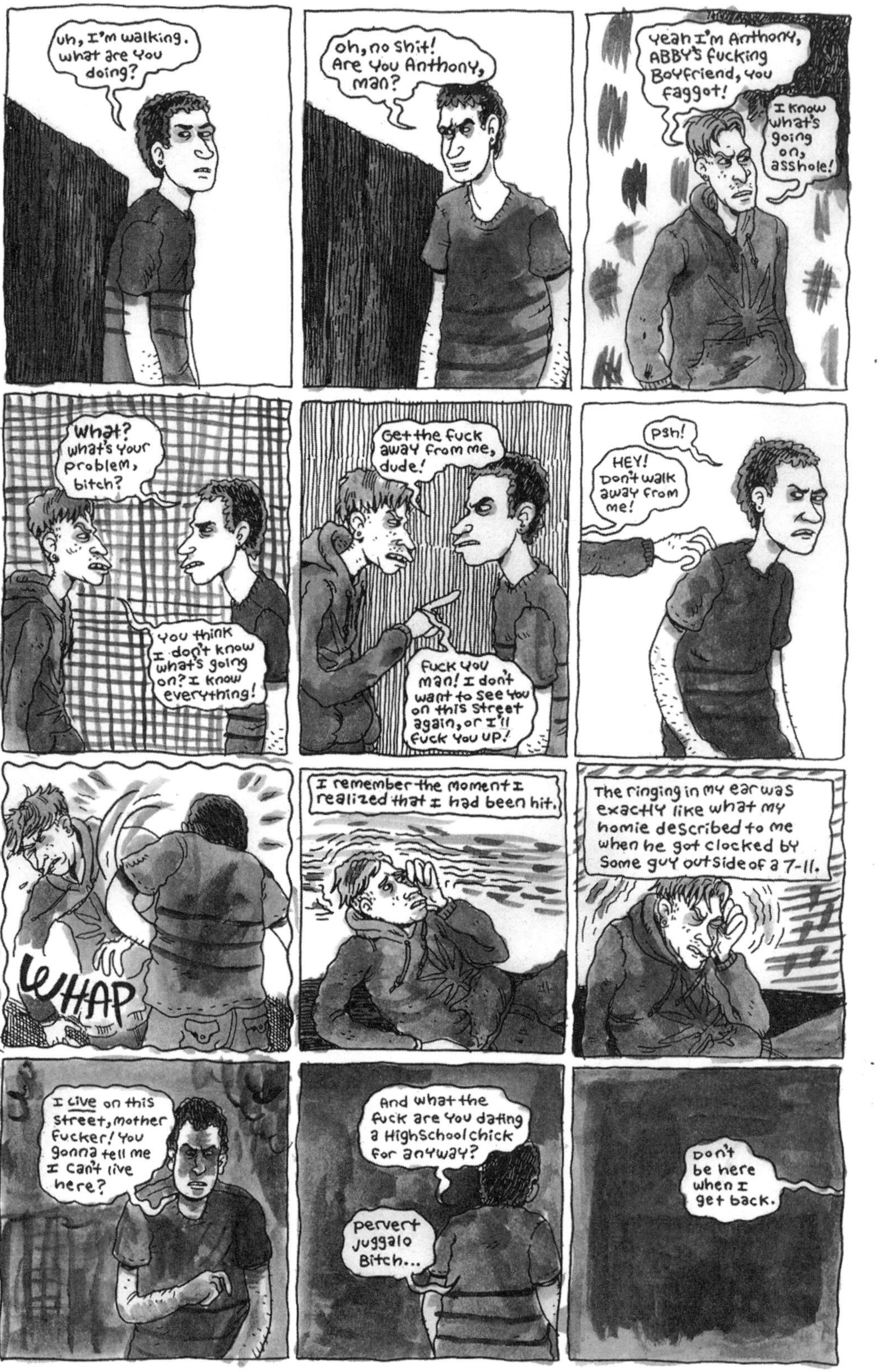
uh, I'm walking. what are you doing?
oh, no shit! Are you Anthony, man?
yeah I'm Anthony, ABBY's fucking Boyfriend, you faggot!
I know what's going on, asshole!
What? what's your problem, bitch?
You think I don't know what's going on? I know everything!
Get the fuck away from me, dude!
Fuck you man! I don't want to see you on this street again, or I'll fuck you up!
Psh!
HEY! Don't walk away from me!
WHAP
I remember the moment I realized that I had been hit.
The ringing in my ear was exactly like what my homie described to me when he got clocked by some guy outside of a 7-11.
I live on this street, mother fucker! You gonna tell me I can't live here?
And what the fuck are you dating a HighSchool chick for anyway?
pervert juggalo Bitch...
Don't be here when I get back.

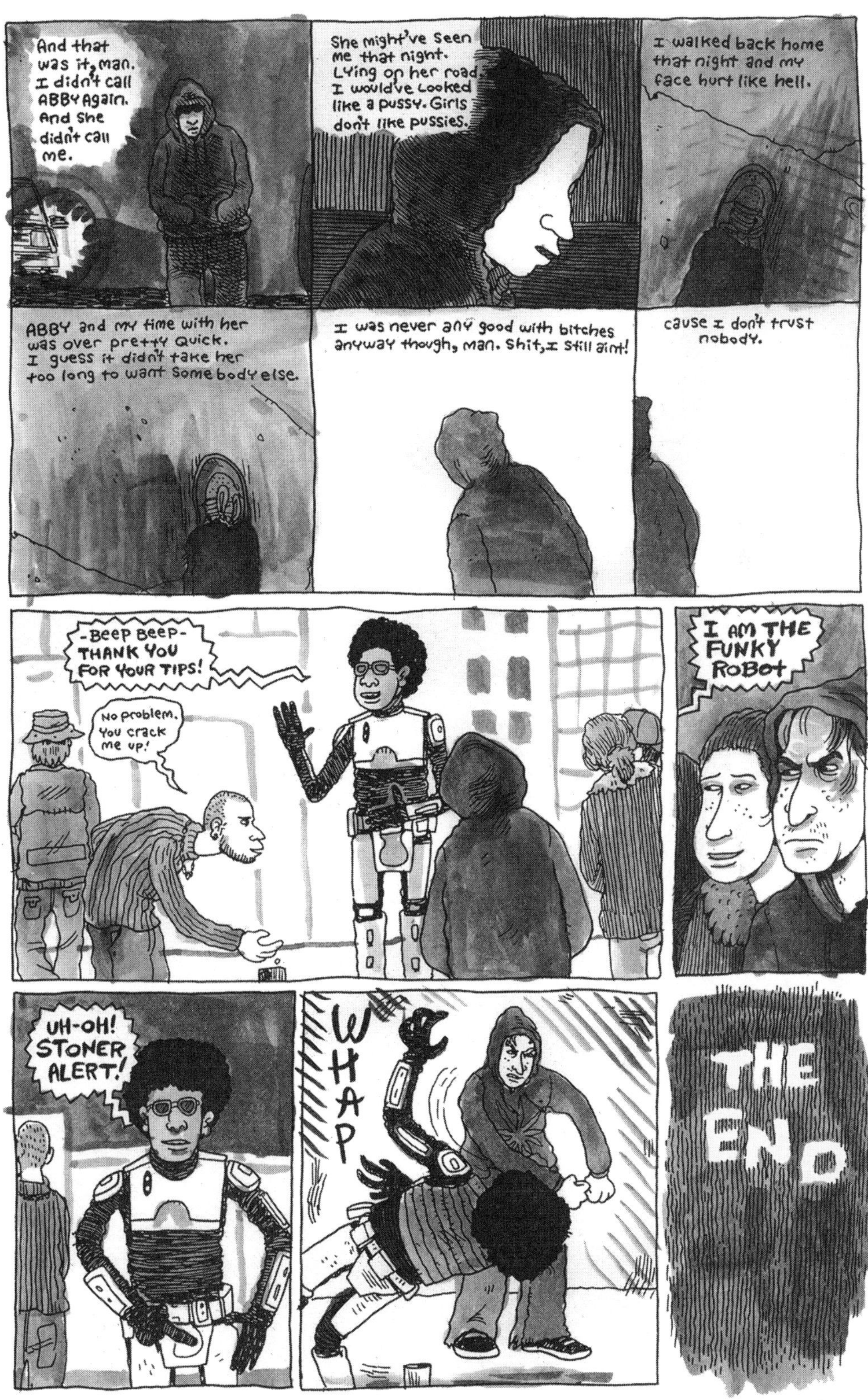
And that was it, man. I didn't call ABBY again. And she didn't call me.
She might've seen me that night. Lying on her road. I would've looked like a pussy. Girls don't like pussies.
I walked back home that night and my face hurt like hell.
ABBY and my time with her was over pretty quick. I guess it didn't take her too long to want somebody else.
I was never any good with bitches anyway though, man. Shit, I still aint!
cause I don't trust nobody.
-Beep Beep- THANK YOU FOR YOUR TIPS!
No problem. You crack me up!
I AM THE FUNKY RoBot
UH-OH! STONER ALERT!
WHAP
THE END

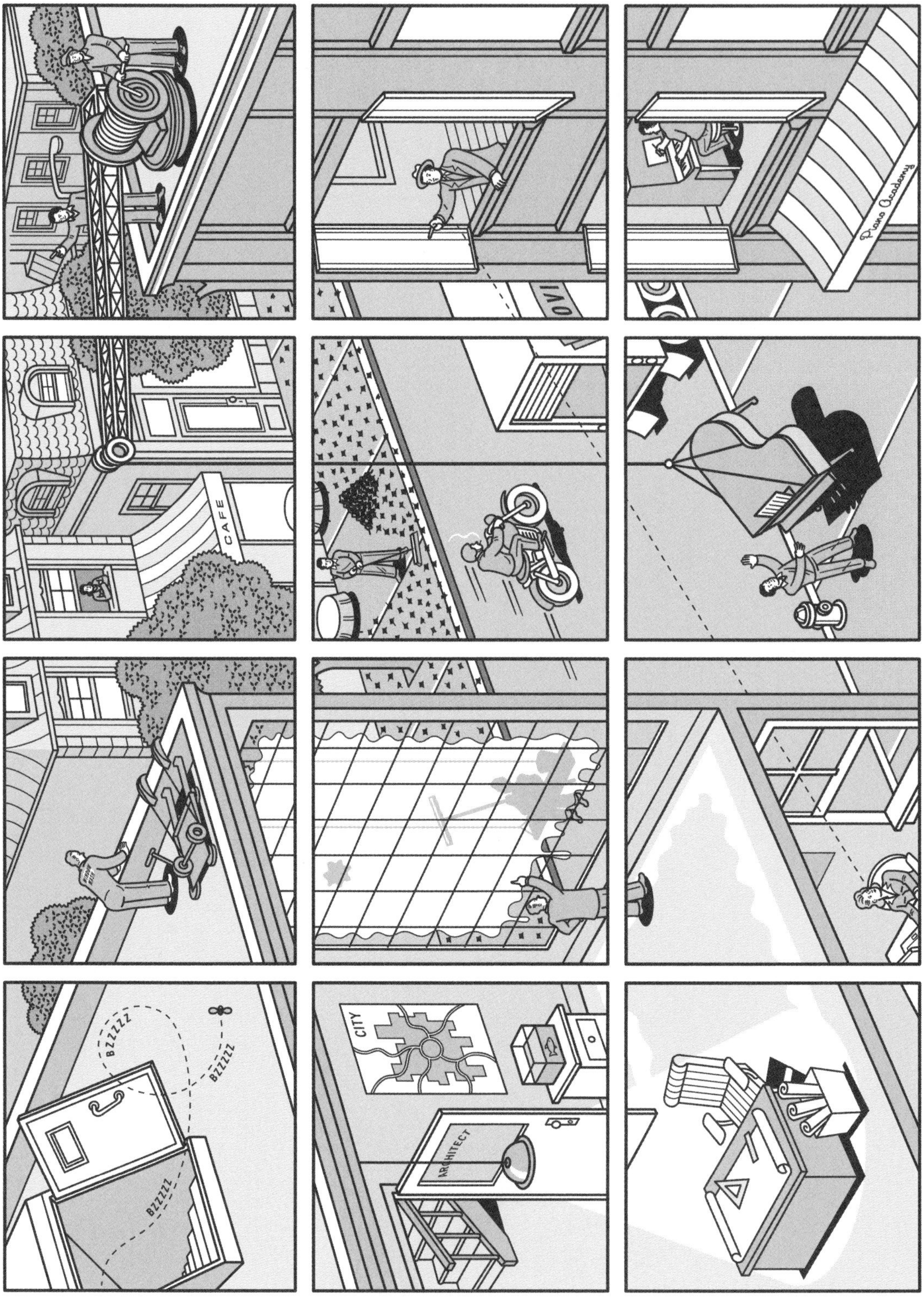

Piano Academy
CAFE
BZZZZZ
BZZZZZ
BZZZZZ
CITY
ARCHITECT

anatomy of a pratfall

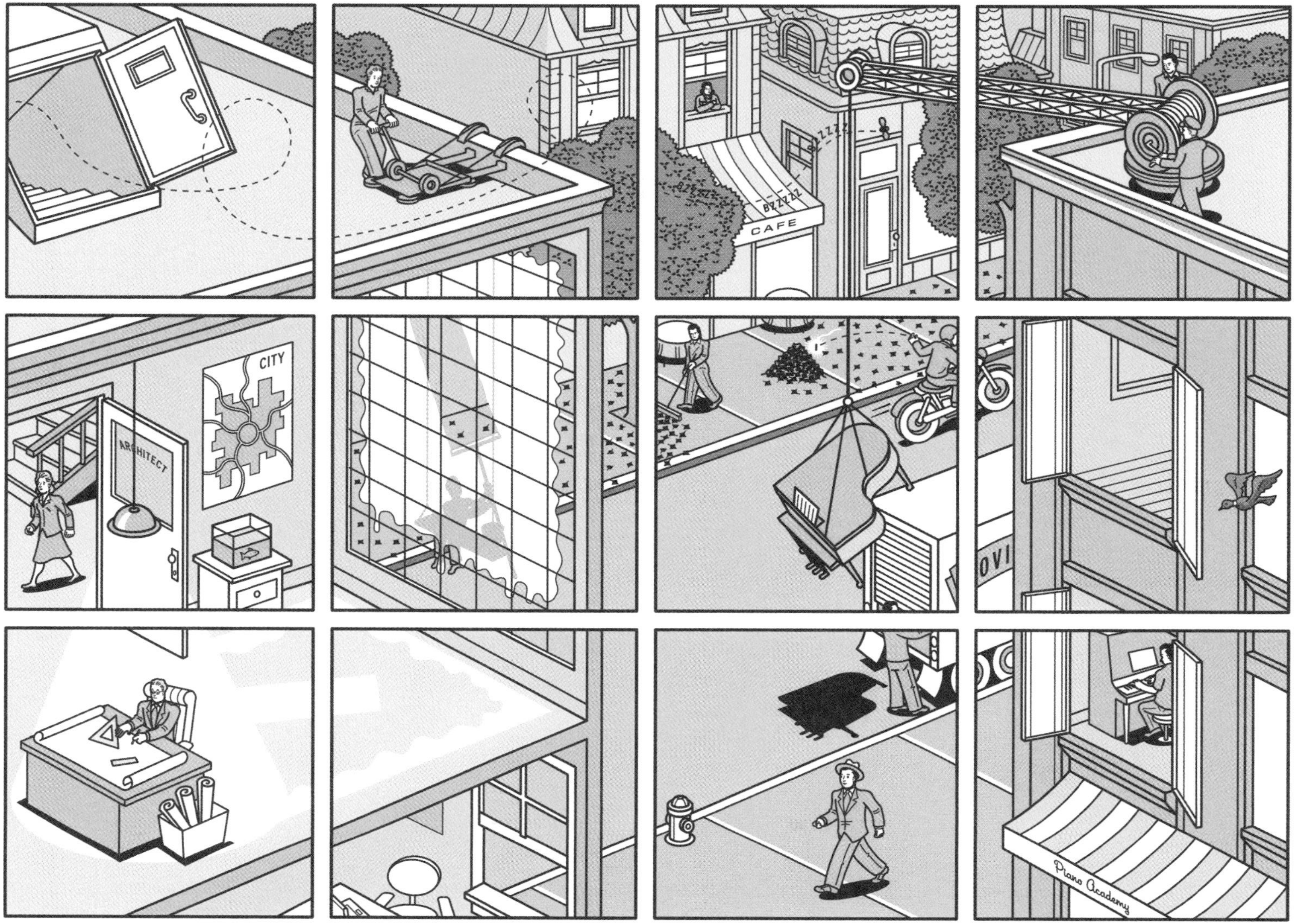
BZZZZZ
BZZZZZ
BZZZZZ
CAFE
ARCHITECT
CITY
OVI
Piano Academy

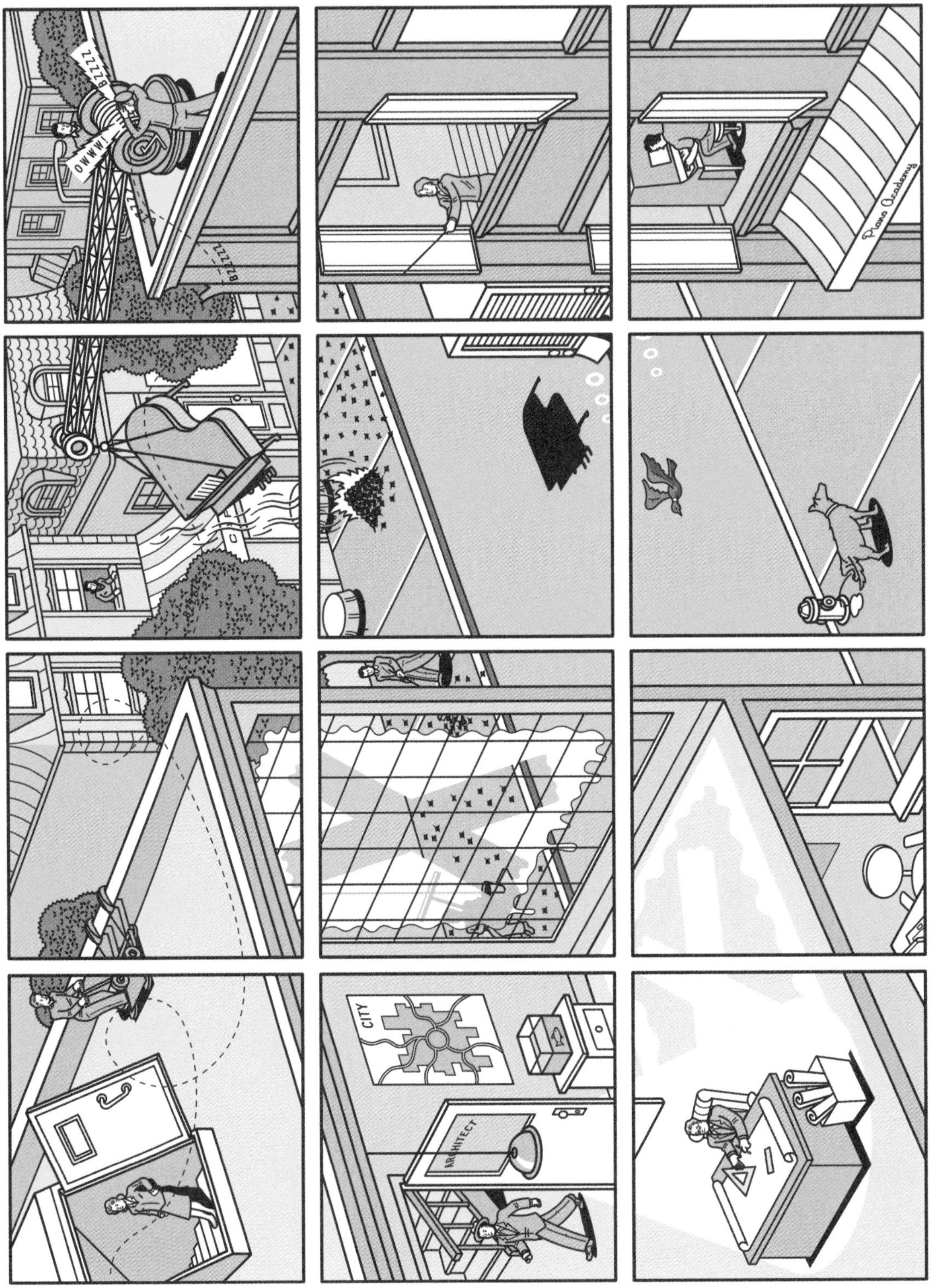
BZZZZ
OWWW!
BZZZZZ
Piano Academy
CITY
ARCHITECT

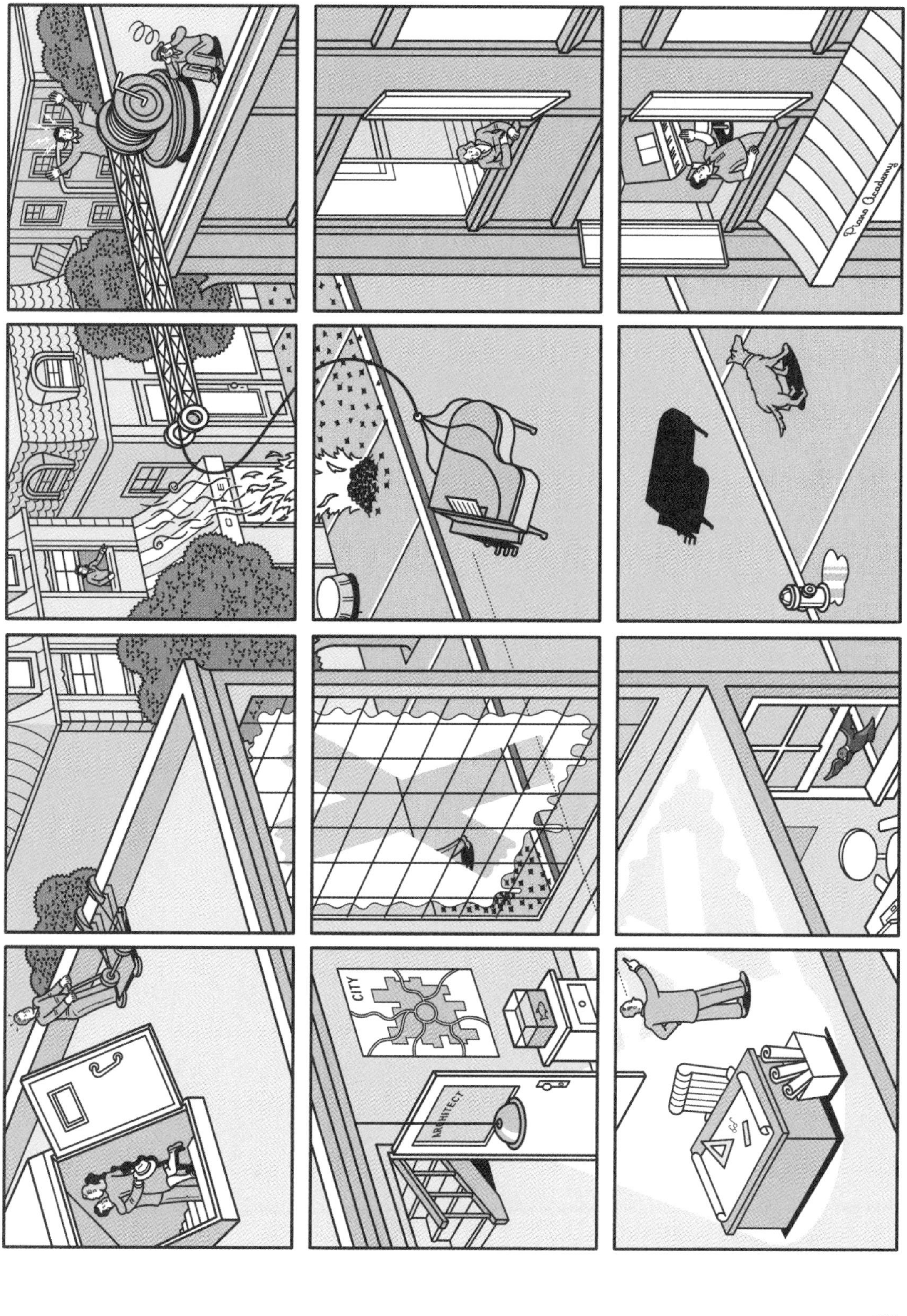
Piano Academy
CITY

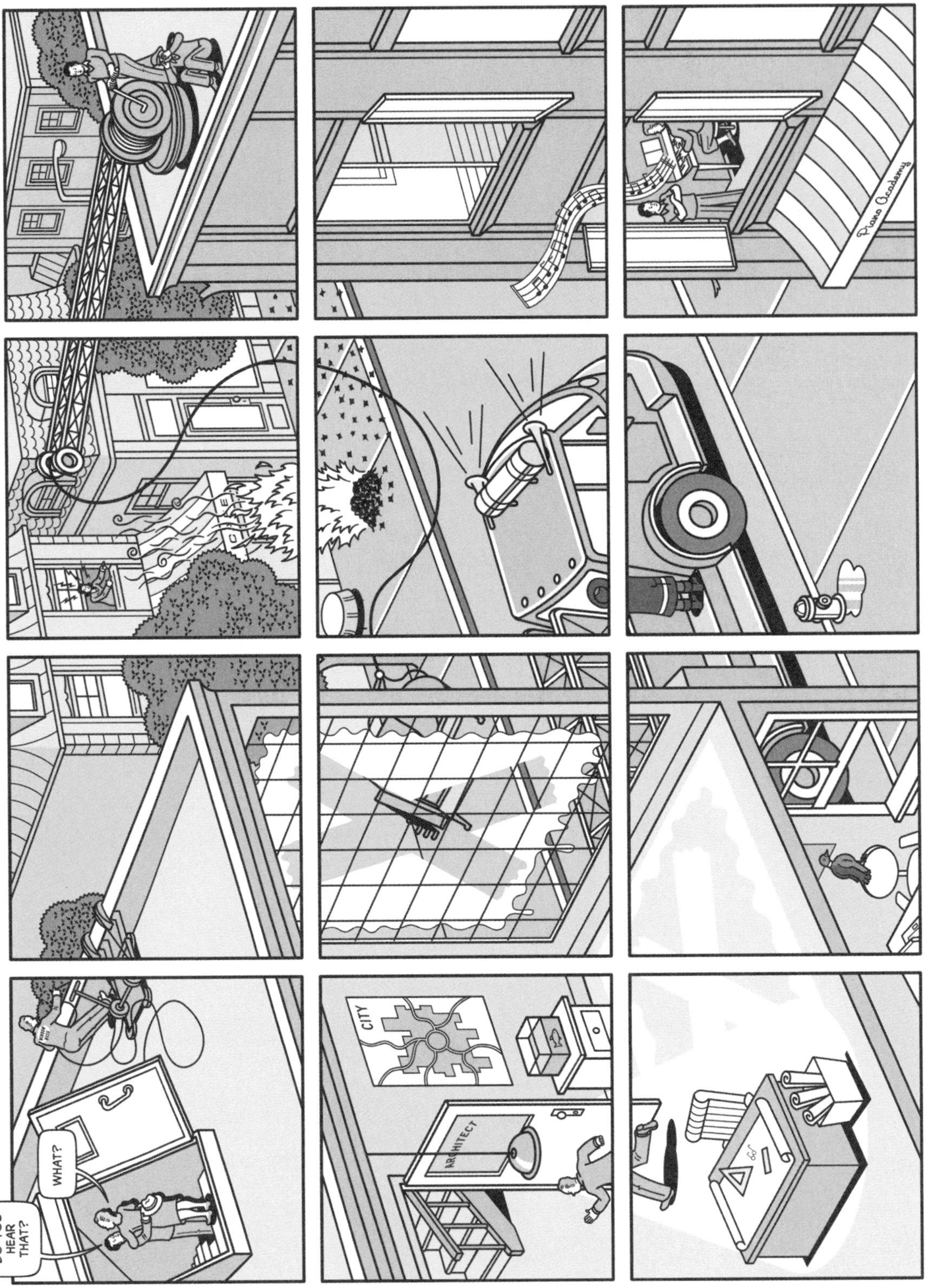

DO YOU HEAR THAT?
WHAT?
Piano Academy
CITY
ARCHITECT

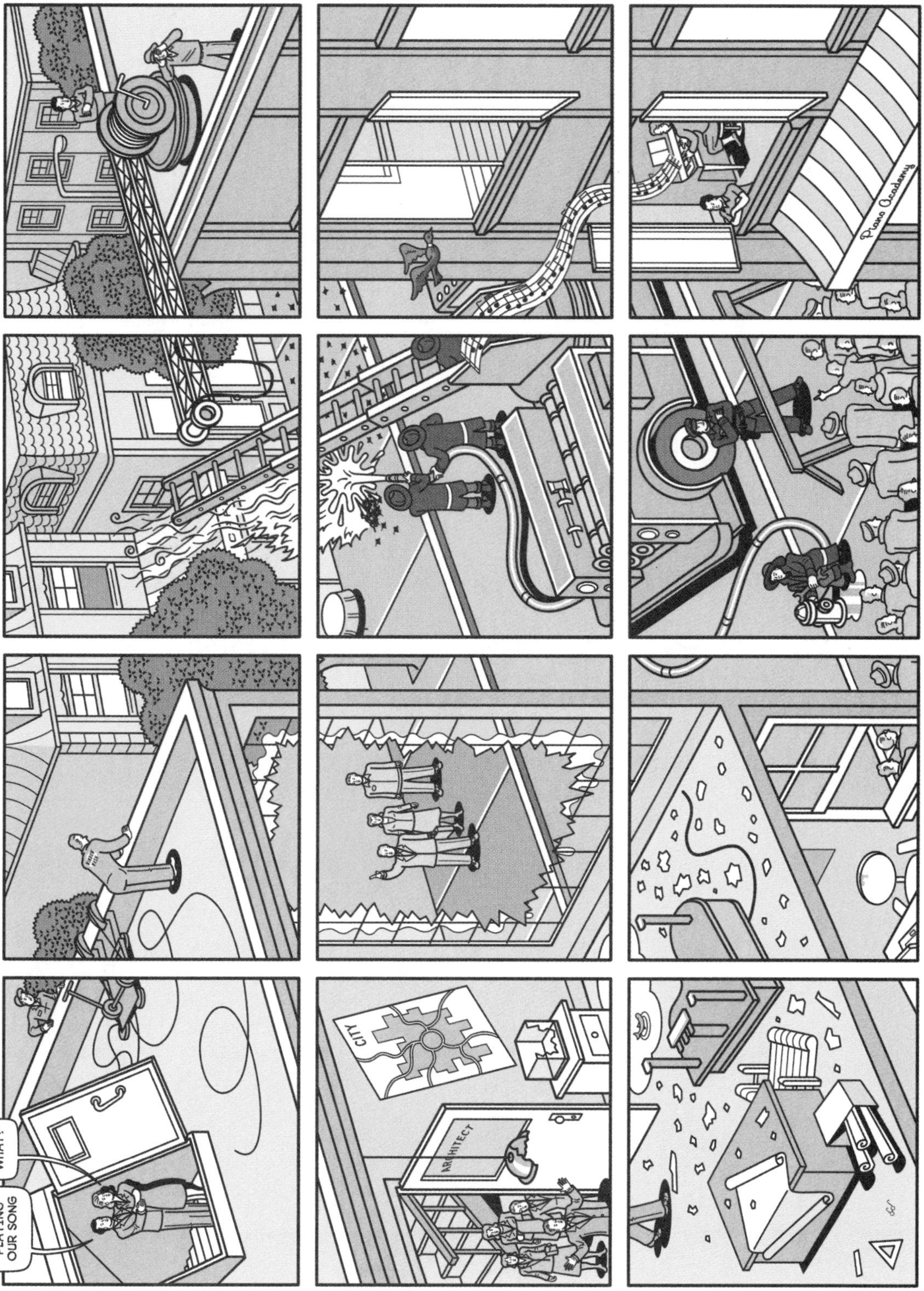
Piano Academy
CITY
ARCHITECT
THEY'RE PLAYING OUR SONG
WHAT?

THE MAD SCIENTIST

excerpt from

RASL

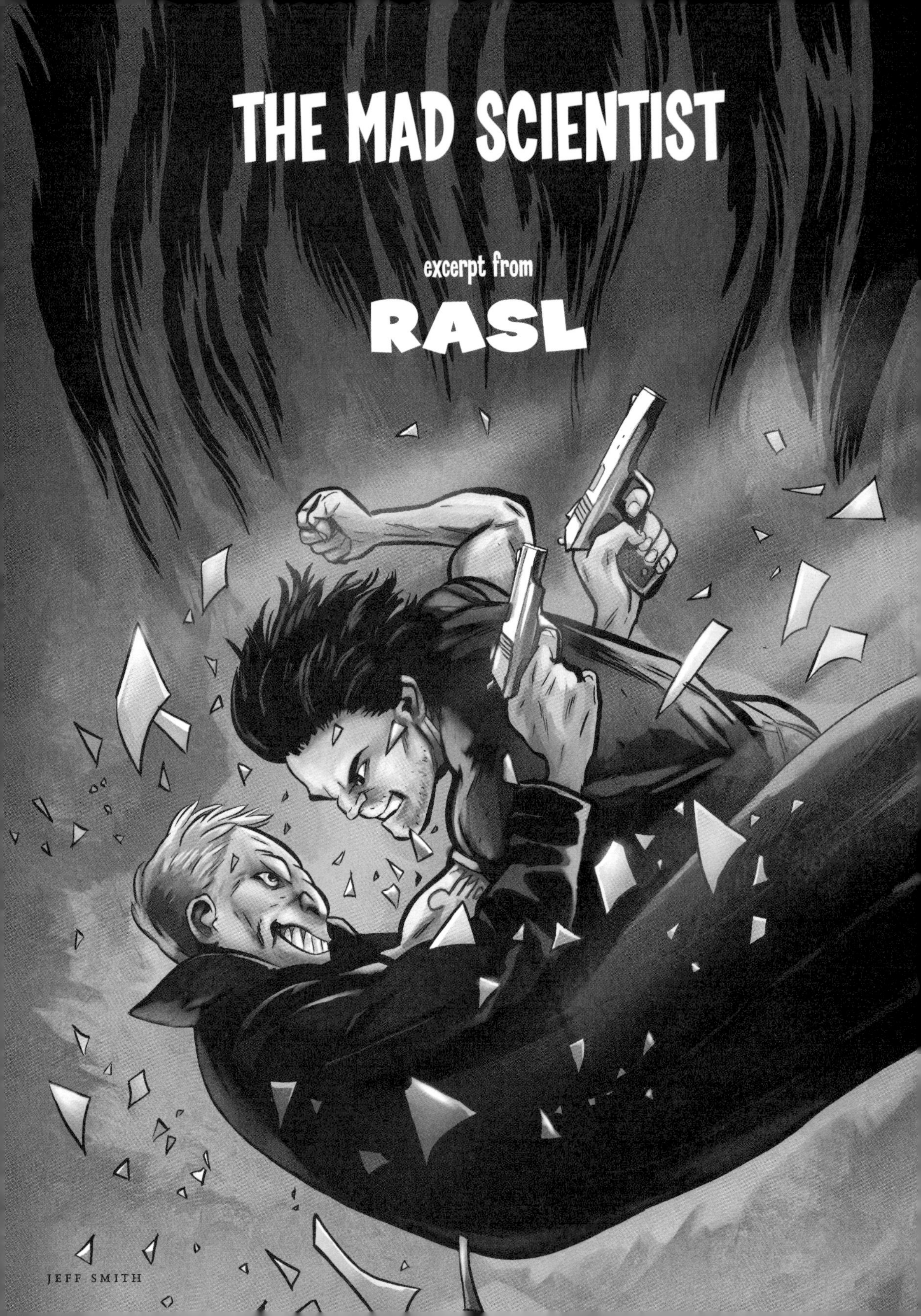

JEFF SMITH

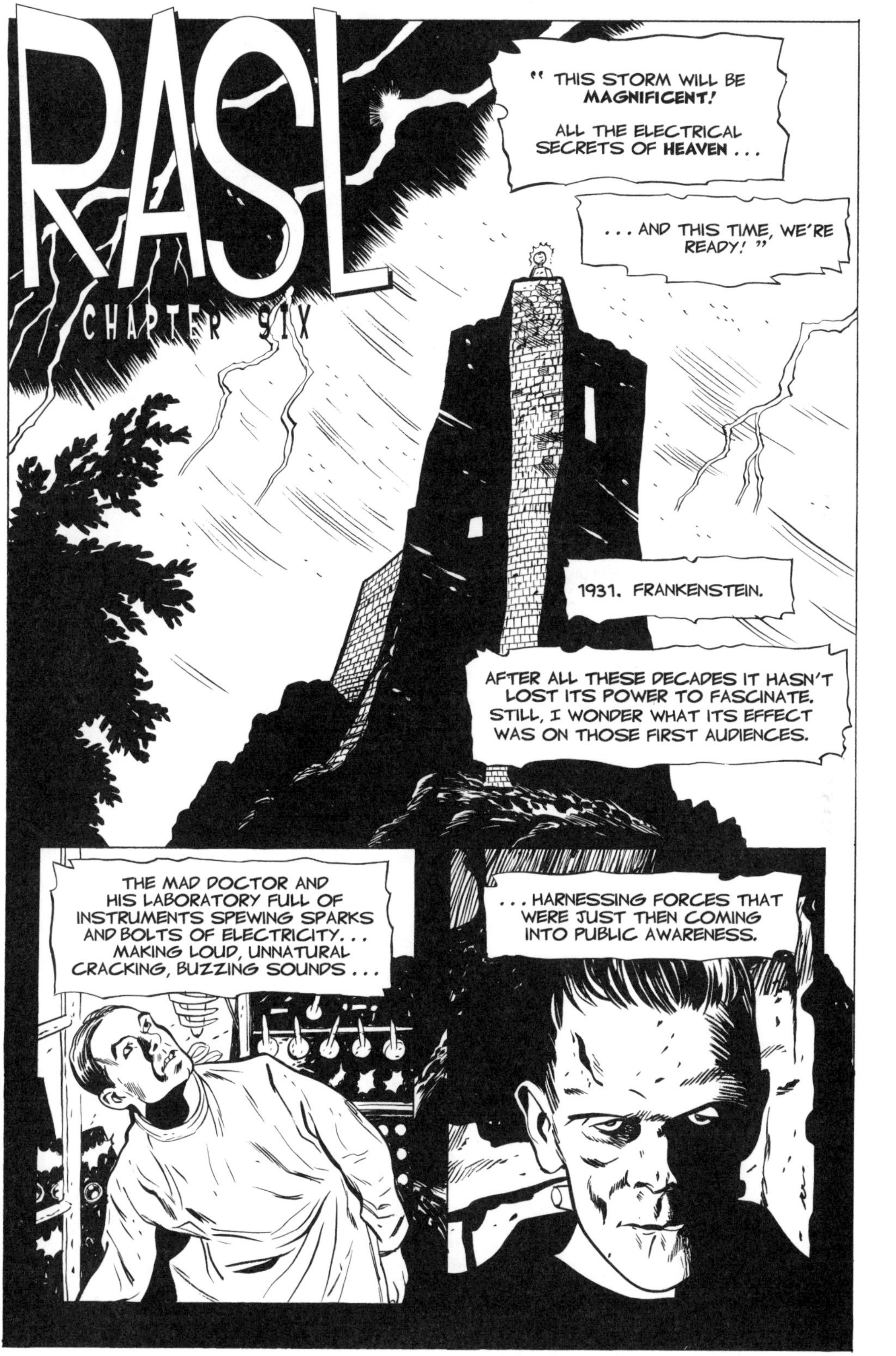
RASL
CHAPTER SIX
" THIS STORM WILL BE MAGNIFICENT! ALL THE ELECTRICAL SECRETS OF HEAVEN . . .
. . . AND THIS TIME, WE'RE READY! "
1931. FRANKENSTEIN.
AFTER ALL THESE DECADES IT HASN'T LOST ITS POWER TO FASCINATE. STILL, I WONDER WHAT ITS EFFECT WAS ON THOSE FIRST AUDIENCES.
THE MAD DOCTOR AND HIS LABORATORY FULL OF INSTRUMENTS SPEWING SPARKS AND BOLTS OF ELECTRICITY. . . MAKING LOUD, UNNATURAL CRACKING, BUZZING SOUNDS . . .
. . . HARNESSING FORCES THAT WERE JUST THEN COMING INTO PUBLIC AWARENESS.

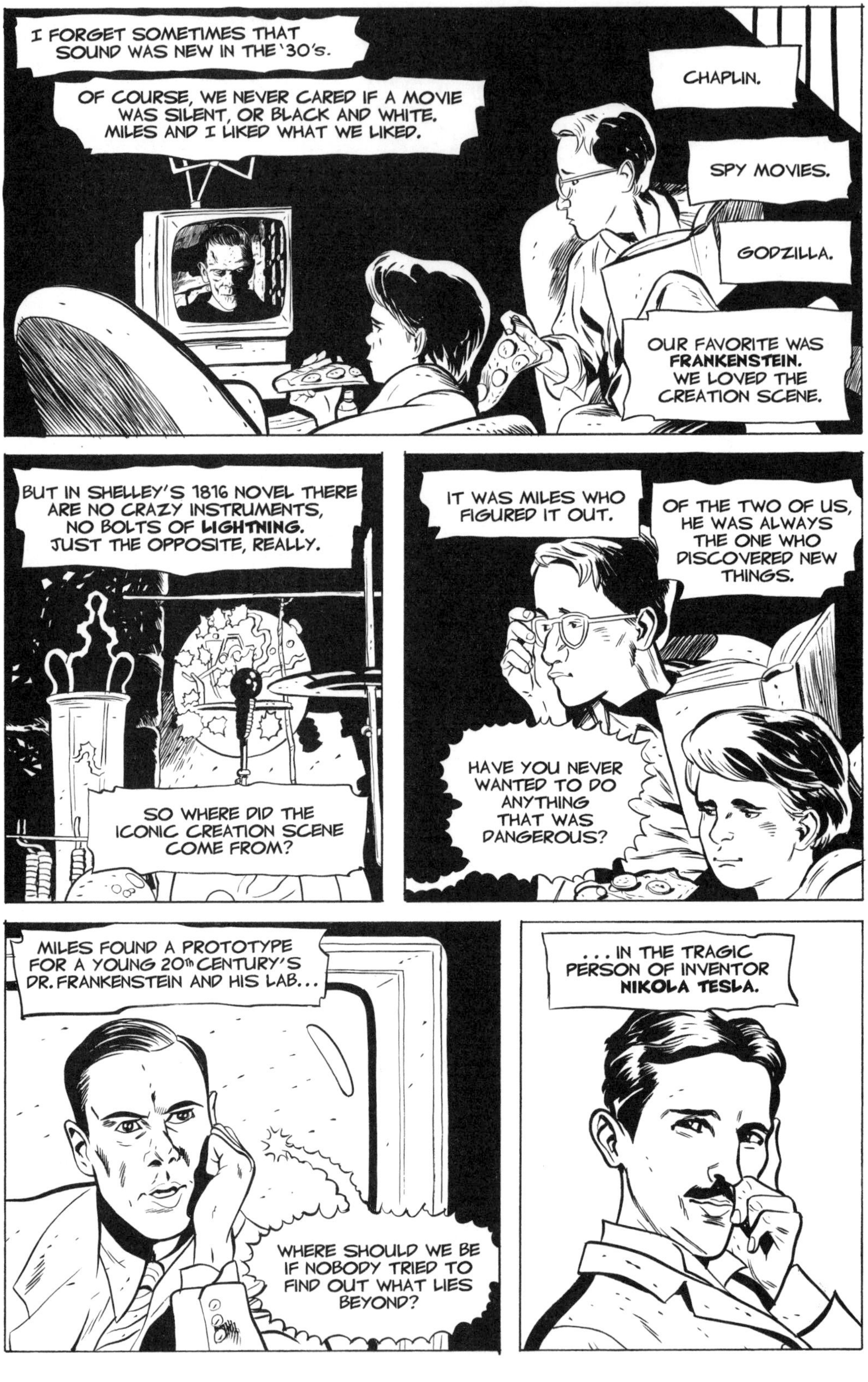
I FORGET SOMETIMES THAT SOUND WAS NEW IN THE '30's.
OF COURSE, WE NEVER CARED IF A MOVIE WAS SILENT, OR BLACK AND WHITE. MILES AND I LIKED WHAT WE LIKED.
CHAPLIN.
SPY MOVIES.
GODZILLA.
OUR FAVORITE WAS FRANKENSTEIN. WE LOVED THE CREATION SCENE.
BUT IN SHELLEY'S 1816 NOVEL THERE ARE NO CRAZY INSTRUMENTS, NO BOLTS OF LIGHTNING. JUST THE OPPOSITE, REALLY.
SO WHERE DID THE ICONIC CREATION SCENE COME FROM?
IT WAS MILES WHO FIGURED IT OUT.
OF THE TWO OF US, HE WAS ALWAYS THE ONE WHO DISCOVERED NEW THINGS.
HAVE YOU NEVER WANTED TO DO ANYTHING THAT WAS DANGEROUS?
MILES FOUND A PROTOTYPE FOR A YOUNG 20th CENTURY'S DR. FRANKENSTEIN AND HIS LAB...
WHERE SHOULD WE BE IF NOBODY TRIED TO FIND OUT WHAT LIES BEYOND?
... IN THE TRAGIC PERSON OF INVENTOR NIKOLA TESLA.

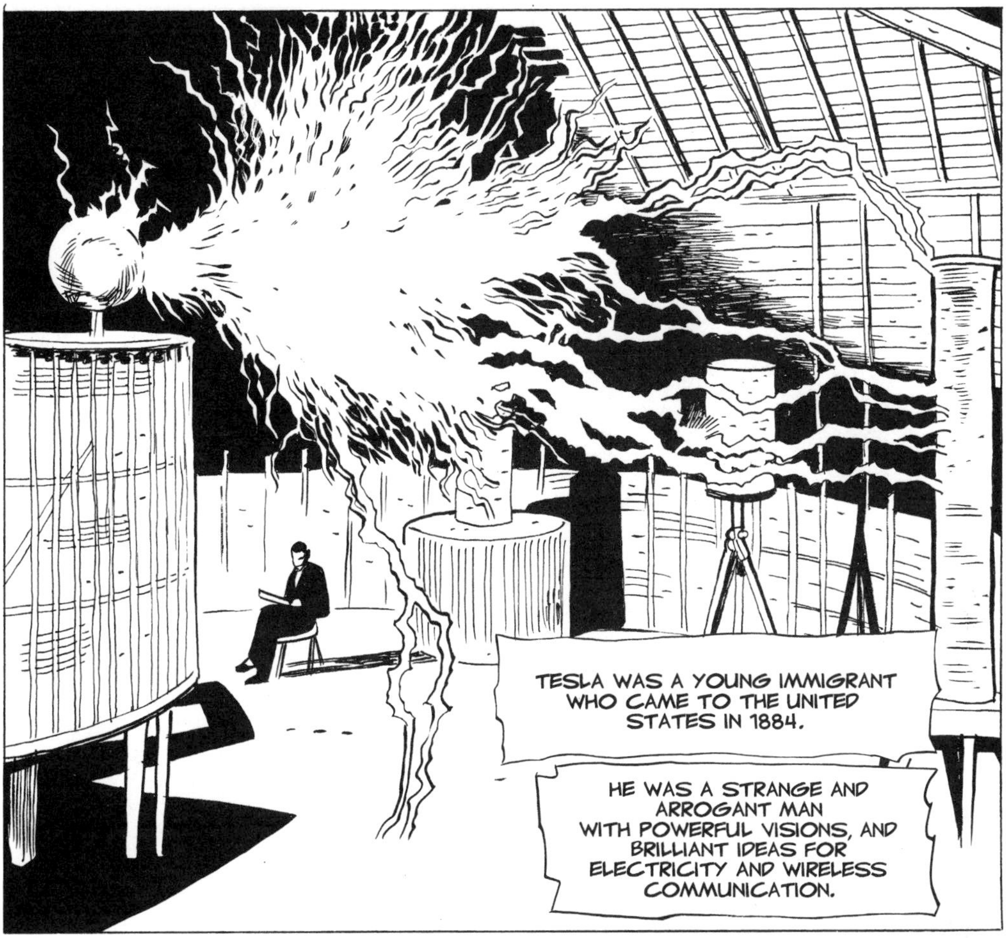
TESLA WAS A YOUNG IMMIGRANT WHO CAME TO THE UNITED STATES IN 1884.
HE WAS A STRANGE AND ARROGANT MAN WITH POWERFUL VISIONS, AND BRILLIANT IDEAS FOR ELECTRICITY AND WIRELESS COMMUNICATION.

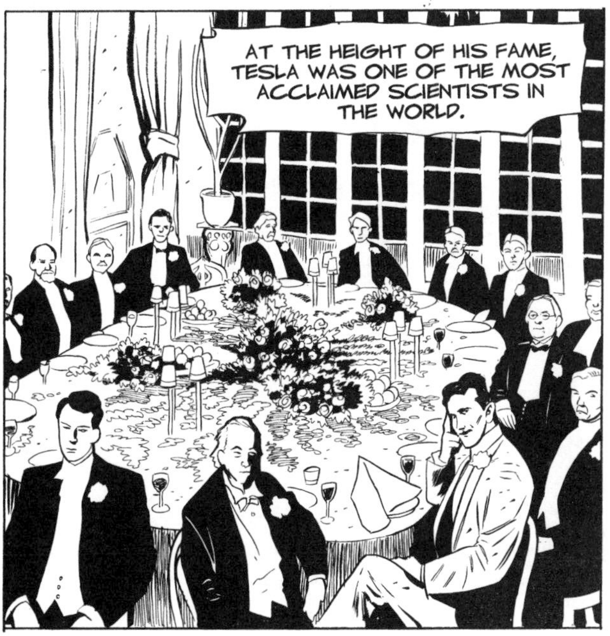
AT THE HEIGHT OF HIS FAME, TESLA WAS ONE OF THE MOST ACCLAIMED SCIENTISTS IN THE WORLD.

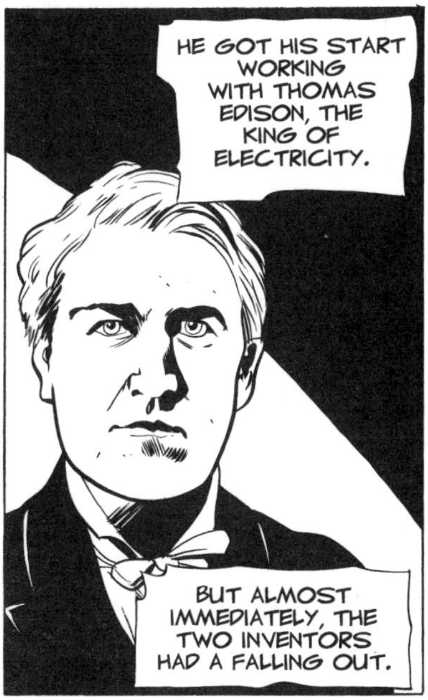
HE GOT HIS START WORKING WITH THOMAS EDISON, THE KING OF ELECTRICITY.
BUT ALMOST IMMEDIATELY, THE TWO INVENTORS HAD A FALLING OUT.

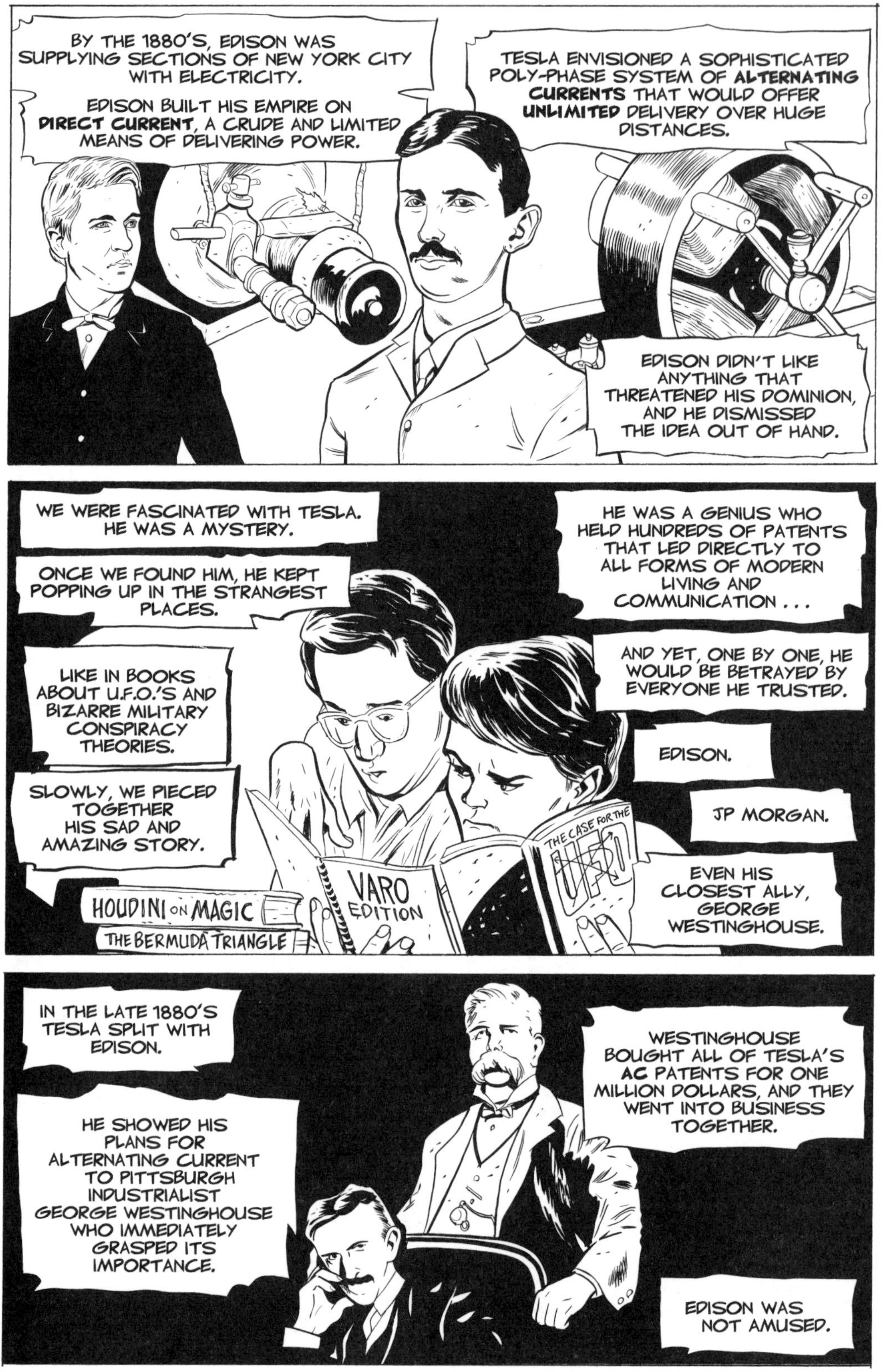
BY THE 1880'S, EDISON WAS SUPPLYING SECTIONS OF NEW YORK CITY WITH ELECTRICITY.
EDISON BUILT HIS EMPIRE ON **DIRECT CURRENT**, A CRUDE AND LIMITED MEANS OF DELIVERING POWER.
TESLA ENVISIONED A SOPHISTICATED POLY-PHASE SYSTEM OF **ALTERNATING CURRENTS** THAT WOULD OFFER **UNLIMITED** DELIVERY OVER HUGE DISTANCES.
EDISON DIDN'T LIKE ANYTHING THAT THREATENED HIS DOMINION, AND HE DISMISSED THE IDEA OUT OF HAND.
WE WERE FASCINATED WITH TESLA. HE WAS A MYSTERY.
ONCE WE FOUND HIM, HE KEPT POPPING UP IN THE STRANGEST PLACES.
LIKE IN BOOKS ABOUT U.F.O.'S AND BIZARRE MILITARY CONSPIRACY THEORIES.
SLOWLY, WE PIECED TOGETHER HIS SAD AND AMAZING STORY.
HOUDINI ON MAGIC
THE BERMUDA TRIANGLE
VARO EDITION
THE CASE FOR THE UFO
HE WAS A GENIUS WHO HELD HUNDREDS OF PATENTS THAT LED DIRECTLY TO ALL FORMS OF MODERN LIVING AND COMMUNICATION . . .
AND YET, ONE BY ONE, HE WOULD BE BETRAYED BY EVERYONE HE TRUSTED.
EDISON.
JP MORGAN.
EVEN HIS CLOSEST ALLY, GEORGE WESTINGHOUSE.
IN THE LATE 1880'S TESLA SPLIT WITH EDISON.
HE SHOWED HIS PLANS FOR ALTERNATING CURRENT TO PITTSBURGH INDUSTRIALIST GEORGE WESTINGHOUSE WHO IMMEDIATELY GRASPED ITS IMPORTANCE.
WESTINGHOUSE BOUGHT ALL OF TESLA'S **AC** PATENTS FOR ONE MILLION DOLLARS, AND THEY WENT INTO BUSINESS TOGETHER.
EDISON WAS NOT AMUSED.

HE HIRED A TEAM OF MEN TO TRAVEL THE COUNTRY AND DISCREDIT AC CURRENT, WESTINGHOUSE AND TESLA.

ONE OF THEIR TACTICS WAS TO PUBLICLY ELECTROCUTE LIVE ANIMALS WITH ALTERNATING CURRENT -- JUST TO SHOW THE GENERAL POPULACE THE DANGERS OF **AC**.

AT ONE POINT THEY EVEN FAMOUSLY MURDERED A CIRCUS ELEPHANT TO PROVE THEIR POINT.

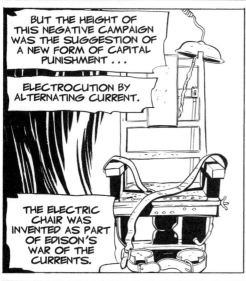

BUT THE HEIGHT OF THIS NEGATIVE CAMPAIGN WAS THE SUGGESTION OF A NEW FORM OF CAPITAL PUNISHMENT . . .

ELECTROCUTION BY ALTERNATING CURRENT.

THE ELECTRIC CHAIR WAS INVENTED AS PART OF EDISON'S WAR OF THE CURRENTS.

THE SMEAR CAMPAIGN WAS BEGINNING TO WORK.

THE COMMITTEE RESPONSIBLE FOR HARNESSING THE GREAT POWER OF NIAGRA FALLS WARNED ALL INTERESTED PARTIES -- AVOID AT ALL COST THE TERRIBLE MISTAKE OF ALTERNATING CURRENTS.

BUT WESTINGHOUSE AND TESLA WEREN'T FINISHED YET.

IN 1893, WESTINGHOUSE UNDERBID EDISON AND ALL COMPETITORS TO LIGHT THE COLUMBIAN EXPOSITION IN CHICAGO. IT WOULD BE THE FIRST WORLD'S FAIR LIT BY ELECTRICITY.

IT WAS A GAME CHANGER. A HUNDRED THOUSAND PEOPLE WATCHED AS THE FAIRGROUNDS EXPLODED IN THE MOST BRILLIANT DISPLAY OF LIGHT THE WORLD HAD EVER SEEN.

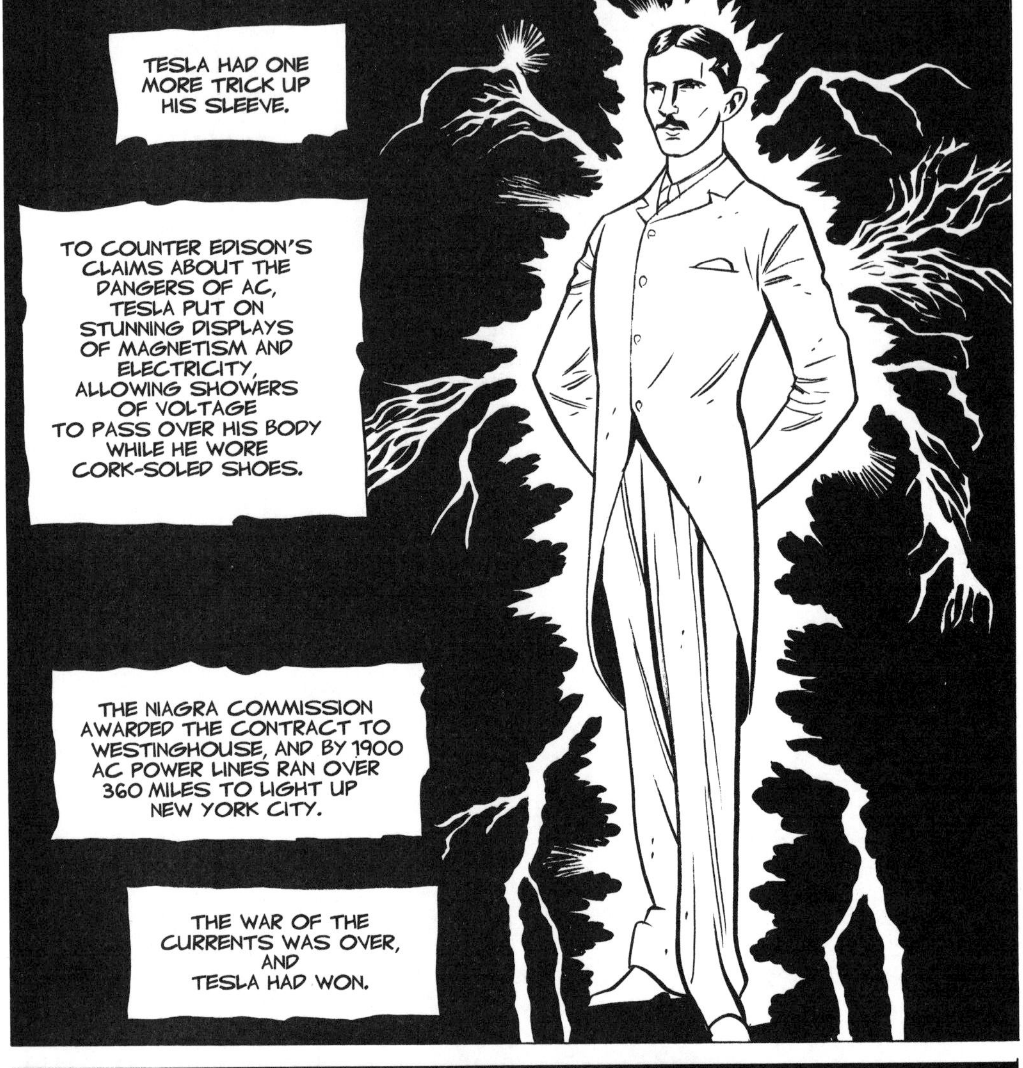
TESLA HAD ONE MORE TRICK UP HIS SLEEVE.
TO COUNTER EDISON'S CLAIMS ABOUT THE DANGERS OF AC, TESLA PUT ON STUNNING DISPLAYS OF MAGNETISM AND ELECTRICITY, ALLOWING SHOWERS OF VOLTAGE TO PASS OVER HIS BODY WHILE HE WORE CORK-SOLED SHOES.
THE NIAGRA COMMISSION AWARDED THE CONTRACT TO WESTINGHOUSE, AND BY 1900 AC POWER LINES RAN OVER 360 MILES TO LIGHT UP NEW YORK CITY.
THE WAR OF THE CURRENTS WAS OVER, AND TESLA HAD WON.

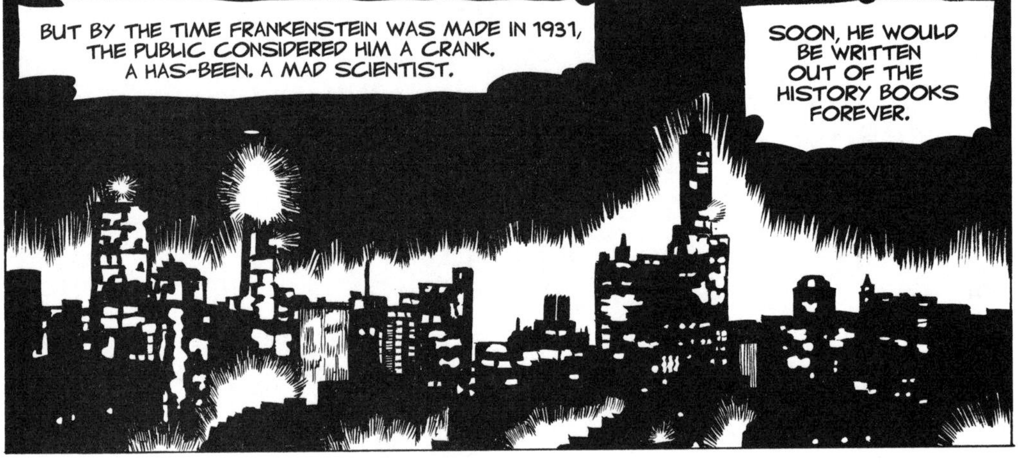
BUT BY THE TIME FRANKENSTEIN WAS MADE IN 1931, THE PUBLIC CONSIDERED HIM A CRANK. A HAS-BEEN. A MAD SCIENTIST.
SOON, HE WOULD BE WRITTEN OUT OF THE HISTORY BOOKS FOREVER.

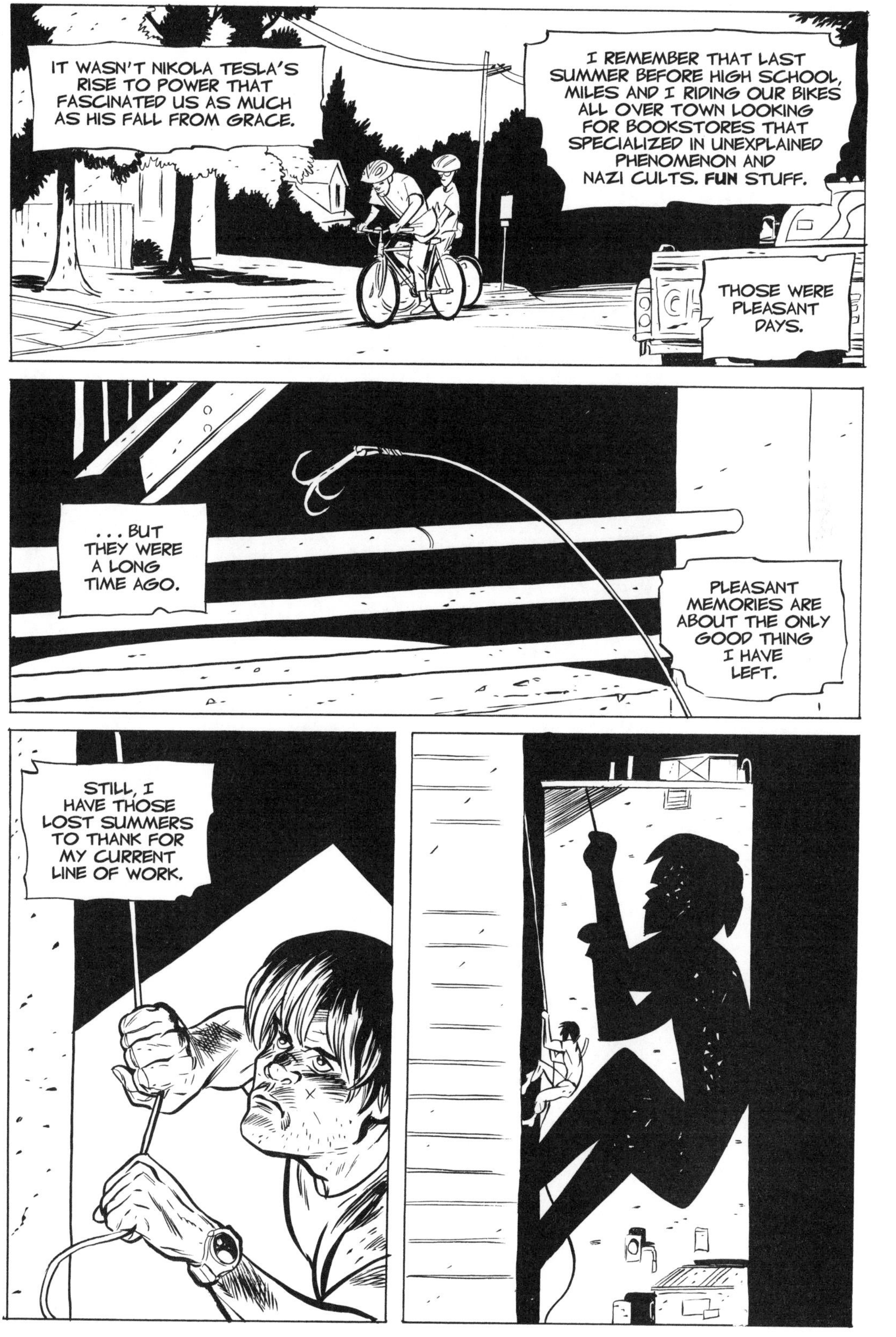
IT WASN'T NIKOLA TESLA'S RISE TO POWER THAT FASCINATED US AS MUCH AS HIS FALL FROM GRACE.
I REMEMBER THAT LAST SUMMER BEFORE HIGH SCHOOL, MILES AND I RIDING OUR BIKES ALL OVER TOWN LOOKING FOR BOOKSTORES THAT SPECIALIZED IN UNEXPLAINED PHENOMENON AND NAZI CULTS. FUN STUFF.
THOSE WERE PLEASANT DAYS.
. . . BUT THEY WERE A LONG TIME AGO.
PLEASANT MEMORIES ARE ABOUT THE ONLY GOOD THING I HAVE LEFT.
STILL, I HAVE THOSE LOST SUMMERS TO THANK FOR MY CURRENT LINE OF WORK.

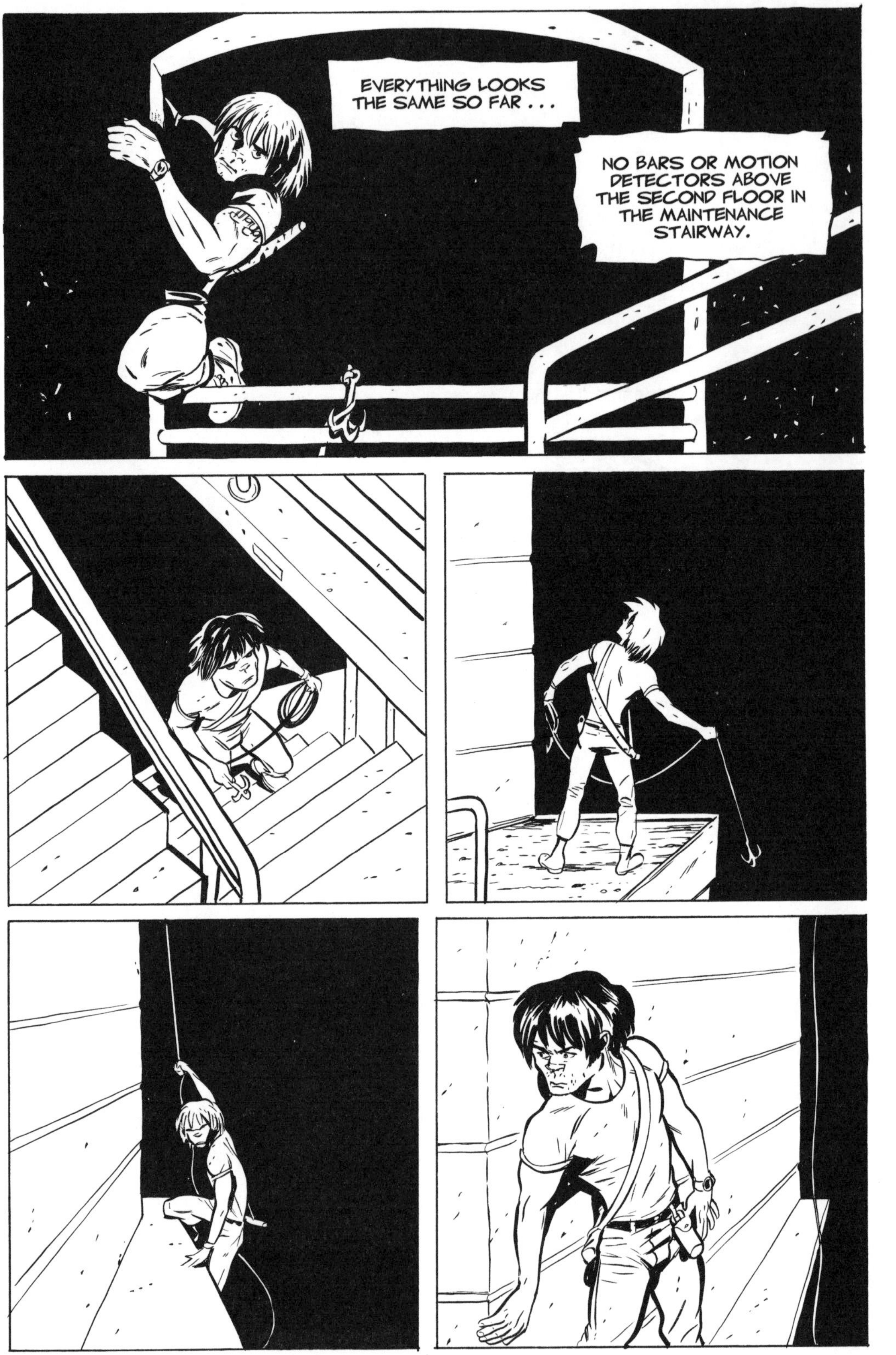
EVERYTHING LOOKS THE SAME SO FAR . . .
NO BARS OR MOTION DETECTORS ABOVE THE SECOND FLOOR IN THE MAINTENANCE STAIRWAY.

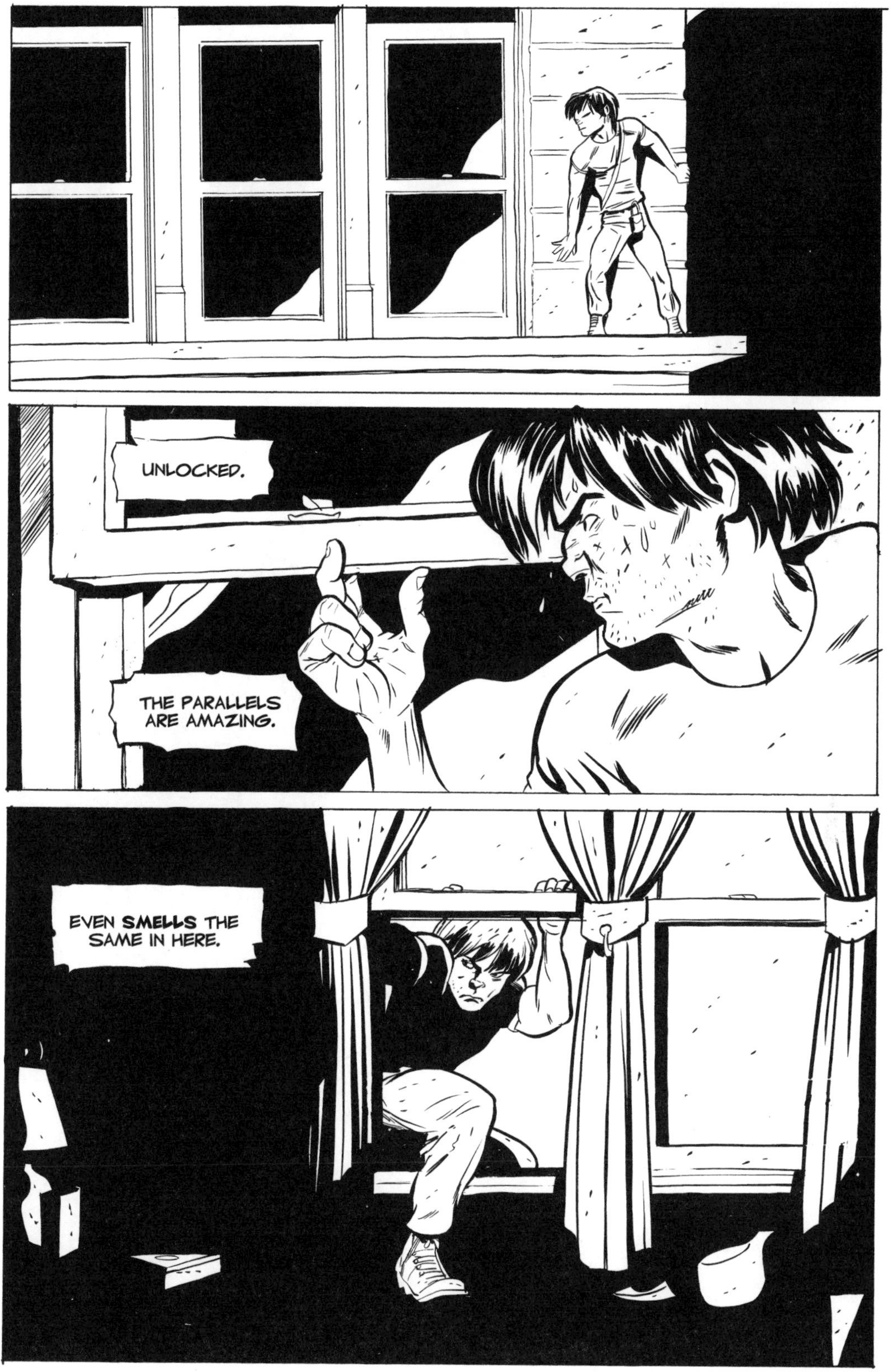
UNLOCKED.
THE PARALLELS ARE AMAZING.
EVEN SMELLS THE SAME IN HERE.

STAY ON YOUR TOES, RASL . . .

NO MATTER HOW IT LOOKS OR SMELLS, THIS **ISN'T** THE SAME PLACE.

THERE **COULD** BE SURPRISES.

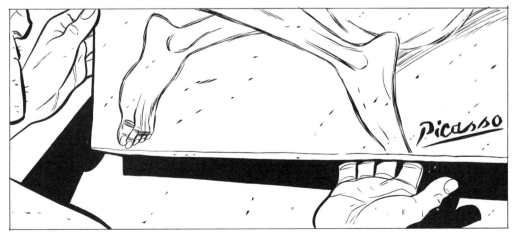

Picasso

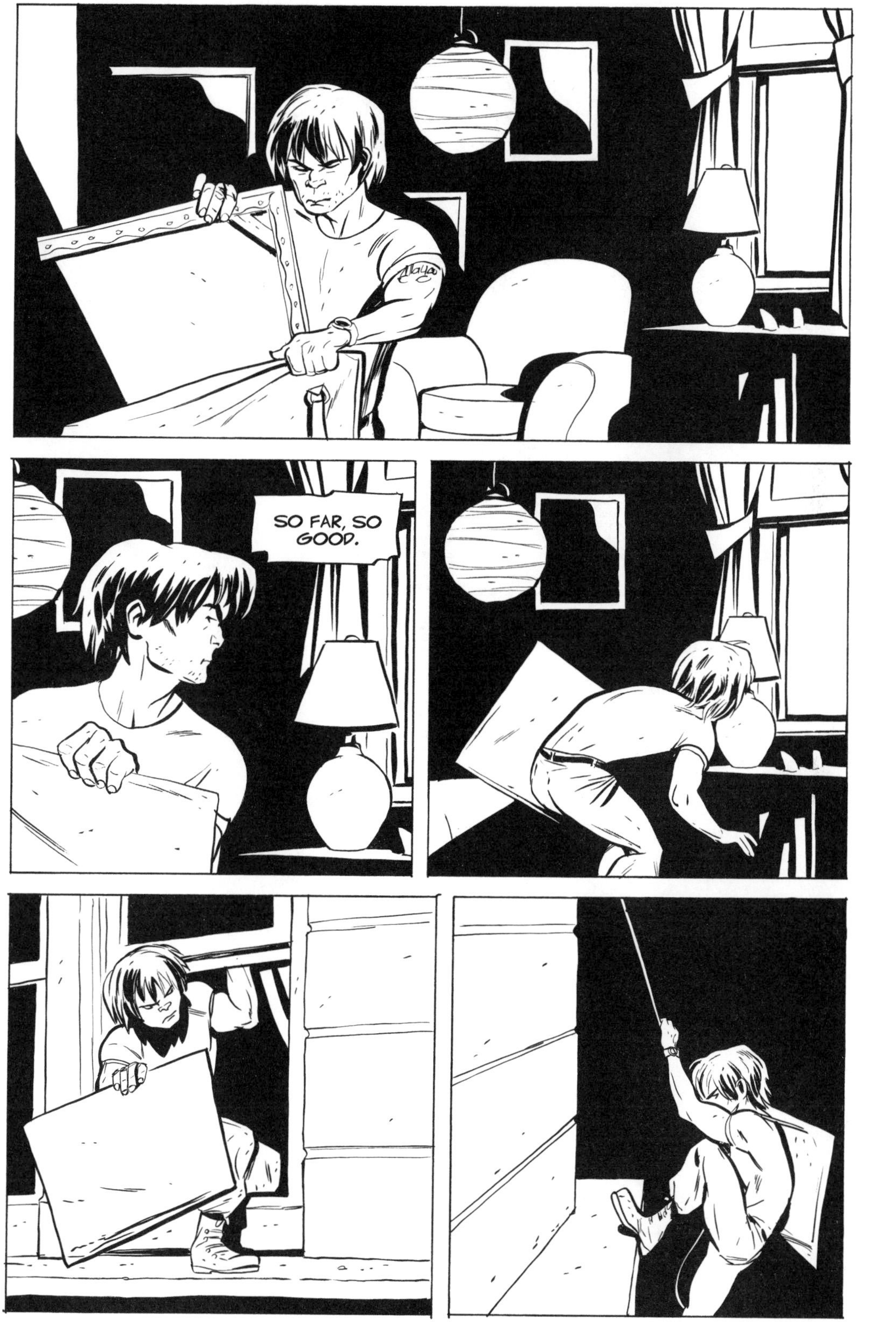
SO FAR, SO GOOD.

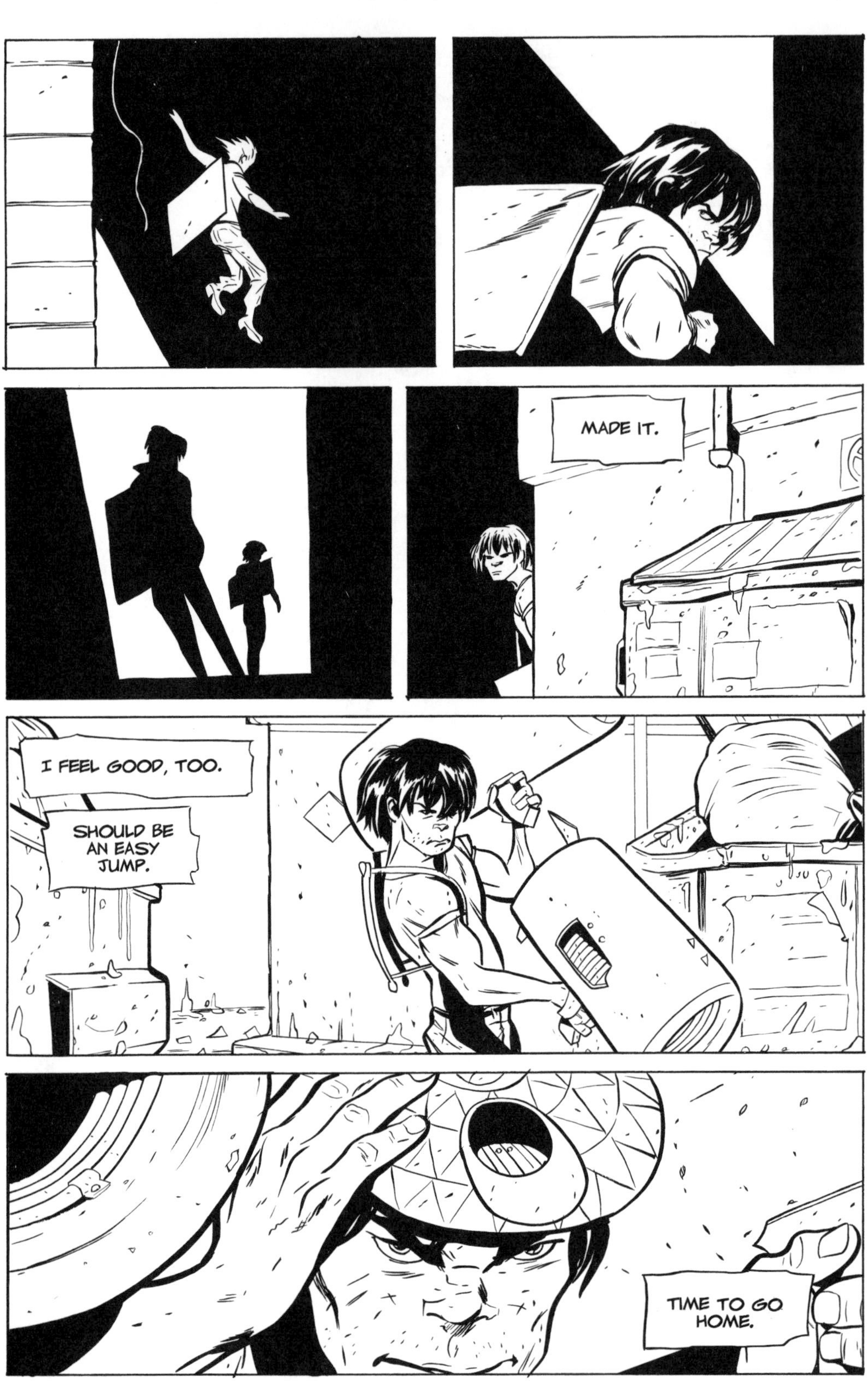
MADE IT.
I FEEL GOOD, TOO.
SHOULD BE AN EASY JUMP.
TIME TO GO HOME.

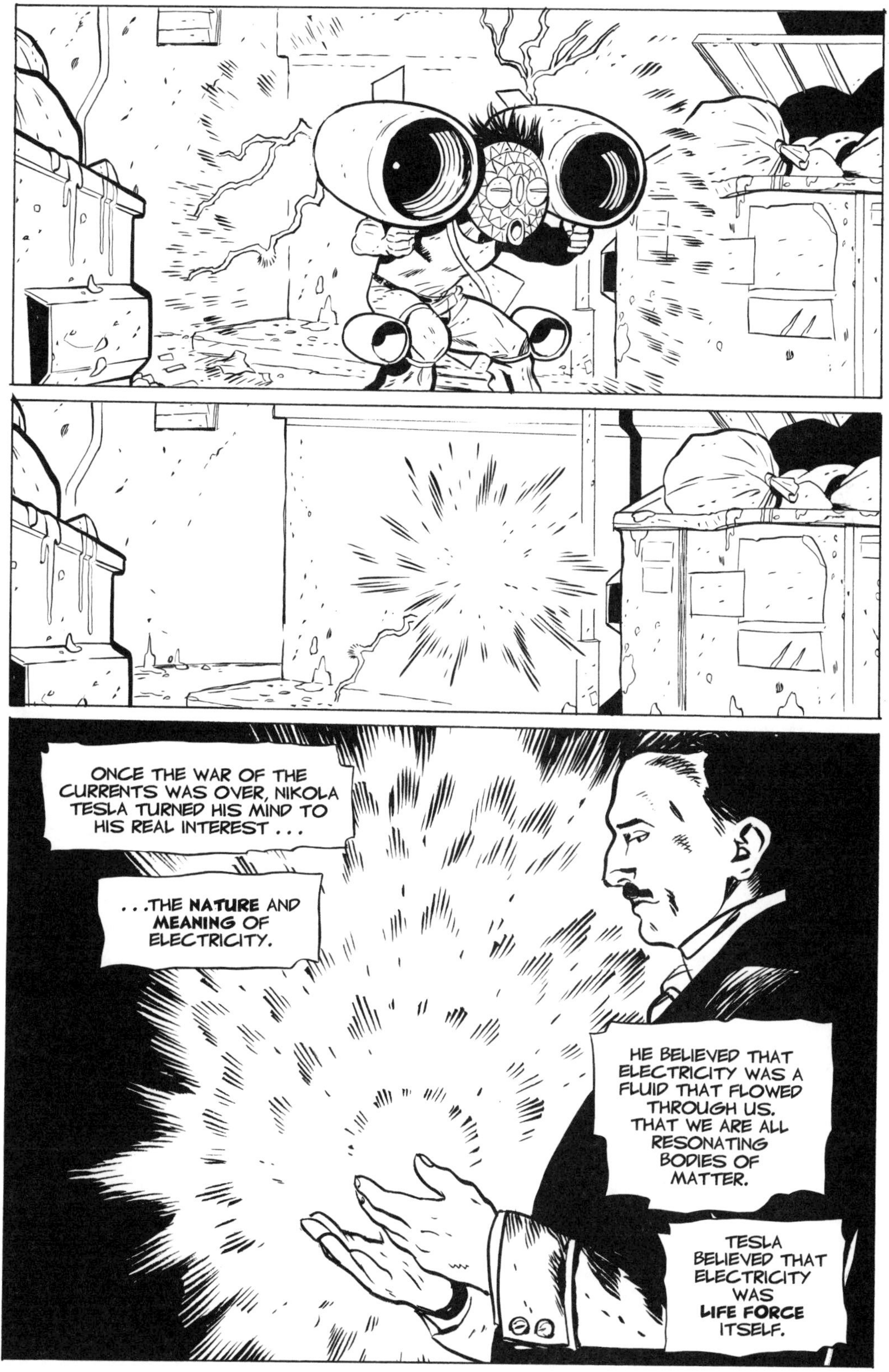
ONCE THE WAR OF THE CURRENTS WAS OVER, NIKOLA TESLA TURNED HIS MIND TO HIS REAL INTEREST . . .
. . .THE **NATURE** AND **MEANING** OF ELECTRICITY.
HE BELIEVED THAT ELECTRICITY WAS A FLUID THAT FLOWED THROUGH US. THAT WE ARE ALL RESONATING BODIES OF MATTER.
TESLA BELIEVED THAT ELECTRICITY WAS **LIFE FORCE** ITSELF.

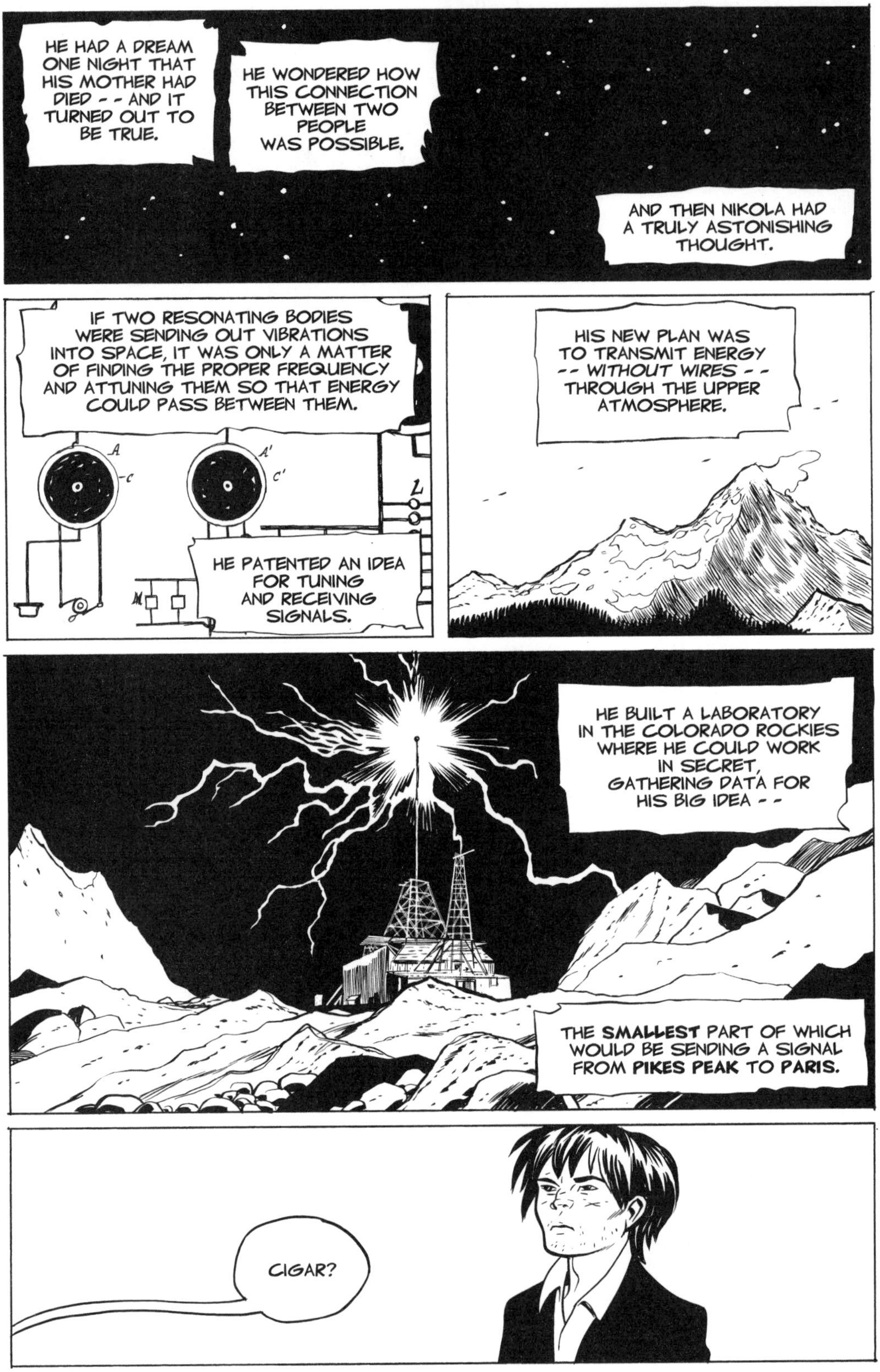
HE HAD A DREAM ONE NIGHT THAT HIS MOTHER HAD DIED - - AND IT TURNED OUT TO BE TRUE.
HE WONDERED HOW THIS CONNECTION BETWEEN TWO PEOPLE WAS POSSIBLE.
AND THEN NIKOLA HAD A TRULY ASTONISHING THOUGHT.
IF TWO RESONATING BODIES WERE SENDING OUT VIBRATIONS INTO SPACE, IT WAS ONLY A MATTER OF FINDING THE PROPER FREQUENCY AND ATTUNING THEM SO THAT ENERGY COULD PASS BETWEEN THEM.
A
C
A'
C'
L
M
HE PATENTED AN IDEA FOR TUNING AND RECEIVING SIGNALS.
HIS NEW PLAN WAS TO TRANSMIT ENERGY -- WITHOUT WIRES -- THROUGH THE UPPER ATMOSPHERE.
HE BUILT A LABORATORY IN THE COLORADO ROCKIES WHERE HE COULD WORK IN SECRET, GATHERING DATA FOR HIS BIG IDEA - -
THE SMALLEST PART OF WHICH WOULD BE SENDING A SIGNAL FROM PIKES PEAK TO PARIS.
CIGAR?

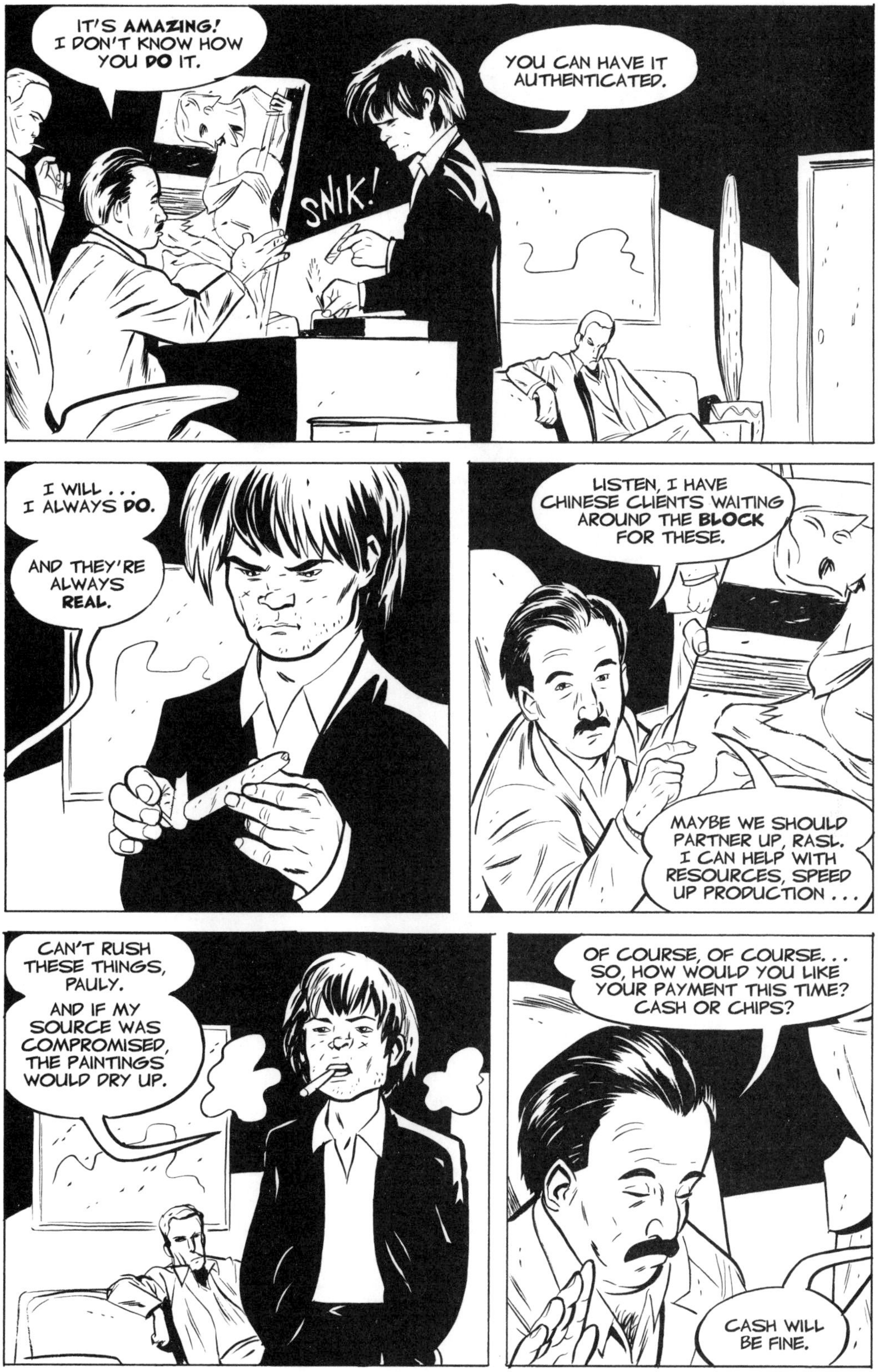
IT'S AMAZING! I DON'T KNOW HOW YOU DO IT.
YOU CAN HAVE IT AUTHENTICATED.
SNIK!
I WILL . . . I ALWAYS DO.
AND THEY'RE ALWAYS REAL.
LISTEN, I HAVE CHINESE CLIENTS WAITING AROUND THE BLOCK FOR THESE.
MAYBE WE SHOULD PARTNER UP, RASL. I CAN HELP WITH RESOURCES, SPEED UP PRODUCTION . . .
CAN'T RUSH THESE THINGS, PAULY.
AND IF MY SOURCE WAS COMPROMISED, THE PAINTINGS WOULD DRY UP.
OF COURSE, OF COURSE. . . SO, HOW WOULD YOU LIKE YOUR PAYMENT THIS TIME? CASH OR CHIPS?
CASH WILL BE FINE.

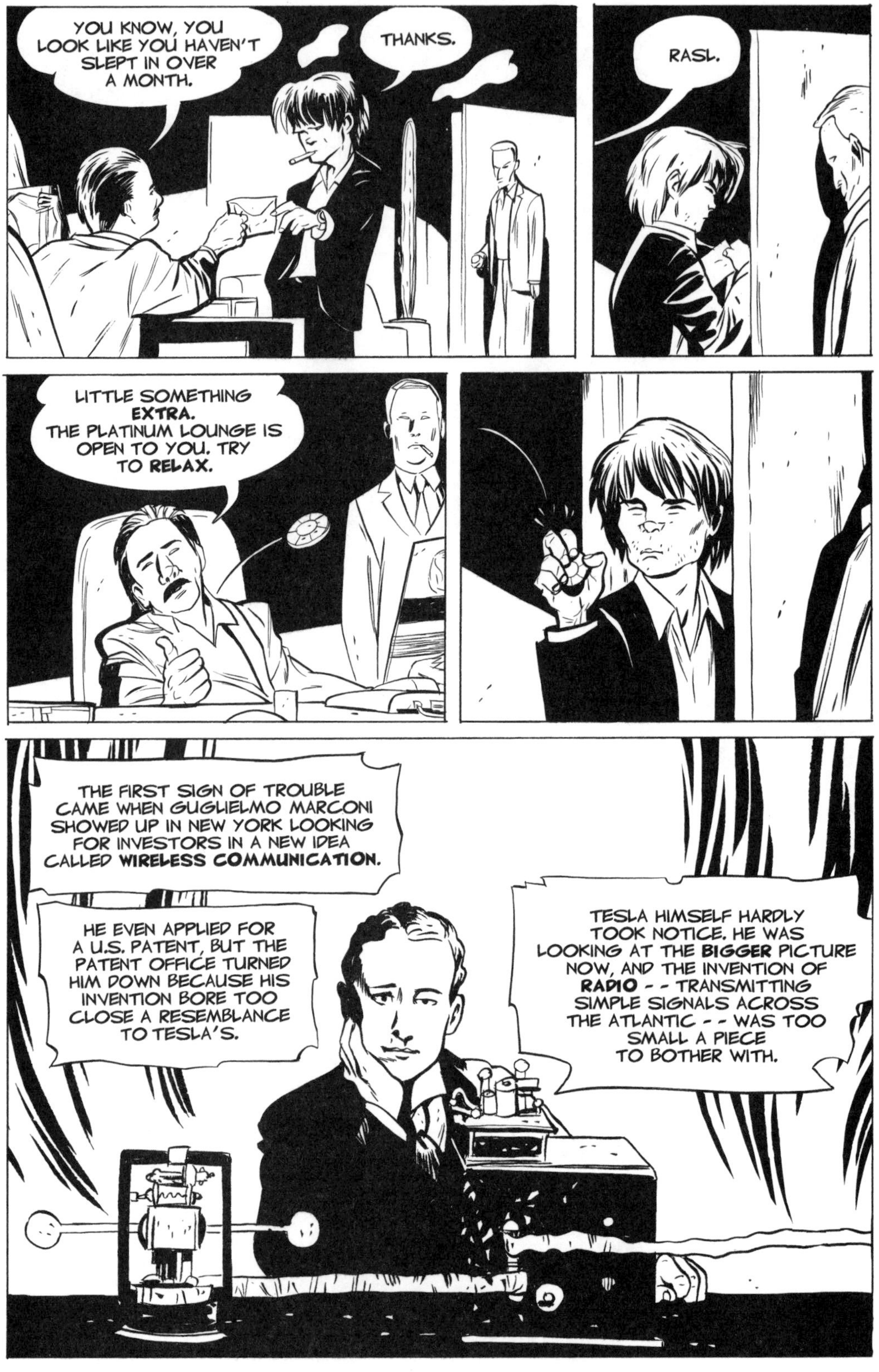
YOU KNOW, YOU LOOK LIKE YOU HAVEN'T SLEPT IN OVER A MONTH.
THANKS.
RASL.
LITTLE SOMETHING EXTRA. THE PLATINUM LOUNGE IS OPEN TO YOU. TRY TO RELAX.
THE FIRST SIGN OF TROUBLE CAME WHEN GUGLIELMO MARCONI SHOWED UP IN NEW YORK LOOKING FOR INVESTORS IN A NEW IDEA CALLED WIRELESS COMMUNICATION.
HE EVEN APPLIED FOR A U.S. PATENT, BUT THE PATENT OFFICE TURNED HIM DOWN BECAUSE HIS INVENTION BORE TOO CLOSE A RESEMBLANCE TO TESLA'S.
TESLA HIMSELF HARDLY TOOK NOTICE. HE WAS LOOKING AT THE BIGGER PICTURE NOW, AND THE INVENTION OF RADIO - - TRANSMITTING SIMPLE SIGNALS ACROSS THE ATLANTIC - - WAS TOO SMALL A PIECE TO BOTHER WITH.

NEXT CAME BAD NEWS FROM HIS GREAT FRIEND AND PATRON GEORGE WESTINGHOUSE.

THE WAR OF THE CURRENTS HAD OVEREXTENDED HIS COMPANY AND WESTINGHOUSE WAS IN FINANCIAL TROUBLE.

IN A GESTURE OF EXTREME LOYALTY, TESLA TORE UP HIS CONTRACT THAT GUARANTEED HIM A ROYALTY ON EVERY HORSEPOWER THAT WAS GENERATED. THE COMPANY WAS **SAVED.**

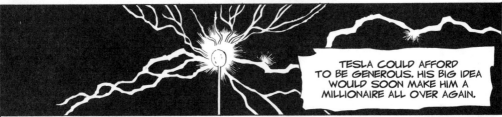

TESLA COULD AFFORD TO BE GENEROUS. HIS BIG IDEA WOULD SOON MAKE HIM A MILLIONAIRE ALL OVER AGAIN.

HOWEVER, AFTER MONTHS OF ALARMING THE LOCAL TOWNSFOLK WITH THUNDER THAT COULD BE HEARD TWENTY MILES AWAY, AND BOLTS OF MAN-MADE LIGHTNING OVER A HUNDRED FEET LONG, THE PEOPLE OF COLORADO SPRINGS HAD HAD ENOUGH.

THEY DIDN'T RUN HIM OFF WITH TORCHES AND PITCH FORKS, BUT IT WAS TIME FOR THE MAD SCIENTIST TO GO.

NO PROBLEM. TESLA HAD WHAT HE WANTED -- KNOWLEDGE THAT WOULD SOON GIVE MANKIND THE POWER OF THE UNIVERSE.

HE HEADED BACK EAST AND SET UP A MEETING WITH THE MOST POWERFUL FINANCIER IN THE WORLD . . .

J. PIERPONT MORGAN.

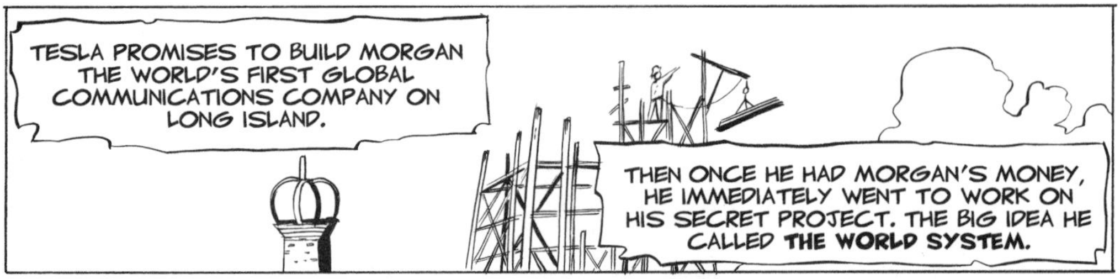
TESLA PROMISES TO BUILD MORGAN THE WORLD'S FIRST GLOBAL COMMUNICATIONS COMPANY ON LONG ISLAND.
THEN ONCE HE HAD MORGAN'S MONEY, HE IMMEDIATELY WENT TO WORK ON HIS SECRET PROJECT. THE BIG IDEA HE CALLED **THE WORLD SYSTEM.**

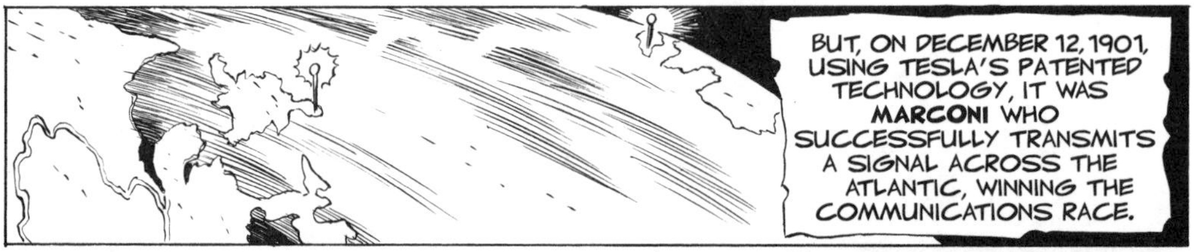
BUT, ON DECEMBER 12, 1901, USING TESLA'S PATENTED TECHNOLOGY, IT WAS **MARCONI** WHO SUCCESSFULLY TRANSMITS A SIGNAL ACROSS THE ATLANTIC, WINNING THE COMMUNICATIONS RACE.

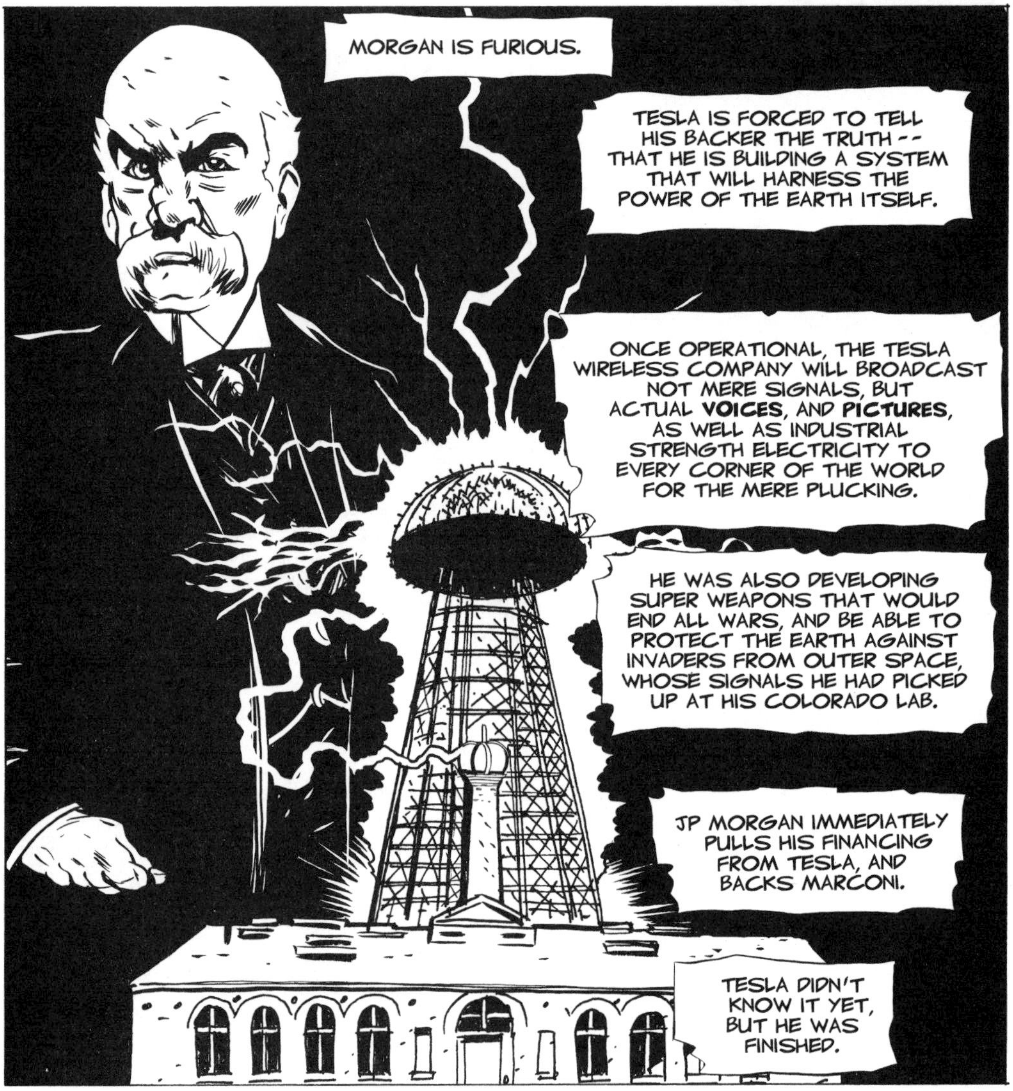
MORGAN IS FURIOUS.
TESLA IS FORCED TO TELL HIS BACKER THE TRUTH -- THAT HE IS BUILDING A SYSTEM THAT WILL HARNESS THE POWER OF THE EARTH ITSELF.
ONCE OPERATIONAL, THE TESLA WIRELESS COMPANY WILL BROADCAST NOT MERE SIGNALS, BUT ACTUAL **VOICES**, AND **PICTURES**, AS WELL AS INDUSTRIAL STRENGTH ELECTRICITY TO EVERY CORNER OF THE WORLD FOR THE MERE PLUCKING.
HE WAS ALSO DEVELOPING SUPER WEAPONS THAT WOULD END ALL WARS, AND BE ABLE TO PROTECT THE EARTH AGAINST INVADERS FROM OUTER SPACE, WHOSE SIGNALS HE HAD PICKED UP AT HIS COLORADO LAB.
JP MORGAN IMMEDIATELY PULLS HIS FINANCING FROM TESLA, AND BACKS MARCONI.
TESLA DIDN'T KNOW IT YET, BUT HE WAS FINISHED.

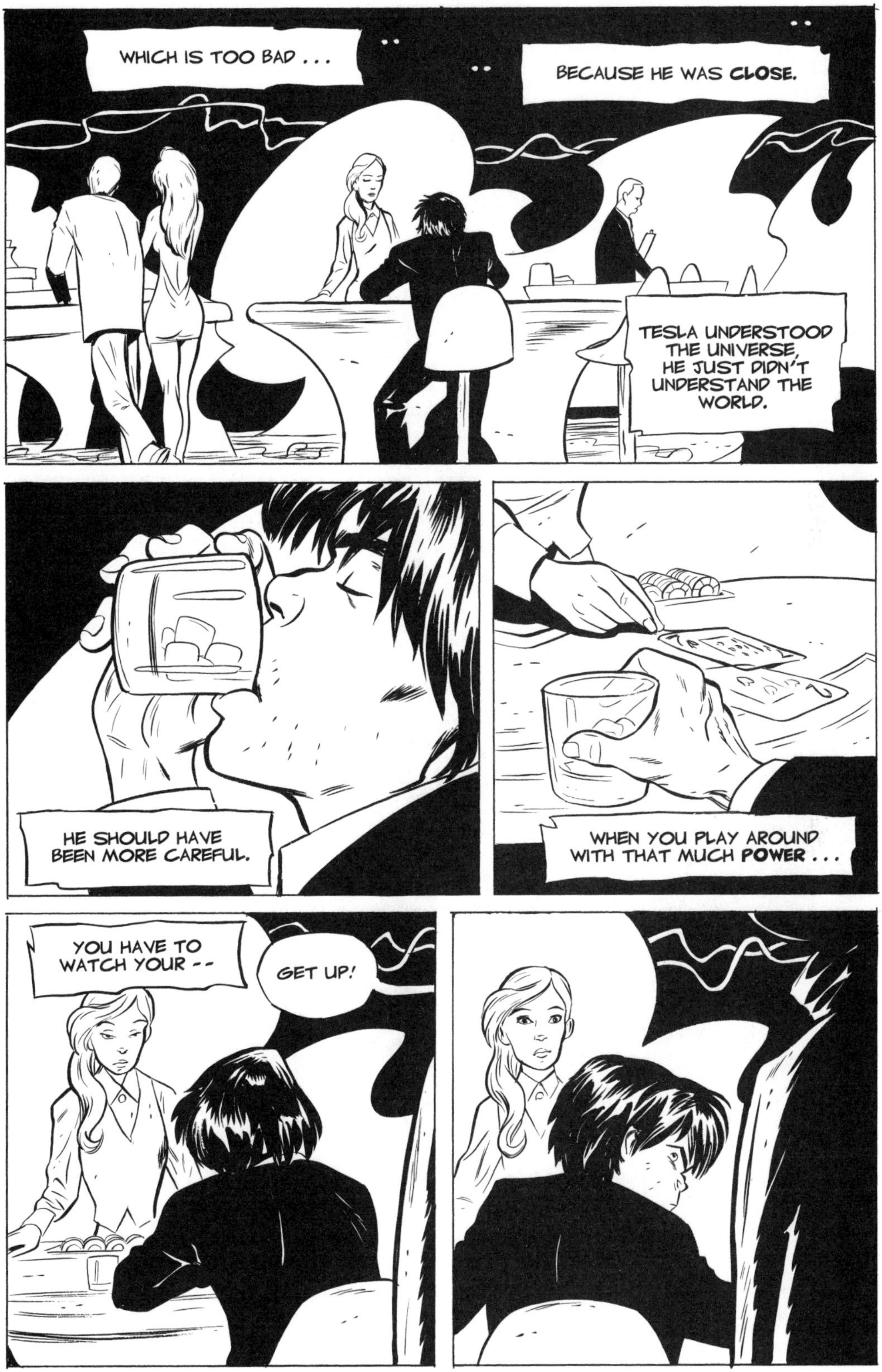
WHICH IS TOO BAD . . .
BECAUSE HE WAS CLOSE.
TESLA UNDERSTOOD THE UNIVERSE, HE JUST DIDN'T UNDERSTAND THE WORLD.
HE SHOULD HAVE BEEN MORE CAREFUL.
WHEN YOU PLAY AROUND WITH THAT MUCH POWER . . .
YOU HAVE TO WATCH YOUR --
GET UP!

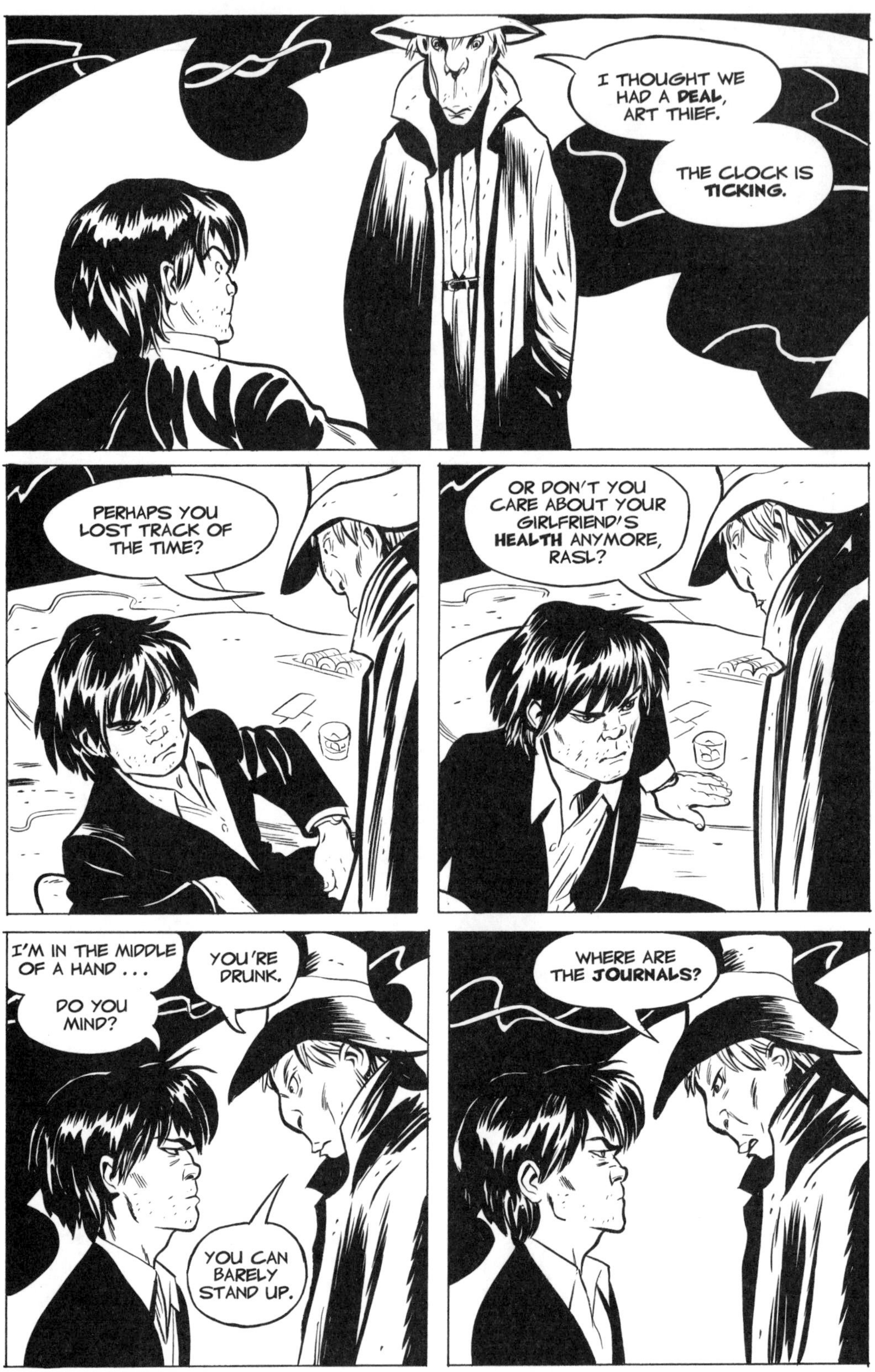
I THOUGHT WE HAD A DEAL, ART THIEF.
THE CLOCK IS TICKING.
PERHAPS YOU LOST TRACK OF THE TIME?
OR DON'T YOU CARE ABOUT YOUR GIRLFRIEND'S HEALTH ANYMORE, RASL?
I'M IN THE MIDDLE OF A HAND . . .
DO YOU MIND?
YOU'RE DRUNK.
YOU CAN BARELY STAND UP.
WHERE ARE THE JOURNALS?

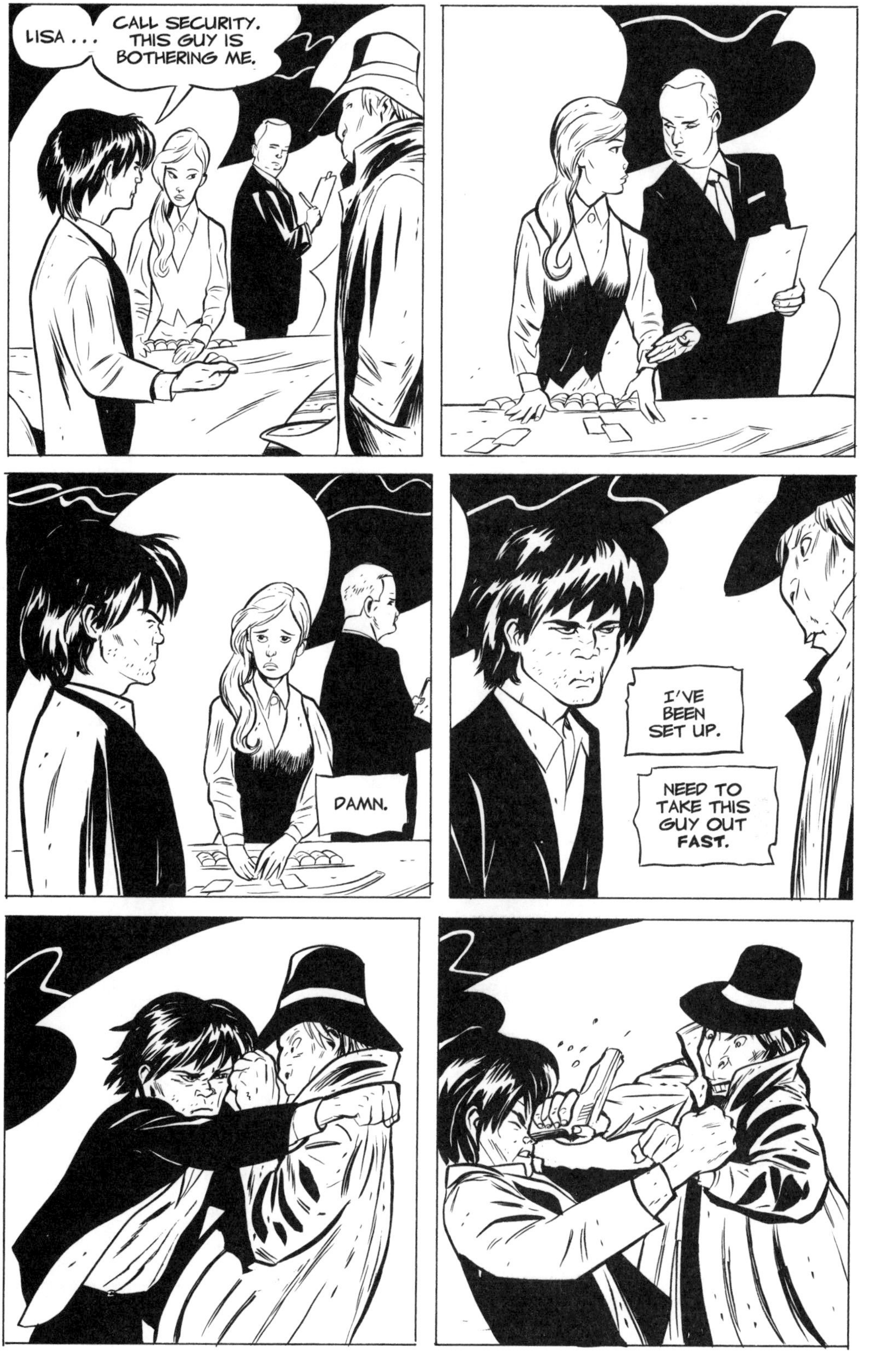
LISA . . .
CALL SECURITY. THIS GUY IS BOTHERING ME.
DAMN.
I'VE BEEN SET UP.
NEED TO TAKE THIS GUY OUT FAST.

CRACK!

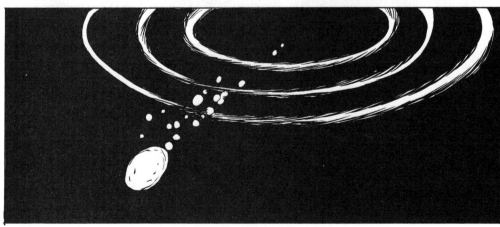

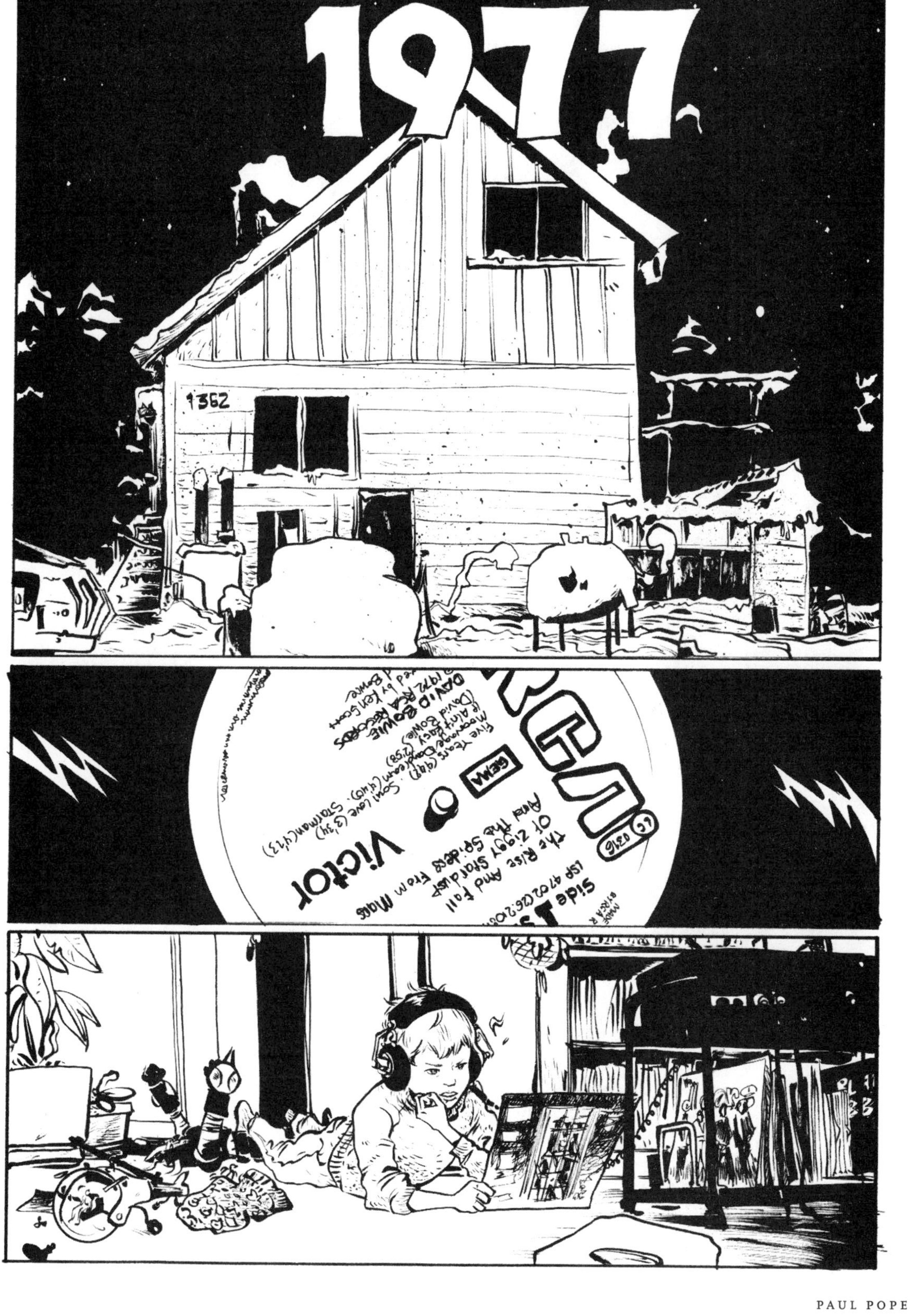
1977
1362
RCA
Victor
Side 1
The Rise And Fall Of Ziggy Stardust And The Spiders From Mars
DAVID BOWIE

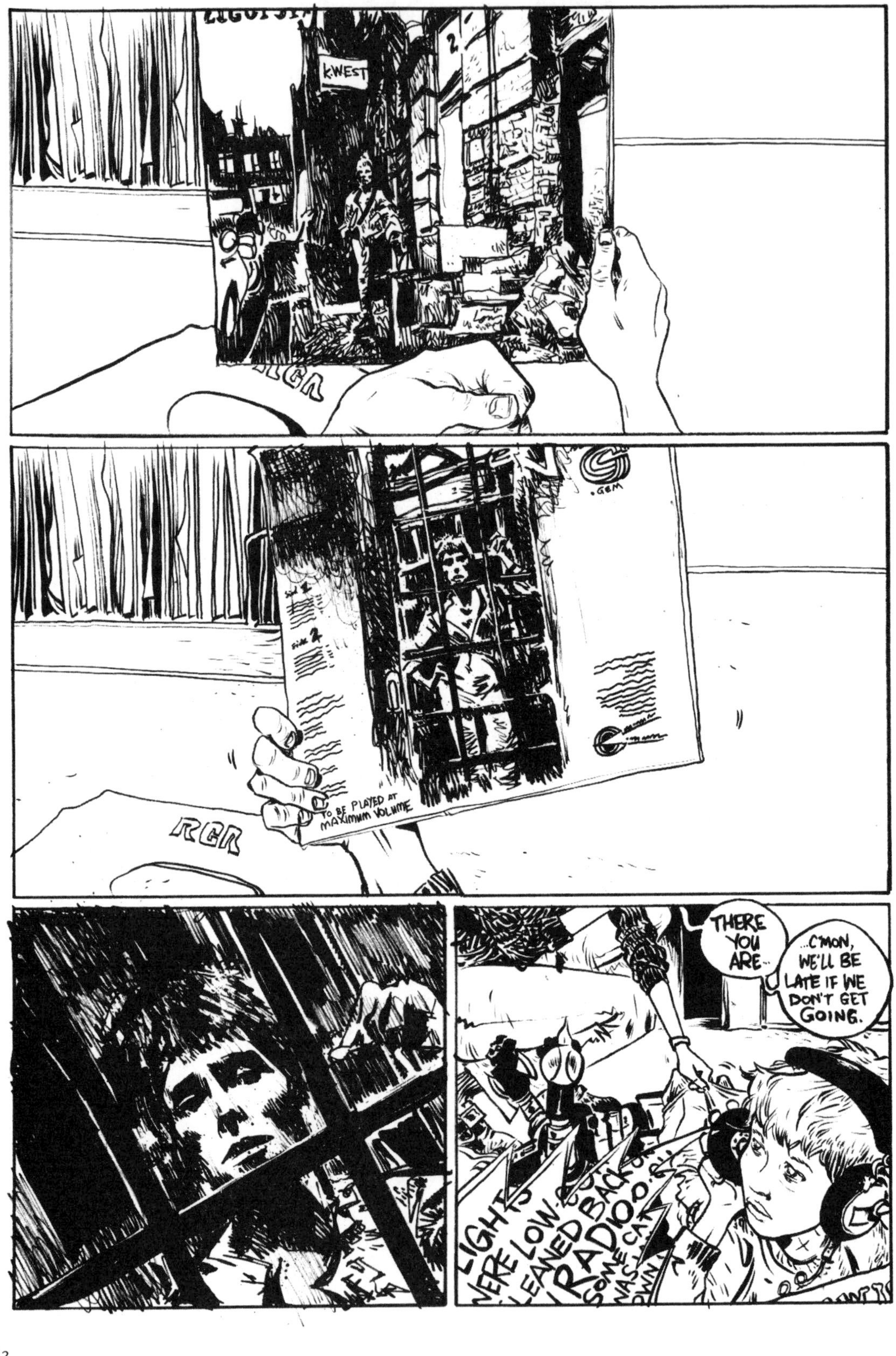
K.WEST
RCA
TO BE PLAYED AT MAXIMUM VOLUME
RCA
THERE YOU ARE..
...C'MON, WE'LL BE LATE IF WE DON'T GET GOING.
LIGHTS
WERE LOW
LEANED BACK
RADIO
SOME CAT
WAS
DOWN

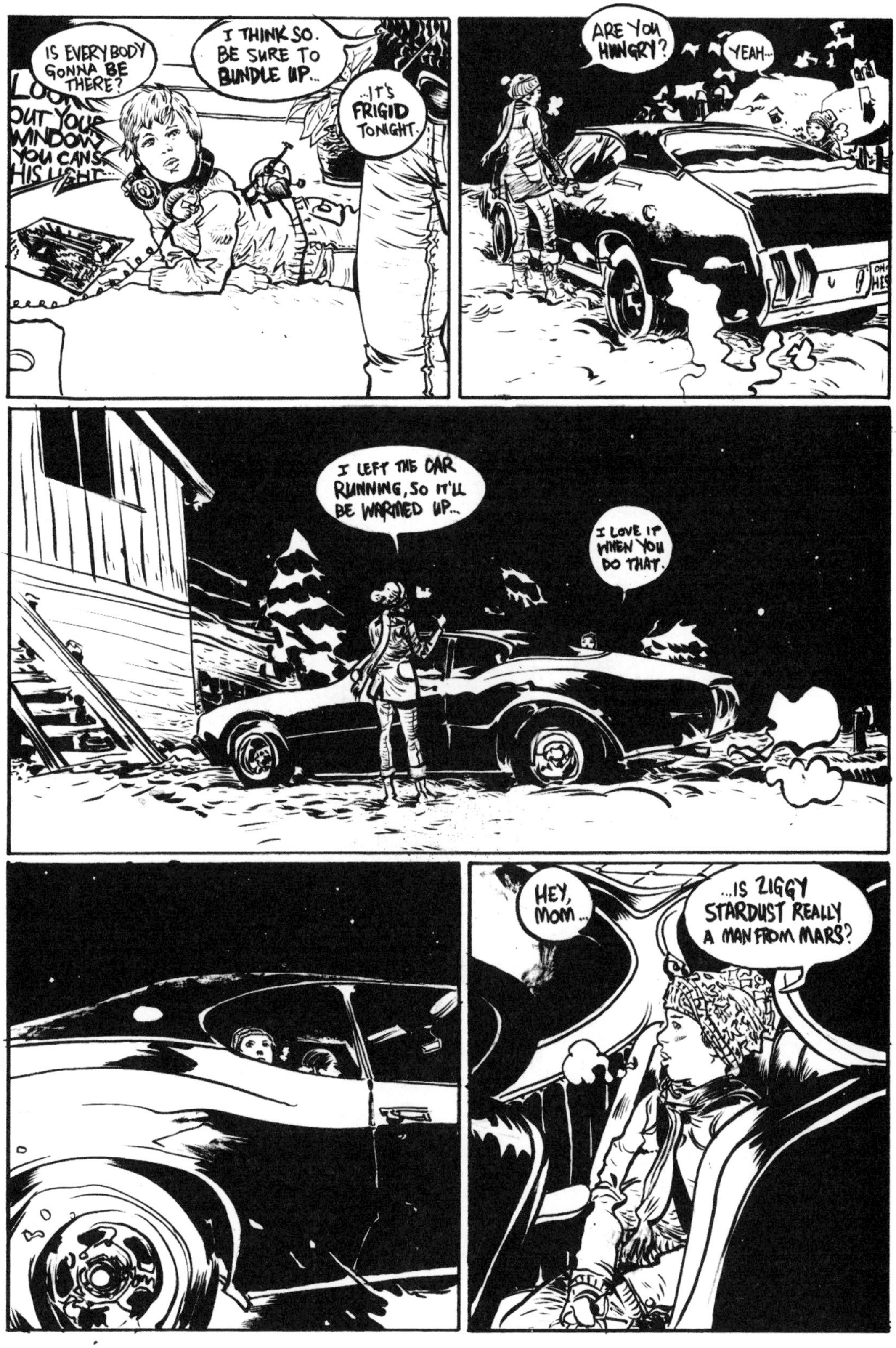
IS EVERYBODY GONNA BE THERE?
I THINK SO. BE SURE TO BUNDLE UP...
...IT'S FRIGID TONIGHT.
ARE YOU HUNGRY?
YEAH...
I LEFT THE CAR RUNNING, SO IT'LL BE WARMED UP...
I LOVE IT WHEN YOU DO THAT.
HEY, MOM...
...IS ZIGGY STARDUST REALLY A MAN FROM MARS?

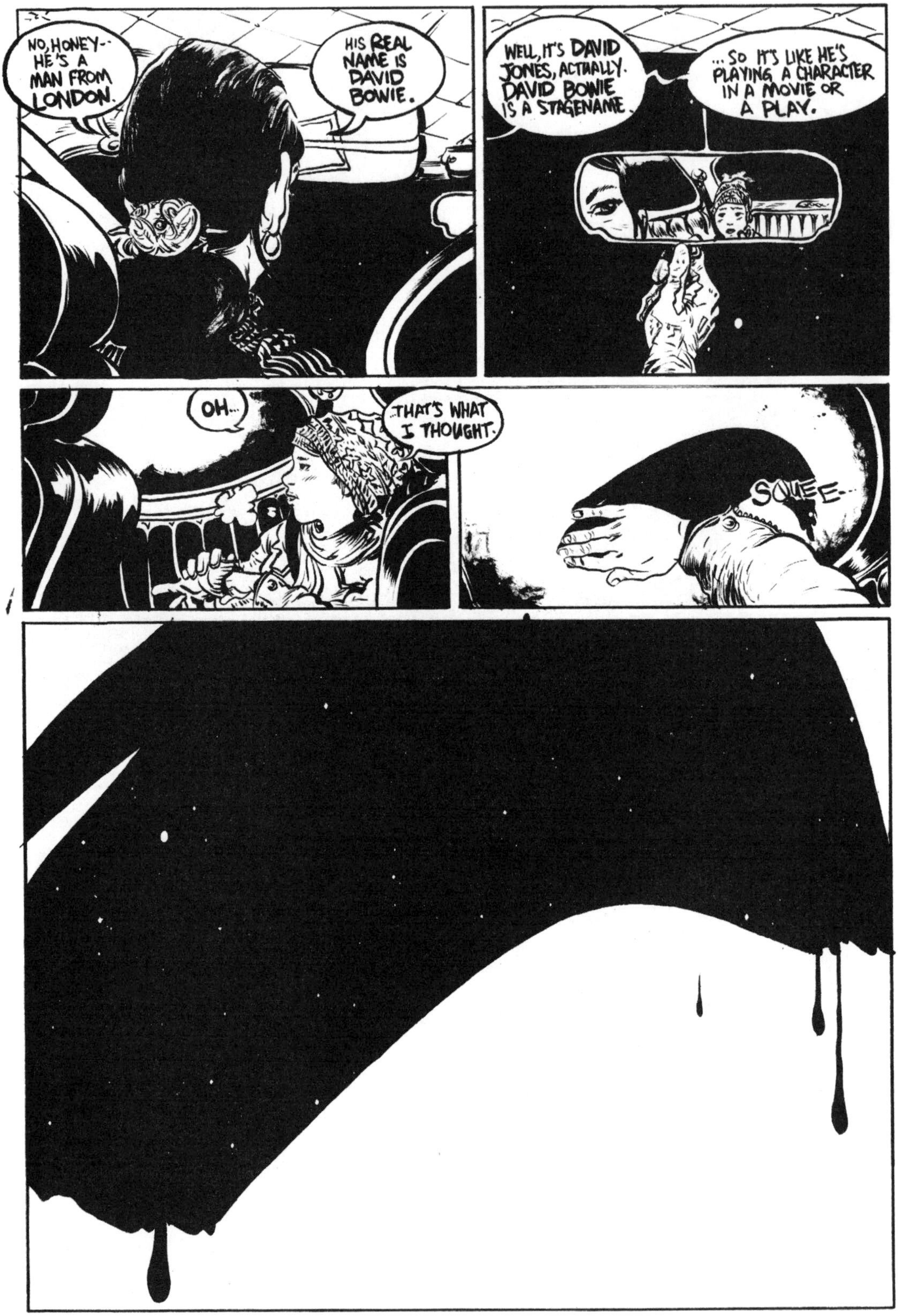
NO, HONEY-- HE'S A MAN FROM LONDON.
HIS REAL NAME IS DAVID BOWIE.
WELL, IT'S DAVID JONES, ACTUALLY. DAVID BOWIE IS A STAGENAME.
...SO IT'S LIKE HE'S PLAYING A CHARACTER IN A MOVIE OR A PLAY.
OH...
...THAT'S WHAT I THOUGHT.
SQUEE--

EXCERPT FROM

THE PTERODACTYL HUNTERS

IN THE GILDED CITY

BRENDAN LEACH

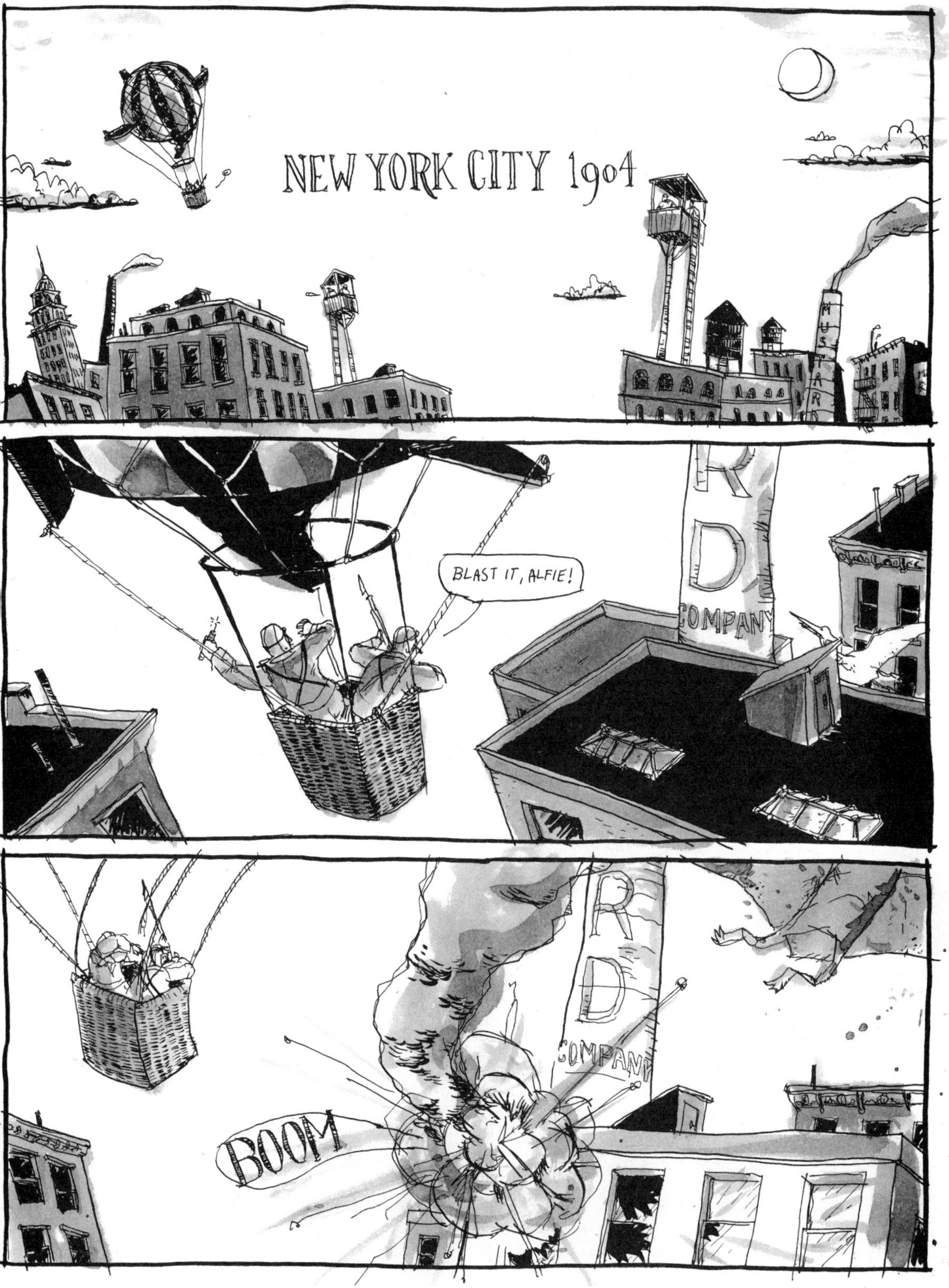
NEW YORK CITY 1904
MUSTARD
BLAST IT, ALFIE!
RD
COMPANY
BOOM

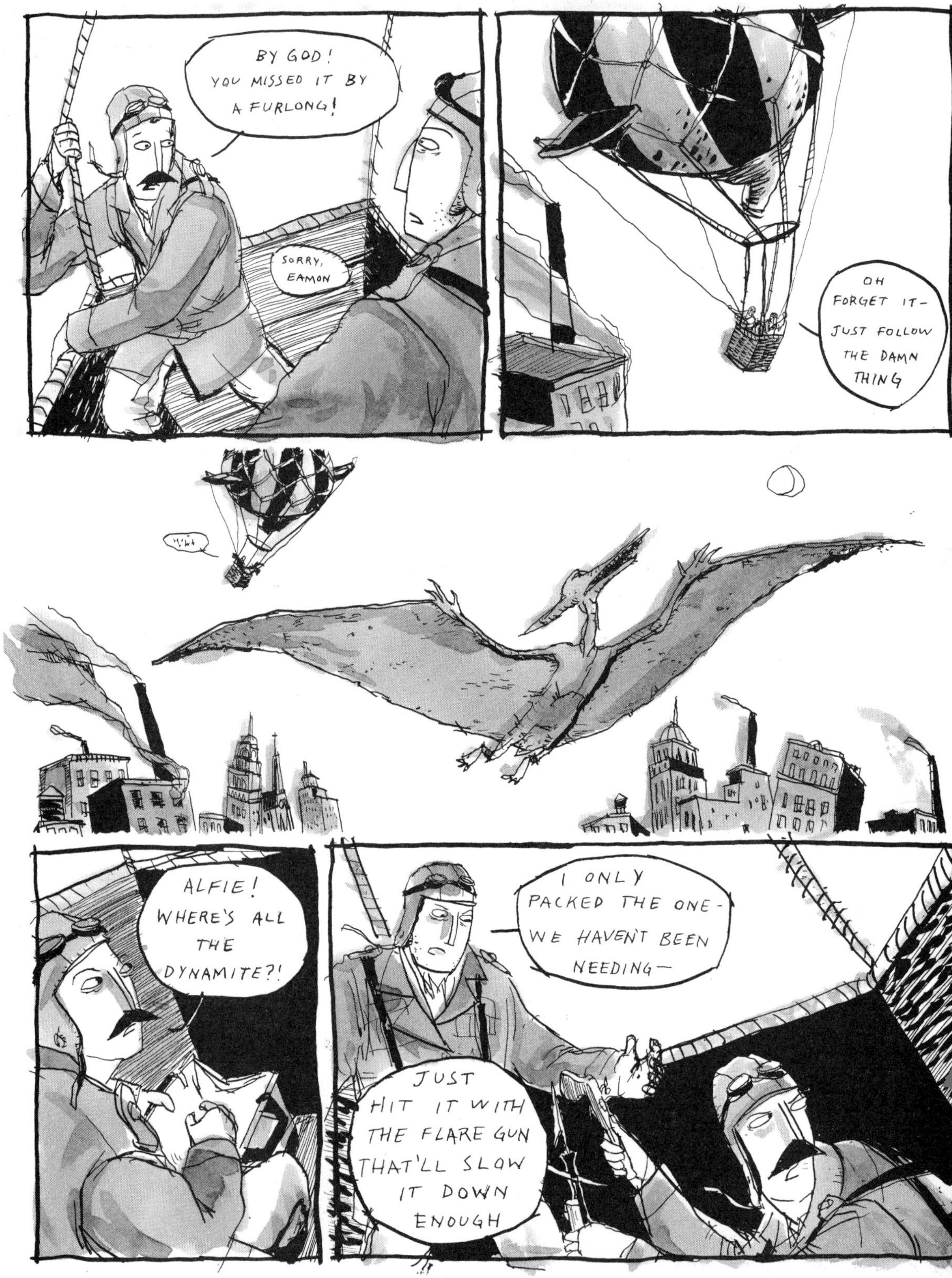
BY GOD! YOU MISSED IT BY A FURLONG!
SORRY, EAMON
OH FORGET IT- JUST FOLLOW THE DAMN THING
ALFIE! WHERE'S ALL THE DYNAMITE?!
I ONLY PACKED THE ONE- WE HAVEN'T BEEN NEEDING-
JUST HIT IT WITH THE FLARE GUN THAT'LL SLOW IT DOWN ENOUGH

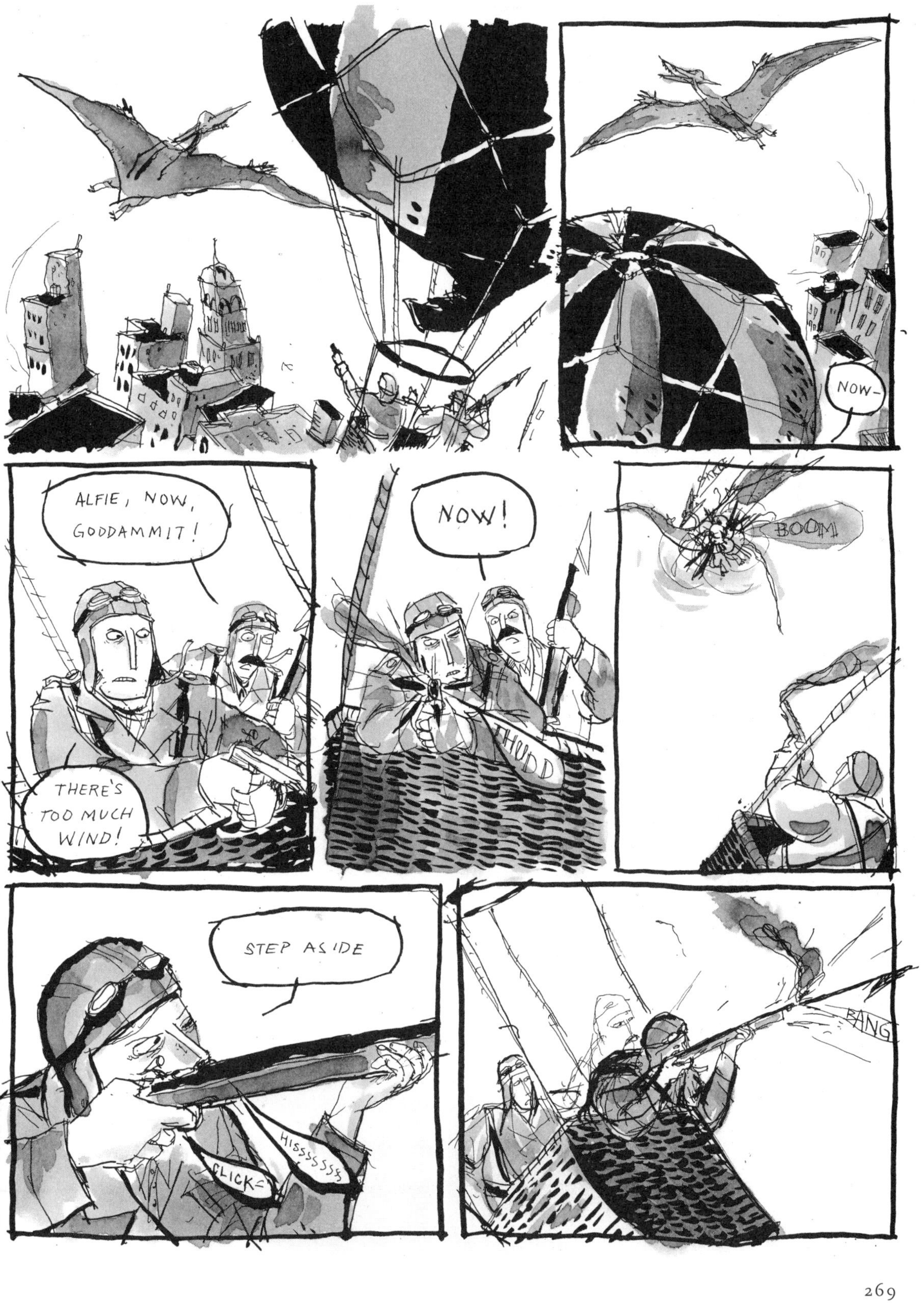
NOW-
ALFIE, NOW, GODDAMMIT!
THERE'S TOO MUCH WIND!
NOW!
THUDD
BOOM
STEP ASIDE
CLICK-
HISSSSSSSS
BANG

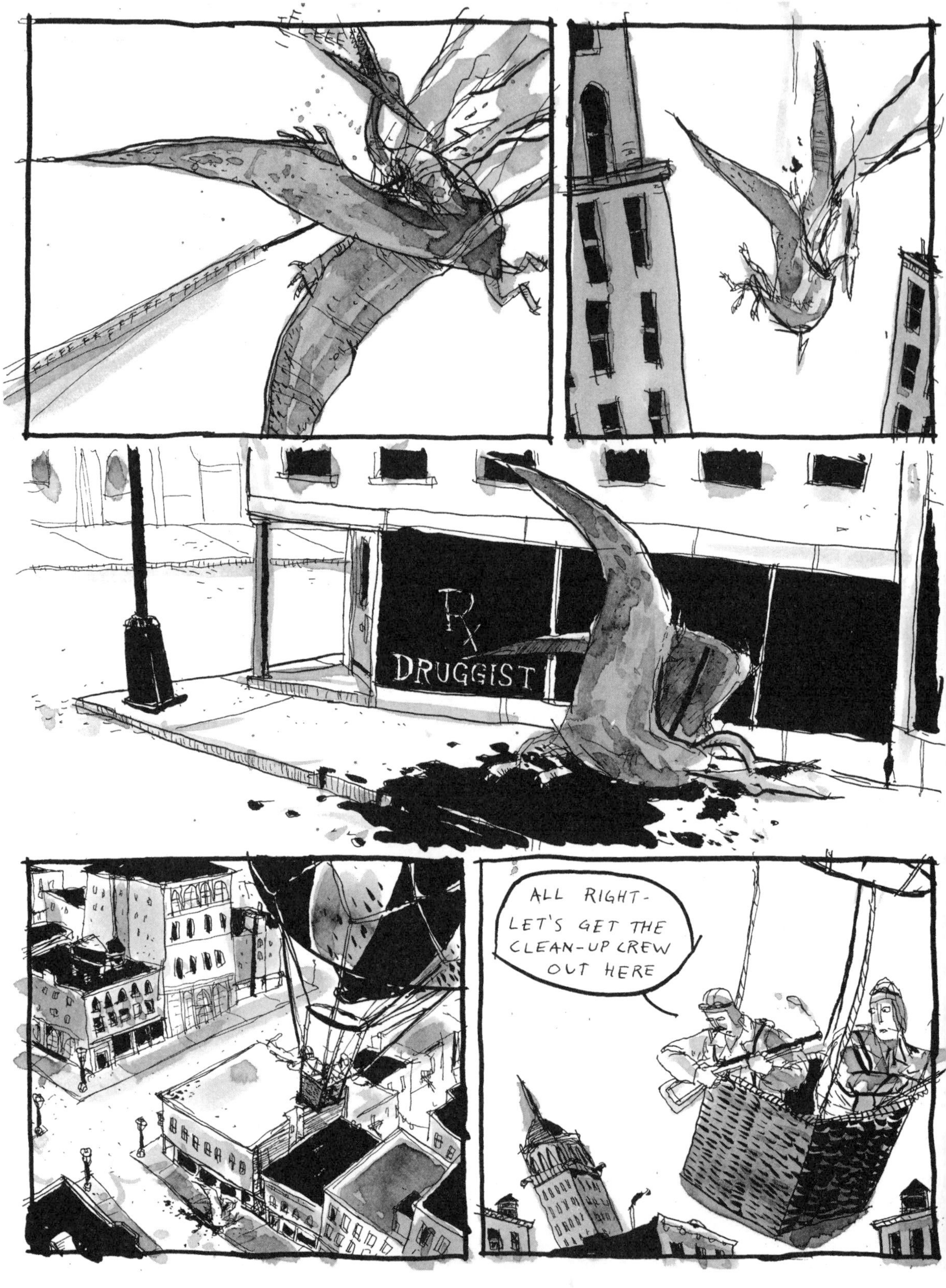
Rx
DRUGGIST
ALL RIGHT-
LET'S GET THE
CLEAN-UP CREW
OUT HERE

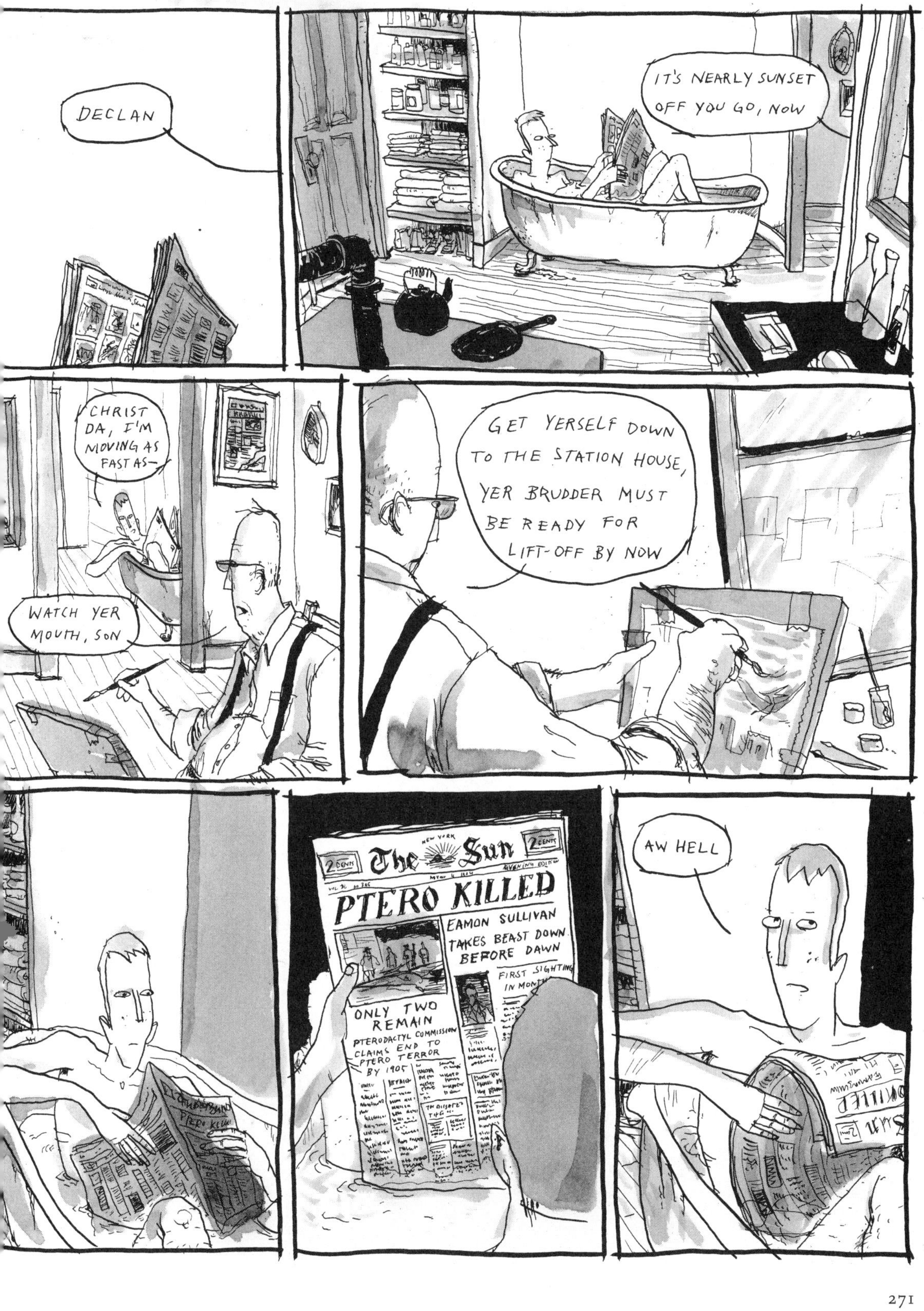
DECLAN
IT'S NEARLY SUNSET
OFF YOU GO, NOW
CHRIST DA, I'M MOVING AS FAST AS—
WATCH YER MOUTH, SON
GET YERSELF DOWN TO THE STATION HOUSE, YER BRUDDER MUST BE READY FOR LIFT-OFF BY NOW
NEW YORK
The Sun
2 CENTS
2 CENTS
EVENING EDITION
PTERO KILLED
EAMON SULLIVAN
TAKES BEAST DOWN BEFORE DAWN
FIRST SIGHTING
IN MONTH
ONLY TWO REMAIN
PTERODACTYL COMMISSION CLAIMS END TO PTERO TERROR BY 1905
AW HELL

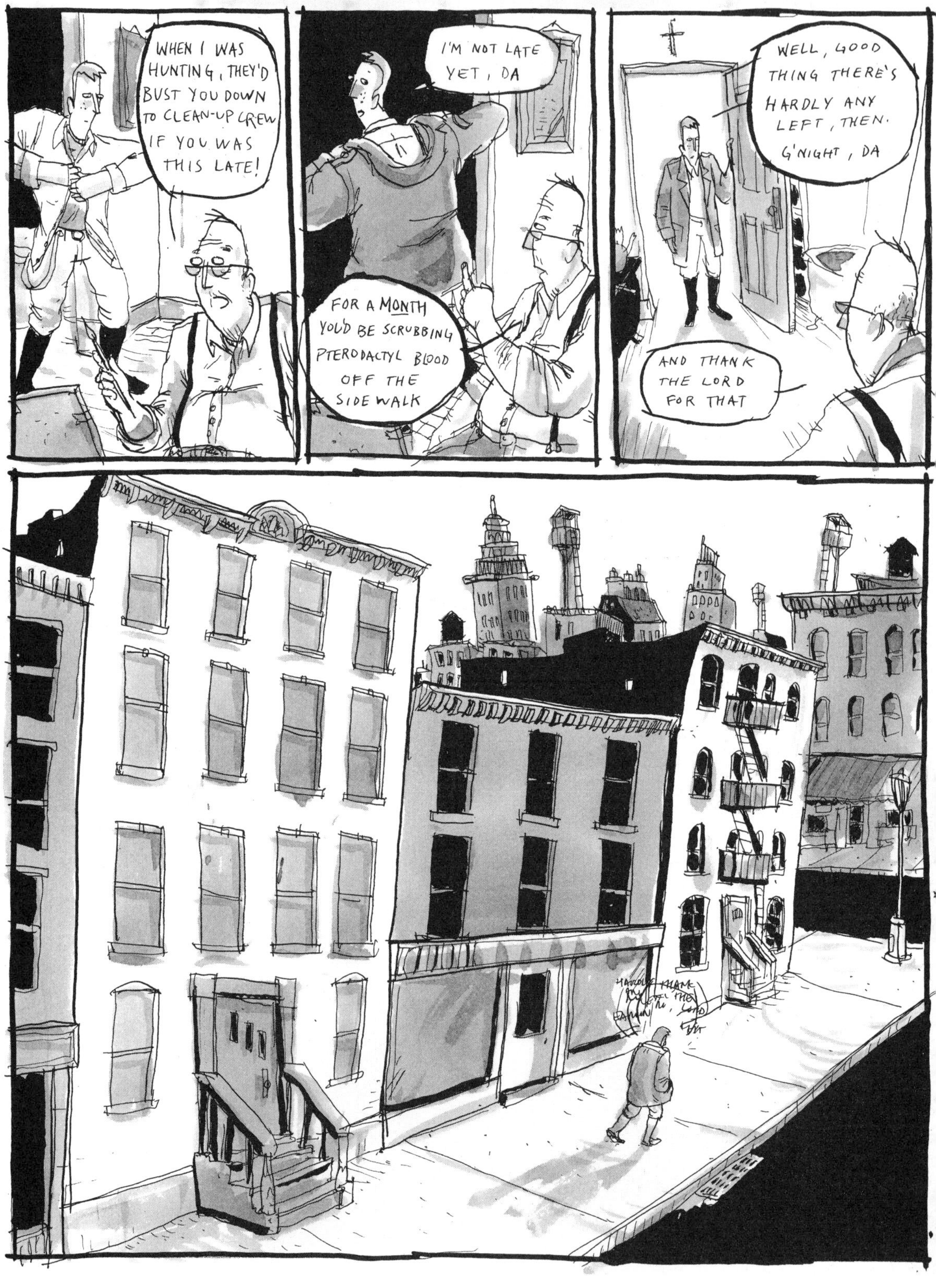
WHEN I WAS HUNTING, THEY'D BUST YOU DOWN TO CLEAN-UP CREW IF YOU WAS THIS LATE!
I'M NOT LATE YET, DA
FOR A MONTH YOU'D BE SCRUBBING PTERODACTYL BLOOD OFF THE SIDEWALK
WELL, GOOD THING THERE'S HARDLY ANY LEFT, THEN. G'NIGHT, DA
AND THANK THE LORD FOR THAT

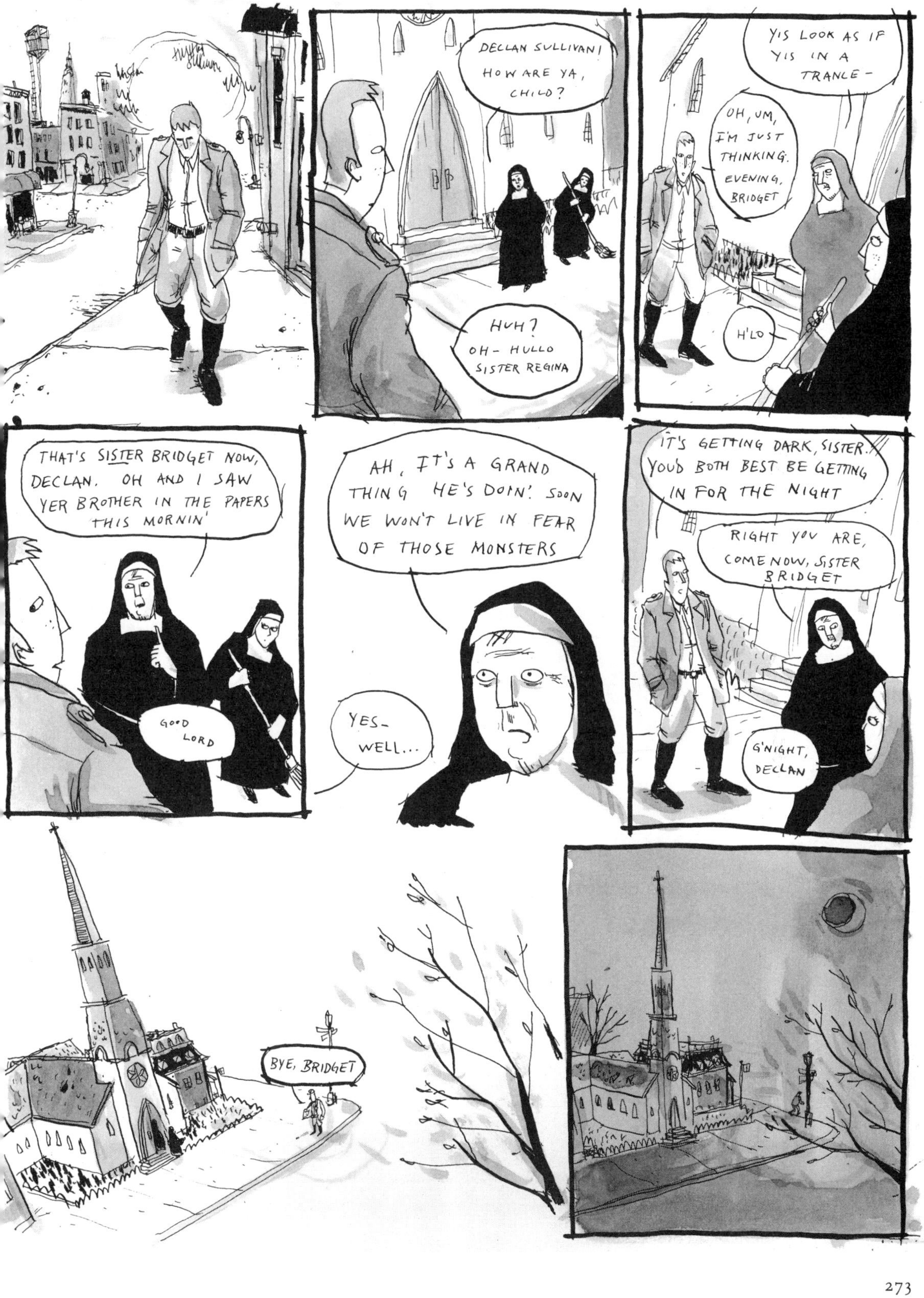
DECLAN SULLIVAN! HOW ARE YA, CHILD?
HUH? OH- HULLO SISTER REGINA
YIS LOOK AS IF YIS IN A TRANCE-
OH, UM, I'M JUST THINKING. EVENING, BRIDGET
H'LO
THAT'S SISTER BRIDGET NOW, DECLAN. OH AND I SAW YER BROTHER IN THE PAPERS THIS MORNIN'
GOOD LORD
AH, IT'S A GRAND THING HE'S DOIN'! SOON WE WON'T LIVE IN FEAR OF THOSE MONSTERS
YES- WELL...
IT'S GETTING DARK, SISTER. YOU'D BOTH BEST BE GETTING IN FOR THE NIGHT
RIGHT YOU ARE, COME NOW, SISTER BRIDGET
G'NIGHT, DECLAN
BYE, BRIDGET

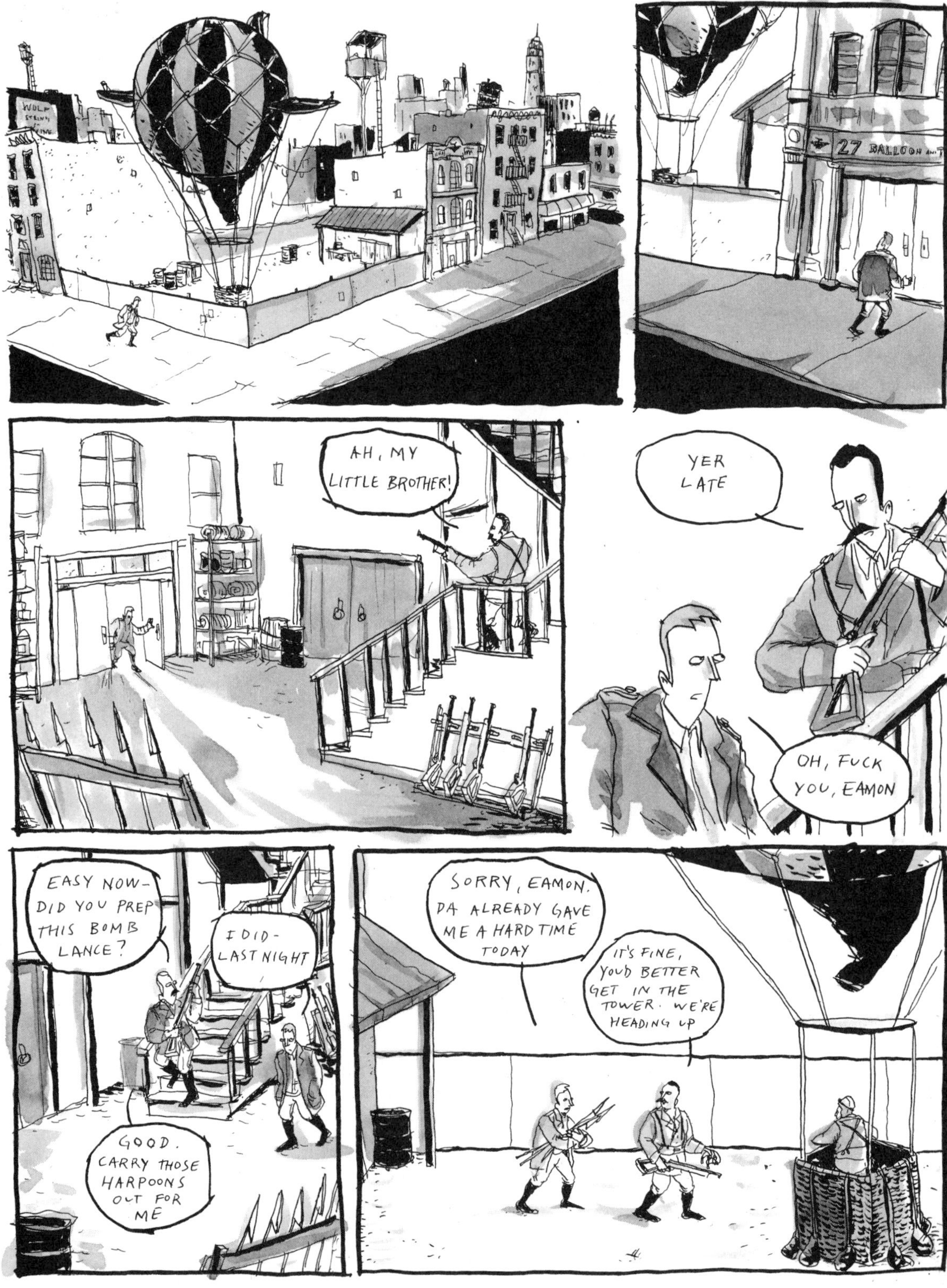
27 BALLOON AND T
AH, MY LITTLE BROTHER!
YER LATE
OH, FUCK YOU, EAMON
EASY NOW- DID YOU PREP THIS BOMB LANCE?
I DID- LAST NIGHT
GOOD. CARRY THOSE HARPOONS OUT FOR ME
SORRY, EAMON. DA ALREADY GAVE ME A HARD TIME TODAY
IT'S FINE, YOU'D BETTER GET IN THE TOWER. WE'RE HEADING UP

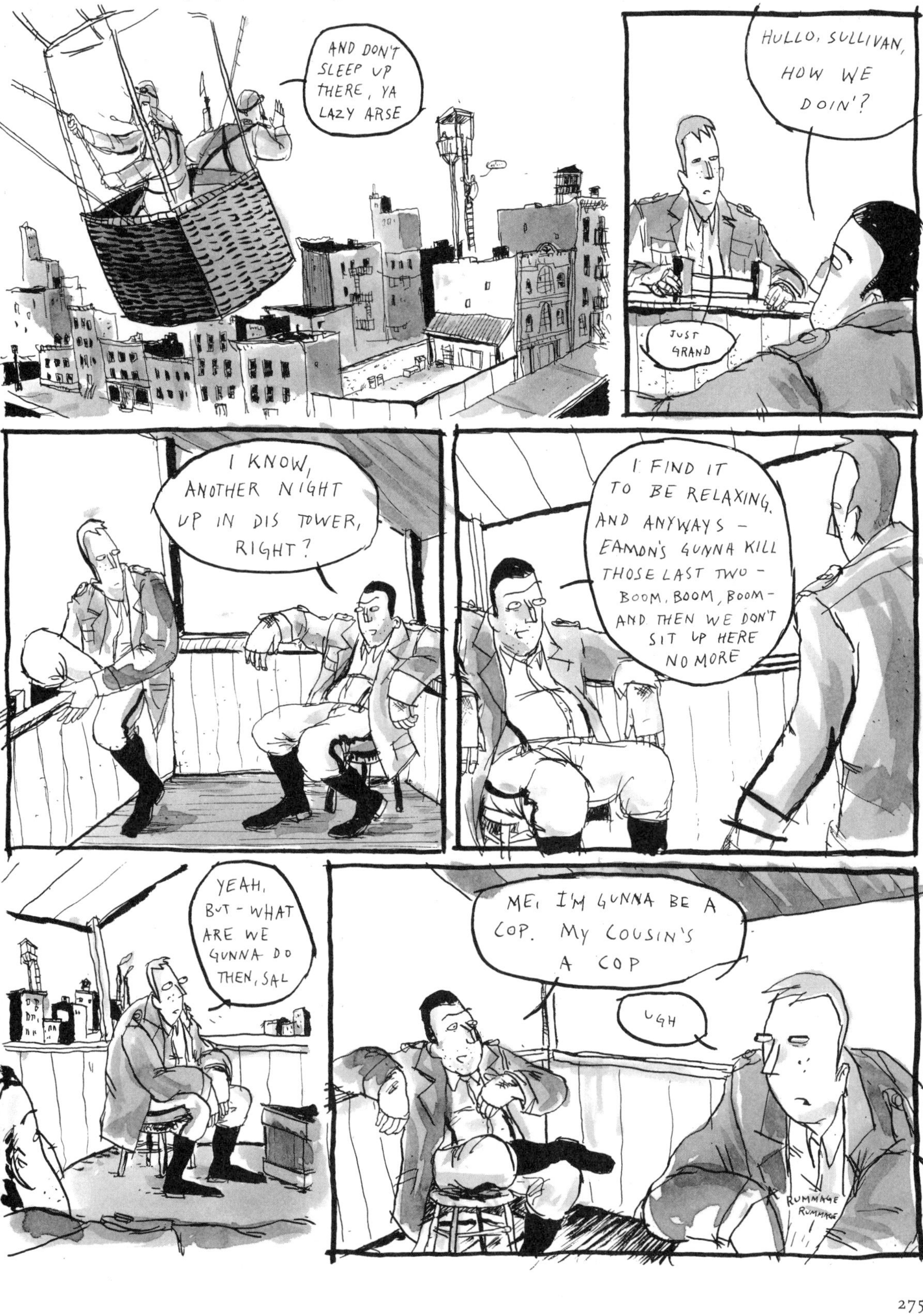
AND DON'T SLEEP UP THERE, YA LAZY ARSE
HULLO, SULLIVAN, HOW WE DOIN'?
JUST GRAND
I KNOW, ANOTHER NIGHT UP IN DIS TOWER, RIGHT?
I FIND IT TO BE RELAXING. AND ANYWAYS - EAMON'S GUNNA KILL THOSE LAST TWO - BOOM, BOOM, BOOM - AND THEN WE DON'T SIT UP HERE NO MORE
YEAH, BUT - WHAT ARE WE GUNNA DO THEN, SAL
ME, I'M GUNNA BE A COP. MY COUSIN'S A COP
UGH
RUMMAGE RUMMAGE

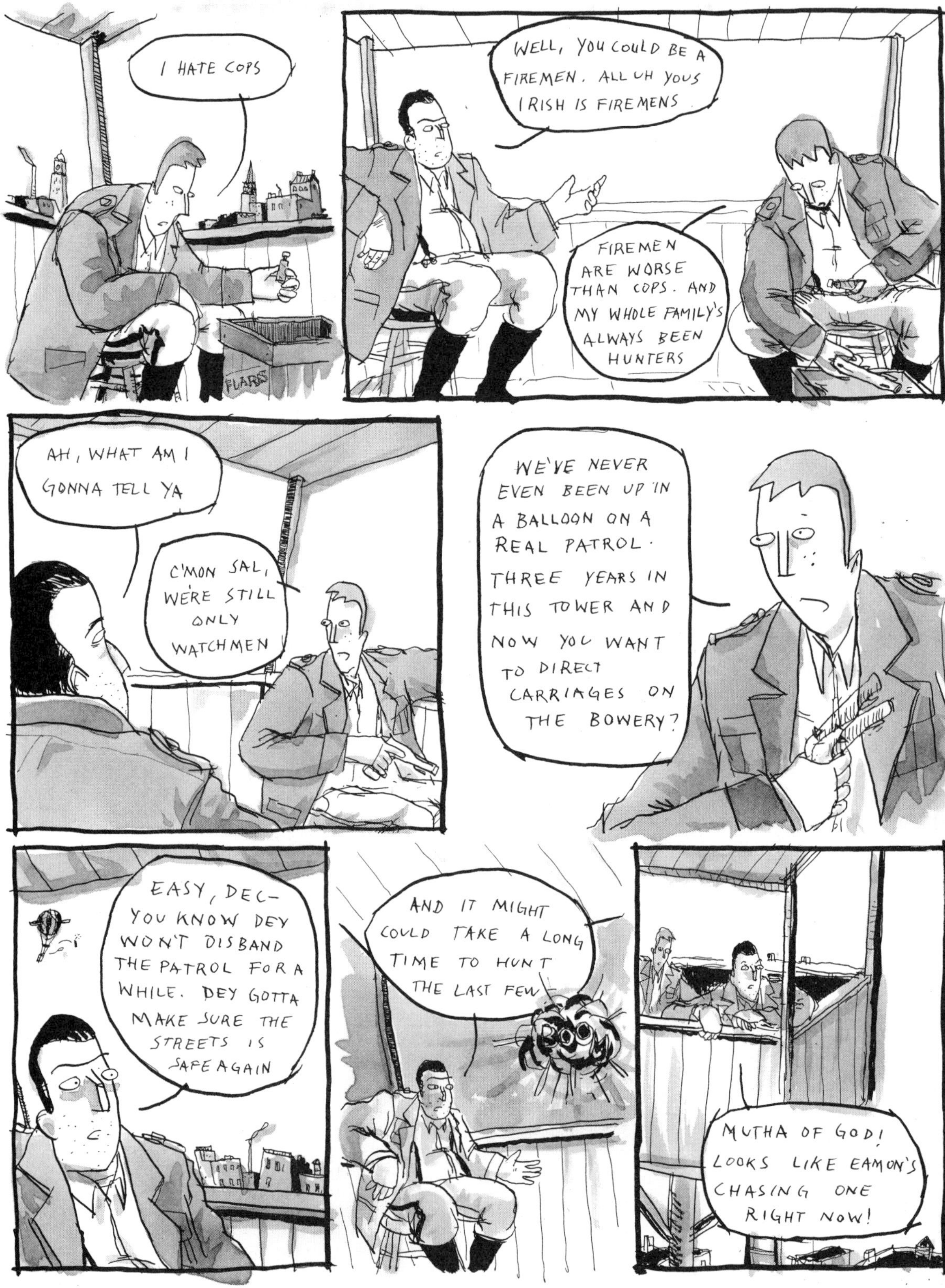
I HATE COPS
FLARES
WELL, YOU COULD BE A FIREMEN. ALL UH YOUS IRISH IS FIREMENS
FIREMEN ARE WORSE THAN COPS. AND MY WHOLE FAMILY'S ALWAYS BEEN HUNTERS
AH, WHAT AM I GONNA TELL YA
C'MON SAL, WE'RE STILL ONLY WATCHMEN
WE'VE NEVER EVEN BEEN UP IN A BALLOON ON A REAL PATROL. THREE YEARS IN THIS TOWER AND NOW YOU WANT TO DIRECT CARRIAGES ON THE BOWERY?
EASY, DEC— YOU KNOW DEY WON'T DISBAND THE PATROL FOR A WHILE. DEY GOTTA MAKE SURE THE STREETS IS SAFE AGAIN
AND IT MIGHT COULD TAKE A LONG TIME TO HUNT THE LAST FEW
BOOM
MUTHA OF GOD! LOOKS LIKE EAMON'S CHASING ONE RIGHT NOW!

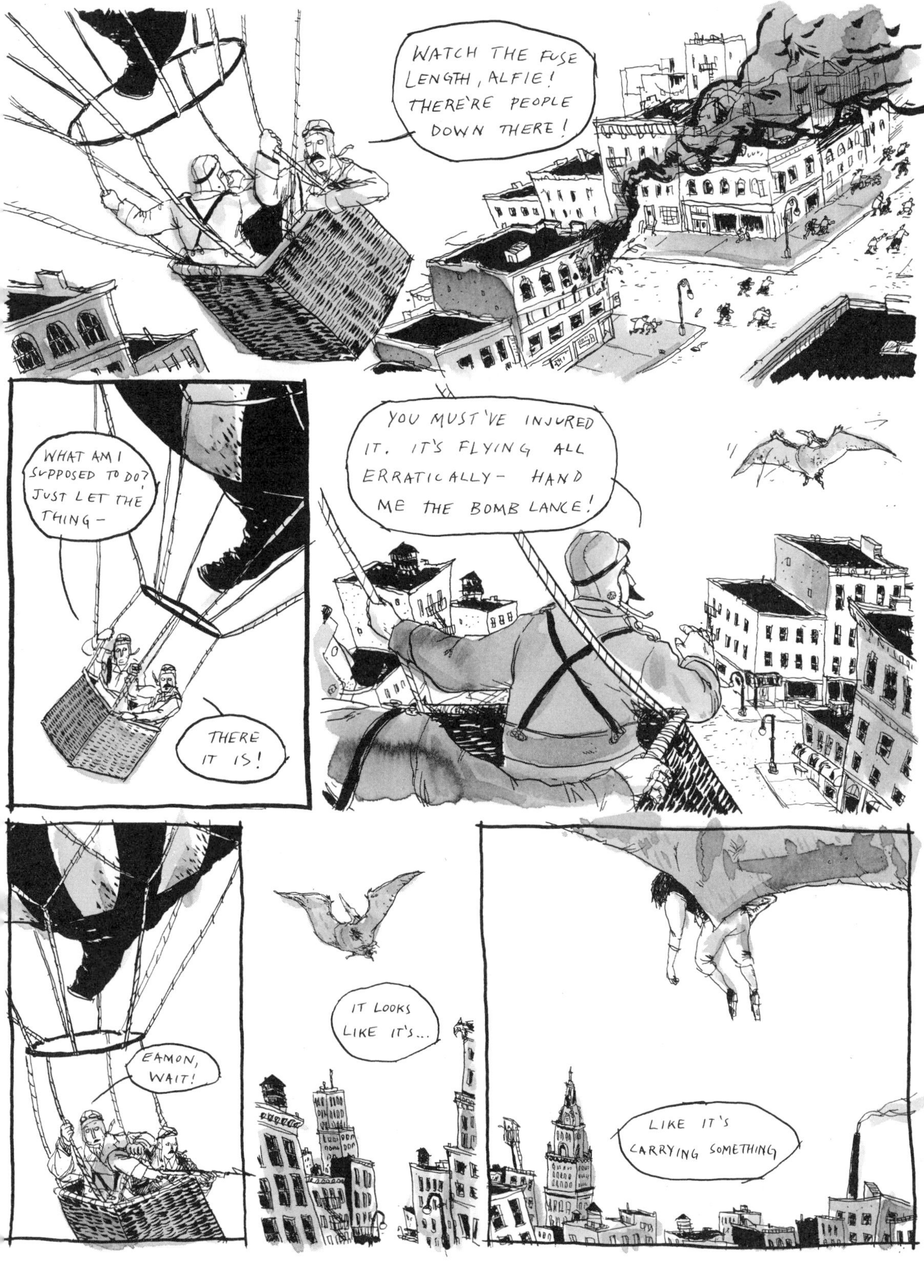
WATCH THE FUSE LENGTH, ALFIE! THERE'RE PEOPLE DOWN THERE!
WHAT AM I SUPPOSED TO DO? JUST LET THE THING-
THERE IT IS!
YOU MUST'VE INJURED IT. IT'S FLYING ALL ERRATICALLY- HAND ME THE BOMB LANCE!
EAMON, WAIT!
IT LOOKS LIKE IT'S...
LIKE IT'S CARRYING SOMETHING

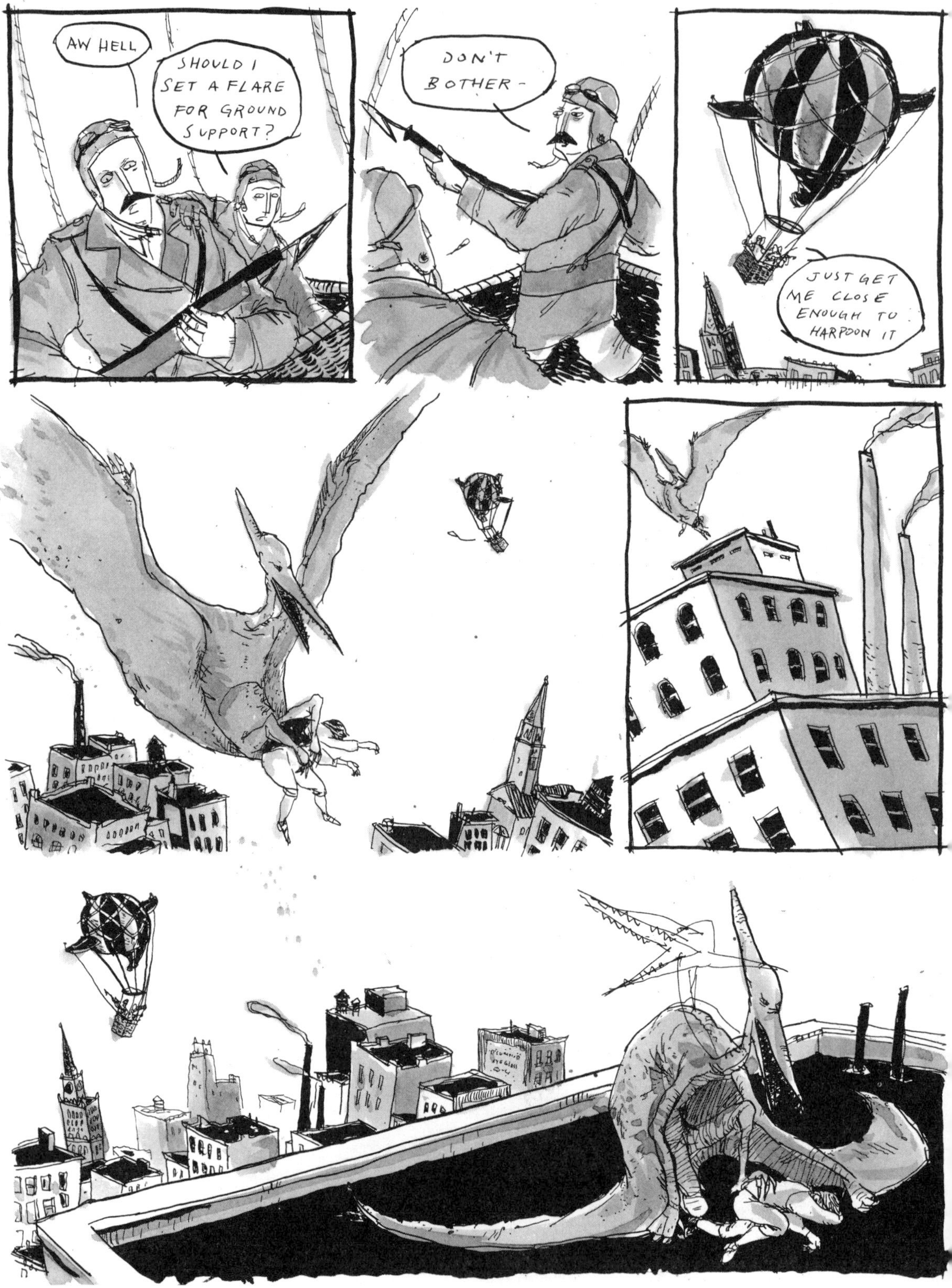
AW HELL
SHOULD I SET A FLARE FOR GROUND SUPPORT?
DON'T BOTHER-
JUST GET ME CLOSE ENOUGH TO HARPOON IT

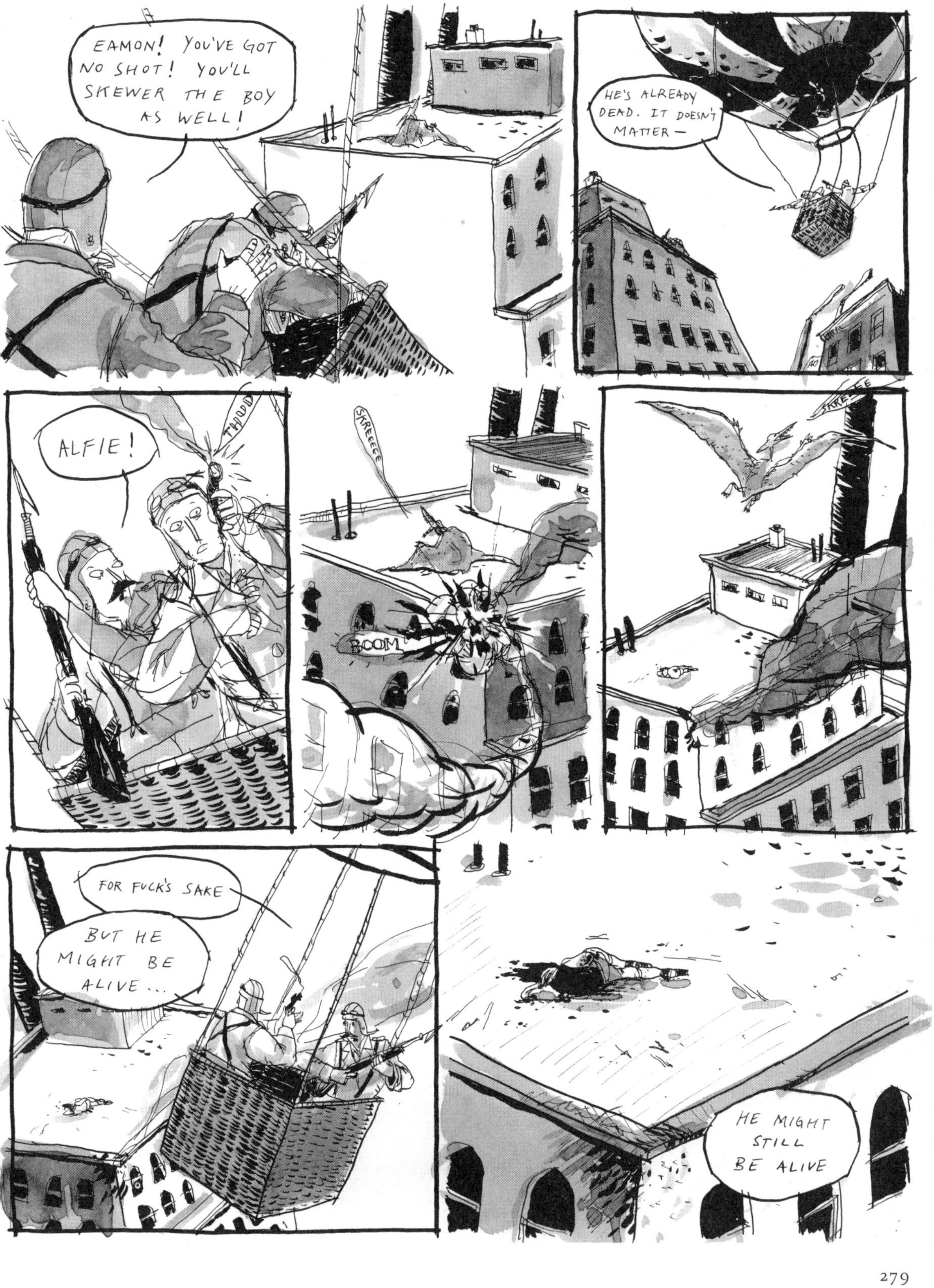
EAMON! YOU'VE GOT NO SHOT! YOU'LL SKEWER THE BOY AS WELL!
HE'S ALREADY DEAD. IT DOESN'T MATTER—
ALFIE!
THOOD
SKREEEEE
BOOM
SKREEEE
FOR FUCK'S SAKE
BUT HE MIGHT BE ALIVE...
HE MIGHT STILL BE ALIVE

Winter

excerpt from

Refresh Refresh

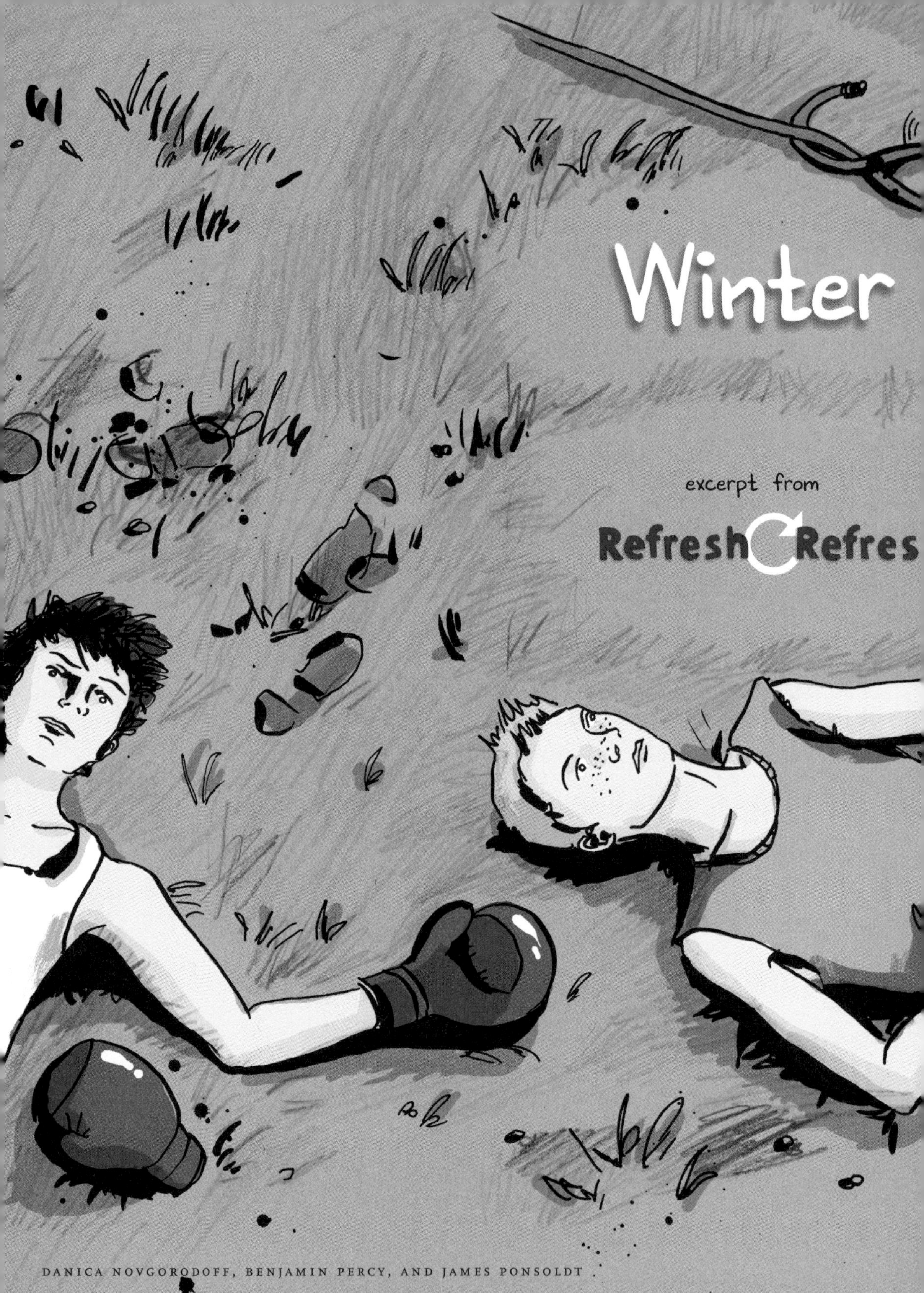

DANICA NOVGORODOFF, BENJAMIN PERCY, AND JAMES PONSOLDT

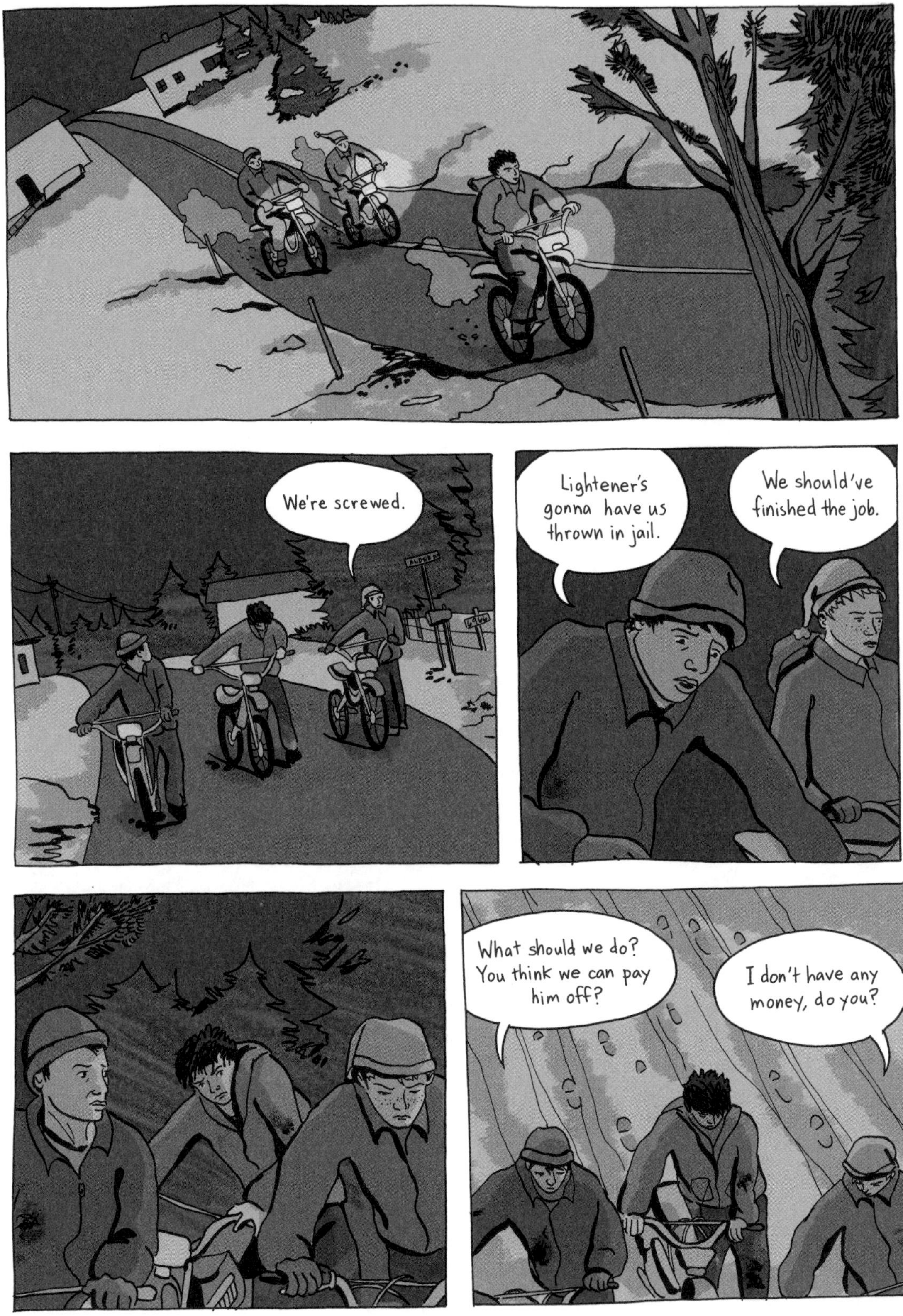
We're screwed.
Lightener's gonna have us thrown in jail.
We should've finished the job.
What should we do? You think we can pay him off?
I don't have any money, do you?

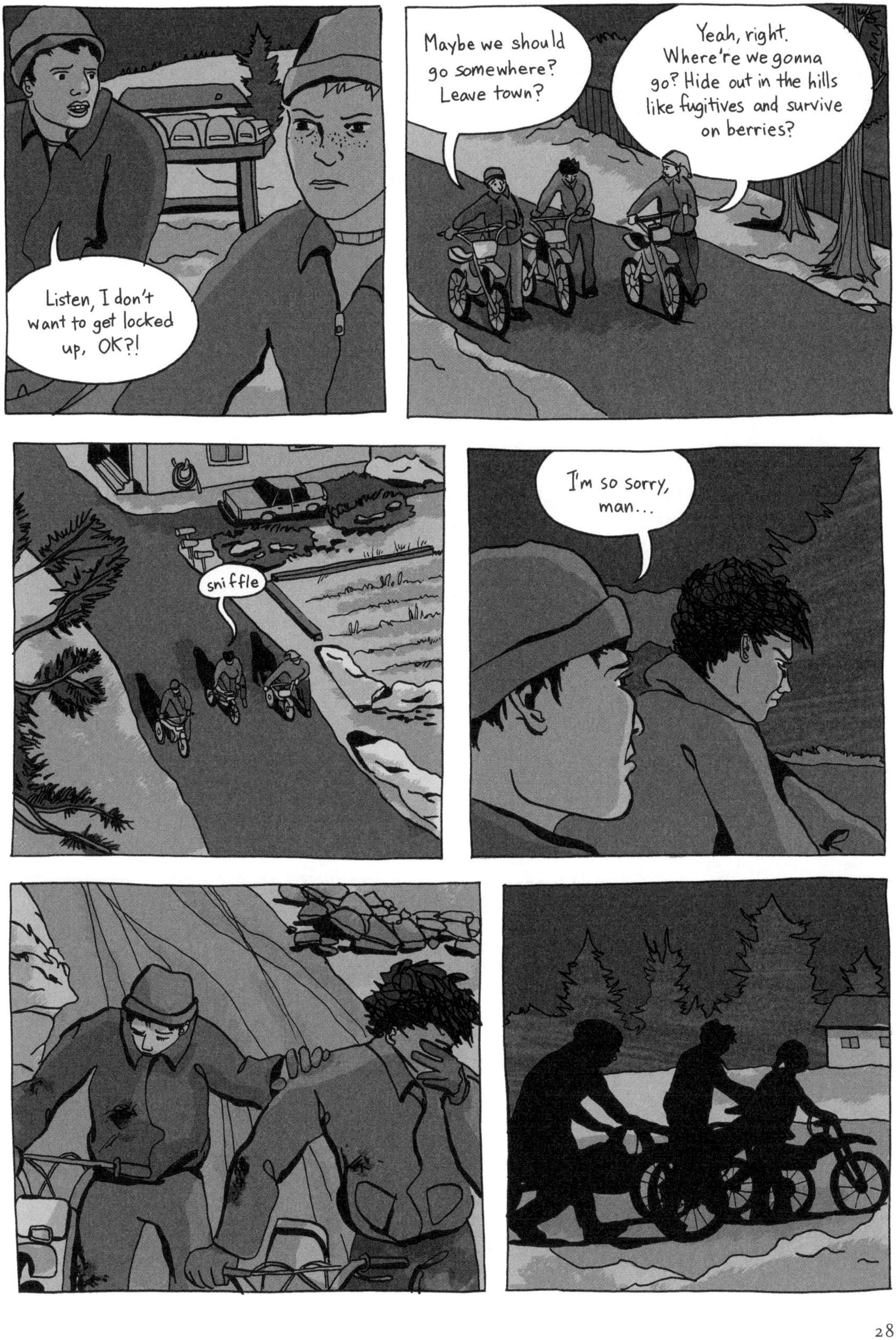
Listen, I don't want to get locked up, OK?!
Maybe we should go somewhere? Leave town?
Yeah, right. Where're we gonna go? Hide out in the hills like fugitives and survive on berries?
sniffle
I'm so sorry, man...

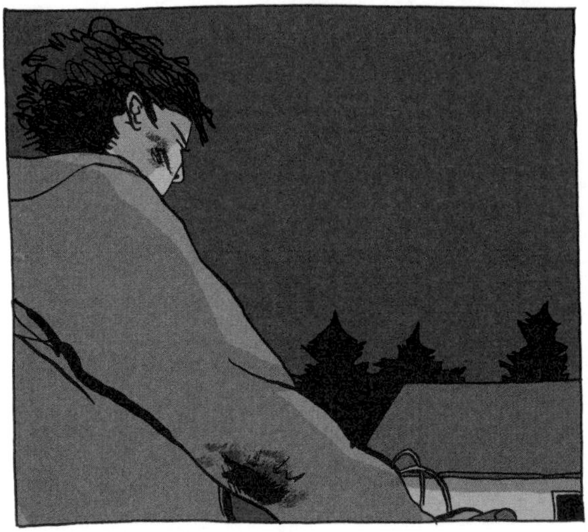

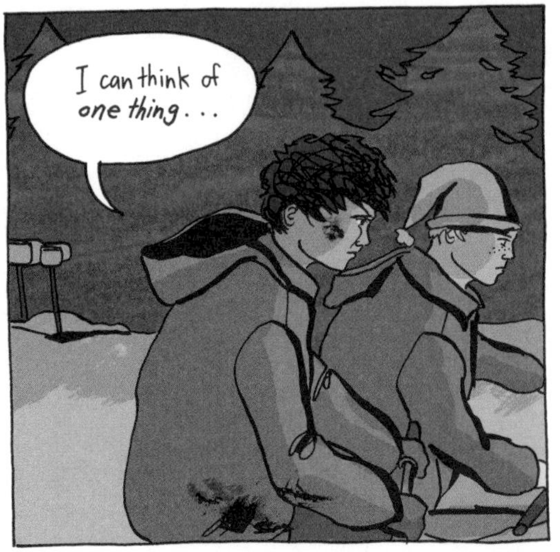
I can think of one thing . . .

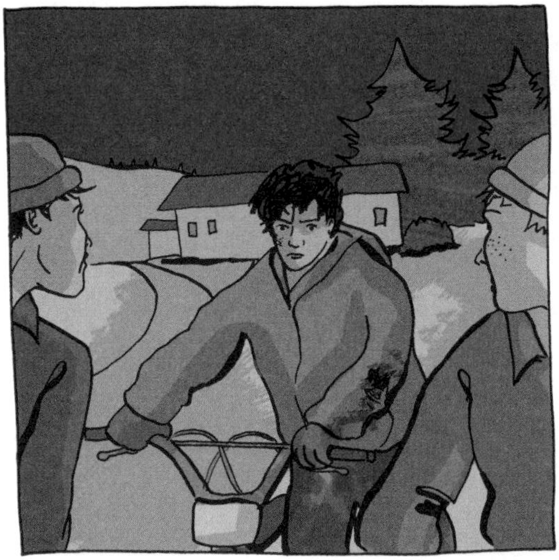

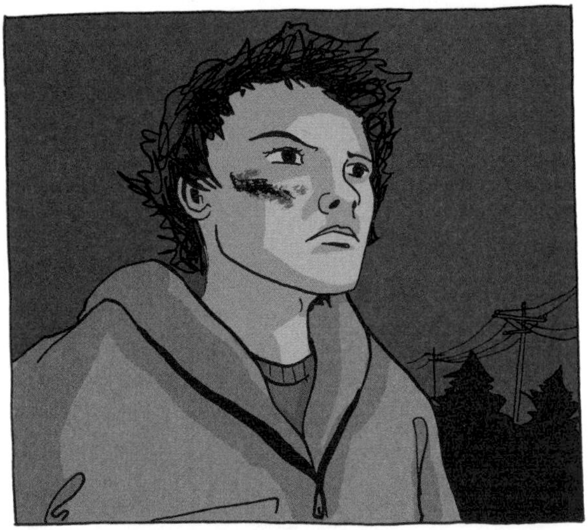

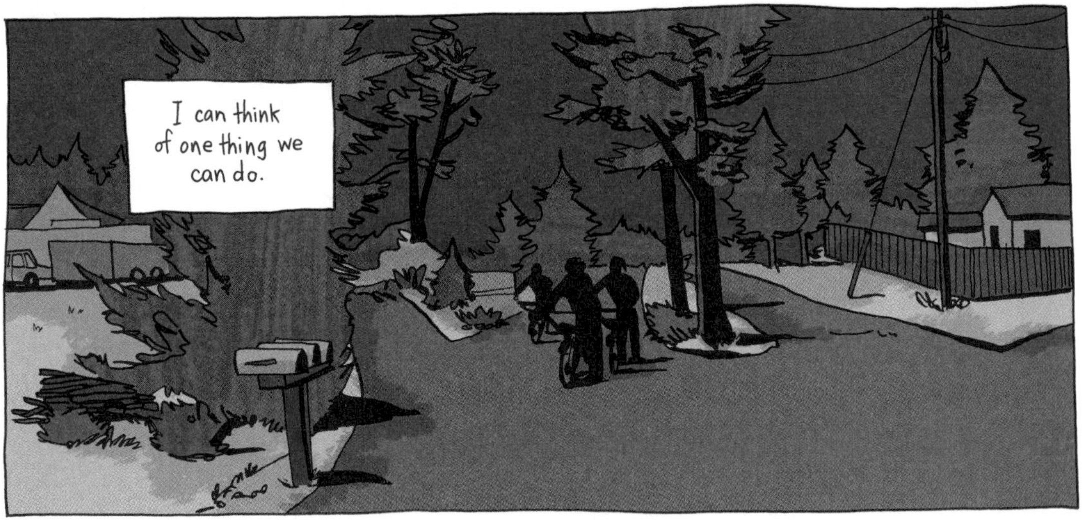
I can think of one thing we can do.

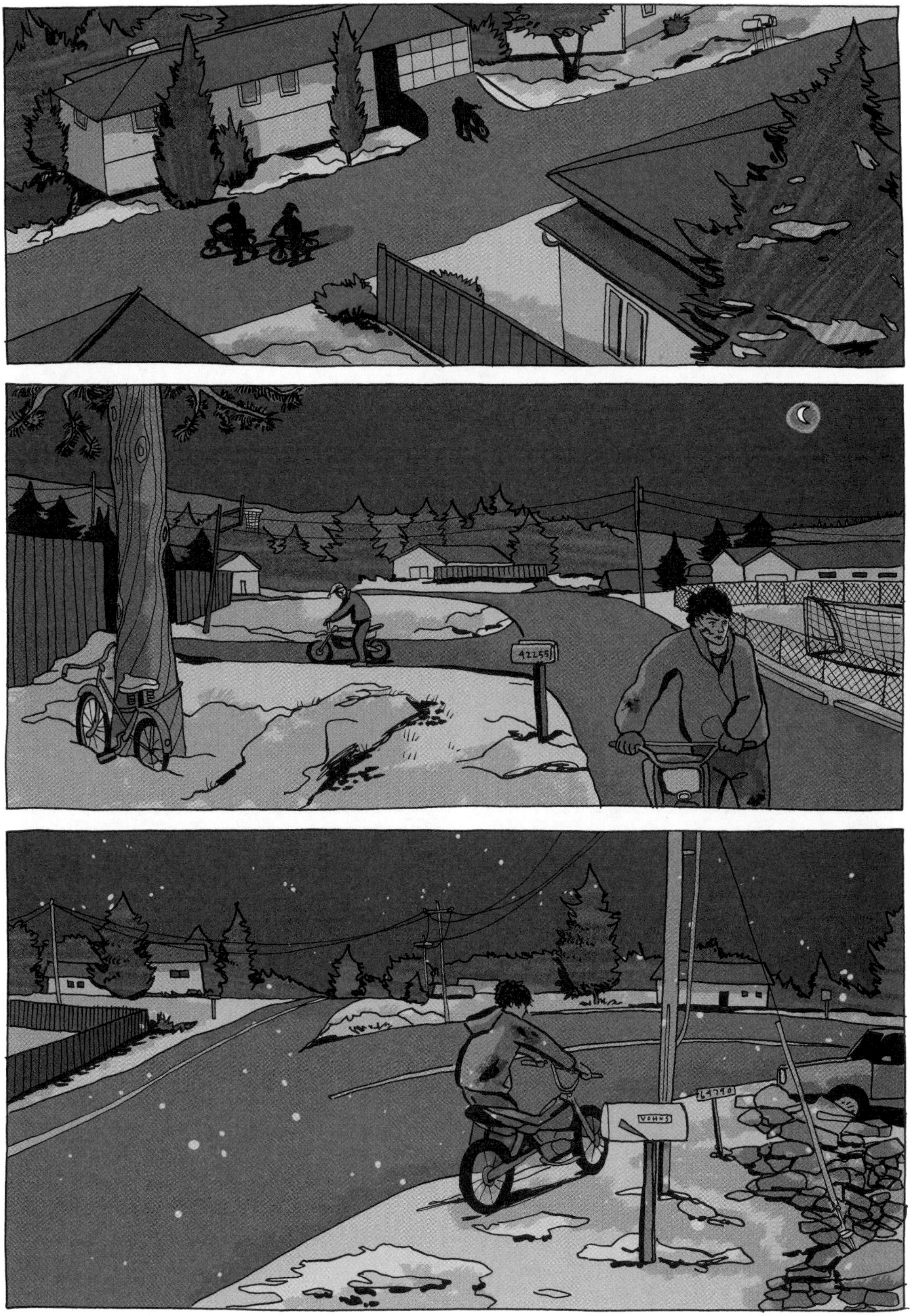
42255
VOHNS
64790

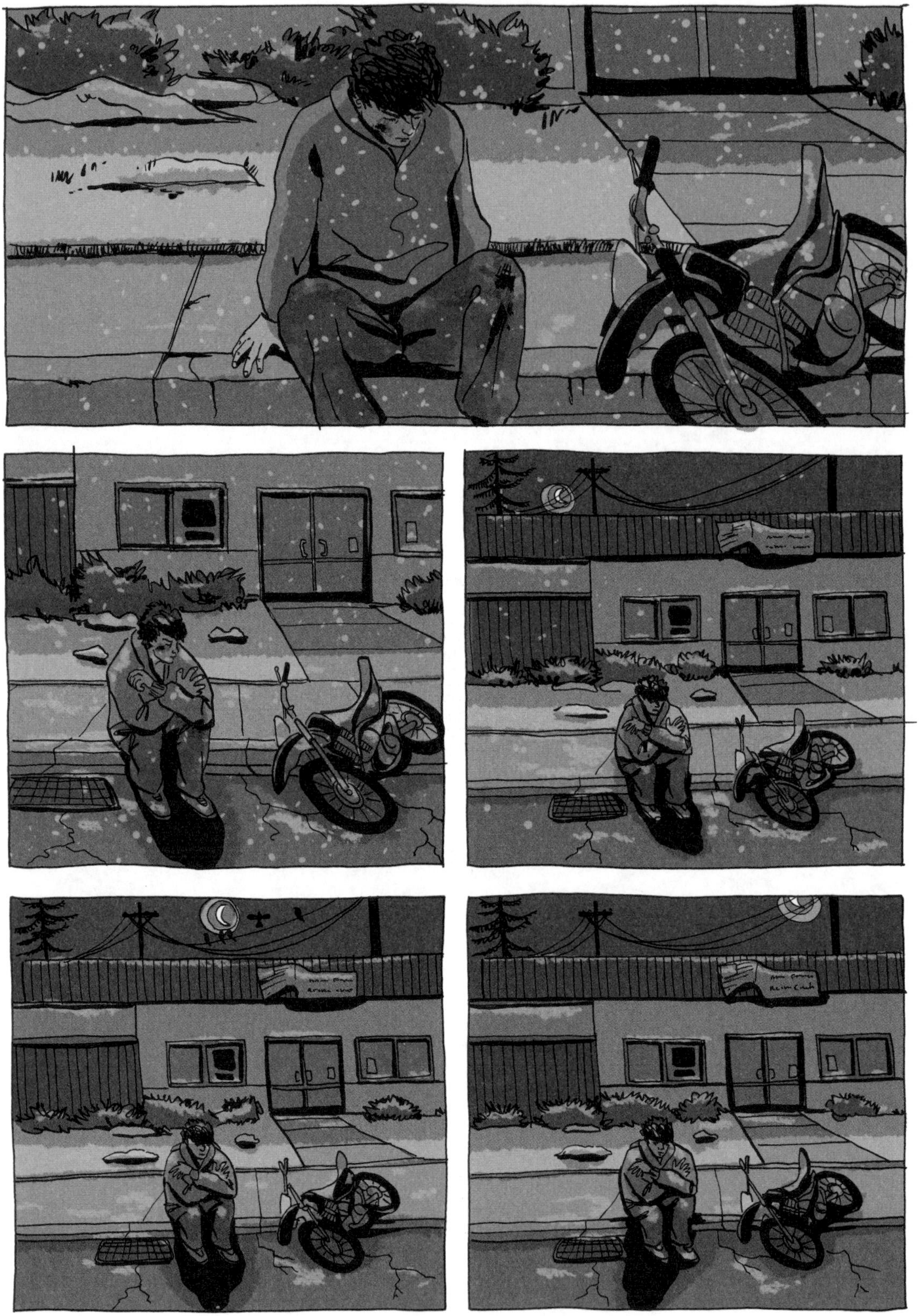

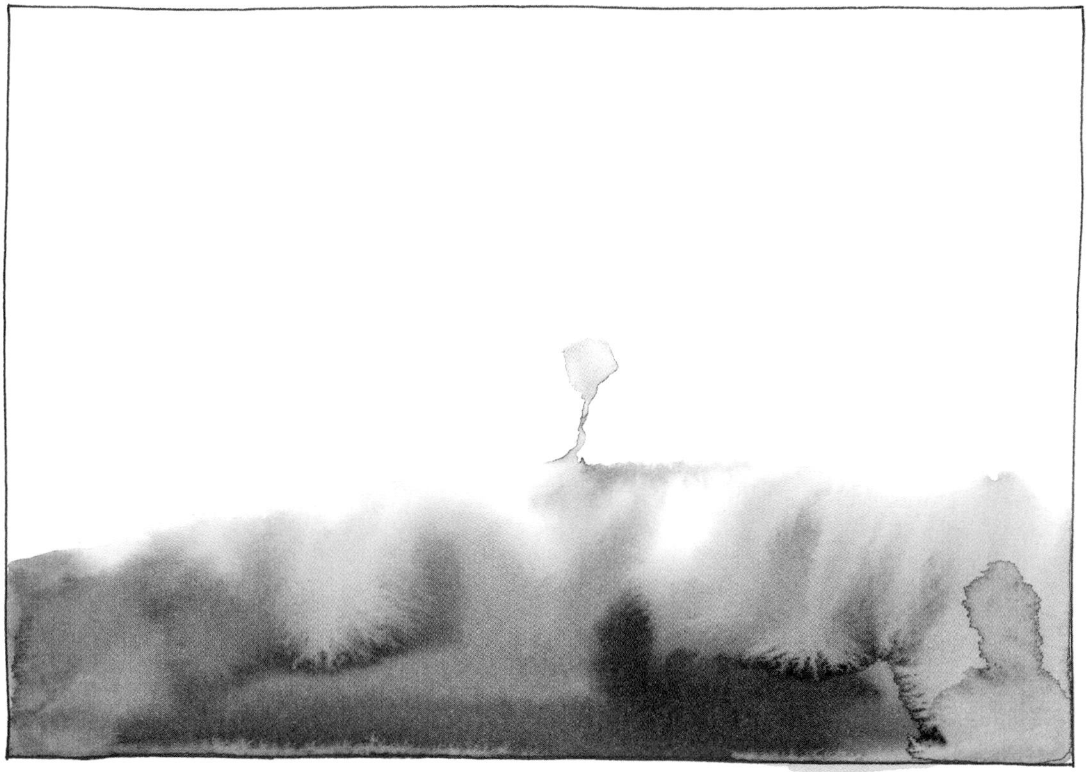

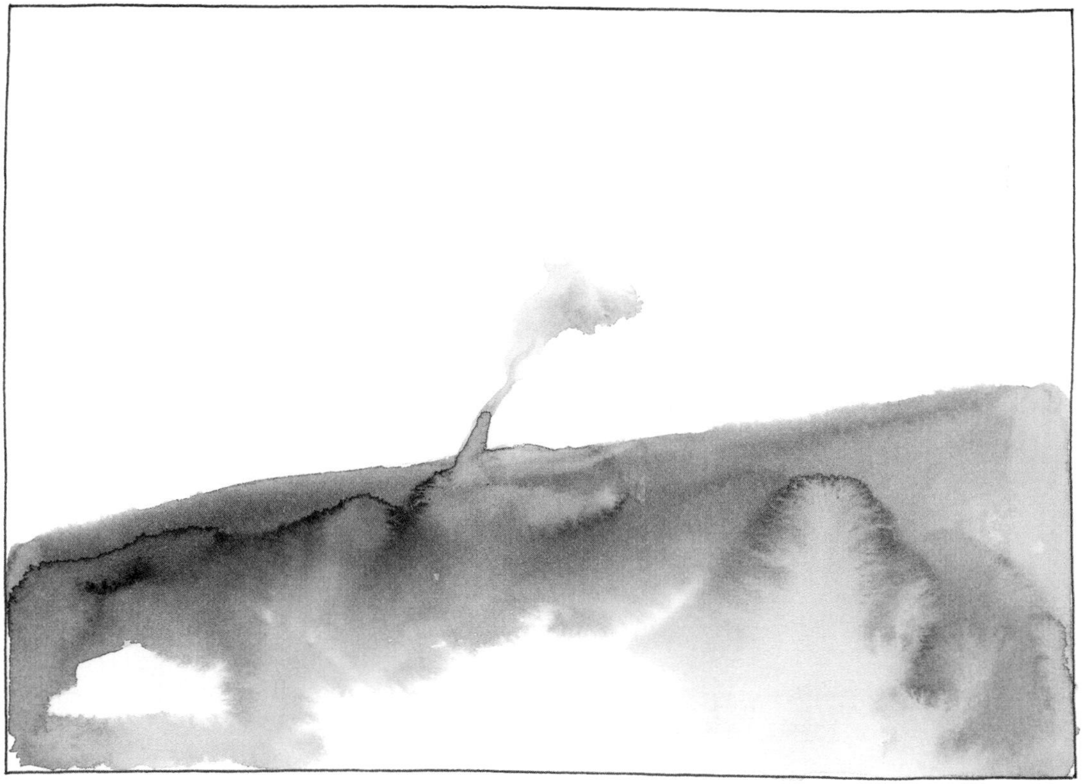

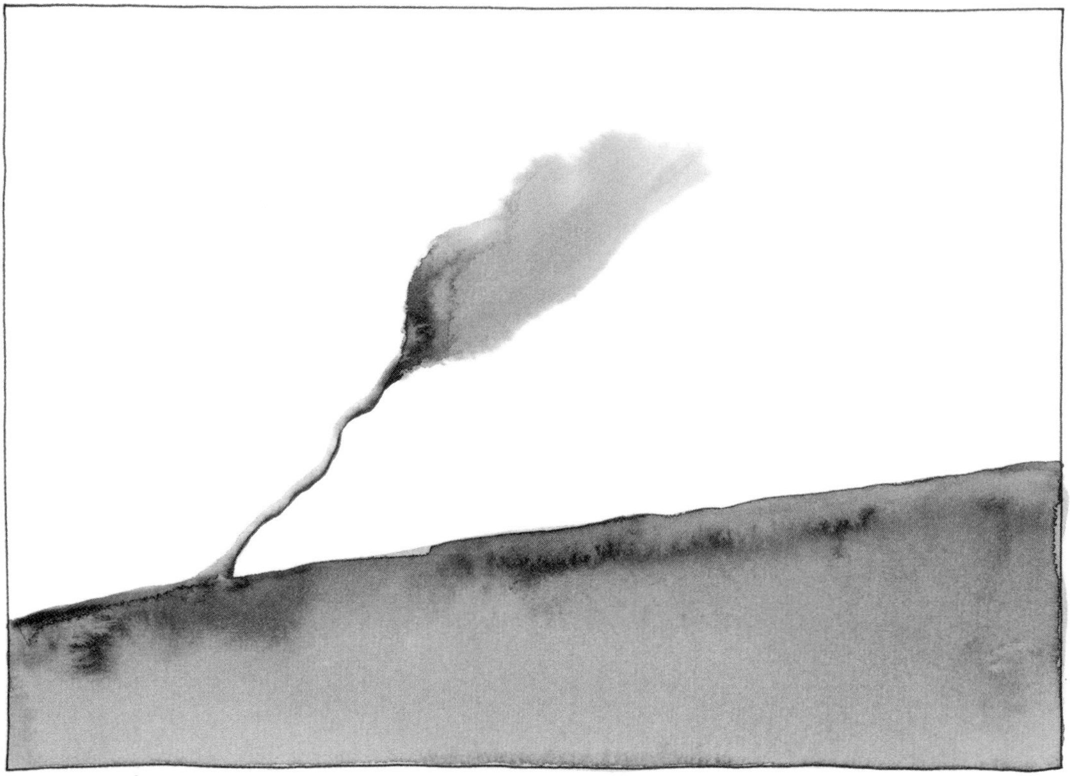

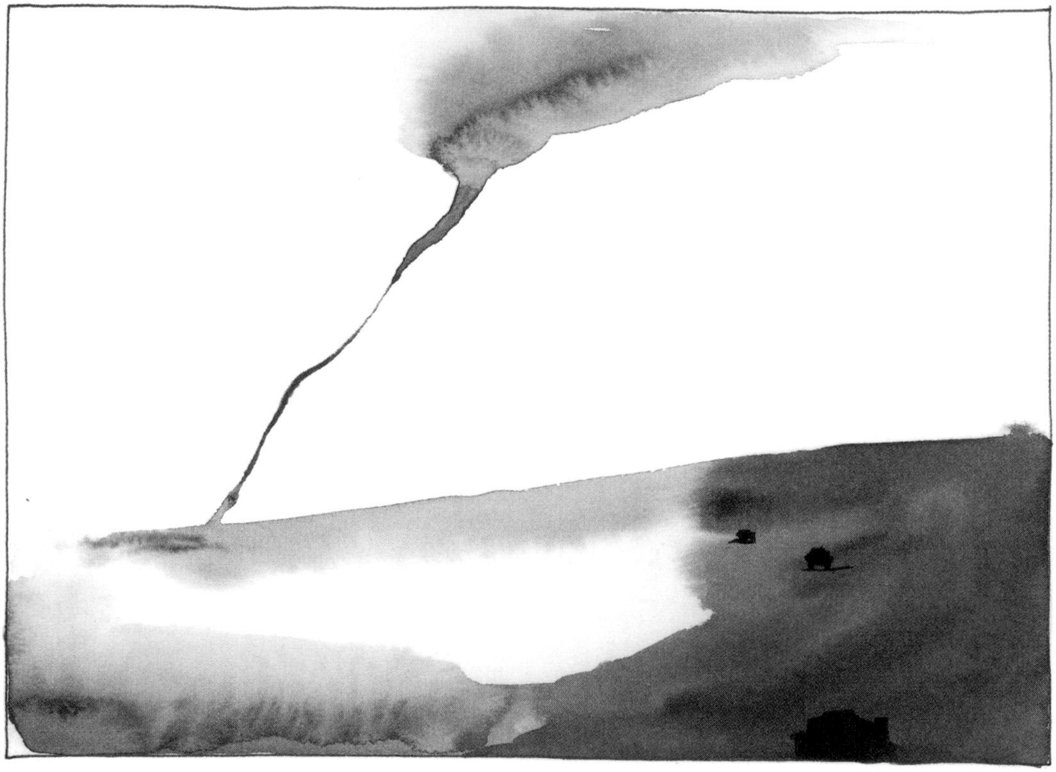

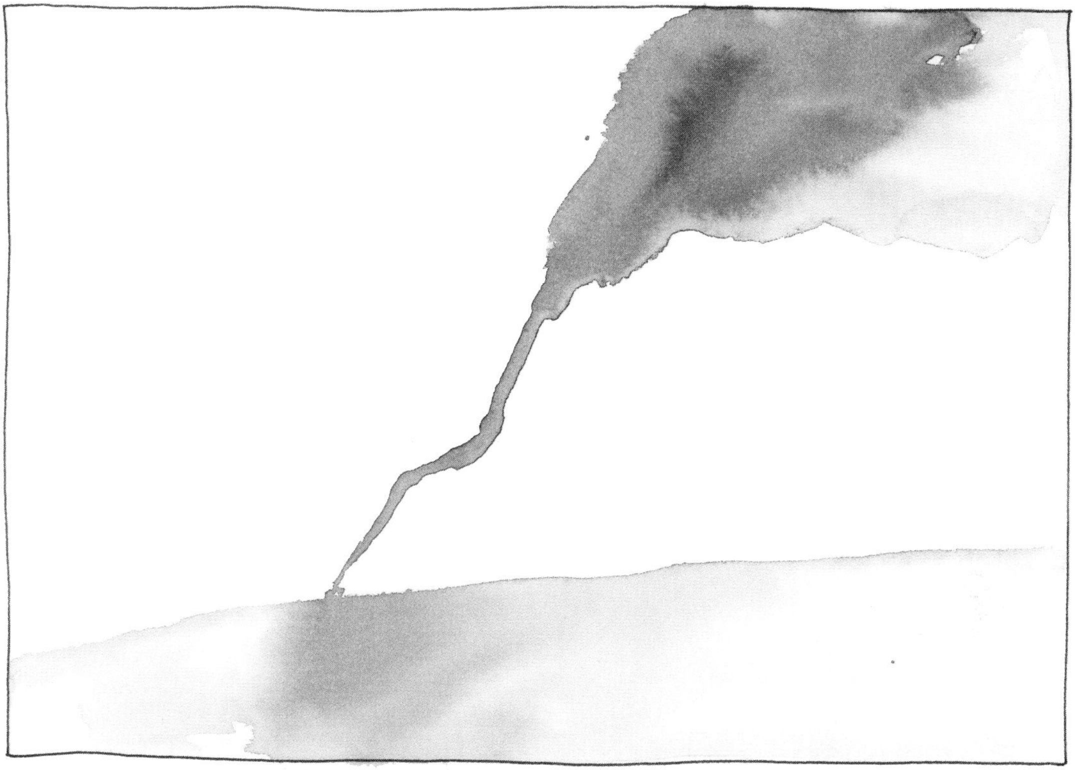

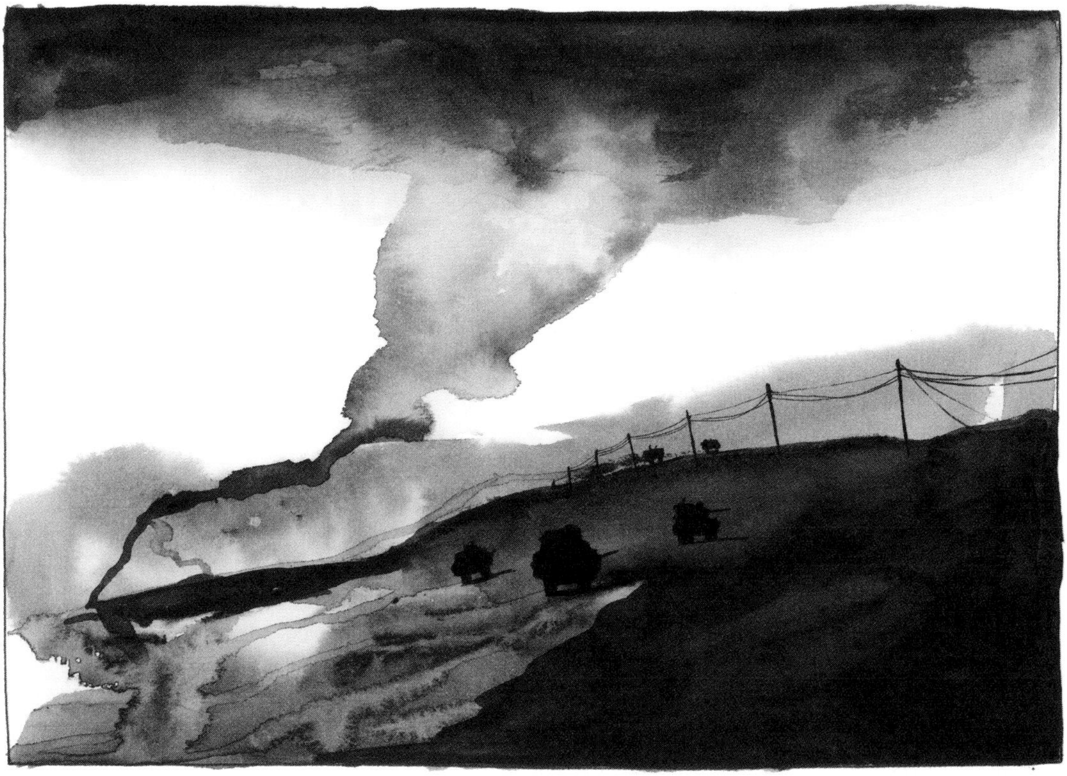

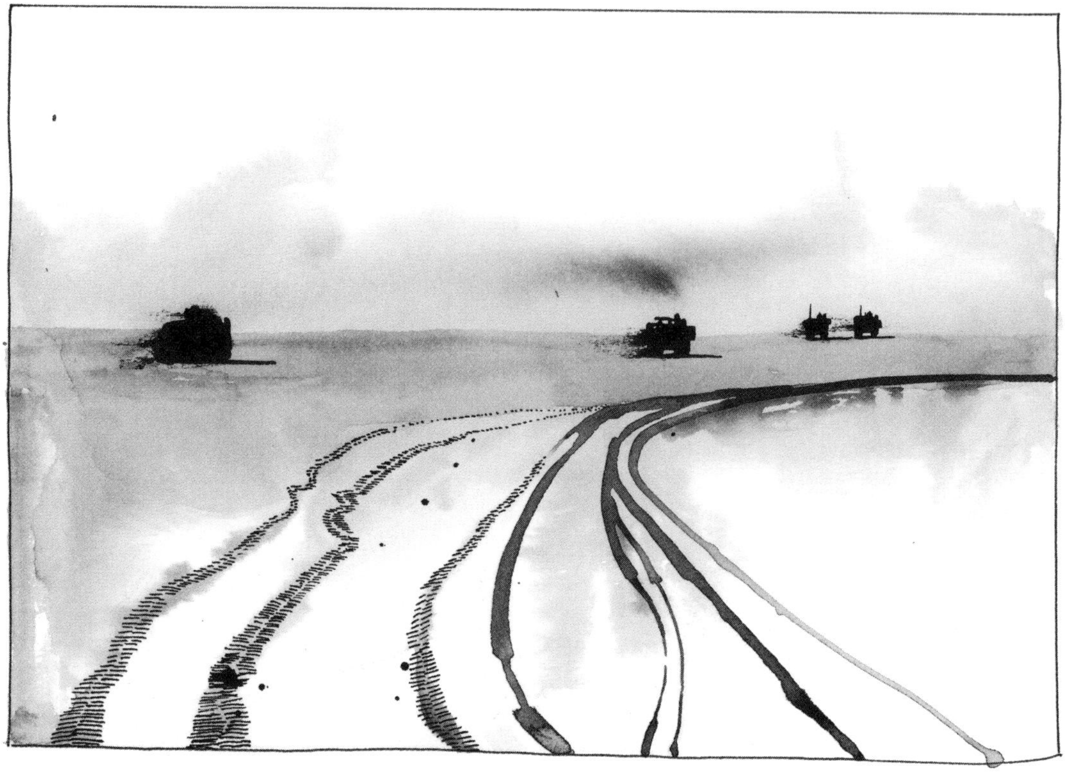

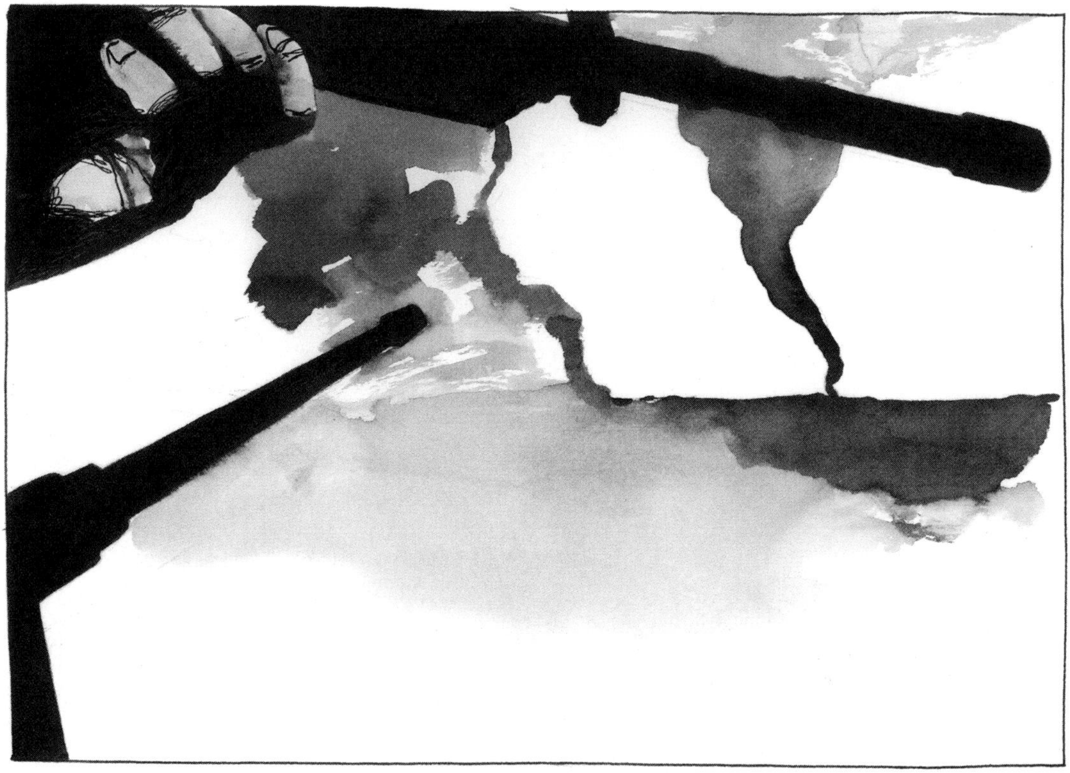

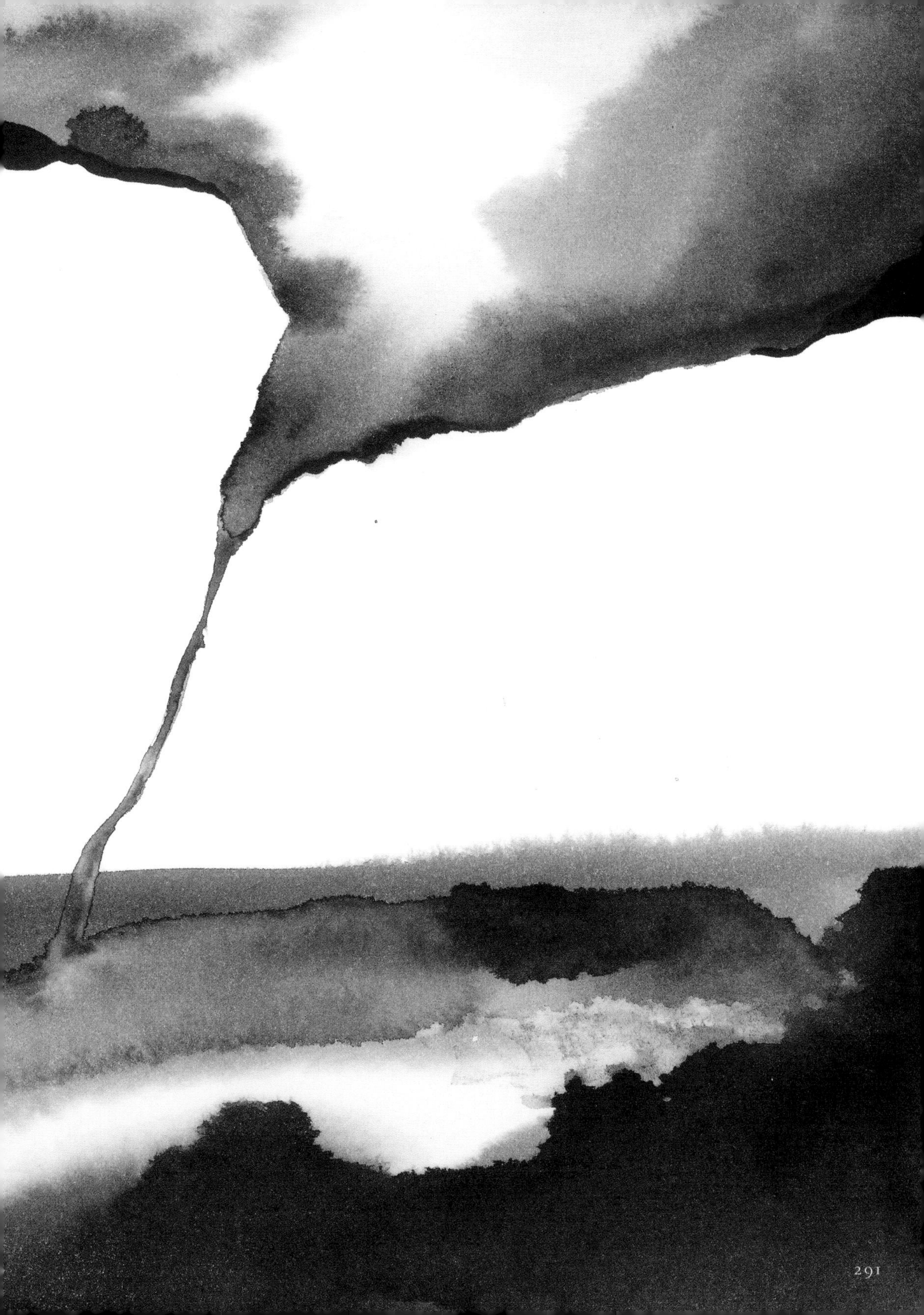

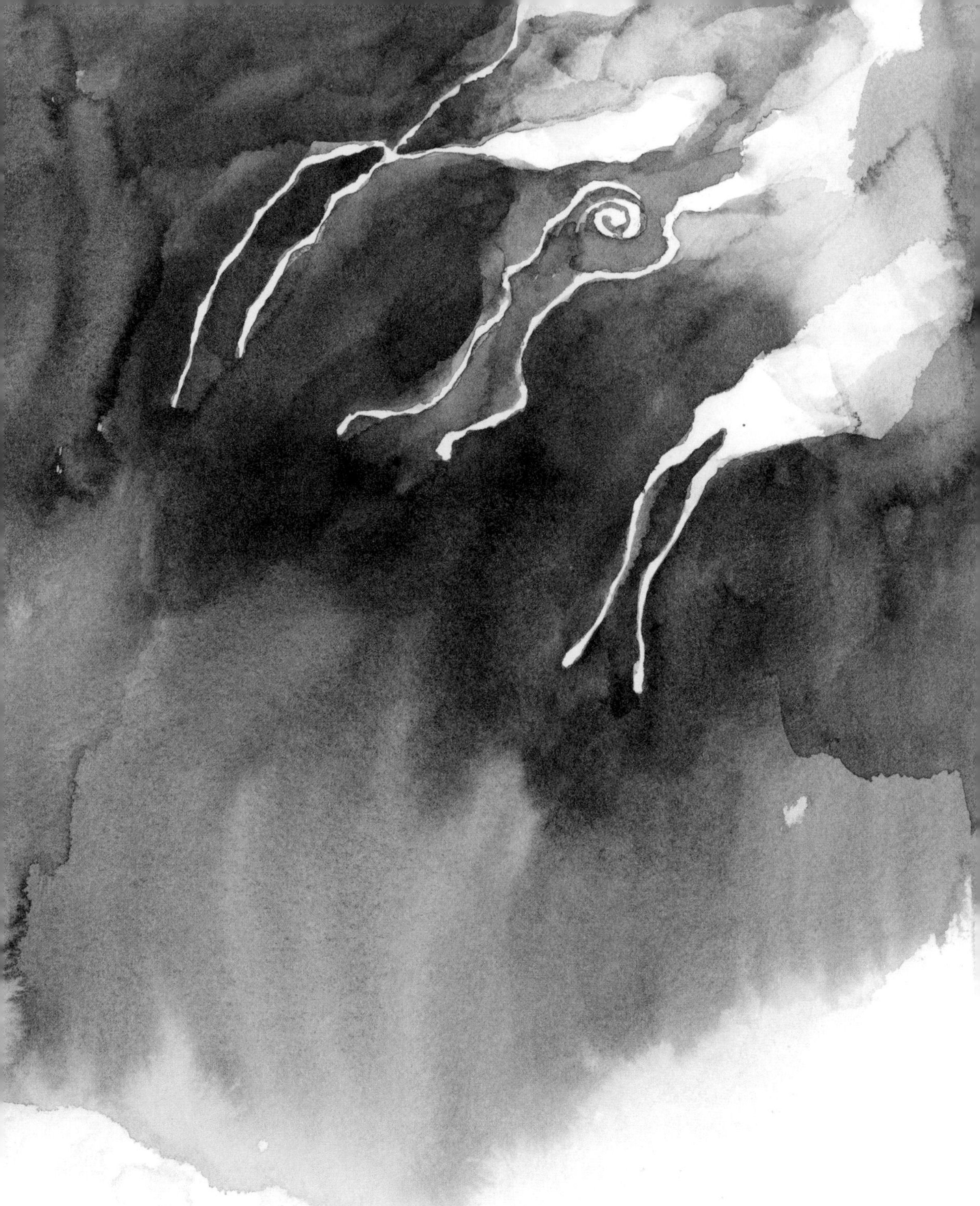

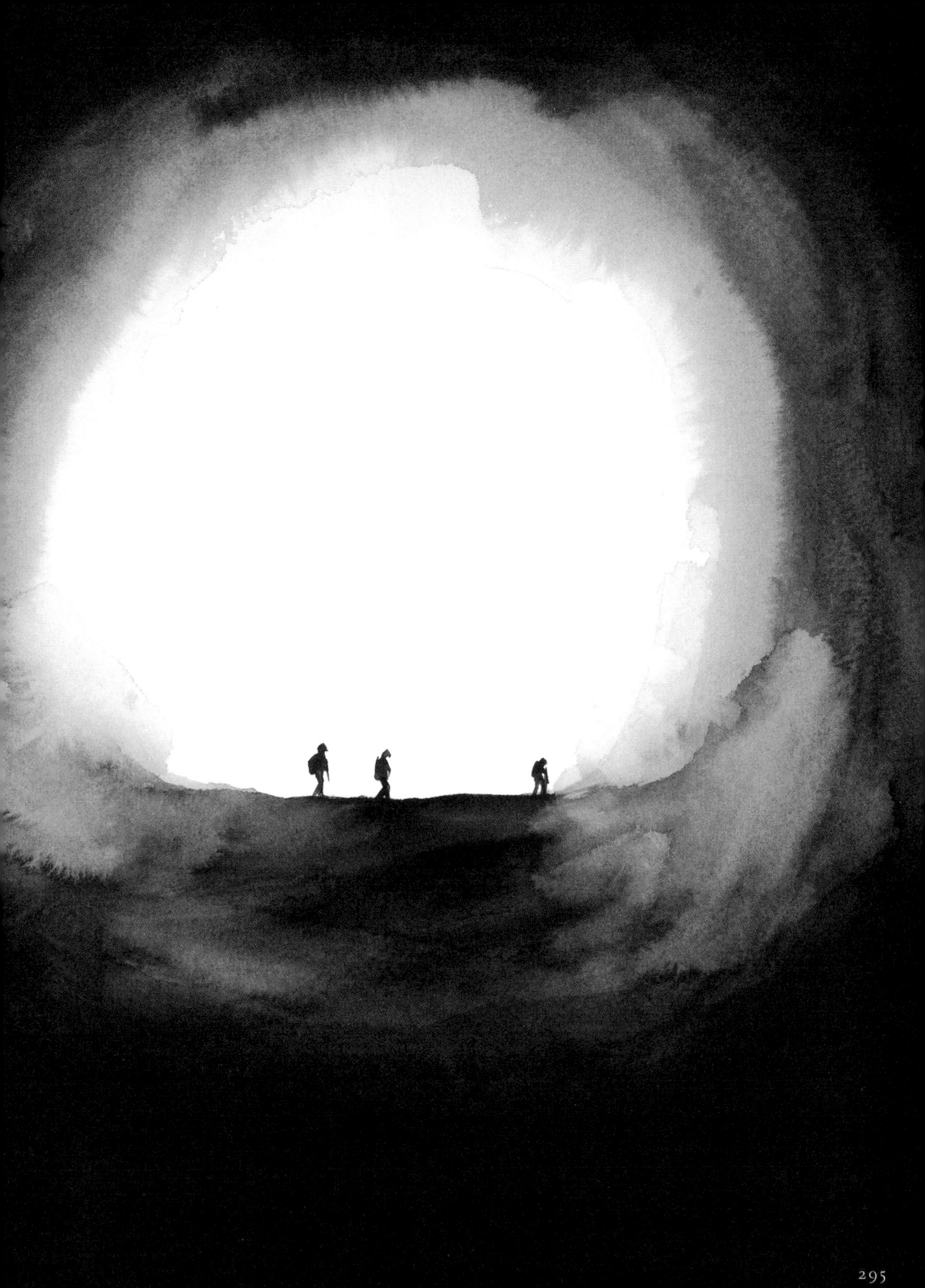

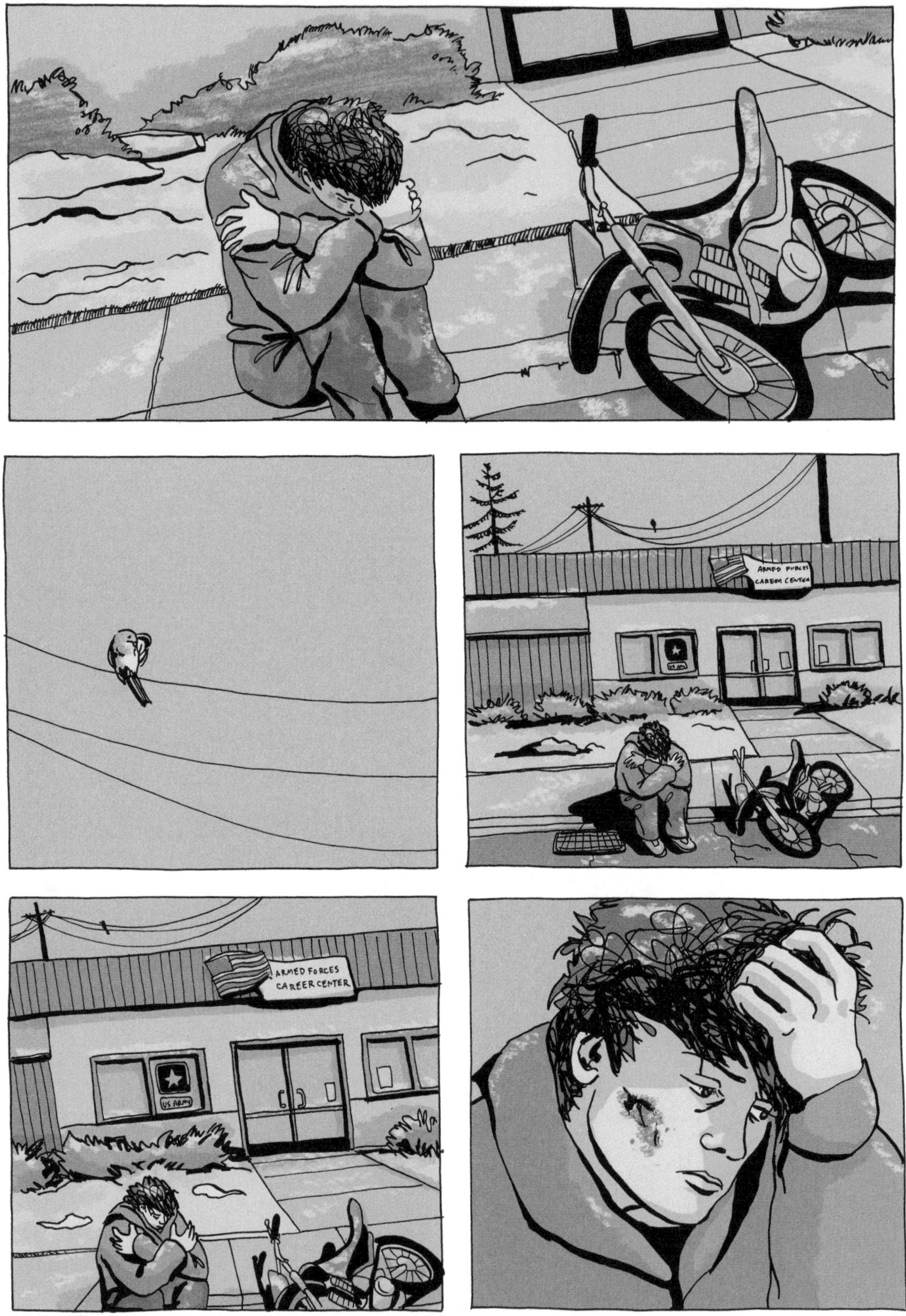
ARMED FORCES
CAREER CENTER
ARMED FORCES
CAREER CENTER
US ARMY

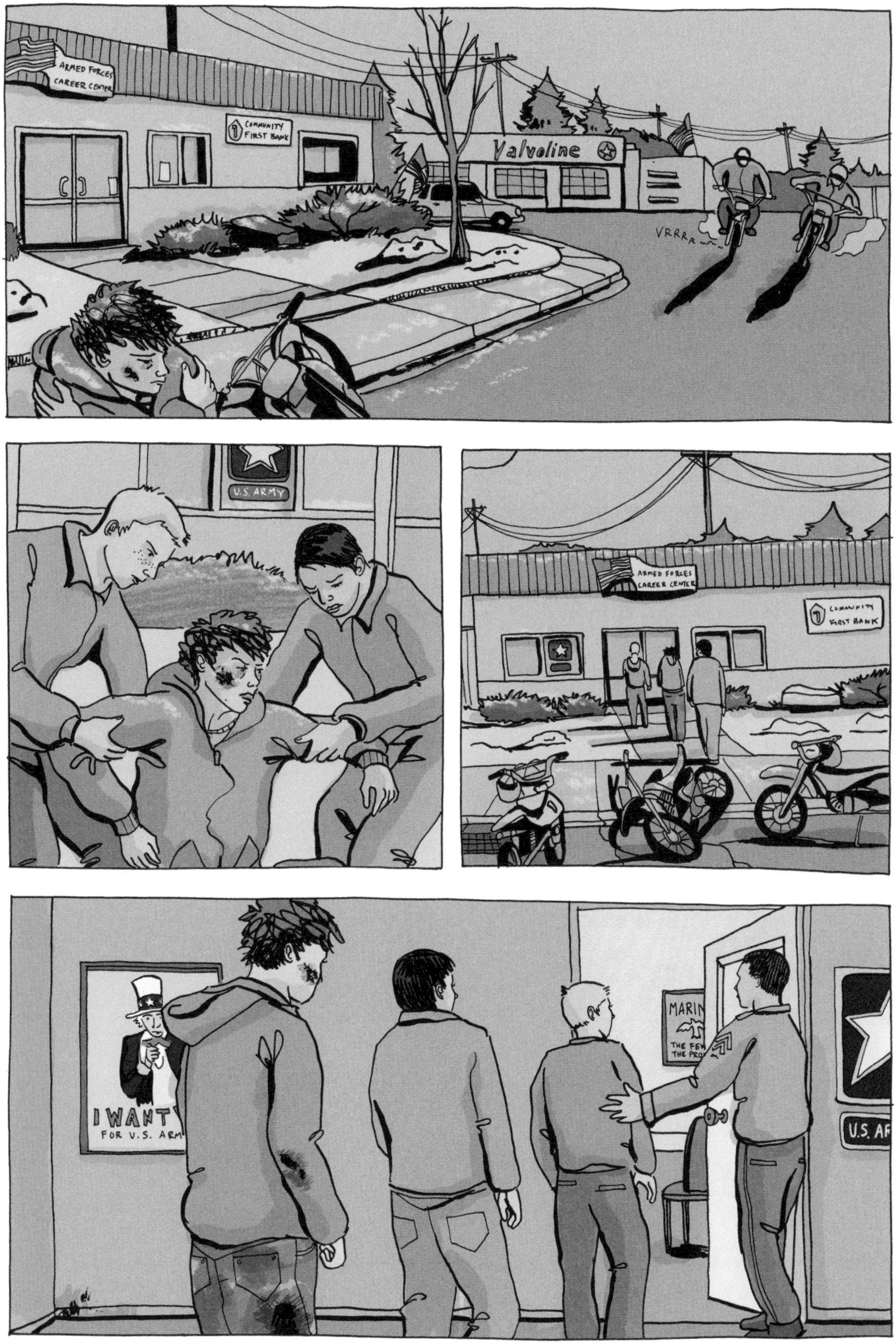
ARMED FORCES CAREER CENTER
COMMUNITY FIRST BANK
Valvoline
VRRRR
U.S. ARMY
ARMED FORCES CAREER CENTER
COMMUNITY FIRST BANK
I WANT
FOR U.S. ARM
MARIN
THE FEW
THE PRO
U.S. AR

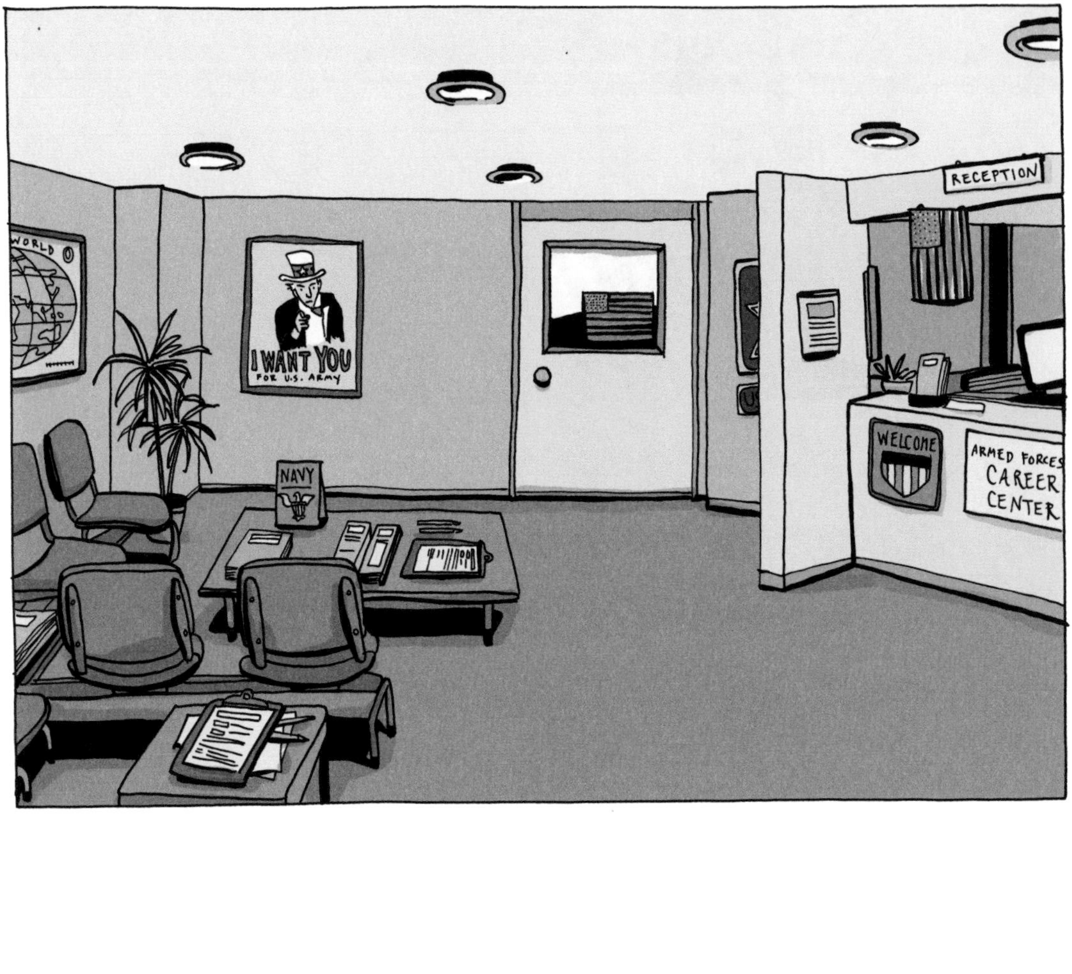

WORLD
I WANT YOU
FOR U.S. ARMY
NAVY
RECEPTION
WELCOME
ARMED FORCES
CAREER
CENTER

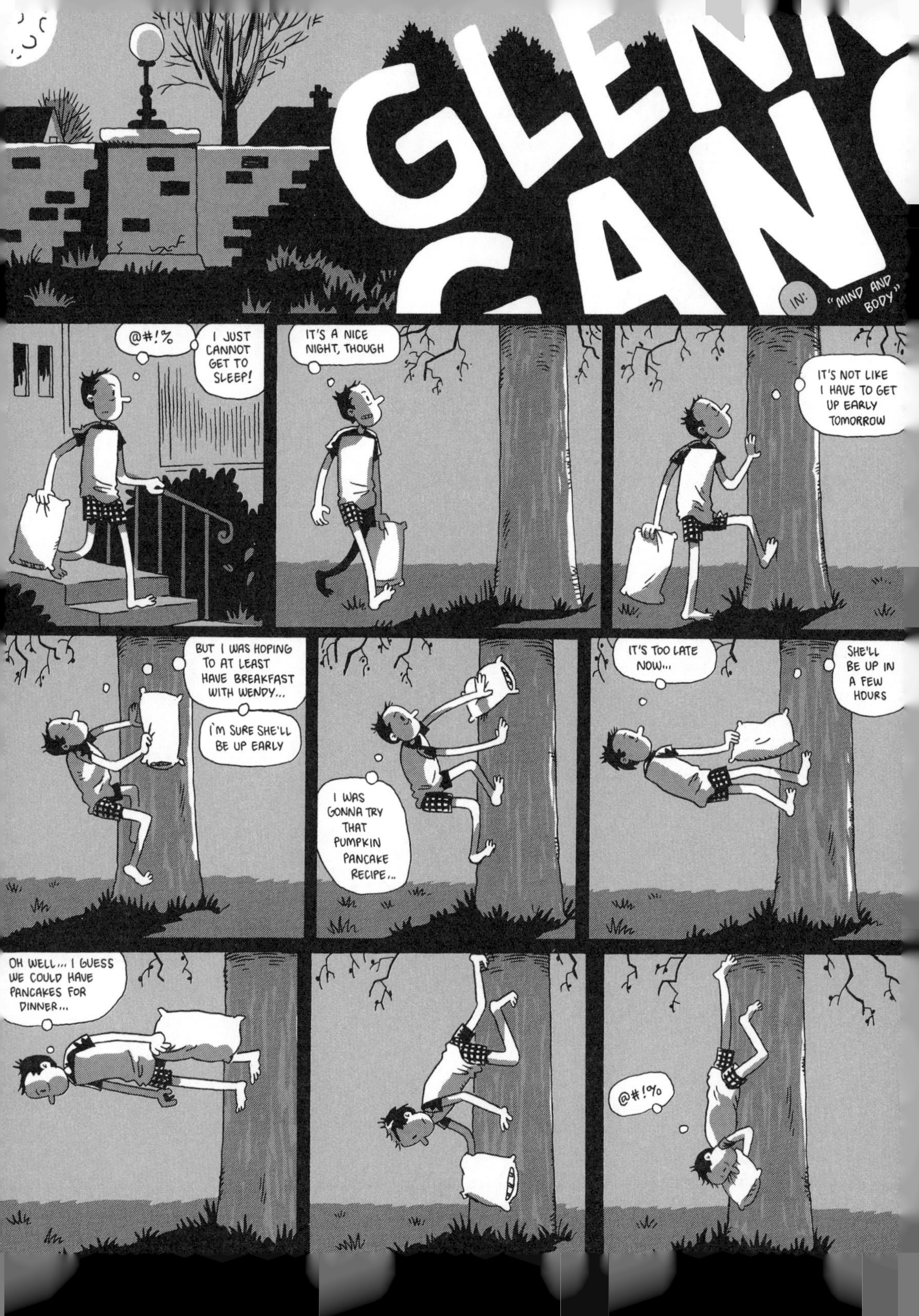

GLENN GANG
IN: "MIND AND BODY"
@#!%
I JUST CANNOT GET TO SLEEP!
IT'S A NICE NIGHT, THOUGH
IT'S NOT LIKE I HAVE TO GET UP EARLY TOMORROW
BUT I WAS HOPING TO AT LEAST HAVE BREAKFAST WITH WENDY...
I'M SURE SHE'LL BE UP EARLY
I WAS GONNA TRY THAT PUMPKIN PANCAKE RECIPE...
IT'S TOO LATE NOW...
SHE'LL BE UP IN A FEW HOURS
OH WELL... I GUESS WE COULD HAVE PANCAKES FOR DINNER...
@#!%

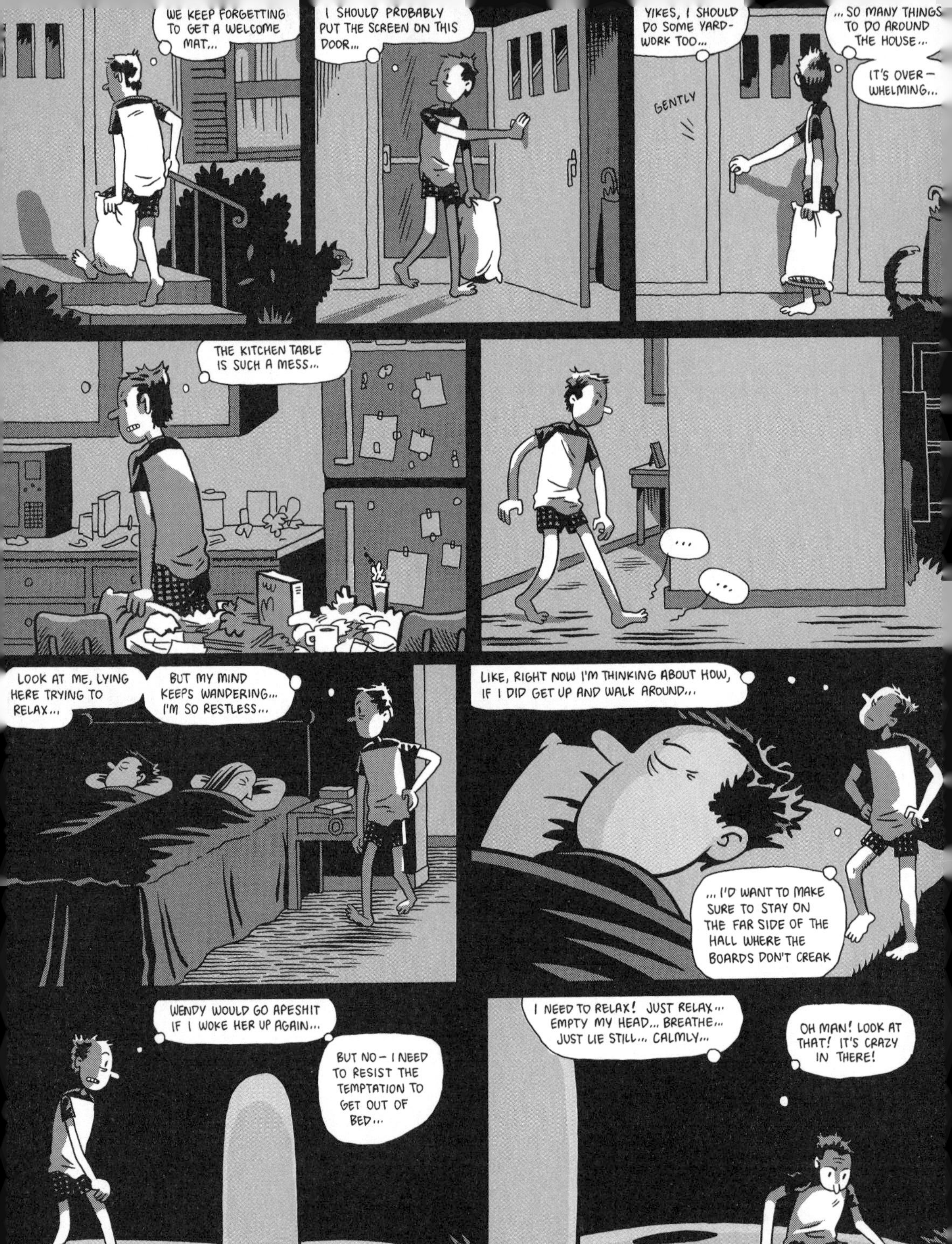
WE KEEP FORGETTING TO GET A WELCOME MAT...
I SHOULD PROBABLY PUT THE SCREEN ON THIS DOOR...
YIKES, I SHOULD DO SOME YARD-WORK TOO...
GENTLY
...SO MANY THINGS TO DO AROUND THE HOUSE...
IT'S OVER-WHELMING...
THE KITCHEN TABLE IS SUCH A MESS...
...
...
LOOK AT ME, LYING HERE TRYING TO RELAX...
BUT MY MIND KEEPS WANDERING... I'M SO RESTLESS...
LIKE, RIGHT NOW I'M THINKING ABOUT HOW, IF I DID GET UP AND WALK AROUND...
...I'D WANT TO MAKE SURE TO STAY ON THE FAR SIDE OF THE HALL WHERE THE BOARDS DON'T CREAK
WENDY WOULD GO APESHIT IF I WOKE HER UP AGAIN...
BUT NO - I NEED TO RESIST THE TEMPTATION TO GET OUT OF BED...
I NEED TO RELAX! JUST RELAX... EMPTY MY HEAD... BREATHE... JUST LIE STILL... CALMLY...
OH MAN! LOOK AT THAT! IT'S CRAZY IN THERE!

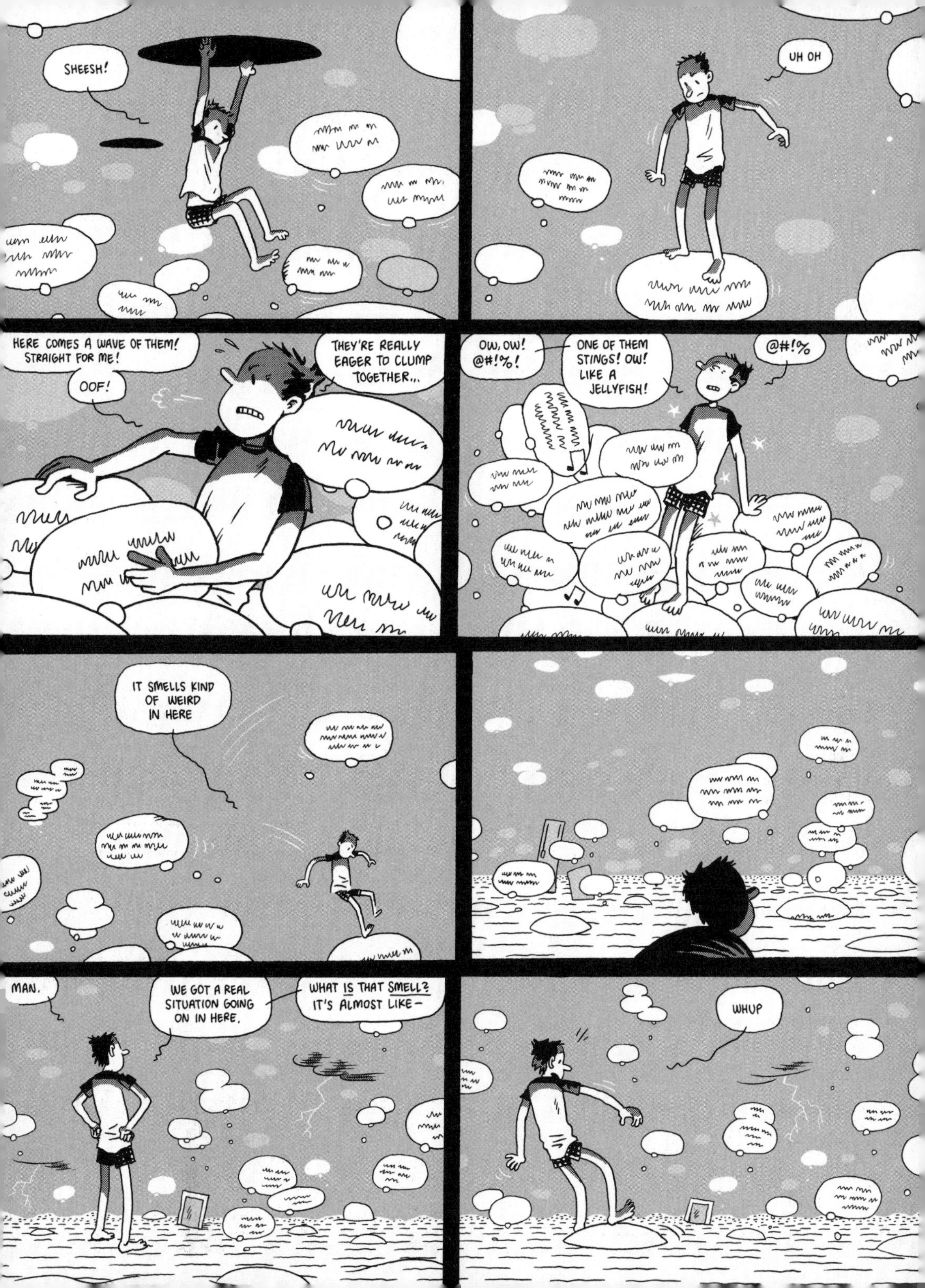

SHEESH!
UH OH
HERE COMES A WAVE OF THEM! STRAIGHT FOR ME!
OOF!
THEY'RE REALLY EAGER TO CLUMP TOGETHER...
OW, OW! @#!%!
ONE OF THEM STINGS! OW! LIKE A JELLYFISH!
@#!%
IT SMELLS KIND OF WEIRD IN HERE
MAN.
WE GOT A REAL SITUATION GOING ON IN HERE.
WHAT IS THAT SMELL? IT'S ALMOST LIKE—
WHUP

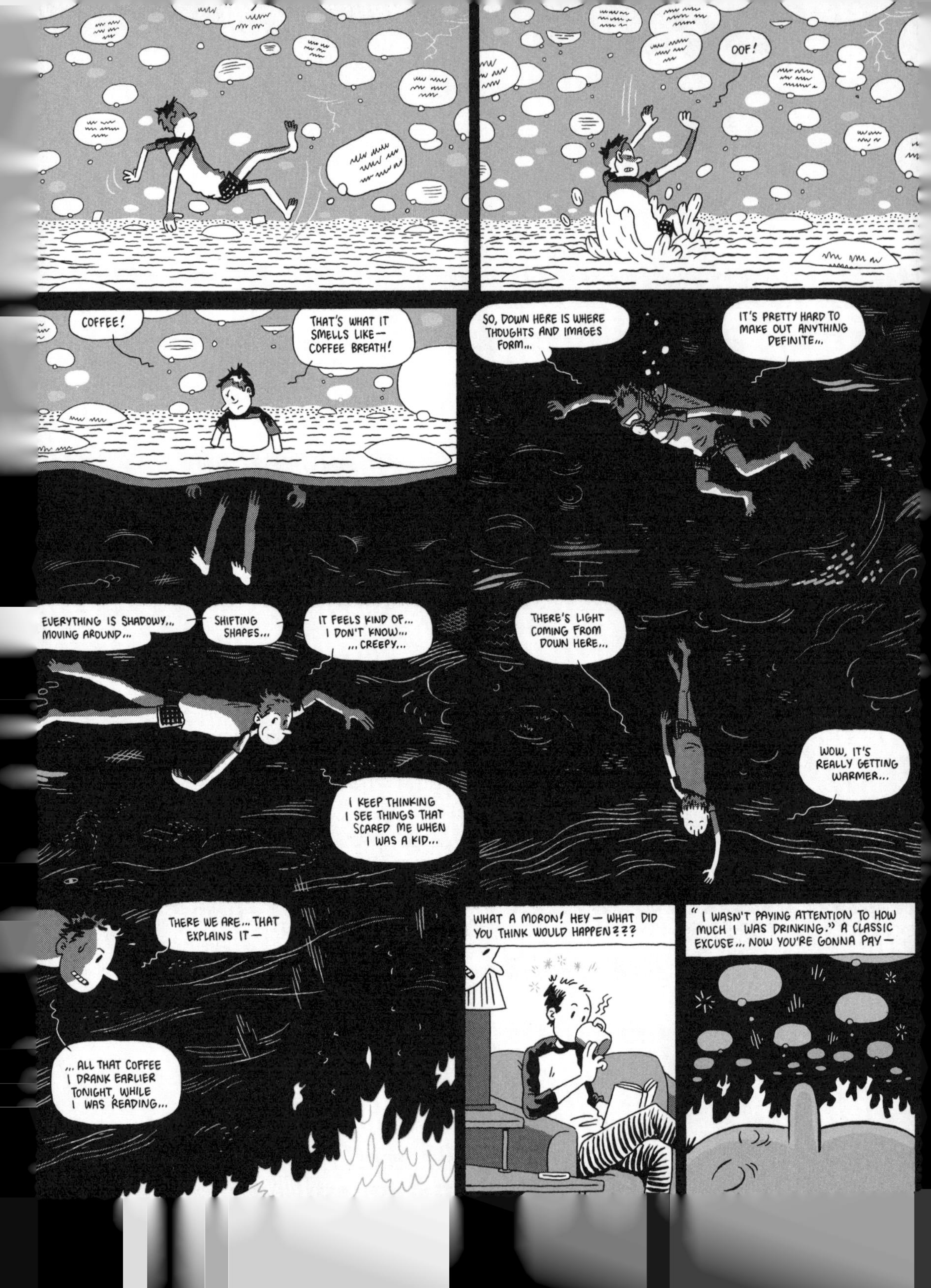
OOF!
COFFEE!
THAT'S WHAT IT SMELLS LIKE— COFFEE BREATH!
SO, DOWN HERE IS WHERE THOUGHTS AND IMAGES FORM...
IT'S PRETTY HARD TO MAKE OUT ANYTHING DEFINITE...
EVERYTHING IS SHADOWY... MOVING AROUND...
SHIFTING SHAPES...
IT FEELS KIND OF... I DON'T KNOW... ...CREEPY...
I KEEP THINKING I SEE THINGS THAT SCARED ME WHEN I WAS A KID...
THERE'S LIGHT COMING FROM DOWN HERE...
WOW, IT'S REALLY GETTING WARMER...
THERE WE ARE... THAT EXPLAINS IT—
...ALL THAT COFFEE I DRANK EARLIER TONIGHT, WHILE I WAS READING...
WHAT A MORON! HEY— WHAT DID YOU THINK WOULD HAPPEN???
"I WASN'T PAYING ATTENTION TO HOW MUCH I WAS DRINKING." A CLASSIC EXCUSE... NOW YOU'RE GONNA PAY—

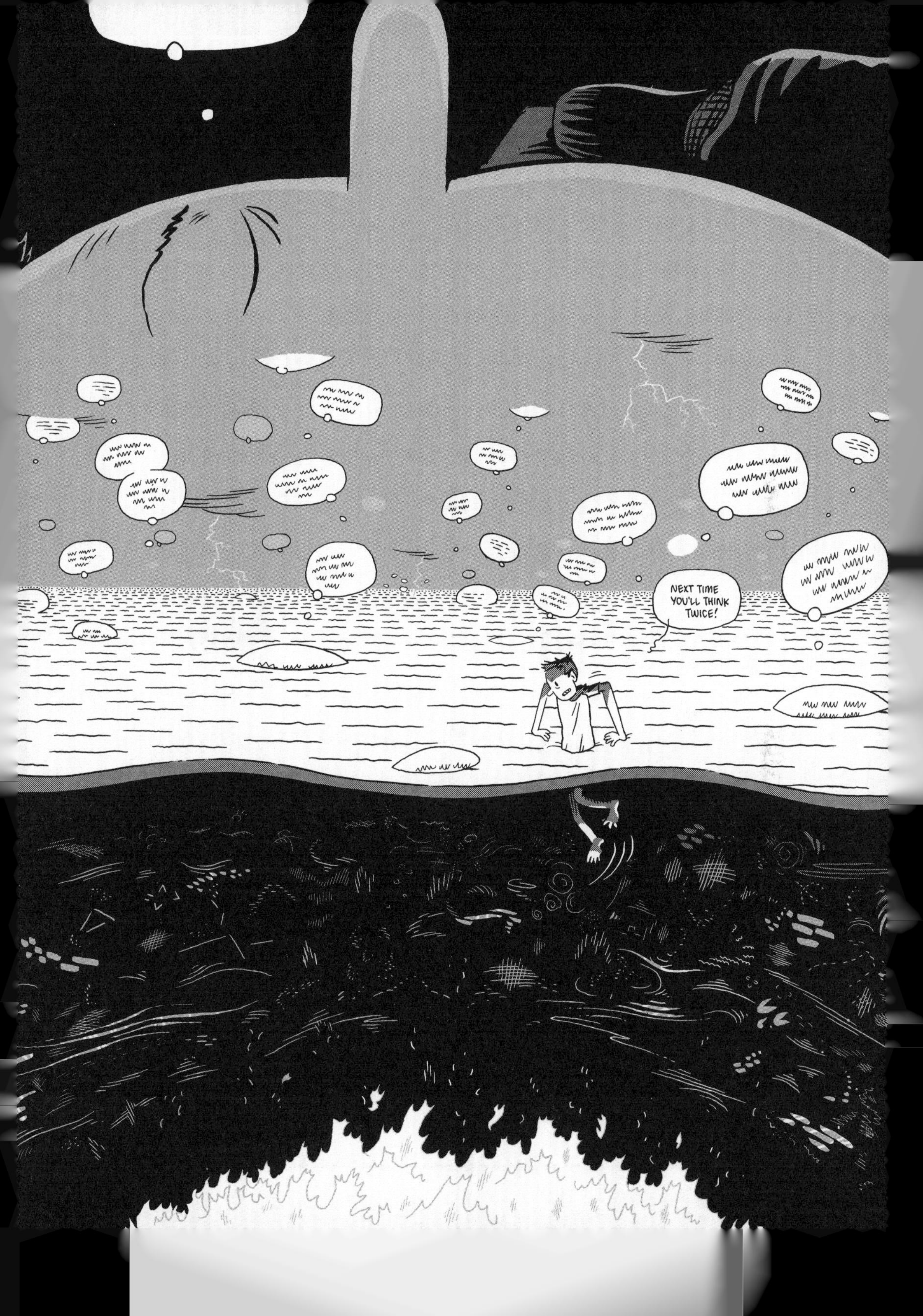
NEXT TIME YOU'LL THINK TWICE!

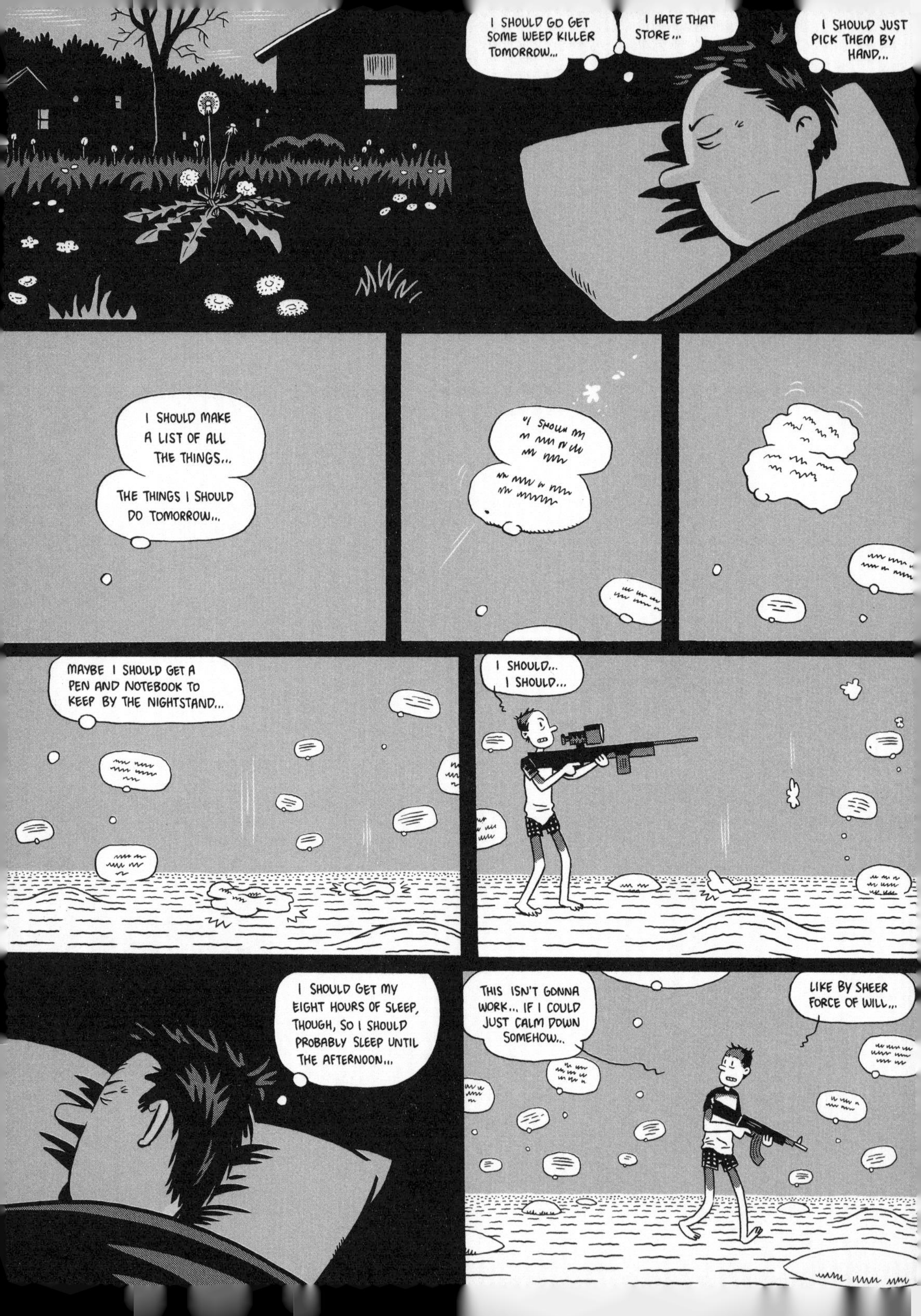
I SHOULD GO GET SOME WEED KILLER TOMORROW...
I HATE THAT STORE...
I SHOULD JUST PICK THEM BY HAND...
I SHOULD MAKE A LIST OF ALL THE THINGS...
THE THINGS I SHOULD DO TOMORROW...
MAYBE I SHOULD GET A PEN AND NOTEBOOK TO KEEP BY THE NIGHTSTAND...
I SHOULD... I SHOULD...
I SHOULD GET MY EIGHT HOURS OF SLEEP, THOUGH, SO I SHOULD PROBABLY SLEEP UNTIL THE AFTERNOON...
THIS ISN'T GONNA WORK... IF I COULD JUST CALM DOWN SOMEHOW...
LIKE BY SHEER FORCE OF WILL...

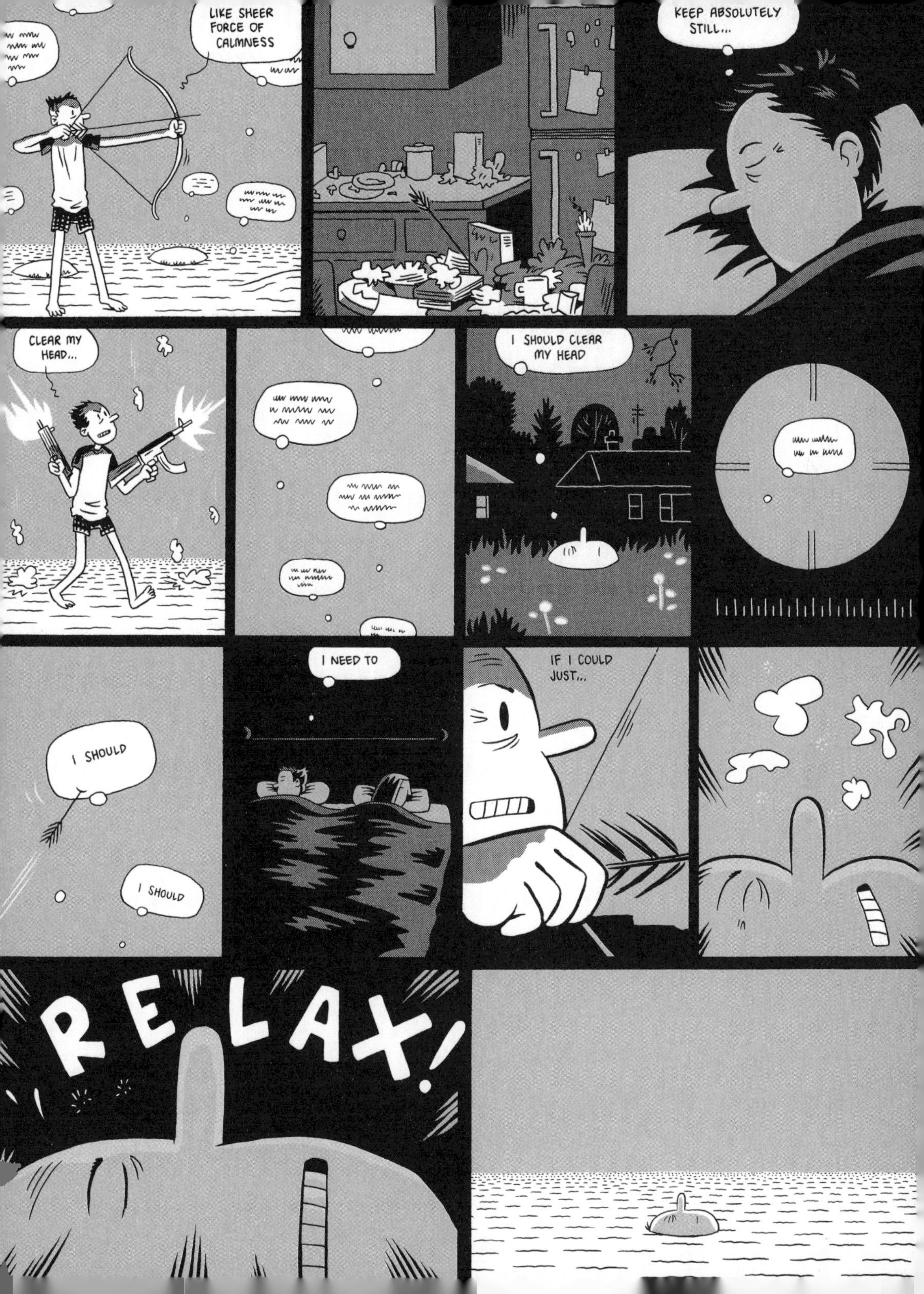
LIKE SHEER FORCE OF CALMNESS
KEEP ABSOLUTELY STILL...
CLEAR MY HEAD...
I SHOULD CLEAR MY HEAD
I SHOULD
I SHOULD
I NEED TO
IF I COULD JUST...
RELAX!

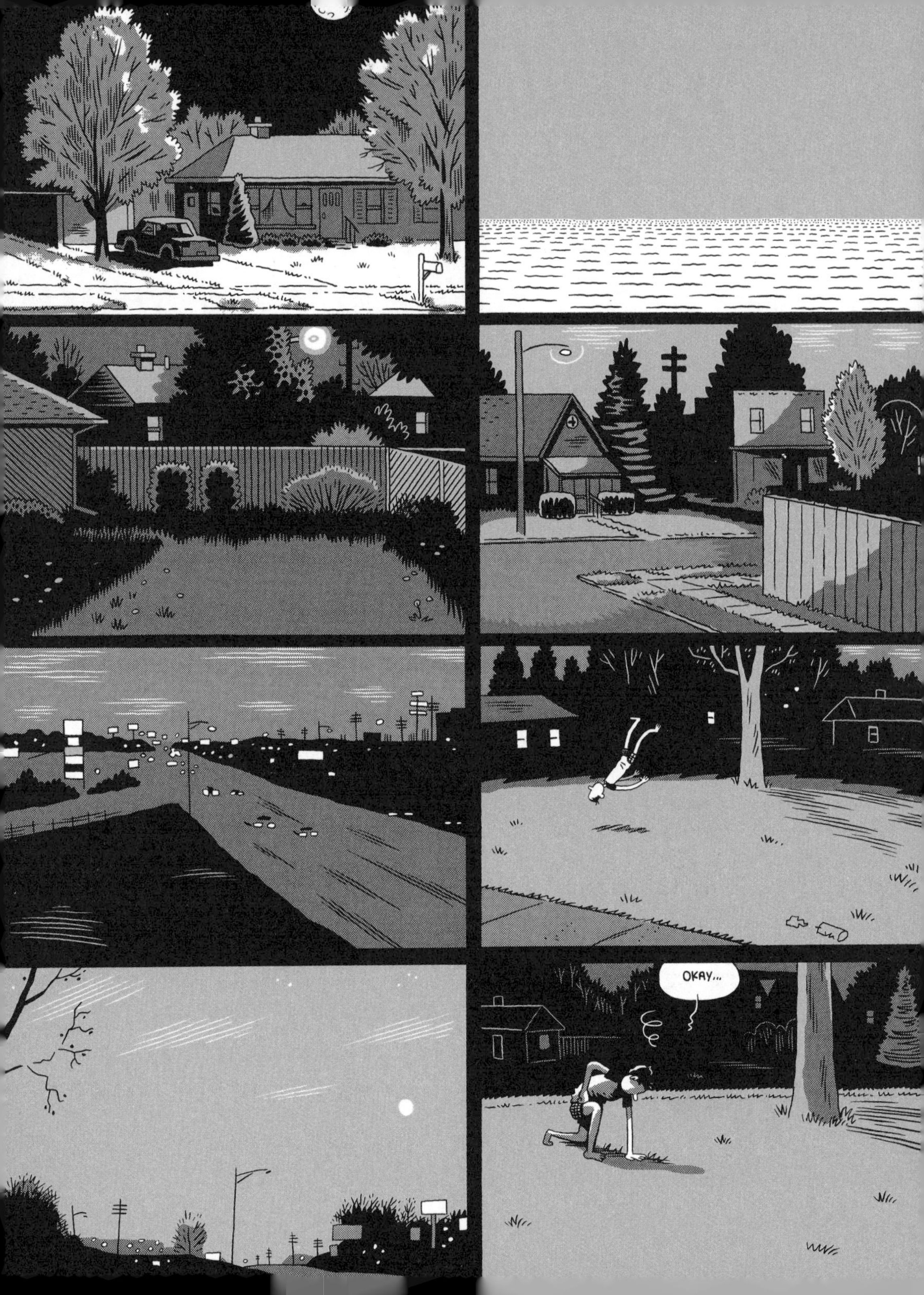
OKAY...

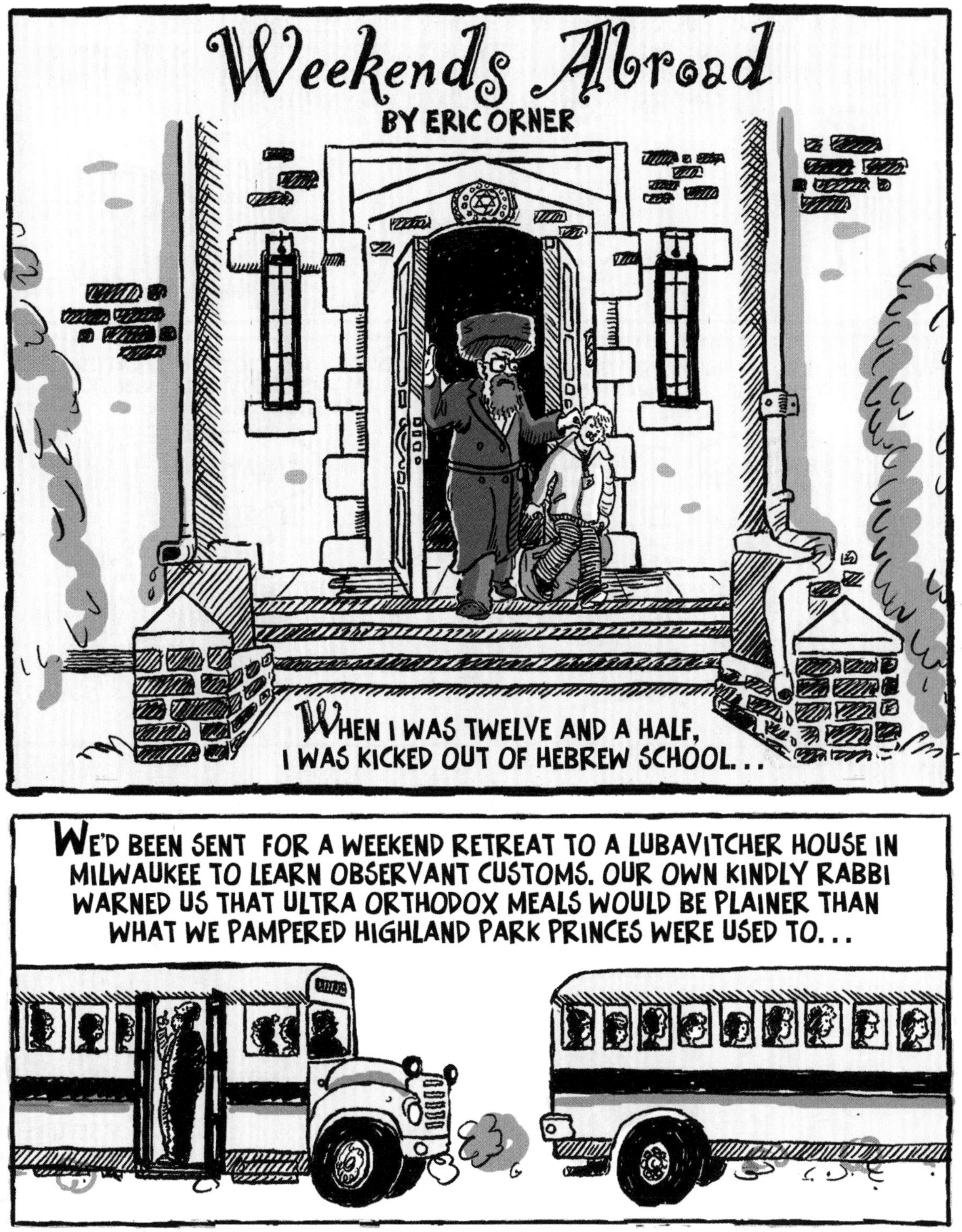
Weekends Abroad
BY ERIC ORNER
WHEN I WAS TWELVE AND A HALF, I WAS KICKED OUT OF HEBREW SCHOOL. . .
WE'D BEEN SENT FOR A WEEKEND RETREAT TO A LUBAVITCHER HOUSE IN MILWAUKEE TO LEARN OBSERVANT CUSTOMS. OUR OWN KINDLY RABBI WARNED US THAT ULTRA ORTHODOX MEALS WOULD BE PLAINER THAN WHAT WE PAMPERED HIGHLAND PARK PRINCES WERE USED TO. . .

In particular, our Rabbi told us that only tap water would be served... we were used to soda, so this sounded pretty gross. At this point I had the first (and so far the last) entrepreneurial thought I've had in my life, which involved hiding a big canister of powdered lemonade in my duffel...

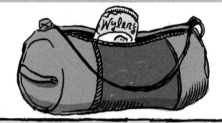

And selling it to my buddies by the scoop. Once we got there, business was brisk on the first night...

HURRY IT UP, MAN, RABBI'S RIGHT THERE...

But on the second I got ratted out by this goody two shoes from another Hebrew school.

CHEATERS!

When my apology to the Lubavitcher Rabbi was deemed insincere...

OK, LOOK, I'M SORRY...

...I WAS SENT HOME EARLY...

MOM HAD TO DRIVE UP FROM CHICAGO. SHE WASN'T DELIGHTED.

...And expelled... and spent the next 2 decades forgetting what little Hebrew I'd learned...

308

Until the last couple of years, which I've spent living, working, and being illiterate in Israel. . .

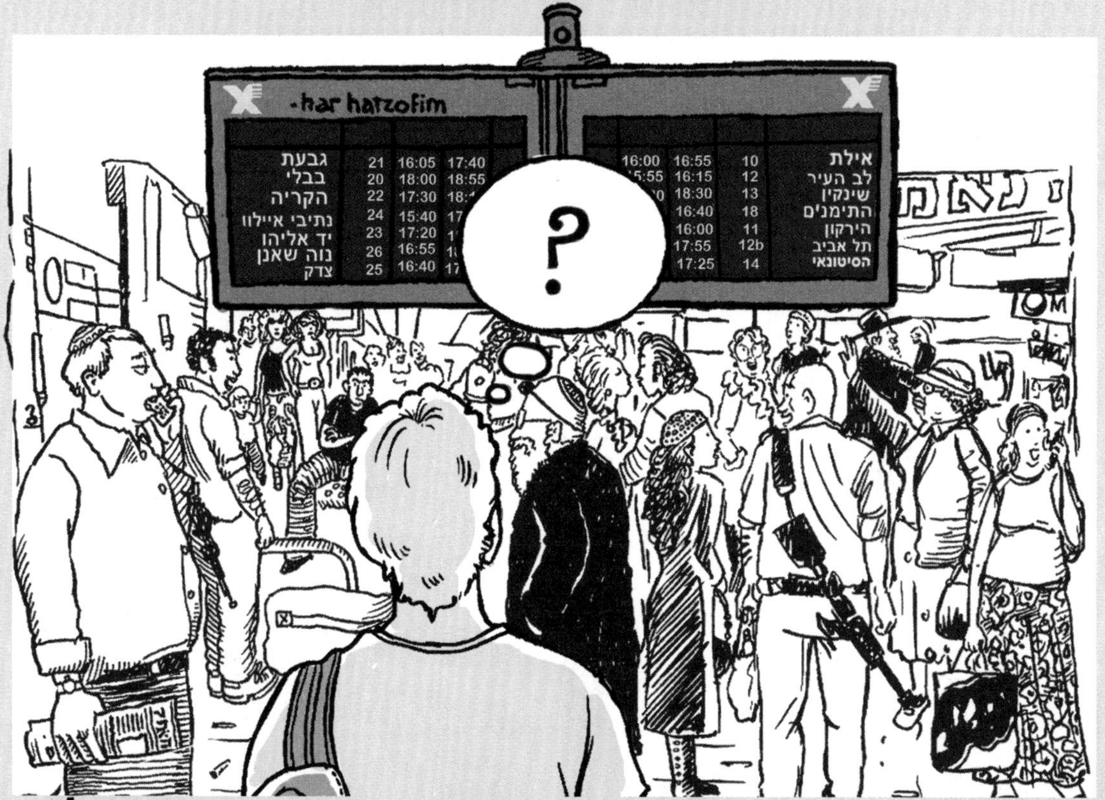
-har hatzofim
גבעת
בבלי
הקריה
נתיבי איילון
יד אליהו
נוה שאנן
צדק
אילת
לב העיר
שינקין
התימנים
הירקון
תל אביב
הסיטונאי
?

My contract was just for 3 months, but they keep renewing it. I'm coming up on 2 years now, but am always thinking the job'll be over soon. So stupidly, I haven't taken the Hebrew course they teach all over the place here at these little schools called "ulpans". What's the point, I keep figuring, if I have to leave soon?

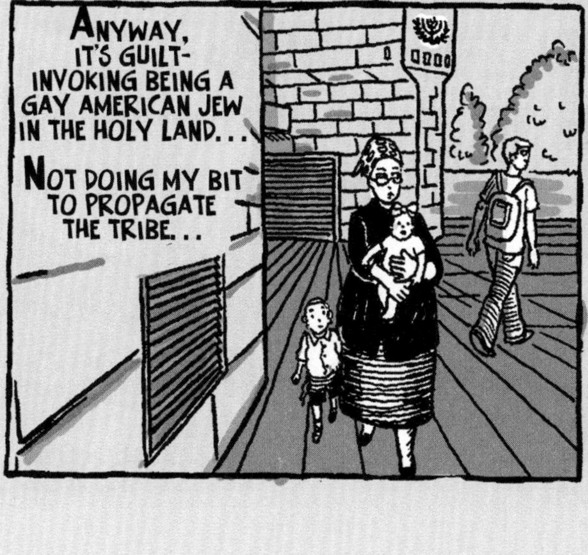
Anyway, it's guilt-invoking being a gay American Jew in the Holy Land. . .
Not doing my bit to propagate the tribe. . .

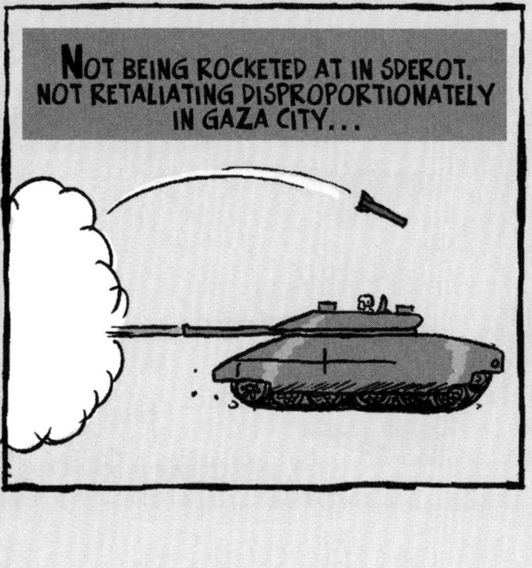
Not being rocketed at in Sderot. Not retaliating disproportionately in Gaza City. . .

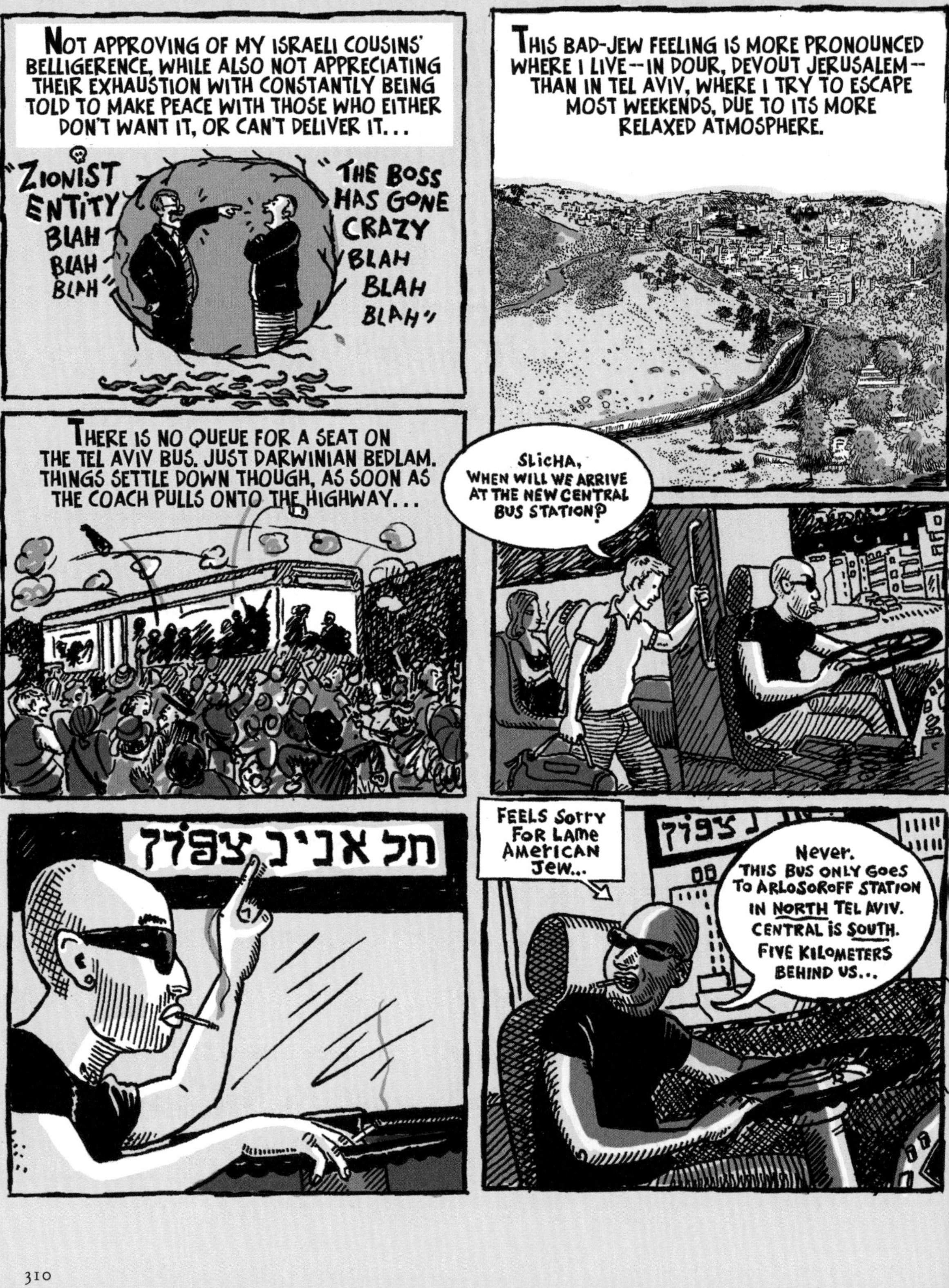
NOT APPROVING OF MY ISRAELI COUSINS' BELLIGERENCE, WHILE ALSO NOT APPRECIATING THEIR EXHAUSTION WITH CONSTANTLY BEING TOLD TO MAKE PEACE WITH THOSE WHO EITHER DON'T WANT IT, OR CAN'T DELIVER IT...
"ZIONIST ENTITY BLAH BLAH BLAH"
"THE BOSS HAS GONE CRAZY BLAH BLAH BLAH"
THIS BAD-JEW FEELING IS MORE PRONOUNCED WHERE I LIVE--IN DOUR, DEVOUT JERUSALEM--THAN IN TEL AVIV, WHERE I TRY TO ESCAPE MOST WEEKENDS, DUE TO ITS MORE RELAXED ATMOSPHERE.
THERE IS NO QUEUE FOR A SEAT ON THE TEL AVIV BUS. JUST DARWINIAN BEDLAM. THINGS SETTLE DOWN THOUGH, AS SOON AS THE COACH PULLS ONTO THE HIGHWAY...
SLICHA, WHEN WILL WE ARRIVE AT THE NEW CENTRAL BUS STATION?
תל אביב צפון
FEELS SORRY FOR LAME AMERICAN JEW...
NEVER. THIS BUS ONLY GOES TO ARLOSOROFF STATION IN NORTH TEL AVIV. CENTRAL IS SOUTH. FIVE KILOMETERS BEHIND US...

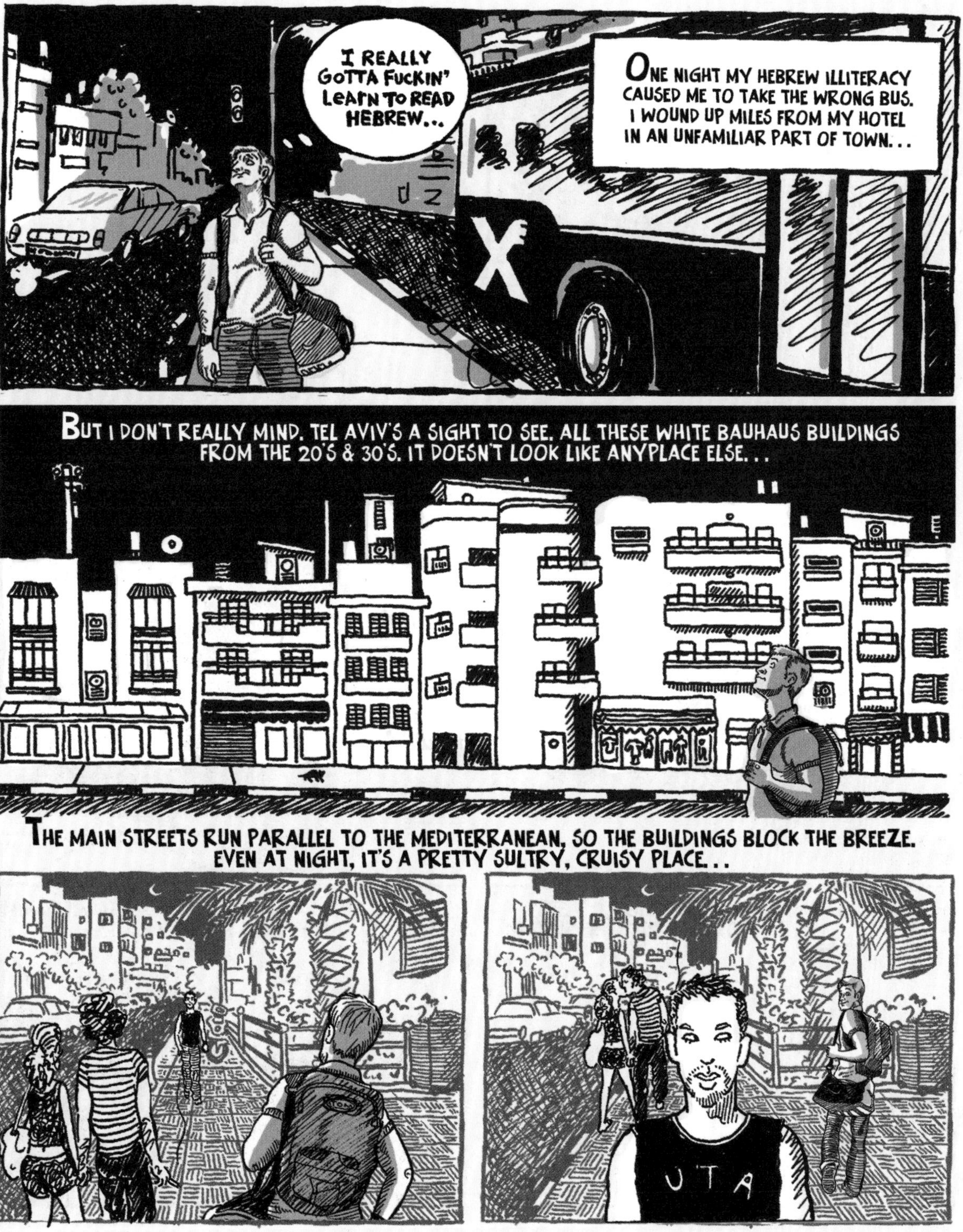
I REALLY GOTTA FUCKIN' LEARN TO READ HEBREW...
ONE NIGHT MY HEBREW ILLITERACY CAUSED ME TO TAKE THE WRONG BUS. I WOUND UP MILES FROM MY HOTEL IN AN UNFAMILIAR PART OF TOWN...
BUT I DON'T REALLY MIND. TEL AVIV'S A SIGHT TO SEE. ALL THESE WHITE BAUHAUS BUILDINGS FROM THE 20'S & 30'S. IT DOESN'T LOOK LIKE ANYPLACE ELSE...
THE MAIN STREETS RUN PARALLEL TO THE MEDITERRANEAN, SO THE BUILDINGS BLOCK THE BREEZE. EVEN AT NIGHT, IT'S A PRETTY SULTRY, CRUISY PLACE...
UTA

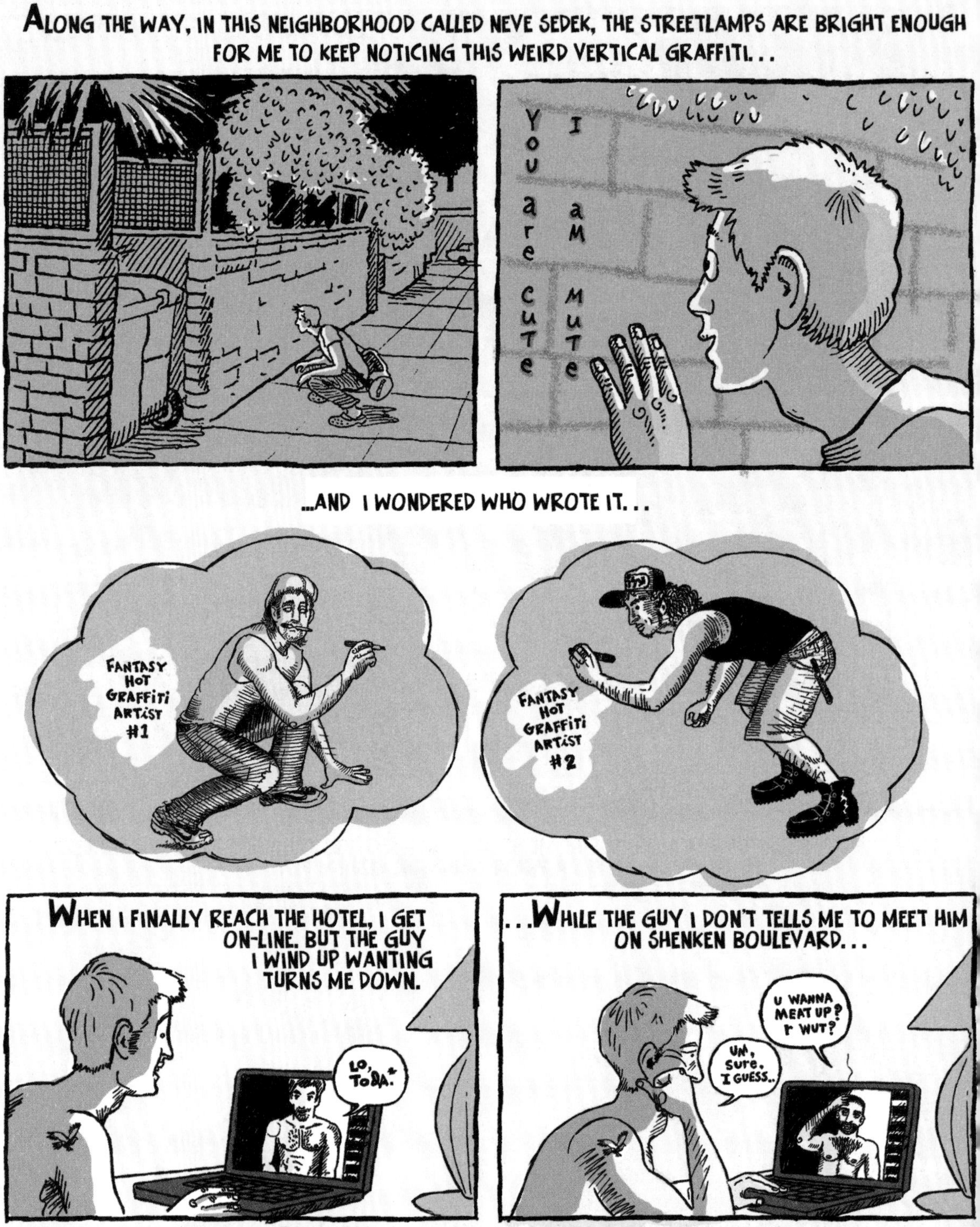
ALONG THE WAY, IN THIS NEIGHBORHOOD CALLED NEVE SEDEK, THE STREETLAMPS ARE BRIGHT ENOUGH FOR ME TO KEEP NOTICING THIS WEIRD VERTICAL GRAFFITI. . .
You are cute
I aM MuTe
...AND I WONDERED WHO WROTE IT. . .
FANTASY HOT GRAFFITI ARTIST #1
FANTASY HOT GRAFFITI ARTIST #2
WHEN I FINALLY REACH THE HOTEL, I GET ON-LINE. BUT THE GUY I WIND UP WANTING TURNS ME DOWN.
LO, TODA.*
. . .WHILE THE GUY I DON'T TELLS ME TO MEET HIM ON SHENKEN BOULEVARD. . .
U WANNA MEAT UP? r WUT?
UM, SURE, I GUESS..

* NO THANKS

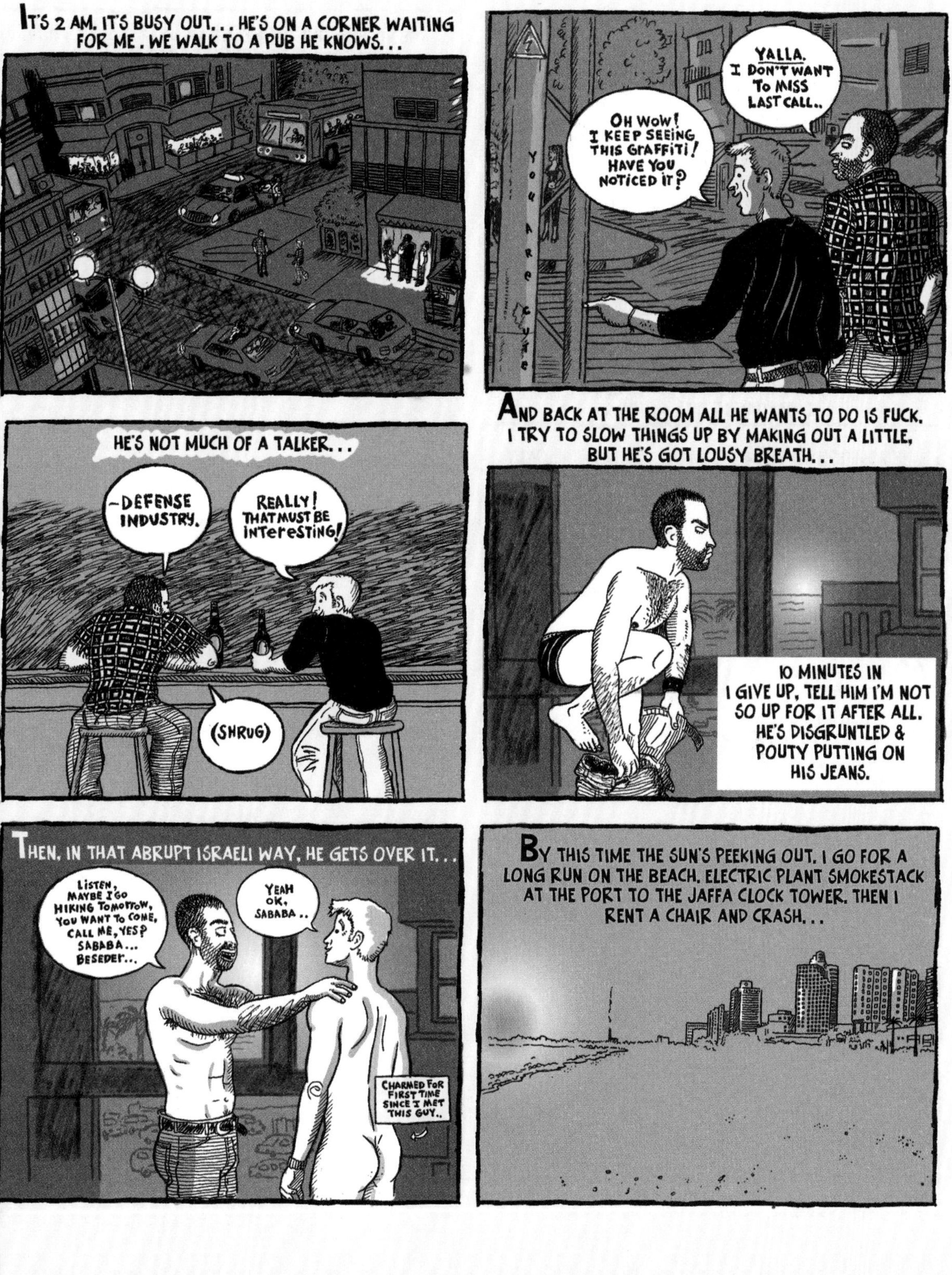
It's 2 AM. It's busy out. . . he's on a corner waiting for me. We walk to a pub he knows. . .
Oh wow! I keep seeing this graffiti! Have you noticed it?
You are cute
Yalla. I don't want to miss last call..
He's not much of a talker. . .
–Defense industry.
Really! That must be interesting!
(Shrug)
And back at the room all he wants to do is fuck. I try to slow things up by making out a little, but he's got lousy breath. . .
10 minutes in I give up, tell him I'm not so up for it after all. He's disgruntled & pouty putting on his jeans.
Then, in that abrupt Israeli way, he gets over it. . .
Listen, maybe I go hiking tomorrow, you want to come, call me, yes? Sababa... Beseder...
Yeah ok, sababa..
Charmed for first time since I met this guy..
By this time the sun's peeking out. I go for a long run on the beach. Electric plant smokestack at the port to the Jaffa clock tower. Then I rent a chair and crash. . .

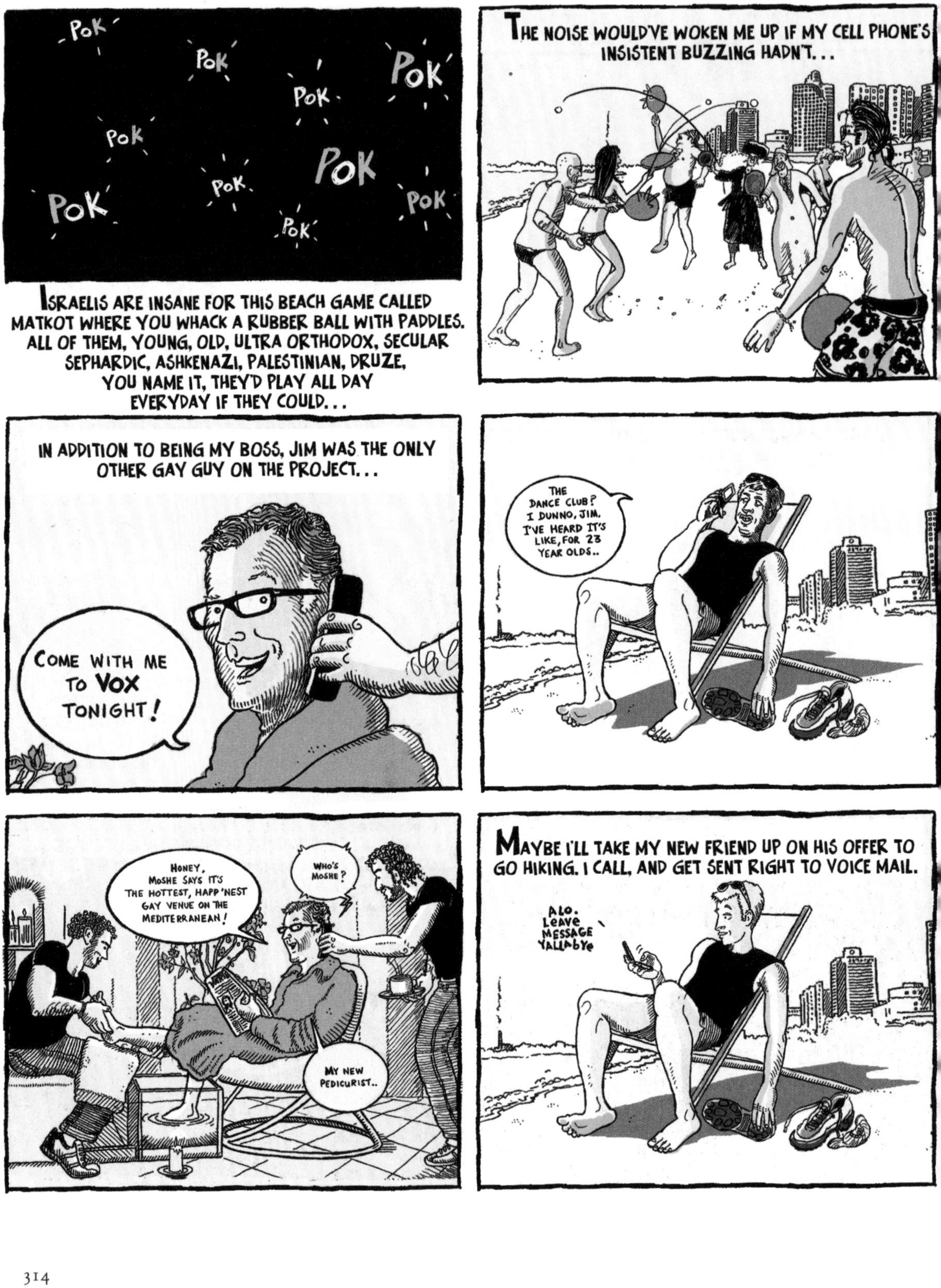
POK
POK
POK
POK
POK
POK
POK
POK
POK
POK
ISRAELIS ARE INSANE FOR THIS BEACH GAME CALLED MATKOT WHERE YOU WHACK A RUBBER BALL WITH PADDLES. ALL OF THEM, YOUNG, OLD, ULTRA ORTHODOX, SECULAR SEPHARDIC, ASHKENAZI, PALESTINIAN, DRUZE, YOU NAME IT, THEY'D PLAY ALL DAY EVERYDAY IF THEY COULD...
THE NOISE WOULD'VE WOKEN ME UP IF MY CELL PHONE'S INSISTENT BUZZING HADN'T...
IN ADDITION TO BEING MY BOSS, JIM WAS THE ONLY OTHER GAY GUY ON THE PROJECT...
COME WITH ME TO VOX TONIGHT!
THE DANCE CLUB? I DUNNO, JIM, I'VE HEARD IT'S LIKE, FOR 23 YEAR OLDS..
HONEY, MOSHE SAYS IT'S THE HOTTEST, HAPP'NEST GAY VENUE ON THE MEDITERRANEAN!
WHO'S MOSHE?
MY NEW PEDICURIST..
MAYBE I'LL TAKE MY NEW FRIEND UP ON HIS OFFER TO GO HIKING. I CALL, AND GET SENT RIGHT TO VOICE MAIL.
ALO. LEAVE MESSAGE YALLABYE

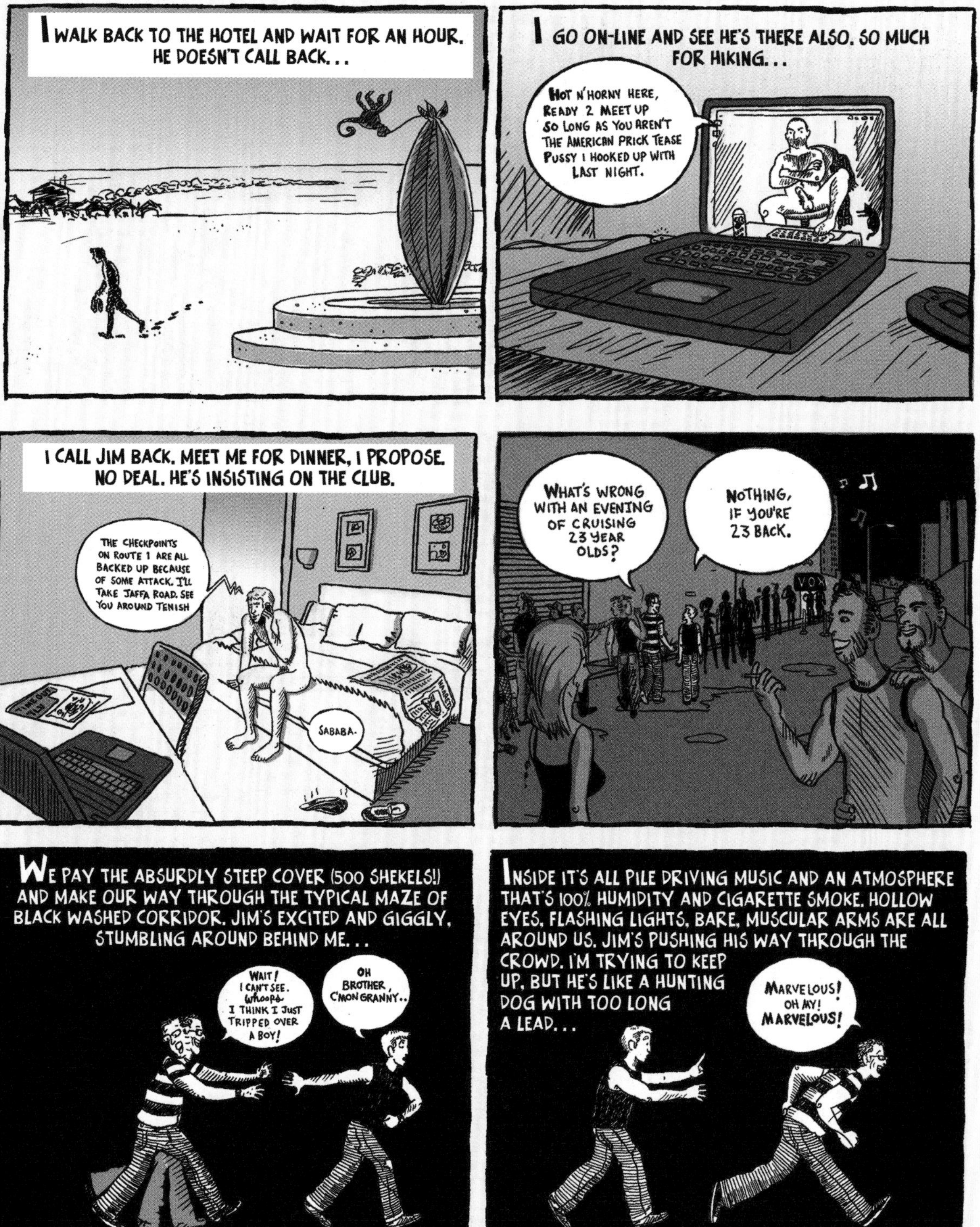
I WALK BACK TO THE HOTEL AND WAIT FOR AN HOUR. HE DOESN'T CALL BACK...
I GO ON-LINE AND SEE HE'S THERE ALSO. SO MUCH FOR HIKING...
HOT N'HORNY HERE, READY 2 MEET UP SO LONG AS YOU AREN'T THE AMERICAN PRICK TEASE PUSSY I HOOKED UP WITH LAST NIGHT.
I CALL JIM BACK. MEET ME FOR DINNER, I PROPOSE. NO DEAL. HE'S INSISTING ON THE CLUB.
THE CHECKPOINTS ON ROUTE 1 ARE ALL BACKED UP BECAUSE OF SOME ATTACK. I'LL TAKE JAFFA ROAD. SEE YOU AROUND TENISH
SABABA.
WHAT'S WRONG WITH AN EVENING OF CRUISING 23 YEAR OLDS?
NOTHING, IF YOU'RE 23 BACK.
VOX
WE PAY THE ABSURDLY STEEP COVER (500 SHEKELS!) AND MAKE OUR WAY THROUGH THE TYPICAL MAZE OF BLACK WASHED CORRIDOR. JIM'S EXCITED AND GIGGLY, STUMBLING AROUND BEHIND ME...
WAIT! I CAN'T SEE. WHOOPS. I THINK I JUST TRIPPED OVER A BOY!
OH BROTHER, C'MON GRANNY..
INSIDE IT'S ALL PILE DRIVING MUSIC AND AN ATMOSPHERE THAT'S 100% HUMIDITY AND CIGARETTE SMOKE. HOLLOW EYES, FLASHING LIGHTS, BARE, MUSCULAR ARMS ARE ALL AROUND US. JIM'S PUSHING HIS WAY THROUGH THE CROWD. I'M TRYING TO KEEP UP, BUT HE'S LIKE A HUNTING DOG WITH TOO LONG A LEAD...
MARVELOUS! OH MY! MARVELOUS!

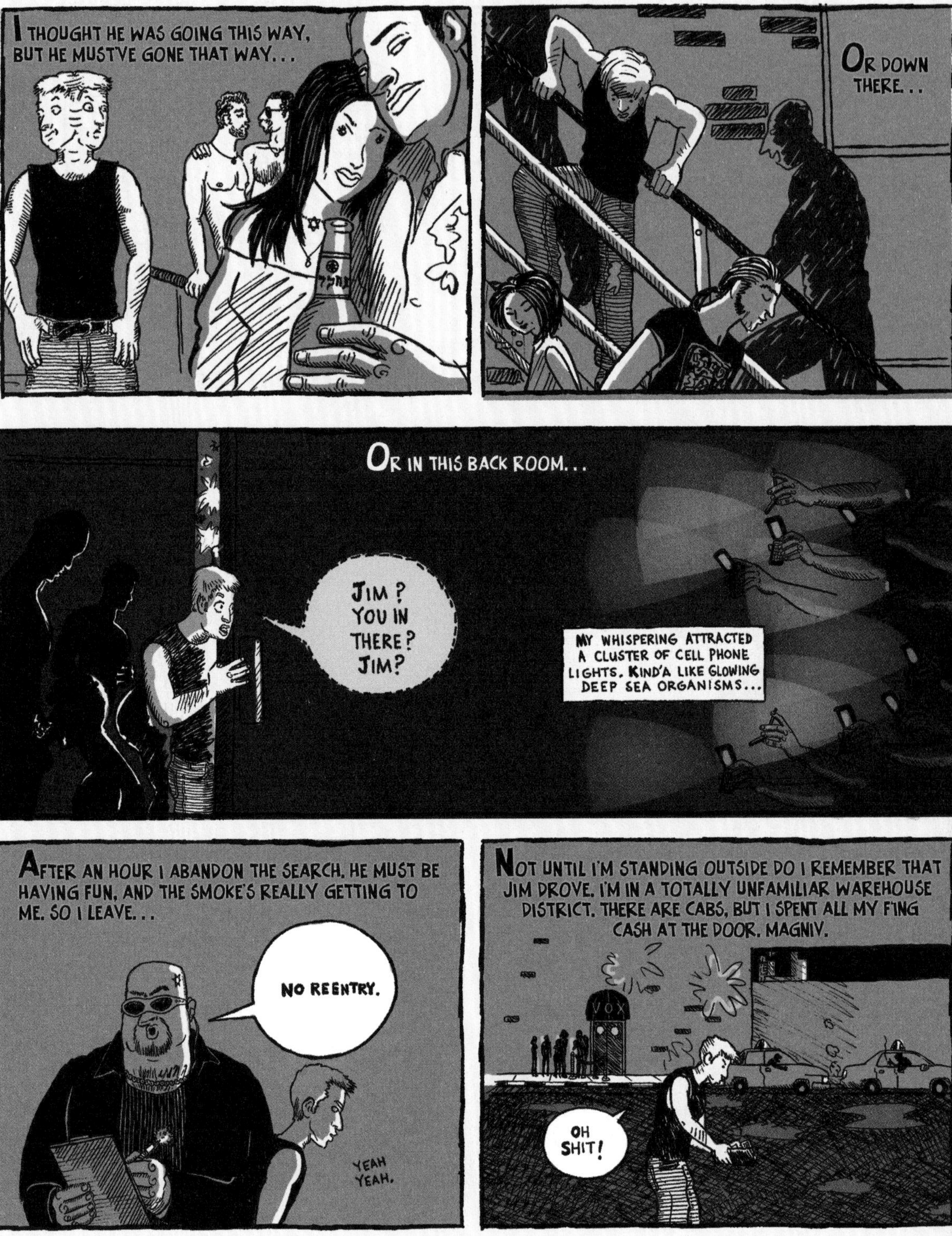
I THOUGHT HE WAS GOING THIS WAY, BUT HE MUSTVE GONE THAT WAY...
OR DOWN THERE...
OR IN THIS BACK ROOM...
JIM? YOU IN THERE? JIM?
MY WHISPERING ATTRACTED A CLUSTER OF CELL PHONE LIGHTS. KIND'A LIKE GLOWING DEEP SEA ORGANISMS...
AFTER AN HOUR I ABANDON THE SEARCH. HE MUST BE HAVING FUN, AND THE SMOKE'S REALLY GETTING TO ME. SO I LEAVE...
NO REENTRY.
YEAH YEAH.
NOT UNTIL I'M STANDING OUTSIDE DO I REMEMBER THAT JIM DROVE. I'M IN A TOTALLY UNFAMILIAR WAREHOUSE DISTRICT. THERE ARE CABS, BUT I SPENT ALL MY F'ING CASH AT THE DOOR. MAGNIV.
VOX
OH SHIT!

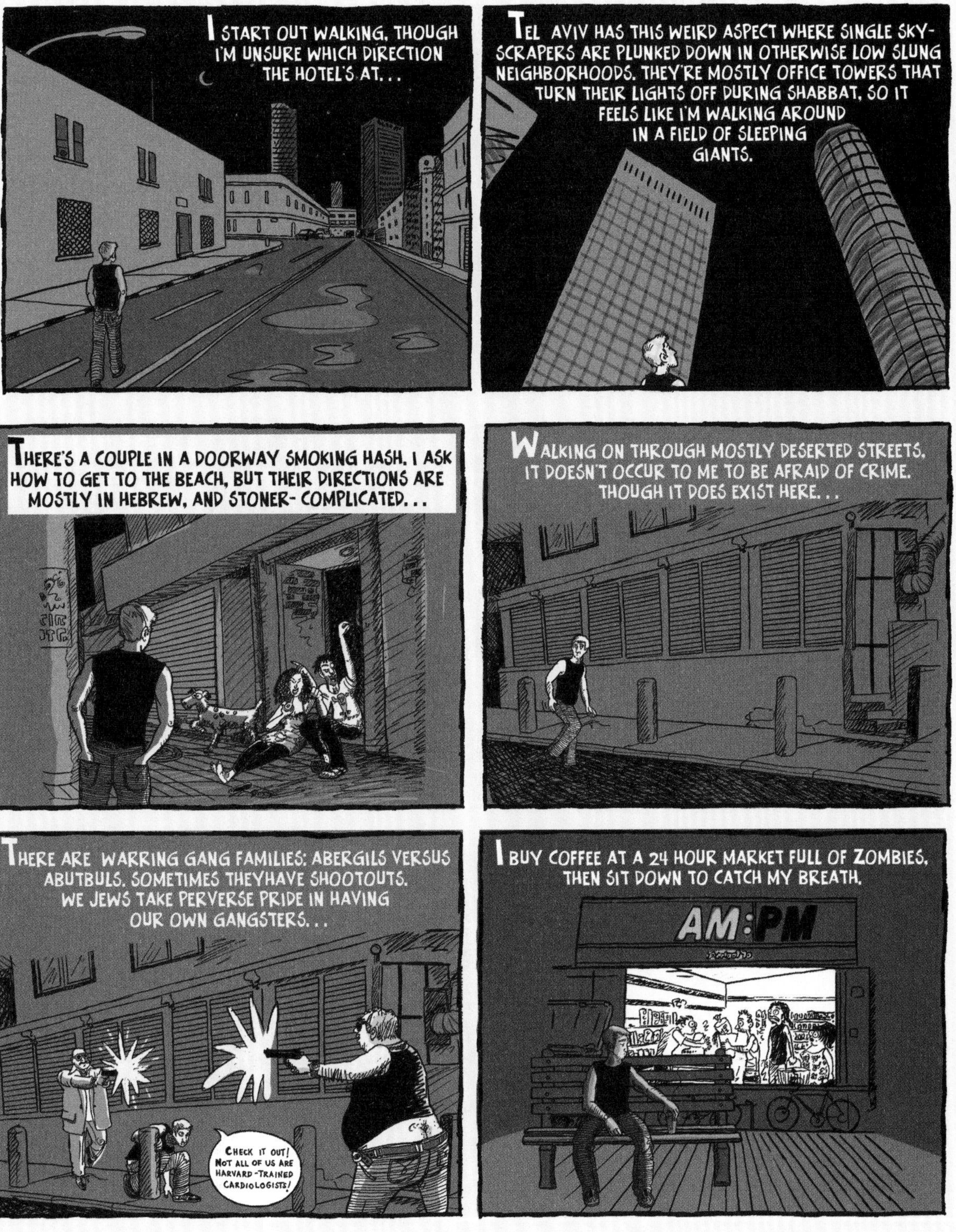
I START OUT WALKING, THOUGH I'M UNSURE WHICH DIRECTION THE HOTEL'S AT...
TEL AVIV HAS THIS WEIRD ASPECT WHERE SINGLE SKY-SCRAPERS ARE PLUNKED DOWN IN OTHERWISE LOW SLUNG NEIGHBORHOODS. THEY'RE MOSTLY OFFICE TOWERS THAT TURN THEIR LIGHTS OFF DURING SHABBAT, SO IT FEELS LIKE I'M WALKING AROUND IN A FIELD OF SLEEPING GIANTS.
THERE'S A COUPLE IN A DOORWAY SMOKING HASH. I ASK HOW TO GET TO THE BEACH, BUT THEIR DIRECTIONS ARE MOSTLY IN HEBREW, AND STONER-COMPLICATED...
WALKING ON THROUGH MOSTLY DESERTED STREETS, IT DOESN'T OCCUR TO ME TO BE AFRAID OF CRIME. THOUGH IT DOES EXIST HERE...
THERE ARE WARRING GANG FAMILIES: ABERGILS VERSUS ABUTBULS. SOMETIMES THEYHAVE SHOOTOUTS. WE JEWS TAKE PERVERSE PRIDE IN HAVING OUR OWN GANGSTERS...
CHECK IT OUT! NOT ALL OF US ARE HARVARD-TRAINED CARDIOLOGISTS!
I BUY COFFEE AT A 24 HOUR MARKET FULL OF ZOMBIES, THEN SIT DOWN TO CATCH MY BREATH.
AM:PM

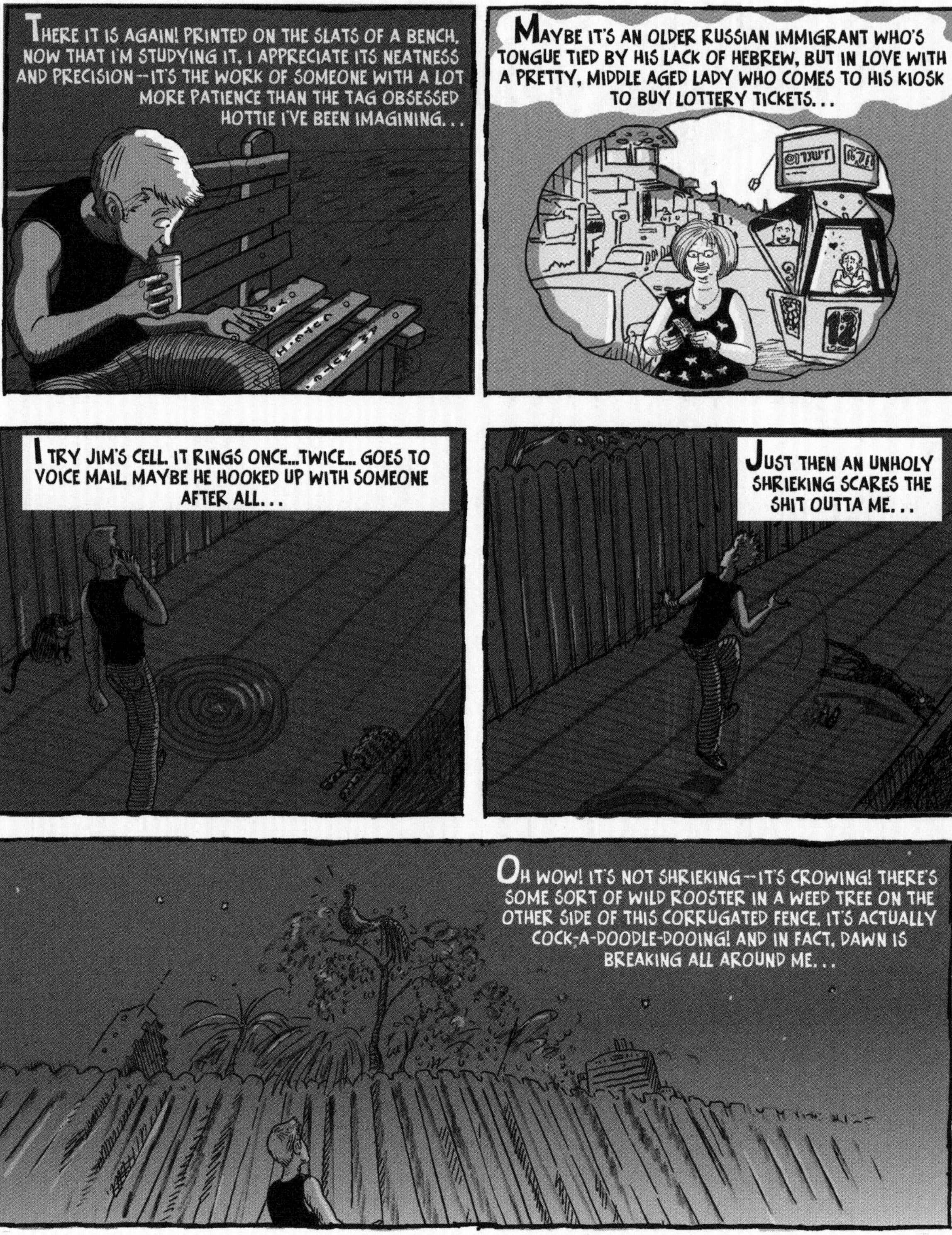
There it is again! Printed on the slats of a bench. Now that I'm studying it, I appreciate its neatness and precision--it's the work of someone with a lot more patience than the tag obsessed hottie I've been imagining...
Maybe it's an older Russian immigrant who's tongue tied by his lack of Hebrew, but in love with a pretty, middle aged lady who comes to his kiosk to buy lottery tickets...
I try Jim's cell. It rings once...twice... goes to voice mail. Maybe he hooked up with someone after all...
Just then an unholy shrieking scares the shit outta me...
Oh wow! It's not shrieking--it's crowing! There's some sort of wild rooster in a weed tree on the other side of this corrugated fence. It's actually cock-a-doodle-dooing! And in fact, dawn is breaking all around me...

I'M A CITY BOY. OR AT LEAST A SUBURBAN ONE. I DIDN'T KNOW ROOSTERS REALLY DID THIS...

IN FRONT OF ME NOW I CAN MAKE OUT A FAINT LINE OF BEACHFRONT HOTELS. FOR THE FIRST TIME IN HOURS, I'M ORIENTED.

JIM CALLS, FULL OF APOLOGIES. SAYS HE LEFT AFTER 15 MINUTES. SAYS HE'S BEEN BACK HOME IN JERUSALEM, IN BED FOR THE PAST TWO HOURS ALREADY...

OH MY GOD IT WAS SOOOO CLAUSTROPHOBIC! HOW CAN YOU EVEN STAND PLACES LIKE THAT?

MY CELL'S RECEPTION ISN'T GREAT AND I'M TRYING TO FOCUS ON OUR CONVERSATION WHILE WALKING TOWARDS THE HOTEL AS FAST AS I CAN. I'VE GOTTA PISS PRETTY URGENTLY.

WAIT! AM I HEARING a ROOSTER? DON'T TELL ME YOU PICKED UP A KIBBUTZIM? OH MY GOD WHAT'S HIS NAME? OH MY MY...

EVEN SO, I'M NOT SO PREOCCUPIED THAT I DON'T NOTICE A YOUNG ETHIOPIAN WOMAN IN A PRETTY SUNDRESS STANDING NEXT TO A LAMP POLE AND RUMMAGING THROUGH HER BAG. A BABY'S SLEEPING ON HER HIP.

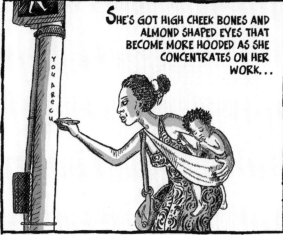

SHE'S GOT HIGH CHEEK BONES AND ALMOND SHAPED EYES THAT BECOME MORE HOODED AS SHE CONCENTRATES ON HER WORK...

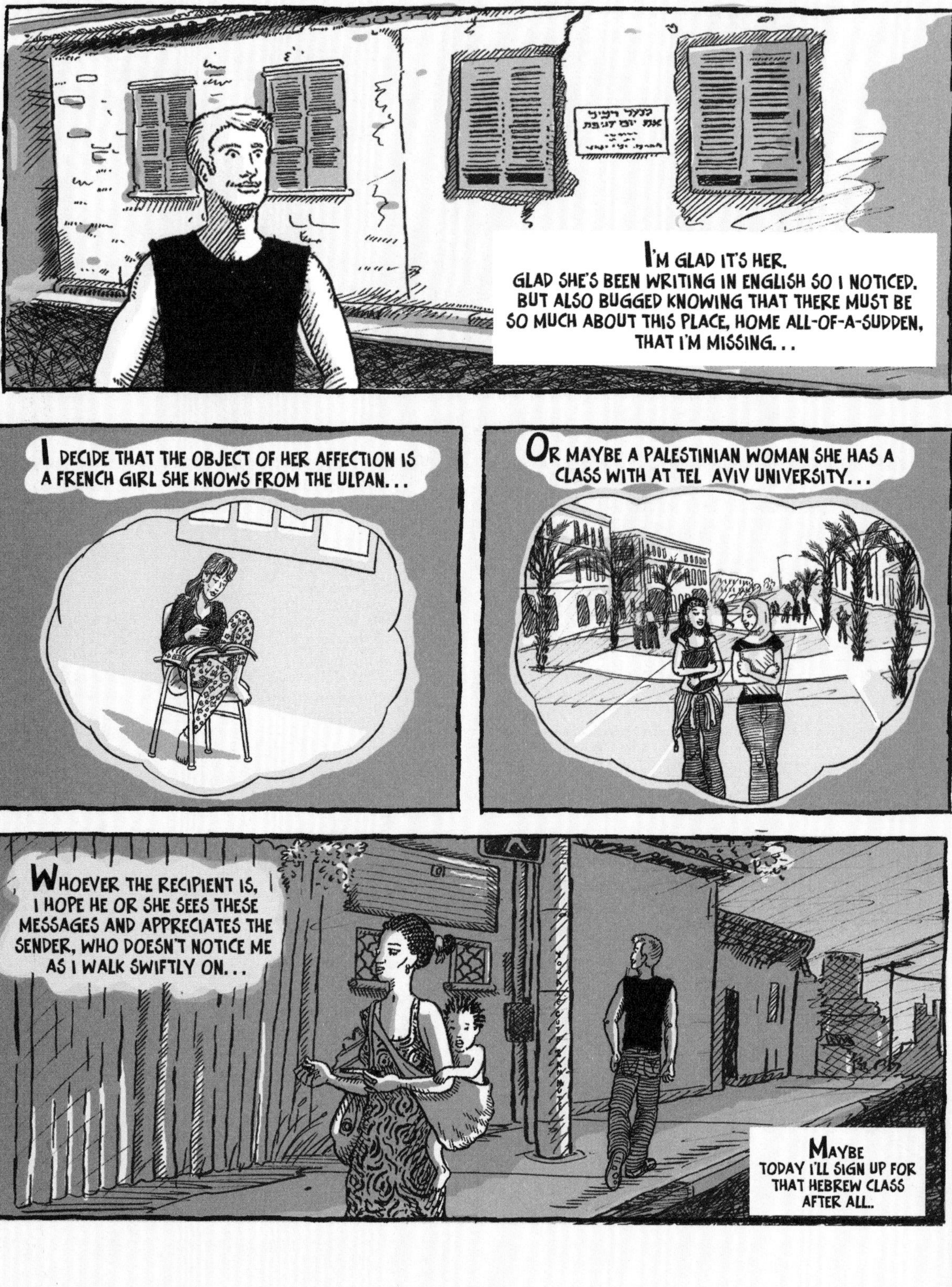
I'M GLAD IT'S HER.
GLAD SHE'S BEEN WRITING IN ENGLISH SO I NOTICED.
BUT ALSO BUGGED KNOWING THAT THERE MUST BE
SO MUCH ABOUT THIS PLACE, HOME ALL-OF-A-SUDDEN,
THAT I'M MISSING...
I DECIDE THAT THE OBJECT OF HER AFFECTION IS A FRENCH GIRL SHE KNOWS FROM THE ULPAN...
OR MAYBE A PALESTINIAN WOMAN SHE HAS A CLASS WITH AT TEL AVIV UNIVERSITY...
WHOEVER THE RECIPIENT IS, I HOPE HE OR SHE SEES THESE MESSAGES AND APPRECIATES THE SENDER, WHO DOESN'T NOTICE ME AS I WALK SWIFTLY ON...
MAYBE TODAY I'LL SIGN UP FOR THAT HEBREW CLASS AFTER ALL.

The Ultimate Graphic Novel

(IN SIX PANELS)

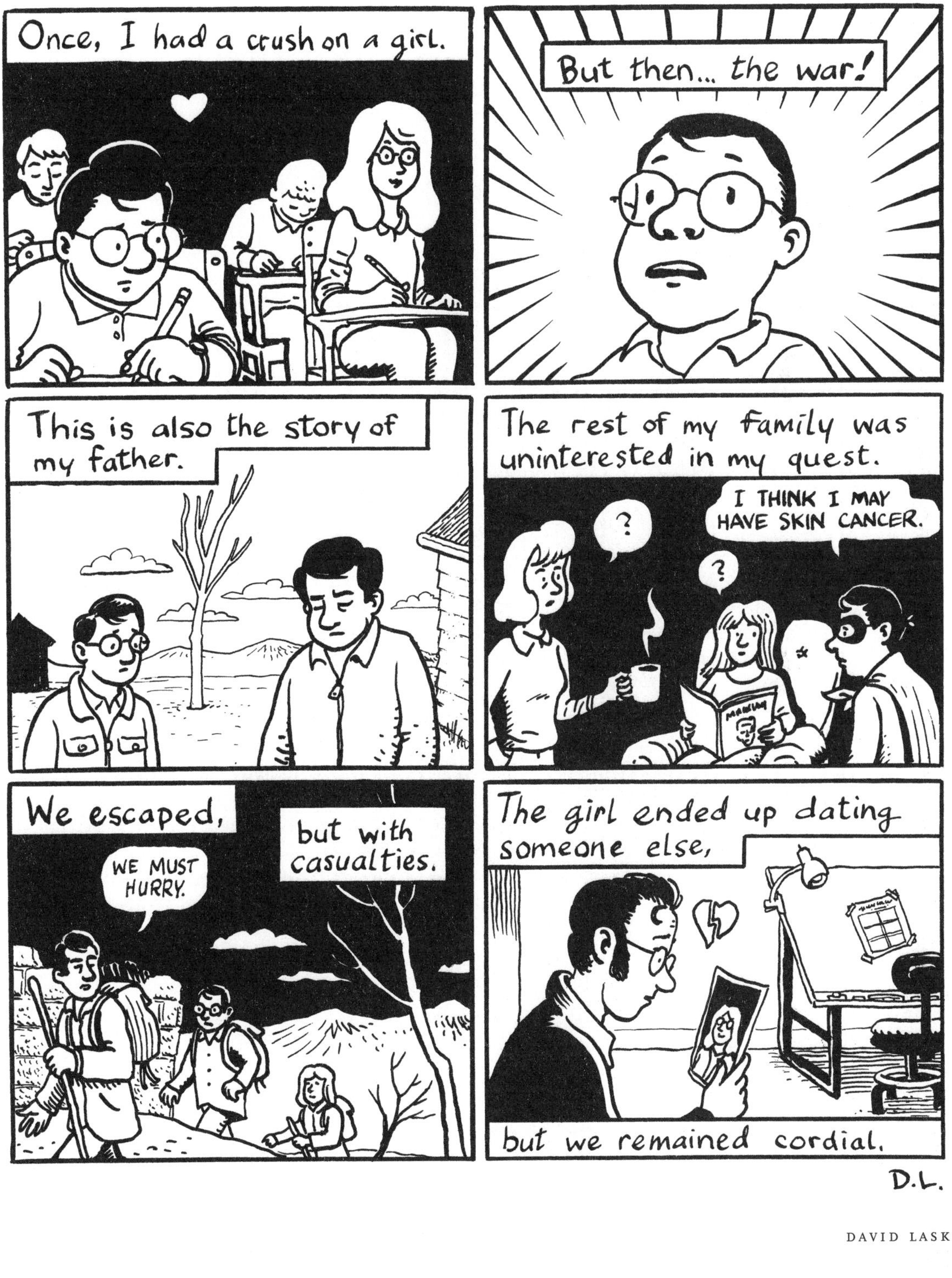
Once, I had a crush on a girl.
But then... the war!
This is also the story of my father.
The rest of my family was uninterested in my quest.
I THINK I MAY HAVE SKIN CANCER.
?
?
We escaped,
but with casualties.
WE MUST HURRY.
The girl ended up dating someone else,
but we remained cordial.
D.L.

DAVID LASKY

Contributors' Notes

Kate Beaton is a Canadian cartoonist who appeared on the comics scene in 2007 with her online work "Hark! A Vagrant." Since then, she has become a fan favorite and has gathered a significant following, with illustrations appearing in places like *The New Yorker, Harper's,* and Marvel's *Strange Tales* anthology. Praised for their expression, intelligence, and comic timing, her cartoons often display a wonderfully light touch on historical and literary topics. The jokes are a knowing look at history through a very modern perspective, and a campaign against anyone with the idea that history is boring.

▪ The best thing about making comics about *The Great Gatsby,* "Great American Novel" contender that it is, is that almost everyone has had to read it at one time or another, meaning the jokes will go over with a much wider audience than, say, a series on *Noli Me Tangere.* Most of us have written a teenage essay on what the green light means, or the eyes of T. J. Eckleburg, or some other thing that breaks the novel down into a stockpile of symbols and themes—it was almost mathematical, in my own high school English class. Theme + theme + symbol = Great American Novel. It's so easy! With all these deep symbols about the American Dream tacking the pages together, it can be easy to forget the real meat of the novel, that is, the insanely selfish and amazing characters who lie, drink, and cheat their way through the Roaring Twenties.

Gabrielle Bell is the author of the books *Lucky* and *Cecil and Jordan in New York* and the popular semi-autobiographical comics blog Lucky (www.gabriellebell.com).

▪ When Shannon O'Leary asked me to submit a comic for her anthology on feminism, I was excited to do it, but I quickly realized I didn't know very much on the subject. I don't think I would have even finished it, but Shannon added pressure by creating some buzz about it. So I have her to thank. But above all I have my mother to thank, once again.

Mairead Case writes fiction for places like featherproof, THE2NDHAND, and The Dil Pickler, plus interviews and criticism for Pitchfork.com, *The New-York Ghost, Punk Planet,* and others. She edited *The Journal of Ordinary Thought, Proximity* magazine, and the books section at *Venus Zine;* taught youth and adults in Chicago libraries and Indiana JJCs; co-organized the 2010 Bronx Museum Book Fair and pitches in at Printers' Ball; coordinates volunteers for Louder Than a Bomb; and put together a radio show about dreams for Neighborhood Public Radio at the 2008 Whitney Biennial. She's working on a manuscript about Antigone.

▪ David and I met in Seattle in 2003, when we worked on *Bandoppler,* the brave, beautiful rock mag started by Jason Dodd, Chris Estey, and Roy Culver. After *Bandoppler* stopped publishing, Chris was working at Light in the Attic Records (lightintheattic.net), and Matt Sullivan asked David and me if we'd be into making a comic for their reissue of Serge Gainsbourg's *Melody Nelson*—an album about a guy in a Rolls Royce who runs over a girl on a bicycle, then falls in love with her. We were! And then we made this one for LITA's *Je T'Aime . . . Moi, Non Plus.* Everything happened long-distance night-owl phone and e-mail, Seattle (David) to Chicago (me). The flip-book concept was David's genius, then I looped the record, read everything I could find, and wrote each half of the script before he drew the images to match. Thanks and congrats to David, an amazing artist and friend, thanks also to the Co-Prosperity Sphere and Istria for letting me use WiFi when I didn't have Internet (and not kicking me out that day when all I bought was coffee!). This one's for RDL.

Ken Dahl is Gabby Schulz, a cartoonist born and raised in Honolulu, Hawaiʻi. He currently lives in Flatbush, New York. All other details can be found at www.gabbysplayhouse.com.

▪ The excerpt here is from *Monsters*, a mostly autobiographical book about having herpes. I drew it not only to appease my masochism, but also to take a little stigma out of having a relatively minor disease that is shared by over 70 percent of the adults I know, in one form or another—which means you probably have it, too.

Michael DeForge was born in 1987 and works as an illustrator in Toronto. His ongoing series *Lose* is published by Koyama Press.

▪ This strip was an early attempt to play around with notions of gender and identity that I am planning to explore with greater depth in some of the longer stories I am currently working on.

Julia Gfrörer is an artist and illustrator from Concord, New Hampshire. She earned her BFA in printmaking from Cornish College of the Arts in Seattle in 2004 and moved to Portland, Oregon, in 2007. Her free-associative fictional autobiography series, "Ariadne auf Naxos," is published by Teenage Dinosaur, and more of her work can be seen at her website, www.thorazos .net. She is a splendid young woman equipped with sharp teeth, roughly 463 freckles on her left hand, and an imposing tangle of shining bright orange hair.

▪ Romance and sexual desire rely on the narratives we create for them to live in, but those narratives are inevitably corrupted by the conflicting physical world. *Flesh and Bone* was inspired in part by the tradition of old ballads eulogizing a dead lover. Because it's not supported by corporeal reality, the affair that the man in my story lives and dies for paradoxically encompasses love in its most pure and most false incarnation. Jadwiga's ambivalence toward this man—she's sympathetic toward him though she also makes fun of him and uses him—is, I think, as close as any of us can honestly get to a conscious understanding of love.

Jaime Hernandez has been creating comics professionally for thirty years and hopes to do it for another thirty.

▪ This was one of those stories that surprised me because every idea seemed to just spill out and land perfectly on the page. It was even more surprising when I found that each scene related to the other, whether it was an important scene or not.

Peter and Maria Hoey are brother and sister illustrators. They have been working together as Coin-Op Studio since 1997. They also produce "Coin-Op" comics and flip-books.

▪ The genesis of "Anatomy of a Pratfall" was the idea of having a story unfold through a gridded street view, with multiple stories cascading across the six pages.

Kevin Huizenga was born near Chicago and now lives near St. Louis. More info about his books and self-published 'zines can be found at www.usscatastrophe.com.

▪ This story is influenced by the old newspaper comics Sunday pages where characters would dream or daydream.

Sabrina Jones is a longtime contributor and coeditor of *World War 3 Illustrated*. She is the author of *Isadora Duncan: A Graphic Biography*, and created comics for *FDR and the New Deal for Beginners*, and Studs Terkel's *Working: A Graphic Adaptation*.

▪ To celebrate the election of President Obama, the editors of WW3 decided to set aside our usual practice of shaking our fists at the powers that be and publish an exercise in positive thinking, an issue called "What We Want." I had come across Jane Jacobs while trawling for women who totally radicalized their field and would be fun to draw—Isadora Duncan was proving to be a tough act to follow. Taking a break from the straight historical comics I'd been doing, I followed the WW3 principle of "tell them up front who you are and why you care about this." Hence this hybrid of auto-bio and hero-worship, with a primer on urban planning and a love note to New York City.

Dave Lapp is a teacher and cartoonist living in Toronto, Canada. He has been doing some form of alternative comics for over a decade. Dave's first graphic novel, *Drop-In* (Conundrum Press), is a collection of stories about his work as an art teacher in one of Canada's poorest neighborhoods. *Drop-In* received Best Book nominations from the Ignatz and Doug Wright awards. Dave's new book, *Children of the Atom* (Conundrum), is a collection of 240 strange, sweet, sorrowful, philosophical strips featuring Franklin-Boy and Jim-Jam Girl, who attempt to distill the very essence of relationships. Dave's next book, *People Around Here*, will be released in 2012 from Conundrum. *People Around Here* collects a decade's worth of cartoons Dave developed using autobiography, life drawing, and overheard conversations. His approach to cartoon realism in *People Around Here* could be regarded as "Pekaresque" as he marvels at and records our quotidian existence.

▪ When you get old enough and you're around teenagers, and you try to act like one, the awkward back step neither amuses nor charms, but something inside hopelessly wishes, yearns to be there . . . again. This is a page from one of Canada's finest literary magazines, *Taddle Creek*, where I am a regular contributor.

David Lasky has been a comics artist off and on since 1989. Besides his series *Boom Boom* and *Urban Hipster* (in collaboration with Greg Stump), he has drawn comics for numerous anthologies (*Kramers Ergot, Hotwire*) and for clients such as King County Public Health ("No Ordinary Flu"). He is currently at work with collaborator Frank Young on a graphic novel biography of country music's legendary Carter family, which will debut in 2012.

▪ My work process begins with observing and absorbing elements of pop culture, literature, film, comics, news stories, anecdotes, and such. I take time to investigate things that interest me. Once this has all had a chance to "stew" in my mind, I begin to concoct a page of comics and look for unexpected coincidences, let happy accidents manifest themselves, and then try to find a way to make it all cohesive.

For "Soixante Neuf," I came up with the format and drew rough thumbnails of the pages, but had not finished art to show writer Mairead Case. I described over the phone what I thought the art was going to be like, and she bravely wrote the words without knowing exactly how they would interact with the pictures. I think the resulting booklet is as much a love poem to Paris in the '60s as it is a romance comic about Serge and Jane.

"The Ultimate Graphic Novel" is the result of reading graphic novels for twenty-five years and noticing patterns in them.

Brendan Leach received a Xeric Foundation grant in 2010 and has been included in comics collections such as *Smoke Signal, Ferocious Quarterly*, and *The Anthology Project*. His illustrations have been recognized by the Society of Illustrators and *3x3* magazine. He has no distinguishing physical characteristics. Brendan currently lives and works in Brooklyn, New York.

▪ *The Pterodactyl Hunters (in the Gilded City)* was done as my MFA thesis project at the School of Visual Arts. The basic concept for the story was in my head for a number of years before I sat down to focus on the writing and draw it out. David Mazzucchelli agreed to act as my thesis advisor and I was lucky to work with him. It took a year to make, and only ten minutes to read.

Kevin Mutch has spent the last twenty-five years as a visual artist, curator, and critic, but comics were his first love. Unfortunately, they were more or less beaten out of him in art school. Eventually, around the time he turned forty, his thoughts began returning to comics and he decided to try his hand at them again. *Fantastic Life,* which is being published this year with the aid of a Xeric grant, is his first graphic novel.

Mutch, who is from Winnipeg, Canada, currently lives in Union City, New Jersey, with his wife and two children. They are all patiently modeling for his next book, *The Moon Prince*, which can be read at his website, www.kevinmutch.com.

▪ *Fantastic Life* began as a short story about a party I went to when I was a young art student (the story was called "Uncertainty Principle" and was published in *Blurred Vision 3*). At the party, someone really stumped me with some unsettling ideas about quantum mechanics—which I'd never heard of before. Eventually, I decided to write a longer piece that would try to address the spooky implications of some of those ideas, which is how the story turned into a graphic novel.

Danica Novgorodoff is a painter, comic book artist, writer, graphic designer, and horse wrangler from Kentucky who currently lives in Brooklyn, New York. She received her B.A. from Yale University in 2002. Her comic *A Late Freeze* (2006) won the Isotope Award and was nominated for an Eisner Award, and her graphic novels *Slow Storm* (2008) and *Refresh, Refresh* (2009) were published by First Second Books.

▪ I started working on *Refresh, Refresh* in 2008, after reading Benjamin Percy's short story by the same name and James Ponsoldt's screenplay adaptation. I realized that there are men fighting in Iraq and Afghanistan who were just getting out of elementary school when the World Trade Center was attacked. The story of kids affected by these wars—kids who can barely remember a time before these wars—seemed like a very important one to tell.

Eric Orner draws cartoons and makes short animated films.

In 2006, his longtime alt-weekly comic strip, *The Mostly Unfabulous Social Life of Ethan Green,* was adapted as a feature film.

He works a day job as a staff counsel for Congressman Barney Frank.

▪ In 2005, I was working as a story artist at Disney on the Tinker Bell movie, where my background as an alt-weekly cartoonist proved pretty much no help at all. Our director wanted Tink to flit lightly across the sky "appealingly," like a hummingbird. Instead, my animated renderings of her lurched from frame to frame like a traffic copter with a bad rotor. Troubled as my experience at The Mouse was, however, it opened doors for me artistically when my boss left to produce an animated feature in Israel and took me with him. The next two years in Jerusalem and Tel Aviv gave me an opportunity to write and draw about how unsettling it is to find oneself living abroad for the first time, which is what my story in this book is about.

Benjamin Percy is the author of two novels, *Red Moon* (forthcoming from Grand Central/Hachette) and *The Wilding*, as well as two books of short stories. His fiction and nonfiction appear in *Esquire, Outside, Men's Journal*, the *Wall Street Journal*, the *Paris Review*, and many other publications. His honors include the Whiting Writers Award, the Pushcart Prize, the Plimpton Prize, and inclusion in *Best American Short Stories*.

▪ In 2005, I read an article about a small town in Ohio that lost a dozen soldiers to an ambush in Iraq. I imagined what kind of cavity that would leave behind on a community—and projected their grief onto my own backyard, central Oregon, punching out a story that later appeared in the *Paris Review* and my second book of short stories. It's been such a pleasure to work with James and Danica on, respectively, the screenplay and the graphic novel, witnessing how they've made the narrative their own.

John Pham was born in Saigon, Vietnam, and raised in Los Angeles, California, where he now works and resides. In 2000, he won a Xeric grant for the first issue of his self-published anthology, *Epoxy*. He is currently working on continuing volumes of *Sublife*, published by Fantagraphics.

▪ "St. Ambrose" was my attempt at trying to encapsulate my parochial school experience into a single, brief comic strip. It branched out to touch upon other related memories (my best friend, Eddie, and my parents, for example), as well as my current experience with the studio space I rent, which coincidentally is located right down the street from the school. Memories relating to my friend Eddie and my parents are sometimes painful for me to address, and I thought that maybe if I clustered them around recollections that weren't as tough or emotionally loaded, I'd perhaps have an easier time returning to them in the future. I'd like to continue making strips like this.

Paul Pope is an award-winning cartoonist/designer/printmaker living and working in New York City. His next big project is a graphic novel called *Battling Boy*, forthcoming from First Second.

▪ "Why don't you ever put me in one of your stories?" my mom asked me once about a year before doing *1977*. I thought about the themes and images for a long time before drawing it; the drawing itself took maybe three days. This story is based on what Freud would've called "mesh memories"—an accumulation of different memory sensations. I like the last panel of this story a lot.

Joe Sacco is a cartoonist. He is probably best known for his comics journalism from the Middle East and Bosnia, but he claims his work will soon move on to fiction, essay, and humor.

▪ The featured excerpts from *Footnotes in Gaza* were my attempt to confront head-on the problematic nature of relying on human memory when trying to reconstruct an event that is decades old. In this case, I was investigating the large-scale killings of Palestinians by Israeli soldiers during the Suez Crisis in 1956.

Joey Alison Sayers lives in Oakland, California, where she draws comics and does other fun things. She is also the creator of the strip *The Machine That Travels Through Time*, which runs in *MAD* magazine. Her weekly comic strip *Thingpart* ran for five years and was translated into Spanish, Italian, and Romanian. Her website is www.jsayers.com.

▪ I wrote "Pet Cat" as I was winding down my real, not-cat-based weekly strip called *Thingpart*. I had been doing that strip for five years and was tired and ready to call it quits. "Pet Cat" was my chance to tell a story whose main character was a comic strip itself; I wanted this fictional strip and all the other characters who came into contact with it to suffer even greater struggles and indignities than *Thingpart* and I did.

Robert Sergel was born in 1982 and currently lives in Cambridge, Massachusetts. His series *Eschew* is published by Sparkplug Comic Books and was nominated for an Ignatz Award in 2010. Additional material is available at www.robertsergel.com.

▪ I started working on this story in early 2009. It took about a year to complete and went through many changes before I was happy with it. I spent a lot of time at first just tracing the static and other odd patterns the console would make. None of those drawings made it into the final version, but that was really the genesis of it.

Dash Shaw was born in Los Angeles, California, and now lives in Brooklyn, New York. He's the cartoonist of *Bottomless Belly Button* (2008, Fantagraphics Books) and *BodyWorld* (2010, Pantheon Books) and the short-story collection *The Unclothed Man in the 35th Century A.D.*, which also includes storyboards and drawings from the animated series of the same name that he wrote and directed for IFC. He's currently working on another comic and a feature-length animated movie. Visit www.ruinedcast.com for drawings and animation work.

▪ *BodyWorld* is the most fun I've ever had making a comic. I was laughing and enjoying myself the whole time. The stuff I'm doing now I think is much better, but it's just not as much fun to do. I wish I could go back.

Jeff Smith is a cofounder of the Self-Publishing Movement of the 1990s and an early adopter of the graphic novel format. He is best known as the writer and artist of *Bone*, an award-winning adventure about three cartoon cousins lost in a world of myth and ancient mysteries. In 2009, Smith was the subject of a documentary called *The Cartoonist: Jeff Smith, Bone, and the Changing Face of Comics.*

Besides *Bone* and *RASL*, his other books include *Shazam: The Monster Society of Evil* and *Little Mouse Gets Ready.*

▪ I wanted to make a science-fiction comic that contained hard science, and fill it with hard-boiled characters. In the world of cutting-edge physics, string theory and modifications of it like M-theory suggest the existence of parallel universes. The idea that a scientist and former employee of the military industrial complex might use experimental equipment to slip into neighboring universes and steal precious artwork for dangerous clients fit my idea of a noir world, and if this scientist's past could be littered with regrettable decisions, well, perfect! The kicker came when I discovered the infamous nineteenth-century inventor Nikola Tesla, whose creations not only underlie all of modern civilization, but form the basis of RASL's technology, and whose own history is strewn with bad choices . . .

Jillian Tamaki is a cartoonist and illustrator. She lives in Brooklyn, New York.

▪ "Domestic Men of Mystery" began as a short story I made when I was creating work for my Drawn and Quarterly petit-livre, *Indoor Voice*. I did few stories about my family and my suburban upbringing. They didn't make it into the book, so the stories remain unpublished. When Aviva Michaelov and Kim Bost at the *New York Times* op-ed page asked me to contribute a comic to their section, I immediately thought of this story about fathers. The original story ended a little more cynically, with us growing into teenagers and ignoring fathers along with everyone/everything else. Given that this was to run on Father's Day (op-art is typically pegged to holidays), something a little more uplifting was necessary. I decided to add the bit about my own father at the end.

Noah Van Sciver is the artist behind the widely praised, Ignatz Award–nominated comic series *Blammo*, published by Kilgore books. His comics have also appeared in *Mome*, *Mineshaft*, *Not My Small Diary*, and regularly in the *Comics Journal*, as well as a slew of other places online and in print. Currently he is working on his first graphic novel, which is called *The Hypo*, about the young Abraham Lincoln, his chronic bouts of depression, and his relationship with Mary Todd. You can find more of Noah at www.nvansciver.wordpress.com.

▪ "Abby's Road" was drawn in a few winter nights on my bedroom floor. I was immediately nervous about publishing it. It was supposed to be a comic about the kind of person you'll see all over America if you're looking for him. The kind of guy that comic artists don't ever draw. An ICP fan. A real American loser. I left it on my floor near a shelf. About a week later, John Porcellino came to visit me. He picked it up off of my floor and read it. John convinced me that I should publish it, and I listened to him, because his OCD would never steer me wrong.

Angie Wang currently resides in Portland, Oregon, where she still draws flowers and girls, and the only straight lines she draws are panel borders. She is working on her first graphic novel.

▪ When I was fourteen I fell for the ubiquitous "we have a great idea and we need you to create art for us—you'll be paid in exposure" line, but for some reason, they asked me to draw mecha and explosions. I was incredulous—up to that point I'd only drawn flowers and girls—but I gave it my best shot. Well! My mecha looked like blocks of tofu, so I gave up on straight lines forever. Some years later, a friend suggested that I conquer my fear of straight lines by combining the things I love to draw (flowers and girls) with the things I hate (mecha), and so "Flower Mecha" was born.

Chris Ware lives in Oak Park, Illinois, and is the author of *Jimmy Corrigan—the Smartest Kid on Earth*. A contributor to *The New Yorker*, his work has been exhibited at the Museum of Contemporary Art Chicago in 2006, and, most recently, at the Gävle Konstcentrum in Gävle, Sweden, in 2010.

▪ Jason Lint (1958–2023) is a character in an ongoing long-form graphic novel, *Rusty Brown*, here appearing both as his own protagonist and biographer. His story is told at the rate of one year per page and was questionably inspired by James Joyce's *Portrait of the Artist as a Young Man*, Rodolphe Topffer's *Albert*, and a short story by John Updike in which a late-middle-aged man notes that despite being assured of his own life's passing with the accepted parade of events one normally expects—marriage, children, deaths, disappointments—he could account for hardly any of it. The same goes for me, though ever since I was a kid, certain odd moments have become emblematic whenever I think of a particular year. Perhaps it's only because I keep pulling them as my mental file labels, but for better or for worse they've come to take on an almost palpable personal iconography. For example: 1971—happily tapping out a regular rhythm with my heels and toes on the tile floor of my grandmother's kitchen. 1975—opening a box of Pink Panther cereal before the groceries were put away to get at the plastic prize, a disappointing clay sculpting tool. 1983—straightening out my otherwise curly hair with a hairdryer under the (mistaken) impression it would make me more attractive to girls. Et cetera.

Notable Comics

from September 1, 2009, to August 31, 2010

Selected by Jessica Abel and Matt Madden

JASON AARON, R.M. GUÉRA, DAVIDE
FURNO, AND FRANCESCO FRANCAVILLA
Scalped: High Lonesome.

WILLIAM AYERS AND RYAN ALEXANDER-
TANNER
To Teach: The Journey, in Comics.

DARRYL AYO
Enemies with Benefits. *anyANYway*, no. 1.

RINA AYUYANG
Arroz Caldo. *Whirlwind Wonderland.*

DERIK BADMAN
20 out of 30 Days.

LIZ BAILLIE
Freewheel, vol. 1.

T. EDWARD BAK
Wild Man Chapter 2: "A Bavarian Botanist in
St. Petersburg," parts 1–3. *Mome*, vol. 17; vol.
18; vol. 19.

ALISON BECHDEL
A Story About Life. *San Francisco Panorama*
(*McSweeney's* Issue 33).

NICK BERTOZZI
Persimmon Cup. *The Act-i-vate Primer.*

JOE BORUCHOW
Stuffed Animals: A Story in Paper Cutouts.

ADAM BOURRET
I'm Crazy.

NICHOLAS BREUTZMAN
You Can't Be Here.

BOX BROWN
Alpha, *Everything Dies* no. 1, Omega, *Everything Dies* no. 2.

ED BRUBAKER AND SEAN PHILLIPS
The Sinners. *Criminal*, vol. 5.

MIKE CAREY AND PETER GROSS
The Unwritten, vols. 1–2.

MARTIN CENDREDA
Copy. *Stories.*

SEAN CHRISTENSEN AND AMY KUTTAB
Labanotation: The Center of Weight.

MARIAN CHURCHLAND
Beast.

SEYMOUR CHWAST
Dante's Divine Comedy.

DANIEL CLOWES
Wilson.

C.C. COLBERT AND TANITOC
Booth.

AL COLUMBIA
*Pim & Francie: The Golden Bear Days {Arti-
facts and Bone Fragments}.*

JOSH COTTER
Migraneur. *Driven by Lemons.*

EVAN DAHM
Rice Boy.

MIKE DAWSON
Troop 142, nos. 1–3.

MICHAEL DEFORGE
Peter's Muscle.

EVAN DORKIN AND JILL THOMPSON
Beasts of Burden: Animal Rites.

JOSHUA DYSART, ALBERTO PONTICELLI,
AND PAT MASIONI
Unknown Soldier: Easy Kill.
Unknown Soldier: Haunted House.

GLENN EICHLER AND NICK BERTOZZI
Stuffed!

CHUCK FORSMAN
Wolf.

ALEXIS FREDERICK-FROST
Courtship of Ms. Smith.
The Voyage.

NEIL GAIMAN AND P. CRAIG RUSSELL
The Sandman: The Dream Hunters.
RICK GEARY
The Terrible Axe-man of New Orleans.
ROBERT GOODIN
The Spiritual Crisis of Carl Jung. *Mome*, vol. 19.
BRANDON GRAHAM
King City, vol. 2.
C. GEOFF GROGAN
Fandancer.
GILBERT HERNANDEZ
The Troublemakers.
JAMES HINDLE
Little Wolves.
Unsettled.
URSULA MURRAY HUSTED
Drawing on Yourself.
CHRISTOPHER HUTSUL
A Very Kraftwerk Summer.
KATHRYN IMMONEN AND STUART IMMONEN
Moving Pictures.
MAT JOHNSON AND SIMON GANE
Dark Rain: A New Orleans Story.
BEN JONES, FRANK SANTORO, AND JOHN VERMILYEA
Chocolate Gun. *Mome*, vol. 16.
TOM KACZYNSKI AND DASH SHAW
Resolution. *Mome*, vol. 17.
MEGAN KELSO
Artichoke Tales.
VICTOR KERLOW
Big Empty Space.
This Is the Story of a Man Who Could Not Die. *Rabid Rabbit's Tall Tales and Magnanimous Myths.*
MATT KINDT
Revolver.
3 Story: The Secret History of the Giant Man.
MICHAEL KUPPERMAN
All About Drainage, Books Are Stupid. *Tales Designed to Thrizzle*, no. 6.
JOSEPH LAMBERT
Tantrum.
TIM LANE
Spike. *Hotwire Comics.*
HOPE LARSON
Mercury.
BRENDAN LEACH
Summer Internship. *Four Comics.*
JASON LITTLE
Bee in . . . The Ramble. *MySpace DarkHorse Presents* (online issue 36).
STUART LIVINGSTON
7:42 a.m. *Popgun*, vol. 4.
JESSE LONERGAN
Joe and Azat.
CATHY MALKASIAN
Temperance.
JAMES MCSHANE
Archaeology.
LANE MILBURN
Death Trap.
TONY MILLIONAIRE
Billy Hazelnuts and the Crazy Bird.
CORINNE MUCHA
Future Dreams. *Is It the Future Yet?*
PRANAS T. NAUJOKAITIS
Beard.
SARAH OLEKSYK
Ivy, chapters 4–5.
BRYAN LEE O'MALLEY
Scott Pilgrim, vol. 6 (Scott Pilgrim's Finest Hour).
ONSMITH
Disposession by Tornado. *Hotwire Comics.*
JASON OVERBY
Untitled. *Shitbeams on the Loose.*
RICHARD POPLAK, ALEX JANSEN, JASON GILMORE, AND NICK MARINKOVICH
Kenk.
JESSE REKLAW
Toys I Loved. *Dope Flounder.*
GRANT REYNOLDS
Where the River Meets the Sea. *Comic Diorama.*
HANS RICKHEIT
The Squirrel Machine.
SEAN MICHEAL ROBINSON
Much of What We Said Wasn't Anything at All. *The Art of Lying.*
JIM RUGG
Rambo 3.5.
JOHNNY RYAN
Prison Pit Book One.
JOE SACCO
The Unwanted, parts 1–2. *Virginia Quarterly Review*, Fall, Spring.
SAM SHARPE
Change Your Name. *Pinstriped Bloodbath.*

DASH SHAW
Blind Date. *Mome*, vol. 16.
JASON SHIGA
Meanwhile.
ANUJ SHRETHSA
True Tales of Kitchkanni, vol 1. *Rabid Rabbit's Tall Tales and Magnanimous Myths.*
DAVID SMALL
Stitches.
ANDREW SMITH
Sausage Hand.
NICK ST. JOHN
How I Came to Work at the Wendy's.
CONOR STECHSCHULTE
Held Sinister.
The Spirit World.
ARON NELS STEINKE
Neptune.
JAMES STURM
Market Day.
SULLY (SHERWIN TJIA)
The Hipless Boy.
RAINA TELGEMEIER
Smile.

C. TYLER
You'll Never Know, Book Two: "Collateral Damage."
CHRIS WARE
Putty Gray. *San Francisco Panorama (McSweeney's* Issue 33).
TRACY WHITE
How I Made It to Eighteen.
MACK WHITE
Roadside Hell. *Hotwire Comics.*
CHADWICK WHITEHEAD
The Myth of Ice Cream and Race Cars. *Rabid Rabbit's Tall Tales and Magnanimous Myths.*
MATT WIEGLE
The Orphan Baiter, *Papercutter,* no. 13.
JIM WOODRING
Weathercraft: A Frank Comic.
BELLE YANG
Forget Sorrow: An Ancestral Tale.
J.T. YOST
Losers Weepers.
JEFF ZWIREK
The Chicago Typewriter. *Pinstriped Bloodbath.*

CREDITS

"Great Gatsbys" by Kate Beaton. First published in *Hark! A Vagrant*. Copyright © 2010 by Kate Beaton. Reprinted by permission of Kate Beaton. "Manifestation" by Gabrielle Bell. First published in gabriellebell.com. Copyright © 2011 by Gabrielle Bell. Reprinted by permission of Gabrielle Bell. "Queen" by Michael DeForge. First published in arthurmag.com. Copyright © 2010 by Michael DeForge. Reprinted by permission of Michael DeForge. "Fear of Fire (Excerpt)" by Julia Gfrörer. First published in *Flesh and Bone*. Copyright © 2010 by Julia Gfrörer. Reprinted by permission of Julia Gfrörer. "Browntown (Excerpt)" by Jaime Hernandez. First published in *Love and Rockets: New Stories*. Copyright © 2010 by Jaime Hernandez. Reprinted by permission of Jaime Hernandez. "Anatomy of a Pratfall" by Peter and Maria Hoey. First published in *Coin-Op #2: Five Stories*. Copyright © 2010 by Peter and Maria Hoey. Reprinted by permission of Peter and Maria Hoey. "Glenn Ganges in 'Mind and Body' (Excerpt)" by Kevin Huizenga. First published in *Ganges*. Copyright © 2010 by Kevin Huizenga. Reprinted by permission of the author. **Fuck The World**. Words and Music by Joseph Bruce and Mike Clark. Copyright © 1999 by Universal Music–Z Songs, Twisted Harmony and Real Beat Music. All Rights Administered by Universal Music–Z Songs. International Copyright Secured. All Rights Reserved. *Reprinted by permission of Hal Leonard Corporation*. "Little House in the Big City" by Sabrina Jones. First published in *World War 3 Illustrated*, Issue #40, "What We Want." Copyright © 2011 by Sabrina Jones. Reprinted by permission of Sabrina Jones. "People Around Here" by Dave Lapp. First published in *Taddle Creek*. Copyright © 2010 by Dave Lapp. Reprinted by permission of Dave Lapp. "The Ultimate Graphic Novel (in Six Panels)" by David Lasky. First published in *The Stranger*. Copyright © 2010 by David Lasky. Reprinted by permission of David Lasky. "Soixante-Neuf" by David Lasky and Mairead Case. First published in *Soixante-Neuf*. Copyright © 2010 by David Lasky and Mairead Case. Reprinted by permission of Mairead Case and David Lasky and Light in the Attic Records. "The Pterodactyl Hunters (in the Gilded City) (Excerpt)" by Brendan Leach. Copyright © 2010 by Brendan Leach. Reprinted by permission of Brendan Leach. "Blue Note" by Kevin Mutch. First published in *Fantastic Life #3*. Copyright © 2010 by Kevin Mutch. Reprinted by permission of Blurred Books. Lyrics from "The Advocate" © 1983 written by Mitch Funk & Jimmy Green of Personality Crisis. All rights reserved. "Winter (Excerpt)" taken from the book *Refresh, Refresh* written by Benjamin Percy. Adapted from the screenplay by James Ponsoldt. Text copyright © 2009 by Benjamin Percy and James Ponsoldt. Illustrations copyright © 2009 by Danica Novgorodoff. Reprinted by permission of Henry Holt and Company, LLC. "Weekends Abroad" by Eric Orner. First published in *Three*. Copyright © 2010 by Eric Orner. Reprinted by permission of Robert Kirkby/Editor-Publisher of *Three*. "St. Ambrose" by John Pham. First published in *Sublife*. Copyright © 2010 by John Pham. Reprinted by permission of John Pham. "1977" by Paul Pope. First published in *THB: Comics from Mars #2*. Copyright © 2011 by Paul Pope. Reprinted by permission of Paul Pope. "Nov. 3, 1956 (Parts One and Two, plus Memory and The Essential Truth)" by Joe Sacco. First published in *Footnotes in Gaza*. Copyright © 2011 by Joe Sacco. Reprinted by permission of Joe Sacco. "Pet Cat" by Joey Alison Sayers. First published in *Papercutter #12*. Copyright © 2011 by Joey Alison Sayers. Reprinted by permission of the author. "New Year's Eve, 2004" by Ken Dahl. First published in *Monsters*. Copyright © 2009 by Gabby Schulz. Reprinted by permission of Gabby Schulz. "Up Up Down Down" by Robert Sergel. First published in *Eschew #2*. Copyright © 2010 by Robert Sergel. Reprinted by permission of the author. Excerpt from *Bodyworld* by Dash Shaw, copyright © 2010 by Dash Shaw. Used by permission of Pantheon Books, a division of Random House, Inc. "The Mad Scientist (Excerpt)" by Jeff Smith. First published in RASL (Chapter 6). Copyright © 2010 by Jeff Smith. Reprinted by permission of Jeff Smith. "Domestic Men of Mystery" by Jillian Tamaki. First published in the *New York Times*. Copyright © 2010 by Jillian Tamaki. Reprinted by permission of Jillian Tamaki. "Abby's Road" by Noah Van Sciver. First published in *Blammo*. Copyright © 2011 by Noah Van Sciver. Reprinted by permission of Noah Van Sciver. "Flower Mecha" by Angie Wang. First published in *Dark Horse Presents, Volume 4*. Copyright © 2011 by Angie Wang. Reprinted by permission of Angie Wang. "Jordan W. Lint (to the Age 65)" by Chris Ware. First published in the *Virginia Quarterly Review*. Copyright © 2011 by Chris Ware. Reprinted by permission of Chris Ware.

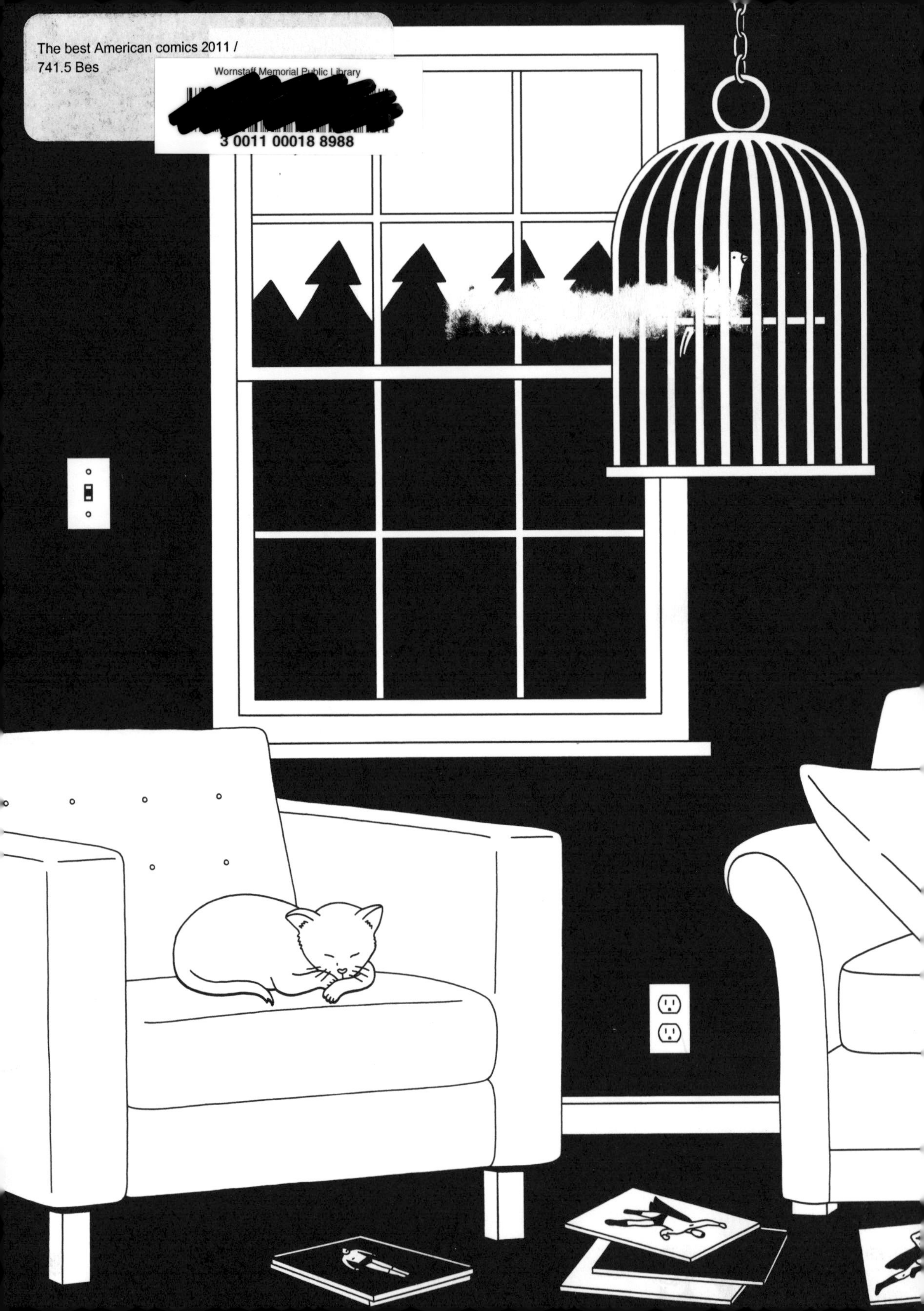